Some Theories of Organization

THE IRWIN-DORSEY SERIES IN
BEHAVIORAL SCIENCE

EDITOR **JOHN F. MEE** *Indiana University*

Some Theories of

ORGANIZATION

EDITED BY

ALBERT H. RUBENSTEIN, Ph.D.
Professor of Industrial Engineering and Management Sciences
The Technological Institute
Northwestern University

AND

CHADWICK J. HABERSTROH, Ph.D.
Professor of Business Administration and Political Science
University of Wisconsin–Milwaukee

Revised Edition, 1966

Richard D. Irwin, Inc. and The Dorsey Press
Homewood, Illinois

First Printing, March, 1966
Second Printing, January, 1969

PRINTED IN THE UNITED STATES OF AMERICA
Library of Congress Catalog Card No. 66–11811

Preface to the Second Edition

It has been more than seven years since the final selection of papers was made for the first edition of this book and almost as long since the essays for the first edition were written. Much progress has been made in the field we call "Organization Theory" in these few years. Evidence for this has been the rapid developments in some relevant aspects of the behavioral sciences—e.g., small group research, simulation, and mathematical modeling; the appearance of several new "inventory" or state-of-the-art books;[1] and the convening of special seminars to examine the field for research opportunities.[2]

On the other hand, we are disappointed that more progress has not been made in further *development, testing,* and *application* of the partial theories represented by the original collection, some of which have been in print now for more than 20 years.

This second edition of our text is still not intended as an inventory or state-of-the-art document. It still focuses on organization theory as an approach to the systematic study of organizational behavior. The essays and articles are designed to expose the reader to a variety of conceptual approaches and research methods, with the emphasis still on empirical studies of real, operating organizations.

Among the changes are 22 new articles (one-half of the total), including two new ones by authors from the first edition. Four of these new articles make up an entirely new section, on Planned Change. This is an area that has been developing rapidly and deserves special treatment in a book attempting to aid in the transition from "pure" social sciences to improved management practice. All of the essays are new and the last one, on Field Study Techniques, has been greatly expanded. It includes discussions of techniques for studying organizations in their natural

---

[1] See, for example: Peter M. Blau and W. Richard Scott. *Formal Organizations.* San Francisco: Chandler Publishing Co., 1962; Theodore Caplow. *Principles of Organizations.* New York: Harcourt, Brace, and World, 1964; Amitai Etzioni, *A Comparative Analysis of Complex Organizations,* Glencoe, Ill.: The Free Press, 1961; Joseph A. Litterer. *The Analysis of Organizations.* New York: John Wiley and Sons, Inc., 1965; and James G. March. *Handbook of Organizations.* Chicago: Rand-McNally, 1964.

[2] Charles Bonini, Robert K. Jaedicke, and Harvey M. Wagner (eds.). *Management Controls.* New York: McGraw-Hill, 1964; and W. W. Cooper, H. J. Leavitt, and M. W. Shelley II (eds.). *New Perspectives in Organization Research.* New York: John Wiley and Sons, 1964.

v

settings and presents examples of the kinds of field studies our students have been doing in the courses in which this book is used.

In the selection of articles, we have tried to incorporate the major schools of thought in this rapidly growing field, as well as providing a picture of the wide diversity of specific approaches.

Albert H. Rubenstein
Chadwick J. Haberstroh

January, 1966

Preface to the First Edition

THIS TEXTBOOK is intended to integrate scientific studies of organization from many of the traditional scholarly disciplines. Its basic premise is that the behavior of organizations and of the individuals who take part in them forms a unified whole worthy of independent study. Although the dominant emphasis is on commercial and industrial organizations, the reader will appreciate that the principles discussed apply to any type of organization, including governmental, philanthropic, military, educational, voluntary, or political. As a discussion of scientific work, its unifying thread is not the *practice of management* in organizations, but rather the *process of research* on organizations. The various theories of organization are presented as results of research or as the impetus to research. As far as possible, the research process is presented whole, with enough discussion of the methods used by the researchers and of the development of ideas in this field to make the reader aware of the potential for new knowledge as well as of the results already achieved.

It has been our intention to deal with the same general subject matter as the book *Organizations* by J. G. March and H. A. Simon. To facilitate cross-referencing, we have, where applicable, included in our index all theoretical terms included in their index. Although the field covered is the same, the objectives of the two books are different. March and Simon present a comprehensive and systematic inventory of the present state of organization theory; we offer an introduction to the research process itself, with the object of showing where it has been, where it is going, and what use can be made of it. These approaches are complementary and we hope that our readers will carry their inquiry into organization theory on through the March-Simon volume and into research reports that are still a-borning.

The idea of preparing a book such as this was generated in the series of graduate seminars on organization theory in the Department of Industrial Engineering at Columbia University, under the leadership of Robert T. Livingston and David B. Hertz. The book itself was developed out of our courses in organization theory given to advanced undergraduate and graduate students of the School of Industrial Management at the Massachusetts Institute of Technology. These courses, and the resulting book, make no assumption as to specific prior preparation of the student, but do assume the degree of intellectual maturity developed from several years of university attendance. The most directly utilizable preparation is in the areas of social science, mathematics, statistics, and accounting.

As the book is intended to be a general presentation of a particular field of knowledge, it is not constrained to any one place in any one curriculum. However, the principal purpose envisioned for it is in a one-semester course in the senior or graduate years of a business administration, industrial management, or industrial engineering program. Such a course might serve as an alternate or supplement to conventional courses in the principles of management. Broadly speaking, it would include the areas of "organization theory" and "human relations" in the business curriculum suggested by R. A. Gordon and J. E. Howell.[1] In our own courses this material has been covered in one semester, although this requires some compression or omission. This way of using it could be broadened, in either of two directions, into a two-semester sequence by preceding it with a semester of managerial psychology or by appending a semester on principles of management or case studies. The creative teacher will undoubtedly find other alternatives as well.

We wish to express our gratitude for the cooperation of the authors and publishers whose works are reprinted herein.

ALBERT H. RUBENSTEIN
CHADWICK J. HABERSTROH

June, 1960

---

[1] Robert A. Gordon and James E. Howell, *Higher Education for Business* (New York: Columbia University Press, 1959), pp. 178 ff., 264–65.

List of Contributors

Conrad M. Arensberg, *Department of Sociology, Columbia University*
Chris Argyris, *Department of Industrial Administration, Yale University*
Chester I. Barnard (Deceased)
Bernard M. Bass, *Graduate School of Business, University of Pittsburgh*
Daryl J. Bem, *Department of Psychology, Carnegie Institute of Technology*
V. Edwin Bixenstine, *Department of Psychology, Kent State University*
Peter M. Blau, *Department of Sociology, University of Chicago*
Theodore Caplow, *Department of Sociology, Columbia University*
Robert L. Chapman, *Hughes Aircraft, Culver City, California*
Kamla Chowdhry, *Ahmedabad Textile Industry's Research Association, Ahmedabad, India*
Michel Crozier, *Centre De Sociologie Europenne, Paris, France*
Richard M. Cyert, *Graduate School of Industrial Administration, Carnegie Institute of Technology*
Melville Dalton, *Department of Sociology, University of California, Los Angeles*
Karl W. Deutsch, *Department of Political Science, Yale University*
Simon Dinitz, *Department of Sociology, Ohio State University*
N. F. Dufty, *Perth Technical College, Perth, Western Australia*
J. M. Dutton, *Graduate School of Industrial Administration, Purdue University*
George Dunteman, *College of Business Administration, University of Rochester*
F. E. Emery, *Tavistock Institute of Human Relations, London, England*
Willard R. Fey, *Sloan School of Industrial Management, Massachusetts Institute of Technology*
Fred E. Fiedler, *Department of Sociology, University of Illinois*
H. G. Fitch, *Graduate School of Industrial Administration, Purdue University*
Frederick G. Frick, *Lincoln Laboratory, Massachusetts Institute of Technology*
Harold Guetzkow, *Department of Political Science, Northwestern University*
Chadwick J. Haberstroh, *School of Business Administration, University of Wisconsin—Milwaukee*
John K. Hemphill, *Educational Testing Service, Princeton, New Jersey*
George C. Homans, *Department of Social Relations, Harvard University*
Alexander B. Horsfall, *Department of Business, Worchester Junior College*
Edwin B. Hutchins, *Association of American Medical Colleges, Evanston, Illinois*
John L. Kennedy, *Department of Psychology, Princeton University*
Nathan Kogan, *Educational Testing Service, Princeton, New Jersey*
Kilburn LeCompte, *Bell Telephone Company of Pennsylvania*
Mark Lefton, *Department of Sociology, Western Reserve University*
Kurt Lewin (Deceased)

William G. Madow, *Stanford Research Institute, Menlo Park, California*

Floyd C. Mann, *Survey Research Center, University of Michigan*

Julius Marek, *Tavistock Institute of Human Relations, London, England*

A. K. Pal, *Ahmedabad Textile Industry's Research Association, Ahmedabad, India*

Benjamin Pasamanick, *Columbus Psychiatric Institute, Ohio State University College of Medicine*

Donald C. Pelz, *Survey Research Center, University of Michigan*

William H. Read, *Graduate School of Business, McGill University*

V. F. Ridgway, *Department of Business Administration, Kansas State University*

Albert H. Rubenstein, *Department of Industrial Engineering and Management Sciences, Northwestern University*

Lee Sechrest, *Department of Psychology, Northwestern University*

Philip Selznick, *Department of Sociology, University of California, Berkeley*

M. Shubik, *Yale University*

Herbert A. Simon, *Graduate School of Industrial Administration, Carnegie Institute of Technology*

George Strauss, *Institute of Industrial Relations, University of California, Berkeley*

W. H. Sumby, *Development Division, Hanscombe Field, Bedford, Massachusetts*

A. J. M. Sykes, *Scottish College of Commerce, Glasgow, Scotland*

P. M. Taylor, *Chamberlain Industries Ltd., Welshpool, Western Australia*

Donald B. Trow, *Department of Sociology, Harpur College, State University of New York*

Stanley H. Udy, Jr., *Department of Sociology, Yale University*

Michael A. Wallach, *Department of Industrial Administration, Duke University*

Richard E. Walton, *Graduate School of Industrial Administration, Purdue University*

Max Weber (Deceased)

Milton G. Weiner, *The RAND Corporation*

Robert S. Weiss, *Department of Sociology, Brandeis University*

Edwin L. Williams, *Raytheon Company, Wayland, Massachusetts*

Lawrence K. Williams, *New York State School of Industrial and Labor Relations, Cornell University*

G. A. Wilson, *Raytheon Company, Wayland, Massachusetts*

Donald Wolfe, *Division of Organizational Sciences, Case Institute of Technology*

Alvin Zander, *Research Center for Group Dynamics, University of Michigan*

Table of Contents

The Nature of Organization Theory

THERE IS little question about the fact that the practice of management has been remarkably successful in harnessing human energy and converting the potentials provided by nature into useful forms for modern society. There are, however, a number of indications of difficulties that managers have in adapting to changes in technology, complexity, growth, and changing environmental conditions. In addition, there are the perennial questions that progressive managements ask themselves:

Can we do better than we are doing?

Can we improve the efficiency of our operations?

Can we develop better employee relations?

Can we learn how to adapt to changes—both anticipated and unanticipated?

Can we make better use of scarce resources?

Can we increase the rate of innovation and receptiveness to change within the organization?

Can we reduce the strain of organization life on the human system?

Are there major opportunities for increased effectiveness that we have not discovered yet?

Are there whole new ways of carrying out the mission of the organization that would involve drastic changes in methods of organizing and operation and that would yield significantly better results?

There is evidence that the rapid changes in managerial information systems and the concomitant requirements for closer coupling of communication and decision making are placing severe strains on existing organizational structures and on individual managers.

It seems possible that answers to some of the above questions may come from the new and exciting field of *Organization Theory*. The emergence of organization theory as an identifiable area of specialization is very recent. Thirty to forty years ago, there were very few people in the contributing disciplines who identified themselves as "organization theorists." Historically, such professionals as the industrial engineer and the anthropologist have been interested in the structure of formal organizations and how they operate. Their interests, however, were adjuncts to their main concerns—i.e., the improvement of operations or an understanding of a given culture, respectively. Some industrial sociologists, economists, and political scientists were also interested in organizations.

Observations and recommendations on organizational phenomena are found in the Old Testament and in documents prior to that. Few of the early writers, however, considered themselves specialists in this field or devoted their professional lives to its study. The number of people contributing directly or indirectly to the field has increased greatly in the past two or three decades—from dozens to hundreds. There are also beginning to emerge professional subgroupings in various professional societies who identify themselves as interested in organization theory—for example, the College on Organization of The Institute of Management Sciences.

Science, as distinguished from a particular scientific theory, is not merely an expression of empirical truths in nature. It is a human enterprise, with knowledge (in the form of scientific theories) as its product. Especially in the case of immature and rapidly developing sciences, the results existing at one point of time are often of less importance than the potential for future results that exists in the scientific community. Since this applies to the study of organization as to all social science, a major objective of the book is to acquaint the reader with the major schools of thought that are contributing to the field, as well as to present some of their results to date. The fantastic increase in the speed and scope of diffusion of information in this field has led to the publication and dissemination *to management and the public* of a large amount of fragmentary and unintegrated ideas about how organizations do or should behave. Hopefully, some systematic preparation will help the student keep track of and interpret this material.

There is not a single, well-defined community of scholars with responsibility for research in organization theory, as there is in physics, psychology, or economics. The criterion for inclusion proposed in this early stage of research on organization theory is: any contribution or potential contribution, deliberate or not, from any field, that increases our understanding of the behavior of people in organizations. Thus, we would include the work of some psychologists, sociologists, economists, mathematicians, anthropologists, statisticians, biologists, ecologists, animal sociologists, and various types of engineers, as well as scientifically minded practitioners such as businessmen and administrators of various kinds.

Members of all of these professional specialties and more have already made contributions, some unwittingly, to our ability to understand, predict, and influence organizational behavior.

In addition to the diversity of disciplinary fields from which contributions to organization theory are coming, it is also interesting to note the diversity of approach or method employed. This is one reason that the field of "organization theory" appears so ununified and disorderly, in terms of common concepts, research methods, and objectives of the researchers.

HOW MIGHT THE ORGANIZATION THEORIST HELP THE MANAGER?

Although the number of direct applications of organization theories to practical design and operation of organizations has been modest up until now, the potential is great. One kind of contribution might be specific organizational design rules—e.g., rules intended to speed the flow of information or to remove inhibitions on the decision process. In addition, many of the research findings of organization theorists can be of value in pointing out potential difficulties and unforeseen consequences of current organization design and operating procedures.

Consider, for example, the design and installation of a new organization-wide data processing system intended to speed information flow and decision making. Many of these expensive installations have been far from successful. A number have failed outright and have been removed from the organization. Few of these failures are due to inadequacy of the mechanical systems themselves. The principal source of difficulty has been the reaction of the people in the organization who must supply information to the system, get information from it, service it, or, in some way, restructure their behavior to accommodate to it.

Organization theorists have been studying problems related to this phenomenon for some time. They have not yet developed any grand theories or universal rules on "how to install data systems," but they have learned a lot about the forms of operating difficulties and resistance to be expected, the reasons for such problems, and some ways of coping with them. Section 4 on Planned Change, which has been added for this second edition, includes examination of this problem of the introduction of new technology.

Aside from the possible direct benefits to specific organizations which attempt to apply organization theory, work in this field has some intrinsic rewards—it can be fun! The problems are intriguing and push the limits of our current analytical ability. Great intellectual challenge lies in questions of how people really behave, why they behave as they do, and the consequences of that behavior for themselves and their organizations.

WHAT ARE THE ALTERNATIVE BASES FOR ADMINISTRATIVE PRACTICE?

Let us visualize a company manager, a school superintendent, a government official, or a military commander who is charged with certain duties and who is expected to act in certain ways in order to perform his duties. How does he learn the proper and the most effective ways of behaving in his job? In other words, what is the basis for administrative practice?

Typically, the major basis for guiding his behavior comes from the administrator's direct experience or from vicarious experience gained as an assistant, colleague, apprentice, or merely an observer of other people performing the same or related duties. In addition, he picks up ideas and information on how to behave through what we call folklore, customs, or "the ropes" of the organization. Many of these are characteristics of his specific job or his specific organization, and they set limits on his behavioral alternatives or suggest certain types of behavior.

If he is "experimentally" oriented, he may evolve appropriate and successful patterns of behavior as a result of conscious trial and error—testing of alternative modes of behavior and evaluating the effect on performance. Usually, however, the opportunity for real experimentation is very limited. In many organizations the new administrator is not left on his own, as the above discussion implies, but is exposed to various formal attempts to teach him how to behave on his job—special training programs, apprenticeships, internships, and so on.

Many of the rules of behavior which are important to the administrator are not readily transferred by formal and deliberate means. They are subtle things which are learned as part of growing up in a society and which become "second nature" to members of that society. Certain modes of behavior seem to be *the* way to do things." It is only when one encounters a society quite different from his own or a situation in which accustomed behavior is ineffectual that these intuitively correct behaviors are questioned.

At this point, one may begin to think that perhaps the behavioral rules he has been following are not the only ones possible or are not adequate ones for varying circumstances. An example of this phenomenon of "culture shock" is the impact on many non-United States students from authoritarian cultures when they first encounter a graduate seminar in the U.S.—where the students seem to be arguing on equal terms with their instructor!

It is interesting to examine, briefly, the major formal means of developing administrators—through general education and training in "management" and "administration." Business and management schools have become an increasing source of administrative talent, to the extent that the opportunity to "work one's way up the ladder" from the production floor or the clerical desk is being drastically reduced. Formal graduate programs and short courses in management are being used with increasing frequency to prepare people for administrative duties. Also interesting is the trend toward integrating more work in behavioral science and organization theory into such programs. The assumption appears to be that the would-be administrator can prepare himself formally with respect to some modes of behavior that will be expected of him—his decision-making process, his communication patterns, and some of his general conduct as an administrator.

Like the physician and the engineer, the administrator may become a better practitioner of his art by studying science. At this stage in the art of administration, however, there is no guarantee that the science-trained administrator will have a clear advantage over his colleagues who have "come up the hard way" and "learned by experience." If the analogy with the other two arts is valid, however, there is high promise that he will eventually have a clear advantage.

As Figure 1 indicates, the role of organization theory in the formal training of the administrator is that of integrating the other behavioral sciences and related specialties as a resource for the improvement of administrative practice. Ideally, the process involves four stages:

1. Developments in behavioral science and other specialties of general theories and propositions.

2. Selection, further development, and general testing of those theories and propositions that are relevant to organizational behavior and administrative practice.

3. Development, adaptation, and testing of new theory-based techniques in specific operating organizations by organizational analysts *within these organizations.*

4. Adoption of the resulting rules and behavioral patterns as standard administrative practice.

As this brief discussion suggests, this is a long and uncertain process. Attempts to select and adapt "decision rules" and behavior patterns directly from the raw behavioral science literature have not been very successful. This is not surprising in view of the disappointing experience in medicine and engineering due to similar attempts to use directly the raw findings of basic research in the sciences, without the essential development, adaptation, and testing. The intermediate development is of two kinds: A) The development of a unified body of knowledge specific to the social phenomena we call organizations; and, B) The integration of this and other knowledge in specific applications to concrete organizational problems. These are the provinces of the organizational theorist, as a be-

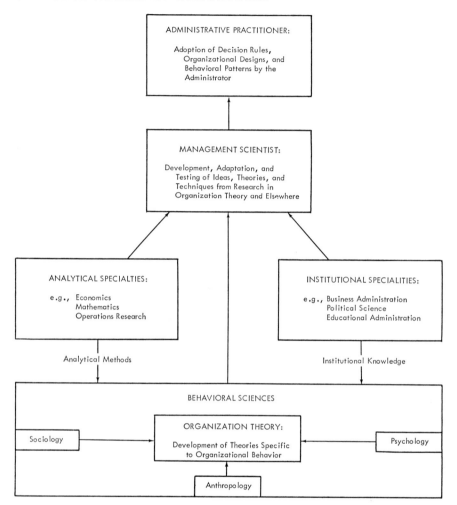

FIGURE 1

THE TRANSITION FROM ORGANIZATION THEORY
TO IMPROVED ADMINISTRATIVE PRACTICE

havioral scientist, and the management scientist as a consultant or staff expert, respectively.

In the universities, there is growing recognition of the importance of organization theory as a discipline. Such labels as "sociology of formal organizations," "industrial sociology," "human relations in industry," "industrial psychology," "organizational psychology," "applied anthropology," and "behavioral theory of the firm," all have in common an orientation to organizations as social entities.

In the field of management consulting and inside most modern corporations and many nonindustrial organizations there are staff groups who have been and are becoming increasingly interested in developing and testing organization theories and applying them to specific organizations. Many of these groups—industrial engineering, organizational analysis, operations research, management science—have had long experience in dealing with organizational problems and attempting to apply systematic methods to their solution. Many of them have not yet appreciated, however, the magnitude of the effort and the time required to make successful use of organizational theories. If one keeps the analogy of the research-and-development engineer in mind, however, there should be an increased realization of the requirements for successful transition from the behavioral sciences, including organization theory, to administrative practice.

The diagram in Figure 1 also emphasizes the three-part foundation required for a useful body of knowledge in organization theory:

The general theories, concepts and research methods of the behavioral sciences—sociology, psychology, and anthropology.

A framework of analytical methods from fields such as economics, mathematics, and operations research. These fields can contribute techniques for model building, data reduction and analysis, simulation and gaming, scaling, and other means of handling data and concepts.

Systematic descriptive and analytical knowledge about specific institutional environments—e.g., business, government, hospitals, and the military.

As in the fields of medicine and engineering, there is an increased interest in exposing practitioners in administration to these foundation areas. In none of the three fields, however, is there an expectation that the practitioner and the basic researcher—the developer of theories and analytical methods—will necessarily be the same person.

WHERE DO PROPOSITIONS IN ORGANIZATION THEORY COME FROM?

Most organization theories consist of one or more propositional statements connecting two or more variables and parameters in a logical or orderly framework. In the readings in this book are examples of many different forms of such statements. One may follow the rules of symbolic logic or a particular geometry in providing a framework for these statements. Typically, propositions in organization theory fall into the general categories proposed by March and Simon(1):

1. Dependence of one variable on another or others—e.g., "the higher the incentive, the better the performance."
2. Qualitative descriptive generalizations—e.g., "administrative decentralization is a growing trend in public school systems."
3. Functional statements (in the physiological rather than the mathe-

matical sense)—e.g., "the use of committees facilitates communication in the firm."

Form 3 is closely related to and can be transformed into form 1 if the variables can be quantitized and a relationship established. For example, such a transformation of the illustration might result in the following form 1 propositional statement: "The more frequently committees are used in an organization, the faster and more accurate the communication in that organization will be." Such a proposition suggests the necessity of a comparative study between organizations with varying frequencies of using committees.

There are a wide variety of sources for specific propositions in organization theory—some very formal, some quite informal. Four major sources are:

1. *Generated from formal models*, based on some simplifying assumptions. For example, there are a number of simple models of two-person cooperating organizations or three-person competing "organizations" (e.g., competing for power or a share of a fixed reward). These types of models are based upon a certain number of initial assumptions about parameters or given conditions of the organization such as: information handling capacity of the participants, available information channels, the kinds of goals held by individuals and shared by the members, and many others. Using a particular formal structure—e.g., symbolic logic, the mathematics of sets, servomechanism theory, or game theory—a number of propositions may be generated about the likely behavior of the members and the consequences for the organization.

2. *Refined from systematic empirical investigation.* A typical starting point for such propositional development is the comment: "Isn't it interesting that . . ." Further thought and attempts to formalize such an observation may lead to a well-structured propositional statement which can be tested in the next round of empirical observations. Many such statements also are suggested in the "wisdom" literature on organization, discussed below. A statement by an experienced manager to the effect that "people in his organization did not resist innovation when it was presented to them in such and such a way" might lead to a general proposition on the order of: "the manner of presenting an innovation to people in an organization affects their readiness to accept it." Further, the various ways of presenting an innovation might be related to each other in some ordinal fashion, with respect to a criterion such as "degree of participation in the implementation." In addition, it may be possible to scale the "degree of readiness" to accept the innovation. When these additional formalizing operations have been performed on the original idea, we may arrive at a set of related, testable propositions about how people in an organization are likely to react to an innovation.

3. *Generated from general subtheories or models* of organizational behavior, developed in another context. For example, research at Northwestern concerning the effects of corporate decentralization on the research and development (R&D) activity (2) has drawn heavily on the bureaucratic theory literature for testable propositions. This has been done in spite of the fact that none of the general bureaucratic theory literature was derived from study in a research and development context. The portion of this literature that appeared particularly relevant was that dealing with response to the demand for control by higher authority.

4. *Based on sudden insights or speculation* about organizational behavior. Some propositional statements that arise in this manner are the result of long or deep experience with a particular set of organizational phenomena and a desire to reach some personal understanding of it. Others are the result of sudden associations with other kinds of phenomena that appear to provide some explanation of observed or supposed organizational behavior. Many propositions of this type appear, to others, to be "pulled off the wall" or "picked out of the air." Unless they can somehow be placed into a systematic and communicable framework so that the work of others can be related to them, such propositions are often rejected by the members of a scientific discipline.

Figure 2 illustrates the general approach taken to proposition formulation and testing in a continuing program of research on the organization of the research and development activity conducted by Rubenstein and his associates at Northwestern University(2). This approach represents a combination of all four sources of propositional statements as a basis for developing subtheories about the R&D process.

In this approach, propositions arising from familiarity with the phenomenon—the R&D process—are juxtaposed with propositions about related phenomena, derived from the organization theory literature. Model building, field testing, and dual validation—empirical and scientific—complete the cycle.

There is a major problem which must be properly handled in the use of this dual approach, although it appears to have greater potential for developing valid and useful organization theories than some of the individual approaches described—e.g., formal models or strictly empirical work. This is the problem of too much initial screening and filtering of potential propositions before they can be completely formulated and tested.

Familiarity with the institutional specifics—the way real organizations and their members actually behave—provides a filter through which propositions must pass before they are formalized. This filter can act as an inhibitor of proposition formulation in the following way: a person very familiar with the real situation will "know" that certain required data are inaccessible and that certain propositions are not intuitively obvious, or

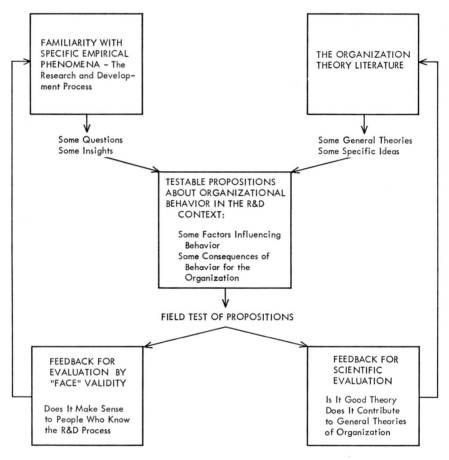

FIGURE 2

An Example of the Use of Multiple Sources for
Propositions about Organizational Behavior

even reasonable. He may have difficulty, therefore, in developing or accepting a proposition that violates his personal knowledge of the availability of certain data or the reality of the phenomena. This is a constant source of concern in the research program mentioned above, and care is taken continuously to keep the empirical and the theoretical sources of proposition in balance.

Some additional questions about this venture of proposition development and testing are:

What criteria does one use for accepting, rejecting, or reserving judgment on a given test of a proposition?

Should one attempt to separate proposition formation from proposition testing? That is, can one effectively engage in a simultaneous or only loosely sequential process of proposition formulation, data collection and analysis, and proposition testing?

These questions are vital, because so far organization theory is essentially a nonexperimental field. Studies in real operating organizations are constrained by limited access, inability to control "other factors," and difficulties of replicating studies in other organizations. Such an integrated approach (theory and field investigation), despite the difficulties, holds great promise for development of the useful theories of organization discussed at the beginning of this chapter.

As in the first edition, the emphasis in the selection of articles for this edition has been on empirical studies of organizational behavior, as compared to speculative essays or abstract formulations. The exceptions are included to provide contrast or to suggest potentially fruitful new approaches. The dominant kind of article is the field investigation in real, operating organizations, although a substantial sample of laboratory experimentation is also included.

It is not yet clear whether the great breakthroughs in organization theory will come from one approach alone, or from a combination of formal, experimental and field approaches. It seems evident, however, that field investigations play a decisive role in the development and application of useful organization theories. The expanded last section on research techniques places primary emphasis on methods of field investigation. Such field studies have been an integral part of courses the editors have conducted in this field at Columbia, M.I.T., Northwestern, and the University of Denver.

Comparative Organization Theory and Common Knowledge

One of the most exciting and potentially powerful aspects of organization theory is the emphasis on comparability between individual organizations and between kinds of organizations. Certainly every organization, like every individual human being, is unique. That is, the total set of characteristics and behaviors of a given organization is seldom duplicated or even approximated in any detail by any other organization. If one were to allow this situation to dominate the search for general theories of organizational behavior, the search would be a short and fruitless one. There is no trick in finding dissimilarities between any pair of organizations.

The remarkable thing is that there are so many *similarities* among organizations—so many characteristics and behaviors that are strikingly similar in essence, if not in detail. It is this faith in the existence of regularities and the possibilities of generalizing between organizations that sustains the organization theorist.

In our field research in organizations over the past dozen or more years, we have studied such diverse organizational types as manufacturing firms, hospitals, government bureaus, judicial systems, military units, research laboratories, schools and school systems, developing countries, service organizations, and many functional divisions of these types of organizations.

In this research, we have been struck repeatedly by the existence of very similar problems, similar attempts at solution, and similar behavioral patterns. For example, many of the organizations we have studied include a group of professionally trained people—researchers, doctors, nurses, teachers, military men. In many of these organizations, similar patterns of conflict are evident between these professionals and the general administrative group which may be viewed as supporting the activities of these professional people. One group frequently feels that the other group does not understand its problems, does not have the good of the organization in mind, or fails to observe proper rules of conduct. Some of the outward manifestations—public accusations, defections from the organization, appeals to higher authority, repeated reorganizations—are noticeable for a wide range of organizations in which such conflict occurs.

Many common reasons for the conflict are also evident across organizational types despite great specific differences in individual organization members and functions of the organizations. To the casual observer or, indeed, to the emotionally-involved participant, such situations are generally attributable to "personalities" and the incompatability of specific individuals. To the organizational theorist, however, such situations are a challenge to discover and explain the nature of the problem and to relate it to more general characteristics of organizations than the specific personalities of its current members.

Traditional organizational "theory" and practice often give the appearance of theoretical statements and have given rise to much speculation and some empirical investigation. A primary example is the notion of "span of control"—the number of people an individual can effectively supervise. Much of the speculation on this notion has consisted of quantitative analyses of the "mathematics" of span of control and the implications of the number of people supervised for the overall size and shape of the organization.

Many such rules of thumb, although initially appealing to intuition, turn out to be counter to intuition and experience when one attempts to apply them. Managers know that the number of people who can be supervised by a given person depends on many factors: the supervisor, the nature of the work, interdependencies among the jobs of those supervised, and, especially, what meaning is attached to "supervisor" in the particular situation. By oversimplifying what really is a very complex phenomenon, contributors to the traditional organization literature have not produced useful theories in the sense that we outline in this book.

In one respect, the selection of material for this book and for the courses in organization theory for which it is intended presented a dilemma. Most students of organization and practitioners of management are already acquainted to some extent with this traditional literature in the field of organization and management. This work is usually focused on the question of "How to Manage." Unfortunately, most of it has not contributed to an ultimate applied science of management through the development, testing, and revision of theories and empirical generalizations. A large segment even helps to perpetuate the belief that management is *by nature* an intuitive art and that the possibility of a science of organizational behavior is not great, if there is a possibility at all.

The dilemma was this: Should a portion of this book (and the courses which use it) be devoted to examining this vast and growing literature? Should a major portion of the reader's (and student's) time be given over to discovering at first hand the inadequacies of much of this material for the purposes of systematic explanation, useful and accurate prediction, and an effective basis for influencing organizational behavior? The essence of this dilemma is that this material is very attractive and very appealing to the intuition. It is often the product of writers with broad, successful experience in management. It is frequently consistent and reasonable, and many readers find it inspiring.

The difficulty is that it is seldom in a form that is subject to empirical testing or communicable in operational form to others. Therefore, not only does it fail to help in developing general propositions or theories about organizational behavior, it is often difficult to teach in a systematic fashion. The dilemma has been resolved in this book by omitting this class of literature and leaving it to collateral or future reading.

As a transition, however, a brief summary of traditional views of organization is presented in Figure 3. This provides a juxtaposition of three sets of notions about organizational behavior, contrasting (1) some of the basic beliefs expressed in much of the traditional literature, (2) some of the tentative conclusions stemming from the work of the behavioral scientists who have been studying organizational behavior, and (3) the organizational traditions of scientists in all fields. As an indication of the profound changes in managerial know-how that may result from the systematic development of knowledge about organizations, the first comparison deserves careful attention. The latter is included as a reminder of the type of social system that has produced our scientific progress to date and as an empirical example of a major social function that does not conform in its organization to the preconceptions of traditional theory.

Some Requirements for Theories of Organization

In many of the papers in this and succeeding sections of the book, the nature of theory is treated in different ways. Some authors begin a description of their research by describing their "theory" or their "work-

FIGURE 3*

Traditional Theory of Industrial Organization	New Direction of Industrial Organization Theory	Organizational Traditions in Science
	1. Wide Participation in Decision Making Rather than Centralized Decision Making	
If the organization has been properly designed, with rational delegation of authority and responsibility and clear and correct specification of tasks and goals at each level, the only important decision making to be done concerns major changes in the organization's course; these are clearly the responsibility of top management; in fact, the whole point of organization design is to reduce the necessity for decision making at lower levels in the organization.	People resist tasks, goals, and changes which are imposed upon them and show a good deal of creativity in developing methods of resistance; *they* want to perform tasks, set goals, and make changes for ends to which they are committed; they are committed only to the kinds of organizations which belong to them—"belong" in the sense that the members have some power of decision in areas that affect them; under these conditions creativity is used for achieving organizational goals rather than for self-defense against organizational rules.	Several traditions in science insure that each scientist has an opportunity to express and argue for his opinion with respect to the usefulness or validity of proposed or generally accepted theory or with respect to other matters, in the forum provided by journals and meetings; he is taught to value independence of thought and creativity, to respect the authority of fact rather than of social power, to set his own goals and tasks, and to change them autonomously: any decisions affecting all scientists are the consequence of the "weight of scientific opinion" rather than of an individual authority.
	2. The Face-to-Face Group Rather than the Individual as the Basic Unit of Organization	
The organization is a pyramid of superior-subordinate relations; responsibility and authority are delegated to individuals; no two individuals should have overlapping responsibility; the term "span of control" refers to the number of individuals supervised, not the size of "group" supervised; groups in any other sense of the term have no place in traditional theory.	The organization is a large group composed of numerous interlocking subgroups; the interdependence of jobs must be matched by an interdependence of the organizational members; the supervisor's main responsibility is maintaining communication between the managerial group of which he is a member and the work group of which he is a member; other overlapping memberships carry similar responsibilities; within each group all problems affecting the group's work must be shared openly; "private" superior-subordinate relations are destructive of collaboration and productive of intrigue.	All messages must be broadcast to the entire scientific community to insure the growth of knowledge and proper attribution of credit; secrecy is anathema and destructive of the scientific group; power resides in the group, not in any individual; it is expressed in the "weight of scientific opinion" and in professional standards democratically determined; informally, importance is placed on small-group discussion as a source of stimulation and criticism.

The organization proceeds on the basis of systematic order-giving and checking from top to bottom of the hierarchy of superior-subordinate relations; the orders are designed to produce behavior which will contribute to the attainment of the organization's goals; hence obedience to authority is the integrative force in the organization.

Mutual confidence refers to a supportive atmosphere and a set of procedures which insure, on the one hand, that individual merit is recognized and, on the other, an absence of intrigue; standards of performance and responsible membership must be group-shared and group-supported; however, this degree of group responsibility can be maintained only if the same degree of confidence and support exists in inter-group relations; that is, the supervisor must be an effective member of both groups.

Several scientific traditions are concerned with the prevention of intrigue and the maintenance of confidence and trust; one is the requirement that all messages be broadcast to insure the proper allocation of credit; another is implicit in the technology of science: controlled, repeatable observation and experiment; honesty, objectivity, respect for facts, and rigorous workmanship are stressed as personal attributes in scientific training; authority does not reside in socially powerful individuals but in observed fact.

4. The Supervisor as the Agent for Maintaining Intragroup and Intergroup Communication Rather than the Agent of Higher Authority

In essence, the supervisor's job is to secure obedience to orders received from his superior; he sees that his subordinates use the proper methods, stick to their jobs, and get the work done.

The supervisor's main jobs are (1) to build a group with a strong sense of responsibility for getting the job done and improving their effectiveness and (2) to be an effective member of management in representing the group he supervises and in representing general organizational needs to the group he supervises.

The scientific community is concerned primarily with intracommunity communication, and the sense of community is maintained by commitment of scientists to the common goal of advancing knowledge; there are community standards which define responsible behavior in science; there is no tradition for maintaining communication between the scientific community and other parts of society; the concept of "management" or "supervision" is absent from and alien to the organizational traditions of science.

5. Growth of Members of the Organization to Greater Responsibility Rather than External Control of the Members' Performance of Their Tasks

Supervision should be production-centered rather than person-centered; the task is central and permanent; people are replaceable; the supervisor's job is to see that people do the job as it should be done.

If the employee accepts responsibility for getting the job done, the supervisor's task is one of giving training and help rather than of policing; hence the supervisor's main responsibilities are to provide a setting in which employees are willing to accept responsibility and to aid them in developing their capacities to the fullest extent possible.

Master-apprentice, teacher-student, senior colleague-junior colleague relations in science all stress the development of the junior member of the pair rather than getting him to perform a particular set of operations.

* Reprinted from Herbert A. Shepard, "Superiors and Subordinates in Research," *Journal of Business*, Vol. XXIX, No. 4, October, 1956.

ing hypotheses" or a statistical hypothesis which is to be tested by the experiment or other empirical study they describe in their article. In later sections, for example, Selznick speaks of: ". . . a reconstruction, which is to say, a theory, of the conditions and forces which appear to have shaped the behavior of key participants"; Argyris says: ". . . we may hypothesize that agents (organizational members) ought to require functions which are so defined that they may fulfill some combination of . . . the broad trends of personality development . . . for individuals in our culture . . ."; Barnard speaks of: "A Theory of Cooperation and Organization"; and Horsfall and Arensberg discuss: ". . . some of the current theories about group structure . . ."

To the student or reader trained in the physical sciences or, indeed, to the one without a scientific background, the use in these articles of the term "theory" and what it implies may be very confusing. To one accustomed to the simplicity and relative lack of ambiguity in physical science theory, the complex formulations and conceptual schemes, the alternative formulations offered for the same set of phenomena, and the preoccupation with definition and redefinition may be disconcerting. Our focus in this book, however, is less on the form in which statements are made than on the substance—the contributions of statements to our ability to understand, predict and influence organizational behavior. We will not, of course, ignore form; on the contrary, we will be very concerned with it as it affects the quality and usefulness of the statements.

Our major criterion for considering the merits of any organization theory is a pragmatic one: Is a given theory, hypothesis, or conceptual scheme potentially *useful* to the practitioner of management? *How* useful is it potentially, and how much time and effort will be required to make the potentiality pay off? If it is useful, then we may call it "good" theory.

Of what value will theory be in the field of organizational behavior or in practicing the art of management? Traditionally, three roles have been assigned to theory. Some sciences have been able to produce theories which can perform all three. Others are limited to one or two. Useful theories of organization should help us to:

1. *Explain* observed organizational behavior. This may not lead to any direct benefits to the practitioner except the satisfaction of knowing why the observed events occurred. It may also make him aware of aspects of the events he would otherwise not have considered.

2. *Predict* future organizational behavior. This can be of extremely high value to both researcher and practitioner. It can provide an opportunity for the researcher to test his ideas about organization and so further improve his theories; and it can help to guide the future actions of the practitioner.

3. *Influence* future organizational behavior. While this may be of least

interest to the basic researcher, it is the essence of the practitioner's interest in learning about organizational behavior. The ability to influence the behavior of people in organizations and the consequences of that behavior are of obvious importance to the success of the manager's job.

To the nonscientist, whose expectations for theory may be based on a few well-known "laws of nature," the uncertainty and tentative nature of theories in this field may be inexplicable, or at best puzzling.

No simple definition of the concept "theory," which is lifted directly from a given physical science, is adequate to cover the kinds of notions, propositions, hypotheses, empirical generalizations, and deductive schemes which may ultimately contribute to theories that can help to explain, predict, and influence organizational behavior. Webster's six alternative definitions spread a blanket over all kinds of intellectual activity from ". . . speculation" and ". . . a guess" to "A body of theorems presenting a clear, rounded and systematic view of a subject . . ."

Philosophical analysts have devoted much attention in recent years to the methodology of scientific theorizing. Their discussions of this question fill volumes, but it is possible here to say somewhat more about theories than that they must be useful to explain, predict, or influence. The earmarks of a theory seem to be that it (1) has empirical reference, (2) contains logical interconnections with other theories, and (3) admits the possibility of rejection. The first point is that some of the terms used in the theory should be directly observable, that is, placed in correspondence with empirical data. The second point is that the theory should be part of a logical structure explaining as many and as different empirical phenomena as possible. The third point is that empirical observations can help us to reject theories, i.e., the theory must enable a researcher to: somehow select for testing from the number of conceivable observations; and, must say that some will happen and some will not. Observation of the excluded possibilities—the events the theory says will *not* happen—would discredit or weaken our belief in the theory.

Reverting to our more fundamental requirement that theories in organization must be useful, we can point out a number of situations in which concepts or formulations that are not theories, according to the above, may nevertheless help to explain, predict, and/or influence organizational behavior:

Is a Model a Theory? Excellent work in the new fields of operations research, statistical decision making, and similar fields has focused management attention on the use of mathematical models. These models are often very useful in influencing organizational behavior and may frequently be adapted to questions of explanation or prediction. Nevertheless, many of them cannot properly be considered theory, in the sense that we have used the term in the preceding discussion.

Although the use of mathematical models in management is a relatively new development, simpler and more obvious types of models have been a characteristic part of the manager's equipment for a long time; and mathematical models have been commonplace in many other fields. A discussion of this question is somewhat confused by variations in usage of the words *model* and *theory* in many fields, but especially in social science and its applications. It is our intention to follow current usage in the philosophy of science, the field to which questions of this nature belong.

To begin with, let us make clear in what sense we are using the term *model*. A model is a system or object that stands in place of another, usually more complicated, system or object. Simple examples are an architect's scale model for a building, or the company telephone directory as one type of model of the organization. A mathematical model is similar. The difficulty that arises is that the mathematical model is likely to be confused with a mathematical theory. The reason for this confusion is the similarity in appearance: both use premises and deduce conclusions in a mathematical manner. To the nonmathematician, one page of symbols may look the same as another. The differences in the two systems, however, partly determine the uses to which they can be put.

The logical structure of a theory is such that the *conclusions* derived from it can be placed into correspondence with (interpreted as) empirical hypotheses and confirmed or refuted by experiments. The logical structure of a model is such that its *premises* are interpreted (i.e., empirical statements), and its conclusions are logical consequences of these. A theory can be refuted by a single contrary empirical finding; a model is not exposed to refutation, but is used as long as any benefit can be derived from it. A model can continue to be useful even though it yields many conclusions which are clearly wrong, provided only that it yields *some* conclusions that are correct (i.e., useful). A theory is expected to yield *only* true conclusions.

In general a model gives intuitive understanding of the object or system modeled. The mathematical model, therefore, serves the same function as the architect's model; it enables its user to grasp the important structure of a problem in a simple and efficient way.

Some of the models in use in a field may contain very useful suggestions for inclusion in theoretical systems. When models have proved successful in a variety of circumstances, that is, when they do not depend completely on the particular circumstances of one case, it may be possible to reformulate key parts in a genuinely theoretical system. Organization charts and job descriptions are examples of models in organization that have provided some concepts of theoretical usefulness. Thus, although models are not theories, they may contribute to theory building.

Is Taxonomy a Theory?   Some natural sciences depend heavily on description as their principal tool. Descriptive botany, zoology, and geology are examples of research fields where major contributions so far have been in the taxonomic (classification) area. Where a taxonomic system begins to produce insights into relationships between classes in the system and to provide a basis for explanation and prediction, it approaches theory. When a set of propositions about, for example, the evolution of species is achieved, the stage of theory has been definitely reached. A taxonomic system in organization which merely labels phenomena, activities, and events may be very useful; but few such systems have approached the level of theory as yet.

Is Measurement Theory? By itself, measurement does not constitute theory. Without it, however, there has been little theorizing in the sciences. It is considered in many fields as a necessary condition for theoretical work, but far from a sufficient one. The basic operations of measuring can be performed on many objects and events without these "measurements" contributing to a theory-building enterprise. Absenteeism, lateness, and output per worker can be measured, but until these measurements are made to contribute to a basis for explaining why they occur in the quantity and time pattern that they do, or until accurate predictions of their future occurrence can be made, they should not be considered a part of a theoretical structure.

Is a Notational System a Theory? It has always been fashionable in many fields to construct elaborate notational schemes which are semantically useful for designating objects, events, and concepts. The use of such schemes for deducing consequences is less common. Here the reader must take care to see whether he is dealing with a completely closed system of definition and metadefinition or whether the scheme has sufficient points of contact with the real phenomena being described to lead to useful results.

The possibility of a scientific, theoretical approach to organizational problems has often been denied on the grounds that the techniques of controlled experiments are not applicable. The opportunity for adequate experimentation with organizations is very rare, and in some cases no proper experiment is feasible. Some very successful natural sciences, however, have not been able to carry out the classical "controlled" experiment, where all factors but the one under study are "held constant" or otherwise accounted for. Despite this, substantial progress has been made in essentially nonexperimental sciences such as astronomy, meteorology, and human genetics. It is true that the experimental sciences have proceeded more rapidly than others in which experimentation is difficult or infeasible. This has not prevented the advance of these latter fields, however, despite the lack of this means of testing their hypotheses and theories.

In spite of this handicap, there are opportunities for experimental testing of theories of organization. Experimental techniques have been developed in psychology for the study of individuals and small groups. As we shall see, the findings are relevant to problems of organization and help to establish the correctness of parts of broader theories. Occasionally, field experiments in organizations have been conducted that permitted comparison between experimental and control conditions, as between different degrees of stress imposed on parallel work groups. Another attempt at an experimental study involving a whole organization is the work of the RAND Systems Research Laboratory discussed in Section Two. This was made possible by advances in computer technology, in this case involving the simulation of environmental inputs.

The readings in this first section are devoted to a general exploration of criteria and methods for discerning or developing useful theories of organization. Lewin discusses one of the major methodological positions developed in the behavioral sciences; it has provided the impetus for a large portion of the active research on human behavior in the past twenty years.

These readings are included to illustrate the kind of very general, philosophical issues that scientists have to resolve, explicitly or implicitly, before they can conduct, criticize or appraise research on human behavior. The time will be well spent on them if it sharpens the distinction between a methodological issue and an empirical one. The essence of scientific progress and the development of useful knowledge is the gradually widening consensus of agreement on empirical issues such as are dealt with in the rest of the book. Consensus on methodological issues is not likely (and to that extent unimportant), because the criterion by which they can be judged is indirect: the usefulness of the resulting empirical research. The issue of differences in methodology will be discussed later in this section.

Homans, in his article in this section, says "The only inescapable office of theory is to explain." He cites the theory of evolution as an explanation of how and why evolution occurs. He argues further that a "theory of a phenomena consists of a series of propositions, each stating a relationship between properties of nature." He also differentiates between all useful statements and statements which can qualify as propositions for a theory.

Bixenstine examines the contrast between two stereotypes of behavior in research—the empirical study, unstructured by prior hypotheses, and the study designed to test or at least explore a specific hypothesis. As implied by our use of the term "behavior in research," the question of approach is an individual matter to be determined by the researcher himself as constrained by the nature of the field, the current state of the art, current practice, and his professional status. Above all, however, the approach is a matter of taste. Despite the many strictures about *the* scientific method, there are alternative ways of developing and testing theories. Appropriateness is determined by usefulness of results, subject, of course, to the requirements for communicability and replicability which the scientific community places on its members. "Private theories" which are not explainable to other members of the scientific community and "private data" which are not obtainable by others, following the same or similar procedures, are generally not accepted as valid. The requirements of scientific method then are as much social as they are logical.

The attempts on the part of the emerging behavioral sciences to conform with the older traditions of scientific method in the natural sciences lead to controversies of the types that are suggestive of the earlier days of natural science and current controversies in medicine. They stem from differences in criteria of relevance and validity among investigators. Much of the data and methodology used by some behavioral scientists is considered "soft" by rigor-inclined colleagues. Questions of operational definition of variables, logical structure of propositions, and methods of measurement continually arise in the study of such variables as attitudes, emotions, values, perceptions, etc. Many of the controversies may be inevitable, because of the inherent difficulty of gaining access to these phenomena. Many of them are the result of distinctly different viewpoints on the nature of theory and research in this field.

Schwab in an interesting essay entitled "What Do Scientists Do," (3) elaborates on the theme that there is no one scientific method of inquiry. He argues four propositions to the effect that (1) there are only a few alternative methods of inquiry, and they can be described; (2) individual scientists are remarkably consistent in their personal choice of an approach; (3) these personal preferences represent a configuration of personality types among scientists which is relatively stable over time and sciences; and (4) the personal factor and circumstances rather than logic or history often determine what is better or best for a given science or scientist at a given time.

Schwab also presents an interesting taxonomy of "decision points" and "choices" apparently made by scientists as reflected in a sample of some 4,000 scientific papers over the past few centuries. His categories (in some cases paraphrased here) are:

1. INVENTION OR SELECTION OF A FORM OF PRINCIPLE FOR INQUIRY:
   a. Reductive Principles
   b. Molecular Reduction
   c. Holistic Principles
   d. Formal-Material Holistic Principles
   e. Rational Principles
   f. Anti-Principles
      (1) Laws of Nature
      (2) Causes
   g. Primitive Principles

2. SELECTION OF CRITERIA FOR THE JUDGMENT OF PRINCIPLE:
   a. Interconnectivity
   b. Adequacy
   c. Feasibility
   d. Continuity

3. SELECTION AMONG ALTERNATIVE EMPHASES FOR DE-
TAILED INQUIRIES:
   a. Reliability
   b. Validity

4. CONSIDERING WHETHER TERMS OF INQUIRY ARE GIVEN BY
THE DISCIPLINE.
   a. Stable Inquiry
   b. Fluid Inquiry

5. SELECTION OF ONE PHASE OF INQUIRY FOR REPEATED EN-
DEAVOR:
   a. Guidance
   b. Empirical
   c. Theorizing

6. PERSONAL ORIENTATION:
   a. To Remedy a Hole in Knowledge
   b. To Use a Research Tool Mastered
   c. To Play the Genius

CURRENT RESEARCH IN ORGANIZATION THEORY

In attempting to classify current research in this area, the following dimensions might also be useful. Each person working in the field might be cross-classified according to several of these dimensions. The suggested dimensions are:

1. *Sources of Data.* This is a continuum ranging from *operational* or *positivistic* toward one end to what might be called *mystical* at the other end. This dimension relates to the source from which the researcher is willing to accept his data. In the first instance, represented best perhaps by the applied anthropologist, he insists that the data he uses be analogous to that employed in the natural sciences. He insists on observability, measurability, communicability, and reproducibility. In doing so, according to adherents to the other end of the continuum, he may be throwing out the baby with the bath water—he may be getting good measurements, indeed, but he may also be getting trivial measurements, while overlooking the important data that are not so scientifically neat.

The counterargument, of course, is that data which is generated in the mind of an individual researcher and which is not subject to replication or testing by other researchers is hardly admissible in the venture called science. And yet, it is clear even at this early stage that some of the most brilliant insights in the behavioral sciences have involved this type of data. Perhaps refinement and further development of our research methods can reconcile the ends of this particular continuum.

2. *Level of Abstraction.* Another set of extremes—on a second continuum—might be called the *relative degree of abstraction* or the *verbal-quantitative* continuum. Here the extremes are represented by, on the one hand, verbal descriptions of phenomena, variables, relationships, and theories. On the other hand are the extreme use of mathematical models and the language of mathematics to represent these same things.

Unfortunately, reconciliation of these extremes is difficult because of the investment that individual researchers have in their own particular language. One group might argue that mathematics is too wasteful of information and sacrifices the richness of data available on the verbal level for the perhaps dubious advantage of precision.

The mathematically-minded will argue, of course, that ordinary English or disciplinary jargon is too loose and *inexact* for any useful analytical purposes. The reconciliation of the people at the extremes is not easy. The great hope lies in people who are competent in both languages and who can translate from one into the other. Such people are being trained in small numbers through the efforts of various universities and foundations, but many more are needed.

3. *Purpose of the Researcher.* A third dimension, where reconciliation of the extremes may be a forlorn hope, at least in some areas, is represented by a continuum we might call *prescriptive . . . to . . . descriptive.* This is not the same sense in which descriptive is often used to connote verbal. Another set of words for this continuum, well known to economists, is *normative . . . to . . . positive.*

The issue here is whether the researcher is primarily interested in stating "theories" or principles which are *prescriptive,* in the sense that they tell people how they *should* behave, or whether he is primarily interested in stating theories that are *descriptive*—merely describing how people *do,* in fact, behave, and leaving it up to the consumer of his theories to make inferences about how he *ought* to behave.

In physical science, this dimension poses little difficulty, since the criteria for theory are clear—does your theory predict actual behavior and can it be tested in a generally accepted, systematic way by any competent researcher? Physicists and chemists do make statements that appear prescriptive or normative, but they are only superficially so. Such a statement, if made properly, will have the form: "You should behave in such-and-such a way because, if you do, these will be the consequences, and they can be demonstrated empirically or experimentally."

This is in sharp contrast with the normative and prescriptive statements which are frequently encountered in the behavioral area. Many of them have the actual form: "You should behave in such-and-such a way because

I tell you to and I know because of my superior experience or reasoning power."

4. *Level of Phenomena.* A fourth dimension, and one that is much less controversial and emotionally charged, might be called a *taste* continuum. It describes the variation in tastes of researchers for the specific *level* of phenomena which they choose to study. Quite often this choice stems from deep conviction that the level chosen is the only *proper* one for an understanding of organizational behavior, but there is no good evidence yet to support such a contention by any group of partisans along this continuum. This is the continuum that unites, rather loosely, so many different disciplines in the study of organizational behavior. It ranges from the detailed study of individual behavior, or even further, the study of the *individual roles* taken by an individual in an organization, through *small face-to-face groups, larger aggregates* that are major parts of an organization, *whole organizations* such as business firms or hospitals, *classes of organizations* such as labor unions, studies of *national societies as wholes,* and, finally, into *international relations.*

People studying all of these levels have already made and continue to make contributions to organization theory, according to the criterion stated above. The fond hope of many of them is that a full understanding of behavior at their level—the individual or the group or the whole organization—will lead to answers at all other levels.

These, of course, have been arbitrarily chosen categories or dimensions. Alternative methods of slicing the field may be equally useful in helping to prognosticate about the future of research in this field and for purposes of overall research strategy.

REFERENCES

1. MARCH, JAMES G., AND SIMON, HERBERT A. *Organizations.* New York: John Wiley and Sons, 1958.
2. RUBENSTEIN, ALBERT H. "A Program of Research on the Research and Development Process." *IEEE Transactions on Engineering Management.* Vol. EM 11, No. 3, September, 1964, pp. 103–112.
3. SCHWAB, JOSEPH J. "What Do Scientists Do?" *Behavioral Science,* Vol. 5, No. 1, January, 1960. pp. 1–27.

1. EMPIRICISM IN LATTER-DAY BEHAVIORAL SCIENCE*[1]

V. Edwin Bixenstine

The mood of behavioral science today is sometimes difficult to assess. There is a rising flow of research, as reported in journals, at regional and national meetings, and at a growing number of invitational conferences. We can only be impressed by the energy and the enthusiasm evinced by the participants. A great deal is being done.

On the other hand, there is an undercurrent of perplexity and doubt. While more persons register at our conventions than ever before, attendance at section meetings for the presentation of papers is embarrassingly thin, and little serious attention is given to the research reported. It is a safe bet that there is now a high inverse relationship between mass of reported works and the attention each receives.

There is a general feeling that we behavioral scientists have less confidence today about our grasp of the field than we had 20 years ago. A reviewer recently commented that the days of the grand theory, à la C. L. Hull or E. C. Tolman, are gone. We now bite off small chunks in specialized areas. Some groupings of behavioral scientists are characterized by inability or lack of desire to communicate with any but the insiders. Sometimes these groupings are established as a result of exclusion; for example, J. B. Rhine and his extrasensory perception group inaugurated a journal because editors refused to publish their work. On the other hand, B. F. Skinner's journal has the mark of aristocracy; it is a product of selective inbreeding.

If our work is often unattractive to all but a few of us, we find little to console us in the recurrently critical judgment of the laity. Public acceptance is far from crucial as regards the intrinsic merit of a research project. On the other hand, can we be sure that lack of lay enthusiasm for projects dear to the hearts of behavioral scientists is always a function of lack of public understanding? Might it be that we have psychic investments in our topics and methods quite different from the need to know, understand, and relate? I think that we do.

Events conspire today to impel the scientist into certain forms of research activity. We have had so few "breakthroughs" in behavioral science that we no longer approach research with the faint but uplifting

* Reprinted from *Science*, Vol. 145, July 31, 1964, pp. 464–67.

[1] This article is adapted from an address delivered in December, 1963, before the psychology colloquium at Kent State University, Kent, Ohio. The author is associate professor in the department of psychology, Kent State University.

hope that *this* time an important, vital insight will result. Number of published works has more to do with status than the importance of the work has. Journal editors have gradually altered their publication policy: reports must be brief, nontheoretical, and on empirical research that is simple both in design and results. Monetary support from granting agencies is likely to go to someone with a "program." This sounds fine, since it encourages systematic development of an inquiry, but inevitably it also means investing in certain kinds of apparatus and in certain procedural and methodological tools which tend to fix the approach and reduce receptivity to new possibilities. No one receives support who says, in effect, I will study X, using procedures a, b, or c, and if my interest in X wanes, I will study Z, using procedures d, e, or f.

The value placed on publication, the editorial policies of journals, and the impact of granting institutions converge in effecting what I call "production-line research." This is research which revolves around a gimmick—a fixed procedural tool or method with which the researcher produces a series of studies, using first one set of variables and then another, systematically plotting some "behavioral space" as defined by the operational coordinates used.

THE SPECIAL IMPACT OF SKINNER

Woven through these developments in the practice of our science is a complementary philosophy and rationale. Disturbed as some of us may be about the way behavioral science is practiced, what is more disturbing is the fact that many others approve, and often talk as if we were approaching the ideal practice of our science. I believe this remarkable complacency can be traced largely to the impact of B. F. Skinner. I suspect that Skinner will emerge historically as one of the most influential behavioral scientists of the mid-20th century. His writings are clear, scholarly, persuasive. He has, as a teacher, great capacity to inspire a loyal following. Add to these attributes the fact that he is a paradox—a man whose preachments are at variance with his practices—and one begins to appreciate the reasons for the kinetic tension he generates in our field.

Let us examine Skinner the paradox. First we note that he *advocates* a "nose-first" style of research. "So far as I can see," he reflects, "I began simply by looking for lawful processes in the behavior of the intact organism" (**5**, p. 80). He proposes that certain unformalized principles actually operate in his, and in most, research. Let us call his first rule the "nose-following" principle: "When you run into something interesting, drop everything else and study it" (**5**, p. 81). Other principles Skinner proceeds to unveil are really subordinate to the first. They are, "Some ways of doing research are easier than others" (**5**, p. 82) (that is, there is no reason to depart from a line of least effort); "Some people are lucky" (**5**, p.

85) (have faith in nose-following); "Apparatuses sometimes break down" (5, p. 86) (there are all kinds of lucky accidents—another reason for relying on nose-following).

Conjecturing, conceptualizing, theorizing, in Skinner's view, are expendable if not harmful preoccupations. The scientist's job is to "smell out" the paths of order and lawfulness—he is obviously an explorer rather than a creator or inventor. Nature is most assuredly "out there," quite distinct from the nature of man the explorer. The model of science Skinner has in mind is clearly that of Newtonian physics. If recent post-Einsteinian developments in physics threaten older modes of thought for physicists, they are of no great moment to Skinner.

He sums up his evaluation of the place of theory as follows (5, p. 69):

Perhaps to do without theories altogether is a *tour de force* which is too much to expect as a general practice. Theories are fun. But it is possible that the most rapid progress toward an understanding of learning may be made by research which is not designed to test theories. An adequate impetus is supplied by the inclination to obtain data showing orderly changes characteristic of the learning process. An acceptable scientific program is to collect data of this sort and to relate them to manipulable variables, selected for study through a common sense exploration of the field.

The foregoing passage brings us face-to-face with the Skinner paradox. His preachment is: do not theorize; rather observe, explore, follow your nose. The admission of a measure of "common sense" need not constitute a contradiction. However, in practice Skinner's "common sense" is far from common! Skinner's own temperament is much more inventive than it is curious. He is startlingly creative in applying the conceptual elements of his—let's be frank—*theory* to a wide variety of issues, ranging from training pigeons in the guidance of missiles, to developing teaching machines, to constructing a model society! For Skinner, not to theorize means not to explicitly define concepts apart from the methods and procedures of one's researches. From one point of view this is excellent. The primary purpose of experimentation is to help us *think* and think *clearly* about our universe, often by providing us with a new vocabulary. It seems to me, however, that to say that thought must be expressed only in terms of experimental procedures is to impose an unnecessary restriction.

That Skinner has operated so effectively under this handicap is a tribute to his talent. I wish we were all as capable. We are not. It is unfortunately much easier to do what Skinner says we ought to do than what he does. I suspect this partially explains the ardor and number of Skinner converts: one can apply Skinner's preachments and thereby gain vicariously a sense of participation in Skinner's practices and accomplishments. Only a few, however, can successfully emulate the master as he really is. My belief is that, while we cannot all think with equal brilliance, we can all endeavor to think to the best of our abilities and with the greatest possible freedom from unnecessary fetters. I believe, further, that such unbridled thinking is desirable and scientifically heuristic, and that Skinner's position handicaps his followers in their exercise of thought.

THE NECESSITY OF THEORY

You may ask, but why think, speculate, and theorize rather than merely search, observe, and catalog? Let us examine the answers that occur to us.

1. *The nature of man*. Skinner notes that "theories are fun," and so they are. They are valuable because we enjoy them and invest our time and identities in them, and because our commitment to research is often a function of our need to remove our doubts regarding these investments. I believe it is human nature to construe, to constantly push understanding in advance of knowledge. Now, with regard to following your nose, our biologist friends tell us that, in the course of evolution, the olfactory sense was undoubtedly the first significant *distance* receptor. But man seems constitutionally averse to depending on his nose. Recent evidence suggests that most of his "smell brain" is not employed in analyzing smells at all; rather, it seems to be involved in complex emotional and dispositional states. Man will never be content with following his nose; he is wholly oriented toward the farthest possible extension of his perception. To theorize is the logical fulfilment of his nature. It is his true "sixth sense."

2. *Minimization of the trivial*. One stands irresolute before the infinite possibilities for scientific observation: where to begin, what to include or exclude, what methods to use, what elements to study, and so on. Skinner would depend on "common sense" to insure that one chooses the important over the trivial. Sidman (4), who shares Skinner's views, appears to be much less sure of "common sense." Sidman concludes a chapter entitled "The Scientific Importance of Experimental Data" by apologizing for wandering "far from the topic under consideration," then explains (4, p. 40):

I have discussed several types of data and several reasons for experimentation. The importance of data is usually judged on these bases, but I have tried (despite my undoubtedly apparent prejudices) to make the point that these bases are not in fact adequate foundations for judgment.

What, then, are we to substitute? Science is supposed to be an orderly logical process, not subject to the whims of prejudice and other human frailties of its participants. If science is to use the importance of data as a criterion for accepting or rejecting an experiment, it must have a set of impartial rules within which the scientist can operate when he has to make evaluations. Do such rules actually exist? The answer is no.

If I have led the student out on the end of a limb and left him to shift for himself, I have done so on purpose. For I cannot take him any further. Whether he likes it or not, he will be on that limb for the rest of his scientific lifetime.

So, we have left only the virtue of realism; for Sidman there just *is* no way to minimize the trivial—not even the way of "common sense." "The cumulative development of a science provides the only final answer to the importance of any particular data . . ." is his conclusion (2, p. 41). No doubt this fosters a kind of stoic optimism; after all, the future may prove the value of work entirely ignored by contemporaries. Conversely, a favorable contemporary evaluation in no way insures that a work will ultimately prevail. Clearly, this point of view is of great comfort to the "production-line" researcher. It enables him to persevere, grimly hopeful that the future will reach forth and touch him with greatness, transforming the trivial into the profound.

All research is a gamble, and we all hope for the "jackpot." Still, have we no better guide than a gambler's intuition—or "common sense"—regarding where we place our "bet"? I submit that it is an essential function of theory to help us do important, significant research to the greatest extent of which we are capable. We theorize in an effort to go beyond our present knowledge and to divine what we may of a distant future. True, the future alone will reveal what is important. But it behooves us to *preview* that ultimate revelation insofar as we can.

3. *Interdependency of theory and "accident."* Sidman and Skinner make much of the accident—the lucky happening. Some wit has declared that the first law of science is that anything which can go wrong *will* go wrong. To be sure there never seems to be a dearth of the accidental, especially of the wrong kind. Certain classes of accident are so commonly encountered that we have evolved elaborate mathematical procedures to help us discriminate between the accidental, in the sense of randomness, and the lawful. It appears, then, that accidents happen frequently and to everyone, so the point is *not* just that "some people are lucky," as Skinner facetiously puts it. Rather, it appears that some people have the perceptiveness to see something worthwhile in "lucky" accidents, while remaining unconcerned with the many irrelevant, "unlucky" accidents.

Take, for example, the accidental discovery of the X ray—quite similar to the equally accidental discovery of the radioactive nature of uranium. The story is familiar (2, 3): in 1896 Antoine Henri Becquerel laid a piece of uranium ore in a drawer containing an unexposed but sealed photographic plate and later was surprised to find a "picture" developed on the plate. Similarly, Wilhelm C. Roentgen a year earlier laid some barium platinocyanide crystals on a table near a vacuum tube which he had constructed. He turned on the current and noticed that those distant crystals were glowing! Like Becquerel, Roentgen knew that here was no accident. He proceeded with a number of experiments on the spot and concluded that the vacuum tube must radiate some kind of energy that was spanning the meter or so of space and penetrating glass, wood, metal, flesh, and other substances to cause a fluorescence in the barium platinocyanide.

Sidman holds (4, p. 10) that the investigator appreciates the importance of these fortunate accidents because he harbors no prior theoretical convictions to narrow his perceptions.

When a hypothesis-bound investigator, after carefully designing his apparatus and experimental procedure to answer a specific question, finds that his equipment has broken down in the midst of the investigation, he is likely to consider the experiment a failure. On the other hand, the simple-minded curiosity tester is likely to look closely at the data produced by the apparatus breakdown.

Here, perhaps, is the greatest virtue of the curiosity-testing school of experimentation. Those who have no hypothesis or who hold their hypothesis lightly are likely to be alert to the accidental discovery of new phenomena.

Was it because Becquerel and Roentgen had no hypotheses cluttering up their sensoriums that they so quickly apprehended the significance of their accidents? Michael Faraday, as early as 1822, was working on the thesis that light was electromagnetic in character, and by 1864 James C. Maxwell had expressed this idea in mathematical form. Faraday had talked of "rays," and Roentgen immediately called his phenomenon "X rays." Becquerel was also fully aware of the electromagnetic theory of light. These men can hardly be said to have been without hypothesis, theory, preconception. It was *because* of their concern with the Faraday-Maxwell hypothesis of a basic energy form—a hypothesis which reached fruition in 1905 with the work of Albert Einstein—that they quickly grasped the meaning of these "accidents."

It is curious that it is psychologists who would so misapply certain concepts basic to the psychology of perception. To be sure, a theory or hypothesis functions as a "set," and *wrong* sets can lead to false perception. But no perception psychologist advocates the eradication of sets in the interest of achieving freedom from misperceptions. The most unexceptional percept is really an integral mixture of expectancy formed, perhaps, mere moments previously and the always partial, incomplete, and momentary data of the senses. Furthermore, without expectancy or set at this elementary level, no perception would develop. In instances where congenitally sightless individuals achieve vision, they are at first, except for a crude response to differentials of illumination and color, functionally blind. As far as vision is concerned, they have yet to learn what follows what, or to form the elementary sets and expectancies through which the disparate, variable, often chaotic flow of visual sense data is integrated into perceptions.

I submit that there is no antagonism between hypothesis and "accident." On the contrary, it is those events which upend expectancy or which appear to confirm our hypotheses in *unexpected* ways which command our attention. Surely, an investigator without hypothesis would fail to be moved at all by such events. There is an epistemological dilemma at the heart of the rule of empiricism in science. The empiricist's mistrust of reason often takes the form of a constant attempt to reduce everything into elements of the "basic sense data." His guiding conviction is that verifiable or true knowledge resides in the raw quantum of sensation. But this is patently nonsensical. Such a reduction would render us as unknowing as the newly sighted person is unseeing! I doubt that there is any serious danger today of a renaissance of seventeenth-century rationalism. But we may be discovering that radical empiricism swings too far in another direction. Neither reason nor the senses alone provide a meaningful body of knowledge. Science is reason tempered by observation, and observation impregnated by thought; it is an orderly construction fitted to the world of the senses, an experiential search for a world of order.

SUMMARY AND CONCLUSION

Let me recapitulate. I am not happy with developments in the behavioral sciences. I wonder whether science does actually stand divorced from the intention, motive, and character of the scientist. I suspect that some of our current philosophies in science, whether so conceived or not, encourage and abet a science of the trivial. I believe we should recognize that, as epistemology, the empirical rule cannot stand alone. The great advances in science are associated with its grand conceptions even more than with its discoveries.

We often mistakenly assume that the rule of objectivity has traditionally divided the character of science from that of the scientist. This is far from true. The objectivity of eighteenth- and nineteenth-century science was believed to be a function not so much of methodology and procedure as of the honesty and integrity of the scientist. Michael Faraday had this to say about the matter (2, p. 233):

It puzzles me greatly to know what makes the successful philosopher [scientist]. Is it industry and perseverance, with a moderate proportion of good sense and intelligence? Is not a modest assurance or earnestness a requisite? Do not many fail because they look rather to the renown to be acquired than to the pure acquisition of knowledge, and the delight which the contented mind has in acquiring it for its own sake? I am sure I have seen many who would have been good and successful pursuers of science, and have gained themselves a high name, but that it was the name and the reward they were always looking forward to—the reward of the world's praise. In such there is always a shade of envy or regret over their minds, and I cannot imagine a man making discoveries in science under these feelings. As to Genius and its Power, there may be cases; I suppose there are. I have looked long and often for a genius for our own laboratory, but I have never found one. But I have seen many who would, I think, if they submitted themselves to a sound self-applied discipline of mind, have become successful experimental philosophers.

Are these issues native only to behavioral science? Earlier, I laid at Skinner's door much of the blame for an unreasonable complacency regarding the disposition of modern behavioral science. In all fairness to Skinner, however, it is only correct to acknowledge that the same problem is evident in other areas of science. Skinner appears to be a spokesman, in the behavioral sciences, for one of those famous "Zeitgeists." Let me quote a series of observations by Paul Weiss, a biologist at the Rockefeller Institute, New York City, from a paper entitled "Experience and Experiment in Biology" (7):

> Without imagination one can contrive infinite variations of experimental set-ups, all of them novel, yet utterly uninteresting, inconsequential, insignificant. The mere fact that something has not been done or tried before is not sufficient reason for doing or trying it. . . .
> But is not scientific history full of instances of accidental discovery of the unexpected? True again, but he who does expect something will be on the alert even for the unexpected, while he who just ambles, looking for nothing in particular, is prone to miss even the obvious. . . .
> We see instruments turning from servants into tyrants, forcing the captive scientist to mass-produce and market senseless data beyond the point of conceivable usefulness—a modern version of the Sorcerer's Apprentice. . . .

Finally, I recommend study of N. W. Storer's article "The Coming Changes in American Science" (6). Storer, a sociologist at Harvard University, feels that prior to 1940 the basic currency in science was professional recognition.

This in turn reinforced certain fundamental values—a high emphasis on communication; dedication of the individual and a tendency to work in small, select groups; a spurning of worldly gain and a proclivity for *basic* research. Today, professional recognition is being replaced by more common currencies—money, power, and worldly prestige. The result is a shift of values in science: numbers are no longer small or groups select; communication and professional recognition are viewed as means to gain money, power, and prestige rather than as ends in themselves; basic research is giving way to a kind of impostor with a thinly disguised commercial goal.

I do not know how to resolve the issues in modern science. It seems to me we may be troubled by the embarrassments of too much success. Will we continue to succeed if we do not change our ways? Maybe, but not as magnificently I am sure as we could if we did change them. We cannot do anything about our numbers—nor would I want us to forswear all worldly possessions. We *can* examine critically and revise certain of our guiding philosophies. We can follow a suggestion of P. H. Abelson (1) and alter granting procedures so that institutions, as well as individuals, are given support. In the end, however, the major force for change resides in the minds and hearts of scientists who share a concern about science.

REFERENCES

1. ABELSON, P. H. *Science,* Vol. 142 (1963), p. 453.
2. GINZBURG, B. *The Adventure of Science.* New York: Simon & Schuster, 1930.
3. POSIN, D. Q. *Dr. Posin's Giants: Men of Science.* Evanston, Ill.: Row Peterson, 1961.
4. SIDMAN, M. *Tactics of Scientific Research.* New York: Basic Books, 1960.
5. SKINNER, B. F. *Science and Human Behavior.* New York: Macmillan Co., 1953.
6. STORER, N. W. *Science,* Vol. 142 (1963), p. 464.
7. WEISS, P. *Science,* Vol. 136 (1962), p. 468.

2. BRINGING MEN BACK IN*[0]

George C. Homans

> A theory of a phenomenon is an explanation of it, showing how it
> follows as a conclusion from general propositions in a deductive system.
> With all its empirical achievements, the functional school never produced
> a theory that was also an explanation, since from its general propositions
> about the conditions of social equilibrium no definite conclusions could
> be drawn. When a serious effort is made, even by functionalists, to con-
> struct an explanatory theory, its general propositions turn out to be
> psychological—propositions about the behavior of men, not the equi-
> librium of societies.

I am going to talk about an issue we have worried over many times. I have
worried over it myself. But I make no excuses for taking it up again.
Although it is an old issue, it is still not a settled one, and I think it is the
most general intellectual issue in sociology. If I have only one chance to
speak ex cathedra, I cannot afford to say something innocuous. On the
contrary, now if ever is the time to be nocuous.

In the early nineteen-thirties a distinct school of sociological thought
was beginning to form. Its chief, though certainly not its only, intellectual
parents were Durkheim and Radcliffe-Brown. I call it a school, though not
all its adherents accepted just the same tenets; and many sociologists went
ahead and made great progress without giving a thought to it. The school
is usually called that of structural-functionalism, or functionalism for
short. For a whole generation it has been the dominant, indeed the only
distinct, school of sociological thought. I think it has run its course, done
its work, and now positively gets in the way of our understanding social
phenomena. And I propose to ask, Why?

THE INTERESTS OF FUNCTIONALISM

I begin by reminding you of the chief interests and assumptions of
functionalism, especially as contrasted with what it was not interested in
and took for granted, for the questions it did not ask have returned to
plague it. If what I say seems a caricature, remember that a caricature
emphasizes a person's most characteristic features.

First, the school took its start from the study of norms, the statements

---

* Reprinted from *American Sociological Review,* Vol. 20, December, 1964,
pp. 809–18.

[0] Presidential Address delivered at the annual meeting of the American Sociological Association in Montreal, September 2, 1964.

the members of a group make about how they ought to behave, and indeed often do behave, in various circumstances. It was especially interested in the cluster of norms called a role and in the cluster of roles called an institution. It never tired of asserting that its concern was with institutionalized behavior, and that the unit of social analysis was not the acting individual but the role. The school did not ask why there should be roles at all.

Second, the school was empirically interested in the interrelations of roles, the interrelations of institutions: this was the structural side of its work. It was the sort of thing the social anthropologists had been doing, showing how the institutions of a primitive society fitted together; and the sociologists extended the effort to advanced societies. They would point out, for instance, that the nuclear family rather than some form of extended kinship was characteristic of industrialized societies. But they were more interested in establishing *what* the interrelations of institutions were than in *why* they were so. In the beginning the analyses tended to be static, as it is more convincing to speak of a social structure in a society conceived to be stable than in one undergoing rapid change. Recently the school has turned to the study of social change, but in so doing it has had to take up the question it disregarded earlier. If an institution is changing, one can hardly avoid asking why it is changing in one direction rather than another.

Third, the school was, to put it crudely, more interested in the consequences than in the causes of an institution, particularly in the consequences for a social system considered as a whole. These consequences were the *functions* of the institution. Thus the members of the school never tired of pointing out the functions and dysfunctions of a status system, without asking why a status system should exist in the first place, why it was there to have functions. They were especially interested in showing how its institutions helped maintain a society in equilibrium, as a going concern. The model for research was Durkheim's effort to show, in *The Elementary Forms of the Religious Life*, how the religion of a primitive tribe helped hold the tribe together.

Such were the empirical interests of functionalism. As empirically I have been a functionalist myself, I shall be the last to quarrel with them. It is certainly one of the jobs of a sociologist to discover what the norms of a society are. Though a role is not actual behavior, it is for some purposes a useful simplification. Institutions *are* interrelated, and it is certainly one of the jobs of a sociologist to show what the interrelations are. Institutions do have consequences, in the sense that, if one institution may be taken as given, the other kinds of institution that may exist in the society are probably not infinite in number. It is certainly one of the jobs of a sociologist to search out these consequences and even, though this is more difficult, to determine whether their consequences are good or bad for the society as a whole. At any rate, the empirical interests of functionalism have led to an enormous amount of good work. Think only of the studies made by Murdock[1] and others on the cross-cultural interrelations of institutions.

As it began to crystallize, the functional school developed theoretical interests as well as empirical ones. There was no necessity for the two to go together, and the British social anthropologists remained relatively untheoretical. Not so the American sociologists, particularly Talcott Parsons, who claimed that they were not only theorists but something called general theorists, and strongly emphasized the importance of theory.

Theirs was to be, moreover, a certain kind of theory. They were students of Durkheim and took seriously his famous definition of *social facts:* "Since their essential characteristic consists in the power they possess of exerting, from outside, a pressure on individual consciousnesses, they do not derive from individual consciousnesses, and in consequence sociology is not a corollary of psycholgy."[2] Since Durkheim was a great man, one can find statements in his writings that have quite other implications, but this caricature of himself was the one that made the difference. If not in what they said, then surely in what they did, the functionalists took Durkheim seriously. Their fundamental unit, the role, was a social fact in Durkheim's sense. And their theoretical program assumed, as he did, that sociology should be an independent science, in the sense that its propositions should not be derivable from some other social science, such as psychology. This meant, in effect, that the general propositions of sociology were not to be propositions about the behavior of "individual consciousnesses"—or, as I should say, about men—but propositions about the characteristics of societies or other social groups as such.

Where functionalism failed was not in its empirical interests but, curiously, in what it most prided itself on, its general theory. Let me be very careful here. In a recent presidential address, Kingsley Davis asserted that we are all functionalists now,[3] and there is a sense in which he was quite right. But note that he was talking about functional *analysis.* One carries out functional analysis when, starting from the existence of a particular institution, one tries to find out what difference the institution makes to the other aspects of social structure. That is, one carries out the empirical program of functionalism. Since we have all learned to carry out functional analyses, we are in this sense all functionalists now. But functional analysis, as a method, is not the same thing as functional theory.

---

[1] George P. Murdock, *Social Structure* (New York: Macmillan Co., 1949).

[2] Émile Durkheim, *Les règles de la méthode sociologique* (8th ed., Paris: Alcan, 1927), pp. 124–25.

[3] "The Myth of Functional Analysis as a Special Method in Sociology and Anthropology," *American Sociological Review,* 24 (December, 1959), pp. 757–73.

And if we are all functional analysts, we are certainly not all functional theorists. Count me out, for one.

The only inescapable office of theory is to explain. The theory of evolution is an explanation why and how evolution occurs. To look for the consequences of institutions or to show the interrelationships of institutions is not the same thing as explaining why the interrelationships are what they are. The question is a practical and not a philosophical one—not whether it is legitimate to take the role as the fundamental unit, nor whether institutions are really real, but whether the theoretical program of functionalism has in fact led to explanations of social phenomena, including the findings of functional analysis itself. Nor is the question whether functionalism might not do so, but whether it has done so as of today. I think it has not.

THE NATURE OF THEORY

With all their talk about theory, the functionalists never—and I speak advisedly—succeeded in making clear what a theory was. It must be allowed in their excuse that, in the early days, the philosophers of science had not given as clear an answer to the question as they have now.[4] But even then, the functionalists could have done better than they did, and certainly the excuse is valid no longer. Today we should stop talking to our students about sociological theory until we have taught them what a theory is.

A theory of a phenomenon consists of a series of propositions, each stating a relationship between properties of nature. But not every kind of sentence qualifies as such a proposition. The propositions do not consist of definitions of the properties: the construction of a conceptual scheme is an indispensable part of theoretical work but is not itself theory. Nor may a proposition simply say that there is some relationship between the properties. Instead, if there is some change in one of the properties, it must at least begin to specify what the change in the other property will be. If one of the properties is absent, the other will also be absent; or if one of the properties increases in value, the other will too. The properties, the variables, may be probabilities.

Accordingly, to take a famous example, Marx's statement that the economic organization of a society determines the nature of its other institutions is an immensely useful guide to research. For it says: "Look for the social consequences of economic change, and if you look, you will surely find them!" But it is not the sort of proposition that can enter a theory. For by itself it says only that, if the economic infrastructure

---

[4] See especially R. B. Braithwaite, *Scientific Explanation* (Cambridge: Cambridge University Press, 1953).

changes, there will be some change in the social superstructure, without beginning to suggest what the latter change will be. Most of the sentences of sociology, alleged to be theoretical, resemble this one of Marx's, yet few of our theorists realize it. And while we are always asking that theory guide research, we forget that many statements like Marx's are good guides to research without being good theory.

To constitute a theory, the propositions must take the form of a deductive system. One of them, usually called the lowest-order proposition, is the proposition to be explained, for example, the proposition that the more thoroughly a society is industrialized, the more fully its kinship organization tends towards the nuclear family. The other propositions are either general propositions or statements of particular given conditions. The general propositions are so called because they enter into other, perhaps many other, deductive systems besides the one in question. Indeed, what we often call a theory is a cluster of deductive systems, sharing the same general propositions but having different *explicanda*. The crucial requirement is that each system shall be deductive. That is, the lowest-order proposition follows as a logical conclusion from the general propositions under the specified given conditions. The reason why statements like Marx's may not enter theories is that no definite conclusions may in logic be drawn from them. When the lowest-order proposition does follow logically, it is said to be explained. The explanation of a phenomenon is the theory of the phenomenon. A theory is nothing—it is not a theory—unless it is an explanation.

One may define properties and categories, and one still has no theory. One may state that there *are* relations between the properties, and one still has no theory. One may state that a change in one property will produce a definite change in another property, and one still has no theory. Not until one has properties, and propositions stating the relations between them, and the propositions form a deductive system—not until one has all three does one have a theory. Most of our arguments about theory would fall to the ground, if we first asked whether we had a theory to argue about.

FUNCTIONAL THEORIES

As a theoretical effort, functionalism never came near meeting these conditions. Even if the functionalists had seriously tried to meet them, which they did not, I think they would still have failed. The difficulty lay in the characteristic general propositions of functionalism. A proposition is not functional just because it uses the word *function*. To say that a certain institution is functional for individual men in the sense of meeting their needs is not a characteristic proposition of functionalism. Instead it belongs to the class of psychological propositions. Nor is the statement that one institution is a function of another, in the quasi-mathematical sense of function, characteristic. Though many functional theorists make such statements, non-functionalists like myself may also make them without a qualm. The characteristic general propositions of functional theory in sociology take the form: "If it is to survive, or remain in equilibrium, a social system—any social system—must possess institutions of Type X." For instance, if it is to survive or remain in equilibrium, a society must possess conflict-resolving institutions. By general propositions of this sort the functionalists sought to meet Durkheim's demand for a truly independent sociological theory.

The problem was, and is, to construct deductive systems headed by such propositions. Take first the terms *equilibrium* and *survival*. If the theorist chose *equilibrium*, he was able to provide no criterion of social equilibrium, especially "dynamic" or "moving" equilibrium, definite enough to allow anything specific to be deduced in logic from a proposition employing the term. I shall give an example later. When indeed was a society not in equilibrium? If the theorist chose *survival*, he found this, too, surprisingly hard to define. Did Scotland, for instance, survive as a society? Though it had long been united with England, it still possessed distinctive institutions, legal and religious. If the theorist took *survival* in the strong sense, and said that a society had not survived if all its members had died without issue, he was still in trouble. As far as the records went, the very few societies of this sort had possessed institutions of all the types the functionalists said were necessary for survival. The evidence put in question, to say the least, the empirical truth of the functionalist propositions. Of course the functionalists were at liberty to say, "If a society is to survive, its members must not all be shot dead," which was true as true could be but allowed little to be deduced about the social characteristics of surviving societies.

Indeed the same was true of the other functional propositions. Even if a statement like "If it is to survive, a society must possess conflict-resolving institutions" were accepted as testable and true, it possessed little explanatory power. From the proposition the fact could be deduced that, given a certain society did survive, it did possess conflict-resolving institutions of some kind, and the fact was thus explained. What remained unexplained was why the society had conflict-resolving institutions of a particular kind, why, for instance, the jury was an ancient feature of Anglo-Saxon legal institutions. I take it that what sociology has to explain are the actual features of actual societies and not just the generalized features of a generalized society.

I do not think that members of the functional school could have set up, starting with general propositions of their distinctive type, theories that were also deductive systems. More important, they did not. Recognizing, perhaps, that they were blocked in one direction, some of them elaborated what they called theory in another. They used what they asserted were a limited and exhaustive number of functional problems faced by any society to generate a complex set of categories in terms of which social structure could be analyzed. That is, they set up a conceptual scheme. But analysis is not explanation, and a conceptual scheme is not a theory. They did not fail to make statements about the relations between the categories, but most of the statements resembled the one of Marx's I cited earlier: they were not of the type that enter deductive systems. From their lower-order propositions, as from their higher-order ones, no definite conclusions in logic could be drawn. Under these conditions, there was no way of telling whether their choice of functional problems and categories was not wholly arbitrary. What the functionalists actually produced was not a theory but a new language for describing social structure, one among many possible languages; and much of the work they called theoretical consisted in showing how the words in other languages, including that of everyday life, could be translated into theirs. They would say, for instance, that what other people called making a living was called in their language goal-attainment. But what makes a theory is deduction, not translation.

I have said that the question is not whether, in general, functional theories can be real theories, for there are sciences that possess real functional theories. The question is rather whether this particular effort was successful. If a theory is an explanation, the functionalists in sociology were, on the evidence, not successful. Perhaps they could not have been successful; at any rate they were not. The trouble with their theory was not that it was wrong, but that it was not a theory.

AN ALTERNATIVE THEORY

Here endeth the destructive part of the lesson. I shall now try to show that a more successful effort to explain social phenomena entails the construction of theories different from functional ones, in the sense that their general propositions are of a different kind, precisely the kind, indeed, that the functionalists tried to get away from. I shall try to show this for the very phenomena the functionalists took for granted and the very relations they discovered empirically. I shall even try to show that, when functionalists took the job of explanation seriously, which they sometimes did, this other kind of theory would appear unacknowledged in their own work.

The functionalists insisted over and over again that the minimum unit of social analysis was the role, which is a cluster of norms. In a recent article, James Coleman has written: ". . . sociologists have characteristically taken as their starting-point a social system in which norms exist, and individuals are largely governed by these norms. Such a strategy views norms as the governors of social behavior, and thus neatly bypasses the difficult problem that Hobbes posed."[5] Hobbes's problem is, of course, why there is not a war of all against all.

Why, in short, should there be norms at all? The answer Coleman gives is that, in the kind of case he considers, norms arise through the actions of men rationally calculating to further their own self-interest in a context of other men acting in the same way. He writes: "The central postulate about behavior is this: each actor will attempt to extend his power over those actions in which he has most interest." Starting from this postulate, Coleman constructs a deductive system explaining why the actors adopt a particular sort of norm in the given circumstances.

I do not want to argue the vexed question of rationality. I do want to point out what sort of general proposition Coleman starts with. As he recognizes, it is much like the central assumption of economics, though self-interest is not limited to the material interests usually considered by economists. It also resembles a proposition of psychology, though here it might take the form: the more valuable the reward of an activity, the more likely a man is to perform the activity. But it certainly is not a characteristic functional proposition in sociology: it is not a statement about the conditions of equilibrium for a society, but a statement about the behavior of individual men.

Again, if there are norms, why do men conform to them? Let us lay aside the fact that many men do not conform or conform very indifferently, and assume that they all do so. Why do they do so? So far as the functionalists gave any answer to the question, it was that men have "internalized" the values embodied in the norm. But "internalization" is a word and not an explanation. So far as their own theory was concerned, the functionalists took conformity to norms for granted. They made the mistake Malinowski pointed out long ago in a book now too little read by sociologists, the mistake made by early writers on primitive societies, the mistake of assuming that conformity to norms is a matter of ". . . this automatic acquiescence, this instinctive submission of every member of the tribe to its laws. . . ."[6] The alternative answer Malinowski gave was that obedience to norms "is usually rewarded according to the measure of its perfection, while noncompliance is visited upon the remiss agent."[7] In short, the answer he gave is much like that of Coleman and the psychologists. Later he added the suggestive remark: "The true problem is not to study how human life submits to rules—it simply does not; the real problem is how the rules become adapted to life."[8]

---

[5] James S. Coleman, "Collective Decisions," *Sociological Inquiry*, Vol. 34 (1964), pp. 166–81.

[6] Bronislaw Malinowski, *Crime and Custom in Savage Society* (Paterson, N.J.: Littlefield, Adams, 1959), p. 11.

[7] *Ibid.*, p. 12.

[8] *Ibid.*, p. 127.

The question remains why members of a particular society find certain of the results of their actions rewarding and not others, especially when some of the results seem far from "naturally" rewarding. This is the real problem of the "internalization" of values. The explanation is given not by any distinctively sociological propositions but by the propositions of learning theory in psychology.

The functionalists were much interested in the interrelations of institutions, and it was one of the glories of the school to have pointed out many such interrelations. But the job of a science does not end with pointing out interrelations; it must try to explain why they are what they are. Take the statement that the kinship organization of industrialized societies tends to be that of the nuclear family. I cannot give anything like the full explanation, but I can, and you can too, suggest the beginning of one. Some men organized factories because by so doing they thought they could get greater material rewards than they could get otherwise. Other men entered factories for reasons of the same sort. In so doing they worked away from home and so had to forgo, if only for lack of time, the cultivation of the extended kinship ties that were a source of reward, because a source of help, in many traditional agricultural societies, where work lay closer to home. Accordingly the nuclear family tended to become associated with factory organization; and the explanation for the association is provided by propositions about the behavior of men as such. Not the needs of society explain the relationship, but the needs of men.

Again, functionalists were interested in the consequences of institutions, especially their consequences for a social system as a whole. For instance, they were endlessly concerned with the functions and dysfunctions of status systems. Seldom did they ask why there should be status systems in the first place. Some theorists have taken the emergence of phenomena like status systems as evidence for Durkheim's contention that sociology was not reducible to psychology. What is important is not the fact of emergence but the question how the emergence is to be explained. One of the accomplishments of small-group research is to explain how a status system, of course on a small scale, emerges in the course of interaction between the members of a group.[9] The explanation is provided by psychological propositions. Certainly no functional propositions are needed. Indeed the theoretical contribution of small-group research has consisted "in showing how the kinds of microscopic variables usually ignored by sociologists can explain the kinds of social situations usually ignored by psychologists."[10]

---

[9] See George C. Homans, *Social Behavior: Its Elementary Forms* (New York: Harcourt, Brace & World, 1961), esp. chap. 8.

[10] C. N. Alexander, Jr., and R. L. Simpson, "Balance Theory and Distributive Justice," *Sociological Inquiry*, 34 (1964), pp. 182–92.

What is the lesson of all this? If the very things functionalists take for granted, like norms, if the very interrelationships they empirically discover can be explained by deductive systems that employ psychological propositions, then it must be that the general explanatory principles even of sociology are not sociological, as the functionalists would have them be, but psychological, propositions about the behavior of men, not about the behavior of societies. On the analogy with other sciences, this argument by itself would not undermine the validity of a functional theory. Thermodynamics, for instance, states propositions about aggregates, which are themselves true and general, even though they can be explained in turn, in statistical mechanics, by propositions about members of the aggregates. The question is whether this kind of situation actually obtains in sociology. So far as functional propositions are concerned, which are propositions about social aggregates, the situation does not obtain, for they have not been shown to be true and general.

EXPLAINING SOCIAL CHANGE

My next contention is that even confessed functionalists, when they seriously try to explain certain kinds of social phenomena, in fact use nonfunctional explanations without recognizing that they do so. This is particularly clear in their studies of social change.

Social change provides a searching test for theory, since historical records are a prerequisite for its study. Without history, the social scientist can establish the contemporaneous interrelations of institutions, but may be hard put to it to explain why the interrelations should be what they are. With historical records he may have the information needed to support an explanation. One of the commonest charges against the functionalist school was that it could not deal with social change, that its analysis was static. In recent years some functionalists have undertaken to show that the charge was unjustified. They have chosen for their demonstration the process of differentiation in society, the process, for instance, of the increasing specialization of occupations. In question as usual is not the fact of differentiation—there is no doubt that the overall trend of social history has been in this direction—but how the process is to be explained.

A particularly good example of this new development in functionalism is Neil Smelser's book, *Social Change in the Industrial Revolution: An Application of Theory to the British Cotton Industry 1770–1840.*[11] The book is not just good for my purposes: it is good, very good, in itself. It provides an enormous amount of well organized information, and it goes far to explain the changes that occurred. The amusing thing about it is that

---

[11] Chicago: University of Chicago Press, 1959.

the explanation Smelser actually uses, good scientist that he is, to account for the changes is not the functional theory he starts out with, which is as usual a non-theory, but a different kind of theory and a better one.

Smelser begins like any true functionalist. For him a social system is one kind of system of action, characterized as follows: "A social system . . . is composed of a set of interrelated roles, collectivities, etc. . . . It is important to remember that the roles, collectivities, etc., not individuals, are the units in this last case." Moreover, "all systems of action are governed by the principle of equilibrium. According to the dominant type of equilibrium, the adjustments proceed in a certain direction: if the equilibrium is stable, the units tend to return to their original position; if the equilibrium is partial, only some of the units need to adjust; if the equilibrium is unstable, the tendency is to change, through mutual adjustment, to a new equilibrium or to disintegrate altogether." Finally, "all social systems are subject to four functional exigencies which must be met more or less satisfactorily if the system is to remain in equilibrium."[12] Note that by this argument all social systems are in equilibrium, even systems in process of disintegration. Though the latter are in unstable equilibrium, they are still in equilibrium. Accordingly they are meeting more or less satisfactorily the four functional exigencies. You see how useful a deductive system can be in social science? More seriously you will see that definitions of equilibrium are so broad that you may draw any conclusion you like from them.

But for all the explanatory use Smelser makes of it, this theory and its subsequent elaboration is so much window dressing. When he really gets down to explaining the innovations in the British cotton textile industry, especially the introduction of spinning and weaving machinery, he forgets his functionalism. The guts of his actual explanation lie in the seven steps through which he says the process proceeds:

Industrial differentiation proceeds, therefore, by the following steps:
   (1) Dissatisfaction with the productive achievements of the industry or its relevant sub-sectors and a sense of opportunity in terms of the potential availability of adequate facilities to reach a higher level of productivity.
   (2) Appropriate symptoms of disturbance in the form of "unjustified" negative emotional reactions and "unrealistic" aspirations on the part of various elements of the population.[13]

I shall not give the other five steps, as I should make the same criticism of them as I now make of the first two. I think they provide by implication a good explanation of the innovations of the Industrial Revolution in cotton manufacturing. But what kind of an explanation is it? Whatever it is, it is not a functional one. Where here do roles appear as the fundamental

   [12] *Ibid.*, pp. 10–11.
   [13] *Ibid.*, p. 29.

units of a social system? Where are the four functional exigencies? Not a word do we hear of them. Instead, what do we hear of? We hear of dissatisfaction, a sense of opportunity, emotional reactions, and aspirations. And what feels these things? Is a role dissatisfied or emotional? No; Smelser himself says it is "various elements of the population" that do so. Under relentless pressure let us finally confess that "various elements of the population" means men. And what men? For the most part men engaged in making and selling cotton cloth. And what are they dissatisfied with? Not with "the productive achievements of the industry." Though some states-men were certainly concerned about the contribution made by the industry as a whole to the wealth of Great Britain, let us, again under relentless pressure, confess that most of the men in question were con-cerned with their own profits. Let us get men back in, and let us put some blood in them. Smelser himself makes the crucial statement: "In Lancashire in the early 1760's there was excited speculation about instantaneous fortunes for the man lucky enough to stumble on the right invention."[14] In short, the men in question were activated by self-interest. Yet not all self-interests are selfish interests, and certainly not all the innovations of the Industrial Revolution can be attributed to selfishness.

Smelser's actual explanation of technical innovation in cotton manufac-turing might be sketched in the following deductive system. I have left out the most obvious steps.

1. Men are more likely to perform an activity, the more valuable they perceive the reward of that activity to be.

2. Men are more likely to perform an activity, the more successful they perceive the activity is likely to be in getting that reward.

3. The high demand for cotton textiles and the low productivity of labor led men concerned with cotton manufacturing to perceive the development of laborsaving machinery as rewarding in increased profits.

4. The existing state of technology led them to perceive the effort to develop laborsaving machinery as likely to be successful.

5. Therefore, by both (1) and (2) such men were highly likely to try to develop laborsaving machinery.

6. Since their perceptions of the technology were accurate, their efforts were likely to meet with success, and some of them did meet with success.

From these first steps, others such as the organization of factories and an increasing specialization of jobs followed. But no different kind of explana-tion is needed for these further developments: propositions like (1) and (2), which I call the *value* and the *success* propositions, would occur in

---

[14] *Ibid.*, p. 80.

them too. We should need a further proposition to describe the effect of frustration, which certainly attended some of the efforts at innovation, in creating the "negative emotional reactions" of Smelser's step 2.

I must insist again on the kind of explanation this is. It is an explanation using psychological propositions (1 and 2 above), psychological in that they are commonly stated and tested by psychologists and that they refer to the behavior of men and not to the conditions of equilibrium of societies or other social groups as such. They are general in that they appear in many, and I think in all, of the deductive systems that will even begin to explain social behavior. There is no assumption that the men in question are all alike in their concrete behavior. They may well have been conditioned to find different things rewarding, but the way conditioning takes place is itself explained by psychological propositions. There is no assumption that their values are all materialistic, but only that their pursuit of non-material values follows the same laws as their pursuit of material ones. There is no assumption that they are isolated or unsocial, but only that the laws of human behavior do not change just because another person rather than the physical environment provides the rewards for behavior. Nor is there any assumption that psychological propositions will explain everything social. We shall certainly not be able to explain everything, but our failures will be attributable to lack of factual information or the intellectual machinery for dealing with complexity—though the computers will help us here—and not to the propositions themselves. Nor is there any assumption here of psychological reductionism, though I used to think there was. For reduction implies that there are general sociological propositions that can then be reduced to psychological ones. I now suspect that there are no general sociological propositions, propositions that hold good of all societies or social groups as such, and that the only general propositions of sociology are in fact psychological.

What I do claim is that, no matter what we say our theories are, when we seriously try to explain social phenomena by constructing even the veriest sketches of deductive systems, we find ourselves in fact, and whether we admit it or not, using what I have called psychological explanations. I need hardly add that our actual explanations are our actual theories.

I am being a little unfair to functionalists like Smelser and Parsons if I imply that they did not realize there were people around. The so-called theory of action made a very good start indeed by taking as its paradigm for social behavior two persons, the actions of each of whom sanctioned, that is, rewarded or punished, the actions of the other.[15] But as soon as the start was made, its authors disregarded it. As the theory of action was

---

[15] Talcott Parsons and Edward Shils (eds.), *Toward a General Theory of Action* (Cambridge, Mass.: Harvard University Press, 1951), pp. 14–16.

applied to society, it appeared to have no actors and mighty little action. The reason was that it separated the personality system from the social system and proposed to deal with the latter alone. It was the personality system that had "needs, drives, skills, etc."[16] It was not part of the social system, but only conducted exchanges with it, by providing it, for instance, with disembodied motivation.[17] This is the kind of box you get into when you think of theory as a set of boxes. For this reason, no one should hold their style of writing against the functionalists. The best of writers must write clumsily when he has set up his intellectual problem in a clumsy way. If the theorist will only envisage his problem from the outset as one of constructing explanatory propositions and not a set of categories, he will come to see that the personal and the social are not to be kept separate. The actions of a man that we take to be evidence of his personality are not different from his actions that, together with the actions of others, make up a social system. They are the same identical actions. The theorist will realize this when he finds that the same set of general propositions, including the success and the value proposition mentioned above, are needed for explaining the phenomena of both personality and society.

CONCLUSION

If sociology is a science, it must take seriously one of the jobs of any science, which is that of providing explanations for the empirical relations it discovers. An explanation is a theory, and it takes the form of a deductive system. With all its talk about theory, the functionalist school did not take the job of theory seriously enough. It did not ask itself what a theory was, and it never produced a functional theory that was in fact an explanation. I am not sure that it could have done so, starting as it did with propositions about the conditions of social equilibrium, propositions from which no definite conclusions could be drawn in a deductive system. If a serious effort is made to construct theories that will even begin to explain social phenomena, it turns out that their general propositions are not about the equilibrium of societies but about the behavior of men. This is true even of some good functionalists, though they will not admit it. They keep psychological explanations under the table and bring them out furtively like a bottle of whiskey, for use when they really need help. What I ask is that we bring what we say about theory into line with what we actually do, and so put an end to our intellectual hypocrisy. It would unite us with the other social sciences, whose actual theories are much like our actual ones, and so strengthen us all. Let us do so also for the sake of our students.

---

[16] Smelser, *op. cit.*, p. 10.

[17] *Ibid.*, p. 33.

I sometimes think that they begin with more understanding of the real nature of social phenomena than we leave them with, and that our double-talk kills their mother wit. Finally, I must acknowledge freely that everything I have said seems to me obvious. But why cannot we take the obvious seriously?

3. DEFINING THE "FIELD AT A GIVEN TIME"*[1]

KURT LEWIN

I. FIELD THEORY AND THE PHASE SPACE

THE HISTORY of acceptance of new theories frequently shows the following steps: At first the new idea is treated as pure nonsense, not worth looking at. Then comes a time when a multitude of contradictory objections are raised, such as: the new theory is too fancy, or merely a new terminology; it is not fruitful, or simply wrong. Finally a state is reached when everyone seems to claim that he had always followed this theory. This usually marks the last state before general acceptance.

The increasing trend toward field theory in psychology is apparent in recent variations of psychoanalysis (Kardiner, Horney) and also within the theory of the conditioned reflex. This trend makes the clarification of the meaning of field theory only the more important, because, I am afraid, those psychologists who, like myself, have been in favor of field theory for many years have not been very successful in making the essence of this theory clear. The only excuse I know of is that this matter is not very simple. Physics and philosophy do not seem to have done much analytical work about the meaning of field theory that could be helpful to the psychologist. In addition, methods like field theory can really be understood and mastered only in the same way as methods in a handcraft, namely, by learning them through practice.

Hilgard and Marquis (7), in a recent publication, quote from a letter of Clark Hull the following sentence: "As I see it, the moment one expresses in any very general manner the various potentialities of behavior as dependent upon the stimultaneous status of one or more variables, he has the substance of what is currently called field theory."

It is correct that field theory emphasizes the importance of the fact that any event is a resultant of a multitude of factors. The recognition of the necessity of a fair representation of this multitude of interdependent factors is a step in the direction toward field theory. However, this does not suffice. Field theory is something more specific.

To use an illustration: Success in a certain sport may depend upon a combination of muscular strength, velocity of movement, ability to make

---

* Reprinted from *Psychological Review*, *50*, 1943, p. 292–310.

[1] This is the third paper given at a Symposium on Psychology and Scientific Method held as part of the Sixth International Congress for the Unity of Science, University of Chicago, September, 1941. The first paper is by Egon Brunswik and the second by C. L. Hull.

quick decisions, and precise perception of direction and distance. A change in any one of these five variables might alter the result to a certain degree. One can represent these variables as five dimensions of a diagram. The resultant of any possible constellation of these factors for the amount of success can be marked as a point in the diagram. The totality of these points then is a diagrammatic representation of this dependence, in other words, of an empirical law.

Physics frequently makes use of such representation of a multitude of factors influencing an event. To each of certain properties, such as temperature, pressure, time, spatial position, one dimension is coordinated. Such a representation in physics is called "phase space." Such a phase space may have twenty dimensions if twenty factors have to be considered. A phase space is something definitely different from that three-dimensional "physical space" within which physical objects are moving. In the same way the psychological space, the life space or psychological field, in which psychological locomotion or structural changes take place, is something different from those diagrams where dimensions mean merely gradations of properties.

In discussing these questions with a leading theoretical physicist, we agreed that the recognition of a multitude of factors as determining an event, and even their representation as a phase space, does not presuppose field theory. In psychology, Thurstone's factor analysis deals with such relations of various factors. Any character profile recognizes the multitude of factors. Field theorists and non-field theorists can both avail themselves of these useful devices, but not everybody who uses them is therefore a field theorist.

What is field theory? Is it a kind of very general theory? If one proceeds in physics from a special law or theory (such as the law of the free-falling body) to more general theories (such as the Newtonian laws) or still more general theories (such as the equations of Maxwell), one does *not* finally come to field theory. In other words, field theory can hardly be called a theory in the usual sense.

This fact becomes still more apparent when we consider the relation between the correctness or incorrectness of a theory and its character as a field theory. A special theory in physics or psychology may be a field theory, but nevertheless wrong. On the other hand, a description of what Hans Feigl calls an "empirical theory on the lowest level" may be correct without being field theory (although I do not believe that a theory on the higher levels of constructs can be correct in psychology without being field theory).

Field theory, therefore, can hardly be called correct or incorrect in the same way as a theory in the usual sense of the term. *Field theory is probably best characterized as a method:* namely, a method *of analyzing causal relations and of building scientific constructs.* This method of analyzing causal relations can be expressed in the form of certain general statements about the "nature" of the conditions of change. To what degree such a statement has an "analytical" (logical, *a priori*) and to what degree it has an "empirical" character do not need to be discussed here.

II. THE PRINCIPLE OF CONTEMPORANEITY AND THE EFFECT OF PAST AND FUTURE

One of the basic statements of psychological field theory can be formulated as follows: Any behavior or any other change in a psychological field depends only upon the psychological field *at that time*.

This principle has been stressed by the field theorists from the beginning. It has been frequently misunderstood and interpreted to mean that field theorists are not interested in historical problems or in the effect of previous experiences. Nothing can be more mistaken. In fact, field theorists are most interested in developmental and historical problems and have certainly done their share to enlarge the temporal scope of the psychological experiment from that of the classical reaction-time experiment, which lasts only a few seconds, to experimental situations, which contain a systematically created history through hours or weeks.

If a clarification of the field thoretical principle of contemporaneity could be achieved, it would, I feel, be most helpful for an understanding among the various schools in psychology.

The meaning of this far-reaching principle can be expressed rather easily by referring to its application in classical physics.

A change at the point x in the physical world is customarily characterized as $\dfrac{dx}{dt}$; that is to say, as a differential change in the position of x during a differential time-period dt. Field theory states that the change $\dfrac{dx}{dt}$ at the time t depends only on the situation S^t at that time t (Figure 1).

$$(1) \qquad \frac{dx}{dt} = F(S^t)$$

It does not depend, in addition, on past or future situations. In other words, the formula (1) is correct, but not the formula (1a).

$$(1a) \qquad dx = F(S^t) + F^1(S^{t-1}) + \cdots + F^2(S^{t+1}) + \cdots$$

Of course, there are cases in physics where one can state the relation between a change and a past situation S^{t-n} (where $t - n$ is a time not immediately preceding t; $|t - n| > dt$). In other words, there are occasions where it is technically possible to write:

$$(2) \qquad \frac{dx}{dt} = F(S^{t-n})$$

However, that is possible only if it is known how the later situation S^t depends on the previous situation S^{t-n}; in other words, if the function F in the equation

(3) $$S^t = F(S^{t-n})$$

is known. Such knowledge presupposes usually (a) that both situations are "closed systems" which are genidentic (11); (b) that the laws are known which deal with the change of all points of the previous situation S^{t-n} and also the laws dealing with the changes in the situations between the previous situation S^{t-n} and the later situation S.

The meaning of linking a change to a past situation by formula (2) might be clarified best by pointing out that it is possible in a similar way to link a present change to a future situation S^{t+n} and to write:

(2a) $$\frac{dx}{dt} = F(S^{t+n})$$

This is possible whenever we have to deal with a "closed system" during the time-period t until $t + n$, and if the laws of the on-going changes during this period are known.

The possibility of writing this functional equation does not mean that the future situation S^{t+1} is conceived of as a "condition" of the present change $\frac{dx}{dt}$. In fact, the same $\frac{dx}{dt}$ would occur if the closed system would be destroyed before the time $(t + n)$. In other words, the change $\frac{dx}{dt}$ depends on the situation (S^t) at that time only (in line with formula [1]). The technical possibility of expressing this change mathematically as a function of a future or a past time does not change this fact.[2]

The equivalent to $\frac{dx}{dt}$ in physics is the concept "behavior" in psychology, if we understand the term behavior to cover any change in the psychological field. The field theoretical principle of contemporaneity in psychology then means that the behavior b at the time t is a function of the situation S at the time t only (S is meant to include both the person and his psychological environment),

(4) $$b^t = F(S^t)$$

and not, in addition, a function of past or future situations S^{t-n} or S^{t+n} (Figure 2). Again, it is possible to relate the behavior b indirectly to either a past situation (S^{t-n}) or a future situation (S^{t+n}); but again, this can be done only if these situations are closed systems, and if the changes in the intermediate periods can be accounted for by known laws. It seems

---

[2] Frequently an occurrence is said to be caused by the "preceding conditions." This term seems to have been misunderstood by psychologists to refer to a distant past situation (S^{t-n}), although it should refer to the present situation, or at least to the "immediately preceding situation" (S^{t-dt}). We will come back to this question.

that psychologists are increasingly aware of the importance of this formula.

III. HOW TO DETERMINE THE PROPERTIES OF A FIELD AT A GIVEN TIME

If one has to derive behavior from the situation at that time, a way has to be found to *determine* the character of the "situation at a given time." This determination implies a number of questions which are, I think, interesting both psychologically and philosophically.

To determine the properties of a present situation or—to use a medical terminology—to make a diagnosis, one can follow two different procedures: One may base one's statement on conclusions from history (*anamneses*), or one may use diagnostic *tests of the present*.

To use a simple example: I wish to know whether the floor of the attic is sufficiently strong to carry a certain weight. I might try to gain this knowledge by finding out what material was used when the house was built ten years ago. As I get reliable reports that good material has been used, and that the architect was a dependable man, I might conclude that the load probably would be safe. If I can find the original blueprints, I might be able to do some exact figuring and feel still more safe.

Of course, there is always a chance that the workmen have actually not followed the blueprints, or that insects have weakened the woodwork, or that some rebuilding has been done during the last ten years. Therefore, I might decide to avoid these uncertain conclusions from past data and to determine the present strength of the floor by testing its strength now. Such a diagnostic test will not yield data which are absolutely certain; how reliable they are depends upon the quality of the available test and the carefulness of testing. However, the value of a present test is, from the point of view of methodology, superior to that of an *anamnesis*. An *anamnesis* includes logically two steps: namely, the testing of certain properties in the past (of the quality, size, and structure of the woodwork) and the proof that nothing unknown has interfered in the meantime; in other words that we have to deal with a "closed system." Even if a system is left untouched by the outside, inner changes occur. Therefore, in addition, the laws governing these inner changes have to be known (see above) if the properties of a situation are to be determined through an *anamnesis*.

Medicine, engineering, physics, biology are accustomed to use both methods, an inquiry into the past and a test of the present. But they prefer the latter whenever possible.[3]

---

[3] There are cases where a historical procedure is preferable. For instance, the hunger of a rat can probably be better determined by the duration of starvation than by a physiological or psychological test of the hunger at time t. This conclusion from the past to the present can be made, however, only during periods and in settings

Psychology has used diagnosis by *anamnesis* rather excessively, particularly in classical psychoanalysis and other clinical approaches to problems of personality. Psychology of perception and psychology of memory have been relatively free from the historical type of diagnosis. Experimental psychology, on the whole, has shown a progressive trend toward testing the present situation.

The method of determining the properties of a situation (S') by testing them at that time t avoids the uncertainties of historical conclusions. It does not follow, however, that this method eliminates considerations of time-periods altogether. A "situation at a given time" actually does not refer to a moment without time extension, but to a certain time-period. This fact is of great theoretical and methodological importance for psychology.

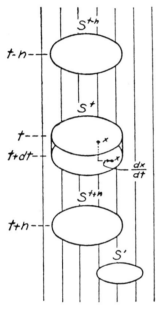

FIG. 1. S during $t - n$ until $t + n$ is a "closed system"; but S is not genidentic with S^t. $\frac{dx}{dt}$ indicates the velocity of x.

It may be helpful to go back for a moment to the procedure in physics. If the vertical lines in Figure 1 represent the so-called physical "worldlines," a "situation" means a cut through these lines at a given time t. A description of such a situation has to include (1) the relative position of the parts of the field at that time; (2) the direction and the velocity of the changes going on at that time. The first task is fulfilled by ascribing certain scalar values to the different entities; the second, by ascribing certain vectors to them. The second task contains a difficulty which I would like to discuss.

To describe the direction and velocity of a change going on at a given moment, it is necessary to refer to a certain period of events. Ideally, a time-differential should suffice for such determination. Actually, one has to observe a macroscopic time-interval or at least the position at the beginning and at the end of such interval to determine that time-differential. In the simplest case the velocity at a given time is assumed to equal the average velocity during that macroscopic time-interval. I will not attempt to follow up the details of this procedure in physics. If sufficient laws are known, certain indirect methods like those based on the Doppler effect permit different procedures.

where a "closed system" (no interference from outside) can be enforced; e.g., for animals which during this period do the same amount of work, which have been on a known diet, etc. The difficulties of this type of control have led Skinner (19) to link the problem of drive strength to properties of present consumption.

However, it remains a basic fact that the adequate description of a situation at a moment is impossible without observation of a certain time-period. This observation has to be interpreted (according to the "most plausible" assumption and our knowledge of the physical laws) in a way which permits its transformation into a statement of the "state of affairs at the time t."

In psychology a similar problem exists. The person at a given time may be in the midst of saying "a." Actually such a statement implies already that a certain time-interval is observed. Otherwise, only a certain position of mouth and body could be recorded. Usually the psychologist will not be satisfied with such a characterization of the ongoing process. He likes to know whether this "a" belongs to the word "can" or "apple" or to what word it does belong. If the word was "can," the psychologist wants to know whether the person was going to say: "I cannot come back" or "I can stand on my head if I have to." The psychologist even likes to know whether the sentence is spoken to an intimate friend as a part of a conversation about personal plans for the future or whether this sentence is part of a political address and has the meaning of an attempt to retreat from an untenable political position.

In other words, an adequate psychological description of the character and the direction of an ongoing process can and has to be done on various microscopic and macroscopic levels. To each "size of a unit of behavior" a different "size of situation" can be coordinated. That the individual in our example is saying "a," can be made sure without taking into account much of the surrounding of the individual. To characterize the sentence as a part of a political retreat, much more of the surrounding has to be considered.

Without altering the principle of contemporaneity as one of the basic propositions of field theory, we have to realize that to determine the psychological direction and velocity of behavior (*i.e.*, what is usually called the "meaning" of the psychological event), we have to take into account in psychology as in physics a certain time-period. The length of this period depends in psychology upon the scope of the situation. As a rule, the more macroscopic the situation is which has to be described the longer is the period which has to be observed to determine the direction and velocity of behavior at a given time (Figure 2).

In other words, we are dealing in psychology with "situational units" which have to be conceived of as having an extension in regard to their field dimensions and their time dimensions. If I am not mistaken, the problem of time-space-quanta, which is so important for modern quantum theory in physics (17), is methodologically parallel (although, of course, on a more advanced level) to the problem of "time-field-units" in psychology.

The concept of situations of different scope has proved to be very helpful in solving a number of otherwise rather puzzling problems. Tolman (20), Muenzinger (16), and Floyd Allport (1), have stressed that a psychological description has to include the macroscopic as well as the microscopic events. Barker, Dembo, and Lewin (2) distinguish and treat mathematically three sizes of units of processes and corresponding sizes of

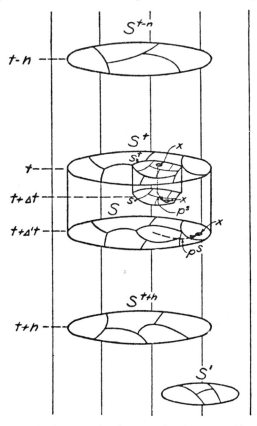

FIG. 2. S during $t - n$ until $t + n$ is a "closed system"; but S is not genidentic with S'. $s^{t,\ t+\Delta t}$ is a small time-field-unit which extends over a relatively small area and includes the relatively small time-period t until $t + \Delta t$. $S^{t,\ t+\Delta't}$ is a larger time-field-unit covering a larger area and including the longer period t until $t + \Delta't$. p^s and p^S indicate the change in position of x during the small and the large time unit.

situations. They have handled certain problems of measuring the strength of frustration during extended periods by referring to overlapping situations in regard to two different sizes of time-field-units. Lippitt and White (15), in their study of social atmosphere, distinguish still larger periods of events. They have shown that the beginning and end of these macroscopic units can be determined rather precisely and with very satisfactory reliability. However, I will not discuss these questions here where we are interested in methodological problems only.

IV. THE PSYCHOLOGICAL PAST, PRESENT, AND FUTURE AS PARTS OF A PSYCHOLOGICAL FIELD AT A GIVEN TIME

The clarification of the problem of past and future has been much delayed by the fact that the psychological field which exists at a given time contains also the views of that individual about his future and past. The individual sees not only his present situation; he has certain expecta- tions, wishes, fears, daydreams for his future. His views about his own past and that of the rest of the physical and social world are often incorrect, but nevertheless constitute, in his life space, the "reality-level" of the past. In addition, a wish-level in regard to the past can frequently be observed. The discrepancy between the structure of this wish- or irreality-level of the psychological past and the reality-level plays an important role for the phenomenon of guilt. The structure of the psychological future is closely related, for instance, to hope and planning (2).

Following a terminology of L. K. Frank (6), we speak of "time perspective" which includes the psychological past and psychological future on the reality-level and on the various irreality-levels. The time perspective existing at a given time has been shown to be very important for many problems such as the level of aspiration, the mood, the construc- tiveness, and the initiative of the individual. Farber (4) has shown, for instance, that the amount of suffering of a prisoner depends more on his expectation in regard to his release, which may be five years ahead, than on the pleasantness or unpleasantness of his present occupation.

It is important to realize that the psychological past and the psycholog- ical future are simultaneous parts of the psychological field existing at a given time t. The time perspective is continually changing. According to field theory, any type of behavior depends upon the total field, including the time perspective at that time, but not, in addition, upon any past or future field and its time perspectives.

It may be illustrative to consider briefly from this field theoretical point of view the methodological problems connected with one of the basic concepts of the conditioned reflex theory, namely, the concept of "extinc- tion." An individual has experienced that after a certain stimulus, let us say the ringing of a bell, food will appear. Being hungry, the individual eats. After a number of such experiences, the individual will show certain preparatory actions for eating as soon as the eating bell rings. The indi- vidual is then said to be "conditioned." Now, the situation is secretly changed by the experimenter and the eating bell is not followed by food. After a while the individual catches on and does not show the preparatory action for food when the bell rings. This process is called "extinction."

"Habits" of a person at a given time can and have to be treated as parts of the present field. Whether they should be represented partly as cogni- tive structure or resistance to change of cognitive structure, partly as a building up or fixation of valences (13), or whether they have to be conceptualized in other ways is not a problem here. Habits of action (18, 14), as well as of thinking, are dealt with in field theoretical research. They are closely related to problems of ideology (9) and expectation.

As Tolman (20), Hilgard and Marquis (7), and others have correctly pointed out, conditioning as well as extinction are both related to changes in the reality level of the psychological future. Field theorists have to distinguish in regard to conditioning and extinction two types of problems. The one type deals with such a question as how expectation is affected by perception on the one hand, and memory on the other. What changes in the perceived structure of the psychological present lead to a change in the structure of the psychological future, and what are the laws governing the interdependence of these two parts of the psychological field? The studies on level of aspiration have provided some knowledge about the factors which influence the structure of the future reality-level. Korsch-Escalona (10) has made a step toward a mathematical treatment of the effect of the future reality-level on the forces which govern present behavior. Study of the level of aspiration has also given us considerable insight into the effect of the psychological past (namely of previous success or failure) on the psychological future. This question is obviously closely related to extinction.

The methodological position of these types of problems is clear: They deal with the interdependence of various parts of the psychological field existing at a given time t. In other words, they are legitimate field theoretical questions of the type $b^t = F(S^t)$.

The second type of questions, treated in the theory of conditioned reflex, tries to relate a later situation S^4, (for instance, during extinction) to a previous situation S^1 during learning or to a number of similar or different previous situations S^1, S^2, S^3, $\cdots$: it relates behavior to the number of repetitions. In other words, these questions have the form $b^t = F(S^{t-n})$ or $b^t = F(S^{t-n}, S^{t-m}, \cdots)$. Here field theory demands a more critical and more analytical type of thinking. One should distinguish at least two types of problems:

(a) How the perceived psychological situation will look at the time S^4 depends obviously upon whether or not the experimenter will provide food and on similar external physical or social conditions. Everybody will agree, I suppose, that these factors cannot possibly be derived from the psychological field of the individual at the previous time, even if all the psychological laws were known. These factors are alien to psychology.

(b) There remain, however, legitimate psychological questions in this second type of problem. We can keep the boundary conditions of a life space constant or change them in a known way during a certain period and investigate what would happen under those conditions. These problems lie definitely within the domain of psychology. An example is the problem of restructurization of memory traces. We know that these processes depend on the state of the individual during the total period S^{t-n} until S^t (Figure 2) and are different, for instance, during sleep and while being awake. Doubtless the experiments on conditioned reflex have given us a wealth of material in regard to this type of problem. They will have to be treated finally in the way which we discussed in the beginning, namely, as a sequence of relations between a situation S^t and the immediately following situation S^{t+dt}.

On the whole, I think the psychological trend is definitely going in this direction. For instance, the goal gradient theory has been formulated originally as a relation between behavior and past situations. Straight, analytical thinking demands that such a statement should be broken up into several propositions (12), one of which has to do with the intensity of goal striving as a function of the distance between individual and goal. This is identical with a statement about certain force fields and is probably correct. A second proposition implied in the goal gradient theory links the present behavior to the past situation S^{t-n}. The specific form is, to my mind, unsatisfactory. But even if it should be correct, it should be treated as an independent theory. Hull's formulation of a "Gradient of Reinforcement Hypothesis" is a step in this direction.

V. PSYCHOLOGICAL ECOLOGY

As an elaboration of our considerations, I would like to discuss some aspects of Brunswik's treatment of the role of statistics (3). I do not expect ever to live down the misunderstandings created by my attack on some ways in which statistics have been used in psychology. I have been always aware that quantitative measurement demands statistics (see Hull's answer to Brunswik [8]). That statement holds also for "pure cases"; i.e., situations where it is possible to link theory and observable facts in a definite way. Since psychology is increasingly abandoning the inadequate objectives of statistics, further discussion might have little pragmatic value.

However, Brunswik has brought into the open new and important aspects, and I feel that their clarification may be helpful for psychological methodology in general.

Within the realm of facts existing at a given time one can distinguish three areas in which changes are or might be of interest to psychology:

1. The "life space"; i.e., the person and the psychological environment as it exists for him. We usually have this field in mind if we refer to needs, motivation, mood, goals, anxiety, ideals.
2. A multitude of processes in the physical or social world, which do not affect the life space of the individual at that time.
3. A "boundary zone" of the life space: certain parts of the physical or social world do affect the state of the life space at that time. The process of perception, for instance, is intimately linked with this boundary zone because what is perceived is partly determined by the physical "stimuli"; i.e., that part of the physical world which affects the sensory organs at that time. Another process located in the boundary zone is the "execution" of an action.

Brunswik states correctly (3, p. 266): "The 'field' within which Lewin is able to predict, in the strict sense of the word, is the person in his life space." Then he proceeds, "But the life space is not to be confused with geographic environment of physical stimuli, nor with actually achieved results in the environment. It is post-perceptual, and pre-behavioral." This statement is partly incorrect, namely, insofar as perception and behavior, to my mind, are legitimate problems of psychology. This view is a necessary consequence of the field theoretical approach according to which the boundary conditions of a field are essential characteristics of that field. For instance, processes of perception which should be related to the boundary zone depend partly on the state of the inner part of the psychological field; i.e., upon the character of the person, his motivation, his cognitive structure, his way of perceiving, etc., partly on the "stimulus distribution" on the retina or other receptors as enforced by physical processes outside the organism. For the same reasons, the problems of physical or social action are legitimate parts of psychology proper.

Brunswik, however, is correct in assuming that I do not consider as a part of the psychological field at a given time those sections of the physical or social world which do not affect the life space of the person at that time. The food that lies behind doors at the end of a maze so that neither smell nor sight can reach it is not a part of the life space of the animal. In case the individual knows that food lies there this *knowledge*, of course, has to be represented in his life space, because this knowledge affects behavior. It is also necessary to take into account the subjective probability with which the individual views the present or future state of affairs because the degree of certainty of expectation also influences his behavior.

The principle of representing within the life space all that affects behavior at that time, but nothing else, prevents the inclusion of physical food which is not perceived. This food cannot possibly influence his behavior at that time under the conditions mentioned. Indeed, the individual will start his journey if he thinks the food is there even if it is actually not there, and he will not move toward the food which actually is at the end of the maze if he doesn't know it is there.

In the past this principle has not always been adhered to in animal psychology but it seems to me so obvious that I had assumed all psychologists agreed on this point. Statements which could be interpreted otherwise I had regarded as loose terminology rather than an expression of differences of opinion until I listened to Brunswik's paper. The discussion following this paper seems to have brought out the issue still more clearly and it will be appropriate, I hope, to refer to this discussion.

According to Brunswik, it is possible to think in terms of laws rather than mere statistical rules if one limits the psychological field in the way described. However, he claims that for this gain one has to pay "the price of an encapsulation" into a realm of problems which actually leaves out the most dynamic aspects of psychology. He wishes to include in the psychological field those parts of the physical and sociological world which, to my mind, have to be excluded. These parts, he states, have to be studied in a statistical way, and the probability of the occurrence of events calculated.

To my mind, the main issue is what the term "probability" refers to. Does Brunswik want to study the ideas of the driver of a car about the probability of being killed or does he want to study the accident statistics which tell the "objective probability" of such an event. If an individual sits in a room trusting that the ceiling will not come down, should only his "subjective probability" be taken into account for predicting behavior or should we also consider the "objective probability" of the ceiling's coming down as determined by the engineers. To my mind, only the first has to be taken into account, but to my inquiry, Brunswik answered that he meant also the latter.

I can see why psychology should be interested even in those areas of the physical and social world which are not part of the life space or which do not affect its boundary zone at present. If one wishes to safeguard a child's education during the next years, if one wishes to predict in what situation an individual will find himself as a result of a certain action, one will have to calculate this future. Obviously, such forecast has to be based partly on statistical considerations about non-psychological data.

Theoretically, we can characterize this task as discovering what part of the physical or social world will determine during a given period the "boundary zone" of the life space. This task is worth the interest of the psychologists. I would suggest calling it "psychological ecology."

Some problems of the "life history" of an individual have their places here. The boundary conditions of the life space during long- as well as short-time periods depend partly on the action of the individual himself. To this degree they should be linked to the psychological dynamics of the life space. The rest of the calculation has to be done, however, with other than psychological means.

The essence of explaining or predicting any change in a certain area is the linkage of that change with the conditions of the field at that time. This basic principle makes the subjective probability of an event a part of the life space of that individual. But it excludes the objective probability of alien factors that cannot be derived from the life space.

REFERENCES

1. ALLPORT, F. H. "Methods in the Study of Collective Action Phenomena," *J. soc. Psychol.*, SPSSI Bulletin, 1942, 15, pp. 165–85.
2. BARKER, R., DEMBO, T., & LEWIN, K. "Frustration and Regression; Studies in Topological and Vector Psychology II," *Univ. Ia Stud. Child Welf.*, 1941, 18, pp. 1–314.

3. Brunswik, E. "Organismic Achievement and Environmental Probability," *Psychol. Rev.*, 1943, 50, pp. 255–72.

4. Farber, M. L. "Imprisonment as a Psychological Situation," Unpublished Ph.D. Thesis, State Univ. Iowa, 1940.

5. Festinger, L. "A Theoretical Interpretation of Shifts in Level of Aspiration," *Psychol. Rev.*, 1942, 49, pp. 235–50.

6. Frank, L. K. "Time Perspectives," *J. soc. Phil.*, 1939, 4, pp. 293–312.

7. Hilgard, E. R., & Marquis, D. G. *Conditioning and Learning.* New York, London: D. Appleton-Century Co., 1940.

8. Hull, C. L. "The Problem of Intervening Variables in Molar Behavior Theory," *Psychol. Rev.*, 1943, 50, pp. 273–91.

9. Kalhorn, J. "Ideological Differences among Rural Children." Unpublished Master's Thesis, State Univ. Iowa, 1941.

10. Korsch-Escalona, S. "The Effect of Success and Failure upon the Level of Aspiration and Behavior in Manic-Depressive Psychoses. *In* Lewin, K., Lippit, R., & Korsch-Escalona, S., "Studies in Topological and Vector Psychology I," *Univ. Ia. Stud. Child Welf.*, 1939, 16, No. 3, pp. 199–303.

11. Lewin, K. *Der Begriff der Genese in Physik, Biologie und Entwicklungsgeschichte.* [The Concept of Genesis in Physics, Biology and Theory of Evolution.] Berlin: Julius Springer, 1922.

12. ———. "The Conceptual Representation and the Measurement of Psychological Forces," *Contr. Psychol. Theor.*, 1938, 1, No. 4, pp. 247.

13. ———. "Field Theory and Learning." In *41st Yearbook of the National Society for the Study of Education*, Part II, 1942, pp. 215–39.

14. ———. *The Relative Effectiveness of a Lecture Method and a Method of Group Decision for Changing Food Habits.* Committee on Food Habits, National Research Council, 1942.

15. Lippitt, R. "An Experimental Study of the Effect of Democratic and Authoritarian Group Atmospheres." *Univ. Ia. Stud. Child Welf.*, 1940, 16, No. 3, pp. 44–195.

16. Muenzinger, K. F. *Psychology: The Science of Behavior.* Denver: World Press, 1939, pp. 270.

17. Reichenbach, H. *From Copernicus to Einstein.* New York: Alliance Book Corp., New York Philosophical Library, 1942.

18. Schwarz, G. IV. Über Ruckfalligkeit bei Umgewohnung. I, II. [On Relapses in Re-learning.] *Psychol. Forsch.*, 1927, 9, pp. 86–158; 1933, 18, pp. 143–190.

19. Skinner, B. F. *The Behavior of Organisms; An Experimental Analysis.* New York: D. Appleton-Century Co., 1938.

20. Tolman, E. C. *Purposive Behavior in Animals and Men.* New York: Century Co., 1932, pp. xiv, 463.

Organization Structure and Process

THEORIZING about organizations can be approached from different points of view. A statesman, a sociologist, or a business executive concerned with long-range planning would be interested in the relations between organizations and in the place of an organization within the entire society. On the other hand, an administrative technician, such as an accountant, personnel officer, production manager, etc., is more interested in the details of a single process in the internal workings of the organization—the way it relates to other areas and the functions performed. Intermediate between these is the general executive, who needs to know how the technical processes are put together to form a whole, capable of successful adaptation to its environment, and how the necessary coordination is achieved. The types of theories that each would find useful would be different but, ideally, interrelated with one another. In this section we consider theories on a relatively macroscopic level, theories of the gross aspects of organization: the organization as an entity, coping with its environment and evolving in accordance with the environmental possibilities and under internal and external pressures.

To the layman, the words "organization structure" bring to mind the organization chart used by most private and public organizations of any appreciable size. The organization chart and any associated position descriptions do provide important information on organization structure. Yet, for the person who wishes to study organizations scientifically, a deeper meaning for this concept is needed. In part, this is because of the commonplace observation that organization charts may not be accurate and do not tell the whole story. The more important consideration, however, stems from the nature of these documents and the way in which they and other aspects of organization structure influence organizational behavior.

An organization chart or position description is a collection of ideas or information. It can impinge on behavior only insofar as it affects the beliefs of the people who conduct the affairs of that organization. A satisfactory conceptual definition of *organization structure*, then, is the pattern of beliefs about the organization that are shared by those individuals who take the coordinated action that we define as *organizational behavior*. It is these beliefs that matter and that provide long-term coherence for the organization regardless of whether their concrete existence occurs in the form of documents, other memory devices, or solely in the perceptions and cognitions of the human participants.

This way of thinking about organization structure derives from some of the key ideas of modern philosophy and social science. Physics is defined by philosophers as shared beliefs of physicists; and culture is defined by social scientists as the totality of shared beliefs of a society. Shared patterns of belief are referred to in social science as institutions. As used below this term refers to any habitual way of thinking, perceiving or evaluating generally shared either by the members of the entire culture or of the organizational subculture.

Much valuable knowledge about organizations consists of the specific institutional structures they have developed. At a theoretical level one seeks for characteristics of these institutions sufficiently general to describe a wide range of specific organizations and yet be useful for the purposes of explaining, predicting, and controlling the behavior of an individual organization. The classical study along this line is that of Max Weber (1864–1920). The essay "Bureaucracy" reproduced in this section shows clearly a grasp of important features of the institutional structure of organizations, their interrelationships and consequences. Weber used a legalistic style of writing, which is no longer fashionable in social science; and this may have led him to arrange the institutional features he discovered in the form of an "ideal type" of organization which he labeled *bureaucracy*. Weber did not use the term "bureaucracy" in the pejorative sense—quite the contrary; rather he used it as a label for a type of organization that was the most modern and technically efficient yet developed.

The reader will note that many of the characteristics enumerated in this essay are a part of his own beliefs concerning proper ways of organizing. As social institutions, they find expression in textbooks of management, in laws and regulations, and in policy manuals of many organizations. Nevertheless, over historical perspective, the structural patterns accepted by a society as good ways of organizing do change; and the bureaucratic type itself appears to have become widespread only in the last 100 years or so. The line of evolution in Western society traced by Weber and other sociologists was a transition from *institutions based on tradition and centrally concerned with persons and their statuses* over to *rationalized institutions centrally concerned with an impersonal task*. The article by

Udy, "Administrative Rationality, Social Setting, and Organizational Development" is a summary of some recent research that bears upon the evolution of modern organizations. It compares specific organizations from various primitive societies in terms of a series of structural elements that progress toward the rationality that is characteristic of Weberian bureaucracy.

In the two articles already mentioned, structural elements are discussed in terms of the part they play in the larger system, the society as a whole. This viewpoint has become dominant in contemporary sociology. It is referred to as a functionalist or structure-function approach. Homans, in his article included in Section 1, explores its meaning and usefulness. Applying this viewpoint to organizations, Weber emphasizes how the bureaucracy behaves as an organ of the society, performing some task that is necessary to the coherence or success of the whole. Likewise, the way in which the structural elements listed in "Administrative Rationality" subserve social functions at each stage of development is highlighted in that article. The functional integration of organizations with their social and economic environment is a key to many significant questions including, especially, the evolution of institutions.

The process of evolution has not stopped with the development of bureaucratic forms. In fact, it can be argued that, in becoming free from the twin anchors of tradition and the primacy of a status system, modern society has lost its main stabilizers. Certainly the rate of technological development, the social unrest, and the vastly enlarged range of possibilities now experienced by mankind are consistent with this thesis. As the social environment changes, pressure is exerted on organizations to evolve in more appropriate directions. Current evolutionary theory posits increasing social differentiation as a functional response to the kind of change that modern society is undergoing (6). Modern experience with organizations appears to illustrate this. Because modern organizations are rationalized and exposed to objective tests of success, they are relatively free to institute and maintain structural patterns deviant from the institutions of a society as a whole. This element of conscious planning in support of goals (*rationalization*) distinguishes formal organizations from other social entities and should enable them to evolve relatively rapidly over short historical perspective under the unsettling effects of environmental change. In order for deviant patterns to persist, the new form would have to be successful in coping with the tasks and problems that it specifically encounters. Thus, different kinds of organization would evolve in different sectors of human activity.

There are at least three types of situations in which the strictly bureaucratic organization does not perform well and where more highly evolved forms do. One is where an environment of rapid and unexpected change affects the success of the organization. The structural response to this is an enriched network of lateral communication and emphasis at every level of the organization on the overall goals toward which the organization is directed (2). A second type is in the growth of the organization to a size where the volume of its traditional activities does not produce sufficient resources to sustain growth. The response here is diversification by means of decentralized decision making (3), where the key operating decisions are made not at the very top but within decentralized units. Third, the complexity of modern technology has required the integration of activities of persons of very diverse, highly specialized competences. The "project" form of organization, which brings these talents together in a single unit dedicated to a particular task, has been a functional response to this need. Perhaps other postbureaucratic examples of organization can be found, but these are already clear and recognized patterns.

Thus, in the course of decades, evolution produces altered patterns of organizing in society as a whole. The managements of individual organizations, in designing formal structures, select and modify the prevailing ideas to suit their immediate purposes. Such design activity occurs intensively in the early history of organizations. Pressures toward adaptation are particularly heavy at that time and the forces that typically oppose adaptation are relatively weak. Nevertheless, mature organizations also experience pressures toward adaptation and must engage in some adaptive activity to survive. As indicated in the last paragraph, adaptive capacity is severely limited in the bureaucratic ideal-type. The function of conscious adaptation is so important in all modern organizations, however, that a special section (Section 4 on Planned Change) is devoted to it.

Here in Section 2 we are also examining the nature of the organizational and environmental forces that affect the behavior of the organization and that, in extreme cases, may require structural adaptation. The most satisfactory general conceptualization of the operation of these forces is due to Chester I. Barnard (1886–1961). An outline of his "Theory of Cooperation and Organization" is reproduced in this section. Whereas Weber emphasized the machinelike structure of the organization, Barnard emphasizes the role of the *membership* (broadly construed to include employees, proprietors and clientele) in determining its behavior. This is implicit in his notion of *efficiency* (the degree to which the organization serves the specifically human purposes of its members) and in the role of the *informal organization* (member-initiated institutions not sanctioned by formal authority) in maintaining a balance of forces or steady state.

As indicated earlier, modern organizations are characterized by their emphasis on the achievement of specific, material goals. Barnard points out that success in achieving these goals (*effectiveness*) is indispensable to the survival of an organization. The choice of what goals to strive for is one of the key decisions in managerial design of structure. A number of important studies (11, 14, 15, 16) have explored the selection or adaptation of organizational goals. Two excerpts from one of these studies (14) are included in this section. "Ideology in Organization" is a theoretical statement of the importance of this choice and of the role of social values shared by all or a powerful segment of the people in a society as a force helping to mold the more limited set of institutions peculiar to any individual organization. "TVA and the Grass Roots: Guiding Principles and Interpretation" summarizes Selznick's methodological commitments in this study, his theory of the dynamics by which the choices are made, and its empirical illustration in TVA.

Selznick's process of *informal co-optation* is one kind of informal organization that illustrates Barnard's ideas. Informal organizations arise in part from limitations and failures in human judgment in the processes of designing the formal structure. Organizations exist in reality; they must cope with the actual environment in which they exist. Formal structure represents the best judgments of those in authority as to characteristics that will cope with the environment they anticipate. Informal extensions and modifications provide one source of adaptive flexibility. They have the additional advantage that they need not be openly admitted or formally approved and the disadvantage that they may defeat the rational designs intended by formal authority and thus impair the technical effectiveness of the organization. Nevertheless, since informal organization is the spontaneous product of direct action by members usually it increases organizational efficiency, at least locally. These features are nicely illustrated in the next two articles.

"Teamwork and Productivity in a Shoe Factory" illustrates some of the findings of the famous studies (13) carried out at the Hawthorne Works of Western Electric Company in the late 1920's and early 1930's, which first pointed out the existence and importance of worker modifications of managerially designed technologies. In the shoe factory, too, the researchers discovered group norms that restricted output. They also found an informally organized work and leadership structure that had been devised to implement these group norms. The dynamics of informal organization are also explored in "Managing the Managers." In this case, however, the informal organization is at the managerial level. Further discussion of this plant and of other plants in which similar phenomena occurred has been collected in a full-length book (5).

This section concludes with two studies from the Systems Research Laboratory of the RAND Corporation. Here an organization of moderate size, an air-defense center, was created under laboratory conditions for the purpose of studying the adaptation of whole organizations in the course of learning to cope with their environment. In this case, the environment was simulated by computer methods and thus could be controlled for experimental purposes. Laboratory studies of this magnitude are expensive. This one was part of a program of research on training methods for the Air

Force. The design has been used in further work on air-defense training by the System Development Corporation, an offshoot of RAND, and by RAND's Logistic Systems Laboratory.

Since 1958 the Logistic Systems Laboratory has undertaken four man-machine simulations on various aspects of Air Force logistics. Two of these exercises (LP I and LP III) were designed to test various policies and systems for the support of aircraft and missile bases. This required the simulation of air matériel areas and base operations. The experiments measured performance in the realization of an assigned program under various operational stresses. LP II and LP IV were intended to develop policies and systems. LP II simulated ICBM squadron and wing organization to study policies on the interaction of operations and maintenance functions. The stresses with which the operating crew had to cope stemmed from variations in equipment reliability and resource availability. LP IV simulated a Strategic Air Command multiweapon base for the purpose of developing a base-maintenance management and information system. These exercises are given careful study by Air Force operating personnel and have been the source of a number of innovations in Air Force management procedures (7).

In this section we are attempting to provide a perspective on some of the most significant features of organizations: the institutionalization of their structures in the matrix of an entire society and the managerial and social processes through which organized behavior occurs. The work surveyed demonstrates viewpoints and theories useful for understanding primitive or historical organizations and also modern organizations such as typical business concerns and even the United States Department of Defense, an organization unique in its size and complexity. Nevertheless, an adequate understanding of the questions raised is only beginning to be attained either by social scientists or by practicing managers. The quality and volume of research in this area has increased greatly in recent years, both on the topics of this section and on the more narrowly defined topics of later sections. The bibliography below and included at the end of other sections will provide an entry to this work and, together with citations in the individual articles, will indicate the periodical sources in which future developments may be found.

REFERENCES

1. BLAU, PETER M., AND SCOTT, W. R. *Formal Organizations.* San Francisco: Chandler Publishing Co., 1962.
2. BURNS, TOM, AND STALKER, G. M. *The Management of Innovation.* Chicago: Quadrangle Books, 1961.
3. CHANDLER, JR., A. D. *Strategy and Structure.* Cambridge, Mass.: M.I.T. Press, 1962.

4. Crozier, Michel. *The Bureaucratic Phenomenon*. Chicago: University of Chicago Press, 1964.
5. Dalton, M. *Men Who Manage*. New York: John Wiley & Sons, Inc., 1959.
6. Eisenstadt, S. N. "Social Change, Differentiation and Evolution," *American Sociological Review*, 29 (1964), pp. 375–86.
7. Geisler, M. A.; Haythorn, W. W.; and Steger, W. A. *Simulation and the Logistics Systems Laboratory,* RAND Corporation memorandum RM–3281–PR, September, 1962.
8. Gouldner, Alvin W. *Patterns of Industrial Bureaucracy*. Glencoe, Ill.: Free Press, 1954.
9. March, James G. (ed.). *Handbook of Organizations*. Chicago: Rand-McNally & Co., 1965.
10. March, J. G., and Simon, H. A. *Organizations*. New York: John Wiley & Sons, Inc., 1958.
11. Massie, Joseph L. *Blazer and Ashland Oil*. University of Kentucky, 1960.
12. Merton, R. K., *et al.* (eds.). *Reader in Bureaucracy*. Glencoe, Ill.: Free Press, 1952.
13. Roethlisberger, F. J., and Dickson, W. J. *Management and the Worker*. Cambridge, Mass.: Harvard University Press, 1939.
14. Selznick, Philip. *TVA and the Grass Roots*. Berkeley and Los Angeles: University of California Press, 1949.
15. Sills, David L. *The Volunteers*. Glencoe, Ill.: Free Press, 1957.
16. Simon, Herbert A. "Birth of an Organization—the Economic Cooperation Administration," *Public Administration Review*, Vol. 13, No. 4 (1953).
17. Thompson, Victor A. *Modern Organization*. New York: Alfred A. Knopf, 1961.

4. BUREAUCRACY*

Max Weber

1. CHARACTERISTICS OF BUREAUCRACY

Modern officialdom functions in the following specific manner:

I. There is the principle of fixed and official jurisdictional areas, which are generally ordered by rules, that is, by laws or administrative regulations.

1. The regular activities required for the purposes of the bureaucratically governed structure are distributed in a fixed way as official duties.

2. The authority to give the commands required for the discharge of these duties is distributed in a stable way and is strictly delimited by rules concerning the coercive means, physical, sacerdotal, or otherwise, which may be placed at the disposal of officials.

3. Methodical provision is made for the regular and continuous fulfilment of these duties and for the execution of the corresponding rights; only persons who have the generally regulated qualifications to serve are employed.

In public and lawful government these three elements constitute "bureaucratic authority." In private economic domination, they constitute "bureaucratic management." Bureaucracy, thus understood, is fully developed in political and ecclesiastical communities only in the modern state, and, in the private economy, only in the most advanced institutions of capitalism. Permanent and public office authority, with fixed jurisdiction, is not the historical rule but rather the exception. This is so even in large political structures such as those of the ancient Orient, the Germanic and Mongolian empires of conquest, or of many feudal structures of state. In all these cases, the ruler executes the most important measures through personal trustees, table-companions, or court-servants. Their commissions and authority are not precisely delimited and are temporarily called into being for each case.

II. The principles of office hierarchy and of levels of graded authority mean a firmly ordered system of super- and subordination in which there is a supervision of the lower offices by the higher ones. Such a system offers the governed the possibility of appealing the decision of a lower office to its higher authority, in a definitely regulated manner. With the full development of the bureaucratic type, the office hierarchy is monocratically organized. The principle of hierarchial office authority is found in

* From *From Max Weber* by H. H. Gerth and C. Wright Mills. A Galaxy Book. Copyright 1946 by Oxford University Press, Inc. Reproduced by permission.

all bureaucratic structures: in state and ecclesiastical structures as well as in large party organizations and private enterprises. It does not matter for the character of bureaucracy whether its authority is called "private" or "public."

When the principle of jurisdictional "competency" is fully carried through, hierarchial subordination—at least in public office—does not mean that the "higher" authority is simply authorized to take over the business of the "lower." Indeed, the opposite is the rule. Once established and having fulfilled its task, an office tends to continue in existence and be held by another incumbent.

III. The management of the modern office is based upon written documents ("the files"), which are preserved in their original or draught form. There is, therefore, a staff of subaltern officials and scribes of all sorts. The body of officials actively engaged in a "public" office, along with the respective apparatus of material implements and the files, make up a "bureau." In private enterprise, "the bureau" is often called "the office."

In principle, the modern organization of the civil service separates the bureau from the private domicile of the official, and, in general, bureaucracy segregates official activity as something distinct from the sphere of private life. Public monies and equipment are divorced from the private property of the official. This condition is everywhere the product of a long development. Nowadays, it is found in public as well as in private enterprises; in the latter, the principle extends even to the leading entrepreneur. In principle, the executive office is separated from the household, business from private correspondence, and business assets from private fortunes. The more consistently the modern type of business management has been carried through, the more are these separations the case. The beginnings of this process are to be found as early as the Middle Ages.

It is the peculiarity of the modern entrepreneur that he conducts himself as the "first official" of his enterprise, in the very same way in which the ruler of a specifically modern bureaucratic state spoke of himself as "the first servant" of the state.[1] The idea that the bureau activities of the state are intrinsically different in character from the management of private economic offices is a continental European notion and, by way of contrast, is totally foreign to the American way.

IV. Office management, at least all specialized office management—and such management is distinctly modern—usually presupposes thorough and expert training. This increasingly holds for the modern executive and employee of private enterprises, in the same manner as it holds for the state official.

V. When the office is fully developed, official activity demands the full working capacity of the official, irrespective of the fact that his ob-

---

[1] Frederick II of Prussia.

ligatory time in the bureau may be firmly delimited. In the normal case, this is only the product of a long development, in the public as well as in the private office. Formerly, in all cases, the normal state of affairs was reversed: official business was discharged as a secondary activity.

VI. The management of the office follows general rules, which are more or less stable, more or less exhaustive, and which can be learned. Knowledge of these rules represents a special technical learning which the officials possess. It involves jurisprudence, or administrative or business management.

The reduction of modern office management to rules is deeply embedded in its very nature. The theory of modern public administration, for instance, assumes that the authority to order certain matters by decree —which has been legally granted to public authorities—does not entitle the bureau to regulate the matter by commands given for each case, but only to regulate the matter abstractly. This stands in extreme contrast for the regulation of all relationships through individual privileges and bestowals of favor, which is absolutely dominant in patrimonialism, at least in so far as such relationships are not fixed by sacred tradition.

2. THE POSITION OF THE OFFICIAL

All this results in the following for the internal and external position of the official:

I. Office holding is a "vocation." This is shown, first, in the requirement of a firmly prescribed course of training, which demands the entire capacity for work for a long period of time, and in the generally prescribed and special examinations which are prerequisites of employment. Furthermore, the position of the official is in the nature of a duty. This determines the internal structure of his relations, in the following manner: Legally and actually, office holding is not considered a source to be exploited for rents or emoluments, as was normally the case during the Middle Ages and frequently up to the threshold of recent times. Nor is office holding considered a usual exchange of services for equivalents, as is the case with free labor contracts. Entrance into an office, including one in the private economy, is considered an acceptance of a specific obligation of faithful management in return for a secure existence. It is decisive for the specific nature of modern loyalty to an office that, in the pure type, it does not establish a relationship to a person, like the vassal's or disciple's faith in feudal or in patrimonial relations of authority. Modern loyalty is devoted to impersonal and functional purposes. Behind the functional purposes, of course, "ideas of culture-values" usually stand. These are *ersatz* for the earthly or supra-mundane personal master: ideas such as "state," "church," "community," "party," or "enterprise" are thought of as being realized in a community; they provide an ideological halo for the master. . . .

II. The personal position of the official is patterned in the following way:

1. Whether he is in a private office or a public bureau, the modern official always strives and usually enjoys a distinct social esteem as compared with the governed. His social position is guaranteed by the prescriptive rules of rank order and, for the political official, by special definitions of the criminal code against "insults of official" and "contempt" of state and church authorities.

The actual social position of the official is normally highest where, as in old civilized countries, the following conditions prevail: a strong demand for administration by trained experts; a strong and stable social differentiation, where the official predominantly derives from socially and economically privileged strata because of the social distribution of power; or where the costliness of the required training and status conventions are binding upon him. The possession of educational certificates—to be discussed elsewhere[2]—are usually linked with qualification for office. Naturally, such certificates or patents enhance the "status element" in the social position of the official. For the rest this status factor in individual cases is explicitly and impassively acknowledged; for example, in the prescription that the acceptance or rejection of an aspirant to an official career depends upon the consent ("election") of the members of the official body. This is the case in the German army with the officer corps. Similar phenomena, which promote this guild-like closure of officialdom, are typically found in patrimonial and, particularly, in prebendal officialdoms of the past. The desire to resurrect such phenomena in changed forms is by no means infrequent among modern bureaucrats. For instance, they have played a role among the demands of the quite proletarian and expert officials (the *tretyj* element) during the Russian revolution.

Usually the social esteem of the officials as such is especially low where the demand for expert administration and the dominance of status conventions are weak. This is especially the case in the United States; it is often the case in new settlements by virtue of their wide fields for profit-making and the great instability of their social stratification.

2. The pure type of bureaucratic official is appointed by a superior authority. An official elected by the governed is not a purely bureaucratic figure. Of course, the formal existence of an election does not by itself mean that no appointment hides behind the election—in the state, especially, appointment by party chiefs. Whether or not this is the case does not depend upon legal statutes but upon the way in which the party mechanism functions. Once firmly organized, the parties can turn a formally free election into the mere acclamation of a candidate designated

---

[2] Cf. *Wirtschaft und Gesellschaft*, pp. 73 ff. and Part II. (German editor's note.)

by the party chief. As a rule, however, a formally free election is turned into a fight, conducted according to definite rules, for votes in favor of one of two designated candidates.

In all circumstances, the designation of officials by means of an election among the governed modifies the strictness of hierarchical subordination. In principle, an official who is so elected has an autonomous position opposite the superordinate official. The elected official does not derive his position "from above" but "from below," or at least not from a superior authority of the official hierarchy but from powerful party men ("bosses"), who also determine his further career. The career of the elected official is not, or at least not primarily, dependent upon his chief in the administration. The official who is not elected but appointed by a chief normally functions more exactly from a technical point of view, because, all other circumstances being equal, it is more likely that purely functional points of consideration and qualities will determine his selection and career. As laymen, the governed can become acquainted with the extent to which a candidate is expertly qualified for office only in terms of experience, and hence only after his service. Moreover, in every sort of selection of officials by election, parties quite naturally give decisive weight not to expert considerations but to the services a follower renders to the party boss. This holds for all kinds of procurement of officials by elections, for the designation of formally free, elected officials by party bosses when they determine the slate of candidates, or the free appointment by a chief who has himself been elected. The contrast, however, is relative; substantially similar conditions hold where legitimate monarchs and their subordinates appoint officials, except that the influence of the following are then less controllable.

Where the demand for administration by trained experts is considerable, and the party followings have to recognize an intellectually developed, educated, and freely moving "public opinion," the use of unqualified officials falls back upon the party in power at the next election. Naturally, this is more likely to happen when the officials are appointed by the chief. The demand for a trained administration now exists in the United States, but in the large cities where immigrant votes are "corraled," there is, of course, no educated public opinion. Therefore, popular elections of the administrative chief and also of his subordinate officials usually endanger the expert qualification of the official as well as the precise functioning of the bureaucratic mechanism. It also weakens the dependence of the officials upon the hierarchy. This holds at least for the large administrative bodies that are difficult to supervise. The superior qualification and integrity of federal judges, appointed by the President, as over against elected judges in the United States is well known, although both types of officials have been selected primarily in terms of party considerations. The great changes in American metropolitan administrations demanded by reformers have proceeded essentially from elected mayors working with an apparatus of officials who were appointed by them. These reforms have thus come about in a "Caesarist" fashion. Viewed technically, as an organized form of authority, the efficiency of "Caesarism," which often grows out of democracy, rests in general upon the position of the "Caesar" as a free trustee of the masses (of the army or of the citizenry), who is unfettered by tradition. The "Caesar" is thus the unrestrained master of a body of highly qualified military officers and officials whom he selects freely and personally without regard to tradition or to any other considerations. This "rule of the personal genius," however, stands in contradiction to the formally "democratic" principle of a universally elected officialdom.

3. Normally, the position of the official is held for life, at least in public bureaucracies; and this is increasingly the case for all similar structures. As a factual rule, tenure for life is presupposed even where the giving of notice or periodic reappointment occurs. In contrast to the worker in a private enterprise, the official normally holds tenure. Legal or actual life-tenure, however, is not recognized as the official's right to the possession of office, as was the case with many structures of authority in the past. Where legal guarantees against arbitrary dismissal or transfer are developed, they merely serve to guarantee a strictly objective discharge of specific office duties free from all personal considerations. In Germany, this is the case for all juridical and, increasingly, for all administrative officials.

Within the bureaucracy, therefore, the measure of "independence," legally guaranteed by tenure, is not always a source of increased status for the official whose position is thus secured. Indeed, often the reverse holds, especially in old cultures and communities that are highly differentiated. In such communities, the stricter the subordination under the arbitrary rule of the master, the more it guarantees the maintenance of the conventional seigneurial style of living for the official. Because of the very absence of these legal guarantees of tenure, the conventional esteem for the official may rise in the same way as, during the Middle Ages, the esteem of the nobility of office[3] rose at the expense of esteem for the freemen, and as the king's judge surpassed that of the people's judge. In Germany, the military officer or the administrative official can be removed from office at any time, or at least far more readily than the "independent judge," who never pays with loss of his office for even the grossest offense against the "code of honor" or against social conventions of the salon. For this very reason, if other things are equal, in the eyes of the master stratum the judge is considered less qualified for social intercourse than are officers and administrative officials, whose greater dependence on the master is a greater guarantee of their conformity with status conventions. Of course, the average official strives for a civil-service

---

[3] "Ministerialen."

law, which would materially secure his old age and provide increased guarantees against his arbitrary removal from office. This striving, however, has its limits. A very strong development of the "right to the office" naturally makes it more difficult to staff them with regard to technical efficiency, for such a development decreases the career-opportunities of ambitious candidates for office. This makes for the fact that officials, on the whole, do not feel their dependency upon those at the top. This lack of a feeling of dependency, however, rests primarily upon the inclination to depend upon one's equals rather than upon the socially inferior and governed strata. The present conservative movement among the Badenia clergy, occasioned by the anxiety of a presumably threatening separation of church and state, has been expressly determined by the desire not to be turned "from a master into a servant of the parish."[4]

4. The official receives the regular pecuniary compensation of a normally fixed salary and the old age security provided by a pension. The salary is not measured like a wage in terms of work done, but according to "status," that is, according to the kind of function (the "rank") and, in addition, possibly, according to the length of service. The relatively great security of the official's income, as well as the rewards of social esteem, make the office a sought-after position, especially in countries which no longer provide opportunities for colonial profits. In such countries, this situation permits relatively low salaries for officials.

5. The official is set for a "career" within the hierarchical order of the public service. He moves from the lower, less important, and lower paid to the higher positions. The average official naturally desires a mechanical fixing of the conditions of promotion; if not of the offices, at least of the salary levels. He wants these conditions fixed in terms of "seniority," or possibly according to grades achieved in a developed system of expert examinations. Here and there, such examinations actually form a character *indelebilis* of the official and have lifelong effects on his career. To this is joined the desire to qualify the right to office and the increasing tendency toward status group closure and economic security. All of this makes for a tendency to consider the offices as "prebends" of those who are qualified by educational certificates. The necessity of taking general personal and intellectual qualifications into consideration, irrespective of the often subaltern character of the educational certificate, has led to a condition in which the highest political offices, especially the positions of "ministers," are principally filled without reference to such certificates.

3. THE PRESUPPOSITIONS AND CAUSES OF BUREAUCRACY

The social and economic presuppositions of the modern structure of the office are as follows:

---

[4] Written before 1914. (German editor's note.)

The development of the money economy, in so far as a pecuniary compensation of the officials is concerned, is a presupposition of bureaucracy. Today it not only prevails but is predominant. This fact is of very great importance for the whole bearing of bureaucracy, yet by itself it is by no means decisive for the existence of bureaucracy. . . .

Even though the full development of a money economy is not an indispensable precondition for bureaucratization, bureaucracy as a permanent structure is knit to the one presupposition of a constant income for maintaining it. Where such an income cannot be derived from private profits, as is the case with the bureaucratic organization of large modern enterprises, or from fixed land rents, as with the manor, a stable system of taxation is the precondition for the permanent existence of bureaucratic administration. For well-known and general reasons, only a fully developed money economy offers a secure basis for such a taxation system. The degree of administrative bureaucratization in urban communities with fully developed money economies has not infrequently been relatively greater than in the contemporary far larger states of plains. Yet as soon as these plain states have been able to develop orderly systems of tribute, bureaucracy has developed more comprehensively than in city states. Whenever the size of the city states has remained confined to moderate limits, the tendency for a plutocratic and collegial administration by notables has corresponded most adequately to their structure. . . .

6. TECHNICAL ADVANTAGES OF BUREAUCRATIC ORGANIZATION

The decisive reason for the advance of bureaucratic organization has always been its purely technical superiority over any other form of organization. The mature bureaucracy compares with other forms exactly as does the machine with the nonmechanical modes of production.

Precision, speed, unambiguity, knowledge of the files, continuity, discretion, unity, strict subordination, reduction of friction and of material and personal costs—these are raised to the optimum point in the strictly bureaucratic administration, and especially in its monocratic form. As compared with all collegiate, honorific, and avocational forms of administration, trained bureaucracy is superior on all these points. And as far as complicated tasks are concerned, paid bureaucratic work is not only more precise but, in the last analysis, it is often cheaper than even formally unremunerated honorific service.

Honorific arrangements make administrative work an avocation and, for this reason alone, honorific service normally functions more slowly; being less bound to schemata and being more formless. Hence it is less precise and less unified than bureaucratic work because it is less dependent upon superiors and because the establishment and exploitation of the apparatus of subordinate officials and filing services are almost unavoid-

ably less economical. Honorific service is less continuous than bureaucratic and frequently quite expensive. This is especially the case if one
thinks not only of the money costs to the public treasury—costs which
bureaucratic administration, in comparison with administration by notables, usually substantially increases—but also of the frequent economic
losses of the governed caused by delays and lack of precision. The possibility of administration by notables normally and permanently exists only
where official management can be satisfactorily discharged as an avocation. With the qualitative increase of tasks the administration has to face,
administration by notables reaches its limits—today, even in England.
Work organized by collegiate bodies causes friction and delay and requires compromises between colliding interests and views. The administration, therefore, runs less precisely and is more independent of superiors; hence, it is less unified and slower. All advances of the Prussian
administrative organization have been and will in the future be advances
of the bureaucratic, and especially of the monocratic, principle.

Today, it is primarily the capitalist market economy which demands
that the official business of the administration be discharged precisely,
unambiguously, continuously, and with as much speed as possible. Normally, the very large, modern capitalist enterprises are themselves un-
equalled models of strict bureaucratic organization. Business management
throughout rests on increasing precision, steadiness, and, above all, the
speed of operations. This, in turn, is determined by the peculiar nature of
the modern means of communication, including, among other things, the
news service of the press. The extraordinary increase in the speed by
which public announcements, as well as economic and political facts, are
transmitted exerts a steady and sharp pressure in the direction of speeding
up the tempo of administrative reaction towards various situations. The
optimum of such reaction time is normally attained only by a strictly
bureaucratic organization.[5]

Bureaucratization offers above all the optimum possibility for carrying
through the principle of specializing administrative functions according
to purely objective considerations. Individual performances are allocated
to functionaries who have specialized training and who by constant practice learn more and more. The "objective" discharge of business primarily means a discharge of business according to calculable rules and
"without regard for persons."

"Without regard for persons" is also the watchword of the "market"
and, in general, of all pursuits of naked economic interests. A consistent
execution of bureaucratic domination means the leveling of status
"honor." Hence, if the principle of the free-market is not at the same

---

[5] Here we cannot discuss in detail how the bureaucratic apparatus may, and
actually does, produce definite obstacles to the discharge of business in a manner
suitable for the single case.

time restricted, it means the universal domination of the "class situation." That this consequence of bureaucratic domination has not set in everywhere, parallel to the extent of bureaucratization, is due to the differences among possible principles by which polities may meet their demands.

The second element mentioned, "calculable rules," also is of paramount importance for modern bureaucracy. The peculiarity of modern culture, and specifically of its technical and economic basis, demands this very "calculability" of results. When fully developed, bureaucracy also stands, in a specific sense, under the principle of *sine ira ac studio*. Its specific nature, which is welcomed by capitalism, develops the more perfectly the more the bureaucracy is "dehumanized," the more completely it succeeds in eliminating from official business love, hatred, and all purely personal, irrational, and emotional elements which escape calculation. This is the specific nature of bureaucracy and it is appraised as its special virtue.

The more complicated and specialized modern culture becomes, the more its external supporting apparatus demands the personally detached and strictly "objective" expert, in lieu of the master of older social structures, who was moved by personal sympathy and favor, by grace and gratitude. Bureaucracy offers the attitudes demanded by the external apparatus of modern culture in the most favorable combination. As a rule, only bureaucracy has established the foundation for the administration of a rational law conceptually systematized on the basis of such enactments as the latter Roman imperial period first created with a high degree of technical perfection. During the Middle Ages, this law was received along with the bureaucratization of legal administration, that is to say, with the displacement of the old trial procedure, which was bound to tradition or to irrational presuppositions, by the rationally trained and specialized expert. . . .

10. THE PERMANENT CHARACTER OF THE BUREAUCRATIC MACHINE

Once it is fully established, bureaucracy is among those social structures which are the hardest to destroy. Bureaucracy is the means of carrying "community action" over into rationally ordered "societal action." Therefore, as an instrument for "societalizing" relations of power, bureaucracy has been and is a power instrument of the first order—for the one who controls the bureaucratic apparatus.

Under otherwise equal conditions, a "societal action," which is methodically ordered and led, is superior to every resistance of "mass" or even of "communal action." And where the bureaucratization of administration has been completely carried through, a form of power relation is established that is practically unshatterable.

The individual bureaucrat cannot squirm out of the apparatus in which he is harnessed. In contrast to the honorific or avocational "notable," the professional bureaucrat is chained to his activity by his entire material and ideal existence. In the great majority of cases, he is only a single cog in an ever-moving mechanism which prescribes to him an essentially fixed route of march. The official is entrusted with specialized tasks and normally the mechanism cannot be put into motion or arrested by him, but only from the very top. The individual bureaucrat is thus forged to the community of all the functionaries who are integrated into the mechanism. They have a common interest in seeing that the mechanism continues its functions and that the societally exercised authority carries on.

The ruled, for their part, cannot dispense with or replace the bureaucratic apparatus of authority once it exists. For this bureaucracy rests upon expert training, a functional specialization of work, and an attitude set for habitual and virtuoso-like mastery of single yet methodically integrated functions. If the official stops working, or if his work is forcefully interrupted, chaos results, and it is difficult to improvise replacements from among the governed who are fit to master such chaos. This holds for public administration as well as for private economic management. More and more the material fate of the masses depends upon the steady and correct functioning of the increasingly bureaucratic organizations of private capitalism. The idea of eliminating these organizations becomes more and more utopian.

The discipline of officialdom refers to the attitude-set of the official for precise obedience within his habitual activity, in public as well as in private organizations. This discipline increasingly becomes the basis of all order, however great the practical importance of administration on the basis of the filed documents may be. The naïve idea of Bakuninism of destroying the basis of "acquired rights" and "domination" by destroying public documents overlooks the settled orientation of man for keeping to the habitual rules and regulations that continue to exist independently of the documents. Every reorganization of beaten or dissolved troops, as well as the restoration of administrative orders destroyed by revolt, panic, or other catastrophes, is realized by appealing to the trained orientation of obedient compliance to such orders. Such compliance has been conditioned into the officials, on the one hand, and, on the other hand, into the governed. If such an appeal is successful it brings, as it were, the disturbed mechanism into gear again.

The objective indispensability of the once-existing apparatus, with its peculiar, "impersonal" character, means that the mechanism—in contrast to feudal orders based upon personal piety—is easily made to work for anybody who knows how to gain control over it. A rationally ordered system of officials continues to function smoothly after the enemy has occupied the area; he merely needs to change the top officials. This body of officials continues to operate because it is to the vital interest of everyone concerned, including above all the enemy.

During the course of his long years in power, Bismarck brought his ministerial colleagues into unconditional bureaucratic dependence by eliminating all independent statesmen. Upon his retirement, he saw to his surprise that they continued to manage their offices unconcerned and undismayed, as if he had not been the master mind and creator of these creatures, but rather as if some single figure had been exchanged for some other figure in the bureaucratic machine. With all the changes of masters in France since the time of the First Empire, the power machine has remained essentially the same. Such a machine makes "revolution," in the sense of the forceful creation of entirely new formations of authority, technically more and more impossible, especially when the apparatus controls the modern means of communication (telegraph, et cetera) and also by virtue of its internal rationalized structure. In classic fashion, France has demonstrated how this process has substituted *coups d'etat* for "revolutions": all successful transformations in France have amounted to *coups d'etat.*

5. ADMINISTRATIVE RATIONALITY, SOCIAL SETTING, AND ORGANIZATIONAL DEVELOPMENT*

Stanley H. Udy, Jr.

ABSTRACT

A scale of structural requisites of administrative rationality is hypothesized, tested with a sample of thirty-four organizations in varied social settings, and interpreted as measuring cumulative specificity of organizational roles and their motivation by internal organizational devices. Institutional correlates of the scale are explored and suggest that independence from the social setting is positively correlated with rationality. Ascriptive elements in the social setting are found to be negatively related to rationality. Certain hypotheses concerning organizational development are proposed in light of the findings.

FEW IF any concepts employed in social science are fraught with so many difficulties as is the concept "rationality." It is used in a bewildering variety of ways, each of which seems to involve its own plethora of philosophical, psychological, and sociological problems. For present purposes we shall let the chips fall where they may and consider social behavior to be *rational* insofar as it is purposefully directed toward explicit empirical objectives and planned in accordance with the best available scientific knowledge.[1] Brushing aside, for the time being, the question of uncertainty—which, though of crucial practical importance, merely complicates the problem in a formal sense—one may say that the most severe difficulties with this concept from a sociological viewpoint seem to appear in situations where it is applied simultaneously to individuals and collectivities in the same context. Historically the classic instance is perhaps the "problem of order" in utilitarian social philosophy; namely, the problem of accounting for the existence of society assuming it to be composed of discrete individuals striving rationally for the same ends in a context of scarce resources. The solution to this problem, of course, as has been widely pointed out, is that neither the individual nor society—particularly the latter—is so rational in its behavior as the utilitarians had supposed. Cultural values distribute ends among categories of persons differentiated in the social structure and, at the same time, motivate "nonrational" behavior in given circumstances.

---

* Reprinted from *American Journal of Sociology*, November, 1962.

[1] Based on Marion J. Levy, Jr., "A Note on Pareto's Logical-Nonlogical Categories," *American Sociological Review*, Vol. XIII (December, 1948), pp. 756–57. The problem of uncertainty of information is, of course, extremely important in other contexts. See, e.g., Herbert A. Simon, *Models of Man* (New York: John Wiley & Sons, 1957), pp. 241–60.

Social integration is hence possible because there is no reason to suppose that it must occur relative to explicit overall objectives. Not all behavior need be rational; indeed, on the societal level it cannot be.[2]

In the analysis of formal organizations, however, the problem of rationality arises again in a somewhat different form. One may define a *formal organization* as any social group engaged in pursuing explicit announced empirical objectives through manifestly coordinated effort and, at the same time, describe an entity that appears to be culturally universal.[3] A striking feature of such organizations is that the individuals in the system qua members as well as the system as a whole are expected to behave in a rational manner. The classical "problem of order" suggests that this state of affairs is by no means easy to attain; we may reasonably expect some formal organizations to come closer to it and, in this sense, to be "more rational" than others. Such "dual rationality" can be approximated in the case of formal organization only because the members of the organization are at the same time members of a larger society where integrative values can find expression independently of administrative structure.

We may thus presume rationality to be present in a formal organization to the extent that role expectations are based on planning for organizational objectives.[4] In a more sophisticated statement, Cyert and March characterize a rational system as being oriented to produce choices through standardized search procedures in such a way as to "maximize the expected return to the system" in terms of "a well-defined preference ordering over possible future states."[5] Two major determinants of the degree of administrative rationality in an organization thus suggest themselves: The first is the extent to which the structure of the organization defines and motivates planned collective behavior; the second is the degree to which behavior in the social setting is independent of behavior in the organization, from the standpoint of the individual member. This paper will thus first attempt to isolate organizational-structural requisites of rationality and to analyze their interrelations. It will be found that the requisites herein isolated form a Guttman scale in terms of which the organizations studied can be compared as to degree of rationality. Second, we shall explore relationships between the rationality scale and the institu-

---

[2] Talcott Parsons, *The Structure of Social Action* (Glencoe, Ill.: Free Press, 1949), pp. 87–94, 697–719.

[3] Stanley H. Udy, Jr., " 'Bureaucracy' and 'Rationality' in Weber's Organization Theory," *American Sociological Review*, Vol. XXIV (December, 1959), p. 792 (hereinafter cited as "*BR*").

[4] Stanley H. Udy, Jr., "Technical and Institutional Factors in Production Organization," *American Journal of Sociology*, Vol. LXVII (November, 1961), p. 248 (hereinafter cited as "*TI*").

[5] R. M. Cyert and J. G. March, *A Behavioral Theory of the Firm* (Englewood Cliffs, N.J.: Prentice-Hall, Inc., 1963).

tional and social settings of the organizations studied, in an attempt to assess the independence from societal ascription of organizations lying at different points on the scale. Finally, we shall propose some hypotheses about the development of rationality in organization.[6]

DATA AND METHODS

Data are drawn from 34 formal organizations engaged in the production of material goods in thirty-four nonindustrial societies; information is based on anthropological monographs and the Human Relations Area Files. The method of cross-cultural comparison was used in order to maximize variation in both internal structure and social setting of the organizations studied. It was also decided to limit the analysis to organizations having three or more levels of authority, inasmuch as previous work suggested that only such organizations would be of sufficient complexity to be of interest for present purposes.[7] The 34 organizations studied are part of a sample of 426 organizations in 150 societies assembled for an earlier, more general study of work organization in nonindustrial culture and were drawn in accord with the criteria set forth by George P. Murdock for his "World Ethnographic Sample."[8] Fifty-six of the original 426 cases proved both to have three or more levels of authority and also to offer sufficient data for purposes of the present analysis. Twelve of them,

---

[6] Rationality is here treated as a *function* of organizational and social structure. In two previous papers we treated rationality as a *structural* category by operationalizing it in terms of presumed structural correlates. In *BR*, Weber's conception of administrative rationality was found to involve limited objectives, a performance emphasis, and segmental participation, as those terms are defined in the present study. In *TI*, degree of rationality was operationalized in terms of the presence or absence of limited objectives and segmental participation, as those terms are herein defined. In view of present considerations these earlier characterizations seem misleading. As indicated below, orientation to limited objectives appears to be the only one of these characteristics that properly forms a part of rationality per se, functionally considered. Performance emphasis, in view of the way it is operationalized, is more properly part of the reward system, and is so considered in *TI*. Segmental participation, along with a new item herein introduced, "specificity of role assignment," may be viewed structurally as an aspect of what one might term "role differentiation and assignment."

These changes, which allow the structural requisites of rationality to cut across the scheme presented in *TI*, suggest some revisions in the model presented there. Briefly, the category "role differentiation and assignment"—with particular reference to its degree of specificity—replaces what is there termed "rationality," and is defined somewhat differently, as indicated above. Assuming more precise ways of measuring it than are presented here, "rationality" could be considered a criterion variable relative to the entire model presented in *TI*. The relationships indicated in *TI* probably remain generally the same despite the change in the one category, although the present results raise some questions about their validity under certain conditions and suggest that some of the operational items are more important than others.

[7] *TI*, pp. 247–54.

[8] George P. Murdock, "World Ethnographic Sample," *American Anthropologist*, Vol. LIX (August, 1957), pp. 664–87.

however, had already been employed in an ex post facto extrapolation of a scale containing four of the seven items used in the scale developed in the present study.[9] Since one of our desires was to test the previous result, these 12 cases were dropped, leaving 44 organizations representing 34 societies. Under the not entirely realistic assumption that organizations in different societies represent independent events while those in the same society do not, only one organization per society was finally used, it being drawn at random when the society offered more than one potentially usable case on the basis of a survey of pertinent ethnographic material. Of the resulting 34 organizations representing 34 societies, 11 are African, 12 North American, and the remaining 11 are distributed over the circum-Mediterranean, insular Pacific, east Eurasian, and South American regions.[10] The geographical distribution of the sample is therefore unfortunately somewhat unbalanced. The extent to which this imbalance reflects the actual distribution of complex production organization as opposed to complete data is not known, except that it may be noted that materials on South American societies are quite sparse.

ADMINISTRATIVE RATIONALITY AND ITS STRUCTURAL REQUISITES

We shall assume that rationality as herein defined minimally involves orientation to *limited objectives*, defined for present purposes as objectives explicitly restricted only to the production of certain products. This simple criterion of rationality is, of course, far from ideal but represents the closest operational approach possible of our data to "explicit announced objectives" or to "a well-defined preference ordering of future states."[11] We shall thus assert that "highly rational" organizations possess limited objectives in this sense, by definition. The problem now becomes one of exploring the structural requisites of an organizational orientation to limited objectives. In an earlier study it had been found that all organizations with limited objectives also involved *segmental participation*—that is, explicit definition of the terms of participation by some mutual contractual agreement—but that not all organizations with segmental participation had limited objectives.[12] Since a reasonable common-sense interpretation of this relationship is at hand (unrestricted

---

[9] Stanley H. Udy, Jr., " 'Bureaucratic' Elements in Organizations," *American Sociological Review*, Vol. XXIII (August, 1958), pp. 415–18 (hereinafter cited as "BE"). In this earlier study, these characteristics were termed "bureaucratic" elements. It has since seemed appropriate to refer to them as aspects of "role differentiation and assignment" associated with rationality, and to treat "bureaucracy" as another dimension of organization entirely (see BR).

[10] Murdock, *op. cit.*

[11] Cyert and March, *op. cit.*

[12] BR.

terms of participation seem likely to invite goal displacement) it was decided to hypothesize that segmental participation precedes limited objectives at the upper end of the rationality scale. Reference was then made to another previous study[13] that found (in a sample different from the present one) the following characteristics to be related to segmental participation on a scale in the following descending order: *Performance emphasis* (expected dependence of the quantity of the reward on the amount and/or quality of work done); *specialization*[14] (the concurrent performance of three or more qualitatively different operations by different members); and *compensatory rewards* (allocation of money or goods in kind by members of higher authority to members of lower authority in return for participation).[15] Reasonable theoretical interpretations seemed possible for these findings as well. Segmental participation would seem to be difficult without some explicit attention being drawn to performance. Similarly, unless roles are specialized relative to one another such that the particular content of each is stable and discretely identifiable, any emphasis on performance would seem tenuous. Specialization, in turn, is always potentially difficult to institutionalize, since it is always at least partially determined by technical considerations. Functionally, compensatory rewards constitute a mechanism whereby specialization can be "artificially" institutionalized by management through its control over the reward system. Furthermore, there is some reason to believe that compensatory rewards constitute the *only* mechanism that can reliably do this. Empirically, there appear to be only two possible alternatives: manipulation of already-existing social obligations, and the use of force.[16] The first of these alternatives presupposes a fortuitous and highly improbable identity of technical activities and social roles; the second is subject to serious limitations as a continuous mode of control, particularly in organizations that are at all complex. If this line of reasoning is correct, compensatory

---

[13] *BE.*

[14] We have elsewhere defined "specialization" as a continuous variable (i.e., the number of different operations performed simultaneously by different members; see my *Organization of Work* [New Haven, Conn.: HRAF Press, 1959], pp. 22–23). In a social context of the type discussed here, however, it seems proper to regard specialization as discontinuous; the number "three" was chosen as the cutoff point because three is the smallest number of roles in one system wherein ego is faced with the problem of defining relationships between two alters in a way independent of ego's relationship with either of them.

[15] See Peter M. Blau and W. Richard Scott, *Formal Organizations* (San Francisco: Howard M. Chandler, 1962), pp. 205–6, 224–25. Blau and Scott regard this characteristic as indicative of "hierarchical dependence." We find that compensatory rewards indeed do represent hierarchical dependence but only one possible form which it may take. Other possible forms would be the use or threat of force, manipulation of approval needs, etc. We would argue that if organization is to be rational it is important that hierarchical dependence be restricted to compensatory rewards.

[16] S. H. Udy, Jr., *Organization of Work* (New York, Taplinger Publishing Co.); chap. vii.

rewards are requisite to specialization, except under extremely improbable social conditions.

A review of pertinent literature on administration revealed that the items so far mentioned are often assumed to be structural correlates of administrative rationality and suggested two further items on which data were available: *specific job assignment* (continuous assignment by management of particular people to particular roles), and *centralized management* (the existence of a single internal source of ultimate authority).[17] The former was placed on the scale between specialization and performance emphasis on the grounds that roles had to be specialized to be assigned and that particular people had to be associated with particular roles to be rewarded for performance in a consistent fashion. Centralized management was placed at the beginning of the scale on the grounds that management could not consistently allocate compensatory rewards without being centralized.

The scale suggested by the preceding arguments was tested over our sample with the results shown in Table 1: "X" denotes the presence of a characteristic, "O" its absence. In general, the results are consistent with the hypotheses proposed.

Since much of the theoretical basis of this scale is probabilistic, one would expect some exceptions. Deviant cases were thus examined in detail, and proved to be of two general types. The first involved the absence of expected specialization or performance emphasis—the apparent loci of most of the deviance. The reason why so much deviation centers on these characteristics seems to be that the presence or absence of each of them, in contrast to the other items, is in part a function of purely technical considerations. Certain kinds of tasks, as for example many involving agriculture or construction, are by nature cumulative and do not lend themselves particularly to specialization, although there is no reason why they cannot be otherwise rationally organized. The Tallensi, Tarahumara, and Camayura cases appear probably to be of this variety. They suggest that rationality involves specialization only where the latter is clearly relevant technologically. Similarly, whether or not rationality involves a performance emphasis appears to be technologically relative. Where activities are highly routinized with a minimum of uncertainty involved, performance seems less likely to be emphasized, despite the presence of other rational characteristics. The Nambicuara, Otoro, and Hopi cases may well be of this variety. In sum, it appears that specialization and a

---

[17] See, e.g., Max Weber, *Theory of Social and Economic Organization* (New York: Oxford University Press, 1947), pp. 225–26; *General Economic History* (Glencoe, Ill.: Free Press, 1950), p. 95; H. H. Gerth and C. Wright Mills, *From Max Weber: Essays in Sociology* (New York: Oxford University Press, 1946), pp. 196 ff.; James G. March and Herbert A. Simon, *Organizations* (New York: John Wiley & Sons, 1958), pp. 12–33; and Chris Argyris, *Understanding Organizational Behavior* (Homewood, Ill.: Dorsey Press, 1960), pp. 12–13.

TABLE 1

ADMINISTRATIVE RATIONALITY IN 34 NONINDUSTRIAL
PRODUCTION ORGANIZATIONS*

Organization	Limited Objectives	Segmental Participation	Performance Emphasis	Specific Job Assignment	Specialization	Compensatory Rewards	Central Management
Iroquois	x	x	x	x	x	x	x
Navaho	x	x	x	x	x	x	x
Paiute	x	x	x	x	x	x	x
Sanpoil	x	x	x	x	x	x	x
Sinkaietk	x	x	0	x	x	x	x
Nambicuara	x	x	0	x	x	x	x
Otoro	0	x	0	x	x	x	x
Hopi	0	x	0	x	x	x	x
Tikopia	0	0	x	x	x	x	x
Kabyles	0	0	x	x	x	x	x
Jukun	0	0	x	0	x	x	x
Tallensi	0	0	x	x	0	x	x
Haida	0	0	0	x	x	x	x
Haitians	0	0	0	x	x	x	x
Dahomeans	0	0	0	x	0	x	x
Tarahumara	0	0	0	x	0	x	x
Turkana	0	0	0	x	0	x	x
Camayura	0	0	0	x	0	x	x
Betsileo	0	0	0	0	x	x	x
Trobrianders	0	0	0	0	x	x	x
Pukapukans	0	0	0	0	x	0	x
Malay	0	0	0	0	x	0	x
Bemba	0	0	0	0	0	x	x
Crow	0	0	0	0	0	x	x
Ifaluk	0	0	0	0	0	x	x
Ila	0	0	0	0	0	x	x
Kikuyu	0	0	0	0	0	x	x
Lobi	0	0	0	0	0	x	x
Papago	0	0	0	0	0	x	x
Sotho	0	0	0	0	0	x	x
Winnebago	0	0	0	0	0	x	x
Dogon	0	0	0	0	0	0	x
Tarasco	0	0	0	0	0	0	0
Tibetans	0	0	0	0	0	0	0

* Coefficient of reproducibility = .95.
For references see Udy, *Organization of Work*, pp. 139–58 ff.

performance emphasis tend in effect not to be a part of rational administration unless their presence clearly contributes to technical efficiency in
the physical sense.

The other class of exceptions may be purely a function of the research
methodology and are thus possibly more apparent than real. A characteristic was coded as "absent" not only when its existence was explicitly
denied but also in instances where it was simply not reported, provided the
context was such that it seemed reasonable to assume that the ethnographer
would have reported it had it been present. This procedure of course

tended to result in "overreporting" absences. On this score the single deviant omissions for the Sinkaietk, Dahomeans, Pukapukans, and possibly the Turkana are dubious; the "absent" characteristics may actually be present. By the same token, the Betsileo case may involve specific job assignments; the description is not entirely clear on this point. General explanations for other exceptions are not apparent.

The results were adjudged to be consistent with the hypothesis, although our interpretation of some of the exceptions suggests the desirability of complicating the model with some contextual variables deriving from technology. We suggest that the scale items indicate a cumulative emphasis on specificity of organizational roles and decision rules such that (1) explicit limits for individual rationality are established and motivated, and (2) interrelated procedures relative to collective rationality are established.

THE INSTITUTIONALIZATION OF RATIONALITY

We now wish to explore and explicate the hypothesis that administrative rationality involves relative independence of the organization from its social setting. Central to this hypothesis is the idea of social involvement, developed in a previous paper. *Social involvement* is defined as the institutionalization of participation and motivation in the organization through expectations and obligations existing independently of the organization in the social setting.[18] One would expect socially involved organizations to be less rational on the grounds that they are less independent of the social setting. The presence in the organization of opportunities to express general social values would inhibit the development of highly specific roles and procedures. In addition, one would expect organizations that are not socially involved to be highly rational under an assumption of structural substitution: that is, if functions are not performed in the setting they would presumably have to be built into the organization.

Rationality was run against a modified version of a social involvement rank order developed in a previous study.[19] The 34 organizations studied were ranked in presumed order of increasing social involvement according to how participation is institutionalized as follows:

1. Participation expected on the basis of voluntary self-commitment and self-defined self-interest.
2. Participation based on voluntary self-commitment defined as a kinship or community obligation.
3. Participation required by compulsory reciprocity.

---

[18] *TI*, pp. 248–49.
[19] *Ibid.*

4. Participation required by compulsory kinship ascription.

5. Participation required by compulsory political ascription, usually sanctioned by bodily punishment.

TABLE 2
RATIONALITY AND SOCIAL INVOLVEMENT*

Social Involvement†	Scale Type							
	0	1	2	3	4	5	6	7
Compulsory political ascription.............2	0	4	3	0	0	0	0
Compulsory kinship ascription..............0	1	1	0	0	0	0	0
Compulsory reciprocity....................0	0	4	1	0	1	0	0
Self-commitment, kinship or community obligation...................................0	0	0	0	6	3	0	0
Voluntary self-commitment, self-defined self-interest.................................0	0	0	0	0	0	2	6

* "Compulsory" social involvement categories collapsed and scale types 0–3, 4–5, and 6–7 combined: $x^2 = 62.79$; $P < .001$; degrees of freedom = 4.
† As indicated by basis of participation.

Results are shown in Table 2. They are consistent with the hypothesis both as to tendency and symmetry, except that the three "compulsory" social involvement categories do not appear to differ from one another in effect.

For further exploratory purposes, the eight *most rational* organizations (those with segmental participation with or without limited objectives) were compared with all other organizations. Another measure of whether or not the organization is institutionalized as independent from its setting is the separation of ownership from management. Table 3 compares organizations having *independent proprietorship* ("ownership" separated from "management" in that control over the ultimate disposition of the means of production is not vested in management) with all other organizations with respect to rationality. All the most rational organizations in the sample have independent proprietorships; most of the other ones do not; the relationship is significant at the .05 level.

TABLE 3
RATIONALITY AND PROPRIETORSHIP*

	Most Rational Organizations	Other
Independent proprietorship......	8	7
Other........................	0	18

$$Q = +1.00$$
$$X^2 = 9.93$$
$$P < .01$$

* One case was omitted owing to lack of data.

We thus conclude that the mechanisms by which rational administration is institutionalized are such as to produce an independence, or segmentation, of the organization from its social setting. As is the case with individual members relative to the organization, so is the case of the organization relative to its social setting; rational administration requires that an "area of discretion" be defined within which manipulative planning is free to occur.

THE SOCIAL SETTING OF RATIONAL ORGANIZATION

The preceding discussion suggests that it is more difficult for rational administration to develop in social settings that emphasize traditional ascriptive relationships. Previous research suggests that this may be especially likely where differences of power and status are ascribed, since such differences seem particularly likely to be part of social involvement

TABLE 4
RATIONALITY AND ASCRIPTIVE ELEMENTS IN SOCIAL SETTING*

	Complex Hereditary Stratification		Hereditary Political Succession		Slavery	
	Present	Absent	Present	Absent	Present	Absent
Most rational organizations.	0	7	4	3	2	6
Other organizations......	10	15	16	7	11	14
	$Q = -1.00$		$Q = -.26$		$Q = -.40$	
	$X^2 = 2.42$		$X^2 = .02$		$X^2 = .29$	
	$P > .10$		$P > .98$		$P > .50$	

* Cases lacking data omitted.

patterns.[20] Accordingly, the settings of the most rational organizations were compared with the settings of all other organizations with respect to three presumed indexes of the general presence of ascription in the society concerned: (1) the presence of a hereditary stratification system with at least three classes or castes; (2) the presence of hereditary political succession; (3) the presence of slavery in any form.[21] Combined results appear in Table 4. The hypothesis is rather weakly confirmed; none of the relationships is statistically significant at the .05 level, but all are in the expected direction, and the stratification relationship approaches significance. None of the most rational organizations in the sample existed in a setting with a complex stratification system. Furthermore, Table 5 indicates what at first glance seems to be a surprising finding—rational

[20] *Ibid.*
[21] Data are drawn from Murdock, *op. cit.*

TABLE 5
RATIONALITY AND GENERAL CENTRALIZED GOVERNMENT*

	General Centralized Government	
	Present	Absent
Most rational organizations..................	1	7
Other organizations........................	12	13

$$Q = -.73$$
$$X^2 = 2.33$$
$$P > .10$$

* One case omitted owing to lack of data.

organization is negatively associated with the existence of a centralized government transcending the local community. The relationship, however, is not statistically significant. We report it because, in the type of society dealt with here, strong central government indicates a hierarchical feudal order wherein political power permeates the entire social order, and is hence probably simply another index of ascription. If so, this result is consistent with our hypothesis.[22]

DEVELOPMENT OF RATIONAL ADMINISTRATION

It is very hazardous to attempt to extrapolate hypotheses concerning organizational evolution or development from cross-sectional data of the type on which this study is based. As our earlier theoretical argument indicates, a scale does suggest a structure of requisite elements. It does not, however, indicate prerequisites. One cannot conclude from our scale, for example, that centralized management must precede compensatory rewards in a temporal sequence of development. Similarly, a scale per se implies nothing about causal relationships among the items in it. It simply describes a modal static state of affairs.

One can, however, use such a scale to predict types of problems that different developmental sequences will probably entail. For example, if specialization should be the first rational characteristic to develop in an organization, the scale implies that such an organization if it is to be stable must immediately develop a centralized management and compensatory rewards. Unless it proves to be the case that rational administrative characteristics are likely to develop simultaneously—and we shall presently see that at least in many cases this is highly unlikely—one may hypothesize that a developmental sequence that follows the scale pattern will probably entail fewer problems and tensions than one which does not.[23]

[22] It should perhaps be pointed out that political conservatives have been alleging this relationship for some time, though the applicability of the present data to such an argument is probably questionable for the reasons suggested.

[23] On the other hand it may be impossible to develop administrative rationality without generating problems and tensions.

It is further possible to infer certain constraints and problems that seem likely to arise at specific points in organizational development. First, the institutional system appears to be markedly discontinuous relative to administrative rationality. An increase in rationality beyond specialization evidently involves a radical change in institutional arrangements; ascriptive social involvement is abandoned in favor of self-commitment. Similarly, an increase beyond a performance emphasis involves another such change— the introduction of the norm of self-defined self-interest in commitment, as well as the separation of proprietorship from management. But between points of discontinuity, it appears possible for rationality to fluctuate independently of the institutional system, provided the requisite pattern suggested by the scale is maintained. Thus, for example, given an institutional adjustment to specific job assignments, performance can either be emphasized or not, with no institutional implications one way or the other. By the same token an organization with no rational characteristics at all can develop a centralized management, compensatory rewards, and specialization without encountering institutional difficulties. But if either of these organizations were to proceed further in rational development, its mode of institutionalization would have to change considerably.

The fact that Table 2 is symmetrical suggests that the converse of the preceding argument may also be valid, insofar as obligation to participate is concerned. It appears that if participation is institutionalized as voluntary commitment based on self-defined self-interest, the organization must at least involve segmental participation plus, in principle, the five other characteristics lower on the scale. Also, participation based on self-commitment in a context of kinship or community obligations implies an organization at least sufficiently rational to possess specific job assignments, together with specialization, compensatory rewards, and a centralized management. On the other hand, where participation is purely ascriptive or based on compulsory reciprocity, no rational elements need necessarily be present.

One may next ask: In what kinds of societal settings is administrative rationality, together with its requisite institutional arrangements, most likely to be found? Owing to gaps in the data, our analysis at this point is necessarily quite fragmentary. In complex hereditary aristocracy, the existence of slavery, hereditary succession to political office, and complex government are viewed as rough indexes of an ascriptive emphasis in the culture concerned. Tables 4 and 5 suggest, as one might suppose, that organizations in settings where ascription is stressed are themselves likely to be highly socially involved, and hence possess nonrational administrative systems. It is particulary noteworthy that complex hereditary stratification is absent from the setting of all the most rational administrative systems. But this relationship is not symmetrical, and the situation with respect to the other social setting variables is not nearly so marked. One infers, therefore, that, to some extent at least, fairly rational organizations can be institutionalized in quite "hostile" settings. Also, it would appear that a propitious setting does not in itself guarantee rational administration. Why might this be so?

We have already seen that certain elements of rationality—notably specialization and performance emphasis—are at least partially functions of technical, as opposed to institutional, influences. If in a more general sense it is the case that administration tends to be no more rational than is technically necessary, one would indeed expect to find instances of relatively nonrational administrative systems in settings where rationality would in principle be possible, merely because in the instances concerned rationality would be technically unnecessary.

A second reason may stem from the type of ascription present in the social setting. Stinchcombe has suggested that where rationality is a general cultural value, ascription may not markedly inhibit rationality in administration, on the grounds that the major effect of ascription is to infuse the organization with general cultural values.[24] It is possible that the Iroquois case in our sample partially illustrates this type of situation. It is known that Iroquois culture placed a high valuation on efficiency and achievement, with socialization measures taken to assure the differential competence of hereditary political officials. And the Iroquois organization in our sample is highly rational, yet exists in a society with a complex government involving hereditary political officials. Complex hereditary stratification is absent, however. Furthermore, participation is based on self-defined self-interest. It may be that a general valuation of rationality simply tends to make possible nonascriptive recruitment in otherwise ascriptive settings. Modern industrial society may largely fit in this category. For even in the presence of a high cultural valuation on efficiency and rationality, ascriptive recruitment can still be disruptive to organizational operations by introducing competing goals and loyalties, however "rationally" they are individually viewed. It would seem that there are limits to the extent to which the effects of ascription on administration can be offset by institutional arrangements.

CONCLUSIONS

In a sample of 34 nonindustrial production organizations, seven organizational characteristics associated with administrative rationality were found to scale in a cross-sectional comparative analysis in such a way as to suggest that rationality involves a cumulative emphasis on specificity of organizational roles and decision rules. The rationality scale was further found to be highly negatively associated with the degree to which the organization is socially involved with its setting; administrative rationality

---

[24] Arthur L. Stinchcombe, "Comment," *American Journal of Sociology,* Vol. LXVII (November, 1961), pp. 255–59

appears to require some modicum of organizational independence. Rationality was somewhat less closely negatively associated to settings having traditional ascriptive elements. From these findings it was possible to infer certain differentials in problems of organizational development under varying conditions.

6. A THEORY OF COOPERATION AND ORGANIZATION*

CHESTER I. BARNARD

1. The individual human being possesses a limited power of choice. At the same time he is a resultant of, and is narrowly limited by, the factors of the total situation. He has motives, arrives at purposes, and wills to accomplish them. His method is to select a particular factor or set of factors in the total situation and to change the situation by operations on these factors. These are, from the viewpoint of purpose, the limiting factors; and are the strategic points of attack.

2. Among the most important limiting factors in the situation of each individual are his own biological limitations. The most effective method of overcoming these limitations has been that of cooperation. This requires the adoption of a group, or non-personal, purpose. The situation with reference to such a purpose is composed of innumerable factors, which must be discriminated as limiting or non-limiting factors.

3. Cooperation is a social aspect of the total situation and social factors arise from it. These factors may be in turn the limiting factors of any situation. This arises from the considerations: (*a*) the processes of interaction must be discovered or invented, just as a physical operation must be discovered or invented; (*b*) the interaction changes the motives and interest of those participating in the cooperation.

4. The persistence of cooperation depends upon two conditions: (*a*) its effectiveness; and (*b*) its efficiency. Effectiveness relates to the accomplishment of the cooperative purpose, which is social and non-personal in character. Efficiency relates to the satisfaction of individual motives, and is personal in character. The test of effectiveness is the accomplishment of a common purpose or purposes; effectiveness can be measured. The test of efficiency is the eliciting of sufficient individual wills to cooperate.

5. The survival of cooperation, therefore, depends upon two interrelated and interdependent classes of processes; (*a*) those which relate to the system of cooperation as a whole in relation to the environment; and (*b*) those which relate to the creation or distribution of satisfactions among individuals.

6. The instability and failures of cooperation arise from defects in each of these classes of processes separately, and from defects in their

* Reproduced by permission of the publisher from Chester I. Barnard, *The Functions of the Executive*, Cambridge, Mass.: Harvard University Press. Copyright 1938 by the President and Fellows of Harvard College.

combination. The functions of the executive are those of securing the effective adaptation of these processes. . . .

An organization comes into being when (1) there are persons able to communicate with each other (2) who are willing to contribute action (3) to accomplish a common purpose. The elements of an organization are therefore (1) communication; (2) willingness to serve; and (3) common purpose. These elements are necessary and sufficient conditions initially, and they are found in all such organizations. The third element, purpose, is implicit in the definition. Willingness to serve, and communication, and the interdependence of the three elements in general, and their mutual dependence in specific cooperative systems, are matters of experience and observation.

For the continued existence of an organization either effectiveness or efficiency is necessary;[1] and the longer the life, the more necessary both are. The vitality of organizations lies in the willingness of individuals to contribute forces to the cooperative system. This willingness requires the belief that the purpose can be carried out, a faith that diminishes to the vanishing point as it appears that it is not in fact in process of being attained. Hence, when effectiveness ceases, willingness to contribute disappears. The continuance of willingness also depends upon the satisfactions that are secured by individual contributors in the process of carrying out the purpose. If the satisfactions do not exceed the sacrifices required, willingness disappears, and the condition is one of organization inefficiency. If the satisfactions exceed the sacrifices, willingness persists, and the condition is one of efficiency of organization.

In summary, then, the initial existence of an organization depends upon a combination of these elements appropriate to the external conditions at the moment. Its survival depends upon the maintenance of an equilibrium of the system. This equilibrium is primarily internal, a matter of proportions between the elements, but it is ultimately and basically an equilibrium between the system and the total situation external to it. This external equilibrium has two terms in it; first, the effectiveness of the organization, which comprises the relevance of its purpose to the environmental situation; and, second, its efficiency, which comprises the interchange between the organization and individuals. Thus the elements stated will each vary with external factors, and they are at the same time interdependent; when one is varied, compensating variations must occur in the other if the system of which they are components is to remain in equilibrium, that is, is to persist or survive. . . .

Organization, simple or complex, is always an impersonal system of coordinated human efforts; always there is purpose as the coordinating and unifying principle; always there is the indispensable ability to com-

---

[1] See definitions in chaps. ii and v, pp. 19 and 55 ff.; also chap. xvi, in C. Barnard, *The Functions of the Executive*, Harvard, 1938.

municate, always the necessity for personal willingness, and for effectiveness and efficiency in maintaining the integrity of purpose and the continuity of contributions. Complexity appears to modify the quality and form of these elements and of the balance between them; but fundamentally the same principles that govern simple organizations may be conceived as governing the structure of complex organizations, which are composite systems. . . .

Historically and functionally all complex organizations are built up from units of organization, and consist of many units of "working" or "basic" organizations, overlaid with units of executive organizations; and the essential structural characteristics of complex organizations are determined by the effect of the necessity for communication upon the size of a unit organization. . . .

Informal organizations and their relation to formal organizations: (1) those interactions between persons which are based on personal rather than on joint or common purposes, because of their repetitive character become systematic and organized through their effect upon habits of action and thought and through their promotion of uniform states of mind; (2) although the number of persons with whom any individual may have interactive experience is limited, nevertheless the endless-chain relationship between persons in a society results in the development, in many respects, over wide areas and among many persons of uniform states of mind which crystallize into what we call mores, customs, institutions; (3) informal organization gives rise to formal organizations, and formal organizations are necessary to any large informal or societal organization; (4) formal organizations also make explicit many of the attitudes, states of mind, and institutions which develop directly through informal organization, with tendencies to divergence, resulting in interdependence and mutual correction of these results in a general and only approximate way; (5) formal organizations, once established, in their turn also create informal organizations; and (6) informal organizations are necessary to the operation of formal organizations as a means of communication, of cohesion, and of protecting the integrity of the individual. . . .

7. IDEOLOGY IN ORGANIZATION*

Philip Selznick

There is a vague and ill-defined quality which, unacknowledged and often poorly understood, represents a fundamental prize in organizational controversy. This is the evolving character of the organization as a whole. What are we? What shall we become? With whom shall we be identified? Where are our roots? These questions, and others like them, are the special responsibility of statesmen, of those who look beyond the immediate context of current issues to their larger implications for the future role and meaning of the group. To pose these questions is to seek more than the technical articulation of resources, methods, and objectives as these are defined in a formal program or statute. To reflect upon such long-run implications is to seek the indirect consequences of day-to-day behavior for those fundamental ideals and commitments which serve as the foundation for loyalty and effort.

"Consequences," writes Dewey, "include effects upon character, upon confirming and weakening habits, as well as tangibly obvious results." And in an earlier passage from the same work: "Character is the interpenetration of habits. If each habit existed in an insulated compartment and operated without affecting or being affected by others, character would not exist. That is, conduct would lack unity, being only a juxtaposition of disconnected reactions to separated situations."[1]

These considerations from the social psychology of the individual provide us with tools for organizational analysis. Organizations, like individuals, strive for a unified pattern of response. This integration will define in advance the general attitudes of personnel to specific problems as they arise. This means that there will be pressure within the organization, from below as well as from above, for unity in outlook. As unity is approximated, the character of the organization becomes defined. In this way, the conditions under which individuals may "live together" in the organization are established, and a selective process is generated which forces out those who cannot identify themselves with the evolving generalized character of the organization. The evolving character, or generalized system of responses, will be derived in large measure from the

---

* Reproduced from *TVA and the Grass Roots*, University of California Press, 1949, pp. 181–85.
[1] John Dewey, *Human Nature and Conduct* (New York: Modern Library, 1930), pp. 46, 38.

consequences of day-to-day decision and behavior for general patterns of integration.

An examination of the logic of this development provides us with a theoretical link between the concept of the character of an organization and that of administrative discretion as discussed elsewhere.[2] The act of discretion permits the administrator to introduce considerations tangential to the formal or stated objectives of the organization. At the same time, by the accretion and integration of modes of response, the officialdom is able to invest the organization with a special character. This special character tends in turn to be crystallized through the preservation of custom and precedent. It is further reinforced by the selective process which rejects those members who cannot fit in, and shapes the personal orientation of those who remain or who are recruited.

In a situation charged with conflict, the process of discretion will be subjected to close scrutiny, and the quality of administrative decision will tend to be infused with a high degree of self-consciousness. The scrutiny of the opposition and self-consciousness of the leadership will alike center upon the question of commitment. What attitudes and what symbols are commanding the loyalties of the staff? What precedents are being established? What alliances are being made? Such issues will be uppermost in the minds of leading individuals during periods when the evolution of the character of an organization is not yet settled. The possibility of stating that some given line of action is the "settled policy of this organization" is one of the strategic objectives in such a controversy. Or, in a field somewhat oblique to questions of policy, there may be conflict over the "heroes" of the group. Laudatory references to a set of individuals as the "fathers" of the organization's policy and outlook may help to define the accepted antecedents of the group; as a result, a whole series of doctrinal commitments are inferred from those antecedents, though not necessarily formally included in the program or objectives of the organization. In such cases, controversy may occur over the question of whether some individual's memory is to be celebrated in the official newspaper or bulletins, or whether certain slogans and symbols, traditionally associated with one general tendency or another, will be included. Conflicts over apparently minor matters of this sort are typically aspects of the struggle to determine the character of an organization.

The internal organizational pressures which drive toward a unified outlook and systematized behavior receive their content, or substantive reference, from the play of interests and the flow of ideas which characterize the organization's social environment. In this way, the internal process of character formation—though generated by needs which may be referable primarily to the organization as such—comes to be stamped with the

---

[2] P. Selznick, *TVA and the Grass Roots*, California, 1949, pp. 64 ff.

typical hallmarks of its own historical period. The general commitments and attitudes of the organization (i.e., its character) will tend to crystallize around value problems which are current in the environment. For an organization whose discretionary power on social questions is broad, there is pressure to make a choice among the "historical alternatives" that are available. Once that choice is made, the organization will tend to reflect in its own character the general sentiments with which it has become aligned.

The struggle over the outcome of this process may extend over a long period, and may be compromised from time to time, but the stake is always all important. The attempt to define an organization's character cannot be divorced from the struggle for leadership or from the possibility of internal convulsion. It is precisely in the struggle over an evolving organizational character that a given leadership having certain personal qualities most easily becomes the receptacle of a social ideal. As such, that leadership—incumbent or proposed—is conceived as indispensable to the goal of stamping the organization as a whole with the desired ideal. A leadership can become indispensable when it has convinced itself and its constituents that some alternative elite cannot be trusted with the exercise of character-defining discretionary powers; whereas the possibility of adequate replacement in the execution of formal executive functions is not normally in doubt. . . .

The thesis thus stated concentrates attention upon organizational dynamics. It is necessary to bear in mind, however, that the evolution of policy may be traced to broader and more general factors than the specific pressures exerted by groups within and around a given organization. In a sense, the forces generated by the process of organization per se may be thought of as the means by which the pressing but more general imperatives of the particular historical period are given effect. Such motives as prestige and survival may adequately impel action; but in general the need to rally forces broader than the small group for whom these motives are effective will make necessary an appeal based on moral or political principles which can be defended on their own level. In this way, the organizational struggle is provided with doctrinal content and a socially acceptable arena. But the price of that strategy involves a commitment to a set of ideas or interests. Hence those ideas and interests are provided with a means of intervention, a driving force which they may not be able by themselves to generate, but which, once generated, can carry them along with it.

To this qualification we may add another: changing historical conditions may seriously affect the choices available to discretionary power. In an administrative agency, controversies over policy may become academic overnight if statutory changes occur. Or the range of choice may be gradually restricted by changing economic conditions—as from a period of depression to one of prosperity, or of relative plenty to relative scarcity—as well as by shifts in the political climate which may make certain choices less expedient at one time than another. As these changes occur, the relative strength of forces within the organization may vary, reflecting needed reorientations. As the new realignment takes place, policy will change, but it might be rash not to look beyond the inner-organizational controversies for the cause of the change. In general, it is suggested that these considerations—which link specific organizational pressures to the more general imperatives and forces of the time—will temper any tendency which may arise from a concentration upon organizational dynamics to ignore the goals and demands provided by a particular historical period.[3]

---

[3] Daniel Bell, in conversation, has made the cognate point that power and the ends of power may not be divorced in a proper sociology. This is an important reminder for all who study the mechanics of organizational interaction.

8. TVA AND THE GRASS ROOTS: GUIDING PRINCIPLES AND INTERPRETATION*

PHILIP SELZNICK

> The entire science considered as a body of formulae having coherent relations to one another is just a system of possible predicates—that is, of possible standpoints or methods to be employed in qualifying some particular experience whose nature or meaning is unclear to us.[1]
> —JOHN DEWEY

IT IS believed that the interpretation set forth in *TVA and the Grass Roots* provides a substantially correct picture of a significant aspect of the TVA's policy at work. Far from remote, or divorced from what is considered pertinent by informed participants, the analysis reflects what is obvious to those who "know the score" in TVA.[2] Of course, this exposition is more explicit and systematic, and the relevant implications are more fully drawn out, but in main outline it can come as no surprise to leading officials of the Authority. This is not to suggest that there are no errors of detail, perhaps even of important detail. The nature of this kind of research precludes any full assurance on that. While much of the material is derived from documentary (though largely unpublished) sources, much is also based upon interviews with members of the organization and with those nonmembers who were in a position to be informed. Care was taken to rely upon only those who had an intimate, as opposed to hearsay, acquaintance with the events and personalities involved. Those who are familiar with the shadowland of maneuver in large organizations will appreciate the difficulties, and the extent to which ultimate reliability depends upon the ability of the investigator to make the necessary discriminations. They will also recognize the need for insight and imagination if the significance of behavior, as it responds to structural constraints, is to be grasped. All this involves considerable risk.

If the use of personal interviews, gossip channels, working papers,[3] and

---

*Reproduced from *TVA and the Grass Roots*, University of California Press, Berkeley and Los Angeles, 1953.

[1] John Dewey, *Problems of Men* (New York: Philosophical Library, 1946), p. 221.

[2] Although responsibility for the analysis rests solely with the author, it should be emphasized that this study was made possible by the willingness of TVA to make its records and personnel available. This is a happy precedent which we may hope will be followed by other organizations, public and private.

[3] Some of the materials quoted in the study are unofficial in the sense that they would be vigorously edited before receiving even the public status of a memorandum sent to another department within TVA. This would be so with comparable documents in any large organization, public or private.

participation[4] opens the way for error, it remains, however, the only way in which this type of sociological research can be carried on. A careful investigator can minimize error by such means as checking verbal statements against the documentary record, appraising the consistency of information supplied to him, and avoiding reliance on any single source. On the other hand, he will not restrict his data to that which is publicly acknowledged.

The possibilities of factual error, however great, are probably less important as hazard than the theoretical orientation of the study. To be sure, an empirical analysis of a particular organization, of its doctrine, of a phase of policy in action, of its interaction with other structures, was our objective. But in order to trace the dynamics of these events, it has been necessary to attempt a reconstruction, which is to say, a theory, of the conditions and forces which appear to have shaped the behavior of key participants.

Theoretical inquiry, when it is centered upon a particular historical structure or event, is always hazardous. This is due to the continuous tension between concern for a full grasp and interpretation of the materials under investigation as history, and special concern for the induction of abstract and general relations. Abstractions deal harshly with "the facts," choosing such emphases and highlighting such characteristics as may seem factitious, or at least distorted, to those who have a stake in an historically well-rounded apprehension of the events themselves. This is especially true in the analysis of individual personalities or social institutions, for these demand to be treated as wholes, with reference to their own central motives and purposes, rather than as occasions for the development of theoretical systems. This general, and perhaps inescapable, source of misunderstanding being admitted, let us review the concepts which have been used to order the materials of our inquiry.

Sociological Directives

The volume has been subtitled "A Study in the Sociology of Formal Organization." This means that the inquiry which it reports was shaped by sociological directives, more especially by a frame of reference for the theory of organization.[5] These directives are operationally relevant without, however, functioning as surrogates for inductive theory itself. That is, while they provide criteria of significance, they do not tell us what is significant; while they provide tools for discrimination, they do not

---

[4] The author spent most of his year's stay at TVA in daily contact with personnel of the agency. A number of weeks was spent in intensive contact with extension service personnel in the field.

[5] For a fuller statement than the summary which follows, see Phillip Selznick, "Foundations of the Theory of Organization," *American Sociological Review*, Vol. XIII (February, 1948).

demand any special conclusions about the materials under investigation.[6] The fundamental elements of this frame of reference are these:

1. All formal organizations are molded by forces tangential to their rationally ordered structures and stated goals. Every formal organization— trade union, political party, army, corporation, etc.—attempts to mobilize human and technical resources as means for the achievement of its ends. However, the individuals within the system tend to resist being treated as means. They interact as wholes, bringing to bear their own special problems and purposes; moreover, the organization is imbedded in an institutional matrix and is therefore subject to pressures upon it from its environment, to which some general adjustment must be made. As a result, the organization may be significantly viewed as an adaptive social structure, facing problems which arise simply because it exists as an organization in an institutional environment, independently of the special (economic, military, political) goals which called it into being.

2. It follows that there will develop an informal structure within the organization which will reflect the spontaneous efforts of individuals and subgroups to control the conditions of their existence. There will also develop informal lines of communication and control to and from other organizations within the environment. It is to these informal relations and structures that the attention of the sociologist will be primarily directed. He will look upon the formal structure, e.g., the official chain of command, as the special environment within and in relation to which the informal structure is built. He will search out the evolution of formal relations out of the informal ones.[7]

3. The informal structure will be at once indispensable to and consequential for the formal system of delegation and control itself. Wherever command over the responses of individuals is desired, some approach in terms of the spontaneous organization of loyalty and interest will be necessary. In practice this means that the informal structure will be useful to the leadership and effective as a means of communication and persuasion. At the same time, it can be anticipated that some price will be paid in the shape of a distribution of power or adjustment of policy.

4. Adaptive social structures are to be analyzed in structural-functional

---

[6] Thus, while approaching his materials within a guiding frame of reference, the author was not committed by this framework to any special hypothesis about the actual events. Indeed, he began his work with the hypothesis that informally the grass-roots policy of working with and through local institutions would mean domination by TVA, because of its resources, energy, and program. After the first two months in the field, however, this hypothesis was abandoned as a major illuminating notion.

[7] For discussion of informal organization, see F. J. Roethlisberger and W. J. Dickson, *Management and the Worker* (Cambridge: Harvard University Press, 1941), pp. 524 ff.; also Chester I. Barnard, *The Functions of the Executive* (Cambridge: Harvard University Press, 1938), chap. ix; Wilbert E. Moore, *Industrial Relations and the Social Order* (New York: Macmillan Co., 1946), chap. xv.

terms.[8] This means that contemporary and variable behavior is related to a presumptively stable system of needs[9] and mechanisms. Every such structure has a set of basic needs and develops systematic means of self-defense. Observable organizational behavior is deemed explained within this frame of reference when it may be interpreted (and the interpretation confirmed) as a response to specified needs. Where significant, the adaptation is dynamic in the sense that the utilization of self-defensive mechanisms results in structural transformations of the organization itself. The needs in question are organizational, not individual, and include: the security of the organization as a whole in relation to social forces in its environment; the stability of informal relations within the organization; the continuity of policy and of the sources of its determination; a homogeneity of outlook with respect to the meaning and role of the organization.

5. Analysis is directed to the internal relevance of organizational behavior. The execution of policy is viewed in terms of its effect upon the organization itself and its relations with others. This will tend to make the analysis inadequate as a report of program achievement, since that will be deemphasized in the interests of the purely organizational consequences of choice among alternatives in discretionary action.

6. Attention being focused on the structural conditions which influence behavior, we are directed to emphasize constraints, the limitation of alternatives imposed by the system upon its participants. This will tend to give pessimistic overtones to the analysis, since such factors as good will and intelligence will be deemphasized.

7. As a consequence of the central status of constraint, tensions and dilemmas will be highlighted. Perhaps the most general source of tension and paradox in this context may be expressed as the recalcitrance of the tools of action. Social action is always mediated by human structures, which generate new centers of need and power and interpose themselves between the actor and his goal. Commitments to others are indispensable in action: at the same time, the process of commitment results in tensions which have always to be overcome.

These principles define a frame of reference, a set of guiding ideas which at once justify and explain the kind of selection which the sociologist will make in approaching organizational data. As we review some of

---

[8] See Talcott Parsons, "The Present Position and Prospects of Systematic Theory in Sociology," in George Gurvitch and Wilbert E. Moore (Eds.), *Twentieth Century Sociology* (New York: Philosophical Library, 1945).

[9] As Robert K. Merton has pointed out to the author, the concept of "basic needs" in organizational analysis may be open to objections similar to those against the concept of instinct. To be sure, the needs require independent demonstration; they should be theoretically grounded independently of imputations from observed responses. However, we may use the notion of "organizational need" if we understand that it refers to stable systems of variables which, with respect to many changes in organizational structure and behavior, are independent.

the key concepts utilized in this study, the operational relevance of this frame of reference will be apparent.

Unanticipated Consequences in Organized Action

The foregoing review of leading ideas directs our attention to the meaning of events. This leads us away from the problem of origins.[10] For the meaning of an act may be spelled out in its consequences, and these are not the same as the factors which called it into being. The meaning of any given administrative policy will thus require an excursion into the realm of its effects. These effects ramify widely, and those we select for study may not always seem relevant to the formal goals in terms of which the policy was established. Hence the search for meanings may seem to go rather far afield, from the viewpoint of those concerned only with the formal program. Any given event, such as the establishment of a large army cantonment, may have a multitude of effects in different directions: upon the economy of the area, upon the morals of its inhabitants, upon the pace of life, and so on. The free-lance theorist may seek out the significance of the event in almost any set of consequences. But in accordance with the principle stated above, we may distinguish the random search for meanings—which can be, at one extreme, an aesthetic interest—from the inquiry of the organizational analyst. The latter likewise selects consequences, but his frame of reference constrains his view: it is his task to trace such consequences as redound upon the organization in question; that is, such effects as have an internal relevance. Thus, only those consequences of the establishment of the army cantonment in a given area which result in adjustments of policy or structure in the administration of the cantonment will be relevant.

There is an obvious and familiar sense in which consequences are related to action: the articulation of means and ends demands that we weigh the consequences of alternative courses of action. Here consequences are anticipated. But it is a primary function of sociological inquiry to uncover systematically the sources of unanticipated consequence in purposive

---

[10] In terms of origins, the TVA's policy—though not the grass-roots doctrine *qua* doctrine—of channeling its agricultural program through the land-grant colleges of the Valley states may be adequately referred to such factors as the nature of the formal agricultural program, the resources available for its implementation, and the administrative rationale which seemed conclusive to leading participants. Moreover, these factors may sustain the continued existence of the policy, and it may therefore seem superfluous when extraneous factors are brought in and somewhat tangential explanations are offered. But when we direct our attention to the meaning of the policy in terms of certain indirect but internally relevant consequences—as for the role of TVA in the agricultural controversy centering on the powerful "farm bloc" in the Congress, we have begun to recast our observation of the policy (taken as a set of events) itself. We are then concerned not with the question, "how did the grass-roots policy come into being," but with the question, "what are the implications of the grass-roots policy for the organizational position and character of TVA?"

action.[11] This follows from the initial proposition in our frame of reference: "All formal organizations are molded by forces tangential to their rationally ordered structures and stated goals." Hence the notion of unanticipated consequence is a key analytical tool: where unintended effects occur, there is a presumption, though no assurance,[12] that sociologically identifiable forces are at work.

There are two logically fundamental sources of unanticipated consequence in social action, that is, two conditions which define the inherent predisposition for unanticipated consequences to occur:

1. The limiting function of the end-in-view. A logically important but sociologically insignificant source of unanticipated consequence exists because the aim of action limits the perception of its ramified consequences.[13] This is legitimate and necessary, for not all consequences are relevant to the aim. But here there arises a persistent dilemma. This very necessity to "keep your eye on the ball"—which demands the construction of a rational system explicitly relating means and ends—will restrain the actor from taking account of those consequences which indirectly shape the means and ends of policy. Because of the necessarily abstract and selective character of the formal criteria of judgment, there will always be a minimum residue of unanticipated consequence.[14]

---

[11] Consequences unanticipated from the viewpoint of the formal structure are not necessarily undesired. On the contrary, the result may be a satisfactory adjustment to internal and external circumstances, upon which the leadership may find it convenient to declare that the results were actually intended, though close analysis might show that this is actually a rationalization. In this type of unintended consequence, some need is fulfilled. The same unintended consequence may fulfill a need for a part of the organization and at the same time cause difficulties for the whole, and conversely. Many unintended consequences are, of course, sociologically irrelevant. For an early statement of this general problem, see Robert K. Merton, "The Unanticipated Consequences of Purposive Social Action," *American Sociological Review,* Vol. I (December, 1936).

[12] Where unintended consequences occur due to error, or to individual idiosyncrasy, they are sociologically irrelevant. However, there is often, though not always, a systematically nonrational factor at work whose presence is manifested by mistakes and personality problems.

[13] This follows, of course, from the hypothetical, and therefore discriminating and ordering, status of the end-in-view. See John Dewey, *Logic: The Theory of Inquiry* (New York: Henry Holt, 1938), pp. 496–97.

[14] The use of the terms "end-in-view" and "anticipated" may easily lead to the fallacy of formulating this problem as one of the subjective awareness of the participants. This is a serious error. What is really involved is that which is anticipated or unanticipated by the system of discrimination and judgment which is applied to the means at hand. This may, and very often does, involve subjective anticipation or its want, but need not do so. Moreover, the system may be adjusted so as to be able to take account of factors previously unpredicted and uncontrolled. This addition of systematically formulated criteria of relevance occurs continuously, as in the recognition of morale factors in industry. In the situation detailed above, the high self-consciousness of the American Farm Bureau Federation apparently led it to anticipate the possible rivalry from a new organization set up under the Agricultural Adjustment Administration, since it took steps to ward off this threat. See p. 161 [of *TVA and*

2. Commitment as a basic mechanism in the generation of unanticipated consequences. The sociologically significant source of unanticipated consequences inherent in the organizational process may be summed up in the concept of "commitment." This term has been used throughout this study to focus attention upon the structural conditions which shape organizational behavior. This is in line with the sociological directive, stated above, that constraints imposed by the system will be emphasized. A commitment in social action is an enforced line of action; it refers to decision dictated by the force of circumstance with the result that the free or scientific adjustment of means and ends is effectively limited. The commitment may be to goals, as where the existence of an organization in relation to a client public depends on the fulfillment of certain objectives;[15] or, less obviously, to means, derived from the recalcitrant nature of the tools at hand. The commitments generated by the use of self-activating and recalcitrant tools are expressed in the proliferation of unintended consequences.[16] The types of commitment in organizational behavior identify the conditions under which a high frequency of unanticipated consequences may be expected to occur:

(i) Commitments enforced by uniquely organizational imperatives. An organizational system, whatever the need or intent which called it into being, generates imperatives derived from the need to maintain the system. We can say that once having taken the organizational road we are committed to action which will fulfill the requirements of order, discipline, unity, defense, and consent. These imperatives may demand measures of adaptation of unforeseen by the initiators of the action, and may, indeed, result in a deflection of their original goals. Thus the tendency to work toward organizational unity will commit the organization as a whole to a policy originally relevant to only a part of the program. This becomes especially true where a unifying doctrine is given definite content

---

the Grass Root]. This is no accidental perspicacity but a result of the systematic consideration of just such possible consequences from the implementation of new legislation. However, the tendency to ignore factors not considered by the formal system—not so much subjectively as in regard to the competence of the system to control them—is inherent in the necessities of action and can never be eliminated.

[15] As in the TVA's commitment to become a successful electric power business; this type of commitment was much milder in the distribution of fertilizer, permitting adaptation in this field by turning over its administration to the county-agent system affiliated with the land-grant colleges and the American Farm Bureau Federation, in return for political support which would contribute to the fulfillment of the prior commitment to electricity.

[16] Our use of the notion of unanticipated consequence assumes that the functional significance of such consequences is traceable within a specific field of influence and interaction. Thus price decisions made by a small enterprise affect the market (cumulatively with others), with ultimate unanticipated and uncontrolled consequence for future pricing decision. This is not an organizational process. When, however, the retailer builds up good will or makes decisions which will enforce his dependence upon some manufacturer, these are organizational acts within a theoretically controllable field, and are analyzable within the frame of reference set forth above.

by one subgroup: in order to preserve its special interpretation the sub-group presses for the extension of that interpretation to the entire organization so that the special content may be institutionalized.[17]

(ii) Commitments enforced by the social character of the personnel. The human tools of action come to an organization shaped in special but systematic ways. Levels of aspiration and training, social ideals, class interest—these and similar factors will have molded the character of the personnel. This will make staff members resistant to demands which are inconsistent with their accustomed views and habits; the freedom of choice of the employer will be restricted, and he will find it necessary in some measure to conform to the received views and habits of the personnel. Thus, in recruiting, failure to take into account initial commitments induced by special social origins will create a situation favorable to the generation of unanticipated consequences. The TVA's agricultural leadership brought with it ideological and organizational commitments which influenced over-all policy. This was a basically uncontrolled element in the organization. It is noteworthy that where the character of any organization is self-consciously controlled, recruitment is rigidly qualified by the criterion of social (class, familial, racial) origin.

(iii) Commitments enforced by institutionalization. Because organizations are social systems, goals or procedures tend to achieve an established, value-impregnated status. We say that they become institutionalized. Commitment to established patterns is generated, thus again restricting choice and enforcing special lines of conduct. The attempt to commit an organization to some course of action utilizes this principle when it emphasizes the creation of an established policy, or other forms of precedent. Further, the tendency of established relations and procedures to persist and extend themselves, will create the unintended consequence of committing the organization to greater involvement than provided for in the initial decision to act.[18] Where policy becomes institutionalized as doctrine, unanalyzed elements will persist, and effective behavior will be framed in terms of immediate necessities. An official doctrine whose terms are not operationally relevant will be given content in action, but this content will be informed by the special interests and problems of those to whom delegation is made. Hence doctrinal formulations will tend to reinforce the inherent hazard of delegation.[19] A variation of this situation occurs when the role of participants comes to overshadow in importance

---

[17] The agriculturists in the Agricultural Relations Department of TVA made vigorous efforts to extend their interpretation of the grass-roots policy to the Authority as a whole; in respect to the federal government, the TVA attempts to have its special interpretation of administrative decentralization become general public policy.

[18] See [*TVA and the Grass Roots*] p. 70 f.

[19] We have reviewed, *ibid.*, pp. 59–64, the unanalyzed abstractions in TVA's grass-roots doctrine—"the people," "working with and through," close to the people," "established agencies," "coordination," "participation"—which are given content and meaning by the pressure of urgent organizational imperatives.

the achievement of formal goals. Action then becomes irresponsible, with respect to the formal goals.[20]

(iv) Commitments enforced by the social and cultural environment. Any attempt to intervene in history will, if it is to do more than comment upon events, find it necessary to conform to some general restraints imposed from without. The organizers of this attempt are committed to using forms of intervention consistent with the going social structure and cultural patterns. Those who ascend to power must face a host of received problems; shifts in public opinion will demand the reformulation of doctrine; the rise of competing organizations will have to be faced; and so on. The institutional context of organizational decision, when not taken into account, will result in unanticipated consequences. Thus intervention in a situation charged with conflict will mean that contending forces will weigh the consequences of that intervention for their own battle lines. The intervening organization must therefore qualify decision in terms of an outside controversy into which it is drawn despite itself. More obviously, the existence of centers of power and interest in the social environment will set up resistances to, or accept and shape to some degree, the program of the organization.[21]

(v) Commitments enforced by the centers of interest generated in the course of action. The organizational process continuously generates subordinate and allied groupings whose leaderships come to have a stake in the organizational status quo. This generation of centers of interest is inherent in the act of delegation. The latter derives its precarious quality from the necessity to permit discretion in the execution of function or command. But in the exercise of discretion there is a tendency for decisions to be qualified by the special goals and problems of those to whom delegation is made. Moreover, in the discretionary behavior of a section of the apparatus, action is taken in the name of the organization as a whole; the latter may then be committed to a policy or course of action which was not anticipated by its formal program. In other words, the lack of effective control over the tangential informal goals of individuals and subgroups within an organization tends to divert it from its initial path. This holds true whether delegation is to members and parts of a single organization, or to other organizations.

These types of commitment create persistent tensions or dilemmas. In a sense, they set the problems of decision and control, for we have identified here the key points at which organizational control breaks down. Operationally, a breakdown of control is evidenced in the generation of observable unanticipated consequences. This is the same as to say

---

[20] The agriculturists were so regarded by others in TVA. *Ibid.*, pp. 205 ff.

[21] In TVA the agricultural interests forced major changes in policies on public land management and conservation, as well as fertilizer distribution.

that significant possibilities inherent in the situation have not been taken into account. The extension of control, with concomitant minimization of unintended consequence, is achieved as and if the frame of reference for theory and action points the way to the significant forces at work.

The problems indicated here are perennial because they reflect the interplay of more or less irreconcilable commitments: to the goals and needs of the organization and at the same time to the special demands of the tools or means at hand. Commitment to the tools of action is indispensable; it is of the nature of these tools to be dynamic and self-activating; yet the pursuit of the goals which initiated action demands continuous effort to control the instruments it has generated. This is a general source of tension in all action mediated by human, and especially organizational, tools.

The systematized commitments of an organization define its character. Day-to-day decisions relevant to the actual problems met in the translation of policy into action create precedents, alliances, effective symbols, and personal loyalties which transform the organization from a profane, manipulable instrument into something having a sacred status and thus resistant to treatment simply as a means to some external goal. That is why organizations are often cast aside when new goals are sought.

The analysis of commitment is thus an effective tool for making explicit the structural factors relevant to decision in organized action. Attention is directed to the concrete process of choice, selecting those factors in the environment of decision which limit alternatives and enforce uniformities of behavior. When we ask, "To what are we committed?" we are speaking of the logic of action, not of contractual obligations freely assumed. So long as goals are given, and the impulse to act persists, there will be a series of enforced lines of action demanded by the nature of the tools at hand. These commitments may lead to unanticipated consequences resulting in a deflection of original goals.[22]

The Coöptative Mechanism

The frame of reference stated above includes the directive that organizational behavior be analyzed in terms of organizational response to organizational need. One such need is specified as "the security of the organization as a whole in relation to social forces in its environment." Responses, moreover, are themselves repetitive—may be thought of as mechanisms, following the terminology of analytical psychology in its analysis

---

[22] The British Labour Party, when it assumed power in 1945, had to accept a large number of commitments which followed simply from the effort to govern in those circumstances, independently of its special program. "Meeting a crisis," in a women's club as well as in a cabinet, is a precondition for the institution of special measures. To assume leadership is to accept these conditions.

of the ego and its mechanisms of defense. One such organizational mechanism is ideology; another, which has been the primary focus of this study, we have termed coöptation. We define this concept as "the process of absorbing new elements into the leadership or policy-determining structure of an organization as a means of averting threats to its stability or existence." Further, this general mechanism assumes two basic forms: formal coöptation, when there is a need to establish the legitimacy of authority or the administrative accessibility of the relevant public; and informal coöptation, when there is a need of adjustment to the pressure of specific centers of power within the community.

Coöptation in administration is a process whereby either power or the burdens of power, or both, are shared. On the one hand, the actual center of authority and decision may be shifted or made more inclusive, with or without any public recognition of the change; on the other hand, public responsibility for and participation in the exercise of authority may be shared with new elements, with or without the actual redistribution of power itself. The organizational imperatives which define the need for coöptation arise out of a situation in which formal authority is actually or potentially in a state of imbalance with respect to its institutional environment. On the one hand, the formal authority may fail to reflect the true balance of power within the community; on the other hand, it may lack a sense of historical legitimacy, or be unable to mobilize the community for action. Failure to reflect the true balance of power will necessitate a realistic adjustment to those centers of institutional strengh which are in a position to strike organized blows and thus to enforce concrete demands. This issue may be met by the kind of coöptation which results in an actual sharing of power. However, the need for a sense of legitimacy may require an adjustment to the people in their undifferentiated aspect, in order that a feeling of general acceptance may be developed. For this purpose, it may not be necessary actually to share power: the creation of a "front" or the open incorporation of accepted elements into the structure of the organization may suffice. In this way, an aura of respectability will be gradually transferred from the coöpted elements to the organization aج a whole, and at the same time a vehicle of administrative accessibility may be established.

We may suggest the hypothesis: Coöptation which results in an actual sharing of power will tend to operate informally, and correlatively, coöptation oriented toward legitimization or accessibility will tend to be effected through formal devices. Thus, an opposition party may be formally coöpted into a political administration through such a device as the appointment of opposition leaders to ministerial posts. This device may be utilized when an actual sharing of power is envisioned, but it is especially useful when its object is the creation of public solidarity, the legitimization of the representativeness of the government. In such circumstances, the opposition leaders may become the prisoners of the government, exchanging the hope of future power (through achieving public credit for holding office in a time of crisis) for the present function of sharing responsibility for the acts of the administration. The formal, public character of the coöptation is essential to the end in view. On the other hand, when coöptation is to fulfill the function of an adjustment to organized centers of institutional power within the community, it may be necessary to maintain relationships which, however consequential, are informal and covert. If adjustment to specific nucleuses of power becomes public, then the legitimacy of the formal authority, as representative of a theoretically undifferentiated community (the "people as a whole"), may be undermined. It therefore becomes useful and often essential for such coöptation to remain in the shadowland of informal interaction.

The informal coöptation of existing nucleuses of power into the total (formal plus informal) policy-determining structure of an organization, symptomatic of an underlying stress, is a mechanism of adjustment to concrete forces. On this level, interaction occurs among those who are in a position to muster forces and make them count, which means that the stake is a substantive reallocation of authority, rather than any purely verbal readjustment. Formal coöptation, however, is rather more ambiguous in relation to *de facto* reallocations of power. The sense of insecurity which is interpreted by a leadership as indicating a need for an increased sense of legitimacy in the community is a response to something generalized and diffuse. There is no hard-headed demand for a sharing of power coming from self-conscious institutions which are in a position to challenge the formal authority itself. The way things seem becomes, in this context, more important than the way they are, with the result that verbal formulas (degenerating readily into propaganda), and formal organizational devices, appear to be adequate to fill the need. The problem becomes one of manipulating public opinion, something which is necessarily beside the point when dealing with an organized interest group having an established and self-conscious leadership.

Formal coöptation ostensibly shares authority, but in doing so is involved in a dilemma. The real point is the sharing of the public symbols or administrative burdens of authority, and consequently public responsibility, without the transfer of substantive power; it therefore becomes necessary to insure that the coöpted elements do not get out of hand, do not take advantage of their formal position to encroach upon the actual arena of decision. Consequently, formal coöptation requires informal control over the coöpted elements lest the unity of command and decision be imperiled. This paradox is one of the sources of persistent tension between theory and practice in organizational behavior. The leadership, by the very nature of its position, is committed to two conflicting goals: if it ignores the need for participation, the goal of coöperation may be jeopardized; if participation is allowed to go too far, the continuity of leadership and policy may be threatened.[23]

---

[23] The analysis of unanticipated consequence and commitment is indispensable to the interpretation of behavior in terms of the coöptative mechanism. The commitments made in the course of action generate unanticipated consequences; in analyzing the function of these consequences we must construct a theory which will explain them as events consistent with the needs and potentialities of the system. At the same time, it must be understood that to formulate such defensive mechanisms as coöptation, is to state possible predicates. For the full understanding of organization it will be necessary to construct a system of such relevant responses which can serve to illuminate concrete cases.

9. TEAMWORK AND PRODUCTIVITY IN A SHOE FACTORY*[0]

ALEXANDER B. HORSFALL AND CONRAD M. ARENSBERG

EDITOR'S NOTE: In the study of social structure and of groups in human organization, much has been said of the need for quantitative verification. With the exception of Eliot Chapple's work on pair interaction and some of the static sociograms of the sociometric school of sociology, studies of interaction and of group dynamics have not yet attained the exactitude of description of common natural science methods.

It is interesting, therefore, to present a pioneer effort to describe and measure the interactions within a group of shoe company workers. They consist of several teams with a common flow of work in a single department of a very ordinary, work-a-day factory. The methods used and developed here are the simplest operations on human interaction. These operations, applicable to all the social sciences, were suggested by Chapple and Arensberg[1] and Chapple and Coon[2] and developed in many studies in industrial sociology. In simple terms, the operations are (1) identification of the persons to be observed, (2) discrimination of the order of interaction (stimulus and response) between them, and (3) timing. "Content" here is eliminated; order is left. The authors describe not what these groups do, but when and how long it takes to do it.

From this description, we get a quantative demonstration of the existence of "informal organization" of the sort that has been so widely discussed in writings on industrial sociology and psychology ever since the publication of *Management and the Worker*.[3]

In this paper, however, emphasis is not on the further demonstration that such teams of "informally organized" workers exist. It is not even on the more interesting point that not all such teamwork serves as a release of "productivity." The factory department under discussion seems to show that there is a limit to the supposed relation between an increase in "informal social relations" and an increase in productivity. The limits on the relationship between "release of spontaneity" and "development of fuller participation," and the changes in other social situations in industry

* Reproduced from *Human Organization*, Vol. 8, No. 1 (Winter, 1949), pp. 13–25.

[0] This study was conducted as a research course in 1938 under the direction of Eliot Chapple. Alexander B. Horsfall, of the College of Business Administration, University of Florida, was the observer and wrote the original paper. Conrad M. Arensberg, Chairman of the Department of Sociology, Barnard College, has since rewritten and enlarged upon the observer's original deductions.

[1] E. D. Chapple, with the collaboration of C. M. Arensberg, "Measuring Human Relations," *Genetic Psychology Monograph*, Vol. XXII, 1940.

[2] E. D. Chapple and C. S. Coon, *Principles of Anthropology* (New York: Henry Holt & Co., 1942.)

[3] F. J. Roethlisberger and W. J. Dickson, *Management and the Worker* (Cambridge, Mass.: Harvard University Press, 1939).

116

(supervision, grievances and communication "up the line," staff-line activity, etc.) still remain to be worked out. The point of interest is that a method of observation is presented that makes the study of these phenomena of social interaction and group structure quantitative, measurable, communicable, verifiable, generalizable.

As a result of this approach to human relations, the science dealing with the dynamics of human interaction—and thus with institutional structure and organization—can begin to make concrete contributions of data and method to studies of organization, incentive, and work-behavior in the engineering and managerial fields, going far beyond present "diagnoses," "understanding," and "art." Quantity is the language of science, and here is quantity in "human relations."

I

IN THE Bottoming Room of the ABC Shoe Company in 1938, four seven-worker teams, each performing the same series of machine operations on shoes, were located side by side. They formed a department group of 28, all in one room.

Like so many other such groups of whom there have been reports since that time, these workers had an informal organization of their own for allocating work, equalizing pay, and spreading and apportioning leisure periods during working hours. This informal organization might be called "restrictive," in that it was outside management rules. The foreman knew of its existence and might have reported it, but it went on independent of him. Led by a few of the older men in the middle teams along the flow of work which united them, the whole group kept the shoes moving through their machines at a pace that kept their pay at a constant level, despite an incentive piece-rate. This meant allocating leisure and apportioning work, holding back while others "caught up," submitting to "informal group controls." Despite the attendant "loss" to individual earners, these controls were in effect in the ordinary run of the department's day. These informal controls, and the group operating under them, broke down only under stress of special hurry orders under management pressure for production. Only then did the workers' interaction revert to the smaller teams of immediate neighbors in the manufacturing process.

The ABC Shoe Company was a manufacturer of inexpensive women's novelty shoes, employing on the average around 1000 persons and producing from 7500 to 10,000 pairs of shoes daily. Ownership and management of the factory had been in the hands of one family since it began as a shoe repair shop 28 years ago. The plant had grown from a one-room establishment to its present size—about 70,000 square feet of floor space—mainly by successive additions to its original buildings.

A large percentage of the employees came from the immediate neighborhood; in many cases there were several from the same family. About 60 per cent of the employees were women. Nearby stores accepted the factory's pay checks as cash, and the factory was an important economic and social element in the community. Many employees had been working in it steadily for 10 years or more. Employee benefits, curtailed somewhat in 1938, still included some medical and dental service, and a trained nurse was employed. In short, the plant was very much a part of the lives of the workers in the neighborhood.

In the ABC Company formal lines of organization were conspicuously absent. Relations between employees and the few foremen allowed for free interchange. The Superintendent had reporting directly to him the Production Manager, to whom in turn the foremen of the various manufacturing process rooms (departments) reported. There were no written periodic reports, everyone being too busy at work. Production was the thing, and the main job of the foremen was to keep it running smoothly, particularly by timing it to prevent bottlenecks or stoppages in the huge, continuous flow of shoes through and out of the factory.

Practically all production was on a piece-rate basis except where a new worker was being trained on a machine, or where a worker was transferred to a machine new to him. In transfers, higher average earnings at a new machine often were regarded as a promotion, and a trainee was paid on a salary basis for the period of his learning. The piece-rate unit was a "case" of 36 pairs, or 72 shoes. Shoes moved through the factory in racks equivalent to this unit. Each rack upon which the shoes were transported from one machine to another contained a "case" of shoes. Thus, in the parlance of the job, both "case" and "rack" indicated the 72 shoes of the piecework unit.

Work was planned and routed through the factory by means of the "checking" and "coupon" systems common to shoe factories. Under the "checking" system, each employee turned in, on a weekly basis, a list of tag numbers. One tag marked the completed rack or case of 72 shoes. Upon these lists, when checked, the payroll was based. The "coupon" system need not concern us here. Only the checking system was used in the Bottoming Room under discussion. Earnings were freely compared by the workers and were common knowledge.

There was no formal inspection of shoes at the various stages of the manufacturing process until the final "treeing" and packing of shoes ready to be shipped out. However, a continual sampling went on whereby a foreman picked shoes from the racks as they passed through his department on the way to another operation. Workers reported damaged or defective shoes to the foreman, providing an equally important check upon production quality. They reported all imperfections, whether due to their own work or to a previous operation. The rack containing the imperfect shoe was then held up and the shoe taken back to be redone by the worker from whom it came. He was identified by his initials on the tag attached to the rack. Usually no penalty was exacted where such damage or defect was faithfully reported, the worker merely correcting the fault in the shoe. But if a damaged shoe were deliberately or carelessly passed on, the worker was charged with its cost. At various stages of processing, racks were counted for missing shoes by the floor boys who wheeled them. Racks with shoes missing also were held up, and a floor girl spent her time in tracing these shoes.

A detailed description of the shoe-making process in the ABC factory need not be given here. It was in the Bottoming Room that the four teams to be described were located.

II

A description of the flow of work into the Bottoming Room, the operations through which the shoes went in the teams, and of the flow of shoes out of the room, follows:

All work came from the Lasting Room and was first processed by the heel-lasters, sitting together on one side of the Bottoming Room. They were then ready for the four teams with which we are concerned, who were located on the other side of the room. In each of the four teams were two trimmers, a pounder, a rougher, a shanker and two cementers.

1. Racks were rolled to the stair-well at the head of the room by the bed laster or toe-laster who had completed the work, and left there.

2. Racks were lined up at the stair-well by the floor boy for the heel-lasters to take when ready. If the racks were piling up, the floor boy might wheel them down to mid-floor, opposite the battery of heel-lasting machines. If the heel-lasters were "caught up" they would stand at the stair-well and take the racks from the bed or toe-lasters as delivered.

3. Racks completed by heel-lasters were pushed to mid-floor, whence they were taken by the rougher or pounder to his particular team's bench. Allocation of the various racks among the teams will be described later in this article.

4. Racks were brought to the trimmers of each team, who removed the shoes to their bench for the first of five main operations performed by the team. These operations prepared the shoe for the attachment of the sole.

(*a*) Trimming. Two trimmer girls started the shoe through each team by trimming off leather which had bunched up at the toe, or any excess of the shank. They removed tacks from the insole. Their two machines were a physical unit and the girls faced each other, one with her back to the window and the other with her back to the aisle. Completed shoes were placed on the pounders' bench.

(*b*) Pounding. The pounder, a man, pounded and ground toes and heels, smoothing the overlapping leather more successfully than had the knives of the trimming machines. He faced the windows, his back to the aisle. He passed his output to the rougher's table at his side.

(*c*) Roughing. A man used a revolving wire brush to roughen the overlapping leather at the bottom of the shoe, preparatory to cementing. He faced the windows. His output went to the shanker.

(*d*) Shanking. This was done by a girl who placed a thin metal strip, previously bent to fit the insole of the shoe, in the center of the instep and stapled it in place. Her output went to the two cementers, and she used the same large bench they did.

(*e*) Cementing. Two girls squirted a layer of cement around the margin of the shoe, which later glued the sole in place. Then a "filler," a small felt pad, was stuck in place at the ball of the foot, and the shoe was placed in a special type of rack having boxes to receive each shoe. These two girls faced the rest of their team, with their right sides to the windows. This work was considered by girls the most desirable in the room. Gaining a position at this machine was considered a promotion. The work required a nicety of skill and was less mechanical in that less depended on the machine, and offered opportunity occasionally to do extra racks requiring a mere cementing operation.

5. In the final step, racks were pushed to the floor by the two cementers of each team, there to be inspected for completeness by the floor boy before being taken to the elevator and finally leaving the Bottoming Room. Incomplete racks were held until the missing shoe had been traced.

III

Observation of activity in the Bottoming Room showed that in addition to the work operations there was activity related in some way to the starting of these work operations in a team. This was a method of allocating racks among the teams according to some order, which was different from the order in which they came from the heel-lasters.

Further observation showed that for each type of shoe in the racks coming from the heel-lasters, there was a corresponding object on one of the four rougher's benches. These objects had come to serve as symbols in an unofficial record-keeping and exchange around the workers' own routing of racks-to-be-done. One might say they were the "coins" of a small economic system. When a rack came to mid-floor from the heel lasters, only the rougher upon whose bench lay the associated object might take it for his team. The sooner he took it, the sooner he could pass the object to the next team and the sooner that team's rougher could take another rack of the same type of shoe. Since the racks were pushed to mid-floor in any part of the room, just as they left the heel-lasters, there was a continual signalling by the roughers of the type of rack which had come to mid-floor. This took the form of shouting the name of the associated object, e.g. "Who's got the bar?" At the signal, the rougher or pounder whose team had the symbolic tool went over and took the rack in exchange for the signal-object and brought it back to the trimmers of his own team. Such exchanges served to pass along the associated object to the next team in a well-defined order of allocation of work by the four teams. The order was: Team No. 4 to No. 3 to No. 2 to No. 1 to No. 4.

Such signalling and exchange took place continuously between the roughers and pounders, the men members of the various teams. In the exchange, since no team in the person of its rougher or pounder took a rack for which it lacked the associated object, and since every team when taking a rack passed along an associated object, it followed that at the end of the day the number of cases done, plus the number of objects held, was the same for each team (within limits determined by the number of objects).

But meanwhile, the racks to be worked on had been routed among the teams in a manner calculated to equalize pay for fast and slow teams alike, and assure that all the workers should score a uniform production of racks. Thus, when work came through rapidly, the exchanges might result in a condition where one team had several racks piled up at its trimmer's machines, together with several exchange objects on its rougher's bench standing for racks routed to other teams.

This condition existed to varying degrees at all times, depending on the differences in the four teams' speed of working. Usually, in other factories the result is that faster teams spend more time "loafing" while waiting for the other teams to catch up. In a typical day in other shoe factories, this unevenness provides the workers with rest periods, scattered and differing in total time for each team, and their earnings are at the mercy of the slower teams for whom they must wait. But here, by the system of exchanges, the work came through so rapidly that it exceeded the limits wherein such waiting and loafing could be tolerated without damming up work in other parts of the factory. The slower teams were bypassed with their consent, and for the time being the other teams worked on the racks passed to them. If the spurt of work was a short one, but longer than a day's limit, then the number of racks the faster of the four teams "owed" the slower ones might be carried over from one day to the next. The exchanges were tallied from the circulated associated objects.

From these exchanges, then, there resulted an allocation of racks so that they were divided equally between the teams, both in number and according to the difficulty of work with the different types of shoes. The method was introduced originally by the roughers. They explained it by saying it made everyone's pay equal over the weeks, that it prevented continued quarrels and insured that one team did not get all the "hard" racks.

It is interesting to note that the explanation did not stress getting "easy" racks, as was the case in other shoe factories where comparable exchanges entitled the workers to alternate between "hard" and "easy" tasks. Desire to equalize pay seemed here as strong as desire to lighten work load. But the reason the roughers, particularly, initiated the practice, and one they did not give explicitly, might have been that with some types of shoes, for instance platform shoes, the roughing step is omitted. Hence, by not having such shoes routed to them, the roughers' weekly earnings might well have been affected.

Examining financial incentive for a moment, it is to be remembered that in the ABC Company, all types of shoes with the exception of suedes were paid for at the same rate. But this equality of rate would not account for the workers' informal organization, for regardless of the rate set by the company, the workers would certainly have found some types of shoes preferable to work on than others. Some workers would have preferred the easier shoes whatever the piece-rate. The motive for informal social organization here, undertaken as it was on initiative of the workers themselves, seemed not so much due to a desire for a steady "take home" pay as to control (eliminate) one of the difficulties inherent in shoe manufacturing.

That difficulty is the scheduling of many inherently different operations altogether, so as to result in a continuous flow of shoes through the factory despite the differences. The difficulty had been heightened in this factory due, among other reasons, to the variety of shoe styles they handled, to a breaking down of operations into machine-processes using unskilled labor to the fullest possible extent, to the haphazard growth of the factory's physical layout and to its small elevator capacity. Among these conditions, the piece-rate method of payment was only one of many factors.

To management here, piece-rate seemed indispensable for, they argued, if all workers were paid by time, the amount of work each team received and completed would be a matter of indifference. However, it is significant that in the face of all these factors outside the control of the workers, the incentive effect hoped for by management in a piece-rate acted instead to produce an organization among the workers for allocation of racks. This gave them a method of adapting their own needs of work-pace and steady pay to a rate of production which still produced shoes for the management, though incentive and control were in reality far more collective than individual.

The following are the objects, the associated style of shoe, and the workers through whose hands a shoe passed, arranged according to the workers' opinion as to degree of difficulty in handling. The most difficult are first.

	Object Name	Shoe Name	Passes Through
1.	Wood (block)	Sandal	All seven
2.	Scraper	Wedge sandal	All seven plus Rg.
3.	Tag	Patent leather	All seven
4.	Bar	Macwelt	All seven
5.	Screw	Wedge (plain)	All seven plus Rg.
6.	Wheel	Platform	T',T,S.
7.	Box (cardboard)	Suede	All seven

IV

The discovery and description of the four teams and their informal organization does not rest solely upon the evidence of interviews with the workers, their foreman and other persons familiar with the room and the ABC Company. It seemed more objective to devise a method of recording the measuring which could check the evidence of interviews against a simple technique of factual, non-verbal observation. The technique developed resulted in a series of observation charts in which minimally-defined, "content"-less, interactions were discriminated according to the persons taking part in them through sample observation periods. These samples followed the hourly and daily interpersonal activity of the 28 persons in the four teams in the Bottoming Room, both in "work" and "non-work" activities of every sort, without regard to such categorization.

Once the record was taken thus, an analysis of the data of the observation charts established regularities of frequency, direction and personal participation which could substantiate objectively the patterns of leadership, team-membership and status, and inter-worker social relations which interviews in the room had revealed in the "subjective" or "unverified" testimony of and about the 28 workers concerned.

The original purpose of the authors was, in fact, to attempt such a verification of current hypotheses about informal organizations.

For observation of human behavior at the social level, an industrial firm offers conditions which are most like a laboratory. Each day the same people come at the same time to the same place and do the same work under essentially the same conditions. They work with the same objects in the same sequence. They have about the same social routine. In short, many factors which are variable elsewhere change, at least, within narrower limits in an industrial concern. This is particularly true where work is with machinery and the job is the production or processing of material objects, as in the ABC Company.

The Superintendent of the ABC Shoe Company[4] had many valid objections to allowing any outsider in the factory for an appreciable length of time. However, once he was satisfied as to the interests of A. B. Horsfall, the observer, what he wanted to do, and how he proposed to do it, he gave his full cooperation. The observer was given a regular employee identification card and the freedom of the factory. The Production Manager was asked to show him the factory, to answer freely any questions that might be asked, and to permit him to come in daily and observe the various processes and workers. At no time did this attitude change, nor was there any let-down in the willingness to allow the observer to go around and ask questions anywhere. Conversely, all actions of the latter were openly explained to the foremen and to interested workers, and his interests and disinterests made clear. The observer was in the factory practically daily for one month—from July 12 to August 13, 1938.

The first few days were spent in going through the factory to get a general idea of the operations performed at various stages in the process of

---

[4] The authors are deeply grateful to the company, its officials and its workers for the privileges here described. The anthropological convention of anonymity prevents our acknowledging them here by name.

making shoes. At this time, it was decided to make observations in the Lasting Room, for the process there seemed to require a clearly defined flow of work in terms of machinery, and a closer dependence of one man's work on that of the previous worker, with a certain amount of essential interaction associated with moving the shoes from one stage of the process to another.

A series of observations were actually made in the Lasting Room, but discovery of the four teams in the Bottoming Room, with their method of allocating work by means of certain of their members passing along objects (which brought to mind the "kula" system of the Trobrianders)— initiated and put into practice by the workers themselves—suggested more possibilities there.

Except as noted above, the observer spent the first two weeks working full time, first with the muller boy, taking uppers from the stitching room and placing them in the muller to be conditioned while the lasts were made up, feeding racks to the assemblers, etc., and then with the floor boy in the Bottoming Room. The former work was simple, manual activity which served as a favorable introduction to the workers and to the activity of the Lasting Room; the latter work enabled him to become familiar with the types and flow of shoes and to identify the employees by sight. At one time or another, the observer tried his hand at most of the machines, and evidence of interest in this way proved to be an excellent way of having his presence accepted. At all times, in fact, the observer's working and making of observations were so mingled that he became one of the group and part of the scenery.

In making observations of the teams in the Bottoming Room after it had been picked as the scene of detailed operations, the objective was to record on paper as accurately as possible the context of the interpersonal, social activity of each event in the room. At first he tried to do this in a literary way, describing the action before him in words and recording conversation. But this procedure soon proved inadequate. It was difficult to write rapidly enough to describe fully the events of the room at the time of their happening, and impossible to do this and keep up with them in their real order and pace of occurrence for an appreciable period of time. In addition, one had to look at one's notebook when writing, and consequently lost out on observing. Words took too long. Moreover, they gave no frame of reference at all, but left that to be described later. The separation of event and frame of reference seemed artificial, as it was always the context of the situation which seemed to lend significance to the event. Lastly, where the objective was to get quantitative data, it was desirable to observe and record all the interpersonal events of any one period of observation. One was forced to make the periods of observation regular lengths of time, as it was not enough to make discrete observations for varying periods of time in a room where the rapidity of events did not permit any adequate description of one event before the occurrence of the next. One had to do full counts of most events of short duration if one was to keep up with the reality of the room.

Thus the observer devised an observation chart which was to be a standard frame of reference, uniform for all periods of observation—at once a spatial representation of the scene of reference and a time coordinate. As observer, standing facing the team, he saw reflected in his notebook the wall, the workers in front of it in spatial arrangements from left to right, and their machines. Without writing a word, he could record every interaction between the workers before him, and in its direction, by striking on his notepad an arrow, going from initiator to responder. On his pad, ruled by minutes, the row of people against the wall was lettered, with a capital for their function, a T for Trimmer; the second row was primed, i.e., T′, C′, and so on.

Final procedure in observation was to stand between two racks (not for concealment, but to be clear of the aisle) about eight feet from a team, approximately in line with its rougher and shanker. From that spot, a whole team from rougher through to the cementers was clearly visible and not shielded by its machines. The observer struck an arrow on his pad for each interaction of any kind, graphically joining the letters for the interacting persons. Occasionally, when he could stand still, he recorded all the conversation possible. But he always made a special attempt to note the first unit of interaction in any conversation, whether or not he recorded any part of it. Noise level due to machinery was high, it should be kept in mind, so even if time had permitted writing down the details of a conversation, often it could only be seen, not heard. But for each bout of it, a line on the pad ran from one party to the next in the order of initiation and response. All workers of a team could easily be observed by facing them this way and every interaction in which members of the team took part was recorded by such a stroke on the pad. All persons in the room had become familiar by sight, and their activity could immediately be recorded by the drawing of a line on their symbols.

No attempt was made to record the duration of each interaction, since the accuracy of such timing with a wristwatch under such conditions would have been small. Moreover, several interactions often occurred at once, overlapping in time. However, any interaction extending over a minute was recorded approximately by drawing on the pad, from the tail of the arrow struck for it, a wiggly line running down the page to the mark of the elapsed minute.

It should be noted that whereas the usual method of making observations in social science is to write a description of the happenings under observation, from which further abstraction of particular facts for quantitative analysis can later be made, here an attempt was made to make primary observations in terms of the simplest operations alone by using these lined pads as charts. What words were written down to reflect the conversation merely served as a supplement to the chart. The chart itself gave all the facts of description. The symbols here are lines and arrows on paper instead of words, and the referents of the lines can only be the discriminated initiations or responses of the people in the room as they were entered. These initiations and responses then were set down in a framework of time, i.e., the minutes, were recorded along the side of the pad; and in a framework of space, i.e., the row of workers listed along the top of the pad from left to right as they stood before the observer. In such recording, then, the referents of words set down on paper are less precise than the arrows and lines that record the initiations and responses. (Words set down are capable of many "meanings"; the arrows and lines are capable of no other distortion than the frailty of the recorder's eye and hand.)

On the completed charts filled in for each period of observation, a system of lines and arrows focuses our attention on the facts. The chart allows direct analysis of primary observations in a form suitable for quantitative analysis.

It should be noted that before the observation periods began it was generally known that the observer was interested in the workers' method of allocating racks by passing objects. There was no suspicion of their being timed for adjustment of piece-rates or the like. Any questions the observer was asked as to what he was doing were freely, if discreetly, answered. It was not generally known that conversation was being recorded. The facts seemed to indicate that the observer's presence did not, as far as he could judge, bias the record or materially change the situation from its normal course.

To give some details of the mechanics of making these observation charts it should be noted that the recording was done in 4″ × 6″ notebook pads which were inconspicuous and easily placed in the observer's trouser pocket when he was pushing racks around between observation periods. The charts were ruled up beforehand. A wristwatch was worn, turned inward to the wrist so that its face was upward as the hand held the notebook, the eyes taking in the dial with the pad. Time was kept accurately by minutes for each 15 minute period of observation. The minute marks were ruled off down the page just before starting the period of observation to save time and to make references to the watch during the recording inconspicuous. The charts thus are accurate as a time record giving the minute of the beginning of each event between people and its end, during 15 minute periods on successive days.

In all this, the foreman was aware that a wristwatch was being used and observation charts were shown to him. The workers were not aware of this last fact, or if they were, asked no questions.

A list of the commoner discriminations made in recording the interactions on the charts is given in Diagram A.

DIAGRAM A
RECORDING CONVENTIONS

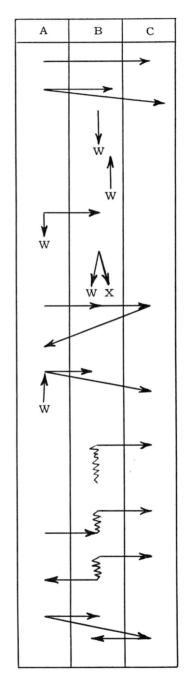

1. An action of A is followed by an   1.
    action of C.

2. An action of A is followed by in-   2.
    dependent actions of both B and C.

3. An action of B is followed by an   3.
    action of W, not a member of the
    group defined for observation.

4. An action of W, not a member of   4.
    the group defined for observation,
    is followed by an action of B.

5. An action of A is followed by in-   5.
    dependent actions by both B and
    by W, not a member of a group.

6. An action of B is followed by   6.
    independent actions by both W
    and X, not members of the group.

7. An action of A is followed by an   7.
    action of B, which action is
    followed by an action of C, which
    action is followed by an action
    of A.

8. An action of W, not a member of   8.
    the group, is followed by an
    action of A, which action is
    followed by independent actions
    of both B and C.

9   An action of B is followed by   9.
    an action of C, which interac-
    tion continues for a period of
    time measured by the length of
    the arrow tail extension.

10. The above interaction is termi-   10.
    nated by an action of A which is
    followed by an action of B.

11 The second above interaction is   11.
    terminated when an action of B,
    during his interaction with C,
    is followed by an action of A.

12. An action of A is followed by   12.
    independent actions of both
    B and C, the next action of C
    being followed by an action of
    B, but not of A.

VI

Observation charts and verbal conversation records covered 120 periods of 15 minutes each; 30 for each of the four teams. It is impossible to give all the data in a report the length of the present one. Both the raw data and the analyses are available and can be consulted. Perhaps at some later date, given the space and resources, it may be possible to bring them all out.

We shall limit ourselves to the measures that demonstrate the existence, characteristics and interrelationships of the teams and that give some picture of the nature of informal leadership in the room.

Our first step will be to see if quantification of interaction does in fact lead itself to a verification of the current hypotheses about interworker social relationships.

First of all, the data does support the hypothesis that such cliquelike groups as these teams show a higher rate of interaction among their members than between their members and outsiders. These teams do show slightly more internal activity (social interaction) than external. But it is interesting that the teams in which the informal leaders of the workroom were members show only a slight preponderance of internal over external interaction. The most active teams (active, that is in social activity within themselves) were not the most productive either in management's hoped-for productivity-per-worker or per-team measures of individual perform-ance, or in leadership in informal organization. Rather, the teams in which the informal leaders of the room were members showed both a slight excess of internal activity over external and a much higher activity of external interaction with out-of-team, cross-team members of the room.

The point is significant, though not surprising. Indeed the foreman said simply enough that the teams that did the most talking and "horsing around" did not get the most work done. The reasons are simple enough, too. In such a set up, and probably in many others, productivity must be some sort of a balance between activity in interpersonal clique relation-ships, out of which zest and color and personal security may develop, and flow-of-work relationships with other workers from whom the work of the division of labor is received and to whom it is passed. Of course, informal leadership must mean, as here, personal traffic across and between the teams if all four teams are to be coordinated and controlled on a scale large enough to include all the 28 people of the room. Such informal, "non-work" activity obviously throws the informal leaders into enough extra-clique, here extra-team, activity to make their teams' score lower, in such a measure as this, than do the teams who only respond in the room's own informal system of allocation and "controls."

The conclusion gives pause to current enthusiasm about encouraging "team work." If team work is merely interpersonal clique activity in working groups it is not by itself a "release" of a productivity damped by the "anomie" of too impersonal, formal and unsocial a working atmosphere in modern industry. It is, instead, a product of more complex social changes in a working situation, not all of them explored so far.

The figures from which such a conclusion can be drawn up tentatively are these:

SUMMARY NO. 1.   EVENTS OF INTERACTION BY CATEGORY, BY TEAMS

	$e(t)$	$e(i)$	$e(x)$	Acts	$I + R$	œ	p-2
Team #1..................	619	402	217	1272	1049	223	34
Team #2+.................	544	286	258	1145	877	268	57
Team #3+.................	450	233	217	949	727	222	49
Team #4..................	583	395	188	1200	1007	193	34
Total................	2196	1316	880	4566	3660	906	174

where the symbols have the following meaning:

$e(t)$ · · · all events.
$e(i)$ · · · all internal events.
$e(x)$ · · · all external events.
Acts · · · all initiations and responses observed in team interactions.
$I + R$ · · · all initiations and responses observed of team members.
œ · · · all open-ends, or initiations or responses made by persons outside the group under observation.
p-2 · · · cumulative total of people over two in each set-interaction.
+ · · · team in which an informal leader is a member.

* * *

VII

Furthermore, the data lends support to some of the current theories about group structure in social science.[6] The measures of interpersonal activity among team members showed a variable amount of participation from one person within the team to the next, but a clustering of higher rates of interactive behavior around only a particular few members of each team. The clustering showed each group, here the team, to be the focus of quite frequent interpersonal activity. The teams here were groups of people who interacted more frequently with one another than with others outside as a result of the controlling effects of the flow of work.

However, in internal structure the teams were not collections of people

---

[6] See the work of the sociometrists of the Moreno school; reference to clique structure in W. L. Warner's *Yankee City Series*, and Davis, Gardner, and Gardner's *Deep South;* and the theory of groups in Chapple and Arensberg's "Measuring Human Relations," *op. cit.*

bound together by quantitatively uniform relationships, in so far as the measured interactive behavior was concerned. The facts were quite to the contrary.

Internally, the teams were collections of relatively inactive persons ranged about clusters of highly interactive persons, only one or two in each team serving as a center or nexus for the rest. Members differed widely in their rates of activity with one another, some of them responsive mostly to immediate neighbors, some of them serving as targets or confidants for a wider circle taking in most of the group, some of them very alert to persons outside. The groups were "structured," then, around only the more active or more widely responsive of their members. Factors, influencing such structuring were by no means uniform as far as could be judged without special study. Central spatial position among the workers of a team vied with leadership function in the over-all organization of the room's allocation system. This was the main reason why in the teams one person or another served as such a focal point. Personality factors seemed to determine whether one was to act as such a nexus in a favorable spatial position, just as personality factors coupled with status difference seemed to indicate why it was that the two informal leaders of the room were among the oldest, most experienced of the men workers, in a room full of less-skilled boys and women.

In any event, summaries of the data (*a*) of intra-team interaction by teams, and (*b*) of rates of interactions within teams, member with member, yield statistical corroboration of the points just made:

DIAGRAM D

SUMMARY NO. 2.   INTRA-TEAM INTERACTION

	T'	T	Team #1 P	R	S	C	T'	T	Team #2 P	R	S	O
T	21			$e(i) = e402$			16			$e(i) = e286$		
	30			$p - 2 =$ 16			51			$p - 2 =$ 6		
				418						292		
P	11	24					8	56				
	12	21					4	22				
R	—	5	23				2	9	3			
	—	3	31				11	18	15			
S	1	4	12	8			0	0	5	5		
	6	3	13	6			4	2	2	2		
C	1	4	0	2	22		—	—	—	1	5	
	4	5	4	5	16		—	—	—	1	6	
C'	—	0	3	2	27	27	1	2	2	0	6	11
	—	4	5	4	26	23	1	4	4	1	1	16

DIAGRAM D (*Continued*)

	Team #3						Team #4					
	T'	T	P	R	S	C	T'	T	P	R	S	O
T	33			e(i) = e233			26			e(i) = e395		
	21		p − 2 =	12			23		p − 2 =	9		
				245						404		
P	14	8					18	10				
	4	4					13	17				
R	11	1	16				2	3	22			
	2	4	15				3	3	9			
S	9	5	4	8			6	4	9	35		
	7	5	1	0			4	1	4	11		
C	2	1	—	2	7		5	3	5	4	32	
	2	1	—	3	4		5	2	5	9	43	
C'	4	3	—	1	9	5	1	0	1	4	16	6
	5	1	—	3	6	14	3	2	1	6	25	2

For example, in Team #1, T' initiated action on T, 21 times, and responded to initiation of action by T, 30 times; there being 51 interactions, or pair relations, between the two of them; and the rate of interaction is 51/30 for each of the 30 periods, or 1.7 per period. Team #1's T' initiated 34 actions and responded to 52 actions in the 30 periods, with other members of Team #1.

For theories of group structure it is interesting to note that in the case of the two less productive teams it was not a dominant or leader-personality which made a person a nexus for this group. Teams #1 and #4, as can be seen from a glance at Summary #3 below, were alike in being structured internally with a secondary sub-clique around one of the women members. This clique existed within the group established by their informal leaders, the men trimmers and roughers who conducted their team's part in the exchanges on the allocation of work and the rerouting of racks. In each case a woman served as a second sub-clique center. In teams #2 and #3, of which the informal leaders of the whole room (the teams' respective roughers and pounders) were members, there was no such development of a secondary women's clique. Teams #2 and #3 were said to be serious and inclined to "stick to work," as befitted their leadership position. Teams #1 and #4, being team receivers rather than initiators in the exchange of work, were known generally to be less serious, more given to talk and horseplay and less "productive," although, of course all had an even output and pay.

The point of personality interest, however, is that those women who acted as secondary centers did not show—in the measures of interpersonal interaction—a high preponderance of initiations over responses in the activity in which they took part. By that measure they were not leaders. Rather they, C' of Team #1, and S of Team #4, Diagram E (Summary #3), were rather highly receptive persons, the one "sympathetic," the other a fat girl, slow, new and inexperienced, a target for advice, abuse, laughter and confidences.

DIAGRAM E

SUMMARY No. 3. RATES OF INTERACTION WITHIN TEAMS*

Table   Spatial Arrangement

Team #1

	T'	T	P	R	S	C
T	1.7					
P	.8	1.5				
R	—	.3	1.8			
S	.2	.2	.8	.5		
C	.2	.3	.1	.2	1.3	
C'	—	.1	.3	.2	1.8	1.7

```
      1.5   1.8
   T → P ← R     C
1.7↓        1.3╱ ↓1.7
   T'          S → C'
                 1.8
```

Team #2

	T'	T	P	R	S	C
T	2.2					
P	.4	2.6				
R	.4	.9	.6			
S	.1	.1	.2	.2		
C	—	—	—	.2	.4	
C'	.1	.2	—	—	.2	.9

```
      ┌──.9──┐
   ↓2.6
   T → P   R   C
2.2↓           ↑.9
   T'    S   C'
```

Team #3

	T'	T	P	R	S	C
T	1.8					
P	.6	.4				
R	.4	.2	1.0			
S	.6	.3	.2	.3		
C	.1	.1	—	.2	.4	
C'	.3	.1	—	.1	.2	.9

```
            1.0
   T    P → R   C
1.8↑
   T'     S   C'
```

Team #4

	T'	T	P	R	S	C
T	1.6					
P	1.0	.9				
R	.2	.2	1.0			
S	.3	.2	.4	1.5		
C	.3	.2	.3	.4	2.5	
C'	.1	.1	.1	.3	1.4	.3

```
      .9    1.0
   T ← P → R     C
1.6↑  ╱   1.9↓ 2.4╱
    ╱1.0
   T'      S ← C'
              1.4
```

---

* Number of interactions, or pair relations, per 15-minute period. The direction of the arrows between persons in the diagrams at the right indicate, from other computations than here given, the preponderance in the pair relations of the one person's initiations over his responses to the other person of the pair, a measure of dominance.

The conclusion one can draw for group structure is that it is the fact of the focusing of attention upon a person, for whatever reason, and by no means as a leader, that makes him or her the center of a group. Or conversely, the group arises out of the history and continuance of a higher rate of interpersonal activity. Perhaps a group's consciousness and its "common interests" are not a precondition of its existence, but a result.

VIII

A final point of interest to be drawn from the data concerns the informal leadership of the allocation of work in the room.

We have already said the interviews revealed that leadership in the exchanges between teams in the room lay with the roughers and pounders of each team, particularly with those of Teams #2 and #3. Measures of interpersonal activity drawn from the observation charts support that evidence.

The significant measures, however, are not so much in higher rates of over-all activity, or in higher percentages of initiation over responses. They are rather in a combination (for such leaders) of high over-all activity with high rates of activity in extra-team relationships (external events) in both of which a relative preponderance of initiations over responses occurs. That means simply that leaders assumed initiative both in inter-team contacts and in contacts within their own teams. Informal leaders, and perhaps all leaders in comparable situations, are thus not necessarily the most active persons, but they do exercise most initiative in first winning and then coordinating the responses of their fellows at home and their opposite numbers abroad. Leaders here initiated activity in relations both with their own team members and with the leaders of other teams.

The point is, of course, not new. But the statistical demonstration of it is. And, more significant, the possibility opened up by the demonstration. With measures of interaction such as these, the way is open to a measurement and a controlled experimentation with the dynamics of changes in human organization.

Computation of the room's informal leadership patterns was possible. First, we computed for each of the 28 workers his rate of total activity (interactions per period) and the percentage of those actions wherein he initiates action $(I/I + R)$. The former was a measure of his share in the total activity of the room; the latter was a measure of the direction of that activity, a description of his role vis-à-vis the others with whom he took part. Then, as any individual might have been active in his own team but inactive in relations outside it, these were calculated as well for internal and external interaction.

In making the count of interactions by individuals, a set event had to be treated as so many simple interactions. The alternatives were to omit a set-event or treat it separately. Going back to the happenings of which the set notation was a representation, we saw clearly that in such happenings a simple interaction had taken place between the person whom we gave as initiating action, and each of the others we noted as responders.

Still, of course, we could not truthfully say that in such set-events, because an action of A was followed by independent actions of both B and C, there was no interaction between A and B or between A and C. It was simply that we could not detect and note it. Unique properties of set-events therefore, had to be neglected; and for the present we have had to treat them simply as so many pair interactions, merely adding them to the pair events. In any case, set-events were few.

Next, to compare one worker with the next we calculated the average rate of interaction and the initiations-percentage for each team and then compared the specific figures for each individual with these team averages, taking the statistically significant deviations (assuming our sample was adequate) as a measure of the differences between the workers in respect to their participation in the social relations of the room. To find these individuals who were relatively active, it seemed sufficient to array the figures for the workers who exceeded their teams' averages. The figures are as follows:

HIGHEST INDIVIDUAL ACTIVITIES*
ALL TEAMS

Total				Internal				External			
Rate		Initiation %		Rate		Initiation %		Rate		Initiation %	
T2	8.7	R2	66	S4	6.3	R2	72	R2	5.3	R2	70
S4	7.1	T2	61	T2	6.0	T2	66	T2	4.0	T'4	69
P1	6.5	R3	60	P2	5.3	T'3	65	R3	3.7	R3	63
C'1	6.1	T'3	54	S1	4.8	P4	59	C1	2.9	P4	61
C4	5.6	C1	53	T1	4.1	C'4	59	C'1	2.9	T2	60
T'3	5.3	T'4	50	C4	4.1	C'3	57	P4	2.6	C2	59
C1	5.3	T1	50	C'1	4.0	S2	57	C4	2.4	P3	56

BY TEAMS

	Team No.1		Team No.2		Team No.3		Team No.4	
	Rate	Initia-tion %	Rate	Initia-tion %	Rate	Initia-tion %	Rate	Initia-tion %
Total.......	P 6.5	C 53	T 8.7	R 66	T'5.3	R 60	S 7.1	P 50
	C'6.1	T 50	P 5.0	T 61	R 4.5	T'54	C 5.6	T'50
Internal.....	P 5.3	T 54	T 6.0	R 72	T'3.8	T'65	S 6.3	P 59
	S 4.8	C 54	P 3.9	T 66	T 2.9	C'57	C 4.1	C'59
External.....	C 2.9	C 48	R 5.3	R 70	R 3.7	R 63	P 2.6	T'69
	C'2.9	C'43	T 4.0	T 60	T'1.9	P 56	C 2.4	P 61

* Average number of initiations and responses per 15-minute period, for each individual.

This array gave us an amorphous spotting of individuals with a relatively high rate of interaction coupled with a relatively high initiation percentage. But it did show the following:

In all teams, the individuals who "led," if taking the initiative in a contact is "leadership," were R2, T2, R3, C'1, C4, C1, and T'3. But next, when these persons were rearranged for their relative ranking in internal and external interaction quite a different set of persons emerged (see above). For example, R2 showed a high rate of external activity, the highest, but he did not appear in the column for persons high in rates of total and internal activity.

The next measure for picking up the pounders and roughers as "informal leaders" of the worker-controlled allocation and production was one which stated the rates of interaction between the teams, person with person, in external events. The measure of external participation picked up as well several individuals who, while not leaders, figured high in external interaction. But when other measures were recombined with this, these persons disappeared from the array once more. The data appears in Diagram F.

DIAGRAM F
SUMMARY No. 4.   RATES OF INTERACTION BETWEEN TEAMS *

	Team #1							Team #2							Team #3						
Team #2:	T'	T	P	R	S	C	C'	T'	T	P	R	S	C	C'	T'	T	P	R	S	C	C'
T'	–	–	–	–	–	.5	–														
T	–	–	–	–	–	1.2	–														
P	–	–	.4	–	–	–	–														
R	–	–	.5	.6	–	–	–														
S	–	–	–	–	–	–	–														
C	–	–	–	–	–	–	–														
C'	–	–	–	–	–	–	.4														
Team #3:																					
T'	–	–	–	–	–	–	–	–	–	–	–	–	–	–							
T	–	–	–	–	–	–	–	–	–	–	–	–	–	–							
P	–	–	–	–	–	–	–	–	–	–	.4	–	–	–							
R	–	–	–	–	–	–	–	–	–	.4	1.3	–	–	–							
S	–	–	–	–	–	–	–	–	–	–	–	–	–	–							
C	–	–	–	–	–	–	–	–	–	–	–	–	–	–							
C'	–	–	–	–	–	–	–	–	–	–	–	–	–	–							
Team #4:																					
T'	–	–	–	–	–	–	–	–	–	–	–	–	–	–	–	–	–	–	–	–	–
T	–	–	–	–	–	–	–	–	–	–	–	–	–	–	–	–	–	–	–	–	–
P	–	–	–	–	–	–	–	–	–	–	.4	–	–	–	–	–	.4	.8	–	–	–
R	–	–	–	–	–	–	–	–	–	–	.5	–	–	–	–	–	–	–	–	–	–
S	–	–	–	–	–	–	–	–	–	–	–	–	–	–	–	–	–	–	–	–	–
C	–	–	–	–	–	–	–	–	–	–	–	–	.4	–	–	–	–	–	–	.5	–
C'	–	–	–	–	–	–	–	–	–	–	–	–	–	–	–	–	–	–	–	.4	–

* All interactions over .3 per 15-minute period, for all charts. The data do *not* show preponderance of initiations over responses *here*.

Taking those persons in Diagram F who took part in external relationships team-to-team, having high rates of occurrence, we were able to compare those with high measures for the initiation of the activity in which they took part with those with low measures of initiation percentages. In such a comparison the women cementers who showed high rates of external participation disappeared.

Only the men R2, P3 and P4 and one woman, T2, remained. These were the leaders. They were located in all the teams, except Team #1. From this analysis the primary leadership of the four teams was centered in Team #2 where the interviews placed it.

In Team #1, P1 figures as third in rank in total activity and highest in his team in internal activity, but he does not seem to have been much of an initiator. His whole team ranks low, and the members characteristically were responding to the initiatives of others, particularly of Team #2.

Thus, picking up the leaders meant discovering them to be persons who were alike in ranking high when the individuals in the room were compared for (1) activity rate in external inter-team relationships, (2) for percentage of initiations over responses in all relationships to their own teams both internal and external, (3) percentage of initiations to responses in internal participation, and (4) percentage of initiations in external participation. As we have said, they were the only persons in the room and among the teams who were active, particularly in extra-team contacts, initiant in contacts with their own teams and initiant as well with the members or (leaders) of the other teams.

The table below gives the ranks for each male and female high in external activity rate in the other measures just described. It documents the sort of "informal leadership" the room exhibited.

IX

In the course of this presentation of quantitative data on the interactions of the members of the Bottoming Room of the ABC Shoe Company, the reader may have been hard put to follow the analysis. Nevertheless, we believe that close attention to the tables and the data will be repaid because through them it is possible to demonstrate, for this department at least, that the facts of industrial organization are not necessarily in accord with the theory. Much has been said about increasing group give-and-take in order to increase production: the most efficient teams indulged least in social activity. This does not mean that there should not be any interaction. The question is to define quantitatively how much is optimum for a given group under what conditions of leadership.

Leadership itself is something which can be defined objectively and differentiated from merely being socially active. It depends upon a frequent and continuous exercise of initiative with reference to the

"Leadership"

Relative rank in the room in several other measures of persons ranking highest in external activity.

(F.: Female; M.: Male)

Person	External Activity Rate	Total Activity Rate	Internal Activity Rate	Initiations % All Events	Initiations % Internal Events	Initiations % External Events
R2 M.	1	–	–	1	1	1
T2 F.	2	1	2	2	2	5
R3 M.	3	–	–	3	–	3
C1 F.	4	–	–	5	–	–
C′1 F.	5	4	7	–	–	–
P4 F.	6	–	–	–	4	4
C4 F.	7	5	6	–	–	–
(P1 M.	–	3	–	–	–	–)

(Leaders are those who appear in two of the three right-hand columns.)

Note: When a rank does not appear in a column, it is of course held by a person not one of the eight of the table. A blank means a higher rank than seven.

constituent individuals in the group. These groups vary in their own internal constitution as a function of personality differences, work flow, and other factors, but they become most effective when they are directly under the control of a leader. Not only did the leaders stabilize the relationships of the four teams to one another. They also gave internal strength and concentration to the teams in which the greater portion of their interaction took place. On what is regarded ordinarily, then, as a single level in industrial organization, the work level, effective leadership developed without the intervention of the first line supervisor. This leadership served to stabilize the manufacturing process, and within the two teams it was dominant to bring about the most efficient performance.

10. MANAGING THE MANAGERS*

MELVILLE DALTON

THIS IS a report and analysis of the inter-managerial relations between the central office (hereafter Office) of a corporation and one of its units, as the managers of the Office imposed a control on those of the unit. The problem is twofold: first, to show the events leading to decisions, and second to follow the interplay between formal groups (representing official fiat) and informal groups (concerned with evading or modifying directives) from a given point to a working adjustment. The problem can best be presented by first tracing actions that led to intervention by the Office.

The Local Plant

Data on the exact size of the plant, the number of departments and executives, and the personnel and financial costs involved in changes must be withheld. But there were about 400 managers spread over more than five levels and many departments, with a total plant population of 9000.

Obstacles to Production

Poor gearing of maintenance activities with those of operation[1] precipitated reorganization of work processes. For years the maintenance shops had compiled the cost records of work done for the various departments, and the record then went to the Auditing Division which entered the charge against the department concerned. Though no complaints were made about the mechanics of clerical recording, the clashes between operation and maintenance groups over the growing volume of unfinished repair work was seen by some officers as indicating a defect in the auditing system. Research[2] showed that this backlog of hundreds of uncompleted orders was spread among the various departments in a way not explainable in terms of plant theory or technology. That is, while some

---

* Reproduced from *Human Organization*, Vol. 14, No. 3 (Fall, 1955), pp. 4–10.

[1] Both *maintenance* and *operation* groups were branches of the line organization—that exercising authority over production. Maintenance executives were in charge of repairing and replacing worn or broken equipment. Operation executives were responsible for volume of production and they, therefore, initiated much action for managers in the other branch.

[2] The writer was a participant observer in this plant. For more details of these initial phases see, "Industrial Controls and Personal Relations," *Social Forces*, March, 1955, pp. 244–49.

departments were abreast of their repair work, others were greatly in arrears. Research indicated that these variations were related to differentials in authority exercised among executives who were of equal formal rank. No scaling of the differentials was attempted because of the conflict and secrecy attending behavior in this area. But instances personally witnessed, and cases reported by intimates, showed that the executives who obtained priority in the shops bullied the maintenance officers concerned and tacitly threatened to interfere with the flow of essential informal favors[3] coming to them if they did not give special consideration to their work. In the drive to meet production, while keeping equipment in top order with replacement parts on hand, such department heads achieved "clean" records at the expense of less influential heads who went "deeper in the hole" from disinclination and/or inability to alter the situation.

Supported by the Office, top local management agreed that changes should be made. There was much debate as to why the maintenance function had collapsed and, not knowing this, what should be done. Without pinpointing cases, some of the executives said bluntly that "politics" was responsible. Others saw "soldiering" and "laying down on the job" by maintenance machinists as the cause—a view taken by several top managers and some of the staff groups. This faction had difficulty thinking that the burden of the problem grew out of supervisory relationships, as suggested by the term "politics." They saw laggard work groups as the source, and hence favored a wage plan to stimulate shop mechanics to greater maintenance effort. But a faction of local and Office administrators decided most aspects of the issue by forcing through their view that the "only solution" was a new control to impersonalize relations at several points between executives of Maintenance and Operation.

STRUCTURE AND OPERATION OF THE CONTROL

Structure

The reorganizers theorized that Operation's orders for maintenance service should pass through a neutral department—to be created—to which all records showing the course of each order and the time charged against it should be returned.

Eventually set up as the Field Work Department (FWD), the new

---

[3] These favors of Operation to Maintenance included: (1) co-operation to "cover up" errors (or at least share responsibility) made by maintenance machinists; (2) defense for the need of new personnel; (3) support (in meetings) against changes recommended by staff groups that in the thinking of maintenance people would disturb currently more desirable arrangements; and (4) sympathetic consideration (and verbal support to top management) of the technological needs of the maintenance group for its survival and success in meeting demands of the operation branch.

entity was manned by about 100 personnel selected from both line branches. Each member had a broad knowledge of plant processes and was also an expert in one or more maintenance specialities such as layout, pipe-fitting, welding, machine operation, brick-laying, motor repair, etc. All were under a divisional superintendent of maintenance who had earlier served in the operating branch. He was aided by several staff experts, including industrial engineers. Orders for maintenance service from Operation executives were clocked in and out of the FWD. By this means and the use of serial numbers, priority of service in the shops was established. The order submitted was circulated among the specialists of FWD who listed essential materials, closely estimated the operations and time required for each job, laid out a route for it to follow among the shop machines and processes, and finally totaled the cost that would be required.

With nominal freedom to bargain first for a smaller or larger estimate, the top departmental executive was required in the end to sign the FWD estimate which gave him no justification for a wide departure. The job then went to the shops to follow a fixed route. The actual time and cost of processing was recorded by the shop clerical group which, like the foremen, was protected by the FWD buffer from coercion by Operation executives. When completed, the record of movements, operations and charges was compiled in the shop, one copy being sent to the Auditing Department and one to the FWD.

In a short time the FWD accomplished the purpose for which it was set up—to open the bottleneck of maintenance orders and keep the stream flowing. But unexpected events followed. FWD records showed increasing variations between its estimates and the reports of actual charges returned from the shops. Some of the executives were greatly exceeding FWD estimates while others were far below—and were getting some jobs completed with no charges against them. Inquiry revealed that the executives formerly without a backlog were now having excessive costs while, for the most part, the other group (heads of the smaller departments) were now much more efficient in terms of cost; several of them had reduced their expenses by half.

This nearly complete reversal of rank in the scale of competent operation was accomplished by hidden collaboration between the long-depressed maintenance foremen and the heads of smaller departments. Each had a score to settle. The foremen had been "pushed around" by the aggressive executives (usually the heads of larger departments) who were now relatively checked by the FWD. On the other hand, the superintendents who had smarted from the implication that their backlogs meant poor management were now in the ascendent. Their reward for not having terrorized maintenance foremen was to find friends among the latter ready to cooperate in charging work time to accounts of the larger departments.[4]

Top local management demanded an explanation of the great discrepancies. The FWD, the shop foremen and their clerical groups, as well as the Auditing Department and both groups of operating executives, each cleared itself logically of all implied malfeasance or collusion. Though top executives did not uncover the informal tie between shop foremen and heads of the smaller departments, they did suspect that unforeseen events had somehow sprung from altered conditions attending the creation of the FWD. Hence the FWD was practically nullified. Then one entire shop was dismantled and its equipment distributed among several of the departments to form centers of departmental maintenance, which succeeded the original division of maintenance. This was a formal reorganization arising from informal action nurtured by friendly ties, antipathies, and the need to escape over-all cost pressures that had not been lessened by introduction of the FWD.

It was soon discovered that the new scheme of departmental maintenance was not a solution because of friction in the department between operation and maintenance personnel, but it was continued on a reduced scale. In the meantime, accumulated dissatisfaction had led the Office to develop its own plan for simultaneously abating Maintenance-Operation friction and bring maintenance costs under rigid control.[5] This plan was now introduced.

With reorganization in the plant, and shift of authority (over much of the maintenance work) from the plant to the Office, the problem changes focus. We need now to examine how formal expectations of the Office initiated informal activity in the local plant, and to follow the interplay between formal and informal to a new adjustment.

PROGRAM OF THE OFFICE

The new plan can be discussed under: (1) cost aspects, and (2) personnel reorganization.

---

[4] Because of having much repetitive work to be done, the larger departments each were given a "standing order number" (subject to annual change) to which such work was charged. In the new informal alignments appearing with the FWD, maintenance foremen found this number to be a useful device (but not the sole one) for rewarding friends and penalizing enemies.

[5] Research in relations between the Office and the local plant was carried on under new limitations. First, the writer had no personal communication with the Office. Knowledge of the Office was derived from: (1) infrequent association with some of its less responsible people who visited the plant; (2) executives in the local plant who had formerly been in the Office and continued to communicate with friends there; (3) a few local executives who made occasional trips to the Office; and (4) intimates who were critically involved in meeting expectations of the Office.

Cost Aspects

The major item in the plan to cut maintenance outlays was a "surplus parts program." This was aimed at compiling a record of all reserve equipment on hand in each department of the plant, and establishing a permanent system for keeping the record up-to-date. Next, the purchase of new parts was to be taken largely out of the hands of local management, though the plan was so introduced that local managers could appear to have a voice in such purchases.

Initially the Office requested a listing of the number of parts on hand that cost $500 or more, and of those parts currently needed or that might be needed by the end of a given period. The intent was to start with the more expensive parts and systematically lower the figure.

Personnel Reorganization

It was believed in the Office that a simple request for such information, to be reported in writing, was unlikely to accomplish its purpose. The realistic move, it was held, would be to create new and specific functions and assign able men to enforce them. After the collapse of the elaborate FWD, however, simplicity and directness were seen as basic to any reorganization, so only two new positions were planned in the local plant.

Conferences concerning the change to be made were held by Office representatives with a few top local executives. Once the department heads learned of the developing plan, those without maintenance backlogs prior to the FWD now wished to influence selection of the officers who would fill the new posts as liaison men between the Office and the local plant. Their superiors, the local divisional executives, supported the movement. Initially, 11 executives worked as what may be called an aggressive horizontal clique (cutting across several departments) to convince Assistant Plant Manager, J. Swain,[6] that the choice should be made entirely by the local plant. (Swain's informal status in the plant gave him greater weight in daily affairs than his superior, the General Manager). Swain clearly regarded the pending control as interference with local authority,

---

[6] All personal names are fictitious. Swain had attained his present position in his late twenties after only a few years in the plant as a chemist. To move so quickly from a *staff* post to such a high *line* position was unique in the plant. He excelled in analyzing obscure and elusive situations, in seizing events useful to himself and in using extraplant social activities to strengthen his position. When necessary he bartered favors and surrounded himself with followers whom he rewarded variously for their support. He was treated as a charismatic figure, though the formal organization was, of course, a complex bureaucracy. He had intimate knowledge of all the executives from having worked with them earlier at their official level. The General Manager had been imported from another unit of the corporation and lacked such personal knowledge.

and agreed with the clique of executives that "we should pick some good men."

The Office, without knowledge of this intent among the group of local managers, was simultaneously searching for a device to soften the impact of its cost plan. Failure of the FWD was seen by the Office as leaving the local managers sensitive about the whole subject of cost control—and even indisposed to be cooperative. Therefore the Office voluntarily asked the local plant for suggestions about suitable candidates from its own ranks to serve as liaison men.

This request precipitated several meetings between Swain and the 11 executives and other less influential officers, to agree on candidates for the positions. Some of the minor officers held for what was requested as "able men" to fill the posts. However, members of the clique, with Swain silent for some time, insisted on two individuals who were regarded as *not* being "able men." Quickly it was seen that the persons chosen were to be amenable to the wishes of the clique. When Swain added his voice the decision was made.

The candidates were R. Jackson and B. Wetzel. When the choice was announced and the candidates accepted by the Office, several of the heads of the smaller departments declared that both were "weak" and "impossible" in the roles given them. Jackson was seen as having been "out-maneuvered" in a recent contest for one of the divisional superintendencies, and, in the thinking of many, this was proof of his unfitness. Jackson's private life was regarded as irregular. His wife had recently divorced him with much commotion in the local community. His heavy drinking, and his repeated defeats in collisions with the union were viewed as further proof of his inadequacy and "willingness to go along with any policy" of his superiors.

Wetzel was nearing retirement on a pension, which he was concerned not to risk losing by displeasing superiors. He was known to dislike responsibilities and repeatedly he was spoken of as being "afraid of his job," i.e., fearful of not being able to meet expectations and of the consequences.

Most of the local staff officers, who were only observers as far as this issue was concerned, saw the selection of Jackson and Wetzel as "manipulation" by local top management "for their own ends."

In his new duties Jackson was to be responsible to no one in the local plant but Swain. And this was a qualified responsibility, for Jackson was expected to communicate freely and directly with the Office, something that not over three of the 400 odd local officers were privileged to do. Jackson's duties were to inspect and approve each "parts report" turned in to his office and to verify its correctness, presumably by personal inspection and count of parts. Officially he was the only officer in the plant with power to authorize the order of new parts.

Jackson was to be assisted by Wetzel. However, Wetzel was responsible only to the Office for his duties. He was to initiate the reports by periodically requesting statements from each superintendent of Operation. Thus he, rather than Jackson, made the face-to-face contacts. After obtaining the statements, Wetzel turned them over to Jackson who certified them with his signature and returned them to Wetzel to be mailed to the Office. The Office then issued the superintendent in question a certificate of authorization which for a specified time enabled him to buy necessary parts from the outside without going through the Office, though each purchase, during any period, required Jackson's approval.

By thus focusing on two individuals, neither of whom had authority over the other and both of whom had direct access to the Office (in order to escape local pressures), the control was regarded as simple, direct and manageable. While no formal statements were made of psychic or other incentives to bind the two officers to their duties, their acceptance by the Office was generally regarded as a high honor.

THE CONTROL IN CHANGE AND ACCOMMODATION

Initial Executive Reaction

Following introduction of the parts program, Wetzel met official expectations by notifying the department heads that he was ready to receive statements. When after two weeks no answers reached his office, he made further requests. A few officers gave excuses of inadequate help, prior problems to be cared for, etc., but no records of parts.

They were restrained by the Swain clique which had expanded and was attempting to coerce all department heads and assistants to adopt a specific approach to the control. The hope was to resist it as long as possible while studying it "to find ways to make it work." Despite the esteem in which Swain was held, several chiefs of the lesser units favored compliance with the Office but feared the outcome of challenging the clique. Skilled in evaluating and exploiting vague situations, clique members advanced arguments and formulas for meeting the Office. They beat down vocal opposition and frightened others into silence.

The arguments used against executives who feared the Office showed the issue to be primarily one of who exercised authority in the plant— local executives or the Office. Swain saw the program as "too inflexible and causing too much trouble." One of the dominant executives long accustomed to initiating action far beyond his official limits declared:

> The thing I've got against the whole damn set-up is procedures. Every time you turn around you run into a rule that stymies you. Some chair-warmer (in the Office) cooks up a crack-pot notion of how things ought to be done. Maybe he was never in the plant but he don't let that bother him. He writes it up and sends it out. Then by God it's up to us to make it work. The way I feel

about it is this: if the set-up is so damned far-fetched that you can't make it work, why bother with it at all? What the hell do they think we're out here for? We know our jobs. If they'd leave us alone we'd never have any trouble.

Verbal reactions of this kind and knowledge of Swain's attitude left no doubt among the resisters that meeting Wetzel's request would be hazardous for their future in the organization.

In the meantime Wetzel was becoming increasingly disturbed by his failure but was helpless to act in the situation. He talked to confidants of how "fidgety" he was getting and of his need "to be doing something." He also considered visiting a psychiatrist. After six weeks of growing distress over his inability to bridge the gap between his expectations of his post and those of local executives (communicated to him anonymously) that he was to do nothing, Wetzel received a letter from the Office asking for a progress report. Accustomed to following official directives as literally as possible—and still having no statements—he notified the Office that the departmental heads "refused to cooperate."

Response of the Office

On learning that Wetzel was unsuccessful with his assignment, the Office sent several investigators to the plant. Tightness of the local informal group limited their findings, but they prepared a statement praising the efforts of Wetzel and censuring the department heads "for failure to cooperate" with him. Copies of the report were distributed at the Office among local top managers.

Wetzel's desperation and resulting action had not been foreseen by the executives. Support by the Office meant that despite Wetzel's docility new devices were necessary to control him. Part of the assumed incentive of his new role was that he would "enjoy" the leisure of what was really a sinecure. But as noted previously, in his dilemma about what to do his leisure was spent in mulling over his anxieties, and thus failed to be a reward.

Swain and others decided to surround Wetzel with more concrete status symbols as an inducement. His quarters were set up in a new office, superior in size and appointments. He was given a secretary and new equipment including filing cabinets and a dictaphone. The need to control the character of his communications to the Office led the executives to reinforce their gifts of the trappings of rank with a flattering personal appeal. To that end several of the managers, accompanied by Jackson, went to Wetzel's office and proposed that "we work this thing out together. After all, we don't want to do anything to stir up trouble."

Whether from the combined inducements or from fear, Wetzel agreed to go along with the executives, whose greatest need was to prevent a count of parts.

Tactics of Escape

Though some of the superintendents continued to be fearful of the Office they cooperated to thwart an accurate count of their surplus elements.

The motivation to hide parts was complex. The satisfaction of outwitting authority was probably much less important than the obscure urge to preserve an accustomed set of "rights" involving command of the plant. But judging from observable actions and spontaneous remarks, the major factor was the assumed need of maintaining a margin of funds to use for ends other than operating costs in the narrow sense. That is, the proportion of parts hidden was much influenced by the daily demands of personal relations[7] as well as those of the organization. Demands requiring expenditures that could not unequivocally be interpreted as maintenance costs could nevertheless be charged to such costs. These demands might include: (1) part- or full-time employment of the relatives or friends of associates from both the plant and the community; (2) a given executive's wish to have materially ostentatious offices in the department; (3) possible emergencies in a period of change; and (4) the need to use plant services and materials to get more cooperation from subordinates and colleagues.

Before the executives showed resistance to the Office, Wetzel's instructions were to make formal requests for an account of parts. Now, to contain the evasion, the Office indicated that Jackson's division of labor would include surprise inspections and count of parts in each department. Both he and Wetzel were alarmed by this new directive, but neither had the courage to carry out the orders as intended. Their adjustment (apparently after conferences with members of the executive clique) was not to make a surprise count but, in advance of the tour, to telephone various key officers informing them of the starting point, time, and route the inspection would follow.[8] Since none of these variables were the same on succeeding inspections, each inspection did appear to be unscheduled.

---

[7] This is to say that *gemeinschaftliche* elements functioned with varying freedom despite restrictions of the *gesellschaftliche* structure, or more correctly that such elements functioned inside and concomitantly with the logical order. Overemphasis on the formal structure by some theorists of bureaucracy amounts to *forbidding the Gemeinschaft* in a planned structure. Tönnies clearly thought a logical organization impossible without a sustaining emotional basis. And Cooley, in viewing human nature (in his sense) as springing from personal relations would, by implication, see it disappear in purely impersonal relations—or absence of personal relations. See H. E. Barnes (Ed.), *An Introduction to the History of Sociology* (Chicago: University of Chicago Press, 1948), pp. 234 and 837. Also R. E. L. Faris, *Social Psychology* (New York: Ronald Press Co., 1952), pp. 338–49. The point labored here is truistic to many sociologists but not appreciated by others.

[8] The physical plant covered over a square mile and was broken into many units and subunits connected by numbered walkways and zoned driveways.

This was not an original device. Use of nominal surprise was common in the plant, and between the plant and the Office in other activities also. For example, visits from members of the parent organization were planned, but given a camouflage of spontaneity that served the needs of both groups. Managers from the Office were thereby spared the unpleasantness of seeing a condition of which they should be officially ignorant, and of feeling embarrassment in possessing knowledge that presupposed corrective action by them. The condition and the potential consequence of action would of course sully the friendly call and hence should be avoided. For their part, local officers reduced the time, cost, and interference with routine, of setting up acceptable appearances by deciding in advance the specific path through the plant that the tour would follow. Then just on the fringes of the entire route, equipment was cleaned and possibly painted, walks and driveways were disencumbered and swept, and everything "put in order."

Nominal surprise was also a conflict preventive in the local plant. For example, the safety inspector (and other inspectors) usually telephoned unofficially in advance of a visit so that he would not see unsafe practices or conditions that he would feel obliged to report. Thus he escaped present embarrassment for himself and avoided incurring the hostility that an offended associate might feel at a time when that officer's good will could be personally helpful in the ongoing and elusive structure of personal claims in which all the executives unavoidably moved.

The fiction of surprise thus enabled all persons involved to maintain official dignity and to give the appearance of following formal procedures despite inevitable obstacles and frequent impossibility.

Notification that a count was under way provoked a flurry among the executives to hide some of the parts. Motor and hand trucks with laborers and skilled workers who could be spared were assembled in a given department. Then the materials not to be counted were moved to: (1) little known and inaccessible spots in the plant; (2) basements and pits that were dirty and therefore unlikely to be examined; (3) departments that had already been inspected and that could be approached circuitously while the counters were en route between the official storage areas; and (4) areas where other materials and supplies might be used as a camouflage for parts.

As the practice developed, cooperation among the chiefs to use each others' storage areas and spare pits became well organized and smoothly functioning. And joint action of a kind rarely, if ever, shown in carrying on official activities enabled the relatively easy passage of laborers and truckers from one work area to another without serious complications for the formal organization.

Reports of surplus parts on hand now arrived regularly in Wetzel's office. Probably in no case, however, were the statements minutely correct. But Jackson approved the papers and Wetzel dispatched them.

Thus an accommodation was reached. The Office received its required flow of documents, and though only roughly accurate, they did allow planning within workable limits; by *de jure* conformity to the Office and *de facto* surrender to the executives, Jackson and Wetzel eluded the tug of cross-claims on themselves; friction between Operation and Maintenance subsided to a low level; and, finally, the superintendents preserved their conception of executive rights, and by their action raised morale in the local organization.

We have followed attempts in the plant, and between the plant and the parent organization, to control human factors interfering with one goal—low maintenance costs. We have seen a sensitive equilibrium reached in the adjustment of local executives to their superiors in the Office. This was accomplished in great part by the rise and dominance of a horizontal clique which worked to resist literal application of the control and to adapt it to their view of local needs. In doing this, the clique saw as crucial the need to select extra-clique members of the executive group to accomplish clique ends. Largely by chance the selection fit in with Office tactics intended to soften introduction of the control.

Conflict over authority between the two entities has been dealt with. But there is also a need to spell out the social-psychological meaning of conflict as a force in shaping the type of personality dominant in situations where covert alignments reduce the certainty of how to act and raise threats both to an individual's current aims and his career objectives if unsuccessful action is taken. And the significance of interaction between formal and informal organizations as a factor in on-going organizational change needs further comment.

11. THE BACKGROUND AND IMPLICATIONS OF THE RAND CORPORATION SYSTEMS RESEARCH LABORATORY STUDIES*

ROBERT L. CHAPMAN AND JOHN L. KENNEDY

The System Studied

It became obvious early in these studies that simulation techniques and techniques for controlling large-scale experiments would have to be pushed beyond their current state of development and that it would be necessary to select a kind of organization that lent itself to being studied with the new techniques. The system selected was suited to these laboratory techniques; it was also of critical importance to the Air Force and one that had enough in common with other systems to give the results generality.

This system was the air-defense direction center, an organization that defends a portion of the United States against enemy air attack. In many ways a direction center is a complete system; it has all the information available about the air traffic in its area and controls weapons for stopping enemy air attacks. What was simulated in the laboratory was a close approximation to a real direction center—a full-scale model manned by a standard crew of 30 to 40 men. Four air-defense experiments were conducted. Each ran for about 200 hours—the equivalent of about six weeks of normal life in a real direction center.

A direction center is a rather complex organization with quite a complex job to do. The laboratory crews had to defend an area of roughly 100,000 square miles. During each experiment there were about 10,000 flights over this area. The air traffic, which increased more than threefold during the experiment, included a wide variety of flights—from commercial air liners on transoceanic flights to cub aircraft hedgehopping from airport to airport. Hostile attacks on targets in the area ranged from single bombers trying to camouflage themselves in the flight-plan traffic to mass raids of as many as 25 hostiles. Symbols containing information about these flights came into the system at an average of 300 a minute—a rate of information input that added up to something like two million symbols during an experiment.

Two conceptual issues, resolved before the experiments started, were crucial ones for making these studies possible. Both of these issues, which were concerned with the kind of organization to be studied, delimited a complicated problem.

---

* Reproduced from RAND Paper P–740, September 21, 1955.

First of all, the air-defense direction center is an organization in which task accomplishment has a well-accepted social value and one whose successes and failures are fairly easy to evaluate at almost any time during its operation. A experimenter can have confidence in an air-defense crew's motivation to defend the country against air attack and in recognition of success and failure. And this motivation is complicated very little by previous personal histories. The complex of values, attitudes, and beliefs that influence this organization's development are derived mostly from the crew's experience with air defense. Because the groups studied were newly assembled, a good part of this happened right in the laboratory.

A second advantage of studying a direction center is that more of the group's activity can be observed than in many other organizations. Much of the crew's behavior in dealing with its task is verbal response to known stimuli—either to other verbal behavior or to task information coming into the system. There is little of importance that can't be seen or heard by the experimenter.

Since these experiments involved groups of nearly 40 men, choosing a system that had these characteristics simplified the problem tremendously. The motivation of the men under study and the means of measuring system effectiveness were both relatively uncomplicated. Most of the group's relevant behavior—and the way this behavior changed—was exposed to view.

The Methods Used

Although a description of the system studied gives some idea of the size and scope of the experiments, the ideas behind these experiments can be put into a larger context and one that is probably more meaningful. Since the effects of equipment modifications were not the object of study, the physical resources were kept constant during each experiment and the task was varied. Any improvements in performance depended entirely on each crew's skill in using the resources it already had.

The Systems Research Laboratory's facilities are used to study human organizations in much the same way a wind tunnel is used in developing new aircraft. In both methods the experimenters manipulate an environment to apply stress to highly detailed models so that the performance of the prototype can be predicted and changes made to improve it. A wind tunnel uses a detailed scale model of the aircraft whose flight characteristics are being studied; the Systems Research Laboratory used a model organization of 30 to 40 men that was practically full scale. By exposing the models to critical environmental conditions over and over again in different combinations, both facilities can be used to expose weak points in the design of the prototype.

Both wind tunnels and this way of studying organizations rely heavily on elaborate measuring devices. And both of them accumulate enormous amounts of data—so much, in fact, that a corps of specialized professional, technical, and clerical workers is needed to handle it.

Research facilities such as the Systems Research Laboratory, again like wind tunnels, are big and expensive, but they may well become as indispensable in designing and improving systems as wind tunnels are in designing aircraft.

But with all these similarities, there is one main difference between wind-tunnel studies of aircraft and large-scale laboratory research with human organizations. In experiments with organizations, the laboratory model changes under stress. It learns. Learning is an invaluable characteristic. It is also a complicating one. Because organizations learn, a formula for predicting their performance, unlike a formula for predicting the behavior of aircraft, has to take into account the way the organization changes under stress.

Although aspiring to study complete man-machine systems is obviously fine in principle, worthwhile results depend on how effectively aspirations are translated into experimental form. An important aspect of this translation is gaining "observational access to the phenomena." "Observational access" is more than being able to get meaningful data—it's primarily a problem of getting worthwhile phenomena to occur at all. If an organization is to be observed under a variety of conditions, it's essential that the men who are being studied function as an organization and not just as a group of individuals and that they are stimulated to develop as an organization—to learn as a group. This failed to happen in the first experiment—the organization learned so much faster than it had been expected to that long before the experiment was over the task that had been so carefully prepared became so easy that the group's performance was no longer worth observing.

Results and Theory

The outstanding empirical result of these experiments was the degree to which an air-defense crew can learn to use its resources more effectively. That a group of human beings can learn is by no means a momentous conclusion—after all, it seems rather obvious to say that the performance of a system can be improved if it has resources of one kind or another that it hasn't used before. What was startling in these experiments was the extent to which performance could be improved by exploiting these unused resources. Although the task load was increased gradually so that it was more than three times as great at the end of the experiment as it had been in the beginning, each of the four crews kept up a highly effective defense of the area against enemy air attack.

Because an organization whose achievement is readily measured was chosen for study, the evidence for saying that organizational development did take place is readily found. Although traffic was continually increased during each experiment to the point where, in the last part of each experiment, it was heavier than the normal air traffic in any part of the United States, each crew's defense against hostile attacks of all kinds continued at a more effective level than we had any reason to expect. (Incidentally there were so many similarities in performance and development among the four crews that crew learning can be considered in the singular, since what happened in any one of the crews was fairly typical of all of them.)

But the scientific significance of the Systems Research Laboratory's work is the way these experiments exposed the process of organizational development.

Just what does an air-defense crew do to maintain effective performance in dealing with a task that keeps getting harder and harder? A rather obvious answer is that it spends its efforts more efficiently. With each increase in the number of tracks the crew had to deal with, saturation seemed imminent because the crew found it more and more difficult to continue handling each track with its current procedures. But each time that saturation seemed imminent, some way of simplifying the job was found.

One way to measure the effort a crew expends is by the number of items of information, such as position reports, it uses to handle the task. There was only a slight increase in the rate of information flow during an experiment. As a matter of fact, during the last hour of the experiment, when the load was more than three times as heavy, the crew used just about the same amount of information it did during the first hour.

It maintained this unexpectedly high degree of success in defending the area by concentrating on traffic that was potentially hostile, spending smaller and smaller amounts on the rest of the tracks. If the crew had spent its efforts at the same rate during the last hour as it did during the first, it would have used nearly 1,300 items of information. Actually, it used only 640—just about half of what would have been necessary if it hadn't changed its ways of handling the task. This is one example of more effective use of the same amount of effort—an illustration of how the crew assigns the kind and amount of effort to task events it considers important. This rough measure of effort expended is the "response model" (Figure 1).

But since there are so many task events, the crew must have some way of deciding which ones are important. It does this by making distinctions between tracks that it has to deal with to accomplish the task and those that it doesn't have to deal with at all. These progressively finer distinctions about which classes of tracks need to be handled make up the "task model" (Figure 2.). Although the number of tracks in the task increased steadily, there was only a slight increase in the number of tracks the crew dealt with. Since it continued to defend the area successfully, even though it dealt with only part of the tracks (about 40 per cent of them in the last hour), these distinctions were obviously effective ones. The important discriminations were between threatening flights (traffic coming from cer-

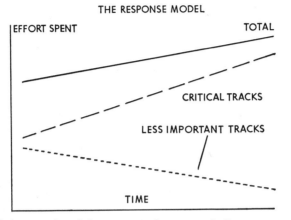

FIG. 1. Although there is only a slight increase in the amount of effort a crew spends during an experiment, more and more of it is spent on critical tracks.

tain directions) and nonthreatening ones (traffic going in other directions).

These models enable the organization to spend its effort more effectively by determining what efforts will be given priority. By making appropriate changes in the models the organization can adapt to changing task circumstances.

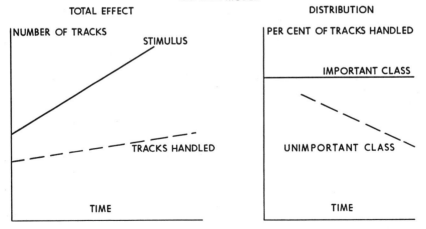

FIG. 2. The number of tracks the crew handles does not increase as fast as the number of tracks in the stimulus (left). This occurs because it handles a smaller and smaller proportion of noncritical tracks (right).

These empirical results seem to indicate that an organization will look for new patterns of behavior when it needs them—when it is under stress. Stress in an organization seems to arise from failure to perform effectively or—for an equally important reason—because it has to work too hard to avoid failure. The first is "failure" stress; the second, "discomfort" stress.

This effect of stress on organizations suggests an analogy between group learning and the familiar description of individual learning: stress, new and appropriate response, reinforcement. Without stress, organizations don't learn. Without reinforcement, they don't learn rapidly.

The results of these experiments indicate that group learning is an essential factor in any equation for predicting organizational effectiveness. From the analogy to individual learning, the main outlines of this theory seem clear—it must include the source of stress (the discomfort and failure that act as pressure to learn), and ways of reducing stress (the priority schemes of the task and response models). Such a formulation should help to predict how fast and how far a system can adapt, to identify what is difficult in the task, and to define the conditions that help an organization use its resources most effectively.

Perhaps the most important result of these experiments is that such concepts as stress, rate of learning, and so on, can be described quantitatively. There are, to be sure, some practical difficulties—the Laboratory now has over 12,000 hours of recordings and some 60 file drawers of supporting information from the air-defense studies. Thus far, some 100,000 IBM cards have been coded for each experiment, with perhaps an equally large amount of information, not yet successfully coded, left over.

These coded data are being used to represent measurable failure and discomfort stress, and the relationship between stress and changes in the task and response models is being explored. This has brought up questions of the place of energy expenditure in group learning and of the sequence of successive steps in adaptation. Adaptation seems to involve a complicated feedback process. When the task becomes more difficult, the crew absorbs some discomfort—making only those changes it can make readily in the task model. But this expedient may well add failure to discomfort. Making further changes that are necessary—in the response model—requires a greater degree of coordination. These changes require additional skill, and the time needed to acquire the needed skill may be another source of failure. As the crew adapts to successive failure and discomfort in this way, the task and response models gradually stabilize, much as an oscillating function damps.

But adaptation is affected by many details not yet fully understood—external conditions in the environment and internal conditions in the organization itself that help or hinder learning. An example of these conditions is the "grease pencils are no damn good" symptom of stress. An organization's first reaction to stress seems to be to blame external conditions, faults of the equipment, and so on. At one point or another during the experiments each crew blamed ineffective operation on the grease pencils it used for marking plots on the big movement board—the pencils were too hard or too soft, they broke too easily, they weren't the right color. But complaints like these disappear when the crew begins to find ways of doing things that lead to better performance.

The analogy between group learning and individual learning suggests the substitution of the organization for the individual as the organism in the classical learning model when organizational adaptation is being considered. In these air-defense experiments the organization has been treated as a unit rather than a collection of individuals, not only in managing the experimental conditions but also in analyzing the data and in building a theoretical framework on the basis of the results. With this kind of formulation the characteristics of individuals—their personality and skill—appear only as qualities of the organization. Such a formulation of group learning seems consistent with much of the data and has some rather definite implications.

Some Implications

There are several implications of this research—most specifically for personnel training and selection and for human engineering. Each of these areas is related to one or more of the others, and in working out their relationships it's not easy to know just where to begin. Although the functions of equipment define the human-engineering problem, just what equipment should do is difficult to specify without the understanding of system operation that comes from intensive examination such as these RAND air-defense studies provide. And so it is with setting personnel-selection standards. They can be set once the system is analyzed to see how much of the work the equipment can take over, but here, too, a thorough study of system operation is needed.

However, some human-engineering and personnel requirements can be described quite generally. Once the importance of group learning is recognized it follows that equipment and facilities should be arranged not just to facilitate operation but also to help the men who operate the system learn to use its full potential most rapidly. Or, more practically, since specifying what these men are to learn is difficult unless the system can be operated under the emergency conditions it was designed for, doing anything that might hinder group learning should be avoided. Communication between members should be made as free and easy as possible. Facilities should be arranged so that each member of the group is given as complete a picture as possible of the task and how the organization is dealing with it—in central displays of some sort if these are feasible. Members of the group should be given a chance to modify their procedures. For example, the members of an air-defense crew develop priority systems for simplifying their task; if information handling is taken over by electromechanical devices, the men who run the system should be free to modify the procedures for using these devices so as to utilize them most efficiently.

Considering a system as an integral unit rather than as a collection of individuals says something about personnel selection. It suggests that, in manning a system, teams rather than individuals should be selected—that matching the individual to the job may be a part of the organizational development process.

The need for system training has shown up in the difficulties of getting today's complex man-machine systems to perform as expected. Reliance on the adaptive capabilities of the operators is implicit in the design of most of these systems, but unfortunately developing these capabilities so that the system will perform adequately in an emergency requires experience under critical stresses equivalent to those of an emergency. These experiments have shown that system training, which can impose such stresses, does result in much more effective use of a system's resources—that it is one way of making the full potential of a system available before an emergency occurs. They have also enabled us to understand enough about how the organizations developed in the laboratory to formulate a useful principle that says: Train the team as a whole in an adequately simulated environment and give it knowledge of results. This technique treats the organization as a unit. It helps the organization develop by providing appropriate stress and the needed reinforcement. Although an organization gets some idea of how well it is doing just by doing it, the more complete the information about the results of its operation it gets, the more it will be reinforced. A training program, therefore, should facilitate learning by providing a factual critique which helps the organization identify its difficulties. This training principle is presently being put to use in a particular training program—the System Training Program RAND is installing in the Air Defense Command.

12. OBSERVATIONS ON THE GROWTH OF INFORMATION-PROCESSING CENTERS*

Milton G. Weiner

The personnel of information-processing centers exist in three inter-related environments: the task, equipment, and cultural environments.

A. The task environment is the set of changing external conditions to which the organization must adjust if it is to achieve the purpose for which it was formed.

B. The equipment environment is the set of equipment and facilities which the organization has available to deal with the task environment.

C. The cultural environment is the set of attitudes, values, and aspirations of the members of the organization relative to the purpose and activities of the organization.

In information-processing centers these three environments are in continual interaction, access to the task environment being mediated by the equipment and the cultural environment affecting the ways in which the task and equipment environment are perceived.

In laboratory investigations, the values at which these environments are initially "set" is established largely by the experimenters. Although the personnel of an organization have usually had some experience with the actual or a related task, equipment, and cultural environment, the early contact with the experimenters involves establishing a set of initial conditions for these environments appropriate to the laboratory. This may take the form of defining the goal or purpose of the organization and the boundary conditions of the equipment and culture. In the following discussion these conditions are presupposed, i.e., a clear statement of the goal of the organization is made, and the limits in the use or change of the equipment and facilities are stated.

Since this section deals with a developmental sequence it is assumed that the values of the initial settings are "low." Specifically, the task environment is not so complex as to overwhelm the organization, the equipment operation is within the capacities of the personnel, and the culture is not rigidly structured. The development for "higher" settings of these values is not to be considered, although the fact that these environments are assumed to be interrelated does imply that marked imbalance in the values may produce different consequences.

With this framework of a defined goal and a set of boundary conditions

---

* Reproduced from RAND Paper P-529, May 21, 1954.

an organization passes through three periods which overlap but can be roughly distinguished.

1. *The basal period*. This period begins with the first meeting of the personnel of the organization. It is marked by a high degree of interaction of the task, equipment, and cultural environments. It terminates with a conception of the ways in which the organization is structured and the relation of the structure to the goal of the organization.

2. *The consolidation period*. This period begins with the acceptance of the organization structure. It is the period during which the organization explores the boundary conditions imposed upon it and the mechanisms for dealing with these boundaries and still preserves the operating efficiency necessary to achieve the goal. The termination of this period is the shift in emphasis from responding to the task environment in the abstract form produced and represented by the equipment to the task environment as sets of changing conditions which are external to the organization.

3. *The organization period*. This period begins with the shift from dealing with the task environment as equipment representations to dealing with the task environment as an external condition. It is the period during which the goal and the task environment become interrelated.

The following presents these periods in greater detail and indicates some of the conditions affecting each period.

The Basal Period

The purpose of all organizations is to deal with a set of externally imposed conditions which the individual is incapable of handling by himself and which require integration of his activities with the activities of others. If the organization is to succeed, the individual must replace his independence and autonomy of function with cooperative actions in dealing with external conditions.

In any organization that is to be effective this implies two initial problems. The individual must be capable of adjusting his sets of values and expectations to include cooperation with others, and he must be able to acquire a set of skills that contribute to the organization. The first is required for becoming a member of the organization and the second is required to remain a member. Both of these problems, the one of the cultural environment and the other of the equipment environment, are influenced by the clarity with which the purpose of the organization is evidenced.

The challenge of the cultural environment is the necessity for relating the general values of the culture and one's individual values and behavior to the purpose of the organization. Wide discrepancies between the value of the work being done by the organization and general values are capable of producing states of conflict that limit the effectiveness of the organization. In the basal period these interpersonal and intercultural problems are paramount since maintaining autonomy of attitude or action violates the premise for existence of the organization and prevents further development.

Statements about the purpose of the organization and what the organization is trying to accomplish represent the initial exchange medium for all personnel. Such statements are perceived by the individual in terms of his previous experiences and attitudes and pose problems for which the solutions that he has formerly employed may not be satisfactory. The interaction of each individual with other members of the organization is an exchange of experience and less frequently of solutions. These exchanges have one common basis, namely, the way in which individuals can contribute to the purpose of the organization of which they are now all members. This basis is sufficient to exert pressure on the individual for agreement on the way in which the purpose of the organization is perceived and understood by the people concerned. It is this attempt to obtain a collective understanding that represents the initial binding forces of the organization.

Any mechanisms that provide for clear understanding of the relations between the goals of the organization and the values of the individual are advantageous. The existence of many channels through which the organization communicates its values and deals with the relation of its values to the general cultural or to individual values tends to increase the involvement of the individual. If the organization also has mechanisms for rewarding the individuals who apprehend and support its values, the developmental pace is accelerated.

The challenge of the equipment environment is the necessity for mastering the capabilities of the equipment and employing them in terms of the goal. The degree to which this acquisition of skill is obtained is of considerably greater significance than is the degree to which the individual masters the specific operations of the equipment. (Optimally, of course, the possession of technical and operational abilities by the individual is desirable, but where this is not possible the choice must be measured in terms of the goal desired.) In the basal period this relationship of equipment means to organization ends is limited. The individual must have sufficient familiarity with the equipment so that he may operate it. At this level, the problems of adequate training, and well-engineered equipment for the operator, are important, but are not the only ones. Emphasis on utilizing the equipment in terms of the goal is, from the organization point of view, critical.

If the operation of equipment is goal-oriented rather than oriented in terms of a specific subtask, it is possible to adapt the equipment operation to the changes of the task environment. This operating "versatility" is a method by which the range of equipment potential is explored and is available for use as the demands of the task change. Most equipment includes some multiple-purpose characteristics usually at the cost of more efficient single-purpose operation. Adhering to single-purpose operation is thus doubly uneconomical.

The integration of the cultural and equipment problems in the basal period shows most markedly in the evolution of the leadership structure. As realization develops that the purpose of the organization (to deal with changing sets of external conditions on a cooperative basis) requires division of labor, the requirements for leadership become clear. This realization, which was one of the conditions for the original formation of the organization, derives new force from the more intimate knowledge of the cultural and equipment environments now available to the organization. In addition to the recognition that a hierarchial structure is an instrumental part of dealing with the task environment, acceptance of any compromise of the values or aspirations of the individual as part of the group is required.

The requirements for leadership are defined in terms of the ability to perceive the relationship between the organization structure and its purpose, the ability to interpret this relationship to other members of the group, and the ability to understand the goal of the organization and to deal with these problems in a stable manner.

As these abilities develop they serve to structure the organization in several ways. On the one hand, individuals offer interpretations of the requirements of the hierarchy. These multiple interpretations serve to delineate further the conditions of the task environment with which the organization must deal. On the other hand, the flow of interpretation in terms of the task environment reduces the pressures of the cultural environment.

It is, in fact, the transition from individuality to division of labor and the acceptance of a hierarchy in the form of a leadership structure that marks the end of the basal period and represents the point at which an "organization" can be said to exist.

The Consolidation Period

The consolidation period is one of exploration and testing in the cultural, equipment, and task environment, and the application of the results of the exploration to the organization's methods of operating. The acceptance of structure which developed in the basal period provides the organization with a framework in which to operate. The framework at this time is not a rigid one: neither the position of individuals in the framework is fixed nor is the limit of the framework determined.

The first portion of the consolidation period is thus a period of movement in a number of directions. The movement occurs both in terms of internal and external demands. For the internal aspect the problems of individual status and responsibility develop.

Since the structure of the organization at this time is diffuse (i.e., it represents nothing more than a series of interpretations), it provides the opportunity for individuals to develop a wide variety of roles. These roles serve both the needs of the individuals who generate them and the needs of the organization in dealing with the environment. The delimitation of these two foci to the single criterion—servicing the organization—occurs through a series of reduction steps. These reduction steps are a necessary part of development because maintaining diffuseness in the roles of the leadership structure is equivalent to maintaining a diffuse operating structure with its consequent inability to distribute responsibility.

The form that these reduction steps take is the production of a series of incidents in which individuals challenge the role-capabilities of each other. The equipment and cultural environments play a part in this competition, the former in terms of the skill with which the various equipments are utilized to attain the goals of the organization, and the latter in terms of the culture that is developing within the organization. The emergence of an "organization culture" is a derivative of the common goal orientation and the developing set of experiences in common that are a part of the basal period.

This culture is marked by value systems, ethical codes, and taboos, which find expression in interpersonal relations. For internal communication the organization may develop a private language. This "meta-language" represents both an economy in dealing with an environment that is sufficiently understood and shared so that it can be codified, and an acceptance of the organization as the unique property of its members.

The definition of limits in these internal relationships is reflected in statements of the responsibilities of the members of the organization, first to each other and then to the goal. The first portion is concerned with confidence and the second with effectiveness. The two become highly interrelated in the leadership structure.

As confidence in the members of the organization develops, and as the conditions of the task environment are effectively met so that the goal of the organization is maintained, the organization stabilizes. Although internal problems may exist they are regarded as "maintenance" problems and not as "survival" problems; i.e., although the organization must deal with them in order to remain effective, they do not threaten the existence of the organization. This is possible because the organization is operating in terms of a generally accepted goal within fairly well defined limits, and with a division of labor that has been accepted on the basis of its effectiveness.

At the same time the external demands continue. The organization responds to these in a similar way by exploring the limits of its own structure and capabilities by "challenging" the environment in which it operates. These are challenges in the sense that they serve as tests of the sensitivity of the task environment and may result in an inability to deal with it. They take the form of modified operating procedures, attempts to surmount equipment constraints, and treatment of the environment in simple rather than in complex terms. They lead to a definition of "effective structure," i.e., the patterns of organization activity capable of dealing with the demands of the environment. With the acceptance of a changing set of external conditions, however, this definition of effective structure is probabilistic, imposed on the organization only for the known set of external conditions.

Since the period of consolidation produces an effective organization for dealing with the problems posed by the task environment, the organization will remain stable in procedures and structure as long as the demands of the task environment do not change markedly. If, however, marked changes do occur—changes such that the existing structure and procedures do not allow the organization to achieve its goal—the organization will undergo modifications to deal with the changes. The first of these modifications marks the beginning of the organization period.

The Organization Period

The "good" organization is one that can adapt to wide variations in the demands of the task environment and still retain a high degree of stability. Thus, good organization is not only defined in terms of the capacity to obtain an adequate "output" for differing sets of "inputs," but also in terms of the ability to accomplish this without becoming unstable.

During the basal period and the consolidation period the organization moves along three dimensions: homogeneity-heterogeneity, global-articulate, and diffuse-specific. The first of these dimensions refers to a process of goal-orientation and involves a progression from a generalized goal-orientation on the part of all members of the organization to a series of individual goal orientations in which each person perceives his activities as a necessary part of the operation of the organization. The second dimension refers to the functions performed by the members of the organization and reflects the change from undefined, or poorly defined, functions to an interlocking series of activities that have meaning in dealing with the task environment. The third dimension refers to the structure of the organization that progresses from general equivalence of responsibilities to a division of responsibility. The stable organization is one that deals with the changing demands of the task environment without losing heterogeneity of goal orientation, articulateness of function, or specificity of structure.

The basal period, in this respect, is pre-organizational in character since it does represent an unstable period. If, following this period, an organization does evolve, then it is considered unstable if the stresses of the task environment produce the same problems that existed at the basal period, i.e., lack of skill in dealing with the environment, questioning the values of the organization, questioning the adequacy of the goal or the techniques developed to achieve the goal. In effect, the unstable organization is one that regresses to a period of high interaction of the task, equipment, and cultural environments. From the regression, of course, it is possible for another organization to emerge, but it can probably be assumed that the new organization will have different goals, leadership structure and methods of operation.

Such a change involves a considerable energy expenditure on the part of the organization. It is the ability of an organization to deal with the variable task environment without this extreme energy expenditure that marks it as a good organization.

To maintain stability under heavy demands from the task environment is possible in at least one way. The organization must solve the problem of the relation of the task environment to the goal of the organization. The task environment, as a set of changing external conditions, and the goal of the organization are interrelated. The inputs to the organization are abstracted portions of the total task environment, some of which have direct consequences in achieving the goal, others having limited consequences.

The good organization develops ordering relationships which allow it to deal with the task environment in terms of the consequences of selecting and responding to one set of demands in preference to some other set. To do this requires treating the changes of the task environment not as equipotential events but as having different potentials for success in achieving the goal of the organization.

The mechanism for separating the inputs into those portions of the task environment directly relevant to the goal of the organization and those portions which are not, is accomplished by utilizing the existing knowledge of the state of the task environment and previous experience with the task environment that has been successful for obtaining the goal, and generalizing this experience to allow for prediction of the effects of various actions of the organization on the goal. This ability to use past and present experience to establish expectations of the future and to undertake action on planning made from this information is the highest order of organizational behavior. It implies a problem-solving ability that the organization employs to deal with variations in the demands made by the environment. Such planning and prediction allows actions to be taken that have high probability of success. By this mechanism the organization is able to "control" the environment and to maintain stability.

The period of organization is characterized by this high-order problem-solving ability that employs past and present experience for predictions and actions to interrelate the task environment inputs to the goals of the organization and allows the organization to maintain its goal without becoming unstable.

The mechanisms and techniques employed by the organization to deal with the demands of the environment in which it exists exclude, by definition, those individual actions which, although part of the behaviors of the personnel, do not serve the organization directly. Such events as the behavior of a member of the organization in obtaining an adequate environment for himself, i.e., making lighting, seating, or ventilation adjustments, are related to the operation of the organization in that they may serve to set the individual for carrying out his functions. Similar activities, such as checking out equipment operation, are part of this group of activities which are considered "performance-related," i.e., they prepare the individual for dealing with the task environment, but are relatively independent of the extent and type of demands that the task environment produces. Such behaviors may be predictable for the individual, but not for the organization.

A second set of mechanisms and techniques are called "programs." These are goal-oriented patterns of coordinated behavior in response to the demands of the task environment. They are the strategies of the information-processing organization for maintaining stability under variable environmental demands and represent procedures which the organization finds effective over a period of time.

That programs are time-related phenomena indicates that they interact with the state of the organization's development. In the basal period and in portions of the consolidation period the main access that the organization has to varying the processing of information is control of the rate and structure of the information. Programs at this early period may be characterized in terms of rate control and structure control. Rate control programs are those patterns of coordinated behavior that modify the time sequence in handling information. Structure control programs are those that modify the form of the information. Sequences of both types of programs may be combined at later stages of development.

The requirements for any program determine the period during which it will appear. If a program involves a particular level of skill in dealing with the equipment environment, heavy reliance on the abilities of others, confidence in their participation, and explicit acknowledgment of the ways in which it helps achieve the goal of the organization, it will not develop until these requirements are met. In this respect programs may tentatively appear at a local level as conditions are adequate and gradually evolve into generalized patterns through a process of testing and revision.

All programs are methods of structuring the task environment and are, therefore, models of the situation external to the organization. That they are models of an external reality leads to the development of another general class of programs. These are the assessment programs.

As structure and rate control programs are being evolved, the organization endeavors to validate the simplified models of external reality that these programs represent. The assessment programs are comparisons of the model with reality at various stages. Assessment programs, in a sense, substitute operating complexity of the organization, a factor over which the organization has some control, for environmental complexity in order to deal with the environment in a simplified form.

Some of the rate control programs evidenced by the organizations under study are:

1. Priority programs. These programs are sets of rules which determine which events will be given preference for representation in the model of the environment. Since every event has a series of characteristics, the establishment of priorities in the high frequency characteristics probably establishes a priority for low frequency characteristics and thus has general consequences for the organization.

2. Storage program. This program represents a limiting condition of the priority program, i.e., information is assigned zero priority at a particular time. A change in conditions may require a reassignment of priority and the information is then processed. This possibility of reassignment distinguishes stored information from discarded information.

Some of the structure control programs evidenced are:

1. "Fact" stipulation. This program is a strategy for applying a structure to the information that is being processed in those cases where the available structure is so ambiguous that definite decisions are not possible. The dynamics of fact stipulation, as well as many of the other programs, lie in the process of "uncertainty absorption." In representing an event as having a higher probability than the existing information merits, individuals allow the organization to continue to operate rather than to "idle" until more definite information is available. It is an integral component of the relation of the individual to the organization since it involves assuming responsibility for the actions taken.

2. Load balancing. Load balancing represents a shifting of tasks from one part of the organization to another as the amount of information being processed increases. This type of shifting restructures the information processing sequences. For such restructuring to exist presupposes both some degree of redundancy in information and some type of equivalence of function, for which the particular requirements depend on the nature of the load balancing.

Some of the assessment programs are:

1. Anticipation. To predict the probable changes in the task environment on the basis of available information and prior experience is a later

development of the organization. It involves a complex process of assigning probabilities to certain events and modifying the operating procedures to cope with the presumed event. Since some aspects of the task environment are usually cyclic, the organization can anticipate these and prepare to deal with any event that is novel in the situation. Exceptions to the expected pattern can then receive immediate processing. By removing the "uniqueness" from some of the events with which the organization has to deal, the model of the task environment is simplified and certain activities become routinized. This process requires continual assessment of the relation of the model to the actual situation to validate the adequacy of the anticipatory sequences.

2. Program shifting. The changing nature of the external situation with which the organization is dealing demands continual modifications of the simplified model which is being used to represent the situation. Perseveration of inappropriate procedures is a step towards instability. One of the mechanisms available to avoid this condition is to shift from one set of procedures to another set that are more appropriate to the goal. This is the strategy of program shifting.

These programs achieve various degrees of formalization in the operating system. They are mechanisms for dealing with the task environment within the constraints imposed by the equipment environment. They require coordination between the personnel of the organization developed out of an appreciation of the common goal and the capabilities of the group. The general nature of any program has significance for many organizations, but the specific application depends upon the set of situations to which the organization must respond. Fixed rules for any program probably require a complete specification of the task environment over a long period of time. For many IPC's this is an impossibility since it would require a knowledge of all possible events. The alternative which the organization develops in the later periods is problem-solving behavior utilizing existing information of the state of the task environment and previous experience with the environment.

Leadership and Morale

A VERY substantial part of the modern literature on the functioning of organizations concerns the reaction of the participant as an individual person to the forces impinging upon him in the organizational context. Most of this is the product of the so-called "human relations" school, now receiving wide currency in managerial applications. The original impetus to this sort of study came from the classical investigation carried out by a research team from Harvard University and the Western Electric Company at the latter's Hawthorne Works in the late 1920's and early 1930's (15). This investigation indicated rather dramatically that psychological factors were dominant in determining the productivity of workers under the conditions existent in the Hawthorne Works, a typical large-scale manufacturing enterprise with a relatively progressive personnel policy for that era. It also indicated that the managerial techniques in use did not secure from the working force a contribution anywhere near the workers' capacity to contribute. These findings were borne out in subsequent studies. The study of shoe factory work teams by Horsfall & Arensberg in Section 2 is typical in this respect, showing the impotence of the management's incentive system in the face of the workers' felt needs for fairness and social solidarity.

These early studies showed clearly the existence and importance in the typical factory of an "unanticipated consequence"—unanticipated, that is, by the management—of the forms of organization employed. The inadequacies centered around management's efforts to control and influence its employees and in the creation of unfavorable attitudes on the part of the workmen toward management, the company, and their work: that is, in management's leadership functions and in the morale of the work force. The implication is that management has failed to understand human nature, failed to develop knowledge and techniques for the exploitation of human resources at all comparable to those developed for material re-

167

sources. The result has been a movement to introduce better psychology into the managerial art.

There are a number of psychological theories of human behavior that have been fruitfully applied in organizational settings. One of these is the theory of motivation due to Abraham Maslow (10). Man has many needs. He behaves in ways that will result in need satisfaction. As needs are satisfied through appropriate behavior, they recede from attention and other needs become prominent. Maslow has provided a set of categories that describe a hierarchy of needs in the sense that those at the beginning of the hierarchy must be satisfied before behavior is directed toward needs at the higher levels. These categories are physiological needs, safety needs, social needs, ego needs, and self-fulfillment needs.

The physiological needs include hunger, thirst, removal of pain, and the like. An honest man will steal food if he is hungry enough, regardless of the dictates of conscience and the threat of jail. Once physiological needs are well satisfied, however, they cease to exert any important influence over behavior. Attention passes, in turn, to the need to gain assurance against future deprivation or against external dangers. The man who is both comfortable and safe looks for companionship. As social animals, human beings are directly gratified by the presence of others. Indeed, relationships with others are an indispensable part of being human. The ego needs refer to one's self-opinion and to the respect that he receives from others. These needs are the most important motivators of behavior in organizational contexts. The needs for self-fulfillment may appear only rarely and perhaps only in the case of exceptional individuals. This need is for the realization of one's full potentialities, for being creative. Self-fulfillment needs remain inactive in persons experiencing deprivation at lower levels in the need hierarchy.

The application of this theory to organizational problems has been especially associated with the work of Douglas McGregor (12). His book points out how many common managerial attitudes and practices are poorly calculated to attain their ostensible objectives of furthering organizational performance. He points out that the carrot-and-stick theory of motivation implicit in common managerial viewpoints is valid only for people motivated by physiological needs and this is an infrequent occurrence, especially in American society. If management is perceived as unpredictable or unfair, its assertion of the right to withhold basic rewards and inflict punishment can be expected to mobilize safety needs and induce activity intended to curtail and resist management's power. McGregor also develops a variety of approaches and illustrations, compatible with a more enlightened view of human nature, that serve to mobilize the ego needs in pursuit of organizational objectives. He recommends a philosophy of self control as opposed to external manipulation.

Other psychological theory that has found application to human behavior in organizations is related to the processes of social interaction, the development of the self, and the fulfillment of the individual's self needs (20). These concepts are very closely interrelated, since it is through our interactions with others that we establish our basic identities, both to ourselves and to others. The most important social interaction in this respect is that within the family. The parent-child relationship is the forerunner of the person's relationships with society as a whole and with specific other persons in positions of power and authority. Outgrowing the childhood state of total dependence and establishing the capacities for independent action and for relationships of interdependence with others is a central factor.

The application of theory of this kind to human relationships in organizations has been a primary concern of Chris Argyris (1, 2). A brief summary of theory and its application in one of his early case studies, *Organization of a Bank*, is reprinted in this section. Argyris' most prominent finding was that the bank tended to draw to it employees of a particular personality pattern, the "right type" for a bank. The "right type" was neat and conventional in manner, polite, quiet and retiring. The stability and security of bank life attracted them, and the bank benefited from their ability to fit into the precise and genteel routine of the work day. This had certain implications for the administrative style of the bank. Employees and officers alike expected a minimum of direct supervisory activity. Neither employees nor officers had much occasion to take the initiative; the bank's activities were either routine or else initiated by customers.

This study and the cases presented by Chowdhry and Pal and by Crozier contain much material relating organizational roles to the self concepts of the various participants. The negative reaction of the bank secretaries to being "pushed around" is a typical finding in situations where work requirements or management philosophy result in a person's activities being initiated for him predominantly by other people (18). The imposition of a high degree of dependence on another person is inconsistent with a self-concept as an adult. Likewise, Chowdhry and Pal point out how, in textile mill **A**, the failure of the managing agent to conform to role expectations of the supervisory staff compromised their identifications with their roles and their statuses in the social system. Similarly, in the French tobacco factories studied by Crozier, the differing patterns of adjustment of the four executives are in large part responses to needs for status, autonomy and achievement.

Two of these categories, achievement needs and status needs, are so important as to require special discussion. The work of David McClelland (11), relates the growth of rational administration and high levels of economic activity to increases in the level of achievement need felt by the general population or in influential segments thereof. The direct relationship between this clinically demonstrated need and a peculiarly organizational characteristic (the realization of specific objective performances) would appear to have singular importance. The need for status, to hold the respect of other people and to occupy a position of worth relative to their standards, also has profound implications for organized activity. As status systems are institutionalized in organizations, individual behavior adjusts to them. Robert Presthus (14) identifies adjustment patterns of the upwardly mobile, those who accept the system and attempt to rise in the hierarchy of status positions; the indifferent, who accept a stable low position in the organizational status system and pursue their central life interests elsewhere; and the ambivalents, who are unable to make a satisfactory adjustment of either kind.

There are many areas other than perceptions of self in which people form their own perceptions by comparison with the views of others. In the area of values, we usually ascribe our beliefs to a reference group such as our nation, our coreligionists, our fellow workers, etc. We likewise check our factual knowledge against the cognitions of others. Thus, coherent patterns of belief and feeling tend to grow up in interacting groups. On the large scale these patterns are institutionalized as social values or traditions, but on a small scale they can appear as group norms or attitudes that may extend no further than a small primary group (5, pp. 566–70).

In organizations or groups, a key attitudinal variable is the value placed on their participation by the members. In the small group, typical bases for the attraction of members are friendship, enhancement of status, perceptions of a common external threat, and the opportunity to attain some mutually attractive goal. The total attraction a group has for its members is referred to in the literature of social psychology as *cohesiveness*. Formal organizations likewise vary in attractiveness to their members and have the same bases of attractiveness as well as others. In organizations, of course, material rewards are of primary importance. However, members may also identify themselves with the moral order of the organization or internalize its values. They may share a common view as to the worth of the organization, endorse its goals and have high regard for its established policies. The value placed on their participation by the members of an organization is usually referred to as *morale*.

The processes of interpersonal comparison of beliefs result in relative uniformity of morale and other more specific attitudes. Nevertheless, there may be significant asymmetries in attitude. Incompatible interests may pull subparts of an organization in different directions resulting in the development of *cliques*.

Imbalance in power is a usual feature of organizations, and there will be significant differences in the relative power of individuals and groups to affect opinion. *Leadership* is the ability to influence the behavior of other members or to gain their acceptance of ideas. The question of leadership in formal organizations is a very complex one. Tradition has it that leadership is inherent in some persons, that they are natural-born leaders. This has led many students of the problem to equate leadership with virtue and to develop long lists of virtuous characteristics that are supposed to inhere in the person of the leader. Unfortunately, although psychologists have devoted a great deal of effort in attempts to confirm this common-sense theory, their results have not been successful (17). The evidence shows only that leaders are somewhat more likely to be tall than short, men than women, intelligent than stupid. Other approaches, however, have yielded significant findings about the process of leadership.

Social power is most appropriately conceived as a relationship among people, not a property of an individual person. French and Raven (6, pp. 607–23) conceive of five bases for power of person O over person P: "(a) reward power, based on P's perception that O has the ability to mediate rewards for him; (b) coercive power, based on P's perception that O has the ability to mediate punishments for him; (c) legitimate power, based on the perception by P that O has a legitimate right to prescribe behavior for him; (d) referent power, based on P's identification with O; (e) expert power, based on the perception that O has some special knowledge or expertness." In this formulation, the influence of any one person is seen to be based in the perceptions and attitudes of other persons, as well as in objective control over resources, sanctions, offices or talent.

Thus, social leadership is a feature of an interacting group. Persons taking leadership roles are implicitly or explicitly recognized by the other members. Leadership status is accorded to those who represent most fully the norms of the group or who display special abilities toward realizing the interests shared by the group. Thus, in the article by Bass and Dunteman, task-oriented people tended to receive recognition as leaders, apparently because of their special contribution to the group task. But when groups were recombined so that persons of like interests were brought together, the leadership pattern changed in ways consistent with the newly established group interest.

Leadership is also a set of functions that must be performed in order for a group to maintain itself and to accomplish its goals. These functions are not always executed by a single person. In fact, psychological studies have shown a tendency for two distinct facets of leadership to be exercised by different persons. These are *task leadership* and *social-emotional* leadership. The task leader produces and evaluates ideas in furtherance of the group's ostensible goals. The social-emotional leader is distinguished by his popularity and tends to see that the members are satisfied, as individuals, with their role in the group. Performance of the functions of task leadership does not necessarily tend to increase a member's popularity. Even where a group process begins with one individual performing both functions, the functions often tend to become split among two members, with the initial leader usually choosing social-emotional popularity over task sponsorship (**5**, pp. 345–46). Some of the problems surrounding differentiation of leadership functions are treated by Hutchins and Fiedler in their article reprinted in this section.

Culturally determined expectations for behavior in organizations operate in favor of a conception of leadership that is at variance with findings like those mentioned in the last paragraph. Systems of legitimate power are the mainspring of influence and action in organizations. Traditional literature on management stresses the principle of unity of command in these systems: that any task group or larger component should have one and only one boss. A structure based on this conception and accepted as settled policy may conflict, not only with other bases of social power, but also with the leadership needs of a work group. Accommodation to such conflicts is an important part of organization process. Much recent literature indicates the existence of a longer-term trend to resolve such conflicts by changing the institutionalized structures that generate them (e.g., **2, 9, 12, 15, 18**).

Patterns of informal organization are one means through which accommodation is reached between the structure of formal authority (legitimate power) and other social considerations. Despite the importance of legitimate power, there remains ample ground for maneuver in any system of organized action. Informal patterns can be worked out that make necessary accommodations or implement leadership functions overlooked by formal authority.

The role of informal leadership appears very prominently in the articles in Section 2 by Horsfall and Arensberg and by Dalton. In the shoe factory, the roughers and pounders put together an informal system of action to subserve a work-group interest almost independently of the intentions of management. In Dalton's factory, the clique leadership both successfully resisted higher management in creating the phony inspection practices and also saw to it that the individual interests of important participants were satisfied in the outcome. In Crozier's tobacco factories, leadership of the maintenance mechanics' interests reinforced the formal position of the technical engineer. This informal system, however, virtually neutralized the influence of the two top plant managers over normal operations.

The morale of an organization and the way in which authority is reacted to are heavily influenced by the existing climate of the organization. Climate in turn is related to the past history of interaction and especially the way in which power figures have behaved. The traditional patterns of management induce a climate of *punitiveness* in organization functioning. Assertion of the right to punish or deprive others and its habitual use generate defensiveness and retaliation. This is well illustrated in Gouldner's analysis of the punishment-centered bureaucracy (**7**). Similar phenomena clearly show up in the case studies by Dalton,

Chowdhry and Pal, and Crozier. The findings of behavioral-science research indicate the superiority of a *supportive* climate in realizing high morale and constructive leadership. This is illustrated by much of the work of the University of Michigan's Institute for Social Research. Their reports give many specific findings of how factors of leadership and organizational design influence the work climate. The article reproduced below by Zander and Wolfe shows how the nature of the performance-reporting practices influences the style of interpersonal relations and the degree of effectiveness of coordinating committees. Likewise, Pelz reviews findings concerning the interaction of supportive behavior and power in determining the degree of acceptance of supervisors by their work groups.

The origins of these and other studies of the Michigan group go back to laboratory studies in group dynamics that were carried out during and after World War II. These findings were that group effectiveness is increased by a democratic process of group leadership and an explicit concern with group process and maintenance of the social system. Democratic group leadership implies that each member participates fully in discussion and work, that each has full opportunity to influence the group's decisions and the outcome of their functioning, and that the relevant needs of all the members as individuals are satisfied in the group. In maintaining the group, the social-emotional leader, preferably with the understanding and help of the group as a whole, must see that the conditions of democratic leadership are maintained and that any malfunction is brought to the attention of the group and worked out before continuation with substantive issues. A failure of the maintenance function shows up in a lowered quality of work as aspects of the task are used in an unacknowledged way to work out emotional problems rather than the reality problem of task achievement.

In a summary of the industrial studies of the Michigan group, Likert (9) emphasizes the need for the work supervisor, if he is to be successful, to assume a role that is sharply differentiated from his workers. This role is seen to be supportive to the work group and to provide a link to the rest of the organization. Thus he must represent the work group in the external system of the organization to generate adequate support for the interests of that group; conversely, he relays the demands of the organization to the group members. He is also supportive of the members individually in their feelings of self-worth and their other felt interests.

The problems of the individual participants in large formal organizations are matters of great interest and concern. In any humanistically oriented society, organizations and their works can only be valued ultimately by what they contribute to the lives of individuals. On the other hand, the contributions of the various classes of individual members are necessary elements toward the—literally—superhuman, organized undertakings that are such an important feature of modern society. This section is primarily concerned with the role of the individual as contributor. It should be clear that, to the individual participant, the organization is an external system of great relevance to his immediate welfare and holds relatively great power over him. The efforts of organizations to bend human resources to the pursuit of collective ends is one of the major moral dilemmas of our time. Whether this shows up as terrorism or brainwashing under a totalitarian government or the manipulation of blind, unthinking conformity under private enterprise in a democracy (19), this dilemma is one of the central concerns of those who study, manage, or participate in large-scale organization.

BIBLIOGRAPHY

1. ARGYRIS, CHRIS. *Personality and Organization*. New York: Harper, 1957.
2. ARGYRIS, CHRIS. *Understanding Organizational Behavior*. Homewood, Ill.: The Dorsey Press, 1960.
3. BASS, BERNARD M. *Leadership, Psychology and Organizational Behavior*. New York: Harper, 1960.
4. BENNIS, WARREN G.; SCHEIN, EDGAR H.; BERLEW, DAVID E., AND STEELE, FRED I. *Interpersonal Dynamics*, Homewood, Ill.: The Dorsey Press, 1964.
5. BERELSON, BERNARD, AND STEINER, GARY A. *Human Behavior*. New York: Harcourt, Brace and World, Inc., 1964.
6. CARTWRIGHT, D., AND ZANDER A. (eds.). *Group Dynamics*, 2nd ed. Evanston, Ill., Row Peterson, 1960.
7. GOULDNER, ALVIN W. *Patterns of Industrial Bureaucracy*. Glencoe, Ill.: The Free Press, 1954.
8. HOLLANDER, E. P. *Leaders, Groups, and Influence*. New York: Oxford University Press, 1964.
9. LIKERT, RENSIS. *New Patterns of Management*. New York: McGraw-Hill Book Co., 1961.
10. MASLOW, A. H. *Motivation and Personality*. New York: Harper Row, 1954.
11. McCLELLAND, DAVID C. *The Achieving Society*. Princeton, N.J.: Van Nostrand, 1961.
12. McGREGOR, DOUGLAS. *The Human Side of Enterprise*. New York: McGraw-Hill Book Co., 1960.
13. PETRULLO, L., AND BASS, B. M. (eds.). *Leadership and Interpersonal Behavior*. New York: Holt, Rinehart and Winston, 1961.
14. PRESTHUS, ROBERT V. *The Organizational Society*. New York: Alfred A. Knopf, 1962.
15. ROETHLISBERGER, F. J., AND DICKSON, W. J. *Management and the Worker*. Cambridge, Mass.: Harvard University Press, 1941.
16. SAYLES, LEONARD R., *Behavior of Industrial Work Groups*. New York: John Wiley & Sons, Inc., 1958.
17. STOGDILL, RALPH M., "Personal Factors Associated with Leadership," *Journal of Psychology*, 1948, Vol. 25, pp. 35–71.

18. WHYTE, W. F. *Human Relations in the Restaurant Industry*. New York: McGraw–Hill Book Co., 1948.

19. WHYTE, JR., W. H. *The Organization Man*. New York: Simon & Schuster, 1956.

20. ZILLER, ROBERT C. "Individuation and Socialization," *Human Relations*, Vol. 17, No. 4 (November, 1964), pp. 341–60.

13. EXCERPTS FROM "ORGANIZATION OF A BANK"*

Chris Argyris

Personality Development versus Organizational Development

One of the basic problems in understanding human organizations stems from the fact that the development of personality of agents tends to be different from the development of organizations. Let us examine this statement in closer detail.

1.0 In a recent review of the literature concerning personality development, the following broad trends of personality development seemed clearly discernable for individuals interacting within our culture.

1.01 People in our culture tend to develop from receiving and incorporating aspects of culture as an infant, to controlling, using, redefining and helping others incorporate these aspects of culture as an adult.

1.02 People in our culture develop from a state of being passive as an infant (i.e., having other people initiate action for them) to a state of being increasingly active as an adult (i.e., they initiate action as much or more than other people towards them).

1.03 People in our culture develop from being capable of behaving only in a few ways and in a rigid manner as an infant to being capable of behaving in many different ways and behaving in a flexible manner as an adult.

1.04 People in our culture develop from being in a subordinate position in the family and society as an infant, to occupying a more equal and/or superordinate position in the family and society, as an adult.

1.05 People in our culture develop from a state of high dependence on others as an infant, to a state of independence and finally to a state of interdependence in their society as an adult.[1]

If we apply the above developmental trends to agents in organizations, we may hypothesize that agents ought to require functions which are so defined that they may fulfill some combination of the above trends. (The exact combination would naturally depend on the specific agent.)

1.1 In order to accomplish this, the agent would require a function in which:

---

*Comprising Appendix D and Chapter 5. Published 1954 by Yale University Labor and Management Center.

[1] Chris Argyris, *Personality Fundamentals for Administrators* (Yale Labor and Management Center, 1952), p. 97.

1.11 he can define for himself a ratio of activity (initiation of action) to passivity where activity is greater than passivity (passivity defined as others initiating action for the agent);

1.12 he can define for himself a position equal and/or superordinate to the other agents with whom he interacts;

1.13 he can define for himself tasks where he is able to provide expression for the many learned ways of behaving that are important to him; (this includes the expression of important abilities, needs, sentiments, and personal goals)

1.14 he can define for himself a sense of fluidity and flexibility that is comparable to his personality fluidity and flexibility;

1.15 he can express feelings of independence and can express feelings of interdependence in relation to the other agents of the organization;

1.16 he can feel that he has the respect of other agents (whom he feels are) important to his life;

1.17 he obtains from his job a degree of creature sufficiency he desires.

1.2 It seems necessary that we pause for a moment and make a few important comments concerning the list just presented.

First, we want to emphasize that the exact combination of these requirements and the degree to which each one of them is to be fulfilled for any given individual can be ascertained only by analysis of that individual case. Thus, it is possible that individual A, for example, requires primarily 1.11, 1.12 and 1.14 with an emphasis on 1.12. On the other hand, individual B may require all the above be fulfilled with an emphasis on 1.15 and 1.16.

It is also conceivable that individual C, for example, may desire (1) *not* to be active (1.11), (2) *not* to have an equal or superordinate position (1.12), (3) *not* to desire to feel independent (1.15), etc. According to our viewpoint this adult would have to be classed as "not mature." He is still at a more childlike stage of development. Psychologists may call him "fixated" at an earlier stage of development. This individual would not require a function which permits him to accomplish the items suggested in 1.11–1.17.

The point we want to emphasize is that we are *not* eliminating individual differences, nor are we imposing our developmental scheme on everyone. This is not a "rose-bud" theory. We are simply suggesting that a normal individual living in and interacting with our culture will tend to exhibit these developmental trends, but in his own unique combination. If the individual does not depict any of these trends, then we would suggest that broadly speaking he is not mature, and that he will tend to be in equilibrium in the kind of a function in which a mature individual will not be in equilibrium.

To summarize, we would suggest that a normal individual in our culture requires a function which permits him to obtain a minimal personality expression and to accomplish this in any given context with the maximum possible success and with a minimum of personality disequilibrium.[2]

1.3 If we turn our attention for the moment to the development of an efficient organization as conceived by the traditional scientific management principles, assuming that the organization is able to express itself as freely as it desires without having to worry about individuals, we find that the following characteristics would tend to arise. Most of the individual agents (excepting the leaders) would be assigned to functions:

1.31 which would tend to permit them little control over their work-a-day world.

1.32 which would tend to place them in a situation where their passivity rather than initiative would frequently be expected.

1.33 which would tend to force them to occupy a subordinate position.

1.34 which would tend to permit them a minimum degree of fluidity and (tend to) emphasize the expression of one (or perhaps a few) of the agent's relatively minor abilities.

1.35 which would tend to make them feel dependent upon other agents (e.g., the boss).[3]

Although this list could be expanded, the important point, in our opinion, is that the developmental processes and end result of the individual and the organization at crucial points are fundamentally different and even antagonistic. This is not to infer that modern organizations are therefore "bad." We are simply saying that this is the way they are. Only by understanding the nature of modern organization can we begin to make some sensible predictions about individuals' behavior in these organizations.

The Steady State of the Trust Department

A. The Workflow Process

1. *Multi-objectives lead to multi-workflows.*

This department, like the bank as a whole, has several objectives and as many discrete workflows. For example, on the basis of data available, we note seven discrete workflows.

---

[2] The last part of this sentence indicates that an individual may modify his desires in order to adapt to a given situation. In other words, if he could not obtain his desired personality satisfaction because his job would not permit it, then, he may, assuming he wants to remain employed, decide to accept the temporary frustrations in order to remain in equilibrium to his working world. Or, he may react differently and become apathetic and attach little importance (potency) to his industrial situation. Or, the agent may be culturally taught not to expect personality gratification in an industrial setting. Finally, the agent may, by the use of psychological defense mechanisms (e.g., rationalization or projection, etc.) adapt to his inability to obtain personality satisfaction in his industrial environment. This does not vitiate the above discussion. In fact, by using the above discussion, we can now understand why the agents use defense mechanisms or why they may attach little potency to their industrial setting.

To put it another way, the exceptions just cited include conditions which are not stipulated above. As such, these exceptions confirm our original ideas.

[3] F. W. Taylor, *Scientific Management* (Harper & Bros., 1947) and R. Urwick, *The Elements of Organization* (Harper & Bros., 1944).

(a) Personal trusts. Some examples are: A court trust fund for the administration of which the organization is made responsible to the court. Voluntary living trusts, i.e., trust funds set up by a customer who thereby turns over his investments and his money to the organization for proper handling. Institutional trusts, i.e., trusts set up for institutions such as churches, Y.M.C.A.'s, etc.

(b) Corporative trusts. The organization acts as a trustee for bond issues. The organization acts as a trustee for pension plans. The organization acts as a fiscal agent for corporations. It pays the corporation's dividends.

These workflows begin, as far as the department is concerned, the moment the customer enters the department and requests to see a trust officer. If the customer has no specific officer in mind, the receptionist guides him to the senior trust officer. At this introductory meeting the services of the department are outlined and the desires of the customer analyzed. As a result, the customer is assigned to a trust officer who is an expert on the customer's problems.

There are several meetings between the customer and the officer in which a detailed study is made of the customer's needs. The officer then spends a good deal of time in trying to find the best possible investment policy for the customer. As soon as the officer in charge is satisfied with an investment policy, he discusses it with the entire officer staff at a departmental meeting. The final form of the investment policy is a resultant of the group's thinking.

This brief description does not give all the details of the workflow. It simply outlines the over-all characteristics. The important point to be noted at this time is that private meetings between the officer and the customer and confidential meetings among the employees constitute the basic framework of the workflow process.

The actual detailed behavior of each meeting cannot be described before hand. It varies as customers and problems vary. Unlike manufacturing workflows, these workflows are comparatively fluid and not rigidly defined. This, we shall see, provides unusual opportunity for the officers to experience a wide variety of emotionally toned events, most of which are related to their personality fulfillment.

The fact that there is fluidity and flexibility does not mean that some stability or "structure" does not exist in the workflows. The workflows have their formal task characteristics defined by organizational policies and by state and federal laws. Thus officers do have some basic definitions of policy expectancies which provides them with a structure for their workflow activity. On the other hand, the actual behavior of people on the workflow (especially the ones contacting the customer) varies considerably from customer to customer and with the same customer at different times.

2. *The critical activity of each workflow is accomplished at the beginning.*

This characteristic of the bank as a whole holds true for the department. The trust services are "sold" by a trust officer at the beginning in the workflow process.

Also, as in the case of the whole, the people in this department who have the functions with greatest power and highest status perform tasks at the beginning of the workflow process. The employees "behind the customer line" receive "products" that have been sold. Their job is primarily the one of recording the sale and maintaining the service.

3. *Workflow pace is not entirely controlled by people from within.*

This is definitely the case as far as the department is concerned. The customer is the "pacesetter." The primary difference is that in the department the *amount* of time spent between employee and customer is greater. This is due to the complicated and personal nature of the services performed. The customer and the employee (usually an officer) interact for longer periods of time than is the case for the employees of the other departments.

Unlike the over-all organizational workflow process, the employees in the Trust Department are unable to predict their "busy" days. One reason is that due to the nature of the transactions, the customers do not come routinely to the department. Also, when the customers do come, they stay much longer. The best that the employees can predict are the busy months, months near income tax returns, quarterly dividends, etc.

Finally, the department's workflows continually place their employees in contact with people outside the organization. They frequently interact with lawyers, doctors, judges, etc., due to the nature of the workflow activities.

4. *The workflow activities have a high human quality.*

In discussing this characteristic we need to differentiate between the people in the department who meet and talk with the customers, and the people who do not. Let us speak of the former first.

The workflow processes in this department is one of the most personal, emotional, confidential, and at the same time technically difficult, workflows in the entire organization. In connection with the last point, the employees report that it is not an easy matter to accept the responsibility of managing other people's money and property and to promise that it will be managed in the best possible manner. Trust work requires much knowledge of legal matters, accounting, investment, and other related activities. In fact, as we have already seen, the workflows are so difficult that groups of experts meet to make decisions on one customer's account.

Nevertheless, the employees report that the human element is most important. No matter how technically competent a trust officer may be, his "personality" is crucial. It is important that people be placed on the workflow who are able to cope with the human problems that are so inexorably woven with the technical ones.

An illustration of the importance of the human characteristics in the workflow activities is found in the following quotations regarding qualifications of trust personnel taken from interviews with officers in the department:

"There must be embedded in each a desire to serve mankind."

"The basic interest is the customer."

"Tact and diplomacy are extremely important. A strong, sound, decent philosophy of life is crucial."

"He must be able to go into a widow's home the day after the husband dies and discuss her very personal problems with her."

"A trust officer is like a doctor."

Not all people in the department experience customer interactions. This does not mean that these individuals do not share some of these experiences. Many of them in describing their activities implied that they "experience" some of these personal interactions by identifying with the information they read when they come into contact with the confidential reports processed in the department. Thus, although they do not have direct contact with the customer, they are still able to experience some of the personal feelings that occur during an interview through the psychological process of identification with the material that they read.

5. *Officers are in the workflow process.*

This is true for this department. As we have seen, the officers are an integral part of the workflow. In fact their position is the most important one in the workflow. It is at the beginning where the selling of the services to the customer is accomplished.

6. *The workflow ties the employees to the customer rather than to the other employees.*

This is primarily true for the officers in the department. They are the ones who contact the customers. The clerical help and technical assistants housed in the "back offices" are linked to the officers rather than to the customers. They supply the officers with the information that the officers desire and type up the reports. The clerical help have no formal reasons to contact the other employees. Thus the characteristic of the workflow not acting to bind the employees with one another still holds true in this department. As was noted previously, this leads to weak informal group activities.

One might suspect that the secretaries who work closely with the various officers might feel closer to the officers and thus to the officer's customer. As far as most of the secretaries (95%) are concerned, neither is true. There are a number of probable reasons for this. First, many of them are in a secretarial pool from which the officers may draw. Thus, the same secretary does not always work with the same officer. Second, no matter how much they interact with the officers, we must not forget that there exists a definite status gap between employees and officers. Thus the girls are forced by the workflow process to interact with officers, while in the remaining organizational processes (i.e., reward and penalty, perpetuation, etc.) they do *not* interact with the officers.

The secretarial pool, although a recent innovation, has another effect upon the relationship. It creates opportunity for the girls to talk to each other. One of the items frequently discussed is the difficulty they have with the officers. Thus, there is beginning to arise an exception to the general characteristic that informal group relationships do not exist. The secretaries are beginning to create informal groupings stimulated by a common feeling that they have common difficulties with the officers.

Finally, it is important to note that there do not exist any departmental workflow processes which would serve to tie the employees in the department into a cohesive unit. Nor is there any workflow process which may serve to tie the Trust Department with the other departments of the organization. There is not much interaction with the employees of the other departments. This tends to create an isolation of this department from the other departments in the organization. The head of the department is keenly aware of this problem and tries continually to weld his department to the "whole" through the use of the organization's identification process. For example, he is continually emphasizing that they are a part of "The Friendly First."

7. *Interrelatedness of workflow to the other processes.*

(*a*) Those employees who contact the customers have tasks in their function representing all the organizational processes. For example, they initiate authority, reward and penalty, perpetuation, etc. tasks. The remainder of the employees (secretaries, clerks, technicians) have primarily formal workflow tasks which are primarily related to the paper work so necessary in the department.

(*b*) The customers, as in the case of the organization's other workflows, are an integral part of the workflow process. In the case of this department we may add lawyers, judges, etc. to the type of "outside" people who become part of the workflow. The customers have formal workflow, authority, reward and penalty, perpetuation and communication tasks in the function which the organization expects them to perform. These tasks are augmented by the customer as he finds it necessary. In fact, due to such identification symbols "Friendly First," "courteous service," etc. the customer finds that he may augment his activities to a considerable degree. The same identification activities also permit the customer to maximize the use of the formal activities expected of him. Finally the same identification activities act to *minimize* and control the inherent authority, reward and penalty, and perpetuation tasks that the officers may have in their function. The unequal balance of power may place internal strain upon the officer and may lead, as one officer put it, "to bite your lip and

smile even if you know you're right." Courtesy, diplomacy, and tactfulness are very important in this type of work.

B. Authority Process

1. *Officers have authority and frequently express it.*

In the analysis of the organization as a whole we note that the majority
of officers do not express directive authority with any substantial frequency. This is not entirely the case in the Trust Department. Three-
fifths of the officers report very frequent daily authority contacts and
two-fifths report moderate daily authority contacts with employees.[4]
Similarly 50 per cent of the employees report very frequent contacts and
15 per cent report moderate authority contacts.[5] This trend, then, is opposite from the one described for the whole organization.

As we have noted in the previous section on workflow, part of the
reason for this frequent expression of authority stems from the fact that
the officers are continually directing their subordinates to obtain specific
types of information which they (officers) will need in order to arrive at
a decision.

The consequences of this "abnormally" frequent expression of authority are interesting. We shall see, for example, that the employees in this
department report (proportionately) more negative feelings about the officers than do the employees in any other department. The employees
directly relate their negative feelings to the "abnormally frequent" authority expression.

2. *There exists a "gap" between officers and employees and also multiple supervision.*

The employees definitely feel that a gap exists between them and the
officers. It is interesting to note that they also feel the gap leads to poor officer-employee relationships. Odd as it may sound, the strongest feelings
about the officer-employees gap come from employees who experience the
most interaction with their officers. These results are congruent with a
previously stated conclusion that the covert or latent relationships are
much more hostile than the overt relationships.

The problem of multiple supervisors is also acute. Secretaries (because
of the pool) are continually being directed to do work by more than one
officer. The technical people find themselves in a similar situation. It arises

---

[4] We remind the reader that unless otherwise indicated the formal tasks referred
to are those of initiation.

[5] We may also remind the reader that the operational criteria for the "degree of
frequency" are as follows:

VF Very frequent (5–10 contacts a day)
M Moderate (2–5 contacts a day)
I Infrequent (1 or less contacts a day, but at least 1 a week)
PN Practically never (less than 1 contact a week)

from the fact that each officer individually manages a certain amount of accounts. He is not expected to know everything about all the services these accounts require. He is expected to ask help from the various technical employees in the department. This results in the employees being directed by more than one officer.

3. *Feelings of self-responsibility are not clearly evident.*

The majority of the non-officer employees do not express feelings of self-responsibility as frequently as do the other employees in the organization. Only the "old timers," who are in the minority, feel that they are their own boss. These results are to be expected, since we know that authority tasks are frequently expressed by the officers. This minimizes the necessity for the employees to create or engage in authority *acts*. The employees, comparing their "lot" with the organization as a whole, interpret their experiences as indicating that they aren't considered as responsible as are the other employees. Seventy-two per cent feel "discriminated against" in the matter of having an opportunity to be their own boss. Sixty-nine per cent believe that if this continues, they should be compensated with higher salaries than those received by other departments. This lends weight to the previously mentioned conclusion that one of the reasons the employees in the *total* organization accept lower wages are the relatively "weak" authority activities.

4. *Inter-relatedness of authority with the other processes.*

(*a*) In the previous chapter we suggest that a "weak" authority process may compensate for low wages. The feelings expressed by the employees in this department about wages do not differ from those expressed by most others in the organization. They feel that the wages are low. But they must find compensations other than a "weak" authority system. In this department, accordingly we find proportionally more employees emphasize that they stay because the work is easier than in any other department. A surprising number admit that they "don't break their neck at work" and add "why should we with what we get paid." Thus, we infer that the employees, realizing that the wages are low and at the same time *not* experiencing a weak authority process as a partial compensation for this situation rationalize or make up for what they perceive to be an "abnormal" situation by working less.

(*b*) As the workflow process in the over-all organizational structure lends support to a "weak" authority process, the workflow, in this department, helps create and reenforce a relatively "strong" authority process. Thus, we have seen that the employees are forced by the very nature of their jobs to receive directions from the officers and in turn, to direct the officers in those matters which they (employees) are experts.

(*c*) The kind of personality type that tends to be perpetuated in the bank finds ideal possibilities for expression under "weak" authority. Since the statistics indicate that the employees in the Trust Department are similar to the "right type,"[6] (i.e., the right type for employment by the bank) we may assume that they also desire a "weak" authority process. Since they do not experience a weak authority process, we may infer that they will tend to express resentment toward the officers. This inference is substantiated by the fact that the comments made by the employees of this department about the officers are the most aggressive and hostile of all comments reported.

(d) Finally, we may also infer that since "strong" leadership goes against the organizational identification codes of "passive leadership," the employees should perceive the officers as deviants from the codes. The employees confirm our inferences and 89 per cent state that this inconsistency leads to even further aggression toward the officers. It also seems to lead to a perfectly rational reason for the employees to project their difficulties onto the officers and blame them for their difficulties.

C. Reward and Penalty Process

1. *Rewards and penalties are hardly ever distributed by the officers to the employees.*

This characteristic holds true for the Trust Department. The fact that it does, leads to problems. The problems arise from, and are directly related to, the frequent authority expression. Since the employees are directed more often, there arises an increased expectation for increased rewards and/or increased penalties. The officers, on the other hand, following the overall organizational reward and penalty pattern, distribute few of either. This results in a discrepancy between the frequency of authority contacts and the reward and penalty contacts that are necessary for the employees to evaluate their relationship with the officer. Thus 75 per cent of the employees feel that they do not know "where they stand" in relation to the officers. They wish the officers would express more reward and penalty activities. This would provide them with a chance to evaluate themselves in relation to the officer.

An interesting problem seems to arise as a result of this. The officers do want to give more rewards and penalties. As to the former, they believe that money rewards are the ones most important to the employees. Compliments, praises, etc. should not be expressed as rewards if they cannot be reenforced by financial rewards. But the financial rewards are not con-

---

[6] The writer infers that some of the more latent characteristics of the "right type" are:

A strong desire for security, stability, predictability in their life.

A strong desire to be left alone and work in relative isolation.

A dislike of aggressiveness and/or hostility in themselves and others.

If these inferences are valid, then we can begin to understand why the people have little difficulty in being retiring, polite, courteous, tactful, conventional, etc. Behaving in this manner tends to minimize the possibility of experiencing aggression from others and/or expressing aggression towards others.

trolled by anyone in the entire department. Thus, the department officers tend to give few rewards of any type.

When it comes to penalties, the officers (with one exception) find it difficult to speak directly to and to discipline the employee. This is due to several reasons. First, they realize that since the rewards are not really in their control, if they were to penalize the employees, they would build up a reward and penalty relationship with them that contained only penalties. This is hardly desirable from their point of view. Another reason is related to the personality type. The "right type" tends to dislike expressing or receiving penalizing sentiments. The officer, coming up from the ranks and/or realizing that the employees do feel this way minimizes the distribution of direct penalties.

However, the employees report penalties are received in an indirect manner. Thus they describe learning how poorly they did some work from another employee who was told "confidentially" by the officer. Sixty-five per cent resent this very much. We will present ample evidence for this when we discuss the over-all employee-officer relationships.

2. *Feeling of "self-responsibility" is not prominent.*

The feelings of self-responsibility are lower than the average expressed in the bank as a whole.

3. *Wages are not considered satisfactory.*

Sixty per cent of the employees feel wages are "poor." Thirty per cent describe them as "terrible" and ten per cent refuse to talk about them.

4. *Feelings about other rewards the organization offers.*

(*a*) Ranking the other factors that are viewed as rewards by the employees, we find that benefits rank highest as most desired and best liked.[7] This is similar to the over-all organizational results.

(*b*) As might be expected—"I am my own boss" is in last place in this department while it is in second place for the entire organization.

(*c*) Working conditions receive a very high second place among factors considered favorable by the employees. This is probably related to the fact that the department's physical quarters were recently renovated.

(*d*) Unlike the organization as a whole, the positive organizational characteristic that "people are nice, they let you alone" is hardly ever mentioned. This is due, we believe, to the fact that the officers do not let the employees alone. It is also due to the officers discussing their feelings about employees with other employees. When the former employees hear about the officer's criticism and that another employee knows about it, they believe that the employee is delving into their personal problems.

Thus we see more evidence of how people's feelings about reward and

---

[7] Included in the benefits are (1) the pension plan, (2) insurance, (3) medical benefits, and (4) vacations with pay.

penalties are interrelated with their feelings about how they are treated in other processes, and how this treatment compares with the one received by the employees in the organization as a whole.

D. Perpetuation Process

1. *Officers hardly ever express perpetuation activities on their own initiative.*

This holds true for the officer-employee relationship in the Trust Department. The figures reported for the entire organization are almost identical.

2. *Feelings of self-responsibility are frequently expressed.*

The feelings of self-responsibility, in relation to the perpetuation process, do exist and are expressed in the same frequencies, as is found in the over-all organizational figures. The feelings of self-responsibility arise from the fact that the officers do not express perpetuation tasks. The employees may therefore substitute perpetuation *acts.*

3. *The director of personnel is seen as controlling the perpetuation process.*

(*a*) The position of the director of the department is weakened.

(*b*) Since he, in turn, is unable to give his subordinate officers perpetuation tasks, their position is weakened.

(*c*) This, in turn, leads to the officers accepting less and less responsibility for the employees in their sections.

4. *The picture of the "right type" hired and developed in the bank as a whole presented in the previous chapter is valid for the Trust Department.*

The employees in this Department perceive themselves as:

(*a*) People who consider themselves more capable of receiving directions (55%) than of directing others (45%).

(*b*) People who feel they are more comfortable if they do not have to initiate actions for others. Only 18 per cent indicate they would feel comfortable in so doing.

(*c*) Finally, 50 per cent prefer to be followers. Thirty-five per cent prefer to be leaders but they qualify "leadership" to mean passive leadership. Only 15 per cent desire to be directive leaders.

E. Identification Process

1. *The officers express few identification activities.*

The conclusions reached with respect to the whole organization are valid for this department as far as this dimension is concerned.

2. *The slogans and phrases which identify the bank hold for this department.*

(*a*) "The Friendly First."

As is the case for the over-all organization, the employees interpret "Friendly First" to be associated with the employee-customer relationship. The extent to which this is felt seems greater in this department. Thus 80 per cent of the employees suggest that "Friendly First" is related to the customer-employee contacts. This increase is understandably accountable, if we recall that—

The customer contacts are especially emphasized in the department.

The abnormally frequent authority interaction rate is related to the employee-officer contacts. Thus these would not tend to be friendly.

Finally, as might be expected, such abilities as "tactfulness," "diplomacy," "patience," are most often mentioned by the employees as the abilities that are required to perform the activities in their department.

(b) The "right type."

The organization's meaning of the identification symbol—the "right type"—definitely exists in the department's identification process. It is interesting to note that some officers (younger ones) are suggesting that the "right type" be changed to mean a more aggressive, go-getting individual. An individual, for example, who will be more active in obtaining new business for the organization. This, they suggest is in line with the organization's desire that this department must expand. However, all report that they are meeting stiff opposition on every side, especially from some of the top officers in the organization.[8]

F. Communication Process

1. *Not all have communication tasks.*

As far as the distribution of communication tasks is concerned, the department is not similar to the total organization. Only half of the employees report formal communication tasks. The other half, who do not, are the clerks and technicians who are continuously at work at their desks doing some sort of "paper work" or "research work." However, this half do report informal communication tasks.

2. *The communications are overtly friendly.*

3. *Covertly, the communications among the employees, and, to a much lesser extent, between the employees and the customers, are not too friendly.*

4. *Communications with officers are officer-centered.*

G. Departmental Evaluation Attitudes and Activities Related to the Steady State of the Departmental Organizational Processes.

To date we have examined the organizational processes individually and those attitudes and activities which are directly related to each of them. We now turn to a discussion of some departmental phenomena which are, as far as we are able to understand, resultants of (1) the steady state of all the departmental processes, and (2) the adaptation problems

---

[8] This is added indirect evidence that the "right type" is as we have described it.

this over-all departmental steady state has with the organizational steady state.

1. *Employee attitudes and feelings about their roles.*

The role of any given individual is the combined complexity of formal tasks, and personal acts, as perceived, interrelated, and organized by that individual.

Clearly, the sentiments that all the people in the department have about their roles will affect the fusion process of each individual in the department. Therefore, it is useful to discuss these attitudes at some length.

(*a*) Perceived Degree of Variety. The employees in the department, as a group, perceive their role to contain more variety than do the other employees in the organization. In classifying the answers in regard to this question, we utilize the following scale.

(1) "My work is routine and monotonous."

(2) "My work is routine, but there is variety in the way I handle the routine." Or to put it another way, "the activities I do are routine but there is variety in the sequence in which I handle the activities."

(3) "My work has variety with a little routine."

(4) "My work is all variety. I never do two things that are alike."

Utilizing this scale the perceived departmental variety is:

Perceived Degree of Variety	Per Cent
1	15%
2	15
3	30
4	30
	100%

(*b*) Perceived Degree of Making Choices. Another dimension that is related to the role is the degree of choice a person believes he has in his working activities. Is there any leeway? Is the work rigidly defined? In classifying the answers to this question, the following categories are used.

(1) I have no alternatives.

(2) I have some alternatives once in a while (i.e., no more than two-three a day or less than what I think is desirable for me.)

(3) I have quite a few alternatives (i.e., more than three, but something less than what the person considers "all that he likes").

(4) I have many alternatives (i.e., all that I want or more than what I want).

Utilizing this scale the departmental results are:

Perceived Degree of Possible Choice	Per Cent
1	10%
2	30
3	45
4	15
	100%

Thus the degree of leeway offered the individual is not considered as high as the degree of variety in the work. This is understandable if we recall that bank tasks are defined by rather rigid rules which do not permit too much leeway in choice. The only digression permitted, and that within limits, is related to *when* (i.e., in what order) the various tasks are done.

(*c*) The Degree of Initiating and Receiving of Action. Another important characteristic of one's work activities is the degree to which one is permitted to initiate action for others. In discussing the concept of initiation of action, it is useful to distinguish two types of initiation of action.

(1) Type "X" (or the "what" type) initiation of action. There is that initiation of action which simply acts as a cue for the recipient of the initiation to perform some task or a set of tasks. For example, A may say to B, "You'd better check Mrs. Smith's account. It is overdue." B then performs the required activities without A having to tell him exactly what to do. We call this type "X."

(2) Type "Y" (or the "how" type) initiation of action. In type "Y" the initiator not only initiates action but he actually defines exactly how the recipient is to perform the action requested. For instance, in the example mentioned above, the initiation of action would be type "Y" if A said to B—"You'd better see about Mrs. Smith's account. It is way overdue. I want you first to do such and such then I want you to do the following, etc." In this example, A defines the exact steps for B.

Before we continue, we want to explain why these data are discussed here. Some students, for example, would place these under the authority process. We do not. An analysis of the interview indicates two interesting results. First, any person who initiates action as a result of formal tasks in his function, theoretically has the power to utilize either "X" or "Y". Second, the data indicate that because of the behavioral content and the existing codes of the organizational processes, it is considered incorrect to utilize type "Y" in this organization. Thus employees who use type "Y" are deviates and as such are disliked. Employees who receive type "Y" feel justified in complaining. Because the evaluation of X and Y type of initiation of action is based on and is a resultant of the several processes of organization, we feel justified in discussing these phenomena at this time.

The reason for the dislike of type "Y" seems to arise from the fact that a type Y initiation of action tends to compound the sense of dependency and submissiveness of the recipient on the initiator. Furthermore, especially as a result of the behavioral activities and codes in the organization's "weak" authority, reward and penalty, and perpetuation processes, the employees interpret type Y to mean that the initiator does not have much faith in them. Thus a type Y initiator of action is described as one who "breathes down your neck" or "one who stands over you all the time."

As one would expect, type Y initiation of action is almost nonexistent in the organization as a whole. New employees being trained are, of course, an exception to the rule. But, the reader may recall that in this department the authority process is used more often than in any other department. Thus, we can hypothesize that if the officers limit their directing to type X, the perceived pressure on the employee's part should be minimal.

Forty-five per cent of the officers report utilizing type X initiation of action while 40 per cent utilize type Y. Of the type Y, 25 per cent are "very frequent" and 60 per cent are "moderate." The remainder report no initiations of actions with employees. Thus, the initiation of action of both types is relatively higher than the rest of the organization.

It is also interesting to note that all the employees who contact customers utilize both type X or Y on these relationships. They report that the customers do likewise. Thus, in the customer-employee relationship, both sides have the power to utilize type X and Y, while in the officer-employee relationships only the former has the power to utilize type Y.

As a result of this, an interesting problem arises for some of the older employees who are experts. They are frequently placed in the position of having to initiate action of the Y type for the officers. For example, as experts they must advise the officers. All the old-timers report this to be a very ticklish situation, since in doing so, they reverse the expected initiation of action pattern. The "expert" employees are cautious lest they be perceived by the officers as "getting too big for their boots," or "getting too bossy," or "as trying to 'show up' the boss' weaknesses."

(*d*) Activities the Employees Like Best. Seventy per cent of the employees say that the activities they like best in their role are those that are related to one or more formal tasks assigned by the organization.

Twenty per cent more state that they like formal and informal activities in their role equally well. They also state that they cannot clearly differentiate the formal from the informal. Only 10 per cent report that they like nothing about their activities.

(*e*) Activities the Employees Like the Least. The "like the least" picture is as positive (from the department's point of view) as are the above data. Thus 25 per cent say that they dislike nothing. Forty-five per cent state that the only thing they like least about their work are "unexpected minor details that crop up once in a while." Twenty per cent state they dislike filing. Ten per cent say that they dislike everything about their role activities.

2. *Perceived respect of work activities.*

Another variable which is a resultant of the steady state of all the organizational processes is the employees' perceived degree of respect that the employees' work activities have within the department and in the organization as a whole.

The results for the department are as follows: Fifty-five per cent believe that other people in the department aspire to and would like to have their job. Forty-five per cent think that no one in the department would like their job.

The perceived picture of respect from the other departments in the organization is brighter. Eighty per cent of the employees believe that people in other departments aspire for work in their department. Fifteen per cent believe not, while 5 per cent are not certain.

Thus the perceived organizational respect for their work activities is high. These data lend weight to the already mentioned notion (see workflow process) that this department's activities are high on the organization's status ladder.

The previously mentioned fact that this department has little contact with other departments partially accounts for the differences between "perceived internal status" and "perceived external status." The people outside probably rank the department according to the organization rules of status (i.e., high status goes to a department with confidential, personal contact with customers). On the other hand, many of the employees within the department rarely experience personal, confidential contacts with customers. They rate their activities according to their experience which tends to be related to officer contacts that are full of hidden conflict and tension.

3. *State of interpersonal relationships in the department.*

(*a*) Employee-Employee Relationships. Forty-five per cent are definitely confident that they "get along well" with others and forty per cent are "almost sure" they get along with others. Only 15 per cent report any negative human relationships. This presents a "rosy" picture and does not jibe with the previously discussed results.

The apparent contradiction is resolved if we also note that 90 per cent of the employees state that they have no close friends in the department in which they work. These data lend support to the previously mentioned phenomena, that human inter-relationships seem happy on the overt level, but they are seething with tension underneath.

(*b*) Officer-Employee Relationships. We have already pointed out that the officer-employee relationships are fraught with covert tension.[9] Let us fill these statistics with human feelings content by presenting some direct quotes.

"I wish they could come out and tell you something. Some officers, when they have some criticism tell others to tell us. Why don't they tell

---

[9] See statistics in discussion of authority processes.

us directly? By the time it gets to us it is distorted and a lot of people think—well I just don't know what they think."

"Another thing, we don't like it when an officer says one thing and then they do another. I know one girl was offered a new job. She didn't like it because of the added work and no increase in pay. She told the officer she'd take it if pay was increased or if the job changed. The officer replied that he doubted if either could be done. So the girl turned the job down. A few weeks later another girl took the job and it *was* changed."

"Why can't we have morning coffee. I can see why the girls in the front office can't—they have to be ready to meet the customers—why can't we have it?"

"Some officers have a lot to do, some have little. It used to be that some girls worked all the time, some didn't. So we changed it. All the extra work is supposed to go to one girl and she gives it to the girls that are not busy. It sounded good. I don't know why, but the officers still take it to their favorite girl."

"Then I wish they could see our point of view. For example, there is a letter with one small error that can be erased. Why should it be re-done?"

"I guess I must sound pretty awful. Let me say something nice. I think the officers are nice. They're polite—they're nice—but it's skin deep. There is a gap between us and the officers. You certainly can't talk to them as if they were a friend."

"The employees don't think too much of them. They resent their attitude. You know, they go around ordering us around. Okay, so we do have to work for a living. But do they have to rub that in?"

"One of the things the girls resent is that they treat customers much better than the employees. Course, the employees are part to blame. They don't really show any interest in their work."

"Then again some of them, especially the junior officers, don't even know how to do the job they're supposed to do. To make matters worse, each one wants his own way. Sometimes they want to do things that are against what the head man wants. It's difficult to keep peace—believe you me!"

"Most of the people think the officers are small. They're so petty. They pick on such small things. They don't insist on the larger things, for example. Their attitude toward us isn't good. I don't hear anything done about that. They forget we're human. Sometimes you feel like banging their heads on the wall."

"And another thing. They never seem to be willing to take the blame. They always blame the underdog. If they were really men, they'd take it."

"We have departmental meetings. Most of the time it's a lecture. The head of the department makes some announcements and then he asked Mr. ——— if he has anything to add."

"No, no one asks our opinion. And if they did, it wouldn't do much good. Most of the people don't say too much anyway. There might be a few brave ones. Not many. Most don't want to make themselves look bad."

"The employees feel they're stuffy. They're not considerate of the help's point of view."

"They're nice to talk to all right. But—I don't know how to say it except that there is a lack of understanding of the employees' points of view."

"They don't realize the pressure we work under. They leave things until the end and then give orders which shows they don't realize how complicated things are."

"We wish they'd tell us something directly when it's wrong. You know something is wrong. You can sense it. But they don't tell you. That—well—that's a deep hurt."

"No, they don't want us to talk. They think if we do, we don't have enough to do. If you spend a minute talking they come up to you and say, 'nothing to do'—and oh, does that burn us up."

"Then there is the pool of girls. In principle it's all right. But the officers don't follow it. Each one thinks I'm his personal secretary. That places us in an awful position since we can't tell him how we feel."

"The people don't respect them. Somehow they don't feel they're qualified men. They're nice as individuals—but they're not qualified. They don't know the work they are doing. Sometimes they're rude. They can—they can—well—they can needle you in a nice sort of way."

14. PRODUCTION PLANNING AND ORGANIZATIONAL MORALE*

Kamla Chowdhry and A. K. Pal°

THIS is a study of the interaction of production planning and management practices, and the effect of these on the morale of the supervisory staff of two Indian cotton textile mills. The two mills are located in a large city, where the main industry is textiles. Both mills are operating in a common social and economic climate, subject to the same type of market fluctuations and to a similar pattern of labor-management relations. In both mills, like the rest of the industry, the top executive control is with the managing agent who acquires the right of control through the Managing Agency Agreement.[1]

The markets to which the goods of these mills go are similar. There are frequent fluctuations in the market due to cotton prices, changes in government policy, consumer demand, etc. A significant difference between the two mills is the policy of the management in meeting these fluctuations in the market. In Mill A the manufacturing program is frequently altered to manufacture types of cloth that the market demands at the moment and that would yield the highest profits at that time. This is the prevalent pattern in the industry. In Mill B, the manufacturing program is relatively stable. There have been no changes for years in the counts spun, and even in the cloth manufactured not many significant changes have been introduced. The mill has emphasized and established a reputation for quality, and their manufactured goods have a steady market demand. Probably only half a dozen of the 65 mills in the city follow this practice.

The object of this study is to examine the implications of the above basic differences in the policy of management on the functioning of the organization. More specifically, we sought (1) to determine in what way this policy is reflected in the organizational structure and in the manage-

---

* Reprinted from *Human Organization,* Vol. XV, No. 4.

° The authors are grateful to Professor Charles A. Myers, Director of Industrial Relations Section, M.I.T., for help in planning the study and discussing the results at various stages. The research was financed in part by funds made available by the Inter-University Study of Labor Problems in Economic Development.

[1] The Managing Agency Agreement allows the transfer of Managing Agency rights to the sons and other members of the joint family. The Managing Agents are generally not salaried people but by contract in the Managing Agency Agreement receive a commission which may be a percentage of profits or gross sales. The Managing Agent and his family are generally the major shareholders in the company.

ment practices prevailing in the two mills, and (2) to examine the effect of the prevailing organizational structure and management practices on the satisfaction of members and the efficiency of each organization.

I. RESEARCH PROCEDURE

Both mills are composite units, with spinning, weaving, dyeing, bleaching and finishing operations. This study was restricted to the spinning and weaving sections only, which comprise the major part of the textile mills. The organization and functioning of these two departments were studied with the help of top management and supervisory staffs. The research staff visited the mills almost daily over a period of three months and observed the activities going on, the interactions and relationships of people, and conducted interviews on certain aspects of organization and management practices. Fixed question–free answer interviews were held with the managing agents, production managers, and twenty-four departmental heads, assistants and supervisors. Mill A and Mill B are compared in terms of formal organizational structure, delegation of responsibility and authority, communication and consultation practices, and the satisfaction and stability of members working in the organization.

II. ORGANIZATIONAL STRUCTURE

The formal organizational structures of Mill A and Mill B are given in Figure 1. The hierarchical levels and their designation in industry are as follows: managing agent, production manager, departmental head, assistant, supervisor, jobber and worker.

Mill A

In Mill A the top executive is the managing agent, and he is in overall charge of the production and the sales of the organization. The next level in the formal structure consists of the production manager, who is the technical adviser to the agent. The third level in the organization is composed of departmental heads, who, however, report directly to the agent. The agent also has direct contact with the departmental heads, but he sometimes passes instructions through the production manager. The departmental heads discuss their problems and difficulties with the production manager, but in a more informal way in the hope that he will be able to present their case to the agent more effectively.

The departmental head reports to the agent once or twice daily in the latter's office. The agent tells them of the changes he wishes to introduce in the manufacturing program, and they in turn inform the agent about efficiency, balance of production, shortage of material and spare parts, labor difficulties, etc.

No clear procedure is followed by the assistant and supervisors about reporting. They report to the departmental head, but they are also asked to report directly sometimes to the production manager or to the agent. The supervisors report to the assistant or departmental head depending on whoever is available, or with whom they have better relations.

It is also clear from Figure 1 that there are more senior personnel

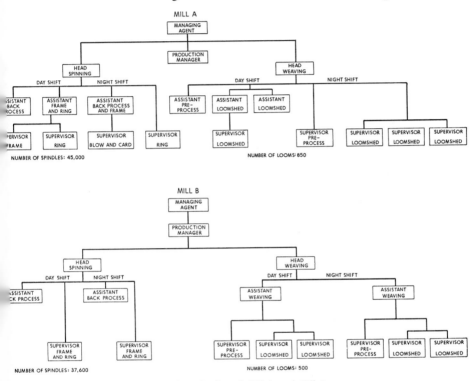

FIG. 1. Organization of Mill A and Mill B

working on the day shift than on the night shift and that the night shift is mainly in charge of junior personnel. Thus, there are two assistants on the day shift in the Spinning Department against one on the night shift. Similarly, in the Weaving Department there are three assistants on the day shift but none on the night shift. This makes the organizational structure very unbalanced in the two shifts. The weaving master says, concerning the senior personnel in the day shift:

It is rather unfortunate that all my assistants are placed on the day shift. It is absolutely necessary to have at least one assistant (of loomshed) on the night shift. I am trying to persuade the agent to transfer X or Y to the night shift.

On the other hand, the spinning master desires to place senior staff on the day shift:

I prefer to keep the assistants on the day shift—otherwise I would not be able to cope with the work. We do all the settings on the day shift. The night shift people only run the machines.

Another feature of the organization of Mill A is that supervisors, and sometimes assistants, are transferred from one shift to another, without a corresponding change in the personnel of the rest of the department. According to factory rules, jobbers and workers change systematically every month from day to night shift. But the assistants and supervisors who are not covered by the factory regulations do not change their shift regularly; they move, but on an *ad hoc* basis, depending on other considerations. This results in the continuity of work relationships being frequently disrupted, in a certain amount of confusion as to who is to report to whom, and in problems of relationships that arise when there is no clear and stable structure of reporting and getting work done.

One loomshed supervisor says:

I don't like this system. I mean no system. I don't know who is my boss, so I have developed a system of working independently.

Another supervisor says:

I like to be with the same group of workers all the time. I like to change shifts with them. You have got to know your workers to get along well with them. But here you don't know where you will be tomorrow.

Mill B

In Mill B, also, the managing agent is the top executive who has overall charge of production and sales of the organization. The next level is the production manager. He is the technical adviser to the agent and also coordinates the manufacturing program of the different departments. The departmental heads mainly report to the production manager. There are no changes in the manufacture of counts in spinning, but if changes in the sorts woven are to be introduced, the sales manager sends direct information to the weaving master or the assistant concerned.

The departmental heads report to the production manager during the latter's round in the department. The departmental heads do not have a daily direct contact with the agent in his office concerning current production problems, as was the case in Mill A. The assistants report to the departmental heads and are not generally called directly by the production manager or the agent for information. The supervisors generally report to the assistants, but sometimes to the departmental head directly.

In Mill B the organizational structures of both day and night shifts are similar. There is the same number of staff in both the shifts and there is an equal distribution of senior staff on the day and night shifts, so that the night shift is not delegated to junior staff as in Mill A. Also, there is a systematic regular change of shift for the assistants and supervisors, with the changeover of shifts for workers and jobbers. The same assistants and supervisors work with the same group of jobbers and workers so that there is stability of relationships from the assistant to the worker level. Work relationships in terms of reporting, making inquiries, etc. with the persons concerned are clear and the channels well established.

As mentioned earlier, there are frequent changes in the manufacturing program of Mill A which necessitate frequent technical changes in the department. Most of these technical changes are made on the day shift resulting in more senior staff on the day shift. Mill B which has a more stable manufacturing program does not have to concentrate its senior staff in the day shift and can consequently afford to distribute its senior staff in the two shifts and have a more balanced structure in each shift.

III. MANAGEMENT PRACTICES

The problems of introducing manufacturing changes do not only affect the formal organizational structure of the mill, but they also influence management practices of delegation of authority, of communication and of consultation.

Mill A

Thus, in Mill A, the managing agent has to give frequent directives for change of counts and sorts. Targets have to be fulfilled and deadlines of delivery dates have to be met since the manufacturing is geared to fluctuating demand in the market. Working under these pressures the agent is constantly checking up on efficiency, production and quality of product. All this tends to result in centralized decision-making and in close and detailed supervision of the departments.

In order that top management can supervise each stage closely, there is a tendency to short-circuit in giving instructions, or in making inquiries about production, quality, adequate flow of material, etc. The agent or the production manager gets directly in touch with the assistants and supervisors for either giving instructions or receiving information.

The resultant pressures on middle and lower management can be seen from some of their remarks quoted below:

Spinning master:

I am leaving the mill soon. I am satisfied with the salary, but I cannot stand the agent's production policy of many changes. These changes are too much to cope with.

Spinning supervisor:

The agent and the production manager call me almost every day to inquire about production and balance of production . . . the constant change of program is responsible for low efficiency. . . . The agent should listen to the technicians and draw up a plan of production according to the existing machines and not according to the whims of the market.

Spinning supervisor:

The thing that worries me most is the agent's policy of constant change of materials. Most of my time and energy is spent trying to keep balance of production. . . . The agent often sends for me to inquire about production targets, shortages and flow of materials. . . .

Almost every member in the Spinning Department expresses his dissatisfaction concerning the frequent changes of manufacturing program and the resultant problems—efficiency, balance of production, and feelings of anxiety and tension. Top management has direct contact with almost every member in the department in order to supervise and inquire about production. The members in the Weaving Department feel the same way about the changes and the frequency of changes introduced in the sorts manufactured as the members in the Spinning Department.

For example, the weaving master says:

The agent's policy is very short-sighted, since his guiding factor is always immediate profit. This policy is reflected in the constant change of sorts. At present all the sorts which were running a month ago have completely disappeared. Such a quick changeover is not economical and it puts the staff into great difficulty. It is almost impossible to retain a high level of production under such conditions and then the blame is put on the technical staff!

The assistants and supervisors especially connected with the loomshed mention the agent's concern about production and quality of production and how they are frequently called into his office to explain the high damages.

Loomshed supervisor:

The agent wants both high efficiency and good quality. I have been called several times to explain high damage. . . . For example, recently a new and a heavy sort was introduced and there was high damage and low efficiency. The agent was very upset and annoyed with everybody, from the weaving master to the workers. I was called to explain the bad working and was fired . . . but no discharge notice was served. It is going too far if the supervisors are held responsible when a bad sort is introduced and there is so much damage.

When new "sorts" (types of cloth) are introduced which the technical staff believes will not yield good efficiency or good quality, then top management feels the need for close supervision to see the working performance of the new sort, and to induce the technical staff to fulfill the targets for production and quality. This type of situation makes it necessary for the agent to maintain close and detailed supervision of the departments. The assistants and supervisors all have to report to him directly, especially when a difficult sort is being run.

The assistant weaving master:

I meet the agent and the production manager. They ask me about the working of the department and I prepare a special report for the agent which I submit every Monday. . . . I am always pressed for better and higher production.

The senior loomshed supervisor:

The agent controls the department himself. I am given instructions by him about new sorts, change in loom speeds, discipline in the loomshed, etc.

Loomshed supervisor:

My duty is to follow the instructions of the agent. . . . He has called me several times to explain about high damages. . . .

These quotations illustrate reactions to centralized decision-making, by-passing in communication, and dissatisfaction and frustration among the staff. The end is a climate of resentment against management and management goals.

An example which indicates the extent to which some members of the management staff in Mill A have lost their sense of identification with management and management goals is given below. It refers to a situation where the agent tried to consult the staff about the advisability of buying a new machine. One of the staff members said:

After the talk by the representative of the company manufacturing machine X was over, the agent asked, "Do you or do you not advise me to buy this machine?" All the members said, "We agree that you should buy the machine." . . . It is his money, let him spend it the way he likes.

Mill B

Let us see the picture in Mill B where the manufacturing program is relatively stable. Some interview comments illustrate the difference.

Spinning master:

The management of this mill is very good and the general atmosphere of working is pleasant. There is no interference from the top in the working of my department. . . . I report to the agent and to the production manager. . . . During the entire period of my work here so far, nobody has asked for the efficiency of the department, but always about quality. . . . I would like to give quality material, so that consumers can say that Mill B has the best spinning.

Weaving master:

The agent and the production manager consult me on technical matters. . . . I am in charge of the department, and the management does not interfere in my work. (All departmental problems concerning damages, spare parts, etc., are solved within the department. No supervisor or assistant mentions that he is called by the office to explain about efficiency, balance of production or high damage rate. Almost everybody mentions that this is a good mill to work in, the management is good, and that there is no pressure about production or efficiency. The impression is that the working of the departments is smooth and there is a high degree of satisfaction of members with management and management practices.)

The change of sorts in Mill B has been commented on by two persons:

Production manager:

The sales manager makes his demands and the production departments have to give way to his requirements. The difficulties of the production departments are not considered. . . .

Weaving master:

If rationalization is to be introduced the mill will have to standardize the type of cloth to be manufactured. Markets should be stabilized by the mills. There is no sense in manufacturing 30 and 32 yards and 40 and 42 in the same sorts. The unnecessary changeover in the department for such differences increases the cost of production.

Even in Mill B there are some protests about the change of sorts demanded by the sales manager, but there is not that feeling of pressure, strain and anxiety in the departments as found in Mill A.

There is also considerable identification with management's goals and a sense of pride in most members about this mill. The satisfaction of members is reflected in their long service in the same mill. Most members have worked in Mill B for from 10 to 25 years, whereas in Mill A, there has been considerable turnover in the senior staff. Within one year, since the completion of the field study, 8 out of 17 of the management staff have left in Mill A.

IV. CONCLUSIONS

In terms of the research questions raised earlier, it is clear that the manufacturing policies of management in Mill A and Mill B influence the organizational structure and the management practices of each case. Thus, in Mill A the picture is one of frequent changes in the manufacturing program, frequent technical and personnel changes in departments, centralized control and decision making, "by-passing" in communication, dissatisfaction of members, resentment against management, especially among the senior staff, and a sense of insecurity and instability among members. In Mill B, the picture is one of a relatively stable manufacturing program, smoothly functioning departments, stable work groups, relative decentralization in control and decision-making, stable communication channels similar to the formal structure, satisfaction with management, and a sense of security and stability in the organization.

There are two further implications of the study that we should like specifically to emphasize:

1. There is an interrelation of management policies and management practices, an interrelation that perhaps stems from an inherent interdependence of these factors. Perhaps the clusters of factors found in Mill A and Mill B are a result of a basic approach, an attitude, a point of view, a frame of mind, and this is reflected in the totality of behavior, whether in policies or practices that a particular management follows. In other words, management involves a certain philosophy, and not merely certain techniques of management.

2. An organizational structure which is based only on the technical needs of the situation can defeat the very purposes of the organization. To function efficiently, management must take into account the social as well as the technical demands of the situation. The organization of Mill A has developed around the technical needs demanded of a manufacturing program of frequent changes. The senior staff has been kept on the day shift to make the necessary technical adjustments. The working of the night shift has consequently been delegated to junior supervisors. In such a system efficiency and quality are affected. There are complaints about the lack of sufficient backstuff and of poor quality, somebody gets blamed in the process, relationships become strained, and there is a constant reshuffling of staff, transferring of personnel from one shift to another to maintain an equilibrium for collaboration and efficient working. These *ad hoc* transfers of supervisors from one shift to another also result in a sense of instability and insecurity. The management does not seem to be aware of this consequence of its production policy. Unless management becomes aware of these reactions to its policy and undertakes to compensate for the continual upheaval, the possible advantages resulting from its policy cannot be realized.

In contrast, the organization of Mill B has also developed around its technical needs, but the technical needs in this case are related to a stable manufacturing program. There are not many technical changes that have to be introduced, the senior staff is equally distributed, and it is consequently possible for management to have a systematic transfer of shifts. All this has resulted in a system promoting stable relationships and close human association at work.

Similar conclusions have been emphasized in a study of 12 industrial organizations sponsored by UNESCO.[2] It mentioned that one of the features peculiar to efficient institutions was found to be:

. . . intimate human association at work. Physical conditions are so arranged that small numbers of people work closely together and can easily communicate with each other. . . . Without the security that comes from the feeling of belonging to a group, the individual is liable to become unadaptable, resentful and socially ill.

[2] Jerome F. Scott and R. P. Lynton, *The Community Factor in Modern Technology*, UNESCO (Paris, 1952), p. 169.

Therefore, in planning an organization's structure, not only have the technical demands to be taken into account, but the social system that underlies a particular technology and work process must also be considered. In an organization where frequent changes in production schedules are contemplated, it is all the more necessary for the organizational structure and the operating practices of management to be such that they can fluctuate with the strains and stresses inherent in a situation of constant changes. A greater degree of attention and emphasis must be paid to problems of organization and organizational practices in such cases. However, it is possible for management to provide a flexible structure and to follow policies which lessen rather than increase the strains and tensions inherent in an organization where constant change is part of the routine.

15. HUMAN RELATIONS AT THE MANAGEMENT LEVEL IN A BUREAUCRATIC SYSTEM OF ORGANIZATION*

Michel Crozier[0]

Comprehensive studies of human relations problems at the management level are usually hampered by two sets of difficulties: first, the complexity of the role structure in modern organizations accounts for a lot of ambiguity and overlapping, making it impossible to match really comparable cases and to use rigorous methods in a meaningful way; second, the general emphasis on status and promotions gives crucial importance to the human relations game and prevents the researcher, therefore, from obtaining reliable data on the central problem of power relationships.

The research we are going to report on provides an interesting situation on both accounts because of, on one side, the very unusual simplicity of the organizational setup and the clear-cut definition of the roles we studied, and, on the other, the general deemphasis on promotions and the concomitant lack of power cliques cutting across functional and hierarchical lines.

Such a blueprint may have its disadvantages, but it gives the social scientist a very good vantage point from which to try to understand the basic organizational givens which characterize human relations at the management level. It is, however, a sort of limit case, and care should be taken to understand it in the proper way; that is, not as a starting point for easy generalizations, but as a more simple example where the relevant variables can be observed in a clearer form.

The field studied is a large-scale multiplant industrial organization operated by the French State under civil service regulations. The study of human relations at the management level was part of a larger research project whose aim was to understand the general functioning of a bureaucratic organization and the impact of bureaucratic rules on the attitudes and behavior of people at the shop and at the management levels. Data on the managers' attitudes and behavior were obtained through two successive processes: first, considerable direct and indirect information was

* Reprinted from *Human Organization*, Vol. 20, No. 2, Summer 1961, pp. 51–64.

[0] Michel Crozier is presently at the Centre De Sociologie Européenne, Paris, France.

The author wishes to express his gratitude to Miss Colette Eichisky who was a most efficient assistant during the research and, for analyzing results, to Miss Miriam Gallagher who gave her warm and skillful help in editing this article in English; also to his colleagues at the Center whose valuable comments enriched a previously too narrow experience.

gathered during an intensive study of three plants where the personnel was systematically interviewed according to elaborate fixed schedules, and where the results of the survey were fed back to the managers as well as to the supervisors and to the representatives of the workers; second, in twenty out of the thirty plants of the organization, the members of the management teams were interviewed also with fixed schedules but with more open questions.

All plants of the organization are run with exactly the same rules and the same very clear hierarchical roles. They are relatively small-size industrial plants dispersed throughout France, and employing from 350 to 500 workers in machine-operating, common labor and service jobs with a rather simple and stable technology. The buildings are usually quite old but production machines are modern; general equipment, however, such as conveyors, raw material processing systems, air conditioning, and sanitary devices are very often lagging behind. For the managers, problems in the organization of the plant concern the preparation and processing of the raw material, for which new types of equipment are looked for; transportation and the flow of work, which must be better standardized and mechanized; the rationalization of maintenance; and the best utilization of machines and equipment in view of the maintenance difficulties. By far the greatest organization worry of the managers, however, is the allocation of jobs and the shifting of workers whenever any kind of change takes place, since no transfer of any worker in any circumstance can contravene the strict seniority provisions of a general national code won over fifty years ago by the unions.

Production workers, two-thirds women, have complete tenure, but no possibilities of promotion. They get fair wages and are protected by a very elaborate seniority code. They showed in the interviews a rather happy pattern of adjustment to the bureaucratic system, but a very demanding kind of relationship with the managers and a strong set of values in opposition to management goals.

Lower supervisors, no more than a dozen in each plant, are recruited by competitive examination. The older ones are usually ex-noncommissioned officers. The younger ones are better educated and more productivity oriented. Their wages are rather poor and their status is low. They are stripped of all direct authority and reduced in fact to a timekeeper and accounting job. They have, in consequence, a very poor morale and seem to adjust reasonably well only if they resign themselves to accepting the workers' values.

There is in the shops still another group, the maintenance workers: in the whole plant, forty to fifty highly skilled people of various trades recruited through difficult competitive occupational tests. They are well paid, at least when they have enough seniority, and very often get more than the supervisors. The younger ones, however, get significantly less than they would get in high-paying wage areas in private industry. Most of the maintenance workers are mechanics, each one of whom is in charge of all maintenance and repair of the three machines he is personally responsible for. They have generally a very happy but also very aggressive kind of adjustment corresponding to their favorable but illegitimate power situation in the shop. Responsible for coping with the only event which breaks a detailed world of rules—machine breakdown—they are the real authority at the shop level but arouse bitter antagonism among the supervisors and a lot of frustration and some rebellion among the workers.

Finally, over the helpless supervisors and the aggressive and hostile maintenance men, there is the authority of the members of the management team. This centralization of authority focuses the attention of the workers on management, but does not help the managers in getting their will done at the shop level. Managers, as a matter of fact, do not have much organization leeway. They can resist workers' demands, but do not have much possibility of initiating action.

More will be said about the human problems within the shop when we discuss the situation and responsibilities of the members of the management team. But, before we proceed, it seems necessary to provide somewhat more detailed background about the management group.

THE CAREER PATTERNS OF THE FOUR MEMBERS OF THE MANAGEMENT TEAM

The management team consists of four members, one director in charge of general coordination, planning and sales,[1] one assistant director responsible for production, one technical engineer responsible for both machine and building maintenance, and one comptroller in charge of supplies, accounting, and personnel administration. The director and the assistant director are part of the same promotional ladder; they are both necessarily graduates of the École Polytechnique, the top theoretical engineering school in France, since by statute the organization can recruit its members of the "engineer corps" (their formal title) only among *polytechniciens*. The future director enters the organization at age 22 to 24; after two years of training at its private "application school" he will be appointed assistant director in one of the plants and, after twelve to fifteen years as assistant director, he will automatically be promoted to a directorship. Then he may later become a General Inspector[2] at the central office and may even

---

[1] Sales is not a very important function since the organization does not deal with private dealers directly but with another public agency; sales problems involve only the planning of deliveries, stockage, and warehouse organization.

[2] The General Inspector's job, however, is not much sought after since it is not very rewarding financially.

be appointed Director-General. The comptroller must have a degree from a law school or a business school. He begins his career as a clerk and after many years will end it as a comptroller if he can get two promotions, which usually are given according to seniority. The technical engineer, finally, is a graduate of one of the minor engineering schools which do not have much prestige; he is appointed technical engineer after having passed a competitive examination and spent some months in training. Like his colleagues, the director, the assistant director, and the comptroller, he is a civil servant with complete tenure, but unlike them his career does not allow for any possibility of promotion; he will quit the organization and get his retirement pension without having had the chance to qualify for another job.

The director is a man of at least forty, usually in his late forties or early fifties, who has spent a good many years in the organization. His promotion has been entirely due to seniority, and the process of his selection may be seen, as a matter of fact, as working against the interests of the organization since at least half of the assistant directors in the past have quit before being promoted, and since the ones who stayed are likely to be those who were afraid they could not succeed elsewhere. On the other hand, the intellectual abilities and the early training of the director make him fit, or make him think he is fit, for a much more important job. This is a man, therefore, who tends to feel superior to his functions but has usually renounced looking for another job. He is not well paid by ordinary business standards, but he gets some tangible fringe benefits—among others, the free use of a large house and of a car and a chauffeur. To these material perquisites, one should add the amount of independence he enjoys and the prestige his way of life still carries: he can use his own time very much as he sees fit; some of the directors pursue their own scientific or scholarly research; some have got permission to assume other administrative duties besides their own, usually as experts; some teach part time in higher institutions. In the past, at least some of the members of the "engineers' corps" have made minor but distinguished contributions in the field of arts and sciences, and generally the freedom of action and the gentlemanly status such a job brings its occupant remind one of the liberal professions in the late nineteenth century.

By contrast, in the plant the role of the director is small. Production goals are narrowly fixed by the central office. Processes are stable and change is extremely difficult. The director does not have the right either to hire or to fire; he does not have even the right to assign workers on jobs. The only people who are really dependent on him are the very weak supervisors' group, and his only chance of making his influence actually felt is to administer the rules in such a way as to diminish the constant squabbling their application brings, and, in that way, to inspire people with more positive attitudes toward production. The great majority of the directors interviewed considered, anyway, that production was mere routine and not interesting at all. Since sales is not a challenge either, the only problem which remains is new construction, remodeling of plant facilities, and general equipment and general planning of future development. Three-quarters of the directors interviewed gave priority to this aspect of their activity; no wonder that some of their critics accuse directors of "building mania"!

The assistant director is a younger man from twenty-five to forty who generally has had to choose a State career because of lack of business connections or because of personal shyness. In the past, graduates of Polytechnique were eager to seek employment in State organizations. Now they tend to choose State careers only as a last recourse.[3]

As a young man fresh from school and with no experience, the assistant director is eager to learn the job of industrial organization. He feels, moreover, that being put immediately in charge of the whole production of a plant is a splendid opportunity to get the experience he seeks and to get it quickly and without risks; he usually will be shifted from plant to plant two or three times, if not more, during his years as assistant director, and this will give him some challenge and some new experience. However, once he feels he has learned everything that can be learned from such a situation, a stage which comes more quickly than he had expected, he will become more and more interested in finding another job. The rate of departure has always been high, but seems now to be increasing still more inasmuch as the spread of economic development provides more and more opportunities for highly trained engineers. The rate is now well over 60 percent.

The comptroller is usually a man considerably past fifty, who has been promoted to the top rank in his own profession after a long wait. He is not likely to have been working a long time in this particular plant, and is not expected to remain long. He has with him younger administrative colleagues of the same "corps," who are impatient for turnover and over whom he has a limited influence. Officially he has important responsibilities, as a financial officer he has to post bond, but his job, in practice, is quite routine; and, but for one or two exceptions, the comptroller does not strike one as having the opportunity to make his personality count.

The technical engineer is alone of his sort in the plant,[4] which means that he has no other man of the same "corps" to talk to—an isolation which

---

[3] Since Polytechnique is a military school, board and tuition are free; but the students have to reimburse the State for all the fees if they do not serve in the Army or in the Civil Service a minimum of ten years. Many private business firms will lend the man they hire the money necessary to repay the State, but this in itself may still raise problems.

[4] Except for the few places where a junior technical engineer is made the assistant to a senior one.

is more than trivial in such a small community. Maintenance of all general equipment, supervision of machines, maintenance and repair, discussion with outside contractors and supervision of their work, keep him constantly busy if not overworked; he feels his job is a challenging one but he knows he will always remain in a situation of subordination and this he resents. He may be younger or older, but there is a good chance that he will be much older than the assistant director and that he will have more seniority in the plant than all other members of the management team, since technical engineers are much less often shifted from one plant to another. His wages are fair but consistently lower than those of engineers with the same amount of responsibilities in private industry. He has no status compensation. Recruitment is therefore apparently becoming very difficult.

The relationship between these four men is governed by a number of detailed rules and statutes, but some ambiguity still remains. The director, of course, is clearly Number One man, but he is obliged to gather a "council" at least once a week and to listen to the advice of the other members of the team. This provision of an old statute is not really enforced now; a few directors make it a point never to hold council, while others hold them as matter of sound business practice rather than as compliance with the rule. There is, however, still a technicality involved in such an institution inasmuch as the technical engineers can participate only if they are especially appointed by the central office to be members of the council; all senior technical engineers are so appointed, but the younger ones are excluded.

The comptroller reports to the director, but, because of his financial accountability, he has to countersign the most important business transactions of the director and has, therefore, the apparent function of checking on him. Practically, there is no question as to his being a subordinate, and the checking is only perfunctory. The only consequence of this ambiguity is some uneasiness and frustration on the side of those comptrollers who think they are entitled to more authority. The assistant director has no direct relationship with the comptroller and there is no problem about determining who should be first. But there is some overlapping of functions and some difficulties in assessing the reciprocal situation of the assistant director and the technical engineer. Theoretically, the technical engineer reports to the assistant director, but this subordination, which is emphasized in the status difference, does not hold consistently in practice. The two men usually will argue on an equal and relatively free basis. Most assistant directors hold a supervisors' conference in their own office two or three times a week; when they can obtain the agreement of the technical engineers they will ask them to attend, but technical engineers, when they do come, tend to act as observers and to avoid appearing as committed participants, a role which would mark their subordination.

Respective age and respective seniority finally are important aspects of the equilibrium of the team. Usually one will find the following combination: the comptroller is the older man, rather aloof in his administrative department where he deals with his own kind of people, not too much involved in the problems of the plant, where he is rather new, and where he does not expect to stay very long. The director will be somewhat younger but already a seasoned civil servant who is likely to have more seniority in the plant than the comptroller but much less than the technical engineer; he is expected to stay for some time and has the final responsibility for what is going on, which means that he has a direct and important commitment to the organization and to its people. The technical engineer's age rank varies considerably, but, unless exceptional, he will have more seniority than any of the others, and, because of his kind of patchup job, will know more and be more competent about plant problems. The assistant director, by contrast, will appear new and inexperienced, and will not be likely to have a great commitment either to the people or to the organization.

Our brief description will already have made clear that such a situation presents some aspect of a sort of laboratory experiment for observing conflict within organizations. We deal with a very well delimited group in the experimental sense; there is no ambiguity about who belongs and who does not; its members are isolated, one might even say cut off, from the outside environment; they have no other persons to talk to among the rest of the staff, since there is an insurmountable gap between them and their subordinates.[5] They are also very far apart from people playing the same role of industrial manager in private organizations, as well as from people having comparable status in the civil service. Executives in private business view them as people with a kind of experience that is not relevant and cannot even be understood, and with whom, therefore, there is no common professional ground. Other civil servants of the same rank may have the same primary interest to defend against their common employer, the national state, and before the same suspicious general public, but the management group of the present study is made up of technicians with organizational responsibilities, a combination whose problems seem utterly peculiar.[6] One can safely assume, therefore, that if they are not in the laboratory vacuum, they are nevertheless much better insulated from outside influence than most people in contemporary natural professional situations. Finally, such a setup is duplicated thirty times, in identical terms, all over France.

---

[5] This is only partially true for the comptroller, whose three or four subordinates hope to be promoted one day to his rank and therefore behave on more equal terms with him. We shall see later that this has some consequences for the comptroller's kind of adjustment.

[6] Technicians in the civil service are professionals in a staff capacity; personal responsibilities are never given to them, and industrial organization has not developed as a recognized technique.

To summarize these background elements, we have four players, separated from the rest of the world and obliged to play together. They do not have the same interests at stake, however, since some expect to quit the game (the assistant director) or can have professional satisfaction outside of it (the director). Finally, their cards (that is, their power) are different.

If our four players had the same stakes and commitments, and no difference in roles, we could work out the prediction of coalitions according to their respective power;[7] however, the much greater interplay of factors must direct us in another way. What it suggests is a less rigorous and more exploratory course: starting the other way round, not with predictions to be tested but with the answers already given to be explained, and the explanations to be used for understanding what may be the relevant variables. This is made all the more easy, since we have a very strange pattern to start with: one major type of conflict keeps appearing consistently in almost all situations observed.

We will, therefore, start with a description of the existing conflicts, in this way analyze how the situation is structured, and from there on study the interplay of personalities with such structured situations, with a view to finally being able to discuss what is the real meaning of the conflict and what are the limits set by social control for its development.

THE EXISTING PATTERNS OF CONFLICT

Out of the twenty cases we were able to study, we found sixteen clear cases of conflict between the technical engineer, on one hand, and the assistant director and/or the director, on the other. Besides this dominant pattern of opposition, there were six or seven cases of assistant director versus director, and two or three of comptroller versus director, the conflicts of these latter types being not only less numerous but also more diffuse and less demanding than the former. The dice, we may assume, are well loaded for only one kind of outcome. Whatever the character of the people who happen to staff the different roles and whatever the peculiar types of combination which may occur in their distribution throughout the thirty different plants, clashes of personality will almost never occur outside of these quite narrow patterns.

Let us now take a closer look and analyze the most relevant characteristics of each pattern.

The Comptroller versus Director Conflict

We have already mentioned the kind of problems raised by the relationship between the director and the comptroller. Interviews showed

---

[7] See, for example, the studies made on coalitions in a triad.

us that comptrollers may be frustrated because of their lack of promotional opportunities and somewhat jealous of their *Polytechnique* colleagues. We occasionally get comments of this sort from a mild-mannered comptroller:

This is not necessary to have a training in advanced maths to be in charge of a factory. . . . I do not understand why a good, serious, and efficient comptroller could not be a successful director.

From a more aggressive and unpopular one:

There are far too many graduates from Polytechnique. They poke their nose into everything. They claim they are administrators with a mathematical training whereas their role should be primarily a technical one.

But it is usually only a casual remark or a way of speaking which marks the uneasiness. In this context they view their financial responsibility, which theoretically entitles them to check on the director, as a very important function. Since they will be held accountable for any commercial decision they must countersign, they may claim the right to discuss its appropriateness and aspire to utilize their signature as a sort of veto power. But withholding their signature would be considered an abuse of position by the central office. Their duty is to check the legality, not the appropriateness, of the decision; they have no leeway and, furthermore, the decisions of the director are in themselves likely to be merely routine. The comptrollers' bargaining power, therefore, is clearly low, and since they are not very strongly committed to the job they are likely to retreat and diminish their stakes, inasmuch as they know they cannot succeed. Some wishful thinking, however, will remain, along with a chance of conflict whenever a poor handling of the prestige problem will have made it impossible for a more aggressive comptroller to settle for some kind of special consideration. But this is relatively exceptional.

The Assistant Director versus Director Conflict

The conflict between assistant director and director is much more commonly expressed and runs somewhat deeper, but it is also a rather natural and acceptable one, since it revolves mostly around these most permanent problems of human society, the training of the younger generation and the stepping aside of the older. Director and assistant director have to work closely together, first because plant production, the domain of the assistant director, represents the core of the directorship responsibilities, and second because the assistant director has to be trained on the job (it is his first job) both for the role of assistant director and for the role of director, since he will become in due time a director himself. The directors are supposed to train their assistant directors and give them gradually a greater part of their work load. But, since this work load is not very heavy and since the assignment which is given first to the assistant director (the problems of personnel and of plant organization) happens to be the most difficult and dangerous one, there is a strong likelihood that conflict will develop around the division of work. Assistant directors will complain that they are maintained in tutelage, and directors will complain that assistant directors are unable to assume any responsibility.

This is more or less what we got in the interviews. But, if there are some traces of opposition in the majority of the cases, actual conflict is rather rare and there are even a few cases of solid partnership.

The following excerpts, matching comments of directors and assistant directors, will show the tenor of the relationship.

First, the usual allusive statements. One director said:

> I now have an assistant but I don't know for how long; since I have been here, I have had four of them; the first one remained three years, which means that I had some help the last two years; but none of the latter ones lasted a year; not only did they not provide help but they took a lot of my time and even that of the technical engineer.

And his assistant director commented:

> The director is quite aloof; I have myself very little contact with him and no possibility of training by learning from him.

Another director said:

> My assistant director has been here two years; for us it is quite a problem; as soon as they are trained, they quit.

His assistant director had this comment:

> My director is a good old man, awfully conservative.

A third director was quite happy:

> My assistant director is very smart, he is a real wonderful guy.

But his assistant director does not follow suit:

> My director always has sweeping ideas and keeps changing them constantly; I must go along without being able to suggest anything to him.

Second, the more conflictual ones. In these cases, the assistant director is usually more aggressive. One said, for example:

> My director is just hopeless; he does not accept that something could be done he has not himself seen before; one has to have his approval for the slightest detail.

And the director, for his part, said:

> My assistant director has neither the technical nor the administrative training required; I am obliged to take care of everything.

Another complained:

My director is very opinionated; he is authoritarian, at least when he can get his way.

And his director echoed:

As regards the assistant director, I will give you my opinion; he has the engineering school disease, theory; he has no training at all and has a lot of trouble getting along.

Third, as an example of a better kind of relationship, this characteristically shorter duet. The director:

I let him try and muddle through; I will only interfere when he needs help.

And the assistant director:

My director is very liberal.

One will notice that the director tends to remain impersonal, to avoid judging directly the behavior of his subordinate, while the assistant director is consistently and outspokenly personal; thus the opposition between generations makes itself felt in style as well. One will also note that the same problem is well laid out in all three groups: the junior man does not want control but needs backing; the senior man does not understand backing without control. One should add that the general feeling in the organization is that a successful adjustment is the exception. The most exuberant assistant director, after having said:

Here I have been able to achieve a lot because the director has given me a real free hand and at the same time has backed me whenever I needed it. [adds immediately] I have had a very extraordinary chance.

The word *extraordinary* comes also to the tongue of two of the other three satisfied assistant directors.

The opposition may be aggravated, too, by the change of outlook of the present young generation, which has shifted away considerably from the more traditional gentlemanly behavior. Young assistant directors seem chiefly interested in efficiency and technique.

The main factor, nevertheless, remains the amount of responsibility. The cases of successful teamwork are also the cases where an important program of rebuilding and technical transformation of the plant gives enough interesting work and responsibility for both the assistant director and the director.

Finally, one should emphasize that the conflict, although diffuse and well argued, is not really very deep. Assistant directors are able to identify with their directors; their anger is the anger of people who have been disappointed. Moreover, the temporary nature of the relationship provides some relief. Assistant directors come and go, and the directors can evade responsibility for them easily; in their turn, the assistant directors know that their situation will change in a not too distant future. There is a definite structure to the situation, but a lot of play is allowed for the protagonists inside it.

The Conflict between Technical Engineer and Assistant Director

Contrary to the foregoing pattern, in the relations between the technical engineers and the members of the "engineers' corps" (director and assistant director) involvement seems very great and the conflict pattern very difficult. Throughout France, our interviewees reported the same problems and almost the same feelings.

This is especially true for the responses of the technical engineers, who express consistently their irritation with and even their hatred for the *Polytechniciens*. But the assistant directors are also quite committed. Most of them, when asked about getting along with other members of the team, will refer to the technical engineer, and often in a violent and passionate way, which shows how central the problem is to their preoccupations.

What strikes us first in the interviews with assistant directors is their constant emphasis on the subordinate position of the technical engineer. They will say:

> He is my subordinate—he must report directly to the assistant director.
> He is responsible for maintenance of machines and equipment according to my planning of the organization.
> He is a subordinate.

But at the same time they know this theoretical statement does not fit the reality, and they worry about it:

> The problem is that the technical engineer has a very special situation, he is a member of the team as well as my subordinate.

Some of them try to explain this difficulty away by complaining about the right of the technical engineer to attend the council, or by deploring that they are given older men as subordinates. But still others will locate the trouble at the training and professional level and admit their helplessness in facing the technical engineer. One will say, for example:

> The school did not prepare us very well for the practical technical problems of the plant; I have to ask the technical engineer constantly for advice; this makes me lose face.

Another, after explaining how inadequate his school preparation was, adds:

> We are not confident of ourselves; this may be the source of the difficulties with the technical engineers.

While a third one recognizes bluntly:

> The assistant director can discuss technical problems only if he can get along well enough with the technical engineer.

The majority of the assistant directors conclude moderately that they do not get along too badly with the technical engineers. Nevertheless, such discrepancy between expectations and reality frequently fosters more violent reactions, such as the three following, which are quite typical of the tone of the discussion and of the arguments presented:

We [assistant directors] think that in the plants it is becoming too much a sort of Mexican army with everybody wanting to be a colonel . . . we do not need technical engineers; a good storeroom manager and a good technical foreman would be quite enough . . . and to run the whole thing, we are here; the central office seems to forget. . . .

One must confess that the technical engineers constitute the most impossible group. . . . One cannot trust a technical engineer . . . and the mere existence of such a job is absurd; the service would be better with a good foreman. When somebody comes from an enginering school he cannot be reduced to a foreman job. I personally think the post should be abolished.

The technical engineer supports the rebellion of the maintenance workers against me. If he could have his way, I could not interfere in the slightest way in what is his own business, that is, everything in the plant. . . . Technical engineers should be suppressed; there is no place for two men; they do not have the tactfulness, the human relations skill to be in charge of the personnel.

Technical engineers may be somewhat less violent than described in these last examples, but they are consistently critical and aggressive. All but three, directly or indirectly, criticized the members of the "engineers' corps," and the only one who was favorable added to his comments this significant understatement:

The temper of the young *Polytechniciens* has changed very much; they do not think they know everything in advance; some of them even are modest.

His colleagues for the most part complained of the haughtiness and the incompetence of their assistant directors and of Polytechniciens in general:

What is so depressing is the lack of technical experience of people whose job it is to be industrial leaders. . . . We have no voice and they just don't know. . . .

Some of them related in allusive details, as one skillful storyteller put it:

. . . [their] unbelievable, terrible mistakes.

But the most widespread frustration concerns the monopoly of the engineer corps over the possibilities of promotion, which is resented as a general conspiracy of the *Polytechniciens*. Only some older and better established technical engineers refrain from what they tend to consider begging for promotion, and say they would like only to strengthen the position of the technical engineer versus the assistant director.

No wonder that the comments on the overall relationship are rather sour:

There is no teamwork possible between the *Polytechniciens* and ourselves. The gap cannot be bridged.

Our bosses are all *Polytechniciens*; it is a feudal system . . . there is not enough work for them . . . one should cut through the services, democratize and suppress the monopoly; it is a sort of Mafia. . . .

The directors for their part, try to avoid making this kind of personal remark; they, of course, benefit from the existence of the assistant director, who acts in a way as a buffer between them and the technical engineer. They tend to answer in more general terms, discussing the problems involved instead of passing judgment.

A few of them, however, usually the ones who have been at some time, or are still, without an assistant director, will present in more reserved terms a similar picture:

My technical engineer is very competent; unfortunately the central office did not give him satisfaction and he thinks I am responsible instead, he is very aggressive and bitter. . . .

My technical engineer is very good but he is also hypersensitive. We are at odds with each other . . . he has no ability to synthesize.

From this brief report, the feelings of the players emerge rather clearly, and some of their motivations already appear. We can now turn to an analysis of the conditions and the rules of the game they are playing.

Theoretically, the technical engineer reports to the assistant director, who is in charge of production, for all his duties, maintenance, repairs, and work contracted for outside, which must be subordinate to the overall imperative of production. But this arrangement is bound to hurt the feelings of the technical engineer, since it is a permanent subordinate situation he himself has no chance to get relief from by occupying in due time the top position, and, at the same time, a situation which does not fit our society's regular expectations about necessary training and competence and which may even contradict some of these expectations, such as those concerning age and seniority.

A permanent "illegitimate" state of subordination will usually produce revolt and retreatism, but this particular one is peculiar in the sense that it does not leave the technical engineer helpless, inasmuch as it gives him so many possibilities for retaliation that he can practically deny his official subordination by making it impossible for his superior to initiate action without his approval.

The process works more or less in the following way:

First, production has become completely routine and it is only maintenance which will raise problems with the consequence that the trouble shooter, the man who can find solutions, will be the technical engineer, and he will defend his position of strength (the impossibility of his superiors getting along without him) by keeping his own domain free from any rationalization.

Second, the assistant director will not be able to control the technical engineer because, while his domain is that of the rule of thumb, he lacks the necessary practical training to learn the tricks of a trade which the technical engineer jealously preserves. Moreover, the official hierarchical decorum which surrounds the "engineers' corps" will protect the technical engineer by making it impossible for the assistant director to undertake a trial-and-error learning process and thus lose face. As a consequence, the assistant director can give formal orders to the technical engineer but cannot control their execution, and the technical engineer who, of course, cannot give orders to him, can, however, control the assistant director's behavior inasmuch as he will be able to set the limits of what is possible and what is not possible for him to do.

Third, the assistant director has a very weak chain of command; the foremen who relay his orders are not very efficient, and he distrusts them. The technical engineer, on the contrary, can rely on a strong group of journeymen who are competent and active. At the shop level, these journeymen, the maintenance workers, are in a position of strength vis-à-vis the foremen, and, for all practical purposes, they are the real bosses. This last element of the situation is naturally strategical. The technical engineer protects the privileges of the maintenance workers, who cannot be controlled by anyone but him, and the maintenance workers, in their turn, make the position of the technical engineer very secure, allowing him to develop and maintain the advantages described in the preceding paragraphs. As one of the technical engineers summarized quite frankly:

> I personally have my journeymen well in hand, and because of that, what I want to do I can do and the director is obliged to go along with what I want. . . .

Finally, any change in the organization of production itself, any move of the assistant director in his own domain, will be liable—because of the position of the maintenance workers as natural leaders in the shop—to the interference of the maintenance department and its all-powerful chief. Another technical engineer explains this in dry terms:

> On top of our duties we are often obliged to take up the work of the assistant director. . . .

This practical success of the technical engineers is bound finally to have some repercussions in the formal setup. It was through this that they won the right to sit at the council, which means that even formally there is an ambiguous situation where, on the one hand, the technical engineer is the subordinate of the assistant director, and, on the other, as a member of the council and usually a senior member he cannot be brushed off easily. As a consequence, the director has become a rather weak arbitrator between a senior and a junior executive. As one assistant director put it very angrily:

> The Council is becoming a soviet . . .

The reaction of the assistant directors to this situation is likely to be bitter. They have as many reasons to feel frustrated as have the technical engineers. They are invested with formal authority but are constantly prevented from exercising it actually. And they have no alternative. Personnel administration is taboo; they cannot initiate any action in the face of the rigid bargaining relationship between the unions and the central office; training, reallocation of jobs, the use of moral and promotional incentives are all made impossible by the strictness of the seniority system. Daily problems of running the plant are completely boring. The only possibility of action, the only challenge for the young assistant director, is the kind of progress which comes from technical improvement and the reorganization that goes with it, and here, too, he must encounter the technical engineer's knowledgeable comments. He may settle for a moderate course, choose the diplomat's way, concede a lot to get a few limited results; this kind of choice is all the more rational since his situation is a temporary one and he can regard himself as being in a learning position. But more frequently, because he is young and self-conscious, he will fight back, try to keep the technical engineer in line. In this case the stage is set for one of those perennial petty wars where the antagonists will not be able to decide any case on its merits, inasmuch as these struggles can be used to weaken the position of the other fellow.

A neat and typical example will illustrate the possibilities in this situation very well, at least as regards the behavior of the technical engineer; the potential opponent in this case is the director, in the absence of an assistant director in the plant at the time.

A new foreman had been brought to the plant a few weeks before the incident; unlike his colleagues he had, through previous industrial employment, some good technical training. An important piece of equipment happens to break down in his shop; the maintenance worker responsible for its repair is called in, fumbles around and reports it is serious and that production will have to stop until further notice. The foreman resents his arrogance and an argument starts immediately; the foreman tells the maintenance worker that he is lazy and incompetent, proceeds to work at the equipment himself and soon discovers the problem is not serious and that the reason for the breakdown is the poor maintenance of one of the parts. Furious, he approaches the second-line foreman to enlist his support in asking for a drastic punishment. This fellow tells him to quiet down and to see the technical engineer first. When approached, the technical engineer does not want to listen; another argument starts and finally the foreman is told that he had no right to interfere with a problem which was not his own responsibility in the first place, and for which he is surely incompetent as all foremen are. Still more furious, the foreman breaks in immediately to the director's office. The director listens to him quietly and carefully, congratulates him for his zeal but tells him with all the tact he can muster that he will have to inquire into the matter further and that he does not think he will be able to impose a sanction because there is not enough proof; then he drops the whole matter. Relating the incident later, the director explained that his decision was the only rational one because he was sure that had he punished the maintenance worker, the whole maintenance group would have immediately struck with the covert support of the technical engineer; they would have been able to shut down the plant, and the central office would never have supported him on such a menial and ambiguous ground. His acting in the case, therefore, would have made him lose face completely. As a corollary, of course, was the unpleasant consequence of discouraging one of the rare foremen who could have been a decisive influence in the plant but instead was led to quit in disgust. But, if it was a painful decision, the director still felt that it was the right one, and was happy in retrospect not to have had an assistant director at the time who, he felt, would surely have capitalized on the case only to make matters worse.

The kind of conflictual situation described in the foregoing appears very well structured. The four exceptions (20 percent of the cases), and the differences among the rest of the cases, raise interesting problems, the analysis of which can teach us a great deal about the range of deviance possible.

The rebuilding and remodeling of a plant, with all the reorganization which is thus made possible, presents the only material factor that can upset the regular pattern. As we have already seen, it gives both the director and the assistant director enough responsibility and initiative to make the relationship between them easier; in addition to this, however, it also gives them a clear lead over the technical engineer. The source of uncertainty in the planning ahead no longer comes from the maintenance and repair problems but from the decisions which director and assistant director will take as regards the new layout and the carrying out of the plans. Two of the exceptions to the regular pattern coincide with the two most important remodeling projects, and in a few other less important cases of transformation we can observe some clear repercussions in the relative bargaining power of the antagonists.

The personality and the ability of the technical engineer makes for a second type of difference. Generally a successful senior technical engineer will be more cautious and less aggressive, which brings a more peaceful relationship. At one extreme of the range of possibilities we have the case of a technical engineer who has succeeded so well in the face of a weak director and constantly changing assistant directors that he is the covertly recognized master of the house. This makes him very tolerant of and friendly to the *Polytechniciens*.[8] At the other extreme we find a technical

---

[8] Contrary to what could be expected, this does not make for less trouble in the plant since the maintenance workers, who have lost their natural protector because of the truce in the daily war, feel more insecure and will fight more bitterly to keep their privileges at the shop level.

engineer who could not stand the strain of his role and seems to have broken down completely, neglecting his own work and retreating in a hands-off policy.

The personality of the assistant director also has some relevance, but never accounts for such extreme differences; it will change the general tone of the relationship but without altering its balance. No assistant director will break down over the situation, neither will any succeed in brushing off the technical engineer except in the cases of plant transformation. This is a tight game, the players are anxious to get the maximum out of it, and, provided there are no special circumstances, there will not be any significant variation in the rules.

THE TECHNICAL ENGINEER'S PATTERN OF ADJUSTMENT

It is not only the technical engineer's relationship with the assistant director that seems to be well structured, but his whole pattern of adjustment and even the salient points of his attitudes toward the job can be quite accurately predicted.

It is amazing indeed to find how the interviews of most technical engineers throughout France so closely match, although these people rarely see each other and thus, surely, cannot be influenced by personal interaction with each other.

First and foremost, the technical engineers love their job. They are very proud of listing the whole series of their duties; they glory in being busy and a good third of them complain of being overworked, of not having the time to look after everything; but even when they claim they are exhausted, they seem to be no less enthusiastic about their "diversified and challenging job"—that job so essential to the functioning of the plant that:

. . . if there is something that does not work in the maintenance department the whole plant will be directly affected.

Jack-of-all-trades, competent and active, the technical engineer thinks of himself as the man on whose shoulders the whole plant relies.

Second, the technical engineers appear to be authoritarian and paternalistic with their subordinates. They are the only ones in the system who take exception to the seniority principle by claiming they would like personally to have the responsibility of rewarding and punishing. They talk of their subordinates and of the workers generally without observing the usual precautions. In the two cases we have been able to analyze most closely, their workers complained of their authoritarianism, although they gave them the most wholehearted support otherwise. The relative harshness of the technical engineer, however, does not mean that he does not communicate; on the contrary, it seems he is more perceptive of the feelings of the workers than are the other members of the management team, and more realistic in his appraisal.

Third, if they are overly paternalistic with their subordinates, the technical engineers are extremely critical of their superiors, ready to pounce on their mistakes with an unfailing jealousy, and they are extremely intolerant of any kind of control. They complain bitterly about the incompetence of the "engineers' corps," and the lack of courage of the people at the central office; they disapprove of the way the system works and seem to hold the *Polytechniciens* responsible for "the whole mess," especially for their poor wages and absence of promotion.

Fourth, the technical engineers are quite realistic; their interviews are more precise than those of the others; their arguments always revolve around practical problems. It seems they would like to give an image of themselves as senior, responsible, overworked people who are constantly on the run to repair the mistakes of intelligent but irresponsible playboys. This self-image fits well enough with the comments made about them by the other members of the team, who see them as intolerant and unpleasant fellows who are, nevertheless, very competent, as well as with the comments by their workers who see them as paternalistically inclined but also efficient leaders.

Finally, this lonely, austere, and bad-tempered man seems to be not only very happy but all the more happy when he has some gripes to express. However paradoxical it may seem, there is a definite tendency for technical engineers to express much less fondness for the job when they cease to be aggressive with other people. To be sure, the relation is not linear, but the association between griping and fondness for the job is more positive than negative.[9]

But now, what about the four technical engineers whose cases did not fit the usual conflict pattern? Their attitudes, of course, are also exceptions to the individual adjustment pattern, but their deviations from this latter pattern are smaller than might appear at first glance.

If we take, first, the three cases of technical engineers who were dominated by the assistant director, we find that these people still said they liked their job and still presented some of the usual complaints. What is gone is their pride, their activism, and their aggressiveness; they are passive and grieve silently; they even seem to have lost their authority over their own subordinates once they became unable to fight their superiors.[10] Such

---

[9] The curve could be of this sort:

[10] We were able to observe the reactions of the subordinates in two out of three cases.

an outcome may help in elaborating the analysis of the situation which the technical engineer has to face; his is a rewarding situation but a situation which brings a lot of strain because of the responsibility and overwork, the loneliness of the job, and the constant fight it requires. Some people are bound to break down, which means becoming a misfit.

At the other extreme, in the one clear case (and in the one or two more dubious cases) of success—where conflict seems to recede because of the dominance of the technical engineer—gripes become less frequent, and the austere technical engineer will mellow a little without, however, losing his caution.

The fight for power seems, in the last analysis, to be the major determinant of the technical engineer's adjustment. And power, in his situation, can only be achieved if he follows a very narrow way. There is no alternative: either he adopts the required behavior of his own social role, or he gives up and loses his self-respect. It is, of course, impossible to ascertain to what extent the situation molds the personality traits and to what extent a self-selection process is operating. Since there is relatively little turnover, it seems, however, that the constraint of the situation is a powerful force.

A last consequence is worth mentioning. As the technical engineer's success in the fight for power comes from the lack of rationalization of his field of action, so it is this lack which gives him the strategic advantage of controlling the only source of uncertainty in an otherwise routinized setup. He will, therefore, try very hard to keep it that way, which means he is likely to adopt a generally conservative attitude on all matters of organization, and that he will devote his innovating abilities to sideline problems, never trying to make progress in the control and predictability of his own field but rather holding to the individual rule-of-thumb way.

THE DIRECTOR'S ADJUSTMENT PATTERN

There seems to be as much variation among directors' reactions as there are similarities among those of technical engineers. Such a contrast may surprise the reader, since both groups participate in the same bureaucratic climate and both have to adjust to a constrained situation where they cannot deviate much from the usual pattern of behavior. But it fits our hypothesis as to the importance of power relationships for individual adjustment very well. The director's situation in this respect is very different from that of the technical engineer. He does not have to adopt a definite pattern of action in order to assert his position. He is given prestige and influence without having to fight for it, but is, at the same time, frustrated in his enjoyment of it, since he has no power to institute change. But unlike the technical engineer, he has no other group to hold directly responsible for his frustration.

We have already described how the director does not have the right to hire and fire, nor even the possibility of putting workers in the place he thinks would be best; nobody depends on him but the weak group of foremen, or supervisors. Production and sales problems are routine. Maintenance is in the skillful hands of the technical engineer. Only new works and general reorganization may present a challenge. The director's kind of leadership is, therefore, more a judicial-administrative than a managerial one.

One could argue, of course, that a judicial-administrative function might be very rewarding and that many people will adjust successfully to it. But, in the present case, such a function is in contradiction to the training and to the prior expectations of the directors, and also, partly at least, to their present values and frame of reference. They are constantly called upon to act as administrators, but they are also reminded that they are industrial managers and therefore responsible for progress and efficiency. They even have within their own organization a few men who are examples of success in this industrial sense, and their prestige is never contested.

The director, therefore, does not get much satisfaction from his professional career. Certainly the prestige of being a member of the "engineers' corps" still has some value, but, in France's more competitive modern economy, it does not carry so much weight anymore. Rewards come only on the formal side, and there is little likelihood of their inspiring a real sense of achievement.

These difficulties of adjustment, however, could not lead to a unique pattern of behavior since, contrary to the technical engineers' group, the directors' group is a dominant group and could only rebel against the whole bureaucratic system. The central office, of which they complain a great deal, is staffed by members of the engineers' corps like themselves and they cannot dissociate themselves too much. They have no common objective for which to fight and, because of their personal freedom, they can find an easy retreat in personal achievements outside the job.

Directors adjust to such a situation in three different and even opposite patterns, which correspond to three distinct ways of life, not to mention a fourth intermediary one.

The first pattern, that of happy, successful adjustment, is very rare. It corresponds to the two or three cases of complete and successful plant reorganization. Certainly the directors who are able to achieve such a result, in the organizational climate which we have described, must have most special qualities. But they also must have had good luck, since, under the actual conditions, it is only possible for the central office to allow the necessary allocation of funds for reorganization to a few directors. Each director, of course, can attempt to attract the attention of the central office to his "sound" project, but, since most plants are in need of change, he must have special and solid ground to win out over his competitors. Regardless of the directors and the sheer value of their plans, certain factories will be considered first simply because of practical, material arguments and certain others because of a long history of precedents. Of course, a director is not appointed to a factory without some consideration of his qualities; he must fit into the possibilities of the situation, although the hazard of seniority may interfere with rational placement.[11] Moreover, since it is difficult for assistant directors and directors to furnish proof of their qualities of leadership, outside of special cases for which certain people have to be chosen, the choices are not choices made according to accomplishments but the more hazardous choices of personalities. As a result, qualities of diplomacy, skill at patching up, at smoothing down, at compromising, tend in the long run to be better appreciated, while the more independent personalities, who could have succeeded well in another environment, tend to be set aside.

Seen through his colleagues' eyes, the happy adjustment of the successful director looks like a matter of luck and favoritism. But, at the same time, its rarity gives it a brilliant aura. For the man himself, it is extremely rewarding since it allows the satisfaction of two contradictory demands, the demand for security and the demand for achievement. And, finally, for the organization this kind of adjustment, rare as it is, has a tremendous importance in that it offers an embodiment of perfection as a yardstick for measuring other performances. Directors themselves, although they usually profess to reject such a standard, are much influenced by its existence.

At the other extreme, in the usual routinelike plant situations, we find two contrasting types of reactions corresponding to two different ways of life.

Directors who choose the first of these claim they have the entire responsibility for everything which might ever happen in the plant. They justify their claim by taking their formal power seriously. When giving the stamp of their authority they pretend they are perfectly free. They happen, of course, consistently to choose certain kinds of solutions, but they explain this by emphasizing their concern for the general interest. They are careful and cautious people who believe that they have to sacrifice short-run advantages for the long-run benefit of the institutions they are in charge of. This constant denying of reality makes for a rather dramatic public character, who can play sometimes with great sophistication the part of an elder statesman, carrying with him the impressive majesty of the public service, however weak his decisions of the moment may be. His own private person seems itself to be influenced. The aura of

---

[11] One man who, because of his special qualities, was well qualified to lead the necessary reorganization of a certain plant was not available when an appointment was to be made there.

glory one sees surrounding him will not leave him at the factory gate. A poised and dignified personality in and around the plant, he shows all the external marks of happy and successful activities.

The colleagues of this type who have chosen a second kind of adjustment appear, on the contrary, to be extremely unhappy. Their solution of their difficulties is not to deny or to sublimate reality but to exaggerate its unpleasant aspects. While the elder-statesman type pretend they are free to do everything they would like to do, that nothing has ever been imposed on them that they themselves had not previously required, these others claim that they do not have the slightest leeway, that they are just transmission cogs with no initiative, and, finally, that their job is completely useless. But this pessimism is more sophisticated than would appear at first glance. By minimizing their professional role, they are preserving the self-respect of their own private lives. If a director does not have any possibility of achievement at all, one cannot accuse him of not having succeeded professionally. He can, therefore, still make a claim to being a brilliant and distinguished citizen, however poor his work achievements are in his own eyes. While their colleagues identify with the successful director, those of the latter type deny the possibility of success.

These two opposite patterns of behavior are, of course, not very often as clear as this description. But a sizable group of directors have reactions surprisingly close to these models, one out of four directors claiming that they are perfectly free and responsible, one out of three claiming that they do not have anything to decide upon.

In between these two so-called unsuccessful groups, there are a variety of different personal adjustments wherein one can recognize traits of both the first and the second pattern. Usually, however, people in this group are more realistic and sensible about their own possibilities, and a number of directors among them might be considered somewhat closer to the successful pattern which we first described. But in certain other cases we find more incoherence than realism, some people claiming, at the same time, that they are all powerful and unable to decide independently.

THE ASSISTANT DIRECTOR'S ADJUSTMENT PATTERN

Assistant directors seem to be able to stand realistic appraisal of their own situation much better than directors. But, if their individual reactions are not as sharply conflicting among themselves as those of their elders, they are still quite diversified and far from being as structured as those of their natural antagonists, the technical engineers.

Such kind of adjustment is well in line with the peculiarities of their own situations. Theirs is at the same time a learning job and a very secure one, so that they do not have too much to worry about; they do not have so much at stake as either the directors or the technical engineers; being lucid about their problems will not endanger their self-esteem.

Their relatively inferior situation in the power relationship is, of course, a strain and it does involve them affectively, but it does not affect their entire outlook. Assistant directors can find scapegoats in the old generation, curse the organization system, and believe that it will eventually change. Whether they wait patiently for their turn to come, or fight back bitterly, or prepare for their departure from the organization, criticism still remains, for most of them, a healthy, enjoyable activity which does not have to become self-derogatory. So one senses, within their interviews and coloring most of their attitudes, a feeling of detachment, a certain freedom of commitment which makes it easier to adjust temporarily, and reasonably well, to a situation, without ceasing to criticize it. Intellectual aggressiveness can still coincide with a rather well-balanced affectivity.

As regards the job itself, however, the conditions for a happy kind of adjustment are narrow. Three different givens on which the assistant director himself has little influence, if any, will determine it entirely; first, the existence of a program of reorganization, or at least of considerable nonroutine activities in the plant; second, the willingness of the director to give him a free hand; and third, the relative helplessness of the technical engineer. Usually all these givens will exist at the same time; when there is a program of reorganization the director is likely to be more broadminded and cooperative and the technical engineer will lose his decisive veto power. In such a situation, the assistant directors are enthusiastic about their jobs and generally much better adjusted.

Such an adjustment, which can be recognized in three or four of our cases, seems to be conducive to more tolerance for the central office policy, and to more moderation and realism in the discussion of the problems. Happy assistant directors, however, still criticize the system of organization and the behavior of their elders; they still think they might eventually quit the organization. But they seem to have a much greater sense of their own responsibilities and more interest in practical problems. Beyond this, they do not appear to share similar personality characteristics.

The difficulties most of the rest of the assistant directors (three-quarters of them at least) run into do not produce a consistent pattern either. We will find, in a general climate of moderate frustration, all sorts of individual adjustment, with some common characteristics, however. First, the generalized hostility to the system of organization and to the older generation which we have already mentioned is common; second, sharp comments on the technical engineer with, at the extreme, the demand to suppress the job; and, third, a general emphasis on technical and organization problems as opposed to human problems.

These common traits would seem to constitute an ideological orientation more than a pattern of adjustment, and surely they are perceived by the assistant directors themselves as coherent reform propositions. But, if one analyzes them as steps in the process of adjustment to the organization on the part of future directors, one will find a different logical thread in them.

When they enter the organization as students at the so-called preparatory school, the assistant directors say almost unamimously[12] that they were attracted to public service, and especially to the organization, because of its liberal tradition. They wanted a job which could give them broad human responsibilities rather than narrow technical ones. When asked how they imagine their role as assistant directors, all of them answered that they wanted to give more importance to their human responsibilities than to their technical ones. They always emphasized in their observations about factory life the importance of being a leader, of assuming a leader's responsibilities toward the workers and toward the community. They see themselves as members of a generation conscious of the human problems of industry and impatient to introduce change in that domain, and they feel they are as much opposed to their elders' timorousness and conservatism as to the engineers' paradise where human beings will have no place, as they feel some of their peers fascinated with technique seem to call for.

A few years later, or at any rate to their colleagues with just a few years' seniority, such opinions will look quite childish. The assistant directors who have more than one or two years' seniority do not have the slightest regard for their role as chief of personnel. Human problems for them are not to be taken seriously. Their only concern is for technique and for the possibilities of achievement which come through the use of technique. When asked about problems of leadership and about the training in "industrial psychology" they had been given at the school, they are generally very bitter. To them, such training does not have any bearing on the hard realities of factory life.

We have no way to prove that such an opposition does not correspond to a change in the mood of two successive generations; but it seems reasonable to assume, in view of the relatively small difference in age of the individuals concerned (five to six years on the average), that this opposition is the outcome of a psychological crisis which the young assistant director has to surmount in order to adjust to his role.

Having held the belief that the older generation was inefficient, weak, and uncaring because they were conservative and old-fashioned, he has now come to realize that the situation does not allow one to be active and successfully efficient. He understands, also, that his human leadership role is only formal and that he cannot influence the workers' behavior, even with the best of intentions. There is no give-and-take possible because

---

[12] We were able to interview the twelve engineers who were studying at the school at the time of the survey.

there is no freedom to compromise on either side. Whatever his own earlier orientation, he has to recognize that the only way to bring change is through technical progress. Technique is his only chance, and he is likely, after some bitter disappointments over problems of personnel to change his own views to fit the situation. Even here, of course, he will not have a great deal of success because of the opposition of the technical engineer. But such a struggle in its more personalized form will be more exciting and eventually more rewarding than the fight against bureaucratic rules. Then, too, there are the examples of the factories where important innovations have been successfully introduced, and with which the assistant directors are much more ready to identify than are the more envious directors.

The assistant directors' ideology, therefore, is not an idle one; under the mask of rationalizing industry, it presents a powerful argument for giving their group a chance to get things done; the obsession with technique may be narrow-minded, but it is producing change and change has become their first goal.

What still looks puzzling, however, is the second reversal that will take place when the assistant director becomes a director. How is it that the same people who once were active and aggressive in pushing ahead technical arguments and in setting aside all other problems, will now be cautious about progress, and will consistently give the lead to human considerations? To understand it we must qualify what we have said about the assistant directors' ideology. It is, to be sure, not an idle philosophy, it is a philosophy intended for action; but it is not the rationale for actual action. Assistant directors cannot and do not introduce significant change outside of the few cases of overall reorganization; they fight for change but do not succeed, and do not even believe completely that they can succeed. Their lack of responsibility and of actual commitment make it possible for them to state their point lucidly, without assuming the burden of the consequences. But when they become director, they have to assume one way or another the responsibility of the system as it is, which means giving priority to human relations since, in a bureaucratic equalitarian organization, these considerations become preponderant. But their view of human relations has now become rather skeptical and conservative, and will become more and more so inasmuch as their own possibilities of achievement will narrow down. Things do not change, they feel, and perhaps ought not to change easily; human problems are the key to everything but it is a key for locking more than for opening up. Humanism in this context will mean recognition of the other fellow's right to oppose change, i.e., acceptance of the status quo.

The entire career development of the members of the *engineers' corps* can be interpreted as a gradual adjustment to the organization as it is, with its principles of seniority and impersonality, with its rigidity of behavior and its resistance to change. In so adjusting, the directors will resign themselves to narrowing down their expectations still more. But they will not abandon, really, their former ideology; they will still look toward change as a positive value which only special circumstances oblige them to discard.

Such an adjustment is in sheer contrast to the aggressive kind of the technical engineers, who can adjust successfully only when they deny the formal order of the organization and, indirectly at least, some of its main principles. One might wonder, however, at this paradox; the leaders of a stabilized, conservative, bureaucratic system profess a philosophy of change in organization patterns, while the "coming men" group opposing them is consistently conservative in that respect.

THE MEANING OF CONFLICT IN A BUREAUCRATIC SYSTEM OF ORGANIZATION

It seems clear that at the root of all the conflicts which we have analyzed there is some kind of fight for power. Such findings are well in line with the results of most recent researches in organizational behavior, which have shown how central the notion of control and power may be for understanding human relations in large-scale organizations.[13] We will not investigate these findings any further here, but we can bear in mind that there are no organizations without power problems and conflicts arising out of them and, moreover, that there are none where these conflicts are not checked by some kind of social control. We will now try to discuss on a more general basis, in terms of the forces operating in all bureaucratic systems of organization, the meaning of the special traits which make these conflicts so acute in the case we have studied and the nature of the social control which still holds the organization together.

What seems most striking when we compare the situation of our management team with the situation of the most common type of organizational hierarchies are two facts: first, that many forces which usually prevent the development, or at least the expression, of conflict are absent; and second, that there is a peculiar balance of power, of prestige and of involvement in the job which makes it necessary and even rewarding for the protagonists to engage in conflict.

On the negative side, i.e., in the absence of the traditional forces which prevent conflict, three main remarks can be made. First, our four group members have perfect security, not only in regard to tenure but even in regard to promotion; so that they do not depend upon one another or upon higher-ups with whom they could line up. They have, in this respect, nothing to fear and can be, if they want, as independent as they please. Second, they have no chance of being materially rewarded or even of

---

[13] See, for example, Dorwin Cartwright (ed.), *Studies in Social Power* (University of Michigan, 1958).

gaining in status by their personal achievements; personal achievements are not even measurable; it is almost a private affair for each individual concerned, so that they are delivered not only from fear but also from hope. Third, the differentiation of their roles and their specification is such that teamwork is not necessary to keep the system going; it surely may help morally and materially in achieving the required goals, but the absence of cooperation does not bring much strain. Our four individuals, therefore, can be considered as completely autonomous in the sense that there is nothing in the system they belong to which requires them to cooperate, to adjust to each other, or to compromise on their conflicting interests. They have little to gain in the long run by teamwork and compromise, since successful performance does not require it and since their future is already set up in advance and will not be changed by the kind of relationship which they have with their colleagues.

On the positive side we will notice that the opposition between maintenance and production, which is at the root of our main conflict, is found in all industrial setups but does not usually stir up much trouble. A rough comparison made with factories producing the same product with the same technology in other countries shows that some of the technical difficulties about which people in France are so worried do not even come to mind in different systems of organization; the human relations and power relations arrangement alone seems to be responsible. According to our findings we can explain the acuteness of the conflict as being due to an unusual distribution of the power of initiating action in the plant, of the official prestige, and of the commitment to the job. The actor whose official prestige is lowest and whose commitment to the job, because of his lifetime involvement with it, is highest is in a position—due to his control of the major source of uncertainty in the routine of factory life—to control also the initiating of action within the usual range of behavior. His antagonists have no way to retaliate effectively, except in special circumstances, but they can adjust to their situation because of a lesser commitment to the job which makes retreat easier.

At a higher level of abstraction, the major elements of our conflict situation appear to be the rigidity of the social roles the organization presents to the individuals, their isolation from one another and the lack of congruence of these roles with the actors' expectations. There are only a few roles, and they are all well structured and do not allow for individual experimentation and innovation. People do not expect to shift from one role to another and do not depend much upon one another for the attainment of their goals. They can therefore take up the cause of their group without either mental reservations or provisions for eventual change of circumstances. If there should be some possibility of an equal enough fight, an otherwise trivial opposition of roles will develop into a basic conflict which will permit the actors to express their own frustrations about their professional situation.

Such an arrangement reminds one of earlier role differentiations in Western societies. Modern professional role systems compared to, say, those of the eighteenth century appear to be characterized by a tremendous diversification of the professional roles and the constant shifting of the individuals from one role to another. As a consequence, lifelong intergroup conflicts have receded considerably; one can argue that the tensions they generated have been at least partially replaced by the tension of interpersonal competition and by the personal anxieties of individuals who have been obliged to internalize some of these earlier role conflicts. But, in any case, people who could conflict on a more permanent basis tend now to be too far apart, and people who are in constant enough contact are much too dependent on each other and know too much of the other fellow's viewpoint to be able to develop such basic conflict.

Does it mean that, as a consequence, the organizational system we have studied can be considered as a conservatory of more ancient patterns of behavior? It is certainly true to some extent, but what is the organizational logic which accounts for such a result?

Three related principles govern the social system of the factories we have studied: first, complete equality between people who are in the same hierarchical ranking and who have roughly the same role, with seniority alone accounting for differences and promotions; second, separate recruitment from the outside for each of these major roles, with abstract competitive examinations as criteria of selection; third, impersonal and detailed rules applying to all possible happenings, so that most uncertainty and concomitant human intervention can be eliminated. There may be some theoretical opposition between the principle of equality-seniority and the principle of outside recruitment, but if one views them both as a way to concur with the common goal of eliminating all human intervention from the organizational machine, they are, on the contrary, mutually reinforcing.

From these principles one could see very well how isolation and rigidity of the role will develop. Strict application of equality and seniority will make interpersonal fights within the group impossible. Outside recruitment will separate the groups and prevent communication. The elimination of uncertainty and human intervention, however, should act as a check insofar as it is intended to suppress power relationship. But our example will have shown that there is always some loophole and that power dependencies and conflicts will grow around them.

It can be argued that these three principles of action are the core of the bureaucratic system of organization and that they are present as tendencies in all large-scale organizations. In private organizations, however, they are checked by the powerful unifying force which is provided by the control of the promotional ladder. But the lower we go down the hierarchical scale, the weaker this control becomes with the result that intergroup fights will tend to develop in the lower echelons. In public administrations such a control becomes more difficult at higher levels as well, especially in the older and more "bureaucratic" ones of which our case is an extreme example. Rigidity of roles and lack of communication between them will make conflict likely to appear in all weak spots of the system.

But even in the case at hand, social control sets limits. Other people's privileges cannot be infringed upon; minimum production standards, order and decorum, status preeminence of the director must be observed. Two sets of forces in this respect seem to be at work. First, the feeling by members of all groups that their privileges depend at a very high level upon the other groups' privileges, which means that the authority of the director as a final arbitrator for keeping peace and order must be recognized; and second, the feeling that the standards of the organization's achievements and practices should be comparable to general expectations in society at large. The first kind of pressure keeps the system working on a routine basis, the second accounts for change and progress which comes from the top down in an impersonal way, with the members of the "engineers corps" as change agents. Occupational or professional roles, however, remain frozen into a very ancient pattern, with no likelihood of internal motivation for change. This alone invites the foreseeing of some kind of crisis when the acceleration of progress will make it impossible for such a system to adjust to modern society.

16. BEHAVIOR IN GROUPS AS A FUNCTION OF SELF-, INTERACTION, AND TASK ORIENTATION*[1]

Bernard M. Bass and George Dunteman

In *Leadership, Psychology and Organizational Behavior* (Bass, 1), three types of group members, self-, interaction, and task oriented, were conceived. It was argued that attempts to lead under specified circumstances would be different among these three types of individuals. The Orientation Inventory (Bass, 1962), 27 triads of questions about personal preferences, values, and projections, was constructed to screen populations for samples of these idealized types. For each triad, subjects indicate which alternative they prefer most, and which they prefer least.

The Orientation Inventory (Ori), in its final form, had the following test-retest reliabilities: self-orientation, .73; interaction orientation, .76; and task orientation, .75. The built-in negative correlations[2] among the three scales and the obtained reliabilities made possible a classification system labeling individuals as of one type or another if they were in the top quartile of a particular distribution. In a classification-reclassification analysis, it was seen that only 6.5% of 84 subjects shifted from one idealized category to another. Most shifts were into and out of the residual category from one of the idealized types (Bass *et al*, 4).

In addition to sex differences, occupational and educational differences were also found in expected directions. For example, engineers earned significantly higher task scores than nonengineers (Dunteman and Bass, 6).

* Reprinted from *Journal of Abnormal and Social Psychology*, Vol. 66, No. 5 (1963) pp. 419–28.

[1] This research was supported by Contract N7 onr 35609, Group Psychology Branch, Office of Naval Research.

[2] Like forced-choice and Kuder inventories, these scales yield ipsative scores. Since the grand mean score is a constant, if an individual is high on one scale, he must be low on another. This accentuates the differentiation in responses of a given individual on the three orientations, making it easier to type him at one extreme or another. Equally important, the forcing fits the conceptualization. We argue that in groups, members are concerned with the task, the interaction, or themselves. If they pay more attention to one, then they must devote less to another. Thus, we suggest that if a person is generally task oriented, then he is unlikely to be interaction oriented. Our measurements follow these restraints. The most uniform negative correlation seems to be between task and interaction orientation. This correlation varies between −.3 and −.5. On the other hand, self-orientation sometimes shows less of a negative correlation with the other scales. Thus, "mixed types" of individuals emerge. A recent suicide was extremely high in task *and* self-orientation and extremely low in interaction orientation. Juvenile delinquents in general tend to be low in task orientation and high in self- and/or interaction orientation. (The interaction oriented get along better in the institution and are paroled more readily.)

At all age levels—early adolescent, late adolescent, and middle age—women were more interaction oriented than men (Bass *et al.*, 4).

Overt choice behavior was found associated in expected directions with Ori scale scores. Subjects with high task orientation scores completed tasks voluntarily more frequently following interruption than subjects with low task scores. Subjects with high task scores volunteered in greater frequency for psychological experiments. Subjects with high interaction scores were more likely to choose to work in a group or to volunteer for discussions rather than working on problems alone. Subjects with high self-orientation scores were more likely to choose to work alone and, of all students, were most likely to shift from nonvolunteering to volunteering for service as a subject of a psychological experiment when an extrinsic monetary reward was added for volunteering (Bass *et al.*, 4).

On a battery of personality inventories and attitude questionnaires, the highly self-oriented subject described himself, to a statistically significant degree, as disagreeable, dogmatic, aggressive-competitive, sensitive-effeminate, introvertive, suspicious, jealous, tense-excitable, manifestly anxious, lacking in control, immature-unstable, needing aggression, needing heterosexuality, lacking in need for change, fearing failure, and feeling insecure. The interaction-oriented subject described himself as significantly in need of affiliation, socially group dependent, lacking in need for achievement, lacking in need for autonomy, needing to be helped by others, tending to warmth and sociability, and lacking in need for aggression.

The task-oriented subject described himself on the other inventories as self-sufficient and resourceful, controlled in will power, needing endurance, aloof and not sociable, sober and excitable, introvertive, radical, not dogmatic, lacking in need for heterosexuality, needing abasement, aggressive and competitive, lacking in need for succorance, low in fear of failure, mature and calm. He also scored higher in intelligence. He was a scholastic overachiever, if above average in ability, compared to equally intelligent subjects lower in task orientation (Bass *et al.*, 4).

PART I

Orientation and Peer Evaluations of Discussion Performance

The present report deals with several independent studies of differential behavior in groups of members assessed by Ori as self-, interaction, or task oriented. Behavior, as rated by peers, of 32 supervisors and 25 secretaries in sensitivity training groups provided two sets of correlated observations. Another study related orientation to observer's appraisals of the leadership potential of 48 candidates for supervisory positions under intensive observation for three days using "country house" techniques. Finally, contrived groups, homogeneous with respect to orientation, or containing specific proportions of members of each type, yielded further evidence on the overall differences in contribution to group life of the task oriented, the interaction oriented, and the self-oriented.

Procedure

Thirty-two members of a management training laboratory were administered Ori at the beginning of the laboratory. They were assembled in "balanced" discussion groups of eight each, matched in educational and occupational level (but without reference to Ori score). Each group met ten times during two weeks for a total of 20 hours of discussion about miscellaneous matters of their own choosing.

Each of the discussions was of the leaderless type. The groups were sensitivity training groups without any formal leader, without any appointed chairman, and without any previously decided agenda of a formal character. Each discussion lasted about two hours, and different from most training programs, *no laboratory staff members were present during the discussion*, although tape recordings were run of the discussions. The discussants were free to talk about anything and everything they wished, constrained only by the other seven members of the group in the room. Prior to these discussions, staff members encouraged participants to experiment in new ways of behaving, to give each other feedback, and to take time during the discussion to analyze its process.

A similar procedure was carried out for 25 professional women secretaries who met in two groups for sensitivity training for one weekend and nine successive evenings once a week. Trainers were present at the regular meetings. The mean age of both secretaries and supervisors was approximately thirty-five with a range from the early twenties to the late fifties. After the tenth meeting, each member of a group rated every other subject in that group on 27 items of behavior. A nine-point scale was used to indicate how much the person the subject was rating exhibited each of the behaviors during the 20 hours of discussion (9 = Completely, 8 = Almost completely, . . . , 1 = Not at all). In addition each subject ranked every other subject in his group according to the extent the subject ranked had successfully led or influenced the group.

The seven ratings received by each subject on each item from fellow members in a group yielded a mean rating on each item which in turn was correlated with the Ori scores of that participant (product moment).

Results

Both among supervisors and secretaries, task orientation and interaction orientation scales tended to correlate much more highly with peer ratings than did the self-orientation scale, and to a much greater degree.

Task orientation was correlated significantly (joint probability at the 1 to .1% level) for both supervisors and secretaries with the following peer ratings: helps members express their ideas (.60, .43),[3] helps group stay on target (.58, .44), helps get to the meat of issues (.57, .38), gives good suggestions on how to proceed (.56, .39), provides good summaries when needed (.52, .44), encourages group to a high level of productivity (.52, .45), takes the lead in selecting topics (.49, .54), works hard (.49, .40), offers original ideas (.46, .37) effectively senses when to talk and when to listen (.45, .38), successfully influences (.44, .43), concerned about successfully completing the group's jobs (.33, .47), and does not run away when faced with a problem (.48, .39).

Task orientation scores of supervisors but not of secretaries correlated significantly at the 1% level with: provides helpful, objective feedback to members (.55) and easy to understand what he is trying to say (.54). Task orientation scores of secretaries but not of supervisors correlated significantly at or near the 5 per cent level with: removal from the group would be a loss (.39), continues to push point even after being blocked repeatedly (.51), annoys others (.37), dominates and imposes her will on the group (.46), makes unjustified assumptions (.40), and blocks the group (.38).

Thus, while task-oriented subjects are seen as exhibiting initiative and aiding the group to achieve its ends, among women secretaries, domineering inflexibility is perceived as going along with helpfulness, initative, and successful influence.

Interaction orientation scores generally revealed a reversed pattern of rated behavior.[4] Among both supervisors and secretaries, interaction orientation scores were negatively correlated (at a joint probability at the 1 or 5 per cent level) with: concerned about successfully completing group jobs (−.36, −.30), dominates and imposes will on the group (−.39, −.49), offers original ideas (−.40, −.31), encourages group to a high level of productivity (−.42, −.32), provides good summaries when needed (−.43, −.32), takes the lead in selecting topics (−.46, −.48), and helps group stay on target (−.51, −.38).

Supervisors only who were high in interaction scores were seen as: running away when faced with a problem (.38) and yielding to group pressures (.26) while highly interaction oriented secretaries were rated highly in making others feel at ease (.30).

Other ratings which correlated negatively in one sample but not the other at the 1 or 5 per cent level included (for supervisors only): easy to understand what he is trying to say (−.43); gives good suggestions on how to proceed (−.44); provides helpful, objective feedback to members

---

[3] The first value in parenthesis is the product-moment correlation for 32 supervisors between task orientation score and peer rating; the second value is the corresponding correlation for 25 secretaries.

[4] This result is inseparable statistically or conceptually from the negative relation between task and interaction orientation.

(—.45); works hard (—.45); helps get to the meat of issues (—.46); helps members express their ideas (—.55). For secretaries only, significant negative correlations at the 5 per cent level were obtained between interaction orientation scores and: annoys others (—.45) and makes unjustified assumptions (—.48).

Interaction-oriented supervisors and secretaries are seen as of little positive help to group work; among supervisors only, as avoiding problems and conflicts; among secretaries, as avoiding being unpleasant and unreasonable.

Self-orientation scores for both supervisors and secretaries were significantly (joint probability at the 5 per cent level) but negatively related with making others feel at ease (—.21, —.20).

PART II

Orientation and Assessed Leadership Potential

A major utility regularly selects journeymen and maintenance workers with promise, according to their performance records and boss' opinions, and sends them to a center for 3 days of intensive observation in various quasi-real group situational tests following OSS procedures and methods usually described as the "country house" technique (see Vernon, 1950). Observers use a five-point scale to pool their ratings into a single overall evaluation of the promotability to supervisory positions of the candidates screened by the situational tests.

Forty-eight of these candidates were given the Ori. The orientation scores, unknown to the assessors, were then compared for the 13 candidates earning the highest "promotability" ratings with the 13 candidates earning the lowest appraisals by the assessment staff. Table 1 shows the mean Ori scores of the 13 high and low candidates. Downgraded candidates were significantly higher (at the 1 per cent level) in interaction orientation and comparably lower in self- and task orientation. Evidently, the lack of initiative of the interaction oriented strongly affected their appraisals, consistent with preceding results obtained for secretaries and

TABLE 1

MEAN ORIENTATION SCORES OF 13 CANDIDATES APPRAISED HIGHLY PROMOTABLE TO SUPERVISORY POSITIONS WITH 13 APPRAISED AS LOW IN PROMOTABILITY

Promotability	Mean Orientation		
	Self	Interaction	Task
High	21.8	23.8	35.5
Low	18.2	29.4	33.4
		$p < .01$	

supervisors. On the other hand, task orientation failed to significantly raise evaluations any more than did self-orientation.

PART III

Recomposed Groups Homogeneous in Orientation

To gain further insight into the behavior of discussants as a function of their orientation, discussion groups were set up of participants, all of a single type. Consistent differences between self-oriented, interaction-oriented, and task-oriented groups, in meaningful ways, were observed for both the supervisors and the secretaries who met once in these recomposed groups.

Procedure

Following the fourth meeting of the regular training groups of supervisors, the groups were recomposed for the next discussion according to members' Ori scores. The members did not know the basis of recomposition. The eight members of the supervisor's laboratory scoring highest on the self-orientation scale were placed in a "Blue" group; the eight scoring highest on the interaction scale were placed in a "Brown" group; and the eight highest on the task orientation scale were placed in a "Purple" group. The remaining eight were not as high as any of the other individuals on any of the three scales and were placed in an "Orange" or "residual" group of individuals, none of whom were high on any of the scales nor low, therefore, on any of the scales. Each of these temporarily recomposed groups held a two-hour meeting, after which they were dissolved and members returned to their original groups.

A somewhat modified plan was followed for the secretaries. After the tenth regular meeting, 22 of the 25 secretaries present from the two regular training groups were recomposed into three groups—Blue, Brown, and Purple—of seven or eight subjects each of the same orientation. No residual Orange group was composed because of the fewer number of subjects available.

Supervisor Analyses

At the end of each of the four preceding two-hour discussions in his regular training group during the first three days of the laboratory, each supervisor had filled out a postmeeting questionnaire. He did the same at the end of the two-hour discussion in the recomposed group.

The questionnaire contained 12 items. Each item was accompanied by a nine-point scale varying from a generally favorable to a generally unfavorable reaction. For example, the first question was, "How do I feel about this group now?" The respondent could indicate a reaction ranging from 1, "worst possible group," to 9, "best possible group."

Results

The recomposed groups behaved as anticipated, although to a degree exceeding expectations.

Table 2 shows the mean extent on each nine-point scale that a recomposed group's discussion was higher in rating by its members than the same members had assigned to the last meeting of the balanced group from

TABLE 2

DIFFERENCES IN EVALUATION OF RECOMPOSED GROUPS OF SUPERVISORS AND THE IMMEDIATELY PRECEDING REGULAR GROUPS FROM WHICH MEMBERS CAME

	Mean Difference in Orientation			
	Self (Blue)*	Interaction (Brown)*	Task (Purple)*	Residual (Orange)*
Postmeeting evaluation				
1. Quality of group	−.5†‡	1.0	−.9‡	−1.2
2. Clarity of group's goals	.4	1.1‡	−1.8‡	−.6
3. Worked hard at task	.5	1.3§	−1.5‡	−.8
4. Practical, realistic discussion	−.4	1.3‡	−2.1§	−.5
5. Discussion about ourselves	−1.9	2.0‡	1.1	−.6§
6. Members out to win own points	−.3	−.9	−1.8	2.2§
7. Group worked at developing itself	−.4	.6	−1.2‡	−1.2
8. I leveled with others	−.5	.8	.5	−1.0
9. I felt joined up	−.6	.8‡	.2	−1.1
10. Tolerated different views	.5	.4	−.9‡	−.8
11. Received help from others	−.5	.5	−.9	−.6
12. Group concerned with content rather than process	−1.5‡	1.4‡	.2	−2.8‡

† A positive value indicates response higher for recomposed group; negative value indicates higher rating of *c* regular group.
‡ $p < .05$, $df = 6$.
§ $p = .01$, $df = 6$.
* Recomposed group.

which they had come. For example, members of the Blue group, on the average, rated their Blue group .5 lower in quality (Item 1) than the various immediately preceding, regular groups. On the other hand, the interaction oriented members gave an average of one point more to their newly formed Brown group than to the various home groups from which they had come. In evaluating these responses, it should be kept in mind that in a management training laboratory of this sort, a great deal of loyalty is developed for one's regular home training group. Most experienced staff personnel will agree that it is difficult to destroy this loyalty by rearranging memberships temporarily. Thus, in general, members were more favorably inclined to their original "home" group with which they had been meeting for the first 3 days than to their newly recomposed temporary group. But there was a striking exception—those who met as the Brown group of highly interaction-oriented subjects.

Interaction-oriented members (the Brown group) felt quite differently about their recomposed group than did any of the other members. They seemed much more favorably disposed towards their recomposed group; and in the informal critique that followed they were rather extreme in this feeling. As noted in Table 2, they reported their recomposed group had clearer goals, worked harder, had a more practical and realistic discussion centered in what was going on in the group. Most significantly in view of the question of loyalties, the interaction-oriented members felt more "joined up" with their new recomposed group than the group they had been meeting with for the past three days.

On the other hand, self-oriented members (the Blue group) tended to rate more favorably the regular training group from which each had come, significantly more so on the first and last of the 12 items.

Some of the differences in reaction between self-oriented and interaction-oriented subjects may be due to the fact that interaction-oriented individuals seem to be much less interested in examining the "whys" and "wherefores" of discussion process than self-oriented persons, who are much more reflective and introverted concerning the process about them. In sensitivity training groups, efforts are made to get the group members to focus in a sophisticated way on the process of their interaction. Interaction-oriented subjects paradoxically seem desirous of avoiding looking deeply into the very phenomena from which they seem to get the greatest enjoyment. Their opinion is often verbalized, as: "People around here are trying to kill the discussion in order to dissect the corpse." The twelfth item illustrates the differences between interaction- and self-oriented groups. In comparison to the regular groups from which they had come, self-oriented supervisors reported their Blue group to be 1.5 lower in concern with content rather than process. In opposite fashion, interaction-oriented subjects noted that their Brown group was 1.4 higher in concern with content rather than process.

As seen in Table 2, like self-oriented subjects, task-oriented subjects also felt less favorably about their recomposed Purple group of only task-oriented members. They judged it was less adequate a group, had less clear goals, worked less hard, yielded a less practical and less realistic discussion. Furthermore, they felt that their recomposed group did not progress in its own development and was more intolerant of different views than the "back-home" regular training group from which each of the members had come.

The "residual" Orange group lived up to its mixed composition. Much more conflict appeared in its discussion, according to its members' negative value on Item 6, "members were out to win own points." The residual members also felt that their recomposed group was much more content oriented than the regular training group from which they had come (Item 12).

Supervisors' critique.   Before announcing the actual basis upon which the groups had been recomposed, a critique was held in an assembly of all 32 subjects after the recomposition experience. Each of the recomposed groups was asked to summarize the content and process of its discussion. Illustrative of the effects of homogeneous grouping was the comment of the spokesman for the recomposed group of highly interaction-oriented members (Brown group);

> . . . In reflecting on our postdiscussion ratings of our group, we felt that they would likely be at the highest level in comparison to what we had been going through during the past two or three days. . . . This gave us a very interesting feeling and we thought you in the laboratory did a remarkable job [in composing our Brown group]. . . . There wasn't a single excuse, argument or a difference of opinion and we all reached the same conclusions.

Secretary analyses.   After meeting in recomposed groups, the secretaries, unlike the supervisors, had not been filling out postmeeting questionnaires after each meeting. So after meeting in the recomposed groups homogeneous in orientation, each secretary completed a single five-item questionnaire. For each question she compared the recomposed with her regular training group on a nine-point scale coded $+4$ to -4. As in Table 2, a positive mean score indicated choice of the recomposed group, while a negative mean score indicated that the item was more true about the regular group. However, the measurement procedure was not directly comparable with the supervisors' ratings. With 5 or 6 df, a value $\pm.5$ generally was likely to be significantly different from 0.

Results

Contrary to expectations, all three groups tended to be more favorable in response to their recomposed group, as can be seen by the high proportion of positive responding to Items 1, 2, 3, and 4 of Table 3 concerning group quality, drive, attractiveness, and mutual interest. The recomposed groups were smaller (7 or 8) in comparison to the regular groups of 11 to 13 members, so direct comparisons may be less important then the relative contrasts between the three homogeneous, recomposed groups. Once again, the interaction-oriented secretaries, like the interaction-oriented supervisors, were most favorably inclined to their newly recomposed group. They felt their recomposed group to be best in comparison to their regular group; they felt it had worked hardest, they preferred the most to return to it rather than their regular group, and felt most compatible.

As before, the group of self-oriented subjects felt relatively more compatible in interests than the comparable assemblage of task-oriented subjects, for relatively more conflict was perceived in recomposed groups homogeneous in task orientation. However, as indicated by the negative values, all subjects saw more conflict in regular than in recomposed groups.

Secretaries critique. Again, in general session, participants were asked to describe their meeting.

The task and interaction groups spent a large portion of their time discussing aspects of the previous weeks' discussions involving the goals of development group training, while the self-oriented group utilized a great proportion of their available time introducing one another and discussing

TABLE 3

DIFFERENCES IN EVALUATION OF RECOMPOSED GROUPS OF SECRETARIES
AND THE REGULAR GROUPS FROM WHICH
MEMBERS CAME

	Mean difference in Orientation		
	Self*	Inter-action*	Task*
Comparative evaluation			
1. Quality of group.............	1.1†	1.3	.9
2. Worked hard at task..........	−.2	1.0	.3
3. Would rather return..........	.1	1.7	−.1
4. Common interests felt........	.8	.9	.3
5. Much conflict................	−1.9	−1.3	−.3

* Recomposed group.

† A positive value indicates a higher rating of the recomposed group; a negative value indicates a higher rating of the regular group.

themselves. Also, the task group spent effort examining the possibility of applying knowledge derived from the laboratory to the working situation. Some individuals seemed aware that each group contained members homogeneous in something, but none could verbalize just what these similarities were.

PART IV

Orientation of the Most Influential Members of the Recomposed Group of Members All High in a Particular Orientation

It is fairly well recognized that the traits of the successful leader depend upon the particular traits of those he leads (Bass, 1, pp. 174–77). Where physical prowess is valued by the group, the leader tends to be above the average in this trait of those he leads; where criminal tendencies are commonplace in the group, the leader is often an archcriminal; where the group is highly frustrated and resentful, the most vocally aggressive individuals are likely to come to the fore.

A working hypothesis was formulated that in a group composed solely of task-oriented members, the most influential member would tend to be outstanding in task orientation relative to the others in his group; in a group of highly interaction-oriented members, the most outstanding member in interaction orientation would tend to be most influential in the group; and in a group of self-oriented members, the most influential member would tend to be most extreme in self-orientation.

The six recomposed groups of supervisors and secretaries provided data for examining the hypothesis. Parallel findings emerged from the two samples of men and women when each subject ranked every other in his recomposed group in influencing the group. The discussant with the highest assigned mean rank by his peers was identified as successful leader of the group.

RESULTS

In the task-oriented group of seven secretaries, the leader was the highest in the group in task orientation, exactly as predicted. In the task-oriented group of eight supervisors, the leader was third highest. Similarly, the most influential secretary among interaction-oriented secretaries and the most influential supervisor among interaction-oriented supervisors were both next-to-highest in interaction orientation in their respective recomposed groups.

A complete reversal (which made sense, after discovery) occurred in parallel fashion for both secretaries and supervisors when the self-oriented discussants were analyzed. The leader of self-oriented secretaries was next-to-lowest in self-oriention while the leader of the self-oriented supervisors was tied for lowest score in self-orientation. . . .

DISCUSSION AND CONCLUSION

Modifications in Conceptualization

The interaction oriented member is now seen as considerably more superficial in his overall approach to group affairs. His concern with maintaining happy, harmonious relations makes it difficult for him to contribute to the group's progress (unless everyone in the group is interaction oriented). The interaction-oriented member's interest in group activities is at a nonfunctional level as far as the group's progress is concerned. Results here fit with unpublished learning data collected by Leo Postman suggesting that in comparison to other subjects, interaction-oriented subjects "speak before they think" in that they have a relatively high error rate coupled with the fastest attainment of an easy criterion of 9 out of 12 correction responses. In comparison, the task-oriented member is ready to examine all facets of group activities including the way members need to relate to each other in order to accomplish the purposes of their group. Despite his concern with the task, the task-oriented member works hard within the group to make it as productive as possible. It is the task-oriented member who is likely to be rated as most helpful to the group and its constituent members—although among women, derogatory feelings may be aroused because of the initiative displayed.

But why did the pooling of only task-oriented members fail to achieve an effective hard-working group? Task-oriented supervisors and secretaries seemed to be relatively less favorable to homogeneous groupings. Several unrelated factors may be involved. First, the task-oriented subject participated the most in his regular group and therefore probably had developed more of a commitment to it. He may have felt the arbitrary recomposition of membership, suddenly imposed by the training staff, to be an intrusion interrupting the work of his regular group to which he was contributing more than other members. Second, assuming that successful leadership is rewarding, the task-oriented member had relatively less opportunity for such reward once placed among other task-oriented subjects. Third, it was suggested in the critique that task-oriented subjects were more inclined to bring into their new recomposed group the particular norms and standards developed in their regular group (which they, no doubt, had been most instrumental in developing). The result was more difficulty in reaching agreement on how to proceed in the recomposed group.

While the task-oriented member emerges as the hero of the training group, as seen in our recomposed groups, for reasons indicated, it by no means leads to the extrapolation that the best group contains only task-oriented members. In addition to the specific situation just discussed, it must be reiterated that while we suggest that some subjects are generally and consistently more task oriented than others over many situations, there are various conditions when the usually task-oriented subject becomes least concerned with the task. Thus, task-oriented subjects are most likely to become apathetic when faced with a dull, irrelevant group chore not providing them a sense of accomplishment, while interaction-oriented subjects might remain content just to have the opportunity to keep interacting. For example, when dyads of subjects of varying combinations of self-, interaction, and task orientation were asked to judge photos during a regular class hour instead of doing classwork, it was interaction-oriented subjects, not the task oriented, who were most favored as partners (Campbell, 5). Yet, when the task for the dyads involved midterm examinations, interaction-oriented subjects proved themselves least agreeable and caused their partners to feel more conflict in two-man discussions about the right answers to the examinations.

As a combination of several factors including the need to dominate as well as to introspect, the self-oriented member is most likely to be rejected by others as well as to be unresponsive to the needs of his group. His concerns with himself are detrimental to his evaluation as a group member by his associates and to his likelihood of modifying his behavior in response to the group's needs in comparison to his own extrinsic demands unrelated to the task at hand. An understanding of his performance may be found in the fact that when given control of a two-way communication system, the self-oriented discussant "turns off" disagreeing partners and "turns on" agreeing ones, behaving in the Hull-Spence tradition, increasing what is immediately rewarding and avoiding what is immediately unpleasant. The behavior of interaction-and task-oriented subjects follows more dynamic theory. Their talking is positively reinforced by agreeable partners. When they can control the systems, they talk more and listen less to agreement; they talk less and listen more to disagreeing partners (Kanfer & Bass, 8). The lack of receptivity of self-oriented subjects is illustrated by a study in progress by Jerry Mendelsohn where he finds in simulated counseling that the more self-oriented the counselor or counselee, the less either agrees on what they talked about during counseling, but the more valuable they thought the counseling session. Lack of modifiability among the self-oriented seems reflected in their tendency to shift their opinions less. Rejection by peers of the self-oriented supervisors and secretaries seems consistent with the tendencies of self-oriented subjects to indicate more defense feelings under ego threat than matched interaction- or task-oriented subjects (Bass, 3) and with their greater tendency to show up as maladjusted clients at counseling centers or in institutions for juvenile delinquents.

Results of these analyses also appear consistent with a most direct exploration by Frye (7) of the proposition developed by Bass (1, pp. 153–57) of how orientation affects attempts to lead under various conditions of success and effectiveness as a leader. Frye studied 48 quartets homogeneous in one orientation or another as they discussed the solutions to a series of nine problems. After each trial, subjects were fed back false information concerning the effectiveness of the group solution as well as their success or failure in influencing others.

First, Frye found that regardless of treatment, interaction-oriented subjects spent significantly more time in discussion than subjects of other orientations, while task-oriented subjects were most attracted to these problem-solving groups after nine trials of experience. Self-oriented subjects talked the least and were least attracted to their groups at the conclusion of the experiment. However, in opposition to what had been suggested by Bass (1), when a subject was told he was influential but the resulting group solution was ineffective, he was significantly more likely to increase his attempts to lead if he was task oriented, and significantly more likely to reduce his attempts to lead if he was self-oriented. Continued failure at the task spurred the task oriented who saw himself as influential, while it deterred the self-oriented. The interaction-oriented subject was most stimulated into increasing his attempts to lead when told that the group was achieving effective decisions, but that he was not successfully influencing the group.

The success of leadership efforts may also depend on orientation. Some research by Fiedler on behavior in small heterogeneous groups indicates that, if a self-oriented subject played the role of a supervisory, authoritative leader, he tended to help the group's performance. On the other hand, a task-oriented subject playing this role tended to hinder the group's performance. If a subject played the role of a participative, permissive leader of a group, the effects were reversed—with self-oriented leaders hindering the group's performance and task-oriented leaders helping.[5]

Minimally, it seems warranted to conclude that identifying group members in advance as self-, interaction, or task oriented is a profitable discrimination that correlates consistently with patterns of leadership and other aspects of group behavior.

REFERENCES

1. Bass, B. M. *Leadership, Psychology and Organizational Behavior.* New York: Harper, 1960.
2. Bass, B. M. *Orientation Inventory.* Palo Alto, Calif.: Consulting Psychologists Press, 1962.
3. Bass, B. M. "Defensiveness and Susceptibility to Coercion as a Function of Self, Interaction and Task-Orientation." *Journal of Social Psychology,* in press.
4. Bass, B. M.; Frye, R. Dunteman, G. Vidulich, R.; and Wambach, H. "Orientation Inventory Scores Associated with Overt Behavior and Personal Factors." *Educational and Psychology Measurement,* in press.
5. Campbell, O. H. "Objective Behavior in Dyads of Self, Interaction and Task-Oriented Members." Unpublished Master's thesis, Louisiana State University, 1961.
6. Dunteman, G., and Bass, B. M. "Supervisory Success and Engineering Assignment Associated with Orientation Inventory Scores." *Personnel Psychology,* in press.
7. Frye, R. L. "The Effect of Feedback of Success and Effectiveness on Self, Task, and Interaction-Oriented Group Members." Unpublished Ph.D. dissertation, Lousiana State University, 1961.
8. Kanfer, F., and Bass, B. M. "Dyadic Speech Patterns, Orientation and Social Reinforcement." *Journal of Consulting Psychology,* in press.
9. Vernon, P. E. "The Validation of Civil Service Selection Board Procedures." *Occupational Psychology,* Vol. 24 (1950), pp. 75–95.

---

[5] Fiedler, F., private communication. Spring, 1963.

17. TASK-ORIENTED AND QUASI-THERAPEUTIC ROLE FUNCTIONS OF THE LEADER IN SMALL MILITARY GROUPS*,[1]

Edwin B. Hutchins and Fred E. Fiedler[2]

Our society expects men to perform many roles either successively or simultaneously. A policeman is a threat to some and a protector to others, and most men play the roles of husband, father, employer and employee all within the same day. Individuals differ in how readily they adapt to these varying role demands. It is also true, however, that certain roles, such as that of career woman and mother, are not easily reconciled and others are inherently incompatible.

The present study concerns two roles which the leader of a small task group is commonly asked to assume. His primary job is the maintenance of productivity. In addition, however, the armed services, as well as many industrial organizations, have urged men to take their personal problems to their immediate supervisors. The leader is thus asked to attend not only to his group's effectiveness but also to the psychological adjustment of his men. In fact, some writers have held that the leader must contribute to the group member's adjustment in order to be effective (10).

There are some indications that the practice of combining the leader's task-oriented and quasi-therapeutic roles may not be wise. Rogers (14), Traxler (18), and Roethlisberger and Dickson (13) have delineated some of the conflicts which arise when an administrator also serves as a therapist or counselor, and these problems have been discussed extensively by Slater (16). Work by Fiedler (6) and his associates indicates that effective task leadership depends on psychological distance from co-workers, while psychologically close relations are characteristic of good psychotherapists (4, 7). Opposite attitudes may thus be demanded by the roles of leader and "therapist," and these roles might then be difficult to combine.

This problem is of obvious importance not only as it contributes to our

* Reprinted from *Sociometry*, Vol. 23, No. 4 (December, 1960), pp. 393–406.

[1] This investigation was conducted under Contracts DA–49–007–MD–569 and MD–2060 with the Office of the Surgeon General, Department of the Army (Fred E. Fiedler, Principal Investigator). We are indebted to Brigadier General Carter, then Commander of the 5th Regional Air Defense Command, and his staff, for permission to test the personnel who participated in the study and their collaboration in the research. We are indebted to Dr. Lee J. Cronbach for his suggestions regarding the treatment of the scores.

[2] University of Illinois. Edwin B. Hutchins is now Research Associate, Association of American Medical Colleges, Evanston, Illinois.

understanding of leadership and group behavior, but also as it affects the management of small groups in industry and in the armed services. Having a man consult his leader about his personal problems might not only retard the man's adjustment, but it may also force the leader into a role which arouses conflicts within him and which could, therefore, be detrimental to group effectiveness.

BACKGROUND OF THE PROBLEM

This study is an outgrowth of two recent research programs which related interpersonal perception measures (Assumed Similarity, AS) to group effectiveness and to informal relations which contribute to personal adjustment. These scores require a subject to describe himself by means of a short personality questionnaire and then to describe others by using the same questionnaire. A comparison of any two ratings of others, or of a self rating and another rating, then indicates the degree of similarity which the subject assumes to exist between the ratees.

Earlier work with AS scores showed that reputedly good therapists assume a higher degree of similarity between themselves and their patients than do reputedly poorer therapists (7). Liked persons are also seen as more similar by the perceiver than are persons he does not like (8). These findings led to the interpretation that high AS indicates feelings of warmth and acceptance of another person.

A second group of studies, utilizing the score Assumed Similarity between Opposites (ASo), was concerned with the leader's influence on group effectiveness. ASo is obtained when we compare the subject's description of the most preferred and of the least preferred co-workers he has ever known. High ASo has been interpreted as indicating a feeling of acceptance toward co-workers, while low ASo presumably indicates psychological distance and reserve, especially to persons who are seen as poor co-workers. The findings have consistently shown that sociometrically accepted leaders with low ASo tended to have more effective groups than those with high ASo (6). These two lines of investigation suggested that the roles required of an effective leader and of a quasi-therapeutic person may be incompatible.

Four specific hypotheses were tested.

Hypothesis I. In groups in which the leader is sociometrically accepted, the leader's ASo will correlate negatively with group effectiveness, i.e., psychologically distant leaders will have better groups than will leaders who perceive similarity to their co-workers.

This hypothesis is essentially an extrapolation of earlier findings to a group setting in which psychological maintenance functions are relatively important. The qualification that ASo will correlate only in groups having sociometrically accepted leaders requires a word of explanation. As has been pointed out in a previous paper (6), the attempt to predict group effectiveness by leader attitudes assumes that the leader's attitude will affect the men who perform criterion-relevant tasks. This is unlikely to occur unless the men are willing to be influenced by their leader. This willingness was here assessed by means of sociometric preference ratings. Since this hypothesis represents a replication of earlier work, it is one-tailed, testing whether the correlation is significantly greater than zero in the negative direction.

The second hypothesis asks whether ASo is related to group adjustment. The "great man theory" of leadership holds that a person with skills in dealing with one set of interpersonal problems will tend also to have competence in other areas of interpersonal relations. Hence:

Hypothesis II. The ASo score of the accepted group leader will correlate negatively with the average personality adjustment scores of his group members.

Previous research has shown that reputedly better therapists perceived their patients as more similar. From ratings made by the group leader we derived an analogous measure, the leader's Assumed Similarity to his group $(\overline{ASg})$. $\overline{ASg}$ indicates the average similarity which the leader perceives between himself and four other members of his group. On the basis of previous work we would, therefore, expect a positive correlation between $\overline{ASg}$ and the personality adjustment of the group. Hence:

Hypothesis III. The $\overline{ASg}$ score of the accepted group leader will be positively related to the group's adjustment.

Finally, we ask whether the person who perceives his actual fellow group members as similar to himself will also have a more effective group. Hence:

Hypothesis IV. The $\overline{ASg}$ score of the accepted group leader is positively correlated with group effectiveness.

PROCEDURE

The data for this study were collected in the context of a larger research program investigating quasi-therapeutic relations among members of small fact-to-face groups (9).

Subjects

Participating in this study were 53 units of an Air Defense Command. Of these, 14 were radar-tracking units and 39 were gun crews. A total of 483 men were tested.

In contrast to most other military units stationed in the United States, these are operational, combat-ready troops. The men live and work together at close quarters, and the stations are frequently located in fairly isolated areas. Each unit is commanded by a senior noncommissioned officer. The unit commander has power to grant or withhold passes, and he sets up work schedules and administers discipline for minor infractions.

The size of the units varied from six to 17 men. The subjects averaged 22.7 years of age and 11.2 years of schooling. Their average Army General Classification Test score was 101.2. Approximately 40 per cent of the men were married. Service in their assignment at the time of testing averaged 6.5 months. While the crews remain in existence over a relatively long time, a group can be composed of entirely different men within a year's time because of the continuous personnel turnover.

The Questionnaires

Measures of leader acceptance as well as of interpersonal perception and personal adjustment were obtained. Cooperation on the part of the men was satisfactory throughout. Only three individuals in 486 declined to cooperate in the study.

Sociometrics. The sociometric rating form contained six questions. Questions 1 and 2 were designed to measure acceptance of the leader on task-oriented functions. These asked the group members to list in order of preference the three men they would prefer (*a*) as leader if their unit were to come under unexpected attack, and (*b*) to have in their unit if they were to go into combat. Questions 3 and 4, designed to measure leader acceptance in a quasi-therapeutic role, asked the subject (*a*) whom in the group he would consult if he had personal problems, and (*b*) whom he considered best in helping a new man get used to the group and the work. Finally, whether the leader played the friendship role was determined by asking the subject (*a*) which man he liked best personally (Question 5) and (*b*) with which man he would prefer to go on a leave (Question 6).

First, second and third choices on these questions were weighted 3, 2, and 1. A group member was defined as "accepted" if he received the highest number of choices within his group on any specific question. We were thus able to dichotomize the formal leaders into those who did and those who did not receive the highest number of choices on a given question. The friendship cluster was discarded since only 10 per cent of the leaders were accepted on Question 5 and 5 per cent on Question 6.

The average percentage of leaders accepted on Questions 1 to 4 was 46, and allows us to discriminate accepted vs. nonaccepted leaders in a proportion consistent with previous findings on groups of this nature.

The *informal leader* (*IL*) role (Questions 1 and 2) involves task-oriented, managerial behaviors on the part of the role occupant which contribute to maximizing group performance. The *therapeutic figure* (*TF*) role (Questions 3 and 4) involves behavior contributing to the psychological well-being of group members. If the formal leader (*FL*) received more choices than any other group member on a given cluster, he was considered as accepted by the group in that role.

Of the 41 crew commanders on whom we had complete data, 18 were accepted both as informal leader and therapeutic figure ($FL = IL = TF$). An additional eight commanders were accepted as informal leaders but were not endorsed as therapeutic figures ($FL = IL \neq TF$). The residual sample of 15 includes crew commanders not selected as the primary occupants for either role ($FL \neq IL \neq TF$). None of the unit commanders was accepted in the therapeutic role without also being accepted as informal leader.

In summary we concern ourselves with these five sociometrically determined samples:

$FL = IL = TF$	$N = 18$
$FL = IL \neq TF$	$N = 8$
$FL = IL$ (Pooled Sample)	$N = 26$
$FL \neq IL \neq TF$	$N = 15$
FL (Total Sample)	$N = 41$

Assumed Similarity Scores. A 20-item graphic rating scale was used to obtain descriptions of self and of others. The form of the scale followed Osgood's Semantic Differential. Examples of the items are given below:

Friendly X___:___:___:___:___:___: Unfriendly
Cooperative X___:___:___:___:___:___: Uncooperative
Stable ___:__X__:___:___:___:___: Unstable

The subject described himself by checking the space which most adequately represented his judgment of himself. He was then asked to describe his most and least preferred co-workers and the four men in his unit with whom he worked most closely, using identical scales.

Basically, Assumed Similarity (AS) scores compare by means of the D statistic (2, 12), two ratings obtained from a single individual. The greater the likeness of the profiles, the higher the degree of similarity the subject presumably sees in the two ratees.

Assumed Similarity between Opposites (ASo). In the above illustration of the scales, let the X represent the subject's description of his most preferred co-worker on each of the items. Thus, the subject marked the first three items toward the positive ends of the scales, giving values of 1, 1, and 2. Let us assume that he described his least preferred co-worker by marking the corresponding items at points 6, 5, and 5. D is obtained by taking the square root of the sum of the squared item differences. In this case, the squared differences would be 25 on the first item, 16 on the second item, and 9 on the third item, yielding a sum of 50. D is the square root of this sum and here equals 7.07.

Note that the amount of similarity assumed by the subject is *inversely* related to the size of the D score. The more similar a leader sees his most and least preferred co-workers, the more his two descriptions of them coincide and the smaller his D score. Thus, a subject referred to here as a *high ASo* leader is one having a *small D* score.

Average Assumed Similarity to the Group $(\overline{ASg})$. An Assumed Similarity score can be computed between any pair of scale sheets completed by the subject. $\overline{ASg}$ was obtained by computing the D *between the self rating and each of the leader's four ratings of his actual co-workers.* The four obtained D's were then averaged. The resulting score, $\overline{ASg}$, was here considered to be conceptually analogous to the Assumed Similarity measure obtained in the client-therapist study (7). The measures ASo and $\overline{ASg}$ were unrelated in our sample (rho $= .10$, $N = 41$).

Reliability of Assumed Similarity Scores. Previous studies on Assumed Similarity have consistently reported adequate reliabilities for these scores. The Spearman rank order relability coefficient of ASo, based on an odd-even item split, was .70. A reliability for $\overline{ASg}$ was obtained by comparing the $\overline{ASg}$ score based on ratings of the first and third co-workers with that based on the second and fourth co-workers. The rank order correlation of these two measures was .75. Since rank order methods were used in computing these reliability estimates, the Spearman-Brown prophecy formula is not an appropriate correction for length. These correlations, therefore, represent the lower bounds of an estimate and appear to be of adequate magnitude.

THE CRITERIA

Two types of criterion measures were required for this study: (*a*) measures of group effectiveness and (*b*) measures of the group members' personal adjustment.

Group Effectiveness

The primary mission of these groups is the defense against aerial attack of their geographical region. Although the crews vary in specific tasks, all are required to (*a*) acquire or locate targets with electronic equipment; (*b*) maintain their radar sets or guns, both of which are highly intricate pieces of equipment, and (*c*) man the equipment with utmost dispatch when required. Because adequate performance scores, which would be comparable for all groups, could not be developed, the main criterion of group effectiveness was based on subjective ratings. Officers in charge of radar areas or gun batteries were asked to make rankings of the crews under their command. These were concerned with target acquisition (radar) or effectiveness (guns) and equipment maintenance. To check the validity of the ratings, we compared, wherever possible, the reliable objective criteria with the subjective ratings. Where this could be done we found substantial agreement.

Reliability of Subjective Ratings. The agreement among raters for each type of rating obtained in each area or battery was assessed by Kendall's coefficient of concordance, W (15). The median W obtained from the twelve sets of target acquisition or effectiveness ratings was .78. The analogous set of maintenance ratings yielded a median W of .75. Each unit's average rank over raters was determined for each of the three criteria, and all scores were then transformed to make ratings in groups with different N's equivalent. These transformed scores, based on the averaged rank scores, comprised our scales of effectiveness and maintenance. These two measures correlated .80 and were, therefore, combined into a single measure of unit performance.

Group Adjustment

Group adjustment was defined in this study as the average personal adjustment score obtained by crew members. Scores from two self-rating inventories and a sick-call index were included in a composite index of adjustment.

The Taylor Scale of Manifest Anxiety. The Taylor Scale is composed of 50 items from the Minnesota Multiphasic Personality Inventory which contains self report items of overt signs of anxiety (17). Forty of these items were chosen for inclusion in the present study. The other ten items were dropped because they demand a verbal level beyond that reached by a substantial number of the subjects.

The General Army Adjustment Inventory. This scale is based on the assumption that an individual who is motivated to remain and succeed in a particular activity is better adjusted to the situation than a person wishing to withdraw. It measures such attitudes as one's willingness to go into combat, satisfaction with army training, feeling that one's job is worthwhile, etc. (11).

The rank order split half reliability coefficient for individual subjects was .82 for the Taylor Scale and .56 for the General Army Adjustment Inventory. Again these correlations represent minimum estimates.

While these scales appeared to have sufficient internal consistency, the reliabilities of the group adjustment means were considerably lower. The rank order correlation between mean Taylor scores based on a random split of group members was .22 (uncorrected). The analogous estimate for the uncorrected reliability of the General Army Adjustment group mean was .18. These lower reliabilities suggest that the leader's influence on adjustment is relatively weak.

Dispensary Visits. On the basis of dispensary visits, the medical officer was asked to judge which of the visits could be considered psychophysiological in origin. Thus, a lower-back pain syndrome with no diagnosed

TABLE 1
SPEARMAN RANK ORDER INTERCORRELATIONS AMONG GROUP MEANS OF THREE
INDICES OF ADJUSTMENT (RHO'S BASED ON $N = 52*$)

	General Army Adjustment Index	Dispensary Visits
Taylor Scale of Manifest Anxiety........37†		.31†
General Army Adjustment Index.........		.02

* One gun crew was dropped from our sample because of insufficient data.
† Significant at the .05 level of confidence.

organic basis was judged to fall into this category, as against continuing visits to have a broken arm dressed. A group measure was obtained by dividing a two-month total of dispensary visits judged psychophysiological in origin by the number of men in the unit. The uncorrected rank order reliability coefficient for this measure, based on a random split of group members, was .60.

Interrelations Among the Criteria of Adjustment. Table 1 presents the rank order correlations among the group means of the three measures outlined above. The matrix of intercorrelations among individual scores was highly similar. The significant correlation between Taylor Anxiety and General Army Adjustment reflects in part the fact that they are both self ratings. The relation between Taylor scores and dispensary visits provides some evidence for the validity of the Taylor Scale. A composite measure of group adjustment was developed by ranking each group on each adjustment measure and then simply adding the ranks. Each measure was, therefore, equally weighted in the composite index which has an estimated reliability of .50.

Interrelations of Group Effectiveness and Adjustment. While we made no formal prediction concerning the relation between group effectiveness and adjustment, the hypotheses imply zero or negative correlations. Indeed low negative correlations were found in the sociometric samples of most concern to the study (Lines 1 and 3, Table 2). The fact that no significant

TABLE 2
SPEARMAN RANK ORDER CORRELATIONS BETWEEN GROUP EFFECTIVE-
NESS AND GROUP ADJUSTMENT FOR VARIOUS SAMPLES
BASED ON SOCIOMETRIC QUESTIONS

Sociometric Sample	N	rho
$FL = IL = TF$............................18		−.25
$FL = IL \neq TF$............................ 8		−.04
$FL = IL$............................26		−.17
$FL \neq IL \neq TF$............................15		.26
FL......................................41		−.13

relationship was obtained between group effectiveness and adjustment has important implications for a "great man" theory of leadership. Leaders who fit the "great man" description presumably should be able to affect positively both group effectiveness and adjustment. If such leaders do in fact exist, they are likely to constitute a small minority. This finding, apparently, does not support the results of a laboratory study by Borgatta, Couch, and Bales (1).

RESULTS

Previous work led to hypotheses concerning relations between the accepted leader's Assumed Similarity scores and (a) group effectiveness and (b) the average level of adjustment attained by group members. This study tested whether the factors which are important to effective leadership would also be important in aiding others to adjust. Two measures of the leader's Assumed Similarity, ASo and $\overline{ASg}$, were, therefore, correlated under various sociometric conditions with the measures of group effectiveness and adjustment.

Relation of Leader's ASo to Criteria of Group Behavior

The ASo score of the accepted leader $(FL = IL)$ correlated negatively with group effectiveness (rho = −.36, Table 3). This result supports Hypothesis I and further extends the validity of previously reported findings. These results again show that the leader must have influence with his men (sociometric endorsement) in order to affect their behavior. The highest correlation (−.66) was found between group effectiveness and the ASo scores of accepted leaders who were not therapeutic figures. A comparison of the effectiveness scores of various sociometric subsamples was made. This revealed no significant differences in performance of

TABLE 3

SPEARMAN RANK ORDER CORRELATIONS* BETWEEN LEADER'S ASo AND THE CRITERIA
OF GROUP EFFECTIVENESS AND ADJUSTMENT FOR
VARIOUS SOCIOMETRIC SAMPLES

Sociometric Sample	N	Group Effectiveness	Group Adjustment
$FL = IL = TF$.........18		−.34	−.08
$FL = IL \neq TF$.......... 8		−.66†	−.19
$FL = IL$................26		−.36†	−.08
$FL \neq IL \neq TF$.........15		−.07	−.02
FL....................41		−.19	−.03

* High Assumed Similarity (small D score) received a rank of 1 as did good effectiveness and adjustment.
† Significant at the .05 level, one-tailed test.

groups which accepted their commanders in a quasi-therapeutic role ($FL = IL = TF$) and those which accepted their leaders only in a task-oriented role ($FL = IL \neq TF$) ($p = .80$). On the other hand, the groups which accepted their commanders were more effective than those which rejected theirs ($FL \neq IL \neq TF$) ($p = .01$). These groups did not differ on the group adjustment criterion. As expected, correlations between ASo and effectiveness were not significant in the residual sample ($FL \neq IL \neq TF$) or in the total sample (FL).

No systematic relations were found between the leader's ASo and group adjustment regardless of the leader's acceptance by the group (Column 2, Table 3). Hypothesis II was, therefore, not supported.

Relation of Leader's $\overline{ASg}$ to Group Behavior

Hypothesis III posited a significant positive correlation between the $\overline{ASg}$ of accepted leaders and the adjustment of their groups. Table 4 shows that this prediction was not supported. Mean $\overline{ASg}$ and group adjustment were correlated significantly only where the formal leader was not accepted either as a therapeutic figure or as an informal leader ($FL \neq IL \neq TF$) (rho = .55). The significance of this finding is probably best understood through an analysis of the simple component scores which comprise the complex, dyadic score, $\overline{ASg}$. The main findings of such a component analysis are discussed below.

The final hypothesis predicted a positive relationship between the $\overline{ASg}$ of the accepted leader and the task performance of the group. Reference to Column 1 of Table 4 shows that positive correlations were obtained for these samples, although only the relationship in the total sample reached statistical significance.

To summarize the results:

(a) No relation was found between group effectiveness and group member adjustment.

(b) The score, Assumed Similarity between Opposites (ASo) of so-

TABLE 4

SPEARMAN RANK ORDER CORRELATIONS* BETWEEN LEADER'S $\overline{ASg}$ AND THE CRITERIA OF GROUP EFFECTIVENESS AND ADJUSTMENT FOR VARIOUS SOCIOMETRIC SAMPLES

Sociometric Sample	N	Group Effectiveness	Group Adjustment
$FL = IL = TF$..........18		.45	.24
$FL = IL \neq TF$.......... 8		.08	−.21
$FL = IL$................26		.34	.00
$FL \neq IL \neq TF$..........15		.36	.55†
FL.....................41		.31†	.13

* High Assumed Similarity (small D score) received a rank of 1 as did good effectiveness an adjustment.

† Significant at the .05 level, two-tailed test.

ciometrically accepted leaders correlated with the group effectiveness criterion in the expected direction $(-.36)$.

(c) A significant positive correlation was obtained for the total sample between $\overline{ASg}$ and group effectiveness $(.31)$.

(d) Contrary to Hypothesis II and IV, no systematic relationship was found between the accepted leader's ASo and $\overline{ASg}$ scores and the adjustment of his group.

(e) For the leader who was *not* endorsed by the group, average Assumed Similarity to actual co-workers $(\overline{ASg})$ correlated positively with the group adjustment criterion $(.55)$.

DISCUSSION

This study presented a further validation of a series of earlier investigations which related the accepted leader's ASo score to group performance criteria. The primary purpose of this investigation was, however, to test whether attitudes which are conducive to group effectiveness are detrimental to group adjustment. While this hypothesis was not confirmed, the opposite point of view, that the attitude which is conducive to group productivity will also aid group adjustment, likewise found no support. In fact, this paper showed that group effectiveness and group adjustment tend to be negatively correlated albeit insignificantly so, when the leader is accepted by his group. This finding is thus not in accord with results of a laboratory study on the "great man" theory by Borgatta, Couch, and Bales (1). However, differences in design and selection of sample might well account for this discrepancy in findings.

A different picture is presented by Table 4, which showed relations of group effectiveness and adjustment with the measure Average Assumed Similarity to Group Members, $\overline{ASg}$. Here we find generally positive correlations which, according to previous research, would indicate that the leader's feeling of closeness to his immediate co-workers is related both to effectiveness and to adjustment criteria.

However, an analysis of the $\overline{ASg}$ score into its components indicated that one component of $\overline{ASg}$, the leader's average rating of others in his group, yielded significant and higher correlations with both criteria for the total sample than did the complex $\overline{ASg}$ score or any of the other components. In other words, the leader's average "esteem" of the four group members whom he rated correlated significantly with group effectiveness (rho $= +.38$, $N = 41$) as well as with group adjustment (rho $= +.33$, $N = 41$). The results of this analytic approach clearly support Cronbach's recent methodological suggestion in this area that complex interpersonal perception scores should be analyzed into their components to provide clearer interpretation of the data (3).

At least two interpretations of these results as substantive findings appear plausible. Since *ASo* correlates more highly with group effectiveness than any of the components we have investigated, the *D* statistic appears to be one possible method for assessing information in the most and least preferred co-worker profiles. We did find, though, that most of the variance in *ASo* can be attributed to the variance between most and least preferred co-workers. This component in turn is heavily weighted with the esteem score on the least preferred co-worker profile. While previous studies spoke of *ASo* as a generalized measure of distance from co-workers, it appears on the basis of these findings that effective leadership requires two divergent attitudes. Distance from group members who are considered to be poor co-workers is required, as well as esteem of or closeness to those co-workers who are both task-oriented and who see themselves as well adjusted. In other words, the effective leader perceived relatively great distance from his least preferred co-workers, but he saw his preferred co-workers as close and acceptable.

Alternatively, the data lend themselves equally well to the interpretation that the score $\overline{ASg}$ is a direct reflection of the group member's adjustment and effectiveness: the leader will rate men more highly if they perform well and if they appear well adjusted.

Our conclusions are, of course, limited by the fact that both criteria of this study leave much to be desired. The group effectiveness criterion was based on officers' ratings. These were in turn based on fairly objective performance criteria and are, therefore, probably fairly accurate. The second criterion measure was a combined adjustment index. This measure was reliable for individual administration, but only about 25 percent of the variance of this measure appeared to be related to group and/or leadership factors. Under these conditions we could not expect to obtain very high correlations between any predictors, such as leaders' Assumed Similarity scores and group adjustment measures. The results of this study strongly suggest, however, that a replication would be highly desirable if more reliable group adjustment measures could be obtained.

SUMMARY AND CONCLUSIONS

A study was conducted to test whether the interpersonal attitudes of a leader of a small military group influenced the group members' adjustment as well as their effectiveness. Leader attitudes were measured by means of two independent Assumed Similarity scores, Assumed Similarity between Opposites (*ASo*) and Assumed Similarity to the group ($\overline{ASg}$). Members of 53 antiaircraft artillery units participated in the study. The criteria of group effectiveness consisted of officers' ratings of units. Personal adjustment was measured by a composite index based on Taylor Manifest Anxiety scale items, the General Army Adjustment Scale, and the average number of dispensary visits per unit.

Previous studies using *ASo* have obtained significant relations between this variable and group effectiveness. This finding has again been confirmed in the present investigation for another group setting, one in which maintenance or sustaining functions are relatively important.

Contrary to theoretical expectations epitomized in the "great man" theory of leadership, no relation was obtained between group effectiveness and group adjustment. Similarly, leader attitudes reflected by *ASo* scores appear to be unrelated to group adjustment in this study.

An analytic treatment of the two interpersonal perception scores used suggested an alternative interpretation of *ASo* as a measure of psychological distance. The effective leader appears to be distant only from poor co-workers, rather than from all of his co-workers.

REFERENCES

1. BORGATTA, E. F.; COUCH, A. S; AND BALES, R. F. "Some Findings Relevant to the Great Man Theory of Leadership," *American Sociological Review,* Vol. 19 (1954), pp. 755–59.

2. CRONBACH, L. J., AND GLESER, G. C. "Assessing Similarity between Profiles," *Psychological Bulletin,* Vol. 50 (1953), pp. 456–73.

3. CRONBACH, L. J. "Proposals Leading to Analytic Treatment of Social Perception Scores," in R. Tagiuri and L. Petrullo, *Person Perception and Interpersonal Behavior.* Stanford, California: Stanford University Press, 1958.

4. FIEDLER, F. E. "An Investigation into the Concept of the Ideal Therapeutic Relationship," *Journal of Consulting Psychology,* Vol. 14 (1950) pp. 239–49.

5. FIEDLER, F. E. "The Psychological Distance Dimension in Interpersonal Relations," *Journal of Personality,* Vol. 22 (1953), pp. 142–50.

6. FIEDLER, F. E. *Leader Attitudes and Group Effectiveness.* Urbana, Ill.: University of Illinois Press, 1958.

7. FIEDLER, F. E., and Senior, Kate. "An Exploratory Study of Unconscious Feeling Reactions in Fifteen Patient-Therapist Pairs," *Journal of Abnormal and Social Psychology,* Vol. 47 (1952), pp. 446–53.

8. FIEDLER, F. E.; BLAISDELL, F. J.; AND WARRINGTON, W. G. "Unconscious Attitudes as Correlates of Sociometric Choice in a Social Group," *Journal of Abnormal and Social Psychology,* Vol. 47 (1952), pp. 790–96.

9. FIEDLER, F. E.; HUTCHINS, E. B.; AND DODGE, J. S. "Quasi-Therapeutic Relations in Small College and Military Groups," *Psychological Monographs,* Vol. 73, No. 3 (1959) (Whole No. 473).

10. GORDON, T. *Group Centered Leadership,* Boston, Mass.: Houghton Mifflin Co., 1955.

11. HAVRON, M. D.; FAY, R. J.; AND GOODACRE, III, D. M. "Research on the Effectiveness of Small Military Units." PRS Report No. 885. Institute for Research on Human Relations, 1951.

12. OSGOOD, C. E., AND SUCI, G. "A Measure of Relation Determined by Both Mean Difference and Profile Information," *Psychological Bulletin,* Vol. 49 (1952), pp. 251–62.

13. ROETHLISBERGER, F. J., AND DICKSON, W. J. *Management and the Worker.* Cambridge, Mass.: Harvard University Press, 1938.

14. ROGERS, C. R. *Client-Centered Therapy.* Boston, Mass.: Houghton Mifflin Co., 1951.

15. SIEGEL, S. *Nonparametric Statistics for the Behavioral Sciences.* New York: McGraw-Hill Book Co., 1956.

16. SLATER, P. E. "Role Differentiation in Small Groups," *American Sociological Review,* Vol. 20 (1955), pp. 300–310.

17. TAYLOR, JANET A. "A Personality Scale of Manifest Anxiety," *Journal of Abnormal and Social Psychology,* Vol. 48 (1953), pp. 285–90.

18. TRAXLER, A. E. *Techniques of Guidance.* New York: Harper & Bros., 1945.

18. ADMINISTRATIVE REWARDS AND COORDINATION AMONG COMMITTEE MEMBERS*

ALVIN ZANDER AND DONALD WOLFE

Members of coordinating committees may develop contrasting and even conflicting intentions: to help their colleagues, to accomplish their individual assignments, and to work on the group's task.

A number of coordinating committees in a large business firm were given an experimental task designed to simulate the conceptual character- istics of their committees. The effects of three different experimental conditions were examined, each conceived as likely to generate one or another of the three motives just described, and each representing a fea- sible emphasis in the reward system of a large organization. The results reveal that the potential rewards for individual success, group success, or both, create quite different styles of interpersonal relations and varied de- grees of effectiveness in collaboration among members.[1]

Alvin Zander is professor of psychology and director of the Research Center for Group Dynamics, University of Michigan, and Donald Wolfe is associate professor of organizational behavior in the Division of Organi- zational Science, Case Institute of Technology.

THE IMPORTANCE of developing coordination among the parts of large organizations has gained increased recognition in recent years. The com- plex interdependence among departments has led to more and more emphasis on organizational teamwork, yet the collaboration desired often cannot be achieved through the workings of the traditional hierarchy. A more direct form of cooperation and mutual facilitation is wanted. We observe, therefore, a growing dependence on coordinating committees.

But participation in a committee frequently poses a dilemma for the member. In an executive committee his unique interests are on one side of this dilemma, the committee's agenda on the other. These contrasting concerns usually create no great conflict, however, because good form requires the member to be attentive to the group's performance and to hold in abeyance his self-oriented needs.[2] In a coordinating committee the dilemma is more complicated and less easily controlled, for the member is expected simultaneously to be helpful on the group's task, to help other

---

* Reprinted from *Administrative Science Quarterly*, Vol. 9, No. 1 (June, 1964), pp. 50–69.

[1] We are grateful to Robert Barnes for his help in the administration of this ex- periment and in the analysis of the results.

[2] Fouriezos N., M. Hutt, and H. Guetzkow, "Measurement of Self Oriented Needs in Discussion Groups," *Journal of Abnormal and Social Psychology*, Vol. 45 (1950), pp. 682–90.

members solve their individual problems, and to be concerned about his own attainments.

An adequate balance among these goals is often hard to maintain. Interaction patterns which are appropriate to helping others or to working on the group task may be (or appear to be) inappropriate to one's own goal-directed activity. The cost to personal success may undermine the very function that coordinating committees are established to perform. To make matters worse, the organization frequently rewards personal achievement more than collaboration.

An opportunity to investigate the effects of such contrasting motives arose in a company's request for a study of their coordinating committees. The company contains 23 geographical districts, each a near duplicate of the others and each having four or five departments. Although the work of each department is specialized, its functioning is contingent upon the others. The heads of the departments within each district meet every month to discuss problems of coordination among their activities. Primary attention is given to changes in the procedures of one department that may be beneficial to one or more of the others.

Each coordinating committee develops its own agenda and elects its own discussion leader. Minutes of the committees' meetings are sent to the company headquarters. Each district level department head is responsible to and evaluated by a different superordinate in the central offices; thus each superior receives copies of all the minutes. Because these reports are a source of revelation about the plans, progress, and collaboration among committee members, extreme care is taken in wording the minutes so that they present the best possible picture of all activities in the district.

The questions posed by the company for this study were broad and general: What goes on in the meetings and why? Why are some committees more effective than others? What can be done to improve their effectiveness? The separate concerns among the members of top management were more specific. Some managers believed that, given interdependence among departments, any decisions a committee might make would tend to improve the effectiveness of each department. Others wondered if the attention devoted to coordination might undermine the effectiveness of the separate departments, since many of the issues which arise in the committees are highly complex and require time and energy on matters extending well beyond the scope of the individual member's responsibility and experience. In general, there was some doubt whether mutual and supportive relationships occurred as much as they ideally should, for each department head was rewarded primarily for the performance of his own department and would therefore wish the record to show he was loyal to his department's favored practices even though such actions might not reduce the problems facing the heads of other departments.

It was apparent from informal visits to a few of the committees as well as from observations and concerns of higher managers that the members of these committees were torn between strategies of collaboration and independent action. It became clear, moreover, that the relative emphasis placed on these strategies by top management and the general reward system of the organization played a major role in the strategic choices of the group members. It became just as clear that one could not gain an adequate understanding of the intragroup processes by observing regular meetings alone. The topics in the separate districts differed in urgency, time depth, importance, and in their demands for collaboration. Without close familiarity of the technical features in the firm's operations, moreover, valid judgments about degrees of collaboration or their appropriateness could not readily be made. A more objective investigation of the conditions under which members are and are not motivated to help one another was required.

A committee "assessment test" was therefore developed in which the motives of the members were conceived in generalizable terms. A standardized task was administered to each committee, designed to contain the conceptual characteristics of a coordinating committee. The task was administered under contrasting conditions, and the different consequences of each were observed. The conditions simulated the essence of the queries made by managers: the effects of interest in personal success, in group success, or both.

RATIONALE AND METHOD

The motives among group members who must coordinate their efforts for the benefit of others as well as of themselves are restated in the following assumptions.

1. A member's standards of behavior in a committee are determined by the criteria a socially powerful person uses when he evaluates the performance of the member. Usually this standard-setter is a superior in the parent organization of the committee.

2. A member whose actions win approval from the powerful person is conceived as attaining a *reward*. A member whose activities generate disapproval is conceived as incurring a *cost*. These terms, *reward* and *cost*, are used in the ways Thibaut and Kelley[3] and Homans[4] have employed them.

3. Each member is motivated to increase his rewards and to reduce his costs. No member wishes to decrease his rewards or increase his cost.

[3] J. Thibaut and H. Kelley, *The Social Psychology of Groups* (New York: John Wiley & Sons, 1959).

[4] G. Homans, *Social Behavior, Its Elementary Forms* (New York: Harcourt Brace & World, 1961).

4. Each participant may to some degree determine his colleagues' rewards and costs. He may be motivated to increase others' rewards and to reduce their costs, to reduce their rewards and increase their costs, or to ignore their rewards and costs, if in so doing he ensures an increase in his own rewards and a reduction in his own costs. The most viable relationship among persons, as proposed by Thibaut and Kelley,[5] is one in which their interactions serve mutually to increase rewards and to reduce costs.

The questions posed by managers may now be rephrased in the above terms. Under what conditions is there greater concern with their own rewards and costs than with the rewards and costs of other persons? What are the further consequences of these conditions for interpersonal relations and individual performance? The standardized task provided an opportunity for participants to create rewards and costs for themselves and others as they wished, and for us to examine the frequency of their choices under different experimental conditions.

The Basic Experimental Task

The conference room in the local offices of each geographical district was used as a laboratory. The committee members were informed by higher management, prior to their testing session, that they were to have an "assessment" of their group and that the testing was to be done by members of the university faculty at the request of the company. The participants were 113 members of the 23 committees, all men, all members of middle management, all at the same level in the company hierarchy.[6]

The members were asked to sit along one side of a large conference table. Across the room was a vertical board 1.5 feet square with two large letters, X and Y, cut out on the face of it. The letters were backed by frosted glass and each could be illuminated red or white by the experimenter (E), making four combinations possible: X white and Y white, X red and Y red, X white and Y red, X red and Y white. Both letters were always lighted simultaneously during the experiment. A predetermined randomized program of illuminations was followed for all trials.

The subjects were informed that this was a test of "work-group intelligence," a vague but important-sounding ability, deliberately undefined for the subjects. Each participant, they were told, was to predict, on a private written ballot, how the X and the Y would be lighted in each of a series of trials. For each correct prediction on either or both letters he would win a given number of points. The points were his

---

[5] *Op. cit.*

[6] The total assessment employed mailed questionnaires, personal interviews, and controlled observations of committee meetings as well as the experimental sessions described below. Only the results of the experiment are presented in these pages.

potential reward, analogous to an approval-winning decision in a regular meeting of the committee.

It was possible, they were informed, for a participant to make his predictions with absolute certainty of being correct. This certainty could be achieved in either of two ways: by obtaining the correct information from E or by obtaining it from another participant. These rules made it possible to introduce both the need and the means for interaction and for this interaction to determine the distribution of rewards and costs among members. The experiment was structured as follows.

Any or all members could request E to tell them ahead of the prediction deadline the correct answer for either X or Y, but not for both. Each subject was provided a small panel at his place containing two electrical switches and two small lights. These were for communication between the subject and E. Shielding over each panel made privacy possible; a subject could send a request for correct information to E and receive it from E without others in the group knowing that he was doing so. If the subject pressed the button marked X, he wished to know what color X would be on the next trial. If he pressed the button marked Y, he wished to know what color Y would be. The experimenter could communicate this information to the subject by lighting, from his control station, either a red or a white light on the subject's panel. When a subject was granted information by E, however, his total number of points was reduced by the amount he would then have won by possession of that information. A unilateral purchase of correct information from E, therefore, provided no more potential reward than cost. Because a member could obtain only half of the correct information via a purchase from E, he was dependent on other members for additional information, and was also in a position to be helpful to others, if he wished to be.

Any member could request from a colleague what color X or Y, or both, would be on the next trial. The request and response, however, had to be in writing and addressed to a specific individual. Three minutes were allowed between prediction deadlines to allow sufficient time for such communication among members. All messages were given to E and delivered by him to the addressee; no oral remarks or other signals were allowed. The messages were later collected by E and serve as a record of intermember interaction.

It was permissible, furthermore, for members to request E to transfer points from their own point totals to the totals of any other persons on the committee. Thus one who desired the correct information could buy it from another for any number of points, provided he could find a colleague who would sell it to him. And, anyone who had the correct information could offer to sell it to colleagues. Such buying and selling of information represented the opportunity a member had to reduce the costs of others (buying from them) or to reduce his own costs (selling to them). Finally each member was allowed to give the information to recipients at no cost, thereby increasing their rewards without either reducing his own costs or increasing theirs. Thus, one member could provide another with correct information (so the latter could make a correct prediction and increase his own rewards), or he could provide him with points (to increase the other's rewards and reduce the other's costs). It should be clear that members were free to collaborate with others as much or as little as they wished. The rules were such, however, that personal scores would benefit from collaborative effort.

Experimental Conditions

All groups were taught the basic experimental task and worked on it for a series of six trials, designated as Test One. The participants were told that the first six trials were to ensure that they understood the rules and the various possibilities for interpersonal collaboration during the test. Their individual scores were reported to them privately after each trial. At the end of the sixth trial the following three experimental conditions, each containing six groups, were introduced. There were five groups in the control treatment. The system for each condition was described to the subjects as "rules for determining scores on the test." Thereafter, the committees participated in six more trials on the task, designated as Test Two.

Group condition. The purpose in this treatment was to motivate members to place more value on the performance of the group as a whole than on their individual outcomes. The members were told that the score obtained by the group as a unit (the sum of the members' separate scores) would be visibly posted after each trial, and that these group scores would be reported to their separate superiors as the results of the test (none of the scores in this or other conditions were ever in fact reported to the superiors).

Consider the implications of these instructions. A single score for a total group indicates to each participant that his own contribution to that score, good or bad, is not visible to persons either outside or inside the group. His public score will be the same as the scores of each of the other members. Thus, a member's interest in enhancing his individual rewards and reducing his costs is likely to be less than his interest in increasing the sum of the rewards or in reducing the sum of the costs of the entire group.

The most efficient procedure, given the desire for a maximally high sum of members' scores, is for one member to purchase information from E about X and for another to purchase information from E about Y. It does not matter who the purchasers are as long as not more than two do the buying (more than two purchases unnecessarily increases the costs among members). The two purchasers then give the information to all others without requiring reimbursement. Such a sequence makes it possible for all members to vote on both letters with certainty and at minimal cost. Two members incur costs, but since this fact is not publicly identified, a poorer performance cannot be attributed to them.

Our prediction is that the posting of a single group score will press the members toward the development of the procedure just described. As a result, the behavior of the members, compared to their performance prior to the group induction and to the behavior of members in control groups, will be more concerned with increasing the rewards and reducing the costs within the group as a whole. More specifically, the number of persons who purchase information from E should be lower, transfer of points to one another should be lower, and providing information to one another should be higher, as a result of the group condition. There should be more providing of information than transferring of points.

Given a concern to maximize the scores of all members, we assume that each will perceive stronger pressures from others to do well, as observed by Thomas.[7] These pressures should generate a stronger desire to earn high scores and a greater readiness to trust the motives of others as reported by Thomas[8] and Deutsch.[9]

Individual condition. The purpose of this treatment was to motivate members to be more concerned about their own individual scores than about the scores of others. The method used to create this motivation was to tell them that the score obtained by each member would be separately and visibly posted after each trial and that these individual scores would be reported to the superiors as the results of the test.

The posting and the intention to report these scores to superiors indicates to each member, we assume, that his own score, good or bad, is visible for evaluation by persons outside and inside the group. Each member's interest in the total score of the committee, therefore, is likely to be lower than his interest in increasing his own rewards and reducing his own costs. In short, a competitive rather than a cooperative orientation is expected.

An efficient procedure to increase his own reward and to reduce his own costs is for each member to avoid purchasing the information from E and to buy it from one who has purchased it for less than the price charged by E. Or, a member may purchase the information from E before others do and offer to sell it widely for less than it cost him, thereby hoping to reduce his own costs and perhaps to make additional profit through the high volume of sales. Of course, one could also operate entirely independ-

---

[7] E. J. Thomas, "Effects of Facilitative Role Interdependence on Group Functioning," *Human Relations*, Vol. 10 (1957), pp. 347–66.

[8] *Ibid.*

[9] M. Deutsch, "The Effects of Cooperation and Competition on Group Process," *Human Relations*, Vol. 2 (1949), pp. 129–52, 199–231.

ently and make a prediction without prior knowledge, relying on chance to yield a profit. Few persisted in this strategy for long. Under this condition there should be little interest in providing information (rewards) to others or in reducing their costs. Given such interpersonal relations, participants should have little trust in one another and little inclination to provide information or to transfer points to other members.

Group and individual condition. In this treatment the intention was to generate a motivation for all members to help one another and at the same time to maximize personal outcomes. The participants were told that both the total sum of the members' scores and the score obtained by each member would be visibly posted, and that all scores, group and individual, would be reported to the superiors.

The properties described in the two previous sections, interest in others' scores and concern with his own personal score, should be operating here simultaneously. Each member, therefore, should be interested in increasing the rewards and reducing the costs of others while simultaneously increasing his individual rewards and reducing his own costs. He should be anxious to help the group do well but not at the cost of his own success. As a result, all should give to one another as fair a deal as possible. The ideal procedure then is for only two persons each to purchase half of the information from E, for them to pass it along directly to others, and for each member to reimburse the purchaser for a share of the purchaser's costs. This method demands planning and division of labor, but properly executed it ensures that all members end up with correct information and all pay an equal share of the costs. Our prediction is that the actions of members in this condition will reflect efficient sharing of information (from the original purchaser to the recipient) but relatively few offers to sell, and that there will be more transferring of points than providing of information.

Control condition. The purpose of this treatment was to maintain all properties in Test Two as they were in Test One. The men were told in this treatment that their scores would be reported to them privately, and nothing was said about reporting these results publicly or to superiors. Any changes during Test Two, compared to Test One, may be attributed to attempts to learn how to improve personal scores.

Measures

A coding scheme was developed, based upon the separate *bits* of information contained in the messages; a *bit* was defined as a distinct idea. The major variables derived from the coded messages and from the records kept by E follow.

1. *Number of purchases from E.* This is derived from records kept by E during the test.

2. *Offer to sell information to colleagues.* This disregards the method seller had used to obtain it.

3. *Information provided to others.* This may be a gift or a sale (the two unfortunately could not be reliably separated).

4. *Points transferred to others.* The size of transfer is irrelevant (the more the number of transfers, the smaller the average size of transfers).

5. *Guess by member.* For this variable, analysis of all information a given person has received indicates that he did not have the correct information at the time of making his prediction and that his bet must have been a guess. This is the most reliable indicator of effectiveness in collaboration among members.

6. *Individual score.* This is derived by taking the total number of points accumulated minus costs incurred from purchases. The validity of this score as a measure of performance is less than perfect because information "flowed" among members via secret signals and undetected copying; there were also a number of lucky guesses when making predictions.

7. *Friendly remarks.* These comments were made to establish, maintain, restore or appeal to "good" interpersonal relations.

8. *Hostile remarks.* These were made to criticize or call into question actions and motives of another member, or to express anger, rejection, lack of trust, and so on.

9. *Procedural negotiation.* This was an action urged on another member, an attempt to determine who should buy from E, or a negotiation over the price of betting information.

Reliability in the coding of messages, the proportion of agreement among two coders on a 25 percent sample of the messages, was .85.

At the completion of Test Two the members were asked to complete a postexperimental questionnaire, introduced as an evaluation of the test so that it might be improved for future testees. The questions were nine-point, Likert-type, rating scales. When the questionnaire was completed the participants were told the true purposes of the study; all deceptions were carefully described and explained. The participants were asked to conceal the nature of the test from friends in other districts until the experiment was finished.

RESULTS

We shall consider changes in the content of interpersonal messages created by introduction of each of the experimental conditions. Our major interest is in how these changes compare with those occurring in the control groups, Test Two contrasted with Test One. We shall also examine the attitudes generated among participants in the separate experimental conditions.

Before examining the results in the experimental conditions, it is useful

TABLE 1

MEAN CHANGES IN BEHAVIOR RELEVANT TO REWARDS AND
COSTS, TEST ONE TO TEST TWO *

	Experimental Conditions				t of Differences	
	Control	Group	Individ-ual	Group & Indiv.	From Control	Among Conditions
		(A)	(B)	(C)		
	(N = 24)	(N = 28)	(N = 28)	(N = 30)		
Change in frequency of message bits per member						
Purchase info. from E...............	−.37	−.89	−.86	−.10	n.s.	n.s.
Offer sale of info. to others........................	+1.00	−.76	−1.00	−1.88	A = 1.71† B = 2.18‡ C = 2.72§	n.s.
Provide info. to others................	+.52	+4.28	−.56	−.42	A = 1.87†	A−C = 2.19‡ A−B = 1.86†
Transfer points to others........................	+.75	+.29	+.43	+1.13	n.s.	A−C = 1.09
Efficiency of coordination						
Guess (mean number trials per member)................	−.67	−1.50	−.10	−1.77	A = 1.76† B = 2.93§ C = 2.42§	A−B = 2.93§ B−C = 3.62§
Individual score, points.........................	+11.50	+19.57	+12.71	+28.53	C = 2.39§	B−C = 2.03‡

* Two-tailed t tests were used in this and Tables 2 and 3.
†p < .10.
‡p < .05.
§p < .02.

to summarize the changes in the control groups from Test One to Test Two. These are shown in the first column in Tables 1 and 2. Scanning these columns suggests that, in general, changes within the Control groups are not large. The greatest changes notable in Table 1 were an increase in offers to sell the correct information to colleagues and an increase in transferring points to colleagues. These were accompanied by an increase in negotiations and by a decrease in friendly remarks, as shown in Table 2. The members of the control groups during Test Two, it appears, became

TABLE 2

MEAN CHANGE IN FREQUENCY OF MESSAGE BITS PER MEMBER CONCERNING
INTERPERSONAL RELATIONS, TEST ONE TO TEST TWO

	Experimental Conditions				t of Differences	
	Control	Group	Individ-ual	Group Indiv.	From Control	Among Conditions
		(A)	(B)	(C)		
Content of Message	(N = 24)	(N = 28)	(N = 28)	(N = 30)		
Friendly remark................	−.83	−.29	+.18	+.20	B = 2.55* C = 1.89†	n.s.
Hostile remark.................	+.08	−.07	+.14	−.07	n.s.	n.s.
Procedural negotiation...........	+1.29	−.04	−.71	+2.53	A = 1.69 B = 2.10*	A−C = 2.54‡ B−C = 2.85*

*p < .05.
†p < .10.
‡p < .02.

more concerned with selling their information and less patient with one another.

Group Condition

In this condition, we have predicted, members will become interested in increasing the rewards within the group. Their message behavior is summarized in Column A of Tables 1 and 2. These results appear to be in accord with the prediction.

Comparing the changes in the group condition, Test One to Test Two, with changes in the control condition, Test One to Test Two, reveals (Table 1) that the participants in the group condition more often decreased their offers to sell information and increased the number of times they provided information. In fact more persons were sending information to one another than was necessary. The p values here are, however, about .10 by a two-tailed test. A rough estimate of the proportion of gifts of information (no charge made for it) among all information provided was possible in this condition. Persons in the control condition decreased their number of gifts by 11 percent while those in the group condition increased by 45 percent (p of difference, $<.05$). The decrease in the number of persons who had to make a guess at the time of placing their prediction because they had not acquired the correct information from any source was greater in the group condition than in the control condition ($p < .10$). The improvement in performance scores was greater in this condition than in the control groups but not significantly so.

The attitudes toward the experience (answers to postexperimental questionnaire) among participants in the group condition were quite different from those in the control groups (see Table 3). In the group condition, members desired a better score ($p < .10$), felt less need for more complete communication with one another, were more aware of the pressures from others to try hard in the test, and were more attracted to the test, than were those in the control groups.

The ways in which behavior in the group condition differed from behavior in the individual condition are noteworthy. Those in the group condition had a greater increase in providing information to others, had more reduction in the number of times members were forced to guess when making predictions (see Table 1), had a stronger desire for a better score, trusted their colleagues more, and felt less strain in interpersonal relations, than did participants in the individual condition (see Table 3).

In sum, the group condition appeared to generate more tendency toward providing rewards for others (perhaps more than was necessary) than toward reducing own costs, more motivation to obtain a good personal score, more trust in others, and considerably less strain in interpersonal relations than did the control or individual conditions. The

TABLE 3
MEAN REACTIONS TO TEST, POST-QUESTIONNAIRE

	Experimental Conditions				t of Differences	
	Control	Group	Individ-ual	Group & Indiv.		
Query	(N = 24)	(A) (N = 28)	(B) (N = 28)	(C) (N = 30)	From Control	Among Conditions
Desired better score[1]...........5.58		6.82	4.68	6.27	A = 1.87*	B−C = 2.49‡ A−B = 3.22‡
Desired fuller communication[2].............4.71		2.82	3.57	5.62	A = 2.40†	A−C = 3.66‡ B−C = 2.58‡
Trusted other members[3]..................7.17		7.43	6.18	7.21	n.s.	A−B = 2.89† B−C = 1.96*
Felt pressure from other members[4]..............7.25		7.96	7.21	6.53	A = 2.64‡	A−C = 4.07‡ B−C = 1.83*
Felt strain in relations[5].........1.64		.99	2.56	1.95	n.s.	A−B = 3.43‡
Felt attraction to test[6]..........5.67		7.46	7.07	6.27	A = 3.25‡	B−C = 1.93*

*$p < .10$.
†$p < .05$.
‡$p < .02$.

[1] *Query:* How important was it to you to do better on the second set of six trials than you did on the first set? (Not at all—Very important).

[2] *Query:* To what extent do you think it might add to a player's enjoyment of the game if he had enough time to communicate fully with all of the other players during the course of the game? (None—Quite a lot).

[3] *Query:* How willing do you think each of the following persons would have been to help you when it might have jeopardized his score to have done so? (Mean rating of all members: Not much at all—Very much).

[4] *Query:* In your opinion, how much did other members of the group expect you to try hard? (Not at all —Very much).

[5] *Query:* Which of the following factors do you believe was most important in restricting the level of the group's performance on this task? (Mean *ranks* assigned to: "feelings which exist between some members of the group" *and* "the amount of competition going on between players," within a list of six items).

[6] *Query:* All things considered, how much did you like being tested in this way this afternoon? (Disliked it—Liked it very much).

reliability of the differences between the group and individual conditions was in general greater than between the group and control conditions.

Individual Condition

The individual condition was predicted to generate a stronger interest in increasing one's own rewards and in reducing own costs than in worrying about others' outcomes. The pattern of results is not quite what was predicted. Rather than becoming interested in own rewards and costs, the participants in this treatment appear to have withdrawn from interaction with others and to have lost interest in own attainments as well. Perhaps they resisted the pressures on them to compete with one another.

Looking down Column B in Table 1, for example, it is evident that members within this condition reduced their tendency to purchase information from E, their offers to sell or provide this information to one another, and showed little improvement in reducing the number of persons who had to guess when making a prediction. They also reduced their procedural negotiating (see Table 2).

In comparison with the changes made in the control groups, participants in the individual condition more often reduced their offers to sell information and less often reduced the number of persons who had to guess answers; they increased the frequency of friendly remarks and showed a drop in their procedural negotiating. But their reactions to the total experience, in Table 3, were not significantly different from those by members of the control groups.

Group and Individual Condition

The motives in this condition were potentially contradictory but attention of each member to others' rewards and costs, described earlier as a fair deal in relations, should have prevented the two motives from having contrasting effects.

The results in this condition, compared to the results in the control groups, indicate that there was a significantly larger increase in personal scores and a decrease in the number of persons who had to guess when making a prediction, as well as a decrease in offers to sell (see Table 1), suggesting that information flowed efficiently among members without much emphasis on selling it. Members transferred points to colleagues often. Members in this condition also increased in the number of friendly remarks ($p < .10$) and the amount of procedural negotiating (see Table 2) more than did those in the control groups. Their reactions after the experience, however, were not significantly different from those in the control groups, as can be seen in Table 3.

Members in the present condition were significantly different from those in both of the other two conditions in several interesting respects. They increased their procedural negotiating, had a stronger desire for more complete information among members, and felt less pressure from other members. These variables, then, describe the ways in which the concomitant presence of the group and individual conditions had unique effects. These results appear to mean that there was more awareness of the need for clarity in making a division of labor in the present condition than in the other two, despite their evident efficiency in earning points. The results in this condition were not similar to one more than to the other among the two experimental conditions previously described; thus we cannot conclude which, the group or the individual aspects of the "both" situation, was more potent in determining behavior within the present condition.

All of the committees in this study had held their present membership for a number of months. Were there previously established interpersonal relations responsible for any of the findings reported here? As part of another study a mailed questionnaire was sent to the members inquiring about their relations with one another in their day-to-day operations. The results from that questionnaire were unrelated to the behavior observed in the separate conditions. Thus the interpersonal relations members brought into the laboratory, as measured by the questionnaire, do not appear to account for the results described.

DISCUSSION

The experimental conditions and the findings in this study are relevant to two separate but similar approaches in research on group behavior.

In one approach the members of a group are assumed to change their interpersonal relations and their group output in accord with the psychological laws of learning. Experimental studies in this approach are devoted to observing behavioral changes as a result of feedback given to members about their performance in the group. The feedback may be a single score for the group, individual scores for members, or both. Berkowitz and Levy,[10] and Berkowitz, Levy and Harvey,[11] have observed that feedback of group scores generated greater involvement in a task and a greater desire for a good performance than did feedback of individual scores. Feedback of group scores, they noted, also stimulated stronger attraction to other members and more interaction among members than did individual scores. Pryer and Bass[12] have reported that feedback of group scores improved the performances of groups more than no feedback of group scores. Zajonc[13] has observed that simultaneous feedback of individual scores as well as the score of the group as a unit was more effective in improving individual performance of members than feedback in which members learned only about the group's score. Hall[14] and Rosenberg and Hall,[15] however, reported that feedback of group scores and individual scores were not different in their ability to generate an improvement of performance, either in the individual members or in the group as a unit; they felt that both types worked equally well. In the context of this learning approach, then, the findings of the present study suggest that feedback of a group score has more favorable effects upon concern for others' outcomes and for pleasantness in interpersonal relations, while feedback of the group and individual scores together has more favorable effects upon the efficiency of collaboration.

---

[10] L. Berkowitz and B. Levy, "Pride in Group Performance and Group-task Motivation," *Journal of Abnormal and Social Psychology*, Vol. 53 (1956), pp. 300–306.

[11] L. Berkowitz, B. Levy, and A. Harvey, "Effects of Performance Evaluations on Group Integration and Motivation," *Human Relations*, Vol 10 (1957), pp. 195–208.

[12] M. W. Pryer and B. Bass, "Some Effects of Feedback on Behavior in Groups," *Sociometry*, Vol. 22 (1959), pp. 56–63.

[13] R. Zajonc, "The Effects of Feedback and Probability of Group Success on Individual and Group Performance," *Human Relations*, Vol. 15 (1962), pp. 149–62.

[14] R. Hall, "Group Performance under Feedback that Confounds Responses of Group Members," *Sociometry*, Vol. 20 (1957), pp. 297–305.

[15] S. Rosenberg and R. Hall, "The Effects of Different Social Feedback Conditions upon Performance in Dyadic Teams," *Journal of Abnormal and Social Psychology*, Vol. 57 (1958), pp. 271–77.

In the other approach to research on groups, the interdependence among members' motives is assumed to have direct and favorable consequences upon interpersonal behavior and performance. High interdependence has been experimentally created among members in this approach by giving the collection of persons one score for the group. Low interdependence has been created by giving members individual scores. These operations are the same as the ones used respectively for the group and the individual conditions in the present investigation. Deutsch[16] and Thomas[17] have reported more cordial interaction and better performance in groups whose members were high in interdependence than in those whose members were low in interdependence. Pepitone[18] and Daniels and Berkowitz[19] have shown, furthermore, that members who are aware that others are dependent on them are likely to work harder for the dependent persons than for others who are not dependent on them.

The contrasting findings from the separate group and individual conditions in the present study appear to be in accord with those from variations in amounts of interdependence in the earlier investigations.

The basic task in the present experiment made it possible for members to collaborate with others or not, as they wished, within rules that assured them greater rewards for collaboration. It is striking then that the individual condition appeared to create enough disinterest in collaboration among members that they avoided coordination in their efforts even when it damaged their own scores to do so. Unfortunately in most industrial organizations specific rewards are almost always given on an individual basis. Rewards for collaboration and for helping others are generally more symbolic or elusive, e.g., informal signs of appreciation or respect. This may account in part for the general lack of concern for the welfare of one's associates observed in many organizations. To the extent that a functional interdependence exists among organizational members—such that coordination or collaboration is required—the individual rewards may also serve as a detriment to organizational effectiveness.

SUMMARY

Twenty-three coordinating committees in a large business firm were given a group of experimental tasks designed to provide an opportunity for maximal or minimal collaboration as desired among members. The rules

---

[16] *Op. cit.*

[17] *Op. cit.*

[18] Emmy Pepitone, "Responsibility to the Group and its Effects on the Performance of Members" (unpublished Ph.D. dissertation, The University of Michigan, 1952).

[19] L. Daniels and L. Berkowitz, "Liking and Response to a Dependency Relationship," *Human Relations,* Vol. 16 (1963), pp. 141–48.

were such that members' scores would benefit from collaborative effort. The subjects were informed that they were taking a test of "work-group intelligence" requested by higher management. After performing the basic task for six trials, one of three different experimental conditions, or a control condition, was given to each group; there followed six additional trials. These conditions described the nature of the test scores to be submitted to higher management and to be posted in the experimental room for each trial: (1) group condition, the sum of the scores of the members in the group; (2) individual condition, the separate scores of each member; (3) group and individual (both) condition, the sum of the members' scores and each individual score contributing to that sum; (4) control condition, no scores reported to management, individual scores reported privately to members.

The group condition, compared to the other conditions, generated more emphasis on providing successful scores for others and less concern about personal rewards or cost involved, more motivation to obtain a good score, more trust in others, and less strain in interpersonal relations.

The individual condition, compared to the other conditions, stimulated more withdrawal from interpersonal interaction, less desire to achieve a good score, less trusting of colleagues, and more strain in interpersonal relations.

The group and individual condition created the greatest improvement in personal scores, accompanied by the greatest increase in procedural negotiating and transferring of points. Efforts to obtain a good group score apparently were modified by personal intentions to ensure that the member himself (and colleagues) did not suffer as a result of his acting for the good of the group. Persons in this condition appeared to be most sensitive to the need for clearly defined divisions of labor and appropriate actions by members.

19. LEADERSHIP WITHIN A HIERARCHICAL ORGANIZATION*

Donald C. Pelz

Introduction

CONCERN with leadership has been central to the Human Relations Program from its beginning. But there have been important shifts in emphasis. Our early concepts and hypotheses drew freely from previous studies on small groups. To discover how the first-line supervisor affected employee attitudes and productivity, the direction of search seemed obvious. One studied the face-to-face interactions between supervisor and work group.

The hard facts of analysis have shown that this approach is incomplete. Leadership in isolated groups is one thing; leadership within large organizations may be something else again. At least, it must be looked at with a fresh view.

The impact of organizational factors on interactions within the work group was suggested by some of our first results. In training courses the supervisor is given this general rule: he should always recognize good work done by employees. He should, for example, recommend deserving employees for promotion. But in the Prudential study supervisors of high producing work groups were found to play one of two roles in the promotion process. Either they made recommendations which generally went through, or they made no recommendations at all. In contrast, the supervisors of low producing work groups often recommended promotions, but these generally did not go through.[1] To recommend promotions was not, as such, related to high employee productivity. A more basic factor seemed to be operating, outside of the sphere of the work group. This factor was the supervisor's power within the larger department The high producing supervisors were more realistic about their power; they entered the promotion process only when they could influence the outcome. The concept of the supervisor's power or influence within his department is central in a recent study, some details of which are given below.[2]

* Reproduced from *Journal of Social Issues*, VII, No. 3, 1951, pp. 49-55.

[1] D. Katz, N. Maccoby, and N. C. Morse, *Productivity, Supervision and Employee Morale, Part I.* (Ann Arbor: University of Michigan, Survey Research Center, 1950.)

[2] D. C. Pelz, *Power and Leadership in the First-Line Supervisor* (preliminary draft). (Ann Arbor: University of Michigan, Survey Research Center, 1951.)

Superficially the results of such studies might suggest that we need one set of theories to account for leadership in isolated groups, and another set of theories to account for leadership within hierarchical organizations. It is our belief, however, that both situations can be incorporated within a single theoretical framework. In fact, it might be possible to use artificial groups and laboratory methods to reproduce some of the variables of an organizational context. Variables such as power and status have been manipulated in several studies done at the Research Center for Group Dynamics.[3] Some elements in a theoretical framework designed to include both leadership situations are discussed at this point.

Basic Postulate: Successful Leadership Depends in Part on Helping Group Members Achieve Their Goals

Empirical studies, as shown in reviews of the literature by Gibb,[4] Jenkins,[5] and Stogdill[6] have failed to find traits that are universal in successful leaders. In different studies, different or contradictory traits in leaders are found related to whatever criterion of success is used. Differences in the situations or in the groups, from study to study, seem to be partly responsible. Gibb concludes that "leadership is relative always to the situation."

But it is not enough simply to say that leadership is relative to the situation. Relative to what aspects of the situation? We must identify those factors which make a given leader behavior "successful" or "unsuccessful."

Recent theories have stressed the *needs of group members* as key aspects of the all-important "situation." The successful or valued or obeyed leader is one who can help group members achieve their goals. This emphasis on group members' needs and goals appears sound, at least is one beginning of a theory of leadership. In any kind of situation, a basic postulate is that *the more the leader (or any member) helps other members achieve their goals, the greater will be the members' acceptance of him.* By "acceptance" is meant that members are willing to follow the leader's suggestions, express satisfaction with the leader's conduct, etc.

This basic postulate is not, by itself, a theory. It does not permit us to

---

[3] Cf. H. H. Kelley, "Communication in Experimentally Created Hierarchies," *Human Relations*, 1951, 4, pp. 39–56; A. Pepitone, "Motivational Effects in Social Perception," *Human Relations*, 1950, 3, pp. 57–76.

[4] C. A. Gibb, "The Principles and Traits of Leadership," *J. Abnormal and Social Psychology*, 1947, 42, pp. 267–84.

[5] W. O. Jenkins, "A Review of Leadership Studies with Particular Reference to Military Problems," *Psychological Bulletin*, 1947, 44, pp. 54–79.

[6] R. M. Stogdill, "Personal Factors Associated with Leadership: A Survey of the Literature," *Journal of Psychology*, 1948, 25, pp. 35–71.

make specific predictions, and this a genuine theory must be able to do. To make predictions, we must be able to state conditions such as: (*a*) Toward what goals are the group members motivated? (*b*) What acts or characteristics of a leader help the members achieve each of these goals? And finally, (*c*) How do specific leaders measure up on these factors? If the first two conditions are known, and if we have measured each leader on the relevant factors, we can begin to predict the acceptance of particular leaders by their particular groups.

Very probably, the basic postulate will apply to leaders within a hierarchial organization, as well as to leaders in simpler groups. But the conditions which we need to know for prediction may be markedly affected by the organizational context. With regard to (*a*), for example, we shall have to give more weight to what we may loosely call "organizational goals" and "group goals." These must, of course, actually function as goals or as sub-goals for the individual members, if the basic postulate is to apply. With regard to (*b*), the organizational context will have much to do with whether certain acts of the leader can or cannot help his group members achieve their goals. The recent study cited above underscores this point. Major features of this research will now be described.

The Point of Departure: Some Puzzling Results in Previous Analyses of the Data

The data for the study were collected early in 1948 from the personnel of a large electric utility, employing well over 10,000 people, and serving a major midwestern manufacturing city and surrounding urban and rural areas. The work of the company covers many different occupations and skill levels. Attitudes of all non-supervisory employees were ascertained through paper-and-pencil questionnaires. Attitudes and practices of all first-line supervisors—each of the people in charge of a work group, the basic unit—were obtained in personal interviews utilizing open-ended questions. The verbatim replies were later coded with the content analysis procedures of the Survey Research Center.

The author's objective was to determine how measures obtained on the supervisors related to attitudes of employees they supervised. What supervisory practices led to employee acceptance of the supervisor? Three separate analyses had to be done, before answers to this question could be formulated. In the process, the importance of organizational factors became increasingly clear.

The first analysis was of a design frequently found in leadership studies. Forty "high employee satisfaction" work groups and thirty "low employee satisfaction" work groups were selected, and the data from their respective supervisors examined on fifty items. While half the differences were in the expected direction, only six differences were statistically significant (at the 5 per cent level of confidence). By chance alone, 2.5 "significant" differences would be expected; the obtained number was little more than twice the chance number.

The inconclusiveness of these results compelled a second analysis. The previous analysis had focused exclusively on the interaction between supervisor and employees in the work group; it had assumed, in all work groups, universal relationships between supervisory practices and employee attitudes. But the evidence on situational effects warns against this assumption. High satisfaction in one group of employees may result from supervisory practices quite different from those used in another well satisfied group. In the second analysis, therefore, different types of employees and situations were handled separately. Separate analyses were performed for men and women, for white collar and blue collar workers, for small work groups and large, for differing educational backgrounds, and for various combinations of these factors.

The results of this analysis were more promising. A direct comparison with the first is not possible—different measures of the supervisory and employee variables were used. It is interesting that statistically significant results numbered seven times chance. But some of these significant results were disturbing; some went *opposite* to predictions based on previous research. One of the supervisory measures, for example, was a scale of "taking sides with employees in cases of employee-management conflicts," based on three intercorrelated items from the interview. In case of disagreement between the employees under him and his own superiors, whose side did the supervisor take? Did he see his job primarily as selling his employees' viewpoint to management, as selling management's viewpoint to employees, or as remaining independent? Previous evidence suggests that group members will think more highly of the leader who "goes to bat" for them, who sides with them in cases of conflict with higher authorities. The results supported this hypothesis in small work groups (10 employees or fewer). But in large white collar work groups, employees were significantly *less* satisfied with such a supervisor; they preferred the supervisor who sided with management. Other supervisory variables showed similar contradictory results.

Why? What was there about the large work group situation that produced relationships apparently opposite to those found in small work groups? Still one more analysis was essential, if we were to resolve this predictive tangle and others like it.

The previous section mentions two general areas within which the third analysis design sought some of the responsible factors. Perhaps employees in the larger work groups had different needs and goals from those in the smaller groups. One step, therefore, was to develop, from existing employee data, crude indices of certain needs.

Or perhaps the same supervisory behavior, in small and in large work groups, might have different results with respect to employees' achieving their goals. At this point, the factor of the supervisor's *power or influence* within the larger department became crucial.

Two Predictions on Influence and Leadership

The type of theory adopted for the third analysis has already been described. The basic postulate is that the supervisor will be "accepted" by his work group if his behavior helps them to achieve their goals. The new concept introduced in the third analysis is that of the supervisor's influence within his department. If the supervisor has considerable influence over events within his department, then his attempts to help employees reach their goals are very likely to succeed. If, on the other hand, he lacks influence, then his attempts toward employee goal achievement are likely to fail.

Two related predictions follow. Given supervisors who are influential, the more they behave so as to aid goal achievement, the more satisfied their employees will be toward them. A positive correlation is predicted between the supervisory behavior and employee attitudes. But given non-influential supervisors, there can be no such relationship. Stronger attempts toward helping employees can produce no rise in employee satisfaction. There might be a drop, in fact. The second prediction, then, is that the correlation between the supervisor's helpful behavior and employee attitudes will be significantly less positive (or more negative) under non-influential supervisors.

If variation in influence does produce these changes in the relationships of supervisory behavior to employee attitudes, then influence may be called a "conditioner" of the relationships, following a useful suggestion by Morris and Seeman.[7] The amount of change—the difference in correlations found under high and low influence supervisors respectively—may be called the "conditioner effect" of influence.

Because of the initial emphasis on the supervisor's interpersonal relations, a variable of his power or influence was not anticipated when the data were collected. But it appeared possible to construct one. A supervisor was considered to have relatively high "influence over the social environment in which his employees were functioning" if he reported having a voice in departmental decisions made by his own superior; if he had relatively little contact with his superior—an indication of more autonomy in running his own work group; and if he had a high salary—indicating higher general status.

Two scales of supervisory behavior appeared to measure "attempts at helping employees to reach their goals." One was the scale previously

---

[7] R. T. Morris and M. Seeman, "The Problem of Leadership: An Interdisciplinary Approach," *American Journal of Sociology*, 1950, 56, pp. 149–55.

described, of "taking sides with employees in cases of employee-management conflict." Another was a scale of "social closeness toward employees," or lack of social distance, based on several items from the supervisor's interview.

Several employee attitudes were used. The most important one was an index of employees' "general satisfaction with the performance of their immediate supervisor." Product-moment correlations between the two supervisory behaviors and the various employee attitudes were computed. These correlations were obtained separately under influential and under non-influential supervisors, in each of seven employee sub-populations, defined according to white collar vs. blue collar occupations, sex, size of work group, and union coverage.

Major Results

The results, in general, confirm the predictions. For the group of high influence supervisors, we obtained twenty-eight correlations between the two supervisory behaviors and the various employee attitudes, in the several employee sub-populations. For the low influence supervisors, we obtained a parallel set of twenty-eight correlations. Nineteen of the correlations under influential supervisors are at least mildly positive, and seven are significantly positive (at the five per cent level of confidence). This is eleven times the chance number (taking direction into account). The first prediction is thus generally confirmed. By contrast, under low influence supervisors, nineteen of the parallel correlations are either zero or slightly negative.

The second prediction concerns the various "conditioner effects" of the supervisor's influence: the difference in each product-moment correlation between a supervisory behavior and an employee attitude, under high and low influence supervisors respectively. Positive differences are found in the majority of the twenty-eight comparisons, and six of them are significantly positive.[8] This number is ten times what chance alone would produce. Thus the second prediction is generally confirmed. It should be noted that none of these conditioner effects could have been foreseen on the basis of previous findings. They are not the product of empirical hindsight.

The results demonstrate, in short, that a supervisor's influence or power within the department does condition the way his supervisory behavior relates to employee attitudes. When an influential supervisor uses these helpful practices, positive correlations are found between his behavior and employee attitudes. But in the case of non-influential supervisors, no cor-

---

[8] The significance of differences between correlations was tested by the use of Fisher's z-transformation for r, as described in Q. McNemar, *Psychological Statistics* (New York: John Wiley & Sons, 1950).

relations (or slightly negative ones) are found between the same supervisory behaviors and employee attitudes.

Implications

In the three successive analyses of our supervisory leadership data, the importance of the organizational context has become increasingly clear. The major variable in the third analysis—the supervisor's power or influence within the department—depends on the supervisor's role within the larger organization. It cannot be measured by observing interactions within the work group. (The power of the supervisor over his group members is not the same variable.)

The findings imply that if an influential supervisor attempts to help employees achieve their goals, his efforts will usually succeed. Concrete results will be achieved. Employee satisfactions will rise. But—the data imply—if a non-influential supervisor tries to do the same, his efforts will often fail. Employee expectations will be frustrated. Their satisfactions will not rise, or may even fall.

This statement does not imply a pluralism in the laws of leadership. On the contrary, we believe that a variety of leadership phenomena might be accounted for in a single theoretical framework. A basic postulate in such a framework—one expressed by several theorists—is that a leader will be accepted by group members to the extent that he helps them to achieve their goals.

This postulate should apply both to isolated groups and to groups in an organizational setting. Specific goals will differ somewhat in the two cases. In the latter, members will emphasize organizational and group goals more than in the former. Moreover, within large organizations the leader's ability to help the group will depend to a much greater degree upon factors outside of the face-to-face group. As the leader's role in the organization varies, our theory leads us to predict sharp changes in the effect of his behavior upon members' goal achievements, and hence upon their attitudes.

SECTION FOUR

Planned Change

As was indicated in Section 2, the modern environment puts a premium on the adaptive capacity of organizations in coping with the technological, economic, political, and cultural changes that have become commonplace. Organizations differ greatly in the amount and nature of their adaptive capacity. As we have seen, there is an evolutionary trend toward organizational structures that are relatively more capable of adaptation, e.g., decentralization.

Central to the problem of adaptation is the process of planning and executing specific changes. Trial and error is too costly a procedure to rely on for evolutionary progress. Effective planned change requires a thorough, science-based understanding of organizational systems. This is an area in which some behavioral scientists are concerned not only with conducting research, but also acting as agents of change through consulting and teaching relationships (3). The processes and problems of change inevitably affect and disrupt the social and individual equilibrium that makes up the organizational system. Behavioral scientists can be especially helpful with these matters.

The content of changes in organizations is either dictated or constrained by organizational imperatives like those dealt with in Section 2. These demands may originate in the environment (e.g., threats from external power sources, economic competition, increased task load) or they may arise from commitments made internally (e.g., to be a research-based or consumer-oriented company). Threats to survival or failure to reach established goals appear to generate search for new and better ways of organizing. Investment in research or other special capability results in a search for worthwhile applications (18). But commitment to change—like any other commitment—can produce unanticipated consequences. Quite frequently these appear in the form of *resistance* to change, as new ways of doing things impinge on established patterns and create repercussions that may spread even to apparently unrelated sectors.

Clearly, the implementation of organizational change requires change in human attitudes, perceptions, cognitions and behaviors. These in turn are properties of whole human beings and play a part in the fundamental equilibrium between the satisfactions of individual participants and the task requirements of the organization. Exploration into the nature of equilibrium in systems of human action has provided valuable insights. In the Lewinian model existing patterns are seen as a resultant of opposing forces; for example, pressures toward high production opposed by the discomfort of working hard (13). In this example, changes in the situation may be produced by altering pressures on either side, either by increasing pressure to produce or by decreasing the associated discomfort. When pressure is increased, change is accompanied by an increase in tension; if pressure is reduced, it is accompanied by a decrease in tension. In general, changes that increase tension are associated with increase in personal anxiety, a tendency to fragment into opposed subgroups, evasive action, attempts to bargain out of the problem, increased rigidity of behavior, or, in the extreme, breakdown into an unstructured state and disintegration of the cooperative system. Many of the psychological forces involved may not be readily apparent. Often, considerable diagnostic activity is necessary to gain sufficient clarification of the problem for remedial action.

The presence of tension in a social system tends to increase pressures to communicate about the sources of tension but at the same time tends to increase reliance on devices to manage tension by suppressing or distorting communication. Intervention to facilitate communication and to overcome the defensive practices helps to make tension function in a way that provides movement and resulting tension reduction.

The attitudes of individual participants are anchored in the social matrix of co-workers, family, friends and reference groups. Classic experiments in social psychology have shown the efficacy of inducing attitudinal changes by methods dealing with natural groups as wholes and involving a high degree of participation on the part of those whose attitude is to be changed. An early experiment by Lewin showed that housewives changed their families' diets to include more variety meats more readily under group participation than under a lecture technique (13). An early and dramatic application in industry demonstrated greater acceptance by workers of changes in work methods and standards by participation techniques as opposed to managerial directives (7).

The techniques found useful in inducing changes in attitudes and beliefs have been taken from many applied fields. Recent efforts have led to a synthesis of these techniques interpreted in the light of sociopsychological theory (4, 8, 14, 15, 19). In addition to Lewinian social psychology, major sources of ideas have been the mental health professions and clinical psychological theories. Clinical work with neurotic and psychotic clients requires the establishment of a relationship between therapist and client in which the client explores the various sectors of his personality with the objective of reducing his internal conflict and thus making himself better able to cope with reality problems. Other contributing fields are more directly concerned with social systems; examples are: community organization, social psychiatry (6), development work in underdeveloped countries (8), and union organizing. A common theme is action by a change agent toward the establishment of communication among the various interests of the client system, reconceptualization of the felt problems, and movement into a new and less conflictful integration of these interests. Pages points out that common aspects of the relationship established by the change agent with the client system include rejection of overt pressure as a motivating device, the communication of diagnoses, encouragement of free expression by the client, and adoption by the change agent of the function of facilitating communication within the client system (4, pp. 168–86). In the case of social systems, techniques for establishing communication may include surveys of affected participants by means of interviews or questionnaires, analysis of existing communication structures, development of sociograms, analysis of goal structure, outside training for key members in the relation of feelings to communication such as T-groups (5), the creation of new communication processes, and direct clinical intervention in groups.

Although a convergence of viewpoint among theorists appears to have been taking place, there remain a variety of approaches to planned change. Psychologically based models of the change relationship represent a significant departure from the traditional managerial or professional formulae of diagnosis of problems by an outside expert, the development of a technically correct solution, and the imposition of this solution by professional or managerial authority. The psychologically based models emphasize involvement of the entire client system in the change process from the very beginning. They emphasize that it is the client system that must do the work that results in change and in adequate resolution of problems. This work will only be forthcoming if the client system fully recognizes the problem and confronts the multifarious implications of change. Thus, the value considerations upon which change is based arise primarily within the client system. The value orientation of the change agent is deemphasized in these models, although practitioners differ in the amount and kind of value orientation which they bring to the change relationship.

Practitioners of planned change have developed a variety of models formulated in developmental terms. These models are generally somewhat more prescriptive or normative than descriptive, since these behavioral scientists have as much an applied as a research interest. The table below

Developmental Models of Planned Change

Author	Source	Phases in Change Process							Time Span
Lewin	(13)	unfreezing present level of group life			moving to the new level		freezing group life on the new level		
Lippitt, Watson & Westley	(14)	development of a need for change	establishment of a change relationship	clarification or diagnosis of the client system's problem	examination of alternative routes and goals; establishing goals and intentions of action	transformation of intentions into actual change efforts	generalization & stabilization of change	achieving a terminal relationship	
Argyris	(1)	change agent's diagnosis		feedback	T-group laboratory training		describe & evaluate results	develop further plans	1 year
Blake	(3)	exposure to behavioral science theory and T-group training	training of work teams	integration between functional groups	goal setting	change agent helps client attain goal	stabilizing the changes		5 years
Pages	(17)	recognition	diagnosis	action					

lists terms describing the phases through which a change process progresses. Although the different models of the developmental process differ in detail, in labeling, and to some extent in emphasis, they have much in common. The beginnings of the change process spring from some sort of exigency that affects the client system. This brings the client to seek help from a change agent, an applied behavioral scientist. The change agent assists in the exploration of the problem, exposing defenses and bringing the human implications of the problem and its proposed solutions clearly into view. This can permit the formulation of a valid diagnosis by the client system with the help of the change agent. Diagnosis leads to change itself, a testing out of possible alternatives; a process of coping with the implications of these changes; and a continuing confrontation of the human implications of progress made, with the help of the change agent. Change is not completed, however, until the major elements of the change have been institutionalized and a new and stable equilibrium attained.

Behavioral scientists, like other scientists, traditionally have undertaken operating responsibility only in research and teaching, which are part of science and without which the scientific enterprise itself would be inconceivable. Acting as change agents, they must necessarily bring to the problem value positions that cannot help but influence the outcome. Their efforts are not ethically neutral. Neither do they, as yet, have the sanction that research and teaching activities have in physical science or that activities in support of health, justice, and religion have in the traditional professions.

Because the values and mores of human beings are a central part of the subject matter of their field, behavioral scientists are sensitive to these questions and generally make their own values explicit. As change agents, they tend to place positive value on openness and free communication in social situations. To some extent, they appear to be biased toward democratic ideals of equality, teamwork, and consideration for the worth of the human being for his own sake. Behavioral scientists differ in the degree and balance of their commitment to these value positions, and client systems differ in their receptivity to these values. Nevertheless, it is clear that most organizations, as systems, have little commitment to value positions of this type. The exploration of these new and different value positions proffered by the change agent is part of the work that must be done by the client system. Part of the success achieved by behavioral scientists as change agents may be due to possibilities for action inherent in these values and discovered by the client system as it attempts to solve its problems.

Even in its strongest forms, the value position of the behavioral scientist is not too constraining. It leaves him plenty of room to come to terms with the fundamental interests of power centers in the client system. So much so, in fact, that social scientists are often accused of being "servants of power" (2, 12). Psychologically oriented studies of planned change show bias in another direction as well. They are primarily concerned with human problems of change rather than with purely technical problems that may be implicit in the major tasks of the organization. Thus, the impulse to change is found in interpersonal tensions.

The relation between these studies and work on economic and technological innovation remains to be explored. The thesis that innovation arises from stressful situations is consistent with Schumpeter's classical formulation, but less so with more recent studies (11,16). It appears from these that much innovation is a routine response to interesting ideas and may occur in successful organizations whose members are well satisfied. Thus, the psychological models may be oriented more toward relatively drastic changes involving the status of participants, the balance of power, and organizational structure. Changes in technological processes or in market strategy may follow quite another pattern.

It is true also that apparently routine actions may create tensions in an organizational system that go undiagnosed in the absence of a competent researcher. Much psychological work has been oriented toward helping relatively peripheral participants (workers and lower management) adjust to the consequences of problems forced on them by purely technical decisions of higher management. In these cases, the client system is a subpart of the total organization. The arena within which change can be undertaken is limited, however; and the fundamental value orientations of the organization as a whole are not exposed to adjustment. In such circumstances, change is likely to be either very minor or very impermanent.

A detailed illustration of how a change can come to naught appears in the work of one consultant (4, pp. 587–91) who was asked by management to help a work group overcome an obvious morale problem. His efforts were successful, but the changes so irritated other people in the plant that top management ordered prior conditions restored. Six of the eight workers and their supervisor decided to seek other employment.

In the studies reported in this section, the initial impetus to change came from top management. The effectiveness of change and its thoroughness, however, depended on management's willingness to permit change to spread beyond its original intentions and to deal with the resulting problems. The utilization of behavioral scientists as change agents, with freedom to pursue change problems to their full resolution, appears destined as an important means of bringing about this result.

REFERENCES

1. ARGYRIS, CHRIS. *Interpersonal Competence and Organizational Effectiveness.* Homewood, Ill., Irwin-Dorsey, 1962.
2. BARITZ, LOREN. *Servants of Power.* Middletown, Conn.: Wesleyan University Press, 1960.
3. BENNIS, WARREN G. "A New Role for the Behavioral Sciences: Effecting Organizational Change," *Administrative Science Quarterly,* Vol. 8, No. 2 (September, 1963), pp. 125–65. This article contains a discussion of Blake's approach.
4. BENNIS, WARREN G.; BENNE, KENNETH D.; AND CHIN, ROBERT. *The Planning of Change.* New York: Holt, Rinehart & Winston, 1961.
5. BRADFORD, LELAND P.; GIBB, J. R.; AND BENNE, KENNETH D. *T-Group Theory and Laboratory Method.* New York: John Wiley & Sons, 1964.
6. CAPLAN, GERALD. *Concepts of Mental Health and Consultation.* Children's Bureau Publications No. 373. Washington, D.C.: U.S. Government Printing Office, 1959.
7. COCH, LESTER, AND FRENCH, J.R.P. JR., "Overcoming Resistance to Change," *Human Relations,* Vol. 1 (1948), pp. 512–32.
8. GOODENOUGH, WARD H. *Cooperation in Change.* New York: Russell Sage Foundation, 1963.
9. GUEST, ROBERT. *Organizational Change.* Homewood, Ill., Irwin-Dorsey, 1962.
10. JAQUES, ELLIOT. *The Changing Culture of a Factory.* London: Tavistock Publications, 1951.
11. KNIGHT, KENNETH E. "A Study of Technological Innovation—The Evolution of Digital Computers." Unpublished Ph.D. thesis. Pittsburgh: Carnegie Institute of Technology, 1963.
12. KRUPP, SHERMAN. *Pattern in Organizational Analysis.* New York: Holt, Rinehart & Winston, 1961.
13. LEWIN, KURT. *Field Theory in Social Science.* New York: Harper, 1951.
14. LIPPITT, RONALD; WATSON, JEANNE; AND WESTLEY, BRUCE. *The Dynamics of Planned Change.* New York: Harcourt, Brace & World, Inc., 1958.
15. MANN, FLOYD C., AND NEFF, FRANKLIN W. *Managing Major Change in Organizations.* Ann Arbor, Mich.: Foundation for Research on Human Behavior, 1961.
16. MANSFIELD, EDWIN. "The Speed of Response of Firms to New Techniques." *Quarterly Journal of Economics,* Vol. 77, No. 2 (1963), pp. 296–311.
17. PAGES, MAX. "The Socio-therapy of the Enterprise." *Human Relations,* Vol. 12, No. 4 (1959), pp. 317–34. Reprinted in (4).
18. PENROSE, EDITH. *The Theory of the Growth of the Firm.* New York: John Wiley & Sons, 1959.
19. SOFER, CYRIL. *The Organization from Within.* London: Tavistock Publications, 1961.

20. A STUDY IN CHANGING THE ATTITUDES AND STEREOTYPES OF INDUSTRIAL WORKERS*

A. J. M. SYKES[1]

THIS STUDY describes an attempt made to change the attitudes of hostility that certain workers held towards their foremen by changing the stereotype on which these attitudes were based. The study covered a period of 14 months in the works. The occasion arose when the author was employed by a large company in the heavy engineering industry to investigate industrial relations in one of its Scottish works. The works had a staff of 680 workers, who, with the exception of the maintenance workers, were all members of the Transport and General Workers Union. The works constituted a complete T & GWU branch in its own right. The secretary, chairman, and committee of the branch were all employed in the works and acted as shop stewards within it, the branch secretary acting as convenor of shop stewards. It may be necessary to point out here that in British trade union practice—as distinct from theory—the post of branch secretary takes precedence over that of branch chairman, and this works was no exception, the branch secretary being the dominant figure to whom the branch chairman and the committee deferred.

METHOD

The aim of the investigation was to study industrial relations within the works and suggest ways in which relations could be improved. The company which owned the works was worried about the bad relations that existed within it: this particular works had frequent disputes, many of which ended in unofficial strikes, whereas other similar works belonging to the same company and situated in the same area were relatively free from disputes. It was known that pay and conditions were not as good in this works as in the other works belonging to the company, and it was thought that this was the reason for the bad relations.

The first step was to see the works manager and explain to him the object of the study and the method to be used. The method consisted of interviewing the shop stewards, the foremen, and a cross section of the workers. These were to be interviewed initially in an office made available by the manager. The interviews were nondirective and the office was in

---

* Reprinted from *Human Relations*, Vol. 17, No. 2, 1964.
[1] A. J. M. Sykes is head of the Department of Management Studies and Sociology at the University of Strathdyde, Glasgow, Scotland.

the works, distant from the administration block and out of sight of the workers on the shop floor. After the initial contact had been made through the formal interviews, informal interviews were held in the canteens, lavatories, and other places where workers congregated to smoke and gossip. The investigator was not a participant observer in the full sense in that he did not do a normal job within the plant and was not a member of the trade union, but he did move about freely within the works, observing activities and speaking to men at their work. As the company had trainee-managers who also wandered freely about the works, this was not regarded as unusual. In the event the workers in the plant soon grew accustomed to the investigator and stopped touching their heads when he appeared in the works—touching the head was the standard signal that a "hat," one of the management, was prowling about the works. The investigator also attended the T & GWU branch meetings by permission of the branch committee.

Good relations with the trade union were established at the beginning of the study. It was believed that if the investigator was first accepted by the shop stewards and the other active members of the branch, this would guarantee acceptance by the workers generally. To this end the branch officials were requested to allow him to attend a branch meeting in order to explain the nature of the study and to answer any questions that the members wished to raise. The officials agreed to this and, since (as in most trade union branches) the normal attendance was very poor, they put pressure on the shop stewards and active members to attend. In all, 33 men attended the meeting, asked questions about the proposed study, and finally expressed themselves satisfied with the answers given by the investigator.

Attitude to the Foremen

The most striking feature of this meeting was the attitude of the trade union members to the foremen in the works. During the course of the meeting several aspects of conditions in the works were criticized. The men complained about wages and conditions, and these complaints were later found to be justified, but the most bitter complaints were made about the foremen. Over half the time spent discussing conditions was occupied in denunciations of the foremen expressed in the most bitter terms:

You'd scour Hell to get their match!
They are a crowd of ignorant bloody men who don't know how to speak to human beings!
They are the worst foremen in Britain, you couldn't get their equal anywhere!
The foremen in here are just slave-drivers, they treat you like dirt!

Such remarks were in contrast with the men's expression of their other grievances which was moderate and reasonable.

Several of the men pointed out that they had complained about the foremen on a number of occasions to the full-time officials of the union, the district and regional organizers, but that nothing had been done. To this, the chairman and the secretary replied that, though they agreed with the members entirely on this question and had brought in the organizer, they had been unable to force the issue because of a lack of concrete evidence, and they asked the members to supply them with details of specific acts committed by the foremen so that they could take the matter up again. Further discussion indicated that this attitude was not assumed to impress the investigator but was held in all sincerity. The men were convinced that the foremen were bad, and believed that the company deliberately chose the most brutal men available to be foremen. It is by no means uncommon for foremen to get a bad name, whether they deserve it or not, but in this case the men showed such bitter hatred of the foremen that it seemed they must have some reason for it. As the trade union officials were moderate, reliable, and accurate in their statements and judgments in other matters it seemed reasonable to suppose they would be equally reliable about the foremen. It did not appear that the men were using the foremen as a scapegoat and were projecting their real grievances upon them, since they did not confine their complaints to the foremen but complained also of pay and conditions in the works. In their relations with management the men complained much more of their other grievances, and it was not realized by management before the research that they regarded the foremen as a major source of grievance.

After the meeting, the research within the works was begun. A check with both management and the union had shown that the 33 men who attended the meeting included all the active members of the T & GWU in the works; it was therefore decided to interview them first. For convenience, these 33 are henceforth referred to as *the active members*. This implies not that they were the only members but that they were the members who took an active part in union affairs. These interviews were interspersed with observation within the works and informal discussions with workers and foremen. The interviews covered industrial relations in general within the works, and the men were allowed to range freely over this field. The information obtained through them confirmed the impression gained at the trade union meeting—that the foremen were extremely unpopular and were regarded as the most objectionable feature of the works.

The Stereotype of the Foremen

During the interviews it became clear that the hostility to the foremen was directed not towards the foremen as individuals but to the stereotype of the foremen accepted by the men. Thus, when the men discussed the foremen they would abuse them in general, and then go on to attack particular individuals among them. Complaints were made about ten foremen: of these, six had retired, the last of the six having retired five years before the investigation. All the 33 active members interviewed complained of two or more of the retired foremen, five complained of two or more of the present foremen, seven of one of the present foremen; the other 21 had no complaints against any of the present foremen. In all, there were complaints about four out of a total of 40 foremen in the works at the time of the investigation.

An extract from an interview with the branch chairman is given below. The pattern it displays—condemnation of the foremen in general, combined with approval of individual foremen—was typical of the interviews as a whole. The branch chairman, a man with 38 years' service in the works, was one of the most bitter critics of the foremen and had pressed the trade union district organizer on several occasions to complain to the senior management of the company about the foremen. The interview began with the branch chairman denouncing the foremen as "a lot of ignorant men, just ignorant, they treat you like jailers!" He then went on to speak of the three he had contact with, the superintendent, senior, and junior foremen in his department, who had been his foremen for fifteen, seven, and five years respectively. The conversation went as follows:

What's A [the junior foreman] like?
He's a very nice bloke, knows his job, got a very nice approach to the men and is always ready to help you; A's a good lad.
What about B? [the senior foreman].
He's all right too, never bothers you. C [the superintendent] is the same, never bothers you if you do your work. He chases some of the men, but it's their own fault, they need chasing, they don't want to work, they only come in here out of the way of the buses. No one who does his job needs to worry about C.

Yet at the end of the conversation he repeated his complaints about "the foremen."

This attitude of hostility to "the foremen," combined with very different attitudes to the individual foremen, was found to be typical of the men interviewed, as well as of the active members. During the period spent in the works a total of 85 men were interviewed in addition to the 33 active members mentioned above (see Table 1). Of these, 79 complained of the foremen in general, the six who did not had all been in the works less than four months; 52 of the men complained about foremen who had left the works, including 17 men who had no direct experience of the foremen they complained of. There were 17 men in departments under one or more of the four foremen about whom the active members had complained—henceforth referred to as the four *unpopular foremen*. Each of the 17 complained of those of the four unpopular foremen he had contact with. Nine of the men made complaints about foremen other than these four, but no two complained of the same foreman. In each case, the shop steward of the department knew of the man's dislike of the foreman and gave reason for it in terms of a specific incident in the past. In three of the cases, the shop steward blamed the foreman; in four, the worker concerned; in two, both foreman and worker.

Thus there was consensus among the men interviewed that "the foremen" were "brutal," and they displayed an attitude of hostility to "the foremen." When dealing with individual foremen there was no general consensus, because *all* the men interviewed did not have experience of *all* the foremen. However, there was consensus among all the men interviewed who had experience of the four unpopular foremen that these were "brutal," and the men displayed an attitude of hostility towards them.

TABLE 1
COMPLAINTS BY WORKERS ABOUT THE FOREMEN

	Of One or More of the Four Unpopular Foremen	Of Other Individual Foremen	Of One or More of the Retired Foremen	Of "The Foremen"	Total Interviewed
By active members.....	12	—	33	33	33
By other workers......	17	9	52	79	85
Total.............	29	9	85	112	118

There was no consensus about the other foremen: there were complaints about nine of them, but only one complaint was made about each of the nine. With the exception of these nine complaints the attitudes the men expressed towards their foremen ranged from acceptance to strong liking.

Origins of the Stereotype

The conclusion that only four foremen were generally unpopular was borne out by the past and present members of the branch committee who had experience of dealing with all the foremen in the course of handling complaints in all departments of the works. When interviewed, each of the committee members named the four unpopular foremen—and only these four—as being generally, and justifiably, disliked. Thus there was a distinct difference between the attitudes of the men to "the foremen" as a collective entity and the attitudes expressed towards individual foremen. This was due to the fact that the attitudes to "the foremen" were a reaction to a stereotype of them; the attitudes to the individual foremen were based on direct experience of them as individuals.

The stereotype of the foremen was apparently based upon the fact that the foremen in the past had been very brutal: on this point the workers, the present foremen, and the management were all agreed. With the outbreak of war in 1939 and the end of unemployment in the area, a distinct improvement had begun, and by the early 1950's all the more brutal foremen had retired and had been replaced by more reasonable men. However, the stereotype of the foremen remained unaltered because the conditions which had led to its creation, the brutality of past foremen, were kept alive by oral tradition in the works. The older workers told the younger ones stories of the behavior of the foremen in the past, how men had to give them money or buy them drink on pay nights in order to keep their jobs, and of their endless bullying and brutal treatment of the men. Some of these stories went back to before the first world war and did not lie within the experience of even the oldest workers, but had been learned by them from a previous generation. Yet the men would become indignant when recounting or listening to these stories and they accepted them as being applicable to the present. In this way, belief in the stereotype was kept alive.

The shop stewards and the men got on well with the foremen as individuals; nevertheless, the existence of the stereotype of the foremen as "brutal" poisoned industrial relations in the works. As they had little contact wih management proper, the men looked on the foremen as the true representatives of the management and the company. Consequently, the attitude of hostility the men had for "the foremen" was projected onto the company and its management, and embittered industrial relations.

Attempt to Change the Stereotype

In the circumstances, it was felt that an attempt should be made to change the stereotype. This was difficult, because it was not considered practicable to make a direct approach to the men and attempt to show them that the stereotype was false. The stereotype was a belief, it was not rational, and it was unlikely to be disproved by logical arguments coming from an outsider. The men were certain to be very suspicious of any direct attack upon the stereotype that seemed to come from the management side. If they became suspicious, then no arguments would prevail, for they would probably refuse to listen and would fall back on the line of argument: "We know, we have experience of them and you haven't"—an argument to which there is no answer.

Thus the situation was that the stereotype had to be submitted to critical examination and analysis if it was to be disproved, and this had to be done by the men themselves. The method chosen was based upon observations made by the investigator during previous research. It had been noted that questions asked in the course of research had the effect of stimulating those interviewed into thinking about, and often questioning, their previous assumptions. Those who had only vague ideas about their work and their attitude to it found that they had to think about these ideas and clarify them before they could answer questions. Even those who already had clear-cut ideas were stimulated to reconsider them while trying to justify them to the questioner, and they were often surprised at the conclusions they reached while doing so. As a result it was noticeable that after research had been conducted in a works or an office, the people in it had much clearer and more definite views on works or office matters than they had previous to the research. Sometimes the ideas of those interviewed changed, sometimes they remained the same, but usually they were clarified. For example, some individuals who had previously held a strong but vaguely defined sense of grievance against the employer now found that they had no real grounds for grievance; whereas others were confirmed in their sense of grievance and were now able to define their reasons for it.

As previous research had produced these results, it was decided to continue with the present study and see whether the research method alone would stimulate the men into analyzing and adjusting their stereotype of the foremen. The research was continued, no attempt was made to argue with the men on the subject of the foremen, and no disapproval was shown of even their wildest denunciations of them. But the men were reminded that, while any justifiable grievance would be taken up and an attempt made to remedy it, they had to *prove* that grievances were justified: statements of opinion were not enough, evidence was required to support them. It was pointed out that this was in the interests of the men, for they had everything to gain by presenting a sound case in support of their claims. The branch committee members in particular saw the point of this and did all they could to collect concrete evidence about their grievances—including that concerning the foremen.

Once the need for evidence had been accepted it was possible to cross-question those interviewed without giving offense. It must be emphasized that this was done in a friendly manner. If a man said the foremen were bad, he was asked how many of those he knew personally were bad, how many good. If he said a particular one was bad, he was asked to give reasons. If he quoted actual cases, he was asked when these occurred, and, if they were prewar as many were, he was asked if the foreman concerned was still in the works, and if he knew of any recent cases of this kind. It was necessary not to harass the men unduly, but at the same time no statement could be allowed to pass unchallenged. It must also be noted that the question of the foremen took up only a part of each interview. Interviews were nondirective and the men were allowed to discuss their work in general. Hence the subject of the foremen did not occupy the whole interview, as may appear from the accounts given above. It occupied an important part, but many other questions of pay, conditions, etc., were also covered. In the circumstances the men had no occasion to feel, and in fact it is known that they did not feel, that any special significance was being placed on the problem of the foremen.

This technique was adopted at a time when the 33 active trade unionists and 26 of the other men had already been interviewed. The investigator had reached the conclusion that the active members created opinion among the men generally, hence they were given informal follow-up interviews using the new technique. This created no problem since the investigator was in constant contact with the active members. The 26 others were not reinterviewed but the technique was applied in all new interviews.

RESULTS

These interviews led to frequent informal discussions among the active members about their grievances, and, at first, to increased discussion with the investigator. However, it became noticeable that the subject of the foremen was soon dropped from these discussions and was deliberately avoided in conversation with the investigator. The first indication of a change of attitude came three months after the active members had been reinterviewed. The branch secretary, hitherto a very bitter critic of the foremen, when discussing with the investigator some recent negotiations with a foreman on pay, praised the foreman for his cooperation and ended his account by saying: "You know we are lucky in here, we have quite a decent sensible crowd of foremen."

However, the other active members remained evasive on the subject of the foremen. It was thought that they might well have ceased or be ready to cease believing in the stereotype but were afraid to declare themselves until they knew the opinion of their group. In short, that the members were in a state of pluralistic ignorance about the group's present stereotype of and attitude to "the foremen." In order to force a public declaration of opinion the investigator raised the question of the foremen with the branch secretary during an informal lunch-time meeting of the branch committee and other active members: a small group of these habitually lunched together in the blacksmith's shop belonging to the works. The branch secretary replied that the men "talked a lot of blethers about the foremen." At this the branch chairman, who had previously been evasive, broke in and told the investigator:

> Don't take too much notice of what the men say about the foremen, they aren't really such a bad lot in spite of what they say; they could have a damn sight worse, in fact, they have had a damn sight worse in this works in the past.

The other men present agreed with him and cited examples of how helpful and cooperative many of the foremen were.

After this incident, there was a marked change of attitude towards the foremen among all the active members who had been present. They were no longer evasive, but discussed the foremen freely and warned the investigator against paying too much attention to the men's complaints about them. The public declaration by the branch secretary of his new attitude to the foremen appeared to have provided the necessary sanction which the other active members had awaited before publicly committing themselves to this new attitude. The active members who had not been present at the meeting remained evasive until the branch meeting a week later, when the branch secretary, without referring to their previous grievances, stated that there had been "a lot of stupid complaints about the foremen by some of the men," and went on to give his opinion that the foremen were "a pretty decent bunch." In this, he was supported by the branch committee. After this event none of the active members was found to be evasive, or to be hostile to the foremen.

In subsequent interviews, none of the 33 active members complained of the foremen generally, although they still complained of the four unpopular foremen. It was noticeable that none of the active members ever admitted that there had been any change of attitude on their part. They said that the men had long had a foolish hostility to the foremen but they, the active members, had never shared it, and had tried to show the men how wrong their view of the foremen was—and from this point on they did discourage criticism of the foremen by the men. At the same time, the active members, and the branch committee members in particular, expressed a view which contradicted their claim that they had always known the foremen were "a good crowd." This view was that the foremen had been *ordered* to be more cooperative. In spite of denials by the investigator, the active members claimed that he must have complained to the management and that they had put pressure on the foremen. As evidence of this, they cited instances of the new cooperativeness of the foremen in handling disputes and grievances; these instances did not include the four unpopular foremen who were still attacked as "men who will never learn." The investigator had found no discernible change in the behavior of the foremen and had not suggested to the management or the foremen that there ought to be any change. In fact the men themselves had cited similar examples of cooperation by individual foremen even when the stereotype of the foremen as brutal was still accepted.

Thus the active members had changed their stereotype of the foremen and had adopted a new attitude towards them. So far as the investigator could discover they realized that a change had taken place but were reluctant to accept that the change had taken place in their own perception of the foremen. They rationalized the situation by claiming: (*a*) that they had always known that the foremen were "all right"; and (*b*) that the foremen had changed their behavior towards the workers.

The rest of the men in the works did not abandon the stereotype and change their attitude to the foremen as rapidly as did the active members. The hostility to the foremen was discernible several months after the active members had changed. That the attitude did eventually change was owing to, or at least was speeded up by, the work of the active members. They became openly critical of any unsubstantiated complaints made about the foremen and, after negotiating on behalf of the men, would return and praise the fairness and moderation of the foremen to them. The long-term effect of this was to create a new stereotype of the foremen and a new attitude towards them.

It is difficult to assess the success or otherwise of such an exercise since it is not possible to measure and compare the various factors involved with any exactitude. From the strictly practical point of view the exercise was a success since it did result in the men adopting a new stereotype of and a new attitude to the foremen. In consequence, relations between the union officials and the foremen improved; as indicated above, these had not been bad before, but they could, and did, improve. The foremen reported that they found the shop stewards more cooperative and less aggressive, and the number of disputes declined considerably; incidents which had formerly led to strikes or at least to disputes which had to be settled at general-manager level were now settled amicably within the department. The subject of the foremen as a major grievance was dropped completely, and the men concentrated on their other grievances, the most important being pay and conditions. As these were *real* grievances which the company could amend, and was willing to amend, this was no disadvantage. In short, an imaginary grievance which could not be settled was replaced by real ones which could—to the satisfaction of the men and the company. It must be emphasized that the grievances about pay and conditions were not tackled until after the active members had changed their attitudes to the foremen, hence there was no question of this change being due to a settlement of their other grievances.

SUMMARY

1. The investigator was asked to study industrial relations in a works and recommend any necessary changes. Relations were found to be bad, mainly owing to the attitude of hostility the men held towards the foremen generally.

2. It was found that this attitude of hostility was based upon a stereotype that the foremen were brutal. The stereotype proved to be false, and the men in general complained of only four out of 40 foremen.

3. An attempt was made to change the stereotype by causing the men to investigate the evidence for their complaints against the foremen. It was hoped that if the stereotype was changed the attitude of the men would change also.

4. As a result, the active members of the union did decide that the stereotype was false but were reluctant to admit this until the trade union leader, the branch secretary, openly stated that it was so. As a result of the

...ange of stereotype, the active members dropped their attitude of hostility to the foremen.

5. The active members never admitted that they had changed their opinion of the foremen but claimed two contradictory things: (a) that they had always known that the foremen were "all right"; (b) that the foremen had changed for the better.

6. The workers in general were much slower in changing their stereotype of the foremen and their attitude of hostility to them, but eventually did so under pressure from the active members.

CONCLUSIONS

It is difficult to draw precise conclusions from a study of this kind because of the vague nature of much of the evidence. However, it is possible to indicate certain general points that were brought out by the research.

1. It has been suggested that where actual cultural differences between groups are small a false stereotype is often due to lack of contact and can be reduced by increasing contact between the groups concerned:

> Contact by itself is a major weapon in the reduction of tension where groups are alike or similar, and where stereotypes are unrealistic (Saenger and Flowerman, 5, p. 237).

In the case described above this was not so; contact alone had no effect. The foremen had the same social background as the workers, they had worked their way up to their present rank within the same works, and they lived in the same small town. There were few or no cultural differences between workers and foremen, and there was frequent contact between them. In spite of this, the stereotype of the foremen as brutal persisted among the workers.

2. Allport has claimed that stereotypes do not create prejudice, but rationalize or justify an existing prejudice:

> Whether favorable or unfavorable, *a stereotype is an exaggerated belief associated with a category. Its function is to justify (rationalize) our conduct in relation to that category* (Allport, 1, p. 187, italics in original).

Saenger and Flowerman have stressed the same point:

> 'Stereotypes are only symptomatic. At most, they reinforce hostile attitudes, are supporting rationalizations' (5, p. 237).

This may be so in many cases, but it is difficult to see how it fits the study described here. In this case the stereotype had fitted the facts: it was agreed by the foremen, management, and office staff, as well as by the workers, that the foremen had been brutal. The retirement of the brutal foremen and their replacement by others who were not brutal created a situation in which the stereotype was false. The workers displayed an attitude of hostility towards "the foremen" who, according to the stereotype, were brutal, but, as Table 1 shows, relatively few men regarded the individual foremen as brutal or displayed an attitude of hostility towards them. In these circumstances it is difficult to see what created and maintained the prejudice against the foremen as a group if it was not the stereotype, particularly as few of the younger men in the works had any direct experience of a brutal foreman. The stereotype did not justify the prejudice against the foremen but *was* the prejudice, and it was justified by an oral tradition in the works which embodied stories of brutal behavior by foremen in the past. In other words, it was justified by myths which formed part of the culture of the works. It may be argued that all workers are prejudiced against foremen because of their role, but even if this is admitted it remains that the prejudice in the works was intensified by the stereotype. In any case there was little prejudice displayed against individual foremen.

Allport further claims that, since the stereotype does not create the prejudice but is only a rationalization of it, removing the stereotype will not remove the prejudice:

> Stereotypes are not identical with prejudice. They are primarily rationalizers. They adapt to the prevailing temper of prejudice or the needs of the situation. While it does no harm (and may do some good) to combat them in schools and colleges, and to reduce them in mass media of communication, it must not be thought that this attack alone will eradicate the roots of prejudice (1, pp. 198–99).

In the case described here removal of the stereotype did end the prejudice against the foremen as a group, and it changed the attitude of hostility the men had towards them. This is not to argue that Allport is entirely wrong, but only that, in cases where a stereotype was once correct but is so no longer, owing to a change in circumstances, then the survival of the false stereotype does in itself lead to prejudicial attitudes, and a change in the stereotype can lead to a removal of prejudice.

It may be argued, from the point of view of Allport, Saenger and Flowerman that the results of the research were misunderstood and that it was the attitude, *not* the stereotype that was changed *initially*. After the attitude had changed the stereotype changed to conform with it. There are two answers to this. First, that whatever did happen, one thing is clear, an attempt was made to change a stereotype, and this led to a change in the stereotype *and* to a change of attitude. Yet Allport argues that a change in a stereotype will not remove a prejudicial attitude. The second point concerns the interdependence of attitudes and stereotypes; to quote Charles L. Stevenson:

The causal connection between beliefs and attitudes is usually not only intimate but reciprocal. To ask whether beliefs in general direct attitudes in general, or whether the causal connection goes rather in the opposite direction, is simply a misleading question. It is like asking, "Do popular writers influence public taste, or does public taste influence them?" Any implication that the alternatives are mutually exclusive can only be rejected. The influence goes both ways, although at times only one direction of influence may predominate (Stevenson, 6, p. 5).

From Stevenson's statement it is possible to construct two hypotheses concerning the attitude change in this study:

(a) That in this particular study the stereotype, the belief, predominated and a change of belief led to a change of attitude. It is not claimed that the belief element *always* predominates, but this study indicates that the belief *sometimes* predominates. Thus the evidence of this research contradicts Allport and Saenger, who are asserting that attitudes *always* predominate and sterotypes are *always* subordinate.

(b) That attitudes and stereotypes are interdependent, without either being necessarily dominant, and a change in one must lead to a change in the other. In this study the stereotype was changed and this led to a change of attitude. However, had the attitude been changed first this would have led to a change in the stereotype.

Further research will be necessary to test these hypotheses. Clearly, however, both contradict the statements of Allport and Saenger.

3. Marrow and French have shown that stereotypes in industry can be changed by inducing those who hold a false stereotype to participate in an inquiry into its validity:

Our experiment at the Harwood Manufacturing Corporation demonstrated that whereas arguments and persuasion had failed to uproot a strong institutional stereotype crystallized into company policy, other methods succeeded. Chief among them were participation of management in research and participation of supervisors in group discussion and decision. Thus, through a process of guided experiences which are equally his own, a person may be re-oriented so that he gradually takes on within himself the attitudes which he would not accept from others (4, p. 37).

The investigator did not know of this study at the time of his own research; nevertheless, the method he evolved was very similar to theirs. Thus, the workers, the active members in particular, were led to inquire into the validity of their stereotype of the foremen with the results shown above. It appears, therefore, that it is possible to remove or reduce prejudice by such methods; however, neither study was precise enough to allow one to draw conclusions as to *exactly* how the change occurred.

4. One interesting fact that emerged during the study was the group nature of the change. The active members did not display any open change

of attitude to the foremen generally until this was sanctioned by the branch secretary and, later, by other committee members who first displayed in public a new attitude and denounced the old stereotype. The workers generally accepted the change only after it was pressed on them by the active members. This appears to support two points raised by Lewin: (*a*) that it is easier to change group standards than to change individual members of the group:

> Perhaps one might expect single individuals to be more pliable than groups of like-minded individuals. However, experience in leadership training, in changing of food habits, work production, criminality, alcoholism, prejudices, all seem to indicate that it is usually easier to change individuals formed into a group than to change any of them separately (3, p. 34);

and (*b*) that in changing "group ideology" and "group action" one should try to change people in "key positions" rather than attempt to change the entire population (*ibid.*, p. 143). This second point, that the approval of prestigeful members of a group may influence group members into changing their attitudes, is supported by Kelley and Woodruff (2) in their study of "apparent group approval of a counternorm communication."

5. A final point that may be of significance is the fact that the men concerned in this study did not admit that they had changed their stereotype of, and attitude to, the foremen. Instead they claimed that they had never held the stereotype of the foremen as brutal and had never been hostile to them; the active members said that the other men had held it; the men generally blamed each other; no one admitted that *he* had ever held the attitude and stereotype; at the same time, the active members claimed that the foremen had changed for the better. In discussing the situation with the active members it was clear that they were ready to resist strongly any attempt to make them admit that *they* had changed. In short, it was easier to bring about a change in their stereotype and attitude than it was to obtain admission of such change. This may seem an obvious point, but it is one that is important in industrial relations: that it may be much easier to make changes in stereotypes and attitudes if one does not insist on an admission that change has occurred, or if the change can be attributed to a fictitious cause—in this case to the supposed change in the behavior of the foremen.

REFERENCES

1. Allport, G. *The Nature of Prejudice*. New York: Doubleday, 1954.
2. Kelley, H. H., and Woodruff, Christine L. "Members' Reactions to Apparent Group Approval of a Counternorm Communication," *Journal of Abnormal and Social Psychology*, Vol. 52 (1954), pp. 67–74.
3. Lewin, K. "Frontiers in Group Dynamics," *Human Relations*, Vol. 1 (1947), pp. 5–42, 143–53.

4. Marrow, Alfred J., and French, Jr., John R. P. "Changing a Stereotype in Industry," *Journal of Social Issues*, Vol. 1 (1945), pp. 33–7.

5. Saenger, Gerhart, and Flowerman, Samuel. "Stereotypes and Prejudicial Attitudes," *Human Relations*, Vol. 7 (1954), p. 217.

6. Stevenson, Charles L. *Ethics and Language*. New Haven, Conn.: Yale University Press, 1960.

21. ORGANIZATIONAL STRUCTURES IN TRANSITION*

KILBURN LeCOMPTE

EDITOR's NOTE: The following article recounts a major organizational change which took place between 1958 and 1962. It was set in motion by a top management concerned (1) to realize development early in their careers of general management personnel, (2) to induce a global, rather than functional, viewpoint for lower-level managers, (3) to improve teamwork at the district levels, and (4) to improve the status and effectiveness of staff functions. Author Kilburn LeCompte served as the change agent. The consultant was Douglas M. McGregor, then Professor of Industrial Management at M.I.T.

BACKGROUND

THE Bell Telephone Company of Pennsylvania is one of the largest in the country. It provides telephone and other communications services within the boundaries of the state of Pennsylvania. The company is fully owned by the American Telephone and Telegraph Company, which also owns a large number of companies similar to the Pennsylvania company. General staff and policy advice is available from the parent company. Since incorporation in the early 1900's, the company has grown steadily in terms of the number of customers it serves, the number of employees on the payroll, and the number of telephones in operation.

Growth has been accelerated within the past fifteen years; in 1961 the company served over 4⅓ million telephones and had more than 32,000 employees on the payroll.

The board of directors is largely an external one, consisting of business leaders from various sections of the state, the president, two vice-presidents of the company, and an officer of the parent company.

The company's rates and earnings are subject to regulation by the State Public Utility Commission. Material, equipment, and supplies necessary for the operation of the business are furnished by the Western Electric Company—also owned by the parent company.

Wages and working conditions for the vocational employees are bargained with several unions at the company level.

Financing required by the company is arranged either through the parent company or on the public market.

The president and his cabinet officers, together with their respective staff groups, form the Headquarters organization of the company; this group is located in Philadelphia, largest city in the state.

* Reprinted from *Organization Theory in Industrial Practice* (ed. Mason Haire), New York: John Wiley & Sons, 1962.

Historically, the company has been divided into three operating areas—known as the Eastern, Central, and Western areas. The headquarters of each of these areas is in the largest city in the area territory. Thus, the headquarters of the Eastern Area is in Philadelphia, together with the company Headquarters organization.

This arrangement, including the Headquarters Department, is shown in Figure 1. Each headquarters department is headed by a vice-president; the

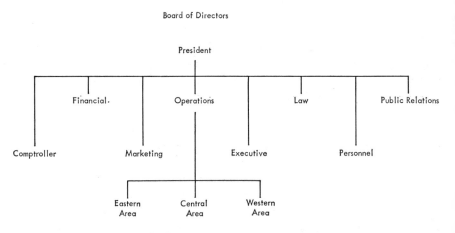

FIG. 1.   Bell Telephone Co. of Pennsylvania

operating areas are each headed by a vice-president and general manager. A typical area structure is shown in Figure 2.

As shown, there are three functional operating departments—Plant, Traffic, and Commercial. Each department has its own personnel and technical staff services. The Plant Department is concerned with construction, installation, and maintenance of the telephone plant. Traffic is responsible for operation of the switchboards; Commercial is broadly responsible for the operation of the business offices, the Sales organization, for billing and collection procedures and the issuance of telephone directories.

The Engineering Department is responsible for the investment side of the business. It is concerned with technical engineering programs, design, and other technical aspects of the business. The Accounting Department is responsible for accounting functions for all departments; and, though located with the area organizations, each area general accounting manager reports to the comptroller at Headquarters.

Each of these five departments is supervised by a fifth-level functional department head. The vice-president and general manager, at sixth level, is the first manager in the line organization for whom interdepartmental supervision is established.

The basic unit of the area organization is the district. A typical operating area has its geography divided into about eight districts. Each district is headed by a district head, at third level, for each of the line

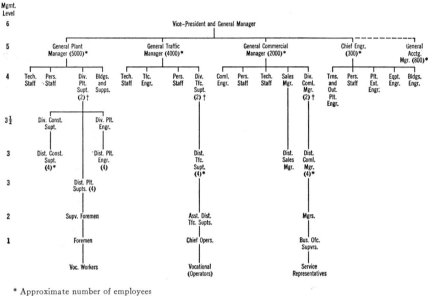

* Approximate number of employees
† Number of titles with similar organizations

FIG. 2. Typical Area Organization

operating departments, with Plant represented by three men. Thus, each district is managed by a district team of five men, with the following titles:

District Plant Superintendent
District Construction Superintendent
District Plant Engineer
District Traffic Superintendent
District Commercial Manager

This team is responsible for total district performance, but each district head reports vertically along functional departmental lines.

This general form of organization has been traditional within the company for many years. With growth, additional vocational workers have been added, together with increased numbers of first- and second-level managers to supervise these people. A few additional district organizations had been created prior to reorganization, but changes above the district level had been minimal.

Historically, a complex system of departmental measurements was used to determine organizational performance. Basically, the same measurement plans are used in all companies owned by the parent company, and internal competition between units is stimulated by monthly comparisons at all levels of the company and also between companies.

THE NEED FOR CHANGE

The president and his cabinet became aware of the need for some change in the company organization several years ago. About 1926, the company was operated on a centralized basis, with all department heads located with the Headquarters groups in Philadelphia. In 1926, the operating groups were decentralized by the creation of four geographic operating areas. During the depression years of the early 1930's, the two areas in the eastern part of the state were combined to make the Eastern Area, which thus became the largest area in the Company. Continued expansion during the next thirty years caused the Eastern Area to grow to a point at which the size of the operation indicated that consideration should be given to forming an additional area organization. Similarly, where operating areas in other companies had grown to the approximate size of the Eastern Area, generally the top management of these companies also moved to create additional area units. Another factor was the growth pattern within the company. Eastern Area, by reason of its location in the economic growth pattern of the state, gave every indication of an accelerated growth pattern in the 1960's, as compared to the other areas. It became evident that, because of current size and future growth pattern, a major change should be considered.

Factors other than size and growth were also apparent. Changes in the telephone art, rapid development of the computer and other forms of mechanization, especially those that appeared to be applicable during the 1960's, gave added weight to the need for change. Broader development of management people to meet the demands of these changes also appeared to be a basic need of the company. In addition, it seemed desirable to move the interdepartmental decision-making level (now at the sixth level) closer to day-to-day operational problems in the districts. Accordingly, it was decided to proceed in the organization planning field.

The Change Agent

In order to assign specific responsibility for implementation of the decision to proceed with organization studies, it was decided to assign an individual on a permanent, full-time basis, reporting to the vice president–personnel. One of the fifth-level department heads, with wide company experience and background, was selected for the job.

In preliminary discussions, the change agent was told that there were no preconceived ideas involving procedures or the end result. No avenues of inquiry were blocked, and every officer of the company was asked to cooperate as requested. Preliminary discussions by the change agent soon disclosed that the various officers held mixed feelings with respect to the need for change, methods of procedure, and particularly with respect to time elements for study and completion of the project.

There were strong indications that some officers felt that the job should be produced in approximately six months; other indicated that the scope and impact of major change would become so involved with human variables that the only way to proceed was on a carefully planned time schedule extending over several years. Another major item seemed to be the need to develop strategies, methods of procedures, and involvement of people which would insure successful operation and, at the same time, produce maximum objectivity for the entire program.

Initial Steps

Shortly after his appointment, the change agent saw two pressing needs: First, the need for information about what other companies owned by the parent company had done with respect to organization planning and change; second, the need for professional guidance and consultation during his task of planning for organization change.

To meet the need for information concerning other companies, the change agent spent several months exploring, in depth, changes made by the other companies. The information was gathered by visits to and discussions with representatives of the parent company, and by on-the-spot interviews with key persons in other companies. The persons contacted were those who had been involved in either the planning or the activation of major organization changes. In addition, visits and discussions were held with outside industries known to be active in organization-planning work.

Meeting the need for professional assistance was a more complex consideration. Several basic decisions had to be made with respect to the nature of the professional help to be sought. Briefly, these decisions involved the following: (1) Whether this assistance should come from a large consulting firm, or from an individual consultant; (2) the extent of professional assistance required; and (3) the degree of familiarity with specific Telephone Company procedures and operation held to be essential. Because of the desire for maximum involvement and participation by company people, it was decided to seek professional help from an independent consultant—preferably with university affiliation—who would serve as a periodic sounding board and guide for general organization study procedure and design. It was felt that a high degree of familiarity with telephone procedures and operation was not vital in view of the expected use of in-company people for planning work.

In retrospect, these seem to have been sound decisions from several standpoints. A widely known, independent expert in organization theory was not viewed by company people as masterminding the future of their business, but rather as a resource person to whom they might turn for help. There was also no hesitancy to accept his advice on face value, since there was no organizational axe of his own to be considered. More important, however, was his ability as an outside expert to work with and contact directly top officers of the company on matters of basic policy and strategy.

A problem already noted concerned the time elements in the minds of top officers of the company for completion of the organization-planning work and for the submission of a recommendation. Here, by way of example, was a major policy decision which could be changed only by these top officers. The change agent and the consultant were convinced that the time limitation mentioned was so short that it would seriously affect both the quality of the planning and the ultimate recommendation. In this regard, the consultant was able, because of his position as an independent expert, to discuss with higher management the potential advantages to be gained from a more lengthy and thorough planning activity, which should result in better understanding and acceptance of change by all parts of the organization. Agreement by the top officers to a longer period for organization planning was greatly facilitated by the role of the consultant as a communications channel to top management.

With the services of the consultant secured and the time limitations eased, the basic question was one of the most efficient and advantageous methods for conducting the organization study. At this point two basic decisions were made. The first concerned the means for conducting the study; the second involved the scope of the activity to be undertaken.

As to the means for conducting the study, it was decided to utilize a task-force approach in *all* areas of the organization study and recommendation preparation. This was felt to be most desirable in order to utilize the best thinking of the company on the problem and to involve persons maximally in building future acceptance of the resulting plan of action. The procedure was, in effect, Telephone people working together to solve a Telephone problem rather than one man or firm solving a Telephone problem for the company by means which would then be imposed on Telephone people.

Examination of the scope of activity revealed that any effective reorganization goes beyond mere shifting of lines and blocks on an organization chart. A basic consideration in any program of organization study and planning should be a reexamination of management philosophy and management control policies. For this reason, it was felt advantageous to have two separate and distinct committees—one to focus its efforts on the problems of organizational structure, the other to explore the current management controls system, whose work could be integrated as the study neared completion. It was realized that there would be some overlap in the deliberations of the two task forces, particularly with reference to management philosophy, but that much would be gained by having a group specifically charged to deal with each of these areas.

The change agent formulated specific recommendations for the conduct of the organization-planning activity. These recommendations were submitted to the president and the cabinet of the company by the change agent in a presentation which reviewed the background work and initial steps he had taken.

The recommendation was that two task forces be appointed with specified level, departmental, and geographic representation. The Planning Committee, focused on organization, was to be headed by an officer of the company with previous or current area general manager experience. The Controls Committee was to be headed by a department head with wide experience. The change agent was to serve as staff for the two committees and to act as liaison between them. The recommendation was accepted by the cabinet, and the committees were appointed.

Planning Committee Operation

The first meeting of the Planning Committee was designed to highlight the importance of the committee's activities to the entire company, and to give the committee members a sense of responsibility and personal involvement in the entire activity. This was accomplished by arranging for a one-week orientation meeting in a location remote from company surroundings. The first day of this conference was devoted to a long meeting with the president and some of his officers. During the discussion, the president pointed out his views and the company's future needs and impressed the group with the importance of their assignment both to the company and to themselves.

Instead of using a prepared agenda or content outline, the chairman played a nondirective role and developed a free, permissive atmosphere to allow full discussion of all subjects advanced by the group. This was considered to be a primary requirement in view of the status barriers contained in a multilevel group. Finally, arrangements were made for individual assignments of information- and data-gathering character to be presented at subsequent meetings planned on a monthly basis.

The change agent worked with the committee chairman in feedback meetings to shape the direction and progress of the committee, and the consultant became available for resource purposes as the meetings developed. Finally, after full discussion of personal viewpoints and experiences, the committee established ground rules and basic assumptions concerning its task. Agreement on the company's basic problems relating to its task—beginning with the basic question of "What is your business?"— started the group on positive problem-solving programs.

For example, some of the objectives and assumptions agreed to, in order to implement the study were:

1. Bring interdepartmental decision level nearer the problem level. (In the traditional organization, the vice-president and general manager, at sixth level, is the first person to supervise several departments.)

2. Keep number of organization levels to a minimum.

3. Reassign departmental functions where increased effectiveness will result, regardless of historical associations.

4. Decentralize those functions which can be performed more effectively if decentralized.

5. Centralize those functions which can be done more effectively on an area or company basis.

6. Improve top management's means of obtaining better evaluation and balance of expense, revenues, and investment by giving greater recognition in the organization structure to "secondary" functions which have become of primary importance due to changes in the character of the business.

7. Assume that labor matters, salary levels, and availability of qualified personnel are not controlling in the design of the organization structure.

The Planning group, by this time, had developed a well-founded objective view of their task; many preconceived and departmental viewpoints began to fade into the background. Earlier attempts to analyze and rearrange organization charts quickly were abandoned in favor of problem-solving approaches.

In order to have authentic, basic data on the current situation available, the committee made arrangements to have every third-level staff employee in all three areas and at Headquarters prepare a function list of his job duties and responsibilities. This material was then sorted and made available for easy reference. This data became the backbone for resource purposes, since any functional realignment would be based upon an analysis of traditional job relationships.

With a view to achieving wider participation throughout the management structure, the group decided to form subcommittees in each of the broad departmental fields and to staff these groups with selected people. Subcommittees were formed in the Western Area for technical staff study, in the Central Area for personnel staff study, and in Headquarters for engineering, directory, and trunk facilities matters. Each committee was staffed with three or four experts in their respective fields with a member of the Planning group acting as chairman of each subgroup. The change agent also participated as a resource person on an occasional basis.

After suitable orientation and several months of work, each subcommittee presented a report to the Planning group—both in conference and in written form. During their study, each subcommittee used the basic function lists and consulted with hundreds of management people at all levels in the organization.

Meanwhile, the Planning Committee was encouraged to proceed with development of several models for the proposed new area; finally, the reports of the subcommittees were tied into the models which were developed. Then a final structure was approved.

At this stage, the Planning group prepared a summary report of their entire activities and included their recommendations to the president of the company. This presentation was made in a two-day conference with the president and his cabinet, with individual committee members presenting various portions of the recommendation. These recommedations included the idea that the new area, if approved, would be regarded as a pilot operation and that no changes would be extended to other areas until

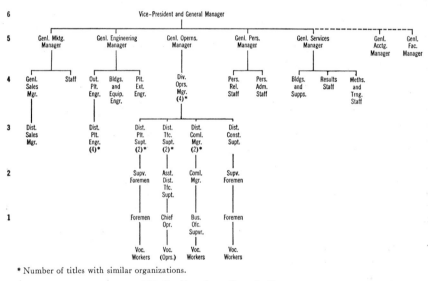

* Number of titles with similar organizations.

FIG. 3.   New Area Organization

evaluation of the pilot operation could be made over a reasonable period of time. By using the pilot approach, subsequent change in the pilot operation could be made without disturbing company operations as a whole.

During this presentation, the outside consultant pointed out that development of a new structure represented only part of the total problem. Completion of this portion of the work presented an opportunity for top management to make changes in managerial strategy, especially in the control and measurement field, which would permit basic objectives and goals to be reached.

A copy of the new organization chart for the new area appears as Figure 3.

Controls Committee Operation

Generally, the formation and orientation for this committee resembled the pattern for the Planning Committee. The committee was formed as a multilevel group; the chairman was a fifth-level department head with wide and varied experience in company operations. Three fourth-level people from various departments were appointed; and, since the final impact of the control and measurement system centered on district operation, three district superintendents from the field line organization were added.

The broad assignment given to the group was:

1. To study the field of controls and measurements that are used in administering the company's internal operations.

2. To work in conjunction with the Management-Planning group and to make recommendations for controls and measurements which could be used in any new area structure that would be recommended by the Planning group.

3. To make any other recommendations in this field that would be helpful to the company's operations.

After several meetings to discuss the problem areas of their assignment, the committee made a basic decision to confine its study to the district level.

It was soon determined that the number and detail of measurements which were in use were voluminous and in great detail. Practically every phase of the district operation was in some form of measurement; standard practice was to publish measurement results in the form of numercial or smokestack charts, whereby every district, division, or area was placed on a comparative basis.

In order to develop an objective frame of reference, it was decided to interview a random sample of company district heads. At the outset, it was thought that the interview could be structured in the area of "What do you, as a district man, need in the way of measurements in order to administer the job to your satisfaction?"

Discussion of this theme with a preliminary sample disclosed that demands varied quite widely and for a variety of reasons. For example, a younger district head expressed a need for most of the existing measurements plus others which he had placed in effect; but an older, more experienced district head might express the opinion that only a few composite measures were needed and that most formal ones could be dispensed with.

One important finding was that the view of the district man's needs and use for measurements was largely determined by the way division heads supervised the district operation and also by the climate created by upper levels of supervision. In some cases, close supervision developed a need for much detailed information—usually on a defensive basis—while in others, just the opposite requirement prevailed. To state it more succinctly: the district head was primarily interested in those things in which his boss displayed an interest.

The data gathered in the interviewing program, sorted by topic and functional department outline, became source material for the committee's use. The committee recorded that there was general recognition by management of the value of measuring tools provided for the company. However, it was apparent that the existence of even a completely adequate system of measurements did not guarantee successful organization performance. Depending upon how they were utilized, measurements could either hinder or help the achievement of company objectives.

The Controls Committee, after a thorough analysis of the data and study of the structure developed by the Planning Committee, prepared a comprehensive report on its assignment. This included a description of its study, detailed data gathered in the interviewing program, an appraisal of the measurement and control systems then in effect in the company, and, finally, proposals and recommendations for changes in the new area organization.

Among these changes, some of the pertinent recommendations included:

1. Elimination, at upper levels, of detailed reports involving district and subdistrict operating units.

2. Minimization of emphasis on comparative data with other district units within the company in favor of emphasis on the units' own past performance.

3. Provision to each level manager of operating data for his unit and for the units immediately below him.

4. Establishment of a pattern of relationship that would provide maximum self-development possibilities for managers in the new organization. This recommendation was developed in detail from the viewpoint of all levels of management.

The theme of the recommendation was that individual performance would be judged in terms of agreed-upon tasks which reflected the goals of higher management.

The report of the Controls Committee was given to the president and his cabinet, who approved the recommendations. Informal meetings between individual officers, the change agent, and the outside consultant were held to implement the report.

Developing Strategy for Acceptance

One major problem faced early in the organization study was that of insuring large-scale acceptance for whatever recommendations might be made. It was felt that two major methods could be used in order to help secure the acceptance and commitment desired. First, it was felt that, at every opportunity, maximum participation by company people from all levels should be secured. Second, periodic announcement concerning the activities and progress of the two committees should be given widespread distribution throughout the company.

The first official announcement concerning activities of the Organization-Planning group came when the two committees were appointed by the president. Up to this point, little or nothing about the organization-planning activity had been promulgated to the various levels of management. It was felt that, with the appointment of these committees, there was an opportunity not only to inform the entire company about the planning activities but also to alert all members of management that they might well be involved in the deliberations which were to follow. For this reason, a letter was sent out over the president's signature to all members in the top four levels of management, with the understanding that they would transmit the information contained in the letter to their subordinates. It should be stressed that such a letter is an unusual occurrence in the company. In sending out such a letter then, maximum attention was focused on the announcement and the activity.

In addition to announcing the specific membership of these two committees, the letter discussed, in some detail, the problems of growth and technological development which had necessitated the organization-planning study. With respect to what might be expected of the organization at large, the letter said, "In carrying out their [the committees'] assignments, it will be necessary to utilize the knowledge and experience of a large cross section of our management people. This means that you, as an individual, will be called upon to contribute to the effort insofar as your particular knowledge and skills may prove to be helpful." This was followed by a statement concerning the importance and the support that the president placed upon this undertaking.

Reference has already been made to the feedback given by the change agent to the president and his cabinet. Here again was a move specifically designed to gain widespread support and acceptance for the undertaking and its ultimate result. It would have been easier perhaps to have reported only to the president, through channels, and for him to have appointed the committees required. It was felt more advantageous, however, to report to the full cabinet. In this manner, it was possible for nominations for committee membership to be solicited from the entire vice-presidential level in the company. This process involved active participation on the part of every officer in the company and, to some extent at least, made him a participant in the future operation.

Reference has also been made to the decision to use a task-force approach. This again was a means of gaining wider participation in the actual study and formulation of recommendations, which would otherwise have been most difficult. This participative approach was carried still one step further with the utilization of subcommittees to work on specific aspects of the organization study. In setting up subcommittees, all departments and all geographic areas of the company were adequately represented as previously described.

When the final recommendation had been prepared, it was presented, by the committee, to the president and his cabinet in a special two-day meeting. Present at this meeting were all vice-presidents of the company, including the vice-presidents and general managers of the three areas, and an officer of the parent company. The presentation was made by the various members of the Planning Committee, each presenting some segment of the material—generally that for which he had been responsible. Here again, it would have been possible to have submitted the report through channels to the president alone, but it was felt that a greater acceptance might be gained through a more widespread presentation.

In this regard, department heads throughout the company (a vital opinion-forming group in the management structure) were presented with a one-day version of the Planning Committee's report and recommendation a short time after it had been presented to the cabinet. The presentation to this group was made on the basis of imparting information. At the conclusion of the meeting, they were asked to submit their reactions and judgments through the vice-president to whom they reported. In this way, top management had the judgments and opinions, both pro and con, to aid them in their consideration of the recommendation.

For some time before the new organization structure officially went into effect, several special issues of the internal house organ were prepared. The first of these—four pages in length—discussed in general terms, and without any organization chart, the difference between the new organization structure and what had been traditionally used in the company. This announcement also stated a timetable for future publicity releases which would be made concerning the activation of the new area.

At the time the new organization officially went into operation, a special issue of the *Telephone News* magazine was distributed. This special issue was entirely devoted to the activation of the new area. It contained a statement by the president, an article on the committee's operation written by the change agent, and a discussion of the new character of structure that had been developed for this pilot operation. It also contained pictures and descriptions of the various management personnel to be involved in the new area.

In these various ways, then, a continued effort was made from the appointment of the committees to the ultimate activation of the new organization structure to provide for participation by the maximum number of people and to inform, as fully as possible, the entire management of the company about each step of the organization activity.

In addition, at the time of announcing formation of the new area to management people, officers of the various unions were told of the arrangements and given the opportunity to arrange further discussion meetings.

Program for Implementation and Support

From the time of appointment of the two task forces until the final reports and recommendations were given to top management, approximately eighteen months' time had elapsed. While the president and his cabinet considered their final decision, plans were made by the change agent to implement formation of the new area. A timetable was prepared for appointing new top area management. For example, it was planned that the new area vice-president and general manager be appointed four months prior to the activation of the area, that his fifth-level department heads be appointed two months ahead, and that the divison (or fourth-level) people be named one month ahead of the activation date. In this way, each level could participate in selecting their subordinates and, as part of their training, could help indoctrinate their own groups.

The task of equipping the new vice-president and general manager with the background and the concept of the management of the area went according to plans prepared by the change agent. Some high lights of this plan included visits with the president, his cabinet officers, the change agent, and the outside consultant. Following this indoctrination, the vice-president and general manager prepared his program for working with his immediate subordinates.

The Management-Planning Committee, by design, did not plan or recommend any organization structure below the third level. Though, as a practical matter, this applied only to the staff groups, it then became the responsibility of the new area administration to plan this portion on their own. This required that they utilize the basic function lists which were used by the Management-Planning group in their study. This arrangement provided not only training for the group but helped also to win commitment and support for the objectives of the committee.

As another practical help to all concerned, several members both of the Management-Planning and the Controls task forces were promoted and assigned to the new area organization. This provided not only local sources for background information but also enthusiastic supporters for the goals of the committees.

Throughout this phase, the change agent was able to feed back to each of the groups information concerning activities of all the interested parties.

In addition, the change agent arranged a series of one-day meetings to middle management groups not only in the new area but also in the other areas of the company and in the headquarters groups. These meetings were held to explain the background of the study and the new organizational relationships which would exist.

In some cases, where new communication patterns would exist, combined meetings between the new area staff groups and their counterparts at headquarters were arranged in order to help establish support at an early date.

Stimulus for New Management Philosophy

The degree of success in attempting to establish a new concept of management is largely related to the behavioral patterns of the top management of the company and the chain of command in the new area, as seen by the area people. In order to aid both groups in this field, the change agent continued to act in the role of an internal consultant for all levels of management. Visits with selected management people which led to discussions of overall objectives and immediate problems provided a basis for insight and understanding of the pilot operation.

SUMMARY

The new area was formally activated by a resolution of the board of directors on October 1, 1960.

By all observable and informal means available, it was noted that a very high degree of interest prevailed throughout the company. Morale and enthusiasm in the new area organization were evidently on a very high plane.

The first month of operation showed that at least six months of operation would be needed to iron out communication and procedural bugs. At least two years of operation would be needed to gather data which would be helpful to the president and his officers for their consideration of the results of the pilot operation. At that time, the decision to extend or modify the new arrangements into the remaining operating areas of the company was to come up for final consideration.

During this interval, the change agent was to collect data from all parts of the new area, in diary form, on a critical incident or observable basis. In addition to all normal company measurements, plans were developed for periodic attitude and morale studies and special interview studies.

POSTSCRIPT

The operation of the new Eastern Area was carried on as planned, with two modifications. Pressures for early improvement in operating results necessitated the abandonment of the objective of modifying some of the control procedures, and the area reverted to the standard control procedures in force elsewhere in the company. Also, the Area was assigned the additional task of introducing a new computer-centered data-processing program. Nevertheless, during 1961, an adequate level of performance was attained. Operations were felt to have become entirely normal by January, 1962.

The morale survey which had been planned was completed in 1961, and all remaining managerial evaluation of the organizational experiment was completed in 1962. The objectives had been substantially achieved. The reorganization had consolidated the responsibility for company investment in the Engineering Department, revenue in the Marketing Department, and expenditures in the Operations Department. The number of middle management positions had been reduced. Staff procedures were considered more effective, better data service was realized, and employee morale continued high.

In 1963, the Company began to reorganize other Areas.

22. SOME SOCIO-TECHNICAL ASPECTS OF AUTOMATION*

F. E. Emery and Julius Marek

This report[1] arises from a series of case studies[2] on the human effects of higher mechanization and automation carried out by the Tavistock Institute of Human Relations, London. Although we are still involved in completing the fieldwork, particularly in collecting data on the economic and managerial aspects, the analysis is at a point where certain observations can be reported and certain questions raised. For the purposes of this paper, we will consider some of the things that happened when a more highly automated power plant was introduced into a large industrial organization. To give a little more depth to our observations, we will make certain comparisons with what was observed when transfer automation was introduced in a light engineering plant.

For ease of communication, we will depart from the logical order of presenting first the assumptions, restrictions, and methods, and then the case data and conclusions. We will instead proceed immediately to discuss the case. Only after this will we come back to the broader issues concerning the value of case studies in this field and the practical difficulties facing the researcher.

The old power plant was built in the twenties, remodelled after the second world war, and replaced by the new one three years ago. The total plant included a water treatment plant, boiler house, and powerhouse. The connection to the national power grid, which in the old plant covered only the export of electricity, has been extended to both import and export in the new power plant. Both the new and the old power plant served the same large industrial complex which engaged in round-the-clock production five and a half days a week. As power plants go, they were not large, having a capacity of the order of 10,000 kw.-hr., but they presented a full range of work and supervisory roles. Insofar as all the men on the new plant had worked on the old one, it was possible to reconstruct in detail conditions that had prevailed there and the history of the transition period.

* Reprinted from *Human Relations*, Vol. 15, No. 1 (February, 1962), pp. 17–25.

[1] This paper was read at the First British Conference on the Social and Economic Effects of Automation, Harrogate, June, 1961.

[2] The series of case studies has been financed by the Human Sciences Committee of the Department of Scientific and Industrial Research, U.K.

THE INTRODUCTION OF CHANGE

The first and most striking observation is the smoothness with which the change was introduced and with which the staff adjusted to their new jobs. The period of transition and subsequently has not been marked by any labor stoppages, bitter disputes, deadlocked negotiations, or deterioration of management-worker relations. We were not able directly to observe the changeover, but were able to interview persons at all levels and particularly those who would have been directly involved in any such disputes. From these interviews, we got a consistent picture of *prior and unhurried negotiation* by representatives of all the parties concerned in the expected conflicts of interest. The beliefs expressed in interviews matched up with the evidence we collected on the dates of meetings, who attended, what was discussed, and what was settled. The sole outstanding point of disagreement concerned methods of payment. The less-automated conditions in the factory allowed for types of incentive payment that could not be given any reality in the new power plant. Naturally, the power plant personnel felt that in some way they ought, as in the past, to share in the financial benefits that were extended to practically everyone else in their firm. This issue was well contained, since both sides understood the real difficulties faced by the other side and some interim adjustments were made by averaging over past bonuses.

Having satisfactorily checked on the validity of this observation, we had to consider why this transition had gone off so smoothly. We were able to establish that it was not due to any absence of active and vigilant trade union representation. Both of these conditions were present, and in any case, if they had been absent one would still have had to explain the absence of deterioration in management-worker relations. There appeared to be several contributory factors:

(*a*) The long term stability of the external economic environment (with respect to outlet markets and to capital requirements).

(*b* The stability of the internal environment owing to the relative absence of the unpredictable fluctuation in orders that characterizes, for instance, engineering. This appears to have contributed to a stable and persistent accommodation in labor-management relations at a very low level of conflict. Connected with and possibly determined by this is the stability of the labor force (mean length of service for male operatives being over 15 years and a high rate of seasonal return to work by women who had been full-time employees before marriage). We feel that these facts taken together help to explain why the negotiations did not become a cover for problems unresolved in the past, nor a struggle for points of potential advantage in the future.

(*c*) The management had proved in their handling of major technological change in other parts of the total plant that they would not accept savings that were made at the expense of sacking staff. In the eyes of their staff, they had a good record for finding other and appropriate jobs within the plant for persons displaced by technological change. This policy did, of course, confront the economic difficulties involved in balancing a low but more or less continuous wastage of staff, with spasmodic reductions in staff requirements. However, these difficulties were considerably lessened by agreements that temporarily reduced normal staff intake and coped by overtime with their self-induced temporary staff shortage.

As we stated, we believe that these factors contributed to the smoothness with which the change in the power plant was introduced. However, these factors, taken singly or together, would not have automatically ensured a smooth change. The critical factor appears to have been that the manager was willing and able to fully utilize the possibilities that were open to him and was consistently guided by his belief that technical and economic considerations were not a sufficient ground on which to time the introduction of major technological change.

It is in the nature of a case study that, though it may give a fairly convincing picture of one way in which things may happen, it does not tell us whether this is the only way. We therefore hasten to add that, on our present evidence, at least one other of our cases had an almost equally smooth changeover, and yet none of the above-mentioned contributing factors was present. Nevertheless, as far as we can ascertain, this contrary case does not contradict what has been suggested above. The contrary case is a transfer technology engaged in light engineering. Here the changes in technology were introduced in a piecemeal fashion and were spread over several years. Although there was some reduction in the staff requirements of each production line, there was no problem of sacking displaced operatives. Owing to a growing market, the number of production lines increased and so did the total size of the labor force. No significant difficulties arose from the changes that were made in the content of the operatives' jobs. In part, this may have been due to the step-by-step character of the changes, but in larger measure it seemed to be due to the fact that, with a relatively high labor turnover, the new jobs went to the new people. The changed content of the jobs was hardly more new to the newcomers than would have been the old jobs. For those of the unchanged staff who were unattracted to the new jobs, there were sufficient jobs on the few remaining production lines of the old batch type. These batch lines were left in existence to cope with short and varied product runs. Of all the staff, the supervisors were most exposed to the human implications of the technological changes. However, for most of these supervisors, the consequences of increased mechanization had been masked by their involvement in the technical challenges of the transition—the constantly recurring teething problems that had to be sorted out on the production floor.

In this case, there was less demand for managerial skill. The variability in market demand could more readily be exported to the labor market, the gradualness and piecemeal nature of the change enabled the lower echelons of management and supervision effectively to carry a considerable share of the problems, and the variety of ordered products enabled a wider and flexible range of technologies to be economically employed side by side. It might well have been otherwise, even with a gradual infiltration of advanced technology, if this had entailed using skills that were in short supply, or if there had not been such a variety of orders as would allow economic use of the old plant.

In selecting our cases, we deliberately set out to avoid instances where there was a prior state of bad management or bad management-worker relations. We felt that in such cases it would be difficult to detect just what effects arose from automation itself. This choice clearly restricts our ability to generalize about the process of transition to higher mechanization and automation. However, within this restriction, it seems clear that there are a great many different conditions that may be successfully exploited to contain the disruptive human and social effects of technical change, and even to turn some aspects of the change to positive advantage. A high degree of managerial skill is not always required, but success is obviously much more likely if it is present and is accompanied by a readiness and ability to time the introduction of the changes on the basis of human factors, not on technical and economic factors alone. As observed in an American case study of the introduction of higher mechanization "An important aspect to the union was the company's early announcement of its plans, and its willingness prior to making the change, to consult the union on issues affecting employment" (U.S. Department of Labor, 3).

CHANGES DUE TO AUTOMATION

Before examining some of the more interesting of the changes brought about by automation, it is necessary to sketch a sort of technological base line.

It is in the nature of power and steam generation that human beings are excluded from the main productive processes—these are accomplished by chemical and physical forces. Similarly, men are excluded from or are unnecessary for all the main transfer operations, except where coal is used as a fuel. The old power plant was coal fired and, although ash was removed manually, the feeding operations had been thoroughly mechanized. Fine motor operations are not extensively required for positioning or guidance of materials and tools, since these requirements are met by the design of equipment (pipes, valves, wiring, etc.). Hence, in these basic respects, the old and new power plants were virtually identical, even though some throttle valves in the old plant had to be judiciously handled. Their main requirements for human participation were limited to the control operations, that is, the operations involving perceptual skills (sensing, measuring, judging), conceptual skills (abstracting, calculating, inferring) and feedback actions (rejecting, rectifying, or resetting of tools or equipment). The effects of the change from the old to the new plant are restricted, therefore, to changes in these kinds of skill and in jobs based on use of these skills. It is important to bear in mind this restriction if any comparison is made between changes observed here and changes observed in cases of transfer automation. In the latter, the technological changes usually involve changes in the degree of human participation in transfer operations and in production operations requiring fine motor skills. Furthermore, the magnitude of the changes in the case of transfer automation is usually much larger.

The major technological changes with the new plant were substantial increases in boiler capacity and operating pressure, and a slight increase in operating temperature. These resulted in 50 percent greater production capacity for fewer boilers, and a 14 percent improvement in thermal efficiency.

In themselves, these facts have no relevance to our problems. They do become very relevant insofar as these changes and results were achieved only by:

(a) Increased complexity of the total process even if measured simply by number of different steps in the process. The decrease in number of boilers affects only the number available on standby, not the number operating. A greater number of steps are needed in the water treatment process in order to achieve the level of purity required for operation at the higher levels of pressure. Rather more steps are also needed in the boiler house in order to feed in fuel, water, and air under the new conditions. All told, there are 62.5 per cent more steps in the new treatment plant and boiler house phases. The main increase in the complexity of the power-house (in the above sense of number of distinguishable steps) derives from the new conception of the utilization of the steam power. The old condensate power units were replaced by back-pressure turbines achieving greater efficiency in the use of the reject heat contained in the exhaust steam. Instead of supplying steam of uniformly high pressure and high temperature to the process work, the steam output from the new plant has been divided into low-pressure and high-pressure flows, both at relatively lower temperatures. The differentiation of electrical power generation from other uses of steam (for process work) resulted in the power plant being placed in a different position relative to the boiler house and the rest of the factory. In the old plant, the powerhouse was simply one of the end-users of the steam, whereas in the new plant the powerhouse is an intermediate user-regulator between the boiler plant and the rest of the factory. The new placement resulted in the installation of additional equipment and in closer cooperation being required of the stokers and the powerhouse operators, especially in cases of wide load variations. The new powerhouse also differed in feeding into and from the outside electricity grid. Unlike the other changes, this was not technologically implicit in the design of the new plant, but rather one of the economic fruits that became attainable.

(b) Decreased tolerance for disturbances. The higher operating capacity and efficiency were achieved only by sacrificing tolerance for impurities in the water, variability in fuel and water temperatures, variability in air flows and power flows. The following table gives a simple indication of how, in the boiler house phase, the number of potential crisis points has almost doubled, and the reaction time decreased.

Reaction Time within Which Disturbance Must be Corrected	Old Boiler House	New Boiler House
5 minutes or less	2	9
More than 5 minutes	3	—
Total No. disturbance points	5	9

As with complexity, there is an additional, economically motivated, change. A decrease in tolerance for disturbances arises from the replacement of high storage capacity in the old plant by high throughput capacity in the new plant. The storage capacity of the old plants in general made it possible to absorb the disturbances in a much easier and much more leisurely manner. Also, under the old system, it was allowable (because technically necessary) for the boiler plant to reduce supply of steam in order to reestablish control. This gave the old system a very considerable tolerance for other disturbances. However, this relief is not so readily available in the new system.

(c) Increased separation of operators from the process. The demands of the new system are in many instances too rigorous to be met by the manually operated controls that satisfied the old system. Only by introducing automatic controls has it been possible to achieve the higher productive efficiency. Thus, at most points in the productive process, the operator is one step further removed from what is going on—he is occupied with monitoring and controlling the controls. The separation is not a simple loss of contact, since the introduction of the automatic sensing and controlling devices has also made it possible to locate indicators of what they are sensing and doing at a convenient and centralized place. With centralized panels of indicators in each of the three main locations, it is now possible for an operator to have conceptual contact with many more steps in the process than previously, and hence to have greater relative knowledge despite the complexity—a source of considerable satisfaction.

The changes in these three dimensions of the technological system affected all the operative roles more or less equally. There was none of the increased heterogeneity of roles that so frequently characterizes increased mechanization.[3] In each of the four operating roles (one on the water treatment phase, two in the boiler house and one in the powerhouse), there was an increase in the complexity of their tasks. They literally had to concern themselves with more things. Thanks to the automated controls, they had normally to do much less about each thing, e.g., less walking to and less manipulation of valves, but they still had to be concerned with the state of affairs at each step in the process. We suspect that there is an unfortunate interaction between these factors. Below a certain level of technical knowledge, it is likely that one can more easily develop and better sustain a map of a complex process when one is constantly moving around the parts of the plant, with habitual operations at the key gauges and manual controls. Under the new conditions there is much more to know and yet the explorations are much more confined to the mental level. For the power plant operator the number of steps in his part of the production process was more than doubled, and to this he had to add the control devices themselves. In the words of one operator, "There always seem to be more things going on [in the new plant]." Similarly, there was reflected in each role the decreased tolerance for disturbance. Thus, not only were there more things for the operator to be concerned about, but he had to be more concerned about a greater number of things than previously. This greater concern was not reflected, as it would have been in the old plant, in more movement around the different parts of the plant, more looking into things, more adjusting and fiddling around with valves, settings, and the like. Instead, it was reflected in waiting and watching for the relevant bit of information in the constant outpouring of so much that was redundant because it said no more than that things were still staying within control. The operators were required to tolerate more waiting and a greater flood of redundant information, while sustaining a greater readiness to respond quickly to crises with more complex, manually operated controls. Phrased in this way, the task sounds rather forbidding. In themselves, these aspects of the task were experienced as only relatively more difficult. The requirement which was in an absolute sense difficult

---

[3] E.g., the range in highly mechanized tube mills from the sheer donkey work of the man plugging the billets to straightforward monitoring of furnace output with a simple rejection function and, at the other extreme, the complex judgmental task of the mill operator; see Walker (4) and P.E.P. (2).

was to remain calm enough at certain of the crises to carry out, on one's own responsibility, the complicated and highly important feedback operations, and only afterwards be free to call in outside technical help. This requirement has become apparent in the several years of operation of the new plant. One of the supervisors stated the issue very clearly. Asked "What is it about a good operator that makes it possible for him to react quickly and in an appropriate manner?" he replied, "It is a question of confidence that comes from knowing himself and knowing his job. I mean you could have a case where a man should be capable, but in an emergency it is not just a question of knowledge but something in the makeup of the man . . . it's born of confidence, ability, confidence in the plant, in himself that he understands the sort of situation, the possible dangers arising, a sort of calculated risk of the job—it's a difficult thing to define."

For the power plant operator, the number of potential crisis points increased from four to seven, and the increase was all in matters that had to be brought under control immediately or at least in less than five minutes. Furthermore, the narrowness of the control limits allowed for less warning than before and placed more stringent demands on the operator when he had to bring them under control manually. At this point, we may well recall that it is no longer as easy to reduce output to the factory, and that he has in many cases no time to call in assistance before acting himself.

The greater separation of the operator from the actual productive processes (from the particular apparatus and machinery within which the processes are going on) has certain effects that have already been noted. It also results in his having to allow for the fact that much of his knowledge is secondhand, i.e., mediated by processes that constitute an imperfect medium (see Heider, 1). This imposes on the operator an additional stress, and checking up on the centralized control instruments is not only a routine duty but one activity that will reflect the individual's sensitivity to stress. At this point, the central concerns of the operator can flow over into his housekeeping chores. These housekeeping chores which are associated with each operative role give the person an excuse to get back amongst the machinery—whether with a grease gun or with a bit of waste—if he organizes his time.

Another important effect is made possible by shifting the operator from the region of process controls, and made necessary by the heightened interdependence of the parts of the process and of the process with its environment. This is that the operator is more heavily involved in responsibility for controlling relations with processes outside his area. Thus the power plant operator has to initiate feedback controls over the boiler house and follow as quickly as possible variations arising from the grid supply and from excess factory demand.

These observations indicate something of the ways in which automation of controls is reflected in job requirements.

The most striking points concerning the effects of automation on the supervisory roles are as follows:

(*a*) With the unification of the operative's role, so that each carries complete authority for the functioning of an integrated phase of production and for "normal" disturbances, the supervisor is able to concern himself with the maintenance of the boundary conditions of the regions under his command. That is, he can spend his time in controlling the overall inputs and outputs of fuel, lubricants, chemicals, personnel, etc., and in checking on the progress of repairs, maintenance, and so on. His task is literally to make the operator's job as easy as possible by minimizing disruptions of the "steady state."

(*b*) The time span of the supervisor's job is considerably extended in correspondence with the sorts of variability with which he is normally coping. Unlike the supervisor in the old plant, he is not primarily concerned with the hour-by-hour control and coordination of the operatives' performances. This function has been replaced partly by automatic coordination of operations. Of greater importance, however, is the fact that the key functions of the operators are performed only in crises and cannot be subjected to routine supervision because of the absence of sufficient warning and the speed with which corrective action must be taken. Only the peripheral tasks such as log keeping and housekeeping are susceptible to routine supervision. Personal differences between supervisors in their attitudes to their roles are perhaps most easily detected in the importance they attach to the routine supervision of the peripheral tasks.

(*c*) The conditions under which the supervisor is called into the operative's task are relatively abnormal, and in consequence:

(i) it tends to be accepted that the supervisor comes on call, not on inspection and control of staff;

(ii) he is required to provide technical advice at a level beyond that possessed by the operatives and in the area of the professional engineer.

In each of these respects, there is a marked contrast to the narrowing of the supervisory role that we have observed in some cases of transfer automation.

Looking at the set of roles, operative and supervisory, it seems that there is greater homogeneity than before in their content. There is much less of the gap in responsibility that usually marks off the wage earner from the salary earner. The need to map at the human level the extensive automatic control system has been met in this case by maximizing the potency of each role in the set rather than by sticking to a narrow concept of what can be expected of wage earners and trying to map the automatic controls by the pattern of close human supervision. Thus, at the point where the task interdependence is most tricky—between water treatment and the boiler house—the difficulty is met not by adding more supervision, but by periodic interchange of roles so that the men in the boiler house are fully skilled in the tasks and problems of the water treatment plant and vice versa.

PROBLEMS OF THE CASE STUDY METHOD

In this brief report we have practically confined our comments to some of the more interesting aspects of a single case. As they stand, these comments illustrate only one sort of question that arises from putting a plant under the microscope. There are two other questions that also arise: how can one generalize from the individual cases to generally useful answers and how can one collect and use this data without harming the interests of the enterprise and the persons studied? We will close with some comments on each of these questions. In our case studies we have, admittedly, been concerned with detailed microscopic examination of individual plants, in some instances quite small ones. However, we believe that the size of the individual unit, as measured by numbers employed, is not in itself highly relevant to the problem of generalizing from these cases.

The relevant issues appear to be:

(*a*) Whether the observed technological changes are representative of classes of technological change that are significant in the general trend towards higher mechanization and automation;

(*b*) Whether one can separate out from the observed changes in human activities those that are meaningfully related to the observed technological changes;

(*c*) Whether the unit studied is, on the one hand, a protected, subordinate part of a concern or, on the other hand, a total enterprise exposed to a relatively uncontrolled environment;

(*d*) Whether the sample of case studies adequately reflects the range of variability to be found in automation.

It is too early to estimate the success with which we have met these criteria, but we have managed to carry out studies on a minimum of two distinct cases within each of several widely differing classes of industrial automation. Theoretically, this design provides possibilities for comparison and cross checking that would not be available in single cases from different technologies or in many cases within the same technology.

Apart from the question of protecting the interests of others, there are several practical considerations that go beyond the obvious steps of obtaining sanction or preserving anonymity. Thus, we have for other reasons felt justified in avoiding plants that are characterized by bad management-labor relations. Additionally, we have found that the level of technological description that is adequate for our purposes enables us to avoid the sort of detail that might fascinate an engineer in a competing firm. The fact that an unidentified firm has bridged an obvious gap between two commonly used machine tools is critical for our report on the study of the production system, but rather uninformative for the "rival engineer" trying to find a technical solution, and of dubious incentive value to the "rival engineer" who has not yet seen the obvious.

It is more difficult, though possible and necessary, to avoid identifying for others to see individual failures or shortcomings. We have naturally been concerned to observe these where they are relevant to the production system, but our scientific interest has been primarily in detecting from these human facts the changes that have occurred in the demands the system makes on its people.

REFERENCES

1. HEIDER, F. "Thing and Medium," in *On Perception and Event Structure.* New York: International Universities Press, 1959.
2. P.E.P. *Three Case Studies in Automation.* London: Political and Economic Planning.
3. U.S. DEPARTMENT OF LABOR. *A Case Study of a Large Mechanized Bakery.* B.I.S. Report 109, 1956.
4. WALKER, C. R. *Toward the Automatic Factory* New Haven: Yale University Press, 1957.

23. OBSERVATIONS ON THE DYNAMICS OF A CHANGE TO ELECTRONIC DATA-PROCESSING EQUIPMENT*

Floyd C. Mann and Lawrence K. Williams

This paper presents findings from an exploratory, longitudinal study of the effects of a change-over to electronic data-processing equipment in a light and power company.[1] As a case study it deals with (1) the general problems of introducing this change, which extended over five years and affected more than sixteen hundred employees in two organizational divisions, and (2) the effects of such a change on organizational structure, policies and philosophy, job structure, and personnel at all levels of the company. Some of the more unique problems of transition to a high degree of automation in the office are indicated.

Floyd C. Mann is program director and Lawrence K. Williams is assistant study director, Institute for Social Research, University of Michigan.

DURING THE past decade social scientists interested in human behavior as expressed in formal organizations have concentrated their research on the determinants of organizational effectiveness. Their primary objective has been the determination of the relationship between individual and organizational goals. Empirically, efforts have been focused on the relationship between individual motivations and satisfactions and organizational measures of effectiveness, and the way these relationships are affected by superior-subordinate relations, work group relations, job content, and organizational policies and practices. Most of the studies have been made in organizations where relatively little change was taking place. Systems undergoing reorganization or accommodation to some major technological innovation have rarely been examined. In an era of accelerating technological surges, it becomes imperative to concentrate more of our energies and resources on the study of organizational change. Such a shift in focus can increase both our understanding of human behavior in an organizational context and our knowledge about the most effective ways of managing change. Studying change facilitates the identification of essential elements and their relationships; attempting to effect change provides crucial tests of our working knowledge of individual and organizational behavior. The introduction of automation in the factory and of electronic data process-

* Reprinted from *Administrative Science Quarterly*, Vol. 5, No. 2 (September, 1960), pp. 217–56.

[1] This article is an elaboration and an extension of a paper given at the Thirteenth International Congress of Applied Psychology, Rome, Italy, 1958.

ing (EDP) in the office has presented social scientists with unique laboratories for investigating the dynamics of organization and processes of change. This paper will summarize some of our findings concerning one such study—a study of the effects of a change-over to EDP equipment.[2]

This study differs from our usual quantitative investigations, in that it is an exploratory, longitudinal study in a single firm over a period of years. We have not attempted to test specific hypotheses but have tried simply to describe the gross, nontechnical, intraorganizational effects on the divisions, the departments, and the individuals involved. The course of events has been followed primarily through informal,[3] on-the-job interviews with key personnel in upper and middle management and occasional interviews with first-line supervisors and their subordinates. The word "observations" is used in the title to emphasize that our findings have no firm quantitative foundation; they are based on materials from over 300 unstructured interviews taken as various phases of the change unfolded.

THE SETTING AND THE CHANGE-OVER

This change-over occurred in a company that produces and sells electric light and power. One of the largest in the United States, it has an international reputation for technical innovation and development in the

---

[2] The principal executives and managers in the company studied deserve a special note of commendation. They have supported this long-term project with time and money in the hope that a careful recording of their experiences would contribute to knowledge about managing major technological changes in white-collar situations. Our policy of maintaining the anonymity of organizations in which we do research precludes detailing our indebtedness to both company and individuals. It is obvious, however, that without their deep and continuing interest the study could not have been made. They were willing to talk with us regardless of the pressures of the moment; they have reviewed this final draft carefully. Grace Beardsley, the editor of the Institute for Social Research, also contributed greatly to the readability of this paper.

[3] The primary impact of this change-over occurred in a group of accounting departments where we had followed changes in work satisfactions of both employees and their supervisors for six years before the change-over began. Thus, we have a continuing account of how 800 employees, 70 first-line supervisors, and their eight department heads felt long before there was any likelihood of a change in the handling of information, records, and accounts within the company. In December, 1954, just at the time of the announcement that new electronic equipment was to be introduced, we asked all three levels to fill out paper-and-pencil questionnaires once again. From that point we followed the change through informal interviews. Now that the conversion is complete, we plan to administer our questionnaires again to all those persons who were at the vortex of the change. The findings obtained from linking this series of surveys will allow us to test quantitatively some observations presented in this paper. Initial and interim statements about our findings have been presented in earlier publications: F. C. Mann, "The Impact of Electronic Accounting Equipment on the White Collar Worker in a Public Utility Company," in *Man and Automation* (New Haven, 1956); F. C. Mann and L. K. Williams, "Organizational Impact of White Collar Automation," *Proceedings of Eleventh Annual Meeting of Industrial Relations Research Association* (Chicago, 1958).

field of atomic power. It is equally well known for its development of new management ideas, especially in the area of "participative management."

Two major divisions are primarily concerned with the accounts of more than a million customers: accounting, the division responsible for all customer billing, bookkeeping, and records; and sales, the division handling all direct contacts with customers relating to service and the payments of their accounts. The 800 accounting employees are located in the company's central offices; most of the 1,500 employees in sales are in district offices spread over a large geographical area. This centralization of the accounting division together with the interdependence of its activities has facilitated the development of an integrated philosophy of management and a unified approach to operating problems. The company's philosophy of superior-subordinate participation in the definition and solution of problems has been elaborated more fully in accounting than in the other major units. The installation of EDP to maintain customers' accounts had an immediate and direct effect on its organization and personnel. The effect on the organization and the work of the sales division was not as immediate nor as extensive. Our study, therefore, concentrated on the change as experienced in the accounting division.

Many of the functions performed in billing and bookkeeping had been transferred to mechanical IBM equipment 15 years before this change-over. This company was one of the first in the utility field to use mechanical equipment. Its earlier change from manual methods to mechanical operations was superimposed on ongoing operations with few major changes in procedures or organization. Conversion to electronic equipment, however, called for a reallocation of functions within the accounting area and between accounting, sales, and other divisions.

The change-over was carried on over a period of about five years with little interruption of daily operations. Changes were made first in organizational alignments and procedures and then in the basic form of the company's records. Essentially, the initial plan recommended four major changes:

1. The consolidation, but not the centralization, of all customer requests for information. Formerly, information flowed into four different types of units which were parts of geographically separated offices. Each unit had its own files for answering customer or intracompany requests for information.

2. The consolidation, but not the centralization, of internal visual customer records. Eight basic records kept in seven locations in five departments were to be replaced by one master record, which was to be maintained at a single location.

3. The consolidation and centralization of all record keeping and cal-

culating work into one data-processing group. This was done through the installation of EDP equipment. All visual customer records became by-products of the magnetic tape system.

4. The consolidation, but not the centralization, of all contacts with the customer on his premises relating to customer accounting activities. Formerly a number of different employees from several different units within the company contacted the customer to reread his meter; to discuss abnormal meter readings, rate problems, lamp quotas; and to collect overdue bills. It was decided that these activities would be handled by a new class of field personnel working out of district offices.

These changes required extensive transfers of functions and employees from one major division to another, and *a major reorganization* within the accounting division. Work section and departmental lines were reorganized, new departments were created, and a level of management was added. With respect to data processing, one master record containing all customer information was placed on magnetic tape for use with the IBM 705.

This brief description indicates some of the unique characteristics of the demand made on an organization and its personnel by this type of technological change. In this case, the conversion to electronic accounting was accompanied by organizational and functional realignments. The problems of introducing a new machine were compounded by changes in the system of relationships among departments and people. The period of transition stretched over five years, during which continuity of operations had to be maintained. The company found itself in the paradoxical position of having to hire a large force of new workers before the staff could be reduced. Not even all of the proposed changes could be carried through during this period; several had to be abandoned or deferred.

In visualizing such a change-over to an electronic data-processing system, it is essential to understand that this type of change is different from a model conversion in an automobile plant, a turnaround in an oil refinery, or the starting up of a new plant.[4] There can be no stock-piling before suspending operations; there is little or no opportunity to make trial runs of new systems without the continual maintenance of the older system.

PHASES AND TEMPO OF CHANGE

In studying a change of this magnitude and duration, it was found useful to identify seven different phases in the sequence of a change-over to EDP: (1) relative stability and equilibrium before the change, (2) preliminary planning, (3) detailed preparation, (4) installation and testing, (5)

---

[4] F. C. Mann and L. R. Hoffman, *Automation and the Worker: A Study of Social Change in Power Plants* (New York, 1960).

conversion, (6) stabilization, and (7) new equilibrium after the change. Activities in the first and last periods were almost unique to a single time period; those in the middle tended to occur simultaneously. The whole process appeared to start off slowly, gradually accelerate to a sustained level of high activity in the installation and conversion periods, and then decelerate until the organization finally arrived at a new state of equilibrium. The change in systems and relationships was thus accompanied by a marked change in the activity level of the organization.

The change was initiated without flourish in October, 1953, when top management announced that a study would be made of the customer accounting and collection function. Electronic accounting equipment was to be considered along with other procedural and policy changes. One year later, after a number of analyses, it was decided to implement the initial recommendations for the reorganization of work within and between the accounting and sales divisions. During 1955 the following changes occurred: (1) functions were transferred between and within divisions, (2) older mechanical IBM equipment was replaced by two small-scale computers (IBM 650) which were used during the early part of the transition, (3) modifications were made in the organization of activities in those departments that supplied work to the EDP unit, and (4) programming of new accounting procedures was initiated. In 1956 detailed program planning progressed, and specially designed and ventilated rooms were prepared for the arrival of the IBM 705 equipment. Activity in all departments mounted as the date for the installation and initial testing of the equipment and programs approached. The machine was delivered in October, 1956—almost three years after the feasibility study was announced. This high level of activity was maintained as personnel at all levels turned their efforts to meeting the date on which the initial conversion was to begin—January 20, 1957.

Pressure mounted during late 1956 until fatigue and stress reached a climax for a number of key personnel. An executive's heart attack dramatized for all both the tempo and the level of tension. The change of records to the new equipment finally began in mid-March, 1957, and continued throughout the year as personnel, equipment, and procedures were tested, found successful, or found wanting and replaced. In late 1957 the difficult economic situation began to affect the ability of the customer to pay his electric light bill. At this time differences between divisions and members of upper management in their understanding and acceptance of the decisions programmed into the system came into focus. For a time the resolution of these differences became a major task for the executives. By early 1958 the system was technically sound and more fully understood and accepted. Attention then turned to the massive task of reassignment and the establishment of permanent jobs and relationships.

This brief resumé gives some indication of the change that occurred in the nature and tempo of work in the departments within the accounting division. It went from a period in which system maintenance was the principal task, through a period when attention was focused on system creation and revision (while still performing all the functions of the old system), to a period in which an equilibrium was being established under the new system.

The seven phases provide both an overview of the change and a framework for the organization of our materials in the remainder of this paper. First we shall discuss the major changes in philosophy, policy, and practice that accompanied these changes. Next we turn to some of the more specific problems of transition. Finally we will describe the problems of reassignment and restructuring and provide an overview of the organization with its new jobs, new structure, and new relationships.

CHANGES IN POLICY, ORGANIZATION, AND PERSONNEL

Reevaluation of Organizational Objectives and Means

Studies of the feasibility of introducing EDP equipment provide an opportunity for a reappraisal of the basic aims of various functions in an organization and of the way in which they are being performed. Members of upper levels of management find themselves in the rare position of being able to review the organization. Long-standing routines can be questioned. Ancillary objectives, which have been added over time, can be reviewed and their contribution to the fundamental purposes of the organization assessed.

Consideration of new equipment also makes possible consideration of a number of major, long-term changes that have been postponed over the years. It is possible not only to review the organization of work within specific divisional areas but to redesign the organization and to take advantage of the climate of change to cut across old divisional lines. Since an "unfreezing" of the organization is going to occur, it is a propitious time to introduce additional changes in the organizational structure.

The scope of the preplanning that precedes the decision to install electronic equipment determines whether such major changes will occur. A limited definition of the problem will result in simply setting the new equipment into old organizational lines and structures. A broad approach may lead to major changes in the total organization, not simply a change in its procedural mechanics. The former can be described as "the hardware approach," the latter as the "system approach."[5]

In this case we observed the combined effects of a reorganization and the introduction of electronic equipment. Many of the economies which accompanied the introduction of EDP probably could have been made

---

[5] Mann and Williams, *op. cit.*

without the equipment *if* the same original and broad-range thinking had been applied to existing operations and equipment.

This reevaluation of organizational objectives and means led to the transfer of bookkeeping functions from district sales offices to accounting and a transfer of meter-reading investigation (a customer contact function) from accounting to sales. All customer contacts were consolidated in sales; all accounting functions were assigned to accounting.

Other structural changes included the combining of several departments within the accounting division, the creation of two new ones, and the addition of a new level of management to direct the change-over activities of this new alignment of departments. As a result of the system approach employed here, a good deal of reorganization took place, and totally new jobs were created.

Early experiences with the new data-processing equipment and a later study of the feasibility of consolidating personnel records by means of electronic equipment raised basic questions about the disposition of final responsibility for such equipment within the company. If the IBM 705 were to change internal operations markedly, then control of this system was seen by some as crucial in terms of the distribution of power within the company. After a good deal of discussion, it was decided that the accounting division would continue to staff and control the machine. The possibility that the control of the IBM 705 and its related data-processing functions should be independent of any one division or group has, however, continued to remain an issue that is periodically reconsidered.

Testing of Management Philosophy

A change-over on this scale provided a crucial test of the corporation's philosophy of participative management. In such a period of upheaval and prolonged transition it was possible to test whether the management philosophy practiced in the past adequately prepared the organization for the change, whether there was actually a common philosophy in the organization, and whether the philosophy was adequate for managing or administering a major change.

The departments in the accounting division appeared to be better prepared for this change than were other units. Over the years much effort had been invested in developing the abilities of the intermediate and first-line supervisors to understand and practice the principles of participative management. Through training courses and by daily example, supervisors had been shown how to work with others, not simply as supervisor-subordinate, but as fellow workers; and further they had been shown how to solve problems through both man-to-man and group discussions. An attitude survey conducted immediately before the announcement of the change indicated a high degree of satisfaction at all levels. The employee good will and trust which had been developed over the years was then available for management to draw upon heavily during the trying period of rapid transition.

From the first announcement about the change, there appeared to be trust in the management and a general acceptance of the impending change in the departments of the accounting division. The quality of the relationship between employees and management had been established well in advance of the conversion, and tolerance for change appeared to be very high. Over the years personnel at all levels had had many opportunities to put to behavioral tests management's verbal pronouncements about their concern for employees as people. The rewards from the investment in management training became apparent again and again as department heads and their supervisors worked together on technical problems of the conversion that required a common management approach toward change. Intraorganizational conflict was kept at a minimum because of the similarity of such values as notifying people in advance of each step of the change, involving subordinates in the development of the plans for their part in the change, and employing other democratic principles in human relations.

When it came time to transfer employees and work from one major division to another and to make the actual conversion to the new procedures of customer billing, it became clear that the communality of the management philosophy in the accounting departments was more unique than had been assumed. In the sales division some of the employees who were found to be affected by the change had not been completely informed. The transfer of groups from one division to another pointed up differences in management practices. These differences reflected on the functioning of the top management group of the organization.

This period of change provided an invaluable opportunity to develop an explicit philosophy of management within the organization. As the conversion process gathered momentum, and as work loads and pressures mounted, the principles for handling change, explicit or implicit, were thoroughly tested in each unit of management. Discussions of how to handle change were no longer seen as dealing with problems that might never be encountered, but were accented with action imperatives of "what do we do tomorrow?" Questions about the rate of change that the organization or individuals could assimilate no longer seemed esoteric but had direct and immediate relevance.

In terms of the problems presented by the change, the limitations of past policies in the recruitment, selection, and promotion of both employees and supervisors became obvious. Making a change of this order was not easy for anyone—employee, supervisor, or department head. A high value was placed on the ability to adjust. Large organizations like government bureaus, private utilities, and insurance companies may be staffed with employees who have less tolerance for accepting changes than those in organizations more vulnerable to competition. As a group they may be more concerned about job stability and security than workers who take jobs in less stable types of organizations. When confronted with a demand to adjust to a major and extended period of change, such a change may loom larger for them than for other workers who have different psychological needs and who have continually experienced such changes during their work life.

The adequacy of the organization's implicit or explicit criteria for promotion to supervision was opened for review. If it is assumed that an effective supervisor has a combination of technical, administrative, and human relations skills, then such a period of change measures the adequacy with which management has been paying attention to the balance of these skills in making promotions in supervisory positions. Supervisors with only technical competence, regardless of the extent of this competence, had trouble coping with the sizable administrative changes of this period. Supervisors with only human relations skills also had difficulty handling the technical changes involved in replacing mechanical equipment with an intricate interlocking system built around electronic equipment.

The change also revealed inconsistencies and inadequacies in the application of the company's philosophy of management. It was easy to retain or even occasionally to advance a questionable employee or supervisor within a framework that seemed to advocate excessive concern for the individual. While such personnel actions were not really consistent with the company's philosophy, such an interpretation of the philosophy could, nevertheless, be used to avoid unpleasant administrative responsibilities. A number of employees and a few supervisors were bypassed, "layered," demoted, or placed in dead-end jobs during the change. While these actions were often attributed to the vagaries of the change, actually they were forced by a new system that stressed and demanded job competency.

Development and Elaboration of Company Policies

The introduction of electronic equipment resulted in the development in elaboration of company policy in a number of areas. Probably the most important concerned employment security of the personnel affected by the change. It was estimated that the consolidation and simplification of records, the mechanization of additional clerical records, and the use of electronic data-processing equipment would result in a marked reduction in both clerical and supervisory work forces. The specter of this eventual reduction could have created a serious morale problem, augmented resistance to reorganization of the system, and even severely retarded the introduction of the new equipment.

Since such technological unemployment could affect not only nonsupervisory and supervisory employees directly involved but members of higher levels of management as well, policies regarding the rights of displaced employees began to be spelled out during this period. The general policy which first evolved was as follows:

Whenever practicable, regular employees whose jobs have been discontinued will be transferred to equivalent assignments for which they are qualified, and at the same rates of pay. It is recognized, however, that permanent assignments to the same rated jobs may not be immediately possible for all employees. When permanent transfers cannot be made, departments are expected to endeavor to provide the most suitable temporary work possible, anywhere in the company. It is the continuing responsibility of the department head to see that such employees are eventually placed in permanent positions —after training if necessary.

It is worth emphasizing that in the development of this type of policy the company went a step further than previously in formalizing its obligation to its permanent and long-service employees. It offered employment security, but not the assurance of a particular job to an employee. The development of this policy was consistent with the prediction of Baldwin and Schultz that companies facing major technological change would develop their own "social shock absorbers"[6]—announced policy of not laying off or downgrading permanent and long-service workers. Such a policy accomplishes several objectives. It demonstrates the organization's concern for the welfare of its personnel, helps ensure the assistance of those on whom the company must rely to accomplish the change-over, and reduces the likelihood of unionization of white-collar workers as they experience a major threat to their livelihood.

Other policy changes were developed because of their expediency during the change-over. Within the accounting division, job posting had previously been restricted to a specific department, and subsequently, if the job was not filled, it was given company-wide posting. Early in the change-over, jobs were opened immediately to bidding by all employees in the five departments of the accounting division that were primarily concerned with the change and whose jobs were the most highly interrelated. This removal of boundaries opened many positions to individuals who normally would not have had such an opportunity on the first posting.

Another policy change resulted in the announcement that all assignments of employees to positions associated with the change were to be considered as temporary. This was done because the completed system was difficult to foresee, and it was necessary to make personnel assignments to the old, the transitional, and the new systems that would maximize the utilization of the available skills of the work force.

[6] G. B. Baldwin and G. P. Schultz, "Automation: A New Dimension to Old Problems," *Proceedings of the Seventh Annual Meeting, Industrial Relations Research Association* (Madison, Wis., 1955), pp. 114–28.

The relationship between the company and the customer was another area in which policy was affected by the change; it was both formalized and routinized. For maximum utilization of the EDP system, it was necessary that the company's practices regarding delinquent bills, cutoff notices, and various customer services be made more uniform throughout the area served by the company. This resulted in greater role prescription in the treatment of customers by employees at individual sales offices. Thus, many of the procedures affecting customer relations became a matter of central policy and not local option.

TRANSITIONAL DEMANDS

Management in the Accounting Division

The demands placed on management during this transitional period were of two types, those that accompany any major change in an organization, such as the extraordinary physical expenditure of energy and time, and those that were unique to the introduction of EDP. Of the latter type, one of the most important was the need to maintain simultaneously three systems of accounting: the old, the conversion, and the new. Manning, operating, and coordinating all three systems was a rigorous test of the abilities and skills of all levels of management in accounting. It was almost impossible for most of them to supervise directly all three phases simultaneously. Therefore, most department heads delegated part or all of the duties of one or more operations. In some departments the senior members of management were primarily responsible for initiating the new system while subordinates maintained the old system; the reverse also occurred. The net effect was a delegation or an assumption of duties that spread responsibility for supervision among a greater number of employees.

An additional demand on managerial energies was the amount of time spent in meetings. With increased interdependency of units and with the possibility that each new change might affect other departments in unknown ways, nearly all decisions had to be reviewed and discussed by representatives from both the accounting and sales divisions. The number of memoranda and other communications during the transition period attest to the high communication rate that was required.

The pressure of the conversion period was augmented by the number of both self-imposed and externally imposed deadlines. The overtime load was very heavy for supervisors and upper levels of management. The proportion of time these men spent in their offices or working at home increased substantially. More and more time was taken from family and community activities and given to the job.

As the organization moved farther into the conversion period, the duties of first-line supervisors became more involved and increasing demands were made of this level. The change-over provided a thorough test of their abilities as well as those of higher management. When change is gradual, supervisors, like employees, become thoroughly familiar with that part of the total work process for which they are immediately responsible. With such a drastic change it was necessary for supervisors to develop a much broader view of the system. Many who had seen the role of supervisor as "a good, not too difficult job," now found familiar routines shattered, and reported themselves as "working harder than ever before."

During this period the effective supervisor not only had to change his perspective of his role, but, along with his superiors, had to be able to draw upon different combinations of skills at different times. Conceptually, we have found it useful to think of three areas of supervisory skills: technical, administrative, and human relations.[7] During a period of change different combinations of these skills are required at different levels in the organization at the same time, and of the same supervisors at different times. In general there is a shift in emphasis from human relations to technical and administrative skills, and back again to human relations skills at the end of the transition period. When an organization is relatively stable, the supervisor has to draw heavily upon abilities that ensure organizational maintenance and effective human relations. By contrast, a transitional period places a heavy stress on the supervisor's technical competence and cognitive skills. The problems of the transition period were basically technical, and only technical knowledge could solve them. Human relations skills were not unimportant, but the job of laying out operationally feasible plans for complex changes in the accounting systems demanded technical competence. Supervisors without adequate resources in all three skill components found their jobs extremely difficult at different periods during the transition.[8]

Training was one of the largest problems continually facing supervisors. Throughout the change period, supervisors complained both about the lack of time for adequate training and about the large amount of time spent in training. Not only were there many replacements on old jobs who had to be trained, but old employees assigned to new tasks also had to be retrained, frequently on overtime. Training for new jobs was particularly difficult. For example, the first employees on new jobs in programming often had to be trained on a process using materials which were unfamiliar to both the supervisor and the trainee.

Management was also faced with another major continuing problem. To be sure that there would be a few experienced and highly competent people manning the old system while the planning and conversion took place, management decided to make all assignments to new jobs on a

---

[7] Mann and Hoffman, *op. cit.*

[8] Mann and Williams, *op. cit.*

temporary basis. Employees on all the new jobs were told that after the conversion had been completed, all assignments would be reviewed and assignments made on the basis of potential as well as actual ability to perform the job. The highly competent, senior employees and supervisors who had kept the old system functioning would have an equal opportunity to compete for all jobs in the new system. This temporary status became a source of insecurity for many employees.

First-line supervisers were faced with quite different morale problems during this period of instability. Some had to try to keep their groups working on activities which all knew would be replaced shortly. Others were trying to develop new job skills in older employees who would have preferred to continue until retirement in the routine they had come to know so well over the years. Still other supervisors were finding it difficult to keep ahead of their subordinates, who were rushing ahead to learn new procedures, nomenclature, and the intricacies of electronic data processing without any inhibiting knowledge about the old system. A few supervisors were encountering problems in introducing white-collar personnel to shift work. Nearly all were able to see the effects of continued overtime and its high cost in terms of fatigue and decreasing productivity.

Another major problem faced by management was the meeting of schedules and principal target dates, which had been set early in the planning phase on the basis of inadequate knowledge. In need of some reference points the tentative dates and schedules soon become fixed goals. Perhaps the most serious psychological stress occurred just before the actual conversion date was missed. It had served well as a goal, but as the target date neared it became increasingly obvious to department heads that the deadline would not be met, yet all were reluctant to make the pronouncement which would indicate failure. As a group they finally were able to acknowledge that the rapidly approaching deadline could not be met. This admission of the failure, without any pinpointing of blame, came as a relief to many. Subsequently, conversion dates and other targets became less public, and more meaningful, smaller segments of change were set as subgoals.

Despite such problems, management was able to continue a high and sustained level of activity without any crippling dissatisfaction or morale problems throughout the transition period. The high degree of involvement, the feeling of personal development, and the sense of team accomplishment undoubtedly did much to maintain satisfaction in what can best be described as a stressful and at times even chaotic period.

Nonsupervisory Employees in the Accounting Division

Nonsupervisory personnel experienced different types of stress at different times during the transition. Before the actual conversion, employees were concerned as to whether they would be able to meet the demands which the change would bring. This was a period of ambiguity and doubt. As soon as the company announced its intention to introduce EDP equipment, some employees began to question their ability to learn the new duties and to be apprehensive about their ultimate place in the organization. Others expressed a desire to "get going and get it over with." During the transition, when management was beginning to spell out in ever greater detail the dimensions of the change through meetings of the key department heads and supervisors in each unit, employees became increasingly concerned about what the final dimensions of the change would be. As top line personnel became more aware of the complexity of the task and began to wonder about their own adequacy to handle it, their subordinates sensed these fears and in turn became more anxious as to when they would be brought in on the plans of the change, how they could actually assist in the transition, and how they personally would be affected.

Once the conversion actually got underway, however, the demands placed upon the employee were those he shared with his superiors and, in contrast to the preconversion periods, were primarily physical demands. Both worked overtime, both lived in an ambiguous, changing work environment, and both were asked to perform at a more rapid rate and in a more devoted manner than previously. While the manager spent his time in managerial meetings, the nonsupervisory employee conferred with co-workers and with his supervisor devising solutions to problems unique to a transition period.

Meeting the deadlines of three systems and keeping activities coordinated required a great deal of overtime work for everyone. Work on weekday evenings and Saturdays became the pattern for many groups as everyone struggled to learn new procedures for either maintaining the old system or initiating the coming system. The overtime problem was complicated by a decision to staff for the change-over with women employees insofar as possible. It was hoped that the high attrition rate for women would alleviate the problem of reducing the staff when the change-over was finally completed. Legal restrictions, however, precluded women working more than two hours of overtime per day. Therefore, much of the heavy load of additional overtime fell on a relatively few men.

Management's decision not to assign any jobs on a permanent basis until the total change process had run its course was at once assuring and disturbing to many employees. They recognized the good intentions implicit in this policy decision, but the resulting uncertainty was hard to live with month in and month out. When the policy was introduced, it was assumed that the change-over would be completed in a relatively short time—two years or three at the most. But as the transition period stretched out, this continuing ambiguity became a greater problem for both employees and supervisors, all of whom were looking forward to a period of system stability and equilibrium.

Not only were employees confronted with a relatively unstructured picture of their long-range future in the company, but the immediate working environment for many was equally ambiguous. Those directly responsible for the introduction of the new system had no guideposts to handle this type of technological change in the office. The few companies with some experience in introducing such EDP equipment had not attempted such a total system change. Supervisors and employees were moving into relatively unknown areas. At times this was doubly disturbing to the employees. Some employees, who did not even remotely understand the system that the managers were hoping to create, found themselves training for a job that no one had really seen in operation. Training and instruction during much of the transition was necessarily at quite an abstract level. It is not surprising that the employees expressed fears about learning the required skills—particularly when the job was subject to frequent modifications on short notice.

During much of the transition, then, the employee operated on faith: faith that the demands placed upon him would be rewarded in the future, and faith in management's ability to effect the new change.

Transitional Problems in the Sales Division

The transitional period posed a much more limited set of problems for the sales division, which was on the periphery of this change in several respects. First, it had little responsibility for implementing the actual change. The IBM 705 was controlled by accounting, and the sales division was primarily a consumer of its services. Secondly, although over 800 people in sales were affected by the change, the tasks performed by the majority of these people were not affected—only part of the information handled was in a new form or from a new source. Finally, most of the members of the division who were affected by the change were both organizationally and geographically farther removed from the decision-making positions relative to the design and control of the system than were members of accounting.

The sales management delegated to one of their staff men the task of keeping the line managers fully informed of developments in the change-over that would affect their units. This assignment of a staff man to a liaison job of this responsibility indicated that sales anticipated a minimal effect on the internal operations of their division. Although the original study regarding the feasibility of converting to EDP was the joint responsibility of one executive from sales and one from accounting, the actual responsibility for effecting the change-over fell primarily on the accounting division. Each division attached different significance to the change. This difference provides a basis for understanding the degree to which their top executives became involved in the process.

For the accounting division, the change was a critical activity. Each department head in accounting saw the conversion to the IBM machine as the principal task facing his unit. The change in the sales division had been predicted to create few internal problems. Department heads in sales delegated the responsibility for the change to subordinates. While the delegation of responsibility was in keeping with the sales division's managerial practices, this disparity in levels at which the change was handled created communication problems between the two divisions. In sales, it also affected authority relationships and delayed upper-level understanding of the problems which were being created by the change. Communication problems already existing between the two divisions were also compounded.

After the change was completed, sales management agreed that the magnitude of the change and particularly its effect on the customers had been underestimated. Alterations in parts of the system had almost unpredictable consequences for personnel in other parts of the system, and inadequate training was a natural consequence. The unpredicted magnitude of the change also meant that a communication system was not established that would enable them to anticipate, identify, and handle expeditiously the many problems of the pressure-laden transition period.

The different significance of the change for the two divisions was also reflected in the means by which the change was communicated to employees. Accounting had more information to communicate. It attempted to give its personnel at all levels as complete an account of the change, its process, and its problems as possible. The sales management, with a larger body of employees, restricted early information about the change to only those they thought would be most directly affected by the change. There were other factors also which affected communication in the two divisions. In announcing the impending change, the same general facts were presented in both divisions; the IBM 705 was described as a system which would improve accuracy at lower costs. It is important to note that these objectives did not have the same significance for sales as they did for accounting personnel. Had the system been presented as a means to better customer service or better and faster handling of customer information, both of which were also among the objectives, much more significance might have been attached to the change by sales personnel.

When the EDP system was put in operation, changes in the way information concerning the customer's account was handled, and in the customer record form and content, presented special problems to the sales nonsupervisory worker. While most sales jobs changed very little, the information with which the employees were familiar was presented in new forms. This in itself was upsetting for some older workers who failed to understand the necessity for new forms. A number tried to translate the new back into the old familiar language rather than to learn to work with the data in its new form. This, of course, reduced effectiveness and productivity. Other individuals were more disturbed because they failed to receive all the information that they formerly had. In some instances there was a real need for this information, but in most cases it was not actually necessary, nor had it ever been necessary for the operation of the system.

Under the EDP system there were new sources as well as new forms of old information. Because some departments or functions were merged with others, part of the problem was learning the new sources. But more important was the fact that many informal information contacts had not been recognized as a part of the former system and consequently had not been incorporated into the new system. Requests for old information from new sources often resulted in the initiator's having to defend his right to the information. Complaints from the sales division that people in accounting would not furnish data or refused to "dig a little" were countered with remarks that supplying such information was not a part of accounting's job. Only after members of each part of the system came to understand one another's duties and after a new set of shared expectations was established were these types of complaints eliminated.

Sales members tended to mistrust either the information, its source, or both. Part of this mistrust stemmed from the notion that the new system would not work and part from their early experiences with frequent errors. For them it seemed reasonable to assume that the accounting division, which appeared remote at best, did not understand their problems and consequently could not be expected to give the needed information even if the system did work.

One attempt by sales to cope with this uncertainty about the information that many had to use in their daily work with customers was referred to as "stockpiling." Old records that were supposed to have been destroyed were maintained in some units. In other instances, information was duplicated, or functions were continued that were supposed to have been eliminated or turned over to others. In still other instances, individuals kept personal notebooks or actual copies of all problem transactions. This was done both as a personal security measure and as an effort to increase efficiency in taking care of the customer.

Taking care of the customer was the principal concern of the average sales employee. His perception of his role in the company was always to be of assistance to the customer—especially when the customer was a victim of the other division. Failure to comprehend fully the new system, continued recurrence of mistakes, and increased dependence on accounting, all pointed to loss of job control. It also represented decreased service to the customer in the eyes of the sales employee and his supervisor and resulted in considerable tension for them.

The new system soon became a prime target for blame. It was seen as accounting inspired and accounting controlled. Many individuals were certain that their jobs had been made more difficult and that in all cases where there was conflict between the needs of the two divisions the machine and the new system were always the winners.

Moreover, at the beginning of the change-over, accounting personnel tended to let the machine be blamed for errors. More and more mistakes were attributed to the machine as a convenient all-purpose scapegoat. When it was recognized that the machine was becoming perceived as an unknown and unpreditable "monster," executives in the accounting division tried to dispel this idea. It was emphasized that, in the IBM 705, mistakes were extremely rare and that errors were attributable to the human beings who controlled the input or its operations. This only shifted the focus of the antagonism from the machine to the accounting division or its members. While the phrase used to identify the change-over was changed from the name of the machine, "the 705 system," to "The Customers Records System," sales members continued to blame those impersonal office workers in the central offices, the programmers, or the management of accounting.

One of the greatest sources of frustration for sales personnel was the repeated error. Errors early in the conversion system had been anticipated, but when the same errors continued to reoccur, even those who had been either neutral or positive at the outset became antagonists of the system. Interviews revealed that many of these individuals first had gone through formally designated channels, and then had tried all other means they could think of to communicate to proper authority the nature of these errors. When they failed to get either the elimination of errors they had pointed out or even confirmation that their message had been received, they gave up and ceased to bring such problems to anyone's attention. Thus, negative attitudes toward the system and its sponsors were first created and then reinforced. Delays in the elimination of errors were explained in part by the geographically and organizationally peripheral position of the sales units and in part by the nature of the IBM 705 system. Communications from sales employees often failed to reach appropriate people in the accounting division, or when they did reach appropriate personnel, they frequently were much too late. Even when it was known that errors were present in certain programs, it was necessary to use them as they were because there was either not enough time or not enough knowledge to modify the program.

The use of bimonthly billing delayed corrections on the customer's bills for three or four months and contributed to the sales employee's conviction that accounting 705 personnel did not care about his problems or at least did not understand them. This belief was reinforced when errors started to disappear as soon as the accounts closest to the home office were converted. The reaction was, "They let us suffer but look what happens when the conversion results in errors for customers who can bring their problems to the direct attention of the key persons in both divisions." In fairness, it should be noted that the system was just becoming stabilized when the more central accounts were being converted.

Some of the errors actually had their origin with the people supplying the information in the sales division, although few sales employees saw it this way. Eventually the top executives of the company became concerned with the errors and their effect on customer relations. Although not attaching blame to any division specifically, the president arranged to have a consulting firm study the new customer accounting system. The consulting firm began by analyzing the errors, tracing them to their source, and also looking at the general billing and accounting procedure.

The work of accounting personnel who had been left with the major responsibility for the change was obviously under critical review. This introjection of outsiders and the uncertainty of the ultimate findings created a great deal of tension for accounting management and the final report of the consultants came as a great relief to accounting personnel. It is noted that there were no more errors than would normally be expected and in effect stated that accounting had done a superior job in creating and installing a totally new system.

One outcome of this consultant's report was to make the sales and accounting divisions jointly responsible for any remedial work that was necessary. The heads of both divisions began to function as a team in discussing and working out solutions to prevailing problems. A series of meetings were conducted with various groups of employees. At each of these meetings the top line people for both divisions were present and assumed active roles in answering questions and working out solutions to problems that were raised.

REASSIGNMENT AND THE NEW STRUCTURE OF THE ACCOUNTING DIVISION

New Policies and the Philosophy of Reassignment

After all company accounts became converted to EDP procedures the transitional period came to an end, and the organization was faced with the task of making the final job assignments in the new system.

The final allocation of the work force presented a type of problem seldom encountered in industrial settings. Management was confronted with a fixed number of jobs and a fixed number of candidates whom they were obligated to place. Earlier commitments to the permanent employees precluded one alternative of the usual selection process, i.e., rejection of the candidate. The problem was one of optimum placement of all employees in a manner that would be best for both the company and the candidate.

New policies for this mass shifting of some 270 employees had to be formulated and announced. The job posting regularly used when a vacancy occurred was supplemented by a procedure which took into account the employee's preferences concerning different jobs. because the new system and equipment had eliminated a number of upper-level jobs, some employees might be forced to accept jobs at grade levels below their permanent job grade. Under the usual job-posting procedures, these candidates would have been required to apply for jobs below their grade level and accept correspondingly lower rates of pay; but if they were assigned to these lower jobs by management they could retain their former pay levels. Since company policy was to avoid reduction in the pay rates of permanent personnel as a result of the change to EDP procedures, the management in accounting was faced with the enormous task of deciding where to assign each employee. It was recognized that if an employee's preference for a job could be met, employee preference would be far superior to arbitrary placement by management. Hence a statement-of-preference form was designed for use as an aid in handling these problems of reassignment.

As a first step in reassignment, each employee was interviewed to determine whether he felt his present assignment was temporary or permanent. The wisdom of this became apparent when some employees argued that they had received permanent raises or assignments, although their records indicated otherwise. In such cases extensive interviewing with previous supervisors, reviews of records, and other similar means were used to determine the individual's actual status. Discrepancies in company records were found in a few instances. Most of the disagreements could be attributed to misunderstandings; a few to deliberate attempts to misrepresent. Had agreement with each employee about his status not been reached early in the reassignment phase, it seems probable that there would have been much more opportunity for misunderstanding and even misrepresentation.

The essentials of the reassignment plans (abstracted from the policy statements) were as follows:

Each department will open for assignment or post its highest graded jobs first. As each vacancy is filled, the next highest of the remaining job grades will be circulated until all jobs from the highest to the lowest have been filled. Like grades for all departments will be posted simultaneously.

Assignment. A notice of job vacancy will be prepared and circulated to employees who have a permanent job grade equal to or higher than the grade of the vacant job. All such employees may indicate their preferences for the available jobs and their interest in being considered for them. Selection will be made from this group on the basis of required qualifications. If any openings remain unfilled after this circulation, the unfilled jobs will be posted for bidding under normal procedure.

Posting. All openings on newly created jobs, modified jobs, and permanent jobs currently filled on a temporary "acting" basis which remain after assignment of qualified employees of a like or higher grade will be posted. All employees who meet the qualifications listed on the notice of job vacancy may apply for the posted jobs.

Selection. Supervisors will be responsible for using an appropriate selection plan. They will review their selections with a department head for approval. In turn department heads will review these selections with their immediate superiors and all selections will be reviewed by the general accountant.

Bases of Selection. Factors to be considered in the evaluation of applicants will include: past and present performance as to quantity and quality of work; work habits; job aptitude and the ability to learn; length of service and attendance record. Job experience acquired by an applicant during conversion will not provide a candidate with a preferential position.

Trial Period. Employees selected for jobs will be given up to six months' trial on the job to determine their ability to do the work. If it is determined that an employee's performance is not satisfactory, his further placement will be reviewed at that time.

One additional policy was formulated later to take care of those instances in which employees had worked on temporary assignments at jobs which were higher rated than their permanent jobs and who could not be allowed to remain in such jobs. The pay of these employees was decreased at quarterly periods and returned to the permanent grade pay by the end of a year.

This total reassignment policy was dictated by a combination of previous commitments, existing circumstances, and the management philosophy of the accounting division. The underlying objectives of this policy were to minimize losses for employees in terms of pay and promotion and at the same time to maintain a staff capable of operating the new system. These goals were often incompatible and compromises had to be made. Seniority was a major factor in selection since only those employees at certain job grades or above were considered during any one assignment phase. From the company point of view, this meant a minimum distortion in pay grades and jobs to which individuals might be assigned. This was done even though it was recognized that seniority and ability did not necessarily accompany each other.

Less obvious was the compromise that developed as reassignments were made and it became apparent that many of the high-grade employees were far from excellent candidates for many of the high-level jobs. Instead of making assignments to maximize the probability of success on the job, many personnel decisions had to be made within the framework of minimizing failure. Trained and sophisticated in the use of good selection procedures, managers were now unable to follow the maxim of "the best man for the job" in its usual sense. Placements were made after consideration of groups or combinations rather than with respect to a single employee. For example, X was obviously the best man for Job 1; he was also the best man for Jobs 2, 3, and 4 that were open simultaneously. On the other hand, there was person Y who had to be placed and who could adequately perform on Job 1 but not on Jobs 2, 3, and 4. The placement of

Y on Job 1 then became imperative even though he was not "the best man for the job." Many hours were spent in working out "best-fit combination assignments."

From an overall company point of view, this approach of trying to find a best fit for all employees was quite acceptable. To the first-line supervisor or department head, who later would be judged by the performance of only his own subordinates, the placing of known-risk candidates and the passing up of better candidates for jobs in his own group were more difficult to accept. While the supervisor or department head had made many compromises concerning his staff during the change period, the acceptance of a marginal employee or the passing up of a superior employee during this final phase had significant long-range implications. It was all too clear that some of these assignments meant the department head and his staff would be burdened with such an employee for a long time. Moreover, these were the employees who presumably would not be able to post out of their present jobs, even if they so desired.

As the reassignment program gained momentum, a review of those individuals who were difficult to place revealed that a few factors—such as age and physical disability—were the principal deterrents to a candidate's placement. It became apparent that some of the old white-collar desk jobs had attracted many individuals with physical disabilities such as speech or hearing difficulties, arthritis, or heart conditions. Some employees had entered the company with such difficulties; others had developed them during their tenure. Many of the new jobs required communication with others including the use of telephones, standing at machines, and a considerable degree of training. Moreover, a larger number of the jobs eliminated were at the higher levels—levels where one found the older members of the work group, many of whom had worked their way up to highly specialized jobs. Some of the most difficult jobs under the new system had to be staffed from a population that had the least potential.

After all individuals had been assigned a job, there was still the problem of coordinating the transfers to these new jobs. An individual who was to work on a new job could not be moved before he had trained his replacement who in turn could not be moved until his replacement could be released. More than six months were required before all of the individuals could actually start on their new jobs.

General Problems for Management

Several of the problems that management faced during the reassignment period were peculiar to the means adopted to reshift employees; others might be expected in any organization as a period of large-scale reorganization is brought to a close.

One of the most pressing problems during this period was the maintenance of a high level of group morale and individual job satisfaction. Every attempt was made to arrive at solutions that would be satisfactory to each individual. While the general policy of reassignment served as guidelines, many unique solutions had to be invented in individual cases. The old problem remained of devising a solution that would meet the employee's personal needs, the company objectives, and still be perceived as appropriate publicly. In many instances an employee upon talking over his particular situation with a supervisor wished to accept an alternative which would appear to be undesirable to co-workers who had not shared the discussion. Other employees in talking about the treatment that such an individual received often evaluated it as a "raw deal." The individual in question did not see it as a bad decision and was actually quite satisfied with the new assignment, but he was reluctant to report all of the information that was shared in his interviews with management. The satisfaction from having arrived at a solution that was acceptable to the individual was quickly destroyed for both the individual and supervisor when they heard reports that it had been described as a "raw deal."

During the reassignment period several other changes were being made that demanded the careful attention of management. They were also directing all of the activities necessary to introduce a new customer bill form and to change the physical location of all departments affected by the innovation. A number of the interviewees noted that either one of these changes would have been highly disruptive, even "traumatic" to some people, at any other period. However, perhaps because of the magnitude and duration of the change they had just encountered and the personal significance that the reassignment process held for each individual, nearly everyone—management and employees—was able to take these other new changes in stride.

The problems involved in shifting personnel and making these additional changes meant that once again various departments in the accounting division were forced to communicate with each other a great deal. During the months just prior to the reassignment, cross-departmental communication had dropped significantly below that of the preceding two years. The problems that each department had been facing were primarily internal; even vertical communications within the departments had diminished. Following the conversion there was not the constant need for department meetings to ensure coordination. This decrease in communication seemed to indicate that the barriers among and within departments were being slowly reestablished. As each group devoted more time to its own problems, its concern for the problems of the total system decreased. This decrease in communication about and concern for operations of the total system pointed toward the need to establish new coordination and "trouble-shooting" roles.

The new system was highly interdependent and a breakdown or bottleneck in one area affected many others. Since some communication channels were being used less and others had ceased to exist altogether, much of the information necessary for coordination was not available at the crucial points in all parts. Formal communication channels were needed to handle that which formerly had been accomplished through informal means. The creation of such channels, however, was not the complete answer. It was necessary to have experts in the system who could monitor the information and translate a work breakdown, for example, into orders and information for other parts of the system. If a breakdown occurred at one point in the system, a different list of people needed to be informed than if some other point experienced a breakdown.

At about this time department heads also had their first chance to evaluate the status of their departments. This meant directing attention once again to such responsibilities as supervisory development, to reactivation of suggestion systems, regulation of absences, and supervision of other activities either ignored or delegated during the more busy period of the change. As top management became more concerned once again with the activities they had delegated, the locus of power and control moved back up the hierarchy of organization. This was also a period when department heads took stock of themselves. In some instances, for the first time in three or four years they appeared to be reviewing their own progress and looking at what the long-range future held for them personally.

Supervisory Problems

While the first-line supervisors had many of the same kinds of problems that upper levels of management had, some problems were unique to this level. Nearly everyone, management and employees alike, had anticipated higher average job grades as a result of the change, but these higher job grades did not materialize. Toward the end of the conversion, an extensive job evaluation and analysis was undertaken by wage analysts and, with the exception of the programming area, there was no significant change in the average job grade. The least interesting and the most menial types of jobs had been eliminated, but so had a number of high-level nonsupervisory jobs. Certain previous job grades in the accounting division had been somewhat higher than similar jobs in other parts of the organization, and for the first time in a number of years it was possible to bring these jobs into line with the rest of the company. Moreover, as might be expected, nearly everyone had at the outset overestimated the complexity of the new jobs because there had been no experience with them.

These final job grades presented particularly difficult problems to the supervisors. As members of management they had no alternative but to support the new job grades, despite the fact that the lower-than-anticipated job grades affected them directly as supervisors. Many had hoped that higher job grades for their subordinates would eventually mean increases in their own salary level. Acceptance of the new job grades was also complicated by the fact that they felt that they had been left out of the job-grading procedure. Prior to this, supervisors had always participated in both job analyses and job evaluations. Although supervisors were interviewed during the analysis phase this time and were consulted occasionally as the job grades were being tentatively established, the objective of aligning job grades across departments and divisions required that coordination and final review of all these jobs take place *above* the first-line supervisory level. The approach to job reevaluation had been streamlined because of the volume of jobs involved. How strongly each supervisor felt about being left out seemed to be directly proportional to his expectation of participation as based on past experience.

Interviewing time was also a considerable burden during the reassignment phase. Every individual who stated a preference for, or who applied for, a job was interviewed by the appropriate supervisor. Candidates who had not initiated an interview but who were seen by management as potential jobholders in a given group were also interviewed. After the selections were made, many of the unsuccessful candidates had to be interviewed again, particularly if they applied for a job that they were on temporarily or if they were now assigned to the supervisor who had rejected them.

Supervisors complained about the amount of time spent in interviewing prospective candidates. They were particularly disturbed, however, about those interviews in which they had to talk to members of their group who were unsuccessful in their applications. Failure to obtain a job could be attributed to poor work habits, attitudes, work history, or recommendations, or to a general or specific lack of ability. The supervisors reported that lack of a specific skill was the easiest deficiency to handle. They reported that often employees were amazed when told that they had a poor work history or poor work habits. In other cases the worker had known he was not a good candidate but, having experienced progress at a satisfactory rate prior to the reassignment phase, had assumed that he would continue to be promoted. The supervisory staff often had the feeling that they were doing the job that should have been done by the supervisor or upper-level management person who in the past had apparently promoted the employee in spite of his undesirable characteristics. In particular, the supervisor found it difficult to rationalize the actions of predecessors who had allowed unsatisfactory workers to be promoted to the top of their pay grade—an indication of satisfactory performance. Now that the organization was confronted with a great number of demanding jobs with little tolerance for poor performance, it was the present generation of first-line supervisors who had to bear the brunt of correcting the accumulated mistakes of a number of years in a very short period of time.

Besides the stresses involved in having to accept high-risk job candidates, there was the accompanying problem of training new members of the work group who were replacing already trained members. Particularly trying for both supervisor and job candidate was the training necessary when the candidate had little background for the job. In many instances the employee had worked in areas which were very different from his present assignment and consequently had to learn a completely new set of skills. Unlike the usual job candidate who anticipates starting at the bottom and learning the fundamentals, the transferred employee often brought several years of seniority with him along with a set of status claims he was accustomed to having met. Even though it was expected that he would rapidly gain proficiency on the job, the necessary training on the elementary and often less challenging tasks of the new job resulted in situations that violated the candidate's self-image. Frustration derived from such situations often severely taxed the supervisor's human relations skills. Such problems appeared to be somewhat less difficult when two or more employees were transferred together. Several individuals could better face these new and frustrating roles as trainees in a new work group under a new supervisor if they could share and evaluate their experiences with others having a common background.

Transferring and retraining the dislocated employee presented a human relations problem about which the supervisor could actively do something. However, employees who had become increasingly marginal and less certain of their future were much more difficult to handle. Having to face and work with employees of this class each day, meant, for the first-line supervisor, eight hours of face-to-face contact with a number of employees who (1) certainly would not be obtaining the jobs they preferred, (2) were anxious about their competence in future assignments, or (3) were being forced to recognize that their age or other factors disqualified them from ever achieving many of their aspirations. The department head could feel sincerely sorry for "good old Joe" who was being bypassed, but he did not have to work with him daily.

Employee Problems

During this same period the employee was confronted with a number of problems related to reassignment and the new job grades. The announcement of the new job grades and the policy for reassignment was made in each work group simultaneously. Care was taken that supervisors would handle these two pieces of information separately. The initial reaction to the placement policy was generally favorable. This was seen as a fair policy, although subsequent interviewing indicated that many individuals did not really comprehend the procedure.

The announcement of the new job grades met with a somewhat different reaction. It was immediately apparent that the new job grades were lower than anticipated. In a few sections there was considerable disturbance over the job grades and a feeling that jobs had been underesti-mated. Some employees contested the grades vigorously. Some blamed management, many the general economic recession. A few noted that management had stated that they were going to effect considerable savings and that these lowered job grades seemed to be how they were going to accomplish this.

As the reassignment process started to affect the majority of the workers personally, more employees became visibly concerned about reassignments. Throughout the study there had been little disturbance or resistance until each change was imminent, and this again was true of the reassignment phase. Immediately after the job grades and reassignment plans were announced, supervisors reported that only a minority showed any signs of psychological distress. The earliest reassignments were made at the highest levels, and, although many individuals were not accommo-dated as they had hoped, there was little change in the behavior of workers as reported by their supervisors. The reaction of employees as reassign-ment of the middle job grades approached was quite different. One of the largest single groups of employees worked at grade 0–9 jobs. The week that the 0–10 jobs were being assigned, supervisors began to report symptoms of nervousness and anxiety, lowered performance rates, and other indications of an agitated work force. A rash of rumors swept accounting that week.

One rumor was that all married women would be asked to leave the company after January 1. Another stated that men sixty years of age or with 40 years of seniority would be asked to retire with either 85 or 100 per cent of retirement pay. The latter idea was widely held; the only argument was as to whether the percentage would be 85 or 100. Another rumor predicted that one thousand men in the organization would be laid off in the immediate future. Although up-the-line communication was generally poor during the reassignment phase, these rumors reached management very quickly, and immediate steps were taken to discount them.

While no systematic records were kept, supervisors generally felt that an individual's performance went up again following a decision on his job assignment, even when the assignment was not favorable for him. Several supervisors reported that the waiting for the decision seemed to be worse for their employees than the decision itself.

THE EMERGING STATE OF EQUILIBRIUM

During the later part of the reassignment period there was a growing realization by personnel at all levels that the organization that was emerging was going to be quite different from the organization they had known. The new patterns of work flow and relationships that were being established contained environmental realities to which both supervisory and nonsupervisory personnel had to accommodate. A brief description of the new organization follows.

Relocation and Centralization of Control and Decision Making

A change-over to EDP appears to accelerate the level of formalization within an organization. The organization of work is further rationalized; rules and regulations are substituted for individual decision making. Programing itself is a large step in this direction. Decisions formerly left to individual employees to handle within the spirit of a general statement of policy are programed into the machine. It is this type of decision with known criteria that can be built most readily into machine programs. With the programing of this area of decision making, important functions and even certain positions within the organization are eliminated. Previously these functions have supported a job occupant's claim to a title and a grade of some status within the system. Such positions are typically perceived as status positions, serving as terminal points for the average employee who rises to these positions through sheer endurance within the system. Occasionally these positions also serve as a proving ground for managerial aspirants.

In this study the elimination of these status positions and the further restriction of the areas of employee decision making was a severe blow to men in these status positions. Employees of long service were stripped of many of their responsibilities at a time when the right and ability to make such decisions was the principal reward of the job. This situation was equally severe for both accounting and sales personnel. The impact of this relocation and centralization of decision making was felt keenly by sales personnel in customer offices when they were prohibited from making certain decisions in their relations with customers and when other decisions which had formerly been theirs were programed for the IBM 705.

The new, more highly integrated work process allowed less autonomy for setting the work pace for both individual employees and work groups. Work could not be held over from one day to the next. Each group had to process a specific number of accounts every day or perform specific operations. Deadlines had to be met, regardless of how the job had been going or how the personnel and equipment were performing. Absences and tardiness became increasingly important because they interfered with the group's ability to complete its portion of the job.

Greater interdependence also resulted in greater vulnerability and a greater need for coordination. A breakdown in one phase of the work flow soon stopped the whole operation. Since a change in one section quickly affected another section's ability to do its job, new procedures and centers for coordination were required. It is significant that the need for coordination became acutely visible during conversion when informal contact systems had been shattered by new departmental and subunit alignments, and when the emerging system was least clear to supervisors and employees.

A different kind of control relocation also occurred as responsibilities for given areas or duties were transferred to other groups, departments, or divisions. Throughout the change period there was evidence that such transfers of responsibility often resulted in control moving either horizontally or to some higher level in the organization to effect a more efficient coordination. Since various subunits contributed to different stages of the input, it was necessary that a central control unit be aware of any deviations that occurred. Consequently, final responsibility and control was vested in a very few positions. This shift toward more centralized control and decision making was required to handle the new level of coordination necessary to maintain what was obviously a more efficient system. On the other hand, such centralization ran directly counter to the company's philosophy of participation—one of its principal objectives being the delegation of responsibility directly to first-line supervisors.

As the change-over progressed, lower levels became more aware of their place in the entire system. When interruptions occurred or where schedules could not be met, these groups often contacted the various units affected directly rather than going through formal organizational channels.

New Jobs and Relationships

The new system resulted in many changes in job structure and in new and differing patterns of relationships. Some of the jobs that were eliminated were taken over directly by the IBM 705. Many of these were the more routine, tedious tasks, requiring employees with relatively low skill; others, however, were of a higher level involving minor decision making. Thus programed activities came from several job grade levels within the organization.

The new equipment also created two major classes of jobs: programers and electronic equipment operators. Early in the change-over the glamor and complexity attributed to the new process affected employees' evaluations of these jobs. Both the jobs associated with the IBM 705 and the other newly created jobs were viewed as more complicated and thus open to higher job grades than the other jobs with which employees were familiar. Much of the subsequent dissatisfaction with the final job grades undoubtedly can be attributed to this exaggerated evaluation of the jobs.

In accounting, the greater number of key punch operators and other machine groups increased the number of employees associated more with the mechanical processing of the data than with the data itself. Because of the obvious distinguishing characteristics of the machine jobs as against the accounting jobs, and because promotion is probably more feasible within rather than between the groups, there is an increasing possibility of a schism between these two groups.

Job enlargement does not necessarily accompany a change-over to electronic accounting. In this instance, however, it did. The work of the nonmechanized accounting groups responsible for the steps preparatory to the machine handling of the customer's account was completely reorganized. The specialized tasks previously done in five separate sections were consolidated into a "station arrangement," and each member of a station was trained to handle all five operations as part of a new, enlarged job. This reduction in job specialization resulted in increased efficiency in the allocation of manpower, and it is believed that most employees and their supervisors were more satisfied with these jobs. The members of each team gained considerable satisfaction from helping train others in their own specialty. Problems, where they did occur, were most prevalent among the older employees.

In addition to creating new jobs and new combinations of old skills, the system required the development of different relationships. With the loss of autonomy and the introduction of more system pacing, groups became more interdependent and individual responsibilities became more obvious and easily evaluated. Individual contributions to input were identifiable. Under the old system, in which a number of individuals shared responsibility for a given phase of the process and a number of checkpoints were relied upon to eliminate errors, it was difficult to control the number of errors or to pinpoint the responsibility for a given error. Under the new system, however, errors were immediately detected within the processing system and responsibility for the error readily traced. Such changes allowed the development of tighter standards of performance, and the increasing costs of errors augmented concern for standards.

In the sense that failures were more easily detected, the machine placed more responsibility upon the individual employee. With greater interdependence of jobs, it was even more important that each individual carry his share of the work. Failure here meant that the work group could not meet its assigned quota or that others had to assume part of the lagging individual's work load. Even before the reassignment phase, supervisors reported individuals who came to them complaining about co-workers who were not "pulling their share." There was practically no record of such occurrences under the old accounting system. Under the new system, each individual was usually more aware of his and others' contributions. During the reassignment phase everyone was being closely watched and evaluated, and there was considerable dissatisfaction with co-workers who were not performing up to standard. While such work group friction was not excessive, it appeared often enough to allow supervisors to note the change in work group relationships between the old and the new systems. The degree to which tensions arising from the several sources of insecurity during the reassignment period found their release in making scapegoats of co-workers cannot be accurately assessed. It should be noted, however, that no supervisor ever reported what appeared to him to be an unjustified criticism of a worker; rather it was that the unsuccessful worker was more in the spotlight than he had ever been before.

SUMMARY

Since this change-over has just been completed, there has been little chance to assess how this extensive period of change will affect the organization eventually, but we have been able to indicate some of the major effects of the change on the organization and its members to date.

Accounting and sales have moved from relatively autonomous departments to a much more highly integrated system. The installation of electronic equipment has brought about changes in policies and procedures that are much more demanding of the individual employee. The level of decision making and control has moved up to fewer and higher positions within the organization. Changes in the job and promotion structure have been quite drastic. For many employees, the experiences of a generation of normal organizational life have been compressed into a few short years.

It has been impossible as yet to determine whether the aggregate effect of these changes has been positive or negative for the individual or the organization. For many individuals this was a period of growth; for others a period of failure and disillusionment. The change severely tested marginal employees and supervisors, while at the same time giving the more experienced and able ones the opportunity to develop and to demonstrate their work potential. The dislocation and the loss of duties and jobs was a serious problem for some employees. In general, the change was a game for the young; for some of the older employees the change meant they were either passed by or failed to rise to the challenge. How each individual, worker, or supervisor feels about this change can now be determined, however, and it is this feeling that we expect to obtain from our attitude measurements made after the change.

The change period gave management at all levels a much deeper understanding of the human resources within their organization. It also increased each supervisor's awareness of how his responsibilities interrelate with other supervisors, superiors, and subordinates. The long period of sharing problems with other managers and the need for extraordinary cooperation at all levels resulted in a greater appreciation and tolerance for other parts of the organization. Employees and supervisors learned to work together in problem-solving groups in a way which neither would have thought possible before the change started. It is already apparent that the principal objectives of this major organizational change are being attained; the new system is permitting a reduction in cost and is sufficiently flexible to encompass further expansion. The final effect on the individual members of the organization who were caught up in this change is still to be learned.

SECTION FIVE

Communication

THE TERM "communication" covers such a vast spectrum of human (and nonhuman) activities that one can readily be confused when told that there is a field of research on "communication." Leaving out the nonhuman areas of communication research, such as telecommunication and the communication aspects of animal sociology, we still have a broad spectrum to consider.

At one extreme, in fields of "micropsychophysiology," researchers are concerned with the chemical and electrical activity associated with the firing of neurons. At another, researchers are examining mass communication such as advertising, propaganda, publishing, and broadcasting.

It is tempting to think of these extremes as ends of a single continuum, or examples of one fundamental phenomenon. In abstract this is a useful concept and has led to worthwhile theory. Operationally, it can lead to the abuse of analogy and the building or extensions of models that are inappropriate to the specific level of communication being examined. Even extrapolation of research results on communication in small groups, (e.g., the articles by Bass and Dunteman in Section 3, Guetzkow and Simon in this section, and Wallach and Kogan in Section 7) to the level of general organizational communication must be done carefully, if it is to be done at all.

There are many suggestive similarities between an experimental small group situation and the communication network of a "natural" organization. For this reason, organization theorists have been very interested in the results of small group research performed primarily by psychologists, sociologists and social psychologists. On the other hand, there are many differences—some of them fundamental. Consider, for example, the status of a particular subset of individuals in an organization; the opportunities to communicate; the secondary role that communication plays in most jobs, relative to working alone; the greater freedom of choice of people with

367

whom one may communicate; the timing and frequency of communication; and many other aspects.

Thus, extrapolation to and inferences about organizational communication from experimental small group research must be done carefully. There has been a limited partnership in this transition between "small-group researchers" and those who carry out empirical studies of communication in natural organizations (as exemplified by most of the articles in this section). However, much more needs to be done in extracting testable propositions from the small group literature for use in describing and predicting communication behavior in natural organizations.

Some writers argue that the essence of organizational behavior is "communication." They claim that an adequate understanding of organizational behavior can be achieved only through an understanding of what is communicated, how it is communicated, and why. Some go even further and imply that a thorough understanding of organizational communication reveals all that is interesting and important to know about organizations. Other enthusiasts and specialists attempt to make similar arguments for decision making, leadership, or other aspects of organizational behavior. Our view is that all of these (and other) aspects are important foci in our studies of the way people behave in organizations. They are all interrelated, and knowledge about one kind of process—e.g., decision making—is necessary for a full understanding of other organizational processes, such as communication, control, and leadership.

Certainly, it is difficult to imagine an organization functioning without some means of communication and without some exchange of information among its members and between them and the external environment.

In What Forms Does Communication Occur in Organizations?

Communication occurs in such variety and volume in most organizations that it is necessary to systematize our examination of this process by developing categories which can help us focus on interesting and significant researchable questions.

One possible set of categories involves a quantitative and qualitative description of the parties to a communication event or a series of communication acts in an organization. If we include the possibility that a person may "communicate" with another or others through some inanimate intermediary—e.g., a book, a report, or a computer—we can visualize in Table 1 communication acts involving sets of "sources" (initiators or senders of a message) and "destinations" (targets for or receivers of a message).

This set of categories of communication events is not, of course, exhaustive of all possible kinds of communication in organizations. It does, however, provide a framework within which to examine current research on organizational communications. Category 1, for example, is the focus of a huge (and growing) research effort in many fields—e.g., computer design and usage, and journal publication. Concomitant with the much publicized "information explosion" of recent years, there are vast efforts underway to improve the generation, transmission and use of information of all kinds.

Major efforts are concentrated in two areas of interest to organization theorists and management practitioners—executive communication and

TABLE 1

FORMS OF COMMUNICATION IN AN ORGANIZATION

Source	Destination	Description or Example of Communication
1. An inanimate intermediary (e.g., book, report, or computer)	An individual	Reading, examining data on a chart or from a computer
2. An individual	An inanimate intermediary	Feeding data to a computer, writing
3. An individual	An individual	A two-person or pair interaction
4. An individual	A small number of individuals	An interaction in a small group situation—one person addressing the group
5. Several individuals	An individual	A group initiating to one person—e.g., a delegation presenting a grievance or a committee reporting to its superior
6. An individual	Many individuals	Mass communication, propaganda, advertising, speaking to an audience
7. Many individuals	An individual	Intelligence gathering, opinion surveying
8. Chains of sources and destinations		A rumor or diffusion system
9. Several individuals mutually linked		A small group situation

scientific and technical information. Although none of the articles in this section deals specifically with either of these two areas, all of them have implications for both. The studies of control tower language (Frick and Sumby) and communication networks (Guetzkow and Simon) deal with two of the many structural elements of an executive or scientific communication system. The specialized languages of computers on the one hand, and of functional specialists or management generalists on the other, strongly influence the design and effectiveness of these systems. Much work is under way in attempting to make these two kinds of languages compatible by either modifying one of them to make it more like the other or developing specialized computer languages such as Fortran, Cobol, and Algol, which are a compromise between natural human languages and machine languages.

The research on network theory and related work on decentralization and theory of teams (5) is aimed at a better understanding of the relations between constraints on communication and certain measures of communication effectiveness and organizational performance. The literature on this subject is growing rapidly as more researchers become interested in the possible effects of computers on organizational behavior (11) as well as in the possible benefits of fundamental changes in interpersonal communication through sensitivity training—or other training in group dynamics (12).

One specific relationship of research on communication networks and information systems to our Category 1 events consists of the danger of the executive or the scientist (in a company's research laboratory, for example) being swamped by the volume and variety of information which can now be supplied to him as a consequence of recent technological advances. These and other developments are increasing the stress on communication systems. As channels become saturated, the normal or planned responses of organizations cannot be maintained. The Mental Health Research Institute has explored the effects of communication overload on organizations and other organized systems (6).

Technological improvements and redesign of organizations can increase information handling capacity, and it is interesting to speculate on the future of these developments. Some observers argue that high-speed digital computers will change the shape of organizations and the location of decision making. Others argue that this is not inevitable and the pendulum of decentralization will not swing back to centralized decision making and control as a consequence of better data processing. So far, however, much of this is in the realm of speculation, since very little is known systematically about the actual effects of "information automation" on organizational behavior.

Among the conflicting speculations are that further mechanization of information handling will (a) eliminate large numbers of middle managers and (b) not affect the *number* of middle managers, but change their job content significantly (4). Valid evidence for either prediction can only come from careful studies of what actually happens in organizations as a consequence of such technological changes. (See the article in Section 4 by Mann and Williams.)

A few words must be said here about a much neglected area of organizational communication—ways of inhibiting it. While it is true that much of organizational life involves interpersonal communication, there are many activities that require contemplation, reading, writing, and other activities that are best carried on alone. The ring of the telephone, which penetrates into the deepest sanctuary of the organization, and the head-in-the-doorway with "have you got a minute," plague the organization member attempting to carry on some of these solitary activities.

In most areas of the organization, a person sitting alone at his desk or gazing out the window in the classical thinker's posture is fair game for a meeting, a conversation, or a telephone call. If he is reading, he is even more vulnerable. In most organizational activities, reading is something relegated to home or the commuter train. Except for brief reports, correspondence, and other business documents, it is not expected that the organization member will do much extensive or "heavy" reading on the job. In many organizations this is even true for the laboratory researcher, whose very job depends on his ability to keep up with the literature.

If these solitary activities are essential for the proper functioning of the organization—e.g., decision making, planning, problem solving, research— then they must be designed for. In the modern organization, design of communication systems emphasizes the active categories of Table 1—those involving interpersonal communication. Meeting rooms, intercom systems, connecting suites, and ease of travel are the foci of the modern "organization communication systems engineer." Perhaps more attention needs to be paid to design for privacy and design for extended periods of the essential solitary activities described above. The familiar comment, "I didn't get anything done today, I was in meetings all day" reflects a need for some careful attention to communication *inhibition* as well as communication *facilitation* in organizations.

What Would We Like to Know about Communication in Organizations?

What are some of the interesting and significant things we would like to know about communication in organizations? Why is the study of communication essential to an understanding of organizational behavior? Let us recall Figure 1 in the introductory essay to Section One, which portrays the relationship between the behavioral scientist, including the organization theorist, the management scientist, and the practicing administrator. Each of these kinds of people will be interested in communication, but from a different point of view.

The *behavioral scientist* may be interested in the phenomenon of small group communication per se. He may focus on the communication configurations possible in a group of five people. He may be concerned with the frequency of use of each possible configuration and, perhaps, the effects of each configuration on speed of problem solution or error rate.

The behavioral scientist interested in organization theory—that is, the organization theorist—may be interested in the results of such small-group experiments on communication for their suggestive value, or he may be able to generate testable propositions about organizational communications from them.

The *management scientist* may be interested in the research findings, concepts, or investigation methods of the behavioral scientist. He may be faced with a problem of organizational design which involves the development of communication networks for planning, control, or decision making. If the literature is useful, even in a suggestive way, he may attempt to apply some of the research findings directly to his design problem.

The *practicing manager* is very unlikely to go directly to the literature of organization theory or behavioral science when he faces a communication problem. He may consult his staff management scientist, an outside consultant, or the management literature for clues on how to resolve or even consider the problem. He seldom mounts a systematic search for such advice, however, unless the problem is critical. Under this condition, he is likely to be in a hurry for some amelioration or quick fix for the immediate problem rather than be interested in a long-term investigation of the underlying phenomena.

Hence, each of these participants in the organizational research and application process is likely to raise different specific questions about communication in organizations.

The *manager* is likely to ask: "Why can't I get reports on time?" or "How can I get research and sales to see eye to eye on this new product?"

The *management scientist* may ask: "How can I design an efficient reporting system?" or "How can I design a smooth transition procedure for new products that are transferred from research to sales?"

The *organization theorist* asks: "What are the factors relating to speed of communication in an organization?" or "Why do technological and organizational changes lead to conflict between functional groups?" Other behavioral scientists may be asking: "What are the limits on the information intake and output of an individual or a small group?" or "How do individuals or groups of people deal with changes in their immediate environment?"

It can readily be seen that all of these people are interested in the same *basic phenomena*, although at different levels, in different contexts, and *for different reasons*. There is great promise for greatly improved understanding of human communication, better design of organizational communication systems, and better functioning of communication in organizations. The latter consequences, however, depend heavily on advances in the former and on an effective means of transferring knowledge among the various kinds of people described above.

The critical link in this transfer currently appears to be the management scientist. He must be able to use the results of the basic research performed by the first two groups and be attuned to the needs of the user of the communication system—the managers and other members of the organization. He must also be in a position to implement the designs he produces and assure that the communication system is kept up to date.

At the present time, this critical role in the improvement of organizational communication is not being adequately performed. Only a few large organizations maintain internal specialists in this field, and only a few of the outside organizations offering these services on a consulting basis have such specialists on their staffs. A trend is evident, however, in the attempts by large organizations to hire, train, or assign people to this important function. In addition, a rapid increase is taking place in the number of people capable of performing this role. These are graduates of programs in industrial management, business, sociology, industrial engineering, and management sciences who have had significant exposure to the behavioral sciences and organization theory. These people could bring about a virtual revolution in organizational communication.

What are some of the questions the organization theorist has about communication in organization? What are the phenomena and events on which he focuses when he embarks on a study of communication in a real, operating organization? Some of these questions are very general—they apply to any organization. Others are very specific, depending on the nature of the organization, e.g., a military unit, a research laboratory, or a school. Here are some of the more general questions:

The communicators
Who are they—what are their roles in the organization?
What are their communication capacities?
What are their communication propensities?
What effects do they have on messages—e.g., distortion, delays?
The messages
What is actually communicated?
What is the information content?
What is the function of classes of messages?
In what languages are messages phrased?
The means of communication
What media are in use and with what relative frequency?
What are the mechanics of information handling?
What is the timing of message flow—the density and time patterns?
What are the capacities of the various communication channels and subsystems available?
The environmental conditions
What volume of messages is required by the organization and its environment?
How do situational factors—e.g., emergencies, organizational growth—affect the communication requirements?
What are the constraints on communication—e.g., the need for secrecy, protocol, speed?
The results of communication
What is the effectiveness of the communication system?
What is the impact of particular classes of messages?
How does communication relate to other organizational functions such as control, decision making, leadership?
How does the communication system adapt to changing circumstances?

Each of these questions has served as a primary or secondary focus for research on communication by organization theorists. In some cases, the major focus was on another organizational process, such as decision making. As indicated earlier, however, it is not possible to study decision making or other organizational processes in an organization independently of the communication system.

How Does Communication Relate to the Study of Other Organizational Processes?

Consider the empirical studies of organizational structure and process in Section 2. The study in the shoe factory (Horsfall and Arensberg) focused on informal organization, group control over productivity, allocation of work, and leadership. The data for inferences about all of these organizational processes was data about the communication behavior of the workers in the factory. The very definitions of some of these processes were in terms of communication frequency and direction.

Dalton's study of the maintenance activity and the articles by Strauss and by Walton *et al* are studies of intergroup relationships—a critical aspect of the communication network in a manufacturing organization. They also concern control systems and informal leadership.

The experimental study of organizational growth and learning at RAND Corporation (Chapman and Kennedy, Weiner) describes the changes in communication patterns as an organization passes through various stages from inception to maturity. In this case, the task of the "organization" being studied *is* a communication task and hence the output is in terms of acts of communication.

Many of the studies of planned change (Section 4) are concerned with the way in which information about new methods of operation and new technology are transmitted between members of an organization. The administration of planned change is a major exercise in organizational communication. It involves the changing of attitudes, work patterns, and other behavior.

The processes of leadership, control and evaluation, and decision making are all heavily dependent on communication. The development of leadership, the legitimization of informal or formal leadership, and the maintenance of the leadership role are all heavily dependent on the "leader's" ability to communicate effectively with his subordinates and other people in his environment. He must learn their needs, transmit knowledge of his needs to them, and persuade them to adopt attitudes or take actions in consonance with common objectives.

Control and evaluation processes depend heavily on communication for transmitting objectives, sensing behavior and its consequences, comparing behavior and consequences with expectations, signaling the need for change, and affirming the effects of the change.

Although some critical aspects of decision making are "solitary" activities—considering alternatives, making judgments, analyzing the probable and actual effects of decisions—the quality of the informational raw material for all of these subprocesses depends on the quality of the organization's several communication systems.

One aspect of decision making that has not been sufficiently studied is the question of time constraints on decision making—the time during which the decision maker has to resolve a decision problem either by selecting a course of action different from the one he is embarked upon or "deciding" not to decide. The role of communication or information seeking behavior in such circumstances may be critical. Consider the time available for decision suggested by Table 2. Here we visualize the jet pilot toward one end of the scale, representing the need for extremely rapid decision. Toward the other end, we may visualize the laboratory research worker. The medical clinician, making decisions about his patient, is somewhere in between.

TABLE 2

TYPICAL ORDER OF MAGNITUDE OF TIME AVAILABLE FOR DECISION

On the Order of Seconds	On the Order of Minutes	On the Order of Hours or Days
e.g., a jet pilot in an emergency situation	e.g., a medical clinician in his consulting room with a patient	e.g., a research scientist in his laboratory

The implications of this concept for the information-seeking behavior of the decision maker are striking. The jet pilot in an emergency has little time to seek information outside his immediate environment. He depends primarily on his instrument readings and other sensory clues from his immediate environment—sound, smells, things he can see from his seat. Many of the "decisions" formerly made by the pilot have been automated for this reason. The medical clinician, engaged in the consulting room with his patient, generally resolves questions of diagnosis, prognosis, etiology, and treatment on the basis of data obtained directly from the patient and his own past experience and knowledge. In a certain percentage of the cases, he will request laboratory tests or other information before making decisions on the above issues. In a large percentage, he makes these decisions in the space of a few minutes, without consulting outside information sources.

The research scientist faces questions of experimental procedure, interpretation of results, or which line of inquiry to pursue. He is under less time pressure to make these decisions than either the pilot or the doctor. He typically consults outside information sources—the literature, colleagues, records of past research he and others in the laboratory have done.

There are many implications of this "time available for decision" for:

information storage and retrieval systems to serve different specialists; training of the specialists and keeping them up to date; design of the organizations in which they work, to facilitate communication; and design of control systems to assure that communication and decision making are being conducted properly.

Despite great increases in the study of communication in recent years and the vast effort being devoted to the design and manufacture of communication *equipment* and *mechanical* information systems, the systematic design of organizations to facilitate communication and information flow is still in a primitive stage. Although some sporadic attempts have been made by industry to "design" their organizations for better communication, much of this effort has been of a "patch on" character. Data-processing equipment has been the major focus of the design effort and organizational considerations have been secondary, if they enter at all.

The military has progressed beyond this stage in several instances, however, with much effort being devoted to design of command and control systems. Such systems have been designed for units from small face-to-face groups, such as squads or platoons, to the entire worldwide military organization. Even in the military case, however, only a few of these design efforts have involved preliminary study phases dealing with the behavioral aspects of communication. Examples of such studies are the RAND experiments with Air Force warning centers (see the articles by Chapman and Kennedy and by Weiner in Section 2). More recent examples are the studies by the Franklin Institute concerning the worldwide communication network of the U.S. Army (2). Tremendous opportunities exist in this area of organizational design for communication. These are opportunities for behavioral scientists and organizational theorists, but most of all, they are opportunities for management scientists and practitioners (see Figure 1 of the introduction to Section 1) to attempt to apply the results already achieved in studies of organizational communication.

In summary, although we do not embrace the suggestion that organization *is* communication, we recognize the crucial role played by communication in all of the organizational processes discussed in the book. In particular, we emphasize the difficulty of studying any of these processes in organizations without the intensive use of communication data.

What Can We Do with Knowledge about Organizational Communication?

Why do we want to know more about organizational communication? What would the organization theorist and the management scientist do with such knowledge? In other words, given a greatly increased understanding of how people in organizations actually do communicate and the consequences of that communication, what actions could be taken to improve the situation?

Three main types of action are available for influencing organizational communication. They are: (1) organizational design, (2) selection of personnel for the organization, and (3) training organizational members.

Organizational Design. Many design features of an organization can be employed to facilitate or control communication. They include: location of personnel; choice of architectural configuration; mechanical connections between individuals and groups (e.g., telephones, intercom systems); and regulation of personnel movement. Two instances of attempts to improve organizational communication through such physical design are:

A large manufacturing company employed over ten thousand people in its headquarters location, scattered in several dozen separate buildings. During one of its periodic reorganizations, a study was instituted to determine which activities and which individuals were required to communicate in order to carry on their mutual business. It was proposed that, in addition to an administrative reorganization, a physical relocation of people and activities might be performed to facilitate essential communication between departments.

Another large company, in the transportation field, was planning its new skyscraper headquarters building. A study was instituted to resolve a basic personnel location dilemma: should department heads be located on the same floor, where they could engage in face-to-face interdepartmental communication, or should each head be with his department, so that he could be in close contact with his subordinates?

In addition to the architectural and organizational aspects of design for effective communication, there is an emerging art of design of information services. This is particularly noticeable in the technical areas of the firm, such as research and development. With the vast increase in information services available to the researcher—indexes, abstracts, retrieval systems, literature searches and summaries—the choice of which repertoire of services to provide becomes a major design question. Although some of the services can be provided and withdrawn with relative ease—e.g., a new journal—many of them require embedding in the organization, learning time, and displacement of other services of activities.

Not too much is known currently about the interaction between the researcher and his information environment (8), but this is a whole new area of investigation for organization theorists and management scientists—one that holds promise of great improvements in the effectiveness of research, development and other technical activities. One line of investigation has been an attempt to experimentally manipulate the information environment of a group of basic researchers (7). Here, the information environment and behavior of the researchers are "calibrated," new information services are introduced, and the effects are measured. Additional studies of this type, in which the actual behavioral changes related to changes in information services are observed, can be of considerable help in designing organizations for more effective use of such communication "software."

Selection of Organizational Members. Specific communication abilities are sometimes included on the list of personal characteristics required for certain jobs—e.g., teachers, salesmen. However, communication skills and traits are generally not made an explicit, formal part of job requirements for most positions. Generally the recruiter or interviewers consider, in an intuitive way, an applicant's ability to express himself or to handle technical information. Some of the personality tests used in recruiting probe for a person's interest in associating with other people and his preferences for working alone or in groups.

Given the importance of communication in organizational life, however, it would seem crucial to employ communication characteristics as a major determinant in the selection of organization members. The difficulty has been that, except for a few specific cases, it is not clear exactly what levels of which communication abilities are needed to perform particular jobs effectively. For example, Chapple (3) has used recorded interview data, based on carefully controlled interviewer behavior, to analyze the interaction behavior of applicants. Among the aspects considered important was the ability to adjust one's interaction rate to that of another person in order to avoid interruptions or awkward gaps in the discussion. Earlier, this approach was attempted as a rough diagnostic tool for interviewing new patients in a mental hospital.

The work of Bales and others in Interaction Process Analysis demonstrates the differential interaction rates among the members of a small face-to-face discussion group. Bales and others have fitted mathematical functions to such curves and have also produced synthetic groups, with the aid of computers (1), which reproduce the same curves, given individual interaction rates as inputs.

The notion of an individual's natural "propensity to communicate" is an intriguing one for the design of organizational subsystems (e.g., committees) and for the recruitment of organizational members. We certainly recognize, intuitively, that people differ with respect to their natural tendency to interact with others. We also note that some people are more likely to initiate interaction than others. Again, intuitively, we select people for particular assignments, such as committees or task forces, with these differences in mind.

For example, in the studies of idea flow in research and development reported by Rubenstein, the role of individual differences in these characteristics is important. Given an idea for a new research project, some people are more likely than others to discuss it with colleagues or superiors. If the idea was originated by individual A and he is generally a "low initiator" of interaction, the idea is less likely to come to the attention of decision makers in the organization than if the idea had been originated by B—a "high initiator"—*other things being equal.* It is in this latter condition that the difficulty is encountered of discovering and using "propensity to communicate" as a design or selection device.

Small-group research and studies of other communication phenomena, such as innovation and rumor transmission, suggest that there are a number of factors which influence the observable communication behavior of an individual, in addition to his natural propensities. Among these are: his relative expertise with respect to the content of the interaction; status differences among the parties to communication events; the interest of the individual in the particular situation being discussed; and physical surroundings and the kind of communication media being used (e.g., some people are more at ease on the telephone than others).

As a consequence, when one is investigating an aspect of communication behavior as part of a proposition about the effects or causes of communication, one has a difficult job of unscrambling these contributing factors. In attempting to predict who will transmit a rumor or who will pass on a technical idea he has heard about, the organization theorist must take into account, at least: the content of the message (rumor or idea); its relevance to the potential transmitter; and some aspects of the circumstances surrounding him and his potential target—e.g., status differences, proximity, and similarity of interests.

Selecting an appropriate measure of interaction or communication rate must also relate to natural propensity. In an observational study of communication in a purchasing department (9), individual buyers were found to vary along two interaction dimensions—frequency of interaction (times per hour) and proportion of time spent in communication. Some buyers were observed to interact infrequently, but for long periods each time. Others engaged in many, very brief interaction events. Since all the subjects were doing essentially the same work in the same environment, it may be inferred that these are "natural" individual differences in communication propensity.

Training.   Finally, knowledge about communication in the organization can serve as a guide to training and retraining programs. Advances in the arts of "group dynamics" and "sensitivity training" have been applied to helping organization members learn how to interact with other people in group situations and become more sensitive to the needs of others, and to removing barriers to communication resulting from misunderstanding and formal constraints, such as status differences.

The interest in "nondirective counselling" and "effective listening" by supervisors reflects the need to control interaction behavior, as well as to stimulate it.

How Do Mathematical Theories of Communication Help in Understanding Organizational Communication?

At the time of the first edition of this book, there was great enthusiasm among organization theorists and other behavioral scientists for the new mathematical theory of communication (generally referred to as "information theory") developed by Shannon (10) and extended by others. It was hoped that this new systematic approach to the analysis of message content and the capacity of communication channels would lead to a breakthrough in understanding about communication between people. So far, these hopes have not been realized in terms of specific research results. That is, the theorems of mathematical communication theory have not contributed directly to our understanding of or ability to design organizational communication systems. The general approach and point of view provided by this new field, however, has stimulated modes of analysis and trains of thought by organization theorists and other behavioral scientists which may yet yield specific useful results. An example is given in the article by Frick and Sumby on "Control Tower Language."

Information theory concerns the efficiency and accuracy of transmission of symbols between a source and a receiver. This is only the first step, however; there is no automatic assurance that the source knows what he is talking about or that, if he does, the receiver understands. These are *semantic* questions of communication. For the communication system to be adequate, there must be a correspondence between the symbols used and the reality being communicated about, and this correspondence must be the property of both source and receiver. Scientific investigation searches for meaningful symbols with which to communicate about the world around us.

The reader will appreciate the importance of the condition that the correspondence between symbols and reality be shared by both source and receiver, especially after reading some of the more technical articles included in this book. This, or any textbook, is partly an attempt to increase the range of shared vocabulary in the culture or in a profession; and its success depends on the number and usefulness of the concepts that can be learned from it.

Even though messages are accurately transmitted, meaningful, and understood, the study of communication cannot yet be concluded. Communication is a purposive act, and most of the interesting problems deal with the pragmatic aspects. Even questions of syntax or semantics have their *pragmatic* aspects. How accurate a transmission system or how extensive a vocabulary will be maintained by a person, organization, or society depends very much on the purposes for which they are to be used. A powerful vocabulary and accurate, fast transmission methods are costly, and the gains from employing them may not justify the costs. Engineers do not generally employ the concepts and mathematics of theoretical physics in routine design problems, and it is not customary to send New Year's greetings over the transatlantic cable.

The most important pragmatic questions do not concern the economics of transmission media or vocabularies. They concern broader questions relating to the purposes of communication. We can illustrate the broader problem by the channel diagram in Figure 1. This shows that a communications act originates for some purpose, is converted into appropriate sym-

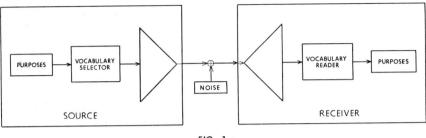

FIG. 1

bols, and transmitted. It is received (more or less accurately), interpreted, and reacted to in terms of purposes, which may or may not be the same as those of the source. As an example, imagine a hungry dog approaching his owner and emitting a pleading whine. The owner hears; realizes the dog is asking for food; and, desirous of continuing to read peacefully in his easy chair, throws a shoe at the dog. The symbol (whine) was in this case appropriately chosen, transmitted accurately, and interpreted correctly. Nevertheless, the dog's communication was not successful, from the viewpoint of the dog.

It is not only the needs at the source that give rise to the communication that are relevant. The needs of those who may act as receiver and those who may relay the message are also relevant. It is easy enough to understand that those who desire to get a certain task accomplished in an organization will initiate communication designed to accomplish it. It is less obvious that information tends to flow in an organization to those points where it is known to be needed for task accomplishment.

REFERENCES

1. BALES, ROBERT F. "A Statistical Model for Simulating Social Interaction." Department of Social Relations. Harvard University. Ditto.
2. BLOOM, JOEL N., MAYFIELD, CLIFTON E. and WILLIAMS, RICHARD M. *Modern Army Communications.* The Franklin Institute, Revised January, 1963.
3. CHAPPLE, E. D. with the collaboration of C. M. Arensberg. "Measuring Human Relations." *Genetic Psychology Monograph.* Vol. 22. (1940).
4. LEAVITT, HAROLD J. and WHISLER, THOMAS L. "Management in the 1980's." *Harvard Business Review.* Vol. 36, No. 6. (November–December, 1958). Also DOMINIC PARISI. "The Impact of Changes in Information Technology on Management Organization Structure, Decision-Making and Interpersonal Relations in a Large Insurance Company." Ph.D. Dissertation. Departments of Business Administration and Industrial Engineering and Management Sciences. Northwestern University, Evanston, Illinois (September, 1965).
5. MARSHAK, JACOB. "Elements for a Theory of Teams." *Management Science.* Vol. 1, No. 2. (January, 1955).
6. MEIER, RICHARD L. "Communication Overload: Proposals from the Study of a University Library." *Administrative Science Quarterly.* 1963, No. 7.

pp 521–544. Also the Sixth and Seventh Annual Reports of The Mental Health Research Institute. 1962 (pp. 30–31) and 1963 (pp. 47–48). Ann Arbor, Michigan.

7. RATH, GUSTAVE J. "Initial Steps Toward Studies of the Information Behavior of Scientists and Engineers." *Information Systems Sciences*. Baltimore, Maryland. Spartan Books, Inc. 1965.

8. RUBENSTEIN, ALBERT H. "Timing and Form of Researchers' Needs for Technical Information." *Journal of Chemical Documentation*. 1962, No. 2, p. 28.

9. RUBENSTEIN, ALBERT H. and SMITH, ROGER. "Communication Measurement in a Purchasing Department." Department of Industrial Engineering. Columbia University. (1953). Unpublished manuscript.

10. SHANNON, CLAUDE E. and WEAVER, WARREN. *The Mathematical Theory of Communication*. (Illinois, 1949).

11. SIEGMAN, JACK. "White Collar Automation: A Study in Technological and Organizational Change." Ph.D. Dissertation, Department of Sociology. University of Illinois, Urbana, Illinois. (January, 1965).

12. STEINER, IVAN D. "Group Dynamics." In *Annual Review of Psychology*. Vol. 15, 1964. Annual Reviews, Inc., Palo Alto, California. pp. 421–446.

24. UPWARD COMMUNICATION IN INDUSTRIAL HIERARCHIES*

William H. Read[1]

THIS STUDY is concerned with communication in large organizations. The particular focus is upon motivational and attitudinal factors which affect the accuracy with which members at one administrative level communicate upward to a higher level.

The majority of studies of communication within hierarchies have dealt with interlevel communication in small groups. Festinger (4) has pointed out that the structuring of groups into hierarchies automatically introduces restraints against free communication, particularly criticisms and aggressively-toned comments by low-status members towards those in higher-status positions. Kelley (7), Thibaut (11), and Back *et al.* (1) have shown that selective screening of information from low- to high-status members is a characteristic of communication in social groups, and serves as a "psychological substitute" for actual movement upward on the part of aspiring low-status members.

More recently, Cohen (2) has emphasized the "instrumentality" of upward communication. The findings of Hurwitz, Zander, and Hymovitch (6) support this instrumental view of communication. They reported that group members tend to perceive those with greater power as instrumental to the need satisfactions of these group members, hence "lows" behave toward "highs" in a manner designed to maximize good relations and minimize feelings of unease in their interactions with high-power persons.

The instrumental nature of communication upward through levels in larger hierarchical organizations such as industrial concerns is usually accepted as a fact of organizational life. Pleasant matters are more likely to be communicated upward than unpleasant ones, achievements are more

* Reprinted from *Human Relations*, Vol. 15, No. 1 (1962), pp. 3–15.

[1] The study reported here was based upon a dissertation submitted in partial fulfillment of the requirements for the Ph.D. degree, University of Michigan, 1959. It was part of a larger project supported by the Foundation for Research on Human Behavior, Ann Arbor, Mich., and directed by Professor Norman R. F. Maier. The writer wishes to express his appreciation for the guidance and inspiration provided by Professor Maier, and is also deeply indebted to Professor Stanley E. Seashore for his supervision of the dissertation during Professor Maier's absence in 1959. (William Read is Assistant Professor in the Department of Psychology at the University of British Columbia, Vancouver, B.C. The research reported in this paper was conducted while Dr. Read was a research assistant in Psychology at the University of Michigan.)

likely to be passed upward than information about errors or difficulties encountered at lower levels. Yet the highly integrated effort required to achieve organizational purposes demands a relatively free upward and downward flow of information, both pleasant and unpleasant, problem-related as well as achievement-related. This screening of information passed upward is likely to be at a maximum when the information content is of a type which might reflect negatively upon the competence and thus, indirectly, upon the security or progress of members of the subordinate level: content such as the problems, current and unsolved, faced by members at this level.

The present study attempts to isolate variables accounting for the accuracy with which subordinate executives at one level of administration in industrial organizations communicate upward a specific type of information—the work-related problems experienced by these subordinates.

Mobility

One such variable is mobility—the mobility aspirations of lower-status members in industrial organizations. Henry (5), in his analysis of the test profiles of executives, and Miner and Culver (9), in a more recent study, attest that the most salient single characteristic of executives in industry is striving for advancement (and its accompanying fear of failure). One would expect that the more the executives are upwardly mobile, that is, the more they value vertical promotion in the hierarchy, the less accurately they will communicate upward "negative" aspects of their work performance. The stronger the mobility aspirations of subordinates, the more will they communicate to their superiors in a way that will maximize positive, and minimize negative, aspects. Thus they would be likely to withhold, restrict, or distort information about the problems, current and unsolved, which they experience in their day-to-day work.

The major hypothesis in this study is that a negative relationship exists between upward mobility of members of industrial organizations and the accuracy with which these members communicate upward in the hierarchy. More specifically, it was predicted that the stronger the mobility aspirations of the subordinate, the less accurate would be his communication of problem-related information to his immediate superior.

Modifying Conditions: Trust And Perceived Influence

It was expected that the relationship between mobility and accuracy in communication would be modified by two conditions, both considered important dimensions of the superior-subordinate relationship. These were *interpersonal trust* of the subordinate for his superior, and the subordinate's perception of his superior's *influence* over that subordinate's career.

Mellinger (8) reported that accurate information between two individuals is less likely to occur under conditions of mistrust than under conditions of trust. He demonstrated that individual A will restrict or distort information about an item X to the extent that he thinks individual B might misuse this item of information (to the possible detriment of A). This finding suggests that the highly mobile subordinate would feel a special threat to his progress in communicating anything "negative," such as information about his unsolved problems, to a superior he does not trust, since this information might be used against him by that superior. It was expected that the predicted negative relationship between mobility and communication would be greater under conditions of low trust (of subordinate for superior) than under conditions of high trust.

The second modifying variable, perceived influence, was also expected to modify the mobility-communication relationship. The study of Pelz (10) has indicated that supervisors, even at the same hierarchical level, vary considerably in the influence they are able to exert in their respective units. Pelz used influence, that is, the supervisor's potential control over the subordinate's work environment, as a modifying variable in the relationship between supervisory practices and employee attitudes. The present study focuses more specifically upon the superior's influence as it directly affects the subordinate's career, particularly his promotion and advancement in the organization.

It was predicted that the greater the influence the upwardly mobile subordinate perceived his superior to have (and thus the stronger that superior's position to satisfy or thwart the subordinate's aspirations), the greater would be the subordinate's tendency to withhold problem-related information from such a superior, or to restrict it. In short, it was predicted that influence would modify the negative relationship between mobility and communication—the greater the degree of perceived influence, the greater the negative relationship between mobility and communication upward.

In summary, the predicted negative relationship between mobility and communication would be conditioned or modified by (a) the subordinate's trust in his superior's motives and intentions, and (b) the subordinate's perception of his superior's degree of influence. These predictions suggest that an extreme condition for barriers to upward communication in industrial hierarchies would be present when a highly mobile subordinate has limited trust in a superior he believes to be powerful or influential.

METHOD

The study was conducted in three major industrial organizations in the U.S.A. One operating unit was selected in each company as a source of subjects. These units were selected on the basis of three main criteria, namely, that the chosen units should (*a*) provide access to executives in a variety of functions, (*b*) be typical of the company in its organizational structure, and (*c*) have a relatively stable history as to executive personnel changes.

A. Selection of Subjects

In each unit of each of the three organizations, subjects were selected at random from the third level of supervision, that is, the supervisory level that was separated from nonsupervisory employees by two intervening levels. For each of the chosen third-level supervisors, a corresponding subordinate was chosen from the *second* level of supervision. In this way, 52 superiors and their 52 respective subordinates were selected, or a total of 104 middle-management personnel from three companies.

B. Descriptions of the Measures

1. Accuracy of Upward Communication. The measure of accuracy of upward communication was derived from interview data provided by exploratory research conducted prior to the present study. These data consisted of descriptions of major problems experienced by 35 middle-level executives, as reported by these executives and, independently, by their immediate superiors. Contrasting descriptions of these major problems had been taken from five industries and utilities in the Michigan area, and the measure of accuracy of upward communication was derived for use in the present study in the following way:

All problems reported in this exploratory study were sorted according to *type*, then edited and combined to form a list representing five major problem types. These were (*a*) coordination and communication, (*b*) budget and cost, (*c*) technical, (*d*) pressures and deadlines, and (*e*) administration and supervision. The most frequently reported problems were listed within each type, making a total of 30 separate problems listed. For example, under budget and cost were listed such items as "handling unforeseen costs" and "deciding upon the feasibility of certain expenditures." Under the technical category were listed items such as "getting enough equipment and supplies."

Because of the striking frequency with which the same problems were reported by the five companies in the exploratory study, together with the fact that these problems covered a very broad range of those encountered by executives, they were considered representative enough to apply to executives in the new settings selected for the present study.

Accuracy of upward communication was operationalized as the degree of agreement between superior and subordinate about the *relative degree of difficulty these problems caused the subordinate,* i.e., the degree to which they *were* problems to subordinates. Low agreement was taken to indicate relatively poor or inaccurate communication of this type of information; high agreement indicated the reverse.

This measure is based on the assumption that the superior's major source of knowledge of his subordinate's current work problems is the subordinate's communication of them in some way to that superior (hence agreement or disagreement between the two would reflect accuracy of upward communication). This was viewed as a reasonable assumption in view of the obviously limited opportunity an executive would have to observe directly the subordinate's experience with day-to-day problems. However, in order to provide a check on other possible sources of feedback the superior might have regarding the subordinate's problems (from peers or from other departments), each member of the subordinate-superior pairs in the sample was asked to state who was in the "best position to know" about the subordinate's problems. All of the superiors and all but two of the subordinates in the sample designated the superior as in the "best position." This was a rough and rather subjective check, but provided at least some assurance that agreement or disagreement between the two about this type of information reflected accuracy of communication between the two, and not the adequacy or inadequacy of some other communication channel.

Both members of the 52 executive pairs were asked to rank order the problems within each category or type according to the difficulty criterion. Using Kendall's *tau*, the two rank orders were correlated for each problem category. A mean *tau* over the five problem categories provided the overall statistical index of agreement for each executive pair.

2. Mobility. Three parallel but independent measures of degree or strength of mobility aspirations among subordinates were used. One measure consisted of a list of two-alternative, forced-choice items, ten in number, representing choices of hypothetical moves to other positions within the organization. One alternative in each pair of alternatives was the choice of a higher-level position, but with an unpleasant condition attached. The other alternative consisted of a hypothetical transfer to a position equivalent to the one presently held, but with a rewarding or pleasant condition attached. This questionnaire was scored simply by adding the total number of promotion alternatives chosen, yielding a possible score range of 0 to 10. This measure represented an attempt to determine strength of mobility aspirations from an indication of the price the individual would pay for promotion upward in the organization. For example, one item posed the alternatives:

Promotion to a high position in which there is a great deal of pressure and stress,

or

Transfer across to an intensely interesting position with little work pressure or stress.

Nine other items such as this provided the measure of the expressed *mobility need* of subordinates.

Two other measures of mobility aspirations were used. These measures were sociological in nature, with the degree of mobility aspiration inferred from the amount of actual vertical occupational movement that the subordinate executives had experienced. These measures were of *work-life* and *inter-generational* mobility.

The study by Warner and Abegglen (12) has shown that the mobility *experiences* of executives, particularly of those who have made the long climb up the occupational ladder, strongly affect their relationships with those above them in the industrial hierarchy. Their study suggested that both work life and intergenerational experiences of progress and advancement are likely to be continuing forces in the executive's behavior even when conscious mobility aspirations may not be expressed.

Work-life mobility was operationalized as the degree to which the subordinate had moved upward through occupational levels from his first job to his present executive position. The second, intergenerational mobility, was the degree the subordinate had moved upward from the position held by his father.

The Detroit Area Study revision of the 1950 U.S. Census Occupational Code provided the scale for measuring both work-life and intergenerational mobility. This scale consisted of seven occupational levels, from "low" to "high" in skill and responsibility, and, except for minor revisions, was identical to the U.S. Census scale.

Scores of 1 to 7 were arbitrarily assigned to the seven levels of occupation on the scale ("laborers" to "professional and kindred"), and these scores were used as measures of both the work-life and intergenerational dimensions of mobility. Thus, for work-life mobility, the subordinate who reported that his first full-time job had been "drugstore clerk" would be assigned a score of 3—he had moved up three levels to his present executive position (the top level on the occupational scale, since all but one or two subordinates were engineers by profession). Likewise, a report of "construction laborer" would be scored 7 on work-life mobility—he had moved from the bottom to the top of the occupational ladder. Scores for intergenerational mobility were derived in an identical way, except that the father's full-time occupation was taken as the base. Thus a subordinate who reported "construction laborer" as his father's occupation would be given an intergenerational mobility score of 7—again, a move from bottom to top, intergenerationally.[2]

3. Modifying Variables: Trust and Influence. The measure of interpersonal trust was derived from four questions, each with five alternative answers, scaled in terms of degree, in the Likert fashion, from "most" to "least" interpersonal trust. By assigning weights of 1 to 5 to these

---

[2] Intercorrelations among the three parallel measures of mobility were: Need and Work life, .22; Work life and Intergenerational, .37; and Intergenerational and Need, .08, indicating quite limited common variance among the measures.

alternatives and summing, the possible score range for the four items was 4 to 20. The questions were intended to reflect the subordinate's trust or confidence in the superior's motives and intentions with respect to matters relevant to the subordinate's career and status in the organization.

The interpersonal trust scale is shown below:

INTERPERSONAL TRUST SCALE

1. Does your superior take advantage of opportunities that come up to further your interests by his actions and decisions?
2. How free do you feel to discuss with your superior the problems and difficulties you have in your job without jeopardizing your position or having it "held against" you later on?
3. How confident do you feel that your superior keeps you fully and frankly informed about things that might concern you?
4. Superiors at times must make decisions which seem to be against the interests of their subordinates. When this happens to you as a subordinate, how much trust do you have that your superior's decision is justified by other considerations?

The intercorrelations among the four trust items for the 52 subordinates were found to range between .39 and .68, indicating relatively high homogeneity of items.

The measure of perceived influence likewise consisted of a four-item scale. These items attempted to assess the subordinate's perception of the degree of *his superior's influence or potential control over four aspects of the subordinate's career*, namely, the subordinate's long-range progress in the company, his reputation as a manager, immediate rewards (wage increases, etc.), and his access to "tools" (equipment, staff additions) needed to perform his job successfully. The perceived influence scale is shown below:

PERCEIVED INFLUENCE SCALE

1. In general, how much do you feel that your superior can do to further your career in this company?
2. To what degree does working for your present superior help your reputation in this company?
3. How much weight would your superior's recommendation have in any decision which would affect your standing in the company, such as promotions, transfers, wage increases, etc.?
4. How often is your superior successful in overcoming restrictions (such as policy or budget) in getting you the things you need in your job, such as equipment, personnel, etc.?

The intercorrelations among the four perceived influence items ranged from −.07 to .62, indicating less homogeneity than with the trust items. However, the existence of only one negative correlation was considered minimum but sufficient justification for summing the separate scores to yield a total perceived influence score.

C. General Procedure

All the questionnaires outlined above were administered in face-to-face interviews with the 52 subjects, thus affording the researcher an opportunity to answer questions, assure anonymity, and clarify the meaning of any item. This questionnaire session was part of a fairly long interview in which other job areas (in addition to problems) were explored as part of a larger study of management communication.

Since the present study focuses upon the subordinate—his attitudes and motives as they affect his upward communication—the only one of the questionnaries outlined above which the superior member of the management pair was asked to fill in was the problem list. He was required to rank order the problems within each category in order of the difficulty they caused the subordinate. These, as stated, were matched against the subordinate's rank ordering of the same problems and *taus* were then computed over the five categories for each pair.

D. Statistical Method

Pearson product-moment correlations were used throughout to test the hypotheses in this study. The relationships between the independent variables (mobility scores) and the dependent variable (the mean *tau* measures of accuracy of upward communication) are expressed as correlation coefficients for an N of 52 cases. To test these same relationships modified by the separate as well as the joint effects of interpersonal trust and perceived influence, the distributions of scores on these conditioning variables were arbitrarily dichotomized into high and low. With the use of r to z transformations, correlations were computed between the independent and dependent variables for conditions of low and high trust, high and low influence, and for the joint low-trust, high-influence and high-trust, low-influence conditions. The correlations between these high and low conditions were in each case compared for the significance of the difference.

RESULTS

The hypothesis of a negative relationship between mobility and accuracy of upward communication was supported for two of the three measures of mobility, need and work life, but was not supported for the third, intergenerational mobility. The correlations are shown in Table 1.[3] The results in Table 1 indicate that, for the group of 52 middle-

---

[3] In reporting the significance of results, p's greater than .20 are shown as "n.s.," not significant. In view of the small N's, differences resulting in p values within the range of .10 to .20 are regarded as worth noting. P values of .10 and less are regarded as statistically significant.

TABLE 1

CORRELATIONS BETWEEN THREE PARALLEL MEASURES OF MOBILITY AND
ACCURACY OF UPWARD COMMUNICATION

Mobility Measure	r	N
Need	−.38*	52
Work life	−.41*	52
Intergenerational	.08	49

* Significant at the .01 level of confidence ($p < .01$).

management executives, the stronger the expressed need to achieve advancement within the organization, as well as the degree of mobility they had experienced from initial job to present one, the less accurate their communication to immediate superiors.

Effects of Modifying Conditions. Analysis of results indicates that the relationship between mobility need and accuracy of upward communication was strikingly modified by the interpersonal trust condition, but very little by the degree of the superior's influence or power (as perceived by the subordinate).

As the data in Table 2 show, the prediction of a greater negative mobility-communication relationship for the perceived influence condition holds only directionally, but is significantly greater in the negative direction when the condition of low trust prevails between a subordinate executive and his immediate superior.

The results in Table 2 also indicate that communication is less accurate under the combined low-trust, high-influence condition, but this

TABLE 2

CORRELATIONS BETWEEN MOBILITY NEED AND ACCURACY OF UPWARD
COMMUNICATION, MODIFIED BY THE SEPARATE AND JOINT EFFECTS OF
TWO CONDITIONING VARIABLES

Conditioning Variables	Comparison of Correlations		p diff.
Trust	High trust	Low trust	
N high = 28	r_{nc}* = −.16	r_{nc} = −.66	<.01
N low = 24			
Influence	Low influence	High influence	
N low = 31	r_{nc} = −.40	r_{nc} = −.55	n.s.
N high = 21			
	High trust,	Low trust,	
Both	Low influence	High influence	
N $h-1$ = 17	r_{nc} = −.07	r_{nc} = −.65	<.05
$N1 - h$ = 10			

NOTE: Correlation between mobility need and upward communication for all cases is −.38.

* Subscript n refers to strength of mobility need, subscript c refers to accuracy of upward communication.

significant result is probably due to the very strong effects of interpersonal trust on the mobility-communication relationship.

The results thus far indicate that, in industrial hierarchies, the stronger the mobility needs among executives, the less accurately they communicate problem-related information; and the less trust they hold for their immediate superiors, the greater is this tendency toward inaccurate communication. There is also some indication that communication inaccuracy is increased when superiors are perceived as high-influence figures and are,

TABLE 3

Correlations between Work-Life Mobility and Accuracy of Upward Communication, Modified by the Separate and Joint Effects of Two Conditioning Variables

Conditioning Variables	Comparison of Correlations		p diff.
Trust	High trust	Low trust	
N high $= 28$	$r_{wc}{}^* = -.37$	$r_{wc} = -.66$	.20
N low $= 24$			
Influence	Low influence	High influence	
N low $= 31$	$r_{wc} = -.40$	$r_{wc} = -.46$	n.s.
N high $= 21$			
	High trust,	Low trust,	
Both	Low influence	High influence	
$N\ h - 1 = 17$	$r_{wc} = -.41$	$r_{wc} = -.49$	n.s.
$N\ 1 - h = 10$			

Note: Correlation between work-life mobility and upward communication for all 52 cases is $-.41$.

* Subscript w refers to degree of work-life mobility, subscript c refers to accuracy of upward communication.

at the same time, not fully trusted. However, unilateral subordinate-superior trust appears to have the greatest single effect upon accuracy of communication.

The analysis of results for work-life mobility is shown in Table 3.

The modifying effect of trust is again evident, though the difference between correlations for high and low trust is only marginally significant. The tendency toward inaccurate communication by the subordinate who has experienced a relatively high degree of vertical mobility during his work life is greater when he has limited trust in his superior's motives and intentions.

A comparison of the remaining correlations in Table 3 suggests, but does not confirm, that both the influence and the combined trust-influence conditions have an effect on accuracy of upward communication.

The results in Table 4 show little or no effect of trust or influence on the mobility-communication relationship.

The lack of any significant results in Table 4 indicates that intergenerational mobility is not a significant determinant of communication accuracy.

TABLE 4

CORRELATIONS BETWEEN INTERGENERATIONAL MOBILITY AND ACCURACY
OF UPWARD COMMUNICATION, MODIFIED BY THE SEPARATE AND JOINT
EFFECTS OF TWO CONDITIONING VARIABLES

Conditioning Variables	Comparison of Correlations		p diff.
Trust	High trust	Low trust	
N high $= 28$	$r_{ic}{}^* = .11$	$r_{ic} = .02$	n.s.
N low $= 21$			
Influence	Low influence	High influence	
N low $= 30$	$r_{ic} = -.04$	$r_{ic} = .10$	n.s.
N high $= 19$			
Both	High trust, Low influence	Low trust, High influence	
$N\ h - 1 = 17$	$r_{ic} = .13$	$r_{ic} = .07$	n.s.
$N\ 1 - h = 10$			

NOTE: Three of the 52 responses to the intergenerational scale were unclassifiable, hence
the total N = 49. The correlation for all 49 cases is .08.

* Subscript i refers to degree of intergenerational mobility, subscript c to accuracy of upward communication.

These overall results for the total sample of 52 subordinate executives
were found to hold fairly consistently for the three different companies
sampled in the study. Table 5 shows a company-by-company breakdown
of the mobility-communication relationship for the three parallel measures
of mobility.[4]

The results in Table 5 show consistency from company to company

TABLE 5

CORRELATIONS BETWEEN THREE MEASURES OF MOBILITY
AND ACCURACY OF UPWARD COMMUNICATION FOR
EXECUTIVES IN EACH OF THREE COMPANIES

Company	Mobility Need N	r
A	16	$-.41*$
B	17	$-.41*$
C	19	$-.22$
	Work-Life Mobility	
A	16	$.04$
B	17	$.17$
C	19	$-.67\dagger$
	Intergenerational Mobility	
A	15‡	$.20$
B	17	$.37$
C	17‡	$-.06$

* Significant at .10–.20 level ($p < .20$).
† Significant at .01 level ($p < .01$).
‡ One response from Company A and two from Company C were unclassifiable, hence were not included.

[4] A further breakdown according to the modifying conditions of trust and perceived influence for each company was not possible because of the relatively small size of the total N.

for mobility need and for intergenerational mobility. Inspection of the differences between mean scores of the variables in the three companies indicated that the total r of $-.41$ (Table 1) between work-life mobility and communication is somewhat inflated owing to clustered sampling. However, the negative direction of two of the three correlations in Table 5 provides some assurance that this overall correlation is not entirely spurious.

DISCUSSION

The results have generally supported the major prediction that, in industrial hierarchies, mobility aspiration among subordinate executives is negatively related to accuracy of upward communication. The findings have paralleled those of small-group studies which have rather consistently shown that individuals in power hierarchies tend to screen information passed upward, and to withhold or refrain from communicating information that is potentially threatening to the status of the communicator. The present study confirms that this tendency prevails in formal, large-scale organizations, is stronger among upwardly mobile members, and is strongly modified by the communicator's attitudes toward those above him in the hierarchy.

More specifically, the present study suggests that two aspects of mobility aspiration are related to inaccurate communication: (a) the expressed present needs of organizational members to advance upward in the hierarchy, and (b) the status-seeking tendencies of members who have experienced a long climb up the organizational ladder during their work lives. One may only speculate on the lack of significant results for the intergenerational aspect of mobility. It may be that the psychological remoteness of one's familial relationship for those well along in their career lives would make it less strong as a motivating force than either one's conscious need or desire to advance, or one's career experiences.

Of particular note is the modifying effect of interpersonal trust on the communication-mobility relationship. This finding not only lends emphasis to the crucial importance of attitudinal factors in communication, but also suggests that free and accurate information exchange may depend significantly upon positive and harmonious relationships between organizational members, particularly those who differ in formal power. It must be pointed out, however, that high mobility aspirations strongly militate against accurate communication of potentially threatening information *even when high trust prevails*. It is only that low trust of the superior's motives and intentions intensifies or strengthens the tendency of highly ambitious subordinates to withhold or in some way prevent accurate upward communication.

The present research has implications for the effective coordination between middle-level executives in industrial hierarchies. The results of this study imply that upward mobility and the associated distortion of communication may introduce strains and imbalance into day-to-day coordination between the two. These strains can perhaps best be traced through in terms of decisions which require maximum information about the subordinate's work problems. First, periodic and important assessments must be made by the superior with respect to the general progress of the subordinate and the quality of his work performance. The findings of this study imply that these assessments are not likely to be made with any clear perspective on the problems and obstacles the upwardly mobile subordinate experiences in his work, unless the superior has other sources of information than the subordinate himself. Thus a judgment about the effectiveness the subordinate has shown in goal achievement cannot be tempered by accurate knowledge of the problems he has encountered in his attempts to achieve the goals.

Second, decisions which the superior must make with regard to the general functioning of his subordinate's work unit or section may well be limited by a lack of awareness by the superior of problems affecting that unit. For example, one would expect that decisions regarding the allocation of manpower within the subordinate's unit would be based on the present problems the subordinate is experiencing with regard to allocation. Third, to the extent that the subordinate insulates his superior from clear knowledge of work-related problems, he has in effect insulated himself from whatever expert knowledge and judgment the superior might apply in solving these problems.

To the extent that the results of the present study hold for all levels of an organizational hierarchy, then the organization, to the degree that it fosters upward aspirations, introduces a system by which problem-related information is filtered through successive levels, and problems that might call for concerted action and decision at the top are effectively blocked at levels below. Perhaps this explains, at least to some extent, the "fog of uncertainty" (Dalton, 3, p. 234) that characterizes executives' work. One can be certain, however, that this potential dysfunction in organizations is not an all-or-nothing affair. Channels other than upward communication exist which can take over when problem information is blocked, and a certain amount of distortion of information can be expected in any organization. Furthermore, some insulation of one level of an organization from another undoubtedly has adaptive value. Inaccurate communication of problems may indicate, at least to some extent, that these problems are being handled at the appropriate level and may reflect effective delegation of duties.

SUMMARY

The purpose of this study was to test hypotheses about the relationship between upward mobility among executives and the accuracy with which they communicate problem-related information upward in industrial hierarchies. This relationship was found in general to be a significant negative one. The relationship was found to be conditioned or modified by the degree of interpersonal trust held by these executives for their superiors, and there is some evidence to suggest that the relationship is also conditioned by the degree of the superiors' influence as perceived by their subordinates.

These results indicate that the motives and attitudes of organizational members strongly affect the manner in which and degree to which they exchange work-related information with each other.

REFERENCES

1. BACK, K.; FESTINGER, L.; HYMOVITCH, B.; KELLEY, H. H.; SCHACHTER, S.; AND THIBAUT, J. "The Methodology of Studying Rumor Transmission, *Human Relations,* Vol. 3 (1950), pp. 307–12.

2. COHEN, A. R. "Upward Communication in Experimentally Created Hierarchies." *Human Relations,* Vol. 11 (1958), pp. 41–53.

3. DALTON, M. *Men Who Manage.* New York: John Wiley & Son, 1959.

4. FESTINGER, L. "Informal Social Communication," *Psychological Review,* Vol. 57 (1950), pp. 217–82.

5. HENRY, W. E. "The Business Executive: Psychodynamics of a Social Role," *American Journal of Sociology,* Vol. 54 (1949), pp. 286–91.

6. HURWITZ, J. I.; ZANDER, A. F.; AND HYMOVITCH, B. "Some Effects of Power on the Relations among Group Members," in D. Cartwright and A. Zander (eds.), *Group Dynamics.* Evanston, Ill.: Row Peterson (1953); London: Tavistock Publications.

7. KELLEY, H. H. "Communication in Experimentally Created Hierarchies," *Human Relations,* Vol. 4 (1951), pp. 39–56.

8. MELLINGER, G. D. "Interpersonal Trust as a Factor in Communication," *Journal of Abnormal* and *Social Psychology,* Vol. 53 (1956), pp. 304–9.

9. MINER, J. B., AND CULVER, J. E. "Some Aspects of the Executive Personality," *Journal of Applied Psychology,* Vol. 39 (1955), pp. 348–53.

10. PELZ, D. "Leadership within a Hierarchical Organization," *Journal of Social Issues,* Vol. 7, pp. 49–55.

11. THIBAUT, J. An Experimental Study of the Cohesiveness of Underprivileged Groups, *Human Relations,* Vol. 3, pp. 251–78.

12. WARNER, W. L., AND ABEGGLEN, J. C. *Big Business Leaders in America.* New York: Harper, 1955.

25. PATTERNS OF INTERACTION AMONG A GROUP OF OFFICIALS IN A GOVERNMENT AGENCY*

Peter M. Blau

The analysis of small groups has received increasing attention in sociological research during recent years. One type of these studies focuses upon the normative orientations that arise in "natural" groups, as exemplified by investigations of restriction of output among factory workers. Another type is primarily interested in developing methods of observation and analysis of interaction, and usually deals with "artificial" groups in laboratory situations.

This paper is concerned with a systematic analysis of the processes of interaction in a "natural" group of officials in a government agency,[1] and the status differences that emerge in this process. It focuses upon three problems: (1) The interdependence between the way an official performs his duties and his interpersonal relations with his colleagues. (2) The usefulness of observable interaction as an index of status in the group. (3) The relationship between interaction in "pair-events," contacts between two individuals, and "set-events," social situations involving more than two participants.

THE SETTING

The peer group studied consisted of 16 agents,[2] who, together with a supervisor and a clerk, composed a department in an agency of law enforcement. Their principal duty was the investigation of business establishments to determine whether any violation of the laws the agency administered had occurred. Each agent worked by himself on the cases assigned to him by the supervisor. Processing a case involved an audit of the books of the firm, interviews with the employer and a sample of employees, negotiation with the employer if violations were found, and writing a full report. Agents spent slightly more than half their working time in the field, and the remainder of it in the large office this department shared with another, similar, department.

---

* Reproduced from *Human Relations*, 7, #3, 1954.

[1] The method of observation used was suggested by E. D. Chapple and C. M. Arensberg, "Measuring Human Relations," *Genetic Psychology Monographs*, Vol. XXII, 1940, pp. 3–147. I am indebted to Professor Arensberg for his helpful comments on the study of social interaction in this group.

[2] Data for only 15 agents are available for most tables.

Problems often arose in the course of making difficult legal decisions. When an agent could not solve such a problem, he was expected to consult his supervisor for advice. However, the supervisor also evaluated the performance of his subordinates on every case, and his annual official rating influenced their promotion chances. Agents were therefore reluctant to expose their ignorance to the supervisor by asking him often for advice. The comment of one of them was typical: "I try to stay away from the supervisor as much as possible. The reason is that the more often you go to the supervisor, the more you show your stupidity."

Officially, agents were not permitted to consult each other; but their need for advice from a source other than the supervisor induced them to ignore this rule. All agents, including the most competent ones, often discussed their problems with colleagues. This unofficial practice reduced their anxiety over making correct decisions and thus improved their performance. The knowledge that he could obtain advice without exposing his difficulties to the supervisor enhanced the agent's ability to make accurate decisions, even when no consultation took place.[3] The existence of this cooperative practice basically influenced the relationships between officials. This therefore is a study of social interaction in a cooperative group.

Social Interaction and Competence

To obtain quantitative indices of interaction, all contacts any member of this department had with anyone else in the office during 30.5 hours of observation were recorded. On the average, an official had 8.3 contacts per hour; 5.1 of these were associations with other agents in this department. Of course, not all of these interactions were consultations. Many, such as greetings or brief private conversations, were not related to official business. Neither the length of the exchange nor its content were given consideration in this count. The total number of contacts observed was 2,189.

Four simple indices can be derived from this record: (1) The total number of contacts an individual had per hour. (2) The number of contacts an individual originated per hour. (3) The number of contacts an individual received per hour, that is, those originated by the other participant in the exchange. (4) The proportion of an individual's total contacts that he originated, which provides an index of his initiative in social interaction.

Competence in performing the duties of an agent was related to par-

---

[3] This practice of unofficial consultation is analyzed in the author's doctoral dissertation at Columbia University, *The Dynamics of Bureaucracy* (Chicago: University of Chicago Press, 1955), a study of this and another agency. A fellowship of the Social Science Research Council, which made this study possible, is gratefully acknowledged.

ticipation in the interaction of this group. The supervisor's rating of the performance of his subordinates provides an index of their relative competence.[4] The more competent agents had a disproportionately large number of contacts, but they did not originate more contacts than others. The positive relationship between proficiency and frequency of interaction was entirely due to the fact that the highly competent agents tended to *receive* more contacts from their colleagues than those who were less proficient,[5] as Table 1 shows.[6]

TABLE 1
CONTACTS RECEIVED PER HOUR
AND COMPETENCE

Contacts Received	Competence High	Competence Low	Total
Many	5	1	6
Few	2	7	9
Total	7	8	15

It is not surprising that the experts were frequently contacted in this situation. They could furnish the best advice, and they were highly esteemed in this group where competence was greatly valued. The rank correlation between esteem and competence was .93.[7] Their colleagues approached these experts disproportionately often, not only to ask their advice, but also to seek their companionship, since associating with a respected person tends to be especially desirable. Their frequent participation in interaction made most experts well integrated members of this group.

Superior ability alone, however, did not assure an integrated position. The two highly competent agents who were considered uncooperative by their colleagues were generally disliked and received only few contacts. To become accepted, an expert had to share the advantages of his superior skill with his colleagues. Provided that he was willing to help others with their problems, the highly competent agent was often drawn into

---

[4] The official rating of the supervisor divided agents into three groups. For purposes of this study, the supervisor ranked agents individually in terms of their competence.

[5] The relation between rank and received contacts corresponds to the conclusions reached by George C. Homans, but the absence of a relation between rank and originated contacts does not. See *The Human Group* (New York: Harcourt, Brace, 1950; London: Routledge & Kegan Paul), pp. 145, 181–82.

[6] All relationships discussed in this paper are significant on the .05 level.

[7] The members of this group were asked to rank their colleagues in terms of their ability as agent. An official's average rank is defined as the esteem he enjoyed among colleagues. In a two-by-two table, the relationship between esteem and competence is perfect.

discussions, and thus became an integrated member of the group without having had to exercise much social initiative.

Competence and Informal Relationships

The less competent agent did not become integrated without special effort. Since he was initially less attractive an associate than the expert, he received fewer contacts, and probably experienced a greater need for improving his interpersonal relationships. As a result, the less competent agents exercised relatively more initiative in their social interaction in the office, as Table 2 shows,[8] and they also cultivated informal relations with colleagues in their free time.

TABLE 2
SOCIAL INITIATIVE AND COMPETENCE

Social Initiative	High	Competence Low	Total
Much	2	7	9
Little	5	1	6
Total	7	8	15

The major opportunity for relaxed informal contacts between agents was provided by the daily lunch hour. Most officials valued this period of companionship greatly, and sometimes returned to the office from the field just before noon in order to join some colleagues for lunch. Since about one half of the agents were usually in the field, even those persons who had regular partners often lunched with other colleagues. An index of the extent of the informal relations of each official was constructed on the basis of a record of all his lunch partners in a two-week period.[9]

Table 3 shows that the least competent agents tended to have more extensive informal relations at lunch than those whose competence was average or high. This appears, at first, to contradict the previous conclusion that most experts were well integrated. However, their less extensive informal relations do not indicate that these experts were excluded from the fellowship at lunch. Generally, they as well as other agents lunched in the company of colleagues.[10] But the greater need of the less competent

---

[8] The less competent agents tended to exercise more initiative than the experts partly because they were more likely to request advice, but also partly because they were more concerned with improving their position in the group.

[9] The agents kept this record themselves at the request of the observer. If a luncheon engagement is defined as eating with one colleague once, the total number of engagements reported (which often included several colleagues on the same day, and the same colleagues on repeated days), divided by the number of days on which the respondent went to lunch from the office, defines the value of this index.

[10] Only two agents, one of the least and one of the most competent members of the group, lunched alone more than once during two weeks of observation (excluding days when agents were in the field at noon).

TABLE 3
EXTENT OF INFORMAL RELATIONS
AND COMPETENCE

Informal Relations	High or Average	Competence Low	Total
Extensive............2	5	7
Less extensive........7	1	8
Total.........9	6	15

agents to improve their position in the group, since they did not become as easily integrated through interaction in the office as the experts, induced them to maintain particularly extensive informal relations with their colleagues in their free time.

Informal Relationships and Social Interaction

The interpersonal relations an agent had established at lunch influenced his participation in social interaction in the office. Most of the agents who had very extensive informal relations received many contacts from others, as Table 4 indicates. On the other hand, neither the total number of con-

TABLE 4
EXTENT OF INFORMAL RELATIONS AND
CONTACTS RECEIVED PER HOUR

Informal Relations	Many	Contacts Received Few	Total
Extensive...........6	1	7
Less extensive........2	6	8
Total.........8	7	15

tacts, nor the number of originated contacts, was related to extent of informal relations.

The more extensive an individual's interpersonal relations are, the better integrated a member of the group he will be. Further, in a group in which most members strive to become highly proficient, and in which they have occasion to appreciate the superior advice experts give them, a close association between integration and competence is to be expected. Since the number of received contacts was the only index of interaction related both to extent of informal relations and to competence, it may be considered an index of integration, that is, of an agent's unofficial status in this group.[11]

---

[11] Why was the total frequency of interaction not related to integration in a cooperative situation? Possibly, because the very knowledge that interaction is integrative induces those members of a group not yet fully integrated but trying to improve their position to originate especially many contacts. For example, the newest member

It will be noted that competence and extent of informal relations, although each was directly related to integration, were inversely related to each other. (Compare Tables 1 and 4 with Table 3.) This suggests the existence of two alternative means of becoming an integrated member in this group. Experts attracted their colleagues through their superior ability, and became integrated by merely being cooperative, without having to exercise much social initiative. Less competent agents were more likely to establish extensive informal relations, since such extensive relations also made an individual a desirable companion for many colleagues, and thus an integrated member of the group. The existence of two alternative mechanisms of integration contributed to the high social cohesion in this department.[12]

The Process of Integration

The preceding interpretation of the relationships between competence, informal relations, and integration raises two questions. First, did these agents actually find their highly competent colleagues particularly attractive? To be sure, their estimation of an individual's ability was closely related to his competence. But was this rationally defined esteem related to social attractiveness? Second, is there any evidence that some agents experienced a need to improve their integration in the group and met this need by establishing especially extensive informal relations in their free time? The analysis of inaccuracies of interview responses concerning lunch partners suggests answers to these questions.

A card with the names of all members of this group was given to each one of them in the course of an interview in his home, and he was asked to divide his colleagues into those with whom he had and those with whom he never had spent a lunch period. Responses from 15 officials were obtained. Every fact, whether two officials had or never had lunch together, was independently reported by two individuals. Of the 105 pairs of statements, 41 did not coincide. This large proportion of discrepancies —39 per cent—indicates that such interview responses provide a very unreliable index of social contacts.[13] However, these very discrepancies

---

of this group (assigned to the department two months prior to observation) ranked third in the number of originated contacts, first in social initiative, but fourteenth in the number of received contacts.

[12] In a competitive group of officials observed in another agency, both mechanisms of integration were greatly impaired. Interaction in the office was largely disintegrative, and the resulting strained relations between officials discouraged them from spending their lunch periods together. As a result, the social cohesion of this group was low.

[13] Accuracy can be somewhat increased by asking for contacts during a limited time only. The number of colleagues who mentioned an agent as their lunch partner seems to provide a valid index of scope of partners, but the number of colleagues named by an agent does not. Only the former index was significantly related to an index of scope of lunch partners based on observation.

do reveal differences in the interpersonal attitudes of these officials and their roles in the group.

Positive discrepancies, the number of colleagues whom an official named but who did not name him, can be considered an index of "role distortion." An individual who claims to have established informal relations with several other members of the group who disclaim these relations has a distorted image of his role in that group.[14] Negative discrepancies, the number of colleagues whom an agent failed to mention but who mentioned him, may be used as an index of "social attractiveness." If an individual does not recall several associations with colleagues which these colleagues report as having occurred, the others are more attracted to him than he is to them.

Table 5 indicates that social attractiveness was related to esteem, as has

TABLE 5
ESTEEM AND SOCIAL ATTRACTIVENESS

Esteem	High	Social Attractiveness Low	Total
High	6	2	8
Low	1	6	7
Total	7	8	15

been assumed. The attractiveness of the esteemed expert, which found expression in his colleagues' remembering occasional contacts with him that he had forgotten, or perhaps reporting associations that had never occurred, induced the others to originate disproportionately many contacts with him. The fact that the expert therefore became integrated without exercising much social effort may well have made his interpersonal relations *appear* less important to him, and thus account for his tendency to forget meetings with colleagues.

Role distortion, on the other hand, was inversely related to extent of

---

[14] It is not known whether a lunch engagement remembered by one agent but not by the other participant actually had taken place, but many positive discrepancies indicate role distortion whether this had been the case or not. Either an individual imagined contacts that never had occurred, or he accurately remembered contacts that had taken place so rarely and so long ago that the other participants had forgotten them. Even the latter indicates that his interpersonal relations have assumed greater significance in his thinking than they warrant. It is also not known whether an individual whose statement was incorrect *remembered* or only *reported* inaccurately. Even if he did not deceive himself, but told the interviewer of contacts that he knew had never occurred, this would indicate that he felt it necessary to present a distorted image of his role in the group to others. The same considerations, *mutatis mutandis*, apply to many negative discrepancies; they indicate social attractiveness, as discussed in the text, regardless of which one of the participants was factually correct.

informal relations, as Table 6 shows.[15] Agents who had established extensive informal relations only rarely reported having lunched with colleagues
who failed to remember such engagements. Those whose interpersonal
relations were less extensive often adapted to an insecure position by main-

TABLE 6
EXTENT OF INFORMAL RELATIONS AND ROLE
DISTORTION

Informal Relations	High	Role Distortion Low	Total
Extensive............2		6	8
Less extensive........6		1	7
Total.........8		7	15

taining a distorted image of their role in the group. This adaptation suggests that these agents experienced a need for improving their position.
The existence of this need helps to explain why the less competent agents,
who were originally less attractive to their colleagues, usually tried to
become better integrated by cultivating informal relations with the other
members of the group.

Interaction in Group Situations

The unofficial status of an agent, indicated by the number of contacts
he received, influenced his behavior in group situations, his interaction
with outsiders, and his performance of his duties.

Departmental meetings, held every other week, were the only occasions when all members of the department were assembled as a group.
These meetings were largely devoted to explanations of new regulations
and changes in enforcement practice by the supervisor, and the discussion
of problems related to new procedures by the agents. Those whose status
was secure, who received many contacts throughout the day, tended to
participate more in these discussions than their less well integrated colleagues, as Table 7 shows.[16]

By raising a question, an agent could clarify an issue that was doubtful
in his mind. By making an intelligent comment, he enhanced his prestige
in the eyes of his supervisor and his colleagues. But by participating in the
discussion he also risked exposing his ignorance and being ridiculed. The
group often responded to a remark with derisive laughter and comments,

---

[15] Role distortion was not related to esteem (and neither to competence), whereas
social attractiveness was not related to the extent of informal relations. This indicates that role distortion and social attractiveness measure two different dimensions.

[16] On the basis of observation during five departmental meetings, agents were
divided into those who spoke three times or more and those who spoke less than
three times per meeting. This index was also positively related to esteem.

TABLE 7
Contacts Received per Hour and Participation in
Discussion at Departmental Meetings

Contacts Received	Agent Participated in Discussion		
	Often	Rarely	Total
Many............5		1	6
Few..............2		7	9
Total.........7		8	15

because it seemed irrelevant or obvious, and the participation of the least integrated agents was most often discouraged in this fashion. In effect, the group permitted only its integrated members to enhance their knowledge and prestige in these discussions.

The superior status of agents who received many contacts also manifested itself in the dominant roles they assumed when a small group of agents was engaged in a joint undertaking. They made most suggestions, and their suggestions were most often followed. For instance, they assumed command on the few occasions when several agents worked together on a project; they usually decided to which restaurant a group went for lunch. The fact that dominance in group situations is associated with the number of received contacts further justifies the use of the latter as an index of status.

Interaction with Outsiders

The better integrated agents had a disproportionately large number of contacts with members of *other* departments.[17] Agents who received relatively few contacts in the course of social interaction tended to confine their associations to members of their own department. An insecure position apparently discouraged ventures into untried social situations. This relationship between status and ease of interaction with out-group members is exemplified by the contacts of agents with stenographers.

Agents could dictate their reports and letters to stenographers, but they did not always avail themselves of the opportunity to do so. Some agents usually wrote their difficult reports in long-hand and had them typed, and some typed an occasional brief report themselves. The extent to which an agent utilized stenographic assistance was related to his status.[18] Table 8 indicates that agents who received many contacts from

---

[17] This is in agreement with William F. Whyte's finding that the leaders of gangs are the channels of communication between gangs. See *Street Corner Society* (Chicago: University of Chicago Press, 1943), pp. 259–60.

[18] The index of utilized dictation time is: the amount of time stenographers spent taking dictation from an agent during an eight-month period, divided by the number of cases he had completed in that period. By holding the number of cases constant,

TABLE 8
CONTACTS RECEIVED PER HOUR AND DICTATION TIME

Contacts Received	Dictation Time		
	Much	Little	Total
Many..............6		1	7
Few...............2		7	9
Total.........8		8	16

their colleagues dictated more often to stenographers than agents who were not as well integrated.

Composing the final report of a complex case was a difficult task, and an enervating one, since this report provided the basis for the supervisor's evaluation of the agent's performance. Two agents explained their failure to dictate some of their reports in the following terms:

If it's exceptionally hard; I actually write it out with pencil and paper, and turn it into the pool for typing . . . It's easier for me to write than to dictate. Often, I don't use quite the right word. I notice it a few seconds later, but I let it go. What shall I do? Ask the girl to go back and change it? I'd rather not. . . .

If I dictate directly, I worry about not getting everything in the report. This way, if I leave something out, I can go back and put it in. It would be a nuisance to tell the stenographer to go back and make such insertions.

An agent found the presence of the stenographer disturbing if he worried about the impression he made on her—for instance, when he had to tell her to correct a mistake he had made. Agents who received social recognition from their peers in the form of being often approached by them, either because their competence was respected or because their company was valued for personal reasons,[19] were relatively unconcerned with the opinion of stenographers. Agents who felt insecure in the peer group, on the other hand, were probably more eager to receive, at least, the respect of the stenographer, and were at the same time less confident of doing so. Their consequent preoccupation with the impression they made on her prevented them from concentrating their thoughts upon composing the report. This disturbance often induced the less integrated agents to forego the advantages of dictating.

Their status in the group also influenced the interaction of agents with the employers of the firms they investigated. Observation indicated that the agents who were well integrated, although not necessarily the most

the amount of dictation time required is roughly held constant. Although the value of this index is influenced by dictation speed, it is primarily a function of the proportion of his reports an agent failed to dictate. Data for all 16 agents were available for this index.

[19] Both esteem and the extent of informal relations were also positively related to dictation time.

effective negotiators, tended to remain more detached in their negotiations with employers. Apparently, the recognition they received from their colleagues made it easier for them to disregard the personal attitudes of clients toward them, and thus to remain unperturbed even in the face of an excitable employer.[20] Such detachment improved the quality of an agent's performance, just as the ability to dictate difficult reports to stenographers enhanced his working efficiency. His status therefore influenced an agent's performance.

Conclusions

Unofficial status and quality of performance were mutually related in this department of a government agency. Superior competence usually produced an integrated status in this group, since its members were especially attracted to those colleagues whose ability they respected. A substitute means for attaining this end, which enabled the less proficient agents also to become integrated, was the establishment of extensive informal relations with colleagues, since this also made many others value the companionship of an individual. Agents who were highly competent, and those who had particularly extensive informal relations, received a disproportionately large number of contacts in the course of social interaction.

The relative number of contacts an agent received from his colleagues constituted the *actual*—to refrain from coining a new term by calling it the "interactual"—expression of their evaluation of his role in the group. It provided him with concrete evidence of his significance for the group. Being approached often gave an agent a feeling of security in social situations which facilitated his interaction with outsiders as well as with members of his own group. In contrast, the insecurity of the agent who was rarely approached by others made his interpersonal relations on the job problematical for him. The number of contacts an agent received per hour indicated his status in the group.

The competence of an agent influenced his unofficial status, which, in turn, influenced the quality of his performance, especially because it affected the social relationships into which he entered in the course of discharging his duties. The concern of the insecure agent with his position in these relationships distracted his attention from his work. On the other hand, the agent whose status gave him confidence in being socially accepted and respected, could concentrate his energies upon the problems of his job, in work situations involving social interaction. Typically, he was more detached in negotiations with clients, less disturbed by the presence of stenographers, and less hesitant to clarify a problem in a

---

[20] For a full report on the relationship between an agent's role in this group and his role as an investigator, the reader is referred to the author's study cited above.

discussion. All of these factors contributed to his efficiency as an agent.

Agents who were disproportionately often approached in the course of interaction between individuals tended to assume the dominant roles in group situations, for instance in the discussions at departmental meetings, or when a small group of officials engaged in a common undertaking. In other words, those agents who *received* relatively many contacts in "pair events" were most likely to take the *initiative* in "set-events."[21] The social recognition an agent received in the form of being approached, often gave him a feeling of security that enabled him to make recommendations freely in group situations. Simultaneously, the same regard for an agent that led others to seek to associate with him also induced them usually to follow his recommendations.

The designation of the frequency of received contacts as index of unofficial status is by no means arbitrary. The recipients of many contacts occupied a superordinate status in the group in the conventional meaning of the term; they could, and did, exercise social control over their colleagues. The members of this group, who were originally peers, became differentiated in status as the result of interacting with each other at different rates. By originating a disproportionately large number of contacts with one of its members, the group expressed their collective regard for and deference to him, and thus bestowed superior status, power as well as prestige, upon him. The frequency of the contacts an agent received therefore not only expressed but also helped to determine his status in the group.[22]

---

[21] Whyte also found that the leaders of a group originated most activities in "set-events"; *op. cit.*, p. 262.

[22] In this group of peers, differences in power, the ability to control others, emerged in the process of co-operative, voluntary interaction. Even here, the intellectual resources of an individual, his competence, influenced his interaction and his status. Initial differences in status, of course, also influence interaction. The conclusions of this paper are not meant to imply that the process of voluntary interaction in a group is the source of all differentials in power. For example, the superior status of the supervisor did not originate in the interaction in this department. It found expression in his interaction with subordinates, and was modified through this interaction, but its source was his official authority over subordinates, including his right to administer sanctions to them. For a discussion of authority, see the author's study cited above.

26. STUDIES OF IDEA FLOW IN RESEARCH AND DEVELOPMENT*

ALBERT H. RUBENSTEIN

THIS IS an example of research in the field of organization theory. It represents a particular view of organization theory and a particular style of research, so that it is not necessarily representative of the increasing amount and diversity of research in this new field.

The viewpoint represented is that of a group of applied scientists—members of the staff and graduate students in our Department of Industrial Engineering and Management Sciences at Northwestern. We view our role in the field of organization theory as that of selecting, refining, and testing theories and notions about organizational behavior. Many of them have been developed or suggested by people in the behavioral sciences who are primarily concerned with theory building per se and who are not necessarily interested in particular organizational contexts. Additional theories and notions have arisen directly out of our own past work or the work of others who are concerned, as we are, with particular organizational contexts.

The particular organizational context that provides the setting for most of our research in organization theory is the Research and Development (R&D) activity. The style of our research involves field studies of operating organizations in their natural settings, but we are not reluctant to attempt building mathematical models of particular aspects of the phenomena or to consider laboratory simulation when it seems appropriate. The purpose of this study is simply stated: it is to increase our understanding of the complex organizational processes which influence the generation, communication, and disposition of ideas for new technical work in an R&D laboratory (12).

Our focus is on the "idea" (Figure 1). We are attempting to study the origins and adventures of (1) ideas or proposals that eventually are accepted and supported as projects by the organization, (2) proposals that are not accepted and supported, and (3) potential proposals which never arrive at a decision point for the organization, but which are disposed of in some other way than outright acceptance or rejection. This latter category, incidentally, entails some difficult conceptual as well as empirical problems. For example, can we properly say that an idea or a proposal "exists" in the organization prior to the time that it is communi-

* Presented to the New York chapter, The Institute of Management Sciences, November, 1963.

cated to someone either formally (such as in seeking official approval and funding for it) or informally (such as mentioning it to a colleague)? Further, if we *can* properly say that it does exist in this precommunication state, how can we gain access to it for purposes of studying its evolution?

The study was initiated in July of 1962. It is being supported by grants from the National Science Foundation and the National Aeronautics and Space Administration, as well as internal fellowship funds.

In this paper, I would like to (1) briefly sketch the historical antecedents of the project, (2) present a highly abbreviated conceptual model of

FIGURE 1

IDEA FLOW IN RESEARCH AND DEVELOPMENT:
DEFINITION OF AN "IDEA"

An *actual* or *potential proposal* for undertaking *new technical work* which will require the *commitment* of *significant* organizational *resources* such as: time, money, manpower, energy.

Typically, if accepted, it will result in a *new project:*

Examples:
1. A new method of synthesizing compound X
2. A study of radiation effects on Y
3. An extension of current work on Z into new areas

Not Examples:
1. A suggestion that the company should "go into electronics"
2. A complaint that Product A needs improvement
3. A plan for reorganizing the lab
4. A modification of an experimental setup on an ongoing project

the organizational processes involved in the study, (3) discuss some of the theoretical structure of the study by illustrating some of the propositions which we are considering testing, and (4) discuss one major methodological issue—the real-time measurement of idea flow behavior in organizations.

Historical Antecedents of the Idea Flow Project

1. *A Study of Team Research* (Columbia University, 1951–53) (7).

We felt that the communication pattern was the key to understanding how a research team or group operates (Figure 2). We made many measurements of the communication behavior of team members, including frequency, direction, participants, and media used.

We realized that we had to know more about the communication events that were being observed and reported. In order to examine the role of communication in the actual work of the research group, we had to have some indication of the motivation for, the content of, and the consequences of communication events.

We measured one aspect of content and one aspect of consequences. We differentiated between "communication events that were relevent to the project" on which the researcher was working and "other communication events." We also determined, through interview and questionnaire, which events, which individuals, and which communication media had provided "information helpful on the current project."

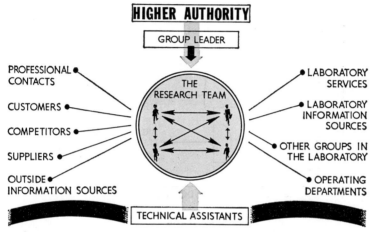

SOURCE: Industrial Laboratories—October, 1952. (From a paper presented at the Third Annual Conference on Industrial Research, Department of Industrial Engineering, Columbia University, June 9–13, 1952.

FIG. 2.   Communication Channels of the Research Team.

2. *A Pilot Study of Sources of Information* (Columbia University, 1953).

This was a follow-up to the Team Research Study, directed toward the motivations for and consequences of "information-seeking" communication events. We asked a sample of researchers to record events in which they sought information from any kind of source—any individual, group, or inanimate reference source. They recorded the problem or question, the source queried, and the answer or result.

This pilot study was not directly followed up until 1963—ten years later—when a series of discussions began within our group at Northwestern about the possibilities of a large-scale simulation attack on the general problem of "information search" by researchers.

3. *Several Theses and Staff Surveys on Project Selection in R&D* (M.I.T. 1953–59) (**16, 5**).

Many criteria were collected from the literature and by interview which purportedly were used by R&D managers for evaluating and selecting projects. In addition, many prescribed procedures for proposing and selecting projects were found. Some came directly from operating organizations, and others were presented by students of the R&D process.

Most of the criteria and procedures encountered in these studies seemed overly formal and rational when compared to actual, observed project selection behavior.

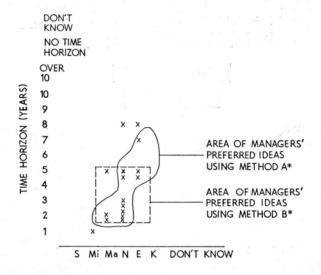

FIG. 3.   Scope and Time Horizon of Managers' Ideas

4. A Study of the Organization of R&D in Decentralized Companies (M.I.T. and Northwestern, 1955–64).

This study was an attempt to examine the effects of corporate organizational structure (in particular, administrative decentralization or divisionalization) on the R&D activity within the company. In order to examine such effects, we needed ways of describing the behavior of the people in R&D laboratories.

We concentrated on two aspects of R&D behavior in this study: (1) The actual set of projects being worked on. We established a set of categories for summarizing this into what we called the "project portfolio." (2) Some indication of the kinds of proposals for projects that were acceptable and not acceptable in the organization. This led us to define an "idea" and attempt to sample the kind of ideas which had recently been and currently were being proposed or communicated in the laboratory.

Here, again, as in the Team Research Study, we were back to studying communication as a key to the operation of an R&D organization—this time at the level of whole laboratories rather than research teams or groups. As part of the study we asked several hundred R&D professionals and managers in a number of laboratories to fill out a detailed questionnaire about ideas in their organization (14). We also conducted follow-up interviews with some of them. Rather than ask them to describe a random selection of ideas, we instructed them to "select the three *best* ideas originated by you during the past year, and the three *best* ideas originated by someone else and transmitted to you (for whatever reason) during the same period."

In contrast to the definition of ideas we are using in the current study— that is, "proposals for new projects"—we employed a more general definition. It included suggestions for "better methods or approaches to ongoing projects" as well as suggestions for "new work that might be undertaken as separate projects."

Analyses of this data, which are still going on, revealed patterns of idea production which could be compared for different hierarchical levels in the laboratory, different levels of education, and other differences between R&D personnel. Figure 3 indicates the approach to categorizing "best" ideas.

This brief historical analysis was intended to indicate the evolution of our present focus on the idea or proposal for R&D work and on certain aspects of the communication process in an R&D activity.

A Flow Model of the Source of Projects in an R&D Laboratory (Figure 4)

Let us conceive of a first approximation to the total list of possible ideas that might be proposed for project status in a particular lab. This is, of course, sheer speculation without a thorough knowledge of the techno-economic environment and capabilities of the organization. That is, in order for an observer to make a reasonably comprehensive list of all of the ideas that *might* be proposed in a given organization at a given time, he would have to know a great deal about the business the company was in, its economic resources, the current state of its technological sophistication, the technical capabilities of its personnel, the states of the various arts that were involved in its field, and so on.

Even with all of this information, however, it still might not be possible for any two experts to agree on a common list. Fortunately, or perhaps as a consequence of this difficulty, the current study design does not require such a list. It does, however, require the *concept* of a feasible list of "Techno-Economic Opportunities" for R&D work by the organization.

This should be a feasible list in the sense that even a casual, if not expert, observer can distinguish between the kind of realistic opportunities that are available to an organization with great technical and economic resources as compared with one that has modest technical and economic resources.

One clue to this feasible list is the behavior of other organizations which are engaged in the same fields as the organization being studied. This notion is being examined in another, separate study where we are attempt-

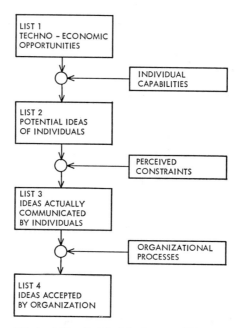

FIG. 4. A Flow Model of the Sources of Ideas or Project Proposals and the Factors Affecting Them

ing to actually establish a rough feasible list for the firms in a particular, narrowly designated market.

The use to which we want to put the concept of such a feasible list is as a starting point in attempting to define an actual list of potential ideas that might be proposed by the individuals in the R&D organization. That is, the interaction between this total feasible list of techno-economic opportunities for R&D projects and the characteristics of the individual members of the R&D organization generates a second list. This second list might be called the list of all potential ideas that actually might be proposed by the individuals in the organization.

As an illustration of the source of a portion of such a list of potential ideas, consider a new researcher entering an organization. He brings with him certain abilities, formal training, skills, knowledge, interests, and experience with certain classes of problems. Upon arrival in the laboratory of his new employer, he learns about the businesses the company is in; the nature of its products, production processes, and services; what is currently going on in the laboratory and elsewhere in the company that relates to R&D; what has been tried in the past; and what people are saying and thinking about future possibilities. Through some "mysterious" psychological process—which we variously call creativity, inventiveness, problem solving, serendipity, etc.—he combines some of his abilities and the information he has collected into what might be called an idea for a potential project. He might, depending on his capabilities and the amount of information he has absorbed, have a number of such ideas over a period of time or at any one time. The sum of these individual lists of ideas may be conceived of as the total list of "potential individual ideas" which "exist" in the organization over a period of time or at a particular time.

In the current phase of our work, we have indeed made an attempt to take a total inventory of such potential individual ideas as well as ideas that have already been communicated to others in the organization. We have attempted a complete inventory among all the professionals in four smaller laboratories (Figure 5) and have taken partial inventories in several larger laboratories. Allowing for the many possible errors in obtaining these kind of data directly from subjects, we believe that we have a fair picture, in the four smaller laboratories, of the kinds of ideas that were in existence at the time we took the inventory.

Once we have this second list of potential individual ideas, we consider a third, reduced list. The ideas on this list are the ones that individuals in the organization actually do communicate to others in the laboratory and, in some cases, formally propose for project status.

The reduction in size from the second list to the third list occurs through another "mysterious" psychological process within the mind of the potential proposer of an idea. This process has to do with his perceptions of the possible consequences for him—as an individual, as an employee, as a professional in his field, and in other possible roles—if he does actually communicate his ideas to other people in the organization. Although we do not intend to and are not equipped to probe very deeply into the motivations involved at this stage, we are attempting to get at some aspects. For example, we are attempting to learn how the individual perceives the constraints placed upon R&D work by the various levels of supervision and management. We are also considering ways of evaluating individual risk propensity as a clue to how far an individual will go in testing the limits of such constraints. When list number two—potential individual ideas—is exposed to this set of factors, we can then expect to find a reduced list, number three, which consists of the ideas that the individual actually does communicate to others.

The factors which tend to reduce the third list to the size of a fourth list—ideas actually accepted by the organization as projects—and in addition, to modify specific ideas on the third list, are the major foci of our study. We call these *organizational processes*. These include, among other things, the communication systems, the power and authority systems, the

		Number of Ideas Reported Company Code				
Stage	Description of Stage	1	2	3	4	Total
1	Not yet communicated to anyone	4	8	11	13	36
2	Communicated only informally	24	13	8	28	73
3	Formally submitted but no consideration yet	6	3	3	7	19
4	Being actively considered but no decision yet	23	14	15	13	65
5	Has been rejected	2	1	2	1	6
6	Has been accepted	30	35	22	35	122
7	Other	13	5	10	8	36
	Total Ideas	102	79	71	105	357
	Number of Researchers Responding	29	11	14	14	68
	Ave. No. of Ideas per Researcher	3.52	7.18	5.07	7.50	5.25

* As reported on "Idea Inventory Form" by all professional researchers in four industrial laboratories.

FIG. 5. Stages of Ideas Used in Preliminary Attempts to Inventory Ideas at a Point in Time*

systems of rewards and penalties, and the decision-making systems. Concentration on these organizational processes has strongly influenced the makeup of our group working on the project. It currently includes one full-time sociologist, one sociology graduate student, one consulting sociologist, one consulting social psychologist, as well as four of our own graduate research assistants with training in various branches of engineering, physical science, and business.

The next section of this paper will provide some illustrations of the possible effects of some of these organizational processes on the transformation of list three into list four, including the modification of specific ideas from their original form.

One comment before this, however, may help to clarify our approach to the often tricky notion of the "originator" of an idea. Although the preceding discussion was couched entirely in terms of the individual as the source of the ideas on the various lists, we know that many ideas originate with groups. We make provision for this in our study design and do not attempt to impose the concept of a single individual as the unique originator upon our data and models.

Some Questions and Propositions about Idea Flow

In organization theory, as in other research areas, there are alternative ways of arriving at potentially testable statements which may ultimately lead to explanatory or predictive theories.

One of these has been used by a number of investigators in the field. They have examined or developed a body of speculative, experimental, and/or logically deduced results about organizational behavior. From these results they have extracted or deduced statements about particular aspects of organization, without necessary reference to specific contexts (e.g., production, governmental operations, executive behavior). These statements are then ready for these investigators or others to apply in a particular context.

Another approach involves the extraction of statements directly from observation of specific phenomena in their natural contexts. Then, depending upon the taste and research style of the investigator, there may follow an examination of the literature to see if there are any previous results that support and increase his confidence in the empirically derived statements.

We have used both of these approaches in a number of studies we have been conducting in our program of research-on-research. In the Idea Flow Study, however, we are attempting to use a third approach, which combines some elements of the other two. From our preliminary work on the phenomenon of idea flow, we have extracted a number of questions which appear relevant to an understanding of what is going on. Most of these questions are not initially in testable form. From our knowledge of the literature in organizational theory and the ongoing work of others, we attempt to relate these questions to an existing substructure of theory about organizational behavior. Within this substructure we attempt to derive successively more specific statements or propositions until we reach a level that can be operationalized and subjected to empirical testing within our contextual situation—an operating R&D laboratory.

I will illustrate with several general questions that have resulted directly from the empirical work so far on the Idea Flow Study, and indicate how we might proceed to develop testable propositions with the aid of existing knowledge about more general but related phenomena.

   I. Question: What kind of ideas is one likely to find in the project portfolio of a given company?

POSSIBLE SOURCES OF THEORY:
    Innovative behavior of organizations (9)
    Resistance to change
    Learning behavior
    Bureaucratic theory
SAMPLE PROPOSITIONS:
    1. Organizations with a tradition of heavy dependence on science are likely to have a more diversified portfolio of projects in terms of time horizon (estimated time to completion) and scope (relation to current products and processes) than organizations lacking such a tradition. Figure 6 presents some empirical evidence related to this proposition, in terms of "time horizon."
    2. Organizations with a history of successful results from R&D are likely to include riskier projects in their portfolios than ones without such a history.

Period in Which Work Started

and Number of Projects

Year Work Started → Month or Period →	Prior to July 1960	1960 7-12	1961 1-6	1961 7-12	1962* 1,2	Row Total
0 - 3	0	2	1	9	3	15
4 - 6	4	5	5	3	3	20
7 - 9	1	1	5	6	4	17
10 - 12	7	2	2	2	1	14
13 - 18	3	6	2	5		16
19 - 24	6	5	1			12
25 - 30	7					7
31 - 36	1		2			3
over 36	12	1	1	1		15
Totals	41	22	19	26	11	119

(Estimated Time to Complete – Months)

median for data from approximately a five year span

*Note: 1962 = 1st 2 months only

●— —● = Median classification over time

FIG. 6. Company 20. Distribution of projects by estimated time to complete versus period in which work started.

Project Management Department*						
Person Contacted	Q 6 Consulted Freq	%	Q 7 Convinced Freq	%	Q 9 Originated Freq	%
1 In Dept.	31	55.3	27	67.8	28	59.5
2 Not R and D/In the same Branch	2	3.6	1	2.3	2	4.3
3 Other Branches	6	10.7	3	7.0	1	2.1
4 Customer	3	5.4	0		4	8.5
5 Vendor	0	0	0			
6 Tech. literature	0	0	0			
7 Consultant	0	0	0			
8 Other R and D Depts.	14	25.0	12	27.9	12	25.5
Totals	56	100	43	100	47	100

Reliability Department †						
Person Contacted	Q 6 Freq	%	Q 7 Freq	%	Q 9 Freq	%
1 In Dept.	62	62	50	61.7	40	64.5
2 Not R and D/In the same Branch	11	11	10	12.3	2	3.2
3 Other Branches	3	3	6	7.4	1	1.6
4 Customer	3	3	2	2.5	6	9.7
5 Vendor	1	1	0	0		
6 Tech. literature	1	1	0	0	1	1.6
7 Consultant	1	1	0	0		
8 Other R and D Depts.	18	18	13	16.0	12	19.4
	100	100	81	100	62	100

Q 6 = Who was consulted about your ideas
Q 7 = Whom did you try and convince about your ideas
Q 9 = Who was the originator of others' ideas

* Men in Dept.: 49; Men Reporting: 31; % Reporting: 63.3%
† Men in Dept.: 54; Men Reporting: 33; % Reporting: 61.1%.

FIG. 7. Consultation Patterns—Number of Mentions

II. QUESTION: To whom is an idea originator most likely to communicate for purposes of seeking advice on his ideas or attempting to convince people of the merits of his ideas?

POSSIBLE SOURCES OF THEORY:

Sociometric patterns in professional organizations (3, 8)
Bureaucratic theory
Small group theory

SAMPLE PROPOSITIONS:

1. Researchers are most likely to consult initially with their peers about their own ideas.

2. Intragroup communication will be greater than cross-group communication in a highly structured organization. Figure 7 presents some data on this, from a very large organization (15).

3. At least one liaison person who can transmit ideas outside the group will be found in each "successful" laboratory group.

III. QUESTION: To whom is an idea originator (O) most likely to: (a) first communicate his idea and (b) ultimately propose it for consideration by the organization?

POSSIBLE SOURCE OF THEORY:

Superior-subordinate relations in work groups (11)

SAMPLE PROPOSITIONS:

1. If O's superior (S) shares O's orientation and has influence with his (S's) superiors at the next level, O will more likely propose his ideas to S than if these conditions did not hold. Some data on the sharing of orientations toward ideas is presented in Figure 8.

2. If S does share O's orientation, but is not perceived by O as having influence with S's superiors, O will seek other channels for proposing his ideas.

IV. QUESTION: What kind of criteria will an individual use in deciding whether to actually propose an idea?

POSSIBLE SOURCES OF THEORY:

Subjective probability
Personality theory
Role theory
Professional orientation (6)

SAMPLE PROPOSITIONS:

A researcher with high "organizational" and low "professional" orientations will tend to propose ideas more closely related to the current, obvious needs of the organization than will a researcher with high professional orientation and either high or low organizational orientation. This relationship is illustrated below:

EFFECT OF ORIENTATION ON IDEAS

		ORGANIZATIONAL ORIENTATION	
		Low	High
PROFESSIONAL ORIENTATION	Low		closest
	High	less close	less close

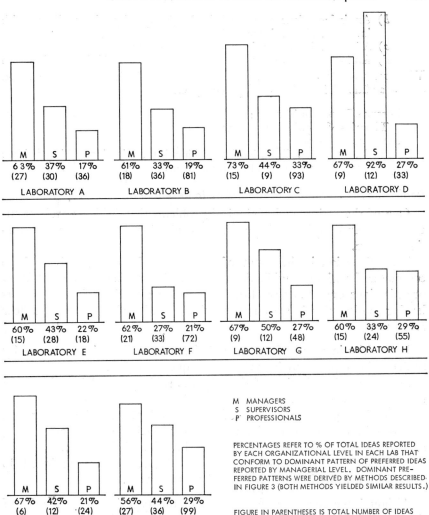

M   MANAGERS
S   SUPERVISORS
P   PROFESSIONALS

PERCENTAGES REFER TO % OF TOTAL IDEAS REPORTED
BY EACH ORGANIZATIONAL LEVEL IN EACH LAB THAT
CONFORM TO DOMINANT PATTERN OF PREFERRED IDEAS
REPORTED BY MANAGERIAL LEVEL. DOMINANT PRE-
FERRED PATTERNS WERE DERIVED BY METHODS DESCRIBED
IN FIGURE 3 (BOTH METHODS YIELDED SIMILAR RESULTS.)

FIGURE IN PARENTHESES IS TOTAL NUMBER OF IDEAS
REPORTED BY INDICATED GROUP

FIG. 8. Patterns of Idea Production: Managers, Supervisors, and Professionals

V. Question: How do patterns of ideas emerge in a laboratory over time?
Possible Sources of Theory:
   Organizational growth (18, 17, 1)
   Theories of enculturation (2)
   Learning theories
Sample Propositions:
   1. R&D groups in a "low-science" environment which are established with a "high-science" charter will tend to drift into proposing ideas of a lower scientific level over time, unless the charter is continuously reinforced.
   2. Reinforcement can occur through combinations of the following kinds of mechanisms:
   a) An early, widely recognized success

       b) An independent source of funds (independent from clients with immediate, low-science problems)

       c) Adequate insulation from outside pressures

       d) An internal, *real* (as contrasted with mere honorific) reward system

VI. QUESTION: What are the effects of rejection of O's ideas on the likelihood of additional ideas being proposed by O?

    POSSIBLE SOURCE OF THEORY:

      Theories of cognitive dissonance

    SAMPLE PROPOSITION:

      If O can successfully rationalize to himself the rejection of his past ideas by the organization, he will continue to propose additional ideas.

Real-Time Measurement of Idea Flow in Research and Development

One of the major methodological problems that field researchers encounter when studying real operating organizations is the temporal distortion of data.

This distortion is the result of a number of factors, and we have encountered various combinations of them in our field studies of R&D organizations over the past dozen years. Some of the principal factors leading to distortion in the current series of field studies on the idea flow are these:

Difficulties in recall of events and the surrounding circumstances by subjects, in response to interviews and questionnaires.

Post hoc rationalization of the way the subject would have liked the events to have occurred.

Distortion of (1) sequence of events and (2) spacing of events.

Loss of the emotional color that accompanied the actual event, e.g., attitudes and interpersonal relations at the time of the event.

Simultaneity of surrounding events and circumstances that might help to explain or bring into better focus the actual event.

Although we encountered problems of this type in our first series of field studies of R&D laboratories—the Team Research Study (13)—the nature of the events we were collecting enabled us to handle the problem in a fairly simple manner. We were merely interested in communication events and wanted a minimum of information about them, such as the participants, the time they occurred, and their relevance to the subject's current project. The "density" of these events—the number per unit time— was sufficiently high and the uniformity was also sufficiently high to permit the use of random sampling techniques.

In contrast, as indicated by Figure 9, the density of "idea-related events" is much lower. Furthermore, these events are much less uniform with respect to the variables we are examining.

In addition, there are questions of economy and "reactivity"—adverse effects on the subjects and deterioration of the subject-investigator relationship. As we have found so far, the typical frequency of idea-related events is something less than one per day (in some cases it is much less—as little as one per week or month for a given subject). We therefore encounter severe problems of economy and reactivity when we attempt to use standard (or modified) time sampling techniques, as we did in the Team Research Study. In that study, we "appeared" in each laboratory one or more times per day and, because of the nature of the phenomena we were investigating, we struck pay dirt almost every time. That is, we did indeed find the subjects engaged in a communication event almost every time we made a visit. This helped us to justify the visit on economic grounds and also appeared to provide some satisfaction—or at least lack of annoyance—for the subject.

FIGURE 9

RELATIVE DENSITY OF VARIOUS LEVELS OF COMMUNICATION EVENTS

Level	Estimate of Frequency
Total communication events*	16 per man day
Information-bearing events*	10 per man day
Idea-related events†	Less than 1 per man day

* SOURCE: Team Research Study (1952)
† SOURCE: Rough estimate based on preliminary field interviews in Idea Flow Study (1963)

In one of the idea flow field studies, on the other hand, we experienced severe diseconomies, plus a near-fatal reaction by the subjects who were tired of being asked what had happened on "idea X" when nothing had happened since the last time (4).

We are still working on this problem and have tried a variety of approaches, including a self-administered instrument and a "remote control" instrument (10).

Summary

An example of field research in organization theory was described—a study of Idea Flow and Project Selection in R&D. A number of previous studies leading up to the present one were mentioned, indicating the development of the present study. A flow model of the source of projects in an R&D laboratory was presented. A number of research questions were presented, along with the possible sources of theory and some testable propositions. Finally, one major methodological problem was discussed briefly—the real-time measurement of idea flow in operating R&D laboratories.

REFERENCES

1. ALPERT, S. B., AND WEITZ, H. "Decision-Making, Growth and Failure," *IRE Transactions on Engineering Management* (September, 1961).
2. AVERY, ROBERT W. "Enculturation in Industrial Research," *IRE Transactions on Engineering Management* (March, 1960).

3. BLAU, PETER M. "Patterns of Interaction among a Group of Officials in a Government Agency," *Human Relations*, Vol. 7, No. 3, (1954).

4. BOLEN, FRANK M. "A Technique for the Real Time Measurement of the Flow of Ideas in Industrial Laboratories." Master's thesis, Department of Industrial Engineering and Management Sciences, Northwestern University, August, 1963.

5. GLOSKEY, CARL R. "Research on a Research Department: An Analysis of Economic Decisions on Projects," *IRE Transactions on Engineering Management* (December, 1960).

6. GOLDBERG, LOUIS C. "Dimensions in the Evaluation of Technical Ideas in an Industrial Research Laboratory." Master's thesis, Department of Industrial Engineering and Management Sciences, Northwestern University, August, 1963.

7. HERTZ, DAVID B., AND RUBENSTEIN, ALBERT H. *Team Research*. Eastern Technical Publications. Cambridge, Mass., 1953.

8. JACOBSON, E., AND SEASHORE, S. "Communication Practices in Complex Organizations," *Journal of Social Issues*, Vol. III, No. 3 (1951).

9. MANSFIELD, EDWIN. "A Model of the Imitation Process," *IRE Transactions on Engineering Management* (June, 1962).

10. MARTIN, MILLES W., JR., "The Use of Random Alarm Devices in Studying Scientists' Reading Behavior," *IRE Transactions on Engineering Management* (June, 1962).

11. PELZ, DONALD C. "Leadership within a Hierarchial Organization," *Journal of Social Issues*, Vol. III, No. 3 (1951).

12. RUBENSTEIN, ALBERT H. "Field Studies of Idea Flow and Project Selection in Industry," *Operations Research in Research and Development* (ed. BURTON V. DEAN), New York: John Wiley & Sons, Inc., 1963.

13. RUBENSTEIN, ALBERT H. "Problems in the Measurement of Interpersonal Communication in an Ongoing Situation," *Sociometry* (1952).

14. RUBENSTEIN, ALBERT H. AND AVERY, ROBERT W. "Idea Flow in Research and Development," *Proceedings of the National Electronics Conference*, 1958.

15. RUBENSTEIN, ALBERT H. AND HANNENBERG, RICHARD. "Idea Flow and Project Selection in Several Industrial Research and Development Laboratories," *Proceedings of the Conference on Economic and Social Factors in Technological Research and Development*, Ohio State University, 1962. In press.

16. RUBENSTEIN, ALBERT H. AND HOROWITZ, IRA "Project Selection in New Technical Fields," *Proceedings of the National Electronics Conference*, 1959.

17. SELZNICK, PHILIP. *TVA and the Grass Roots*, Berkeley and Los Angeles: University of California Press. 1949.

18. WEINER, MILTON G. "Observations on the Growth of Information-Processing Centers." In *Some Theories of Organization* (eds. A. H. RUBENSTEIN AND C. J. HABERSTROH). Homewood, Ill.: Richard D. Irwin, Inc., and The Dorsey Press, 1960. (See his article in this book, pp. 157–66)

27. THE IMPACT OF CERTAIN COMMUNICATION NETS UPON ORGANIZATION AND PERFORMANCE IN TASK-ORIENTED GROUPS*

HAROLD GUETZKOW AND HERBERT A. SIMON[0]

BAVELAS, Smith and Leavitt[1] have posed the problem: what effect do communication patterns have upon the operation of groups? To study this problem they designed a laboratory situation that is a prototype of those occurring in "natural" organizations existing in government and business. Each member of the group is given certain information. Their task is to assemble this information, use it to make a decision, and then issue orders based on the decision. This design provides a situation stripped of the complexities of large-scale social groups but retaining some essential characteristics of the organizational communication problem. In it we can examine how the communication net affects simultaneously (a) the development of the organization's internal structure, and (b) the group's performance of its operating task.

Leavitt made certain deductions from Bavelas' model of communication nets,[2] but his empirical studies[3] did not confirm the derivations. Leavitt explains the discrepancies in terms of such concepts as "different kinds of messages require very different clock times," and the failure of his subjects "to gravitate to the theoretically 'best' operating organization."[4] It is the purpose of this paper to present an alternative theory of these miniature organizations, and to test this theory by new empirical data and by comparison with Leavitt's original empirical findings.

The proposed explanation requires that a sharp distinction be made between: (a) the effects of communication restrictions upon performance of the operating task; and (b) the effects of the restrictions upon a group's ability to organize itself for such performance. That is, instead of

---

* Reproduced from *Management Science*, Vol. 1, Nos. 3 and 4, April–July, 1955.

[0] This work was supported by a grant from the research funds of the Graduate School of Industrial Administration. Grateful thanks are due to Messrs. Wm. Dill, K. Hellfach, A. D. Martin, and F. Metzger, and to Mrs. Martha Pryor and Miss Anne Bowes for aid in the conduct of the investigation and help in analyzing its results.

[1] A. Bavelas, "Communication Patterns in Task-Oriented Groups," *Jour. of Acoustical Soc. of Amer.*, 1950, 22, pp. 725–30.

[2] A. Bavelas, "A Mathematical Model for Group Structures," *Appl. Anthrop.*, 1948, 7, pp. 16–30.

[3] H. J. Leavitt, "Some Effects of Certain Communication Patterns on Group Performance," *Jour. of Abnorm. and Soc. Psychol.*, 1951, 46, pp. 38–50.

[4] Leavitt, *ibid.*, pp. 46–47.

regarding the group's problem as unitary, it appears essential to separate the operating or "substantive" task from the organizational or "procedural" problem. Our hypothesis may be stated thus: Imposition of certain restrictions on the communication channels available to a group affects the efficiency of the group's performance, *not directly* by limiting the potential efficiency of task performance with optimal organization in the given net, *but indirectly* by handicapping their ability to organize themselves for efficient task performance.

Our empirical study involves basically a replication of Leavitt's work, but with essential modifications to permit us to study separately the group's performance of its operating task and its organizational task.

Each of 56 groups operated in the laboratory for about two hours, during which time the task was repeated twenty times. A fifteen minute pre-experimental training period was employed to reduce the task problem to a mere routine before the experiment with each group began. Each of the twenty task trial periods continued until the task was completed, the time required for completion varying from six minutes to less than one minute. Intertrial periods of not more than two minutes between successive trials provided the groups with an opportunity to solve the organizational problem. By signalling arrangement, the subjects were allowed to terminate the intertrial periods at any time they wished before the end of the two minutes allowed them.

The alternation of task trials with interpolated intertrial periods was suggested by analogy with the traditional "trial-after-trial" design employed in learning experiments in individual psychology. In terms of this analogy, the intertrial periods may be interpreted as "learning" periods, during which the subjects may work on their organizational plans. The task trial periods are then "test" periods, in which the progress of the group is tested by measuring the speed and efficiency of task performance.

Except for the explicit separation of trial and intertrial periods, our procedures paralleled those used by Leavitt and Smith. As will be indicated later, our results substantially replicate their findings.

In Section I, we shall set forth the theory from which our central hypothesis is derived. In Section II, we shall test the hypothesis with the new empirical data we have obtained. In Section III, we shall compare our findings with those of Leavitt.

I. SEPARATION OF OPERATING TASK FROM ORGANIZATIONAL PROBLEM: THEORETICAL CONSIDERATIONS

Description and Analysis of the Operating Task

Simon, Smithburg and Thompson argue that communication in a decision-making organization is two-fold:

Communications must flow to the decision center to provide the basis for decision, and the decision must be communicated from the decision center in order to influence other members of the organizations whose cooperation must be secured to carry out the decision.[5]

The Bavelas-Leavitt-Smith problem requires both processes. In the operating task each person must record which one symbol of six is held in common by the five members of the group. The same six symbols are used on each trial. At the beginning of each trial, each person is given a card on which is printed five symbols; the other symbol is missing. Each individual is lacking a different symbol. The problem on a given trial is to have the group discover and record the one symbol that no one is lacking. The variation in distribution of the symbols from trial to trial in this investigation followed the schedule used by Leavitt.[6]

Note the two-fold communication process involved in this line task:

(a) Information Flow: At the beginning of a trial each participant knows only one of the missing symbols—his own. The participant need not know all of the missing symbols for solution of the problem. Each group member needs to know only the answer to record it, or to "carry out the decision." There must, however, be sufficient exchange of information so that one or more persons can form the solution, or "make the decision."

(b) Decision Flow: Once an answer is formed by one or more persons in the group, it must be communicated to those who are unable to, or do not, make the decision themselves.

Before proceeding with the analysis, let us explain the mechanics of the experiment.[7] The subjects, seated around a circular table, were separated from each other by five vertical wooden partitions (Figure 1). They were able to pass messages to each other through interconnecting slots. During the operating trials, they interchanged messages written on pre-coded cards which contained places for information and answers. During the intertrials the subjects were free to write to each other uncoded messages on blank cards about their organizational arrangements. This meant the group could determine who would send information to whom, who would make the problem-decision, who would send the decision-order to whom.

When a subject had recorded the problem-decision, this fact was immediately conveyed to the experimenter. When all five persons had re-

---

[5] H. A. Simon, D. W. Smithburg, and V. A. Thompson, *Public Administration*, (New York: Knopf, 1950) p. 220.

[6] Leavitt, *op. cit.*, Figure 2, p. 40.

[7] Further details about the procedures of the experiment are available, and can be obtained from American Documentation Institute, 1719 N Street, N.W., Washington 6, D.C.

corded the solution, the trial automatically ended and the intertrial period began. The subjects were silent throughout the experiment, communicating only through pre-coded cards during the operating task trial and by written "free" messages during the intertrial periods. This enabled us to obtain a complete record of their communications.

Two hundred and eighty male freshmen engineering students at Car-

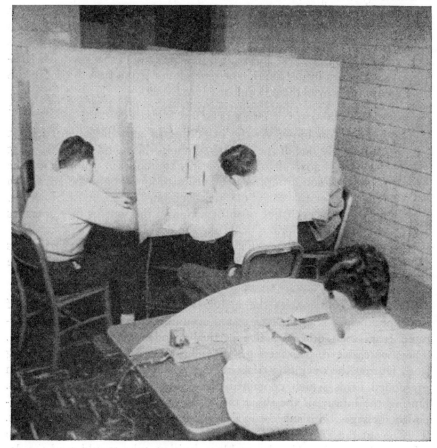

FIG. 1. Experimental Set-up

negie Institute of Technology served as subjects for the experiment. The two hours devoted to the experiment were a required substitute for one class and an out-of-class assignment in a required freshman course. Most subjects were not very well acquainted with each other. Each group was composed of one man from each of the Carnegie Tech quintiles of the American Council on Education Psychological Examination; scores were available on all subjects. This insured an equating of groups with respect to intellective ability.

Given this task, how will a five-man group divide the labor involved in completing it? (1) It is possible either for everyone to *exchange information* with everyone else, or to have the missing symbol information collected by a single person. (2) It is possible either for everyone to *form the solution*, or to specialize to the extent that only one person forms the solution. (3) It is possible either to complete the problem without *circulation of answers* (since each may form the solution by himself), or to have the answer relayed from a single central source. But which organizational arrangement will be adopted? To what extent does the choice depend upon communication restrictions?

In replicating Leavitt's experiment, we have used two of his restrictions —those constituting his extreme cases: the "Wheel" and "Circle." In addition, we established groups that were entirely free of restrictions, using an "All-Channel" pattern. The three communication nets are illustrated in Figure 2. Our initial problem is to discover how the net restric-

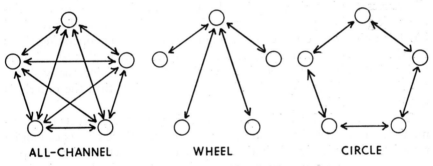

ALL-CHANNEL   WHEEL   CIRCLE

FIG. 2. Open Channels Used in the Three Nets

tions imposed upon the various groups determined the organizational patterns used in performing the operating task.

Consider first the Wheel net: If the task is divided so that the "spokes" send their information to the "hub," the latter can make the decision and in turn return answers to the spokes. We will call this pattern a "two-level hierarchy." Next, consider the Circle net: If two neighbors send their information to their opposite neighbors, who in turn relay this information with their own to the fifth member of the circle, this "key-man" can make the decision and relay the answer back through the "relayers" to the "endmen." We will call this pattern a "three-level hierarchy." In the All-Channel nets, either one of these procedures—or others —may be used. It can be shown that the arrangements just described are the most efficient of those available. Although the use of the relays in the three-level hierarchy involves time delays, the minimum number of messages required by the two- and three-level hierarchies is the same—eight.

A channel-usage analysis, as suggested by Bavelas' model, misleads one into supposing that the two-level hierarchy is twice as efficient as the three-level hierarchy; for the two-level arrangement obviates the need for relaying, both when sending information and when sending answers. But the task is more than one of merely sending messages—messages must also be received, collated, and prepared. To compare efficiencies we need an estimate of the time required to perform *all* these task elements, and in proper sequence. To provide such a comparison of "limiting" efficiencies, of the two-level and three-level hierarchies, Hellfach made a methods-time measurement analysis of the task.

Methods-Time Measurement is a time-study procedure used widely in industry.[8] It involves identification of the basic motions that must be used to perform the operating task, and assignment of standard time values to these basic motions. Hellfach analyzed each position in the five member group both when arranged as a two-level hierarchy and when arranged as a three-level hierarchy. Then he drew up a composite analysis of the operation for the two types of arrangement, making appropriate allowances for idle time required by the sequential nature of task elements (e.g., a "relayer" cannot transmit information until he has received it). His estimates are presented in Figure 3. He predicts operating times for the two-level hierarchy of .445 minutes; and for the three-level hierarchy of .437. The difference between these times (which actually shows the three-level hierarchy to be slightly more efficient than the other!) is not consequential.

These theoretical considerations argue that, whatever effects the communication nets may have upon task performance, these effects cannot be traced to the objective limitations imposed by the net restrictions upon the groups. If a group can discover and use the optimal organizational pattern among those permitted it by the net restrictions, the minimum time achieved by a Circle group should be substantially the same as by a Wheel group. Even more interesting, the analysis leads to the conclusion that there is no difference in the limiting times for task performance between groups in the unrestricted net (the All-Channel groups) and those in the restricted nets (the Wheel and Circle groups).

Description and Analysis of the Organizational Problem

The theoretical discussion to this point supports our hypothesis that the communication restrictions affect the task performance of the groups not directly, but only indirectly by influencing the ability of the members to organize themselves for optimum performance in their line operation. Now let us examine in more detail the way in which the nets pose organizational problems.

Twenty of our 56 groups were allowed to operate without any imposed

[8] H. B. Maynard, G. J. Stegmerten, John L. Schwab, *Methods-Time Measurement* (New York: McGraw-Hill), 1948.

restrictions on their internal communication. The other groups operated within communication restrictions that reduced the number of channels for communication to approximately half of those available in the unrestricted groups. The two sets of restrictions differed from each other, however, in their effects upon the ease with which the groups might develop interaction patterns. The 15 Wheel groups were restricted in such

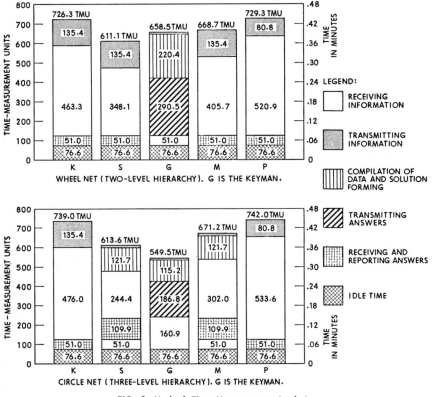

FIG. 3. Methods-Time Measurement Analysis

a way that their organizational problems should be minimal. The 20 Circle groups were restricted with almost the same degree of severity (in terms of number of open channels), but in a way that made their organizing tasks comparatively difficult.

The three variations in the nets had different relationships to the organizational problem:

(a) The "All-Channel" Net: The organizational problem for an All-Channel group is not simple. The group has an advantage in that each member can communicate with the others, so that no relaying of messages through a "second party" is required. Yet the lack of communication restrictions means an open field with almost too many opportunities—a total of 20 one-way channels. Accordingly, each All-Channel group has the difficult job of developing its own restrictions—deciding that certain available channels will *not* be used. In addition, each of the members is equipotential with respect to his place in the communication net; no one member has initial advantages from his place in the net with respect to the functional requirements of the task.

(*b*) *The "Wheel" Net:* The Wheel groups are in a net in which the communication restrictions reduce the difficulty of the organizational problems to a minimum, yet hold the requirements of the operating problem constant. If the task is divided so that the spokes send their information to the hub, the latter can solve the problem and in turn send answers to the spokes. There would be no need for relay through a "second party." All the "unnecessary" channels have been blocked, so that their elimination is no longer part of the organizational problem. This reduces the number of open channels from 20 to 8, some 60 per cent. The existence of a hub means that the positions in the net are not equipotential—the four spokes are disadvantageously situated. Should a spoke attempt to become the solution former, he would need to depend upon the hub for relaying both information and answers. In addition, in such a situation, the organizational problem as to which of the four equipotential spokes would become the problem-solver would need to be handled. But, if the hub becomes the solution-former, the wheel requires a minimum of organizing effort for solving the operating task.

(*c*) *The "Circle" Net:* This net retains the symmetry of the positions in the free situation but restricts drastically the number of communication opportunities. Simultaneously it makes imperative the use of a relay system, or three-level hierarchy, within the organization. No potential solution-former has immediate access to the other four missing symbols. His two neighbors need to relay their information and that of their other neighbors to him. Along with this impediment to organizing, there is the added difficulty that no one position is more or less advantageously situated for handling the solution-forming requirement. The reduction of available channels in this net is from 20 to 10, just 50 per cent.

A comparison of the way in which the three characteristics of the net differ from net to net is diagrammed in Table 1. From this display it is

TABLE 1
COMPARISON OF THE THREE NETS
Characteristic Differences among the Three Nets

Characteristics	All-Channel	Wheel	Circle
Number of Open Channels	20	*8*	*10*
Number of Symmetric Positions	5	*4*	5
Minimum Number of Relays Necessary	0	0	*2*

(The italic entries indicate the points at which the Wheel and Circle nets contrast with the All-Channel net.)

possible to make rough estimates of the difficulty of the organizational problem for groups in each type of net. The Wheel groups would have the least difficulty, for they have no channels to eliminate, no relays to establish, and already have one person occupying a dominant position in the net. The All-Channel groups would have the next grade of difficulty, since the elimination of excess channels and the evolution of one person as solution-former are both required, yet relays need not be established. The Circle groups should have the most difficulty, for they need both to establish relays and to evolve an asymmetrical arrangement among the positions. They also must do some eliminating of unneeded channels, although this last requirement is minimal. The difficulty of the organizational problem in the different nets varies as follows:

$$\text{Wheel} < \text{All-Channel} < \text{Circle} \,.$$

This analysis of the organizational difficulty yields a surprising outcome in indicating that an unrestricted net (All-Channel) in itself involves difficulties, and that restrictions in communication may be helpful (Wheel) or harmful (Circle) in the evolution of organizational structures, depending upon the nature of the relation of the restriction to the organizing and operating tasks.

This concludes our theoretical analysis. It develops our basic hypothesis by arguing that the communication restrictions have no direct effect upon performance of the operating task. It argues that the communication pattern has important effects upon the difficulty the group will encounter in organizing itself—but that the restricted patterns do not necessarily make for more difficulties than the unrestricted patterns. Now let us examine the empirical data to determine whether they support or refute our theoretical analysis.

II. THE EMPIRICAL FINDINGS

Performance Times in Operating Task Trials

As far as the subjects were concerned, the time required for each trial was the central focus of the experiment. In the instructions they were told, "Your team is competing with the other five-man groups to see which group is fastest at getting the answer. The shorter the time, the better your team score."

The average time per trial for the three types of groups is presented in Figure 4. The Circle groups are clearly slower than the Wheel groups after the first trial. The All-Channel groups occupy an intermediate position. A statistical check of the differences between the types of groups was made on the cumulative time required for the 20 trials as shown in Table 2. This table also includes the averages for the three fastest trials within each type of group. Although the Circle groups are significantly different from the Wheel and All-Channel groups for both measures, there was a significant difference between the Wheel and All-Channel groups on only the "total time" measure.

The effects of the communication nets upon the time criteria were

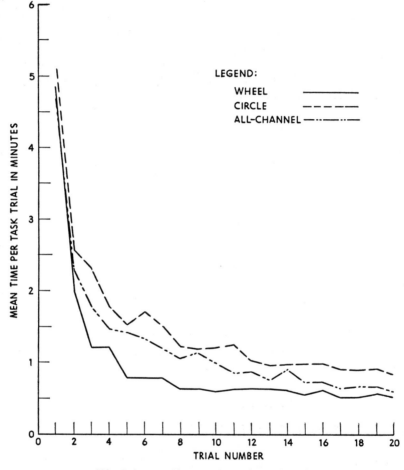

FIG. 4. Average Time per Group for Task Trials

marked. During the 8th trial, the Wheel groups had already reached the levels eventually attained by the All-Channel groups in their last few trials. At the end of the 20 trials, the Circle groups were using some 60 per cent more time than the Wheel groups in performing their operations. During the course of the twenty trials, there were performance differences between the All-Channel and Wheel groups that eventually disappeared.

These findings hint that the Wheel groups, with the least difficult or-

TABLE 2
TIME OF TASK TRIALS
(Minutes)

Net	TOTAL TIME		AVERAGE OF THE THREE FASTEST TRIALS	
	Mean	Standard Deviation	Mean	Standard Deviation
All-Channel ($n = 20$)	24.38	4.82	0.54	0.15
Wheel ($n = 15$)	19.12	3.09	0.46	0.08
Circle ($n = 21$)	29.45	5.08	0.73	0.15

Significance of Difference Between Nets

	Total Time	Average of the Three Fastest Trials
Wheel—All-Channel	$t = 3.06$ $p < .01$	t is not significant
Circle—All-Channel	$t = 3.17$ $p < .01$	$t = 3.96$ $p < .001$
Wheel—Circle	$t = 6.20$ $p < .001$	$t = 5.69$ $p < .001$

ganizational problem, organized earliest; that the All-Channel groups, with a more difficult job, organized more slowly, but were eventually performing as well as the Wheel groups; that the Circle groups had difficulty in organizing, not reaching optimum performance within the 20 trials allowed. These differences correspond to the variations in organizational difficulty imposed by each net. The more difficult the organizational job, the less rapid was the evolution toward efficient task performance.

But are these differences actually due to the organizational arrangements, or are they (contrary to our theory) due to differences in task operation times in the optimal arrangements? An answer to this question requires an analysis of the organizational arrangement developed by each group. What are the message sending and receiving patterns that developed in the groups over the course of the twenty task trials? To examine the growth of miniature organizations, it is necessary first to determine whether there *is* a definite pattern; this is the *stability* problem. Then, if there is a pattern, we can examine how the message sending became differentiated into a particular *organizational arrangement*.

Organizational Stability

The *interaction pattern* is defined for a given trial in terms of whether or not one or more messages were sent from a particular person to another —that is, which of the open channels in the net were used, and in which direction, by the five persons constituting the group. Because a message card might have two or three units of information on it, the actual number of cards sent over a channel was of no literal significance.[9]

The *stability* of the interaction among the five persons is defined as the extent to which a given pattern persisted over a sequence of trials. An analysis was made of every trial for each group, contrasting the pattern of information messages with the pattern of answer messages. Then each sequence or "segment" of four trials within each group was classified as to stability of the pattern of channels used. The five segments chosen coincided with questionnaire periods: trials 1 to 4, 5 to 8, 9 to 12, 13 to 16, and 17 to 20. Information and answer messages were analyzed separately.

In making the analyses, we diagrammed the stability of the segment by using a solid arrow for those channels which were always used or never used, respectively, during the four trials constituting the segment. We employed a broken arrow for those channels which were used once, twice, or three times during the four trials. This notation is illustrated in the examples of Figure 5. Three degrees of stability were defined as follows:

1. Stable: A segment was termed "stable" with respect to its information or answer messages, if only one or two of the channels were used "intermittently," i.e., once or twice, or three times during the segment, regardless of the number of channels available. See the examples a, b, and c in Figure 5.
2. Semi-Stable: A segment was termed "semi-stable" with respect to its information or answer messages when three to one-half of the total open channels were used intermittently. As noted previously, there were 20 open channels in the All-Channel, but only 8 in the Wheel and 10 in the Circle nets. See examples d, e, f in Figure 5.
3. Unstable: A segment was termed "unstable" with respect to its information or answer messages when more than half of the open channels were used intermittently. See examples g, h, i in Figure 5.

These criteria were developed after considerable exploratory work with other ways of setting the boundaries between classes.

The results of the classification of the segments are presented in Table 3. The groups in All-Channel nets are significantly less stable than those

---

[9] Because of our use of pre-coded message cards, it was easy for the senders to include more than one piece of information on each card. For example, a subject might have forwarded to his neighbor in a single message not only his own missing symbol but also information about what one, two, or three other persons were missing. Examination of the messages suggested we would lose little in the analysis of counting the number of message cards exchanged during the course of the experiment rather than tallying each item. A sample of the messages received by each of the 220 subjects during a single trial was checked for correspondence between the number of items of information and the number of message cards involved. The sample was drawn evenly from all 20 trials for all three types of groups. The product-moment correlation between items and cards was $+.84$. This reliability was considered satisfactory, obviating the labor involved in a count of items.

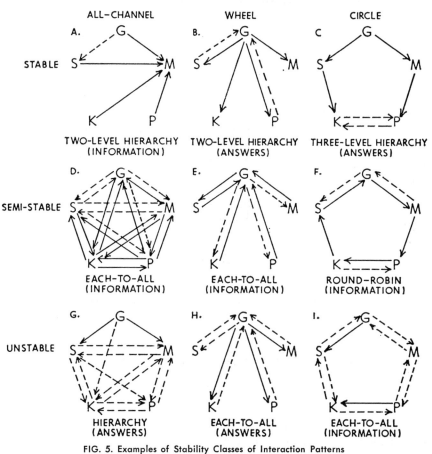

FIG. 5. Examples of Stability Classes of Interaction Patterns

placed in more restricted nets. The Wheel groups are more stable than the Circle groups. Thus, the more restrictions imposed on the communication channels, the more stable the groups. The stability level reflects the number of open channels (see Figure 2), although the difference between the All-Channel and Circle groups fails to approach a 20 to 10 ratio.

Organizational Arrangement

Now it is possible to characterize the organizational arrangements embodied in the semi-stabilized and fully stabilized interaction patterns. Qualitative analysis of the diagrams obtained from the stability analysis of the segments indicates that some groups operated without much division of labor or specialization of positions, utilizing all available channels. Others developed a more highly differentiated group structure.

1. *All-Channel groups.* These groups fell into two types of patterns in *exchanging information.* Three groups stabilized their information ex-

TABLE 3
PERCENTAGE DISTRIBUTION OF SEGMENTS INTO STABILITY CLASSES

Net	Stability Classes	Information Exchange	Answer Exchange	Total Exchange
		%	%	%
All-Channel Segments ($n = 200$)				
	Stable	40	28	34
	Semi-Stable	45	37	41
	Unstable	15	35	25
Wheel Segments ($n = 150$)				
	Stable	90	91	91
	Semi-Stable	10	9	9
	Unstable	0	0	0
Circle Segments ($n = 210$)				
	Stable	81	21	51
	Semi-Stable	17	29	23
	Unstable	2	50	26

Significance of differences in stable vs. combined semi-stable and unstable segments between nets

	Information		Answer		Total	
Wheel–All-Channel	$x^2 = 43.3$	$p < .001$	$x^2 = 68.7$	$p < .001$	$x^2 = 45.5$	$p < .001$
Circle–All-Channel	$x^2 = 36.2$	$p < .001$	x^2 is not significant		$x^2 = 11.5$	$p < .01$
Wheel–Circle	$x^2 = 2.8$	$p < .10$	$x^2 = 85.1$	$p < .001$	$x^2 = 64.2$	$p < .001$

change with each person sending messages about his missing symbols to all others. Such an "each-to-all" pattern (semi-stable in this case) is illustrated in Figure 5d. By the end of the experiment, the other seventeen groups had clearly differentiated into two-level hierarchies, like the one illustrated in Figure 5a.

The All-Channel groups displayed more variety in the organization of their *answer exchanges*. One group, in which each person had given information on his missing symbol to every other person, exchanged almost no answers. Another group developed an each-to-all pattern; still another developed a relatively unstable but clearly differentiated hierarchy in exchanging answers. Six groups developed quite stable three-level hierarchies in exchanging answers. The remaining eleven groups used two-level hierarchies, the inverse of the patterns they used in exchanging information.

In the All-Channel groups, taken as a whole, there is approximately the same kind of organization in the information exchanges as in the answer exchanges and both showed considerable differentiation.

2. *Wheel groups*. The imposition of the Wheel net resulted in the use of very stable two-level hierarchy patterns for information and answer exchanges after the first three or four trials.

During the initial trials in four Wheel groups, the *information exchanges* were of the "each-to-all" type, the person in the hub sending out information to all participants, as in Figure 5e. In the other eleven groups, the hubs during the initial trials sent information to only one or two persons, and ceased to send out any information about their own missing symbols after the fourth or fifth trial.

In *exchanging answers*, all of the fifteen groups very rapidly developed a two-level hierarchy in which the person at the hub alone sent messages to the others in the group. Seven of the groups used this pattern for all twenty trials; another seven groups contained persons who sent answers to the hub during the early trials, as in Figure 5b. One group during its first four trials sent no answers back and forth, inasmuch as each person used his "information-received" to come to a solution independently.

There was early and very rapid development of the organizational arrangement in the Wheel groups, the information exchange being mirrored by the answer exchange.

3. *Circle groups.* The groups placed in Circle nets had much difficulty in organizing their structures. Although the groups *in toto* were not as unstable as the All-Channel groups there was still considerable variation in channel usage. The Circle groups tended to organize in the more "primitive," each-to-all patterns, as in Figure 5i.

The bulk of the Circle groups—13 out of the 21—used each-to-all patterns in exchanging their *information* messages. Eight groups used somewhat more differentiated patterns. A first step toward differentiation is found in four groups which evolved semi-stable "round-robins" in which information is passed around the circle, as illustrated in Figure 5i. A fifth group used a round-robin from trials 2 to 10, but in trial 11 one of the participants stopped forwarding his information, reconstituting the round-robin pattern into a chain. Three other groups developed the most specialized information exchange structures of all the Circle groups—ending their last three trials in three-level hierarchies.

The Circle groups differentiated more decidedly in their *answer exchange* patterns. Only one group remained in an each-to-all pattern. Ten of the 21 groups temporarily organized into special patterns, exhibiting much fluidity. Their answer exchange fluctuated from one form of a hierarchy to a semi-stable "each-to-all" to another form of hierarchy, often ending in a semi-stable each-to-all. The remaining ten groups differentiated into three-level hierarchy arrangements as in Figure 5c.

There was considerably more differentiation among the answer exchange patterns than among the information patterns. But by and large, there was a marked tendency for the Circle groups to remain primitive and undifferentiated. Almost half of the stability and semi-stability reported above (Table 3) for these Circle groups was gained by the consistent use of each-to-all patterns.

Table 4 displays the development of the differentiation throughout the course of the experiment for all three types of groups. The bulk of the organization of differentiated patterns is accomplished by the end of the 12th trial in the All-Channel groups. The imposed net helped the Wheel groups to achieve their organizations by the end of the 4th trial. The relative lack of differentiation in the Circle groups is vividly portrayed in Table 4;

TABLE 4

DEVELOPMENT OF ORGANIZATIONAL STRUCTURES
(Percentage of Segments Differentiated)

		SEGMENT				
Net	Type of Organization	Trials 1–4	Trials 5–8	Trials 9–12	Trials 12–16	Trials 17–20
		%	%	%	%	%
All-Channel Segments (n = 200)						
	Differentiated*	5	42	78	85	88
	Each-to-All	28	20	10	8	7
	Undiscernible	67	38	12	7	5
Wheel Segments (n = 150)						
	Differentiated*	77	100	100	100	100
	Each-to-All	23	0	0	0	0
	Undiscernible	0	0	0	0	0
Circle Segments (n = 210)						
	Differentiated*	14	26	33	48	48
	Each-to-All	52	40	33	38	36
	Undiscernible	34	34	34	14	16

* "Differentiated" means using such patterns as the two- or three-level hierarchy, round-robin, and chain.

their high variability from one pattern to another is also reflected in the fluctuation of the percentage of differentiation from segment to segment.

The Critical Observations

We are now in a position to subject our central hypothesis to a clear-cut test. It follows from the hypothesis that groups placed in different nets will experience different degrees of difficulty in attaining an efficient organizational arrangement (say, a two-level or three-level hierarchy); further that the *speed of task performance will be approximately the same in all groups that do in fact attain an efficient arrangement, regardless of the net in which they are operating.* Finally, the average time required for task performance in the efficiently organized groups should, at least approximately, be that predicted by the M-T-M analysis.

Either a two-level hierarchy or a three-level hierarchy (or both) was a possible organizational arrangement within the nets studied. The empirical data indicate that three or more groups within each of the nets actually did organize themselves into one or the other type of hierarchy either for information exchange or answer exchange or both. *When the groups were so organized, they performed their operating tasks efficiently.*

The fifteen Wheel groups (all of which we may regard as "efficiently organized") averaged .46 minutes for their three fastest trials (cf. Table 2). This is almost identical with Hellfach's estimate of .45 minutes in his M-T-M analysis (*supra*, p. 237).[10]

The data for the organized Circle and All-Channel groups are decisive in confirming the hypothesis. The average speeds in the three fastest trials in the 17 All-Channel groups that developed two- or three-level hierarchies in both information and answer sending ranged from .34 to .68 with a mean of .489 minutes. The corresponding range for the three Circle Groups which developed a three-level hierarchy was .40 to .52 minutes, with a mean of .472 minutes. The differences between the means of the organized All-Channel and Circle groups and Hellfach's estimate are not statistically significant; nor are the differences between the means of these groups and the mean of the Wheel groups.

The correctness of the other half of the hypothesis—the relative difficulty in achieving efficient organizational arrangement in different nets —follows immediately. Only groups working within the Wheel net were able to achieve a hierarchical organization with ease. As already reported, all fifteen such groups did so, and usually during early trials. Of the twenty All-Channel groups, seventeen did so, but generally later in the sequence of trials. Only three of the 21 Circle groups developed hierarchies. These findings confirm the theoretical analysis (*supra*, p. 240), which predicts that the difficulty in organizing will be greatest in the Circle groups, next in the All-Channel groups, and least in the Wheel groups.

Thus, both parts of our basic hypothesis are confirmed: The communication nets affected the efficiency with which the groups performed only through the influence they exerted upon the ability of the groups to develop adequate organizations.

III. REPLICATION OF LEAVITT'S EXPERIMENT

Our experimental procedure used the Wheel and Circle nets in common with Leavitt. We ran our groups 20 trials, in contrast with his 15 trials. He

---

[10] It is perhaps worth emphasizing that Hellfach's estimate does not in any way derive from the data of the experiment. The standard times he used for the task elements were derived from M-T-M tables drawn up from industrial time and motion studies. Although Hellfach was acquainted with the results of the experiment, his estimate was built up from data expressed in hundredths of hours, rather than minutes; he converted his totals to minutes as the last step. Hence, there was little opportunity for the experimental data to influence his estimate, even unconsciously.

did not match his groups on the basis of intellective ability. In his experiment, the task and non-task messages were written contemporaneously during the operating trial itself, without benefit of a pre-coded task message card; we had the non-task messages written during an intertrial period.

Despite these differences, our empirical results in the main are a forthright confirmation of the work that was replicated. Leavitt found the fastest trial in his Wheel and Circle groups to average .53 and .83 minutes respectively.[11] His figures are comparable to those presented in Table 2. The Wheel groups in both his and our experiments took a little more than 60 per cent of the time taken by the Circle groups for completion of their fastest task runs. The absolute differences in times between the two experiments may be artifacts produced by apparatus dissimilarities and by the fact that Leavitt's data include the time used for sending non-task messages.

Leavitt's figures on volume of messages are comparable to the sum of our task *and* intertrial messages. In the Wheel nets our groups sent an average of 177 messages per group during the first 15 trials compared with Leavitt's 166, our average being about 7 per cent greater. In the Circle nets our groups sent an average of 389 messages over the first 15 trials and intertrials compared with Leavitt's 372, ours being about 2 per cent greater. These differences are not statistically significant. The ratio of information messages to answer messages in the two experiments is similar. Thus, our use of an intertrial period seems not to have disturbed the situation as originally designed by Bavelas, Leavitt, and Smith.

Despite our ability to replicate Leavitt's results as far as the time and volume of messages are concerned, there is a striking difference with regard to the extent to which our Circles organized. Leavitt says, "The *circle* showed no consistent operational organization. Most commonly messages were just sent in both directions until any S(ubject) received an answer or worked one out."[12] Although our Circle groups were much less differentiated than groups in the other two nets, many consistent patterns evolved. The latter difference between our results and Leavitt's cannot be ascribed to the fact that we ran twenty rather than fifteen trials. At the end of the 15 trials, as Table 4 demonstrates, some 48 per cent of the segments had already differentiated into stable or semi-stable interaction structures. We cannot explain these differences.

Our results on the Wheel groups are identical with those obtained by Leavitt. All of his groups, like ours, used the same interaction structure, the information pattern being the inverse of the answer pattern. Like our groups, his evolved the organization by the fourth or fifth trials.

---

[11] Leavitt, *op. cit.,* Table 2, p. 43.
[12] Leavitt, *op. cit.,* p. 42.

IV. SUMMARY

This replication and extension of the work of Bavelas, Leavitt, and Smith on communication patterns in task-oriented groups enabled us to separate the effect of communication nets upon the performance of an operating task by the group, and upon the ability of the group to organize itself for this operating task. The particular nets we explored did not create differences among the groups with respect to the time needed for handling the operating task when an optimal organization was used. These same nets did introduce important differences in the organizing difficulties encountered. In this way we obtained an estimate, which can be refined through further experimentation, of the relative difficulties introduced by demanding the establishment of non-symmetric "keyman" roles, the organization of relay points, and the elimination of unnecessary channels.

The current management literature on the topic of communication leaves one with the expectation that certainly a reduction in communication restrictions should lead to a more adequately functioning organization. Yet, our findings in this experiment indicate that assertion of a one-to-one relationship between effective functioning and freedom in communication is unwarranted. Had our analysis not separated the organizational problem from the operating problem, it would have seemed paradoxical that complete freedom of communication is at times more limiting than restricted communication. The findings warn the practical communications expert working in industry or government that a change in communications structure may have quite different consequences for the efficiency of immediate day-to-day operations, and for the ability of the organization to handle changes in its own structure.

28. A STUDY OF CONFLICT IN THE PROCESS, STRUCTURE, AND ATTITUDES OF LATERAL RELATIONSHIPS*

R. E. Walton, J. M. Dutton and H. G. Fitch[1]

ABSTRACT

This paper is a report of a comparative field study of managers interacting in six plants of a decentralized manufacturing firm. This study is part of a larger projected investigation which embraces the formulation and testing of a theory of lateral relationships in organizations, including the antecedents and consequences of conflict and collaboration in lateral relationships in over a dozen plants of a large industrial firm.

The study presented here is confined to a theoretical and empirical examination of the internal characteristics and dynamics of the lateral relationship itself and in particular the manifest conflict and collaboration. The theory postulates a relationship among measures of the joint decision process between units, the structure of interunit interactions, and certain attitudes toward the other unit. The authors provide statistical evidence of these relationships in the covariance among aspects of relationships measured from the field study.

INTRODUCTION

How do departmental managers who are functionally interdependent, such as production and sales officials, relate to each other behaviorally? These lateral relations are not shown on the typical organization chart, because there is no authority or accountability bond between them. Yet this lateral relationship is often one which greatly preoccupies the participants. These relations often have crucial influence for the quality of the performance of each unit and for the performance of the larger organization. Moreover, the maintenance of this relationship is more difficult precisely because it has to be fashioned in the absence of an authority relationship.

Just as one may distinguish between different styles or patterns of influence in superior-subordinate relations, one can observe differences in patterns which develop between managers in their lateral relations. A relatively large amount of organizational literature has treated vertical relations, but fewer attempts have been made to focus on lateral relations.

---

* The authors wish to acknowledge the support for study provided by Purdue Research Foundation and the comments of D. C. King of the Department of Psychology, Purdue University.

[1] Purdue University, Lafayette, Indiana.

Work on lateral relations includes Blau (1954), Burns (1954), Shepherd and Weschler (1955), Gregson (1957), Simpson (1959), Dalton (1959), Chapple and Sayles (1961), Crozier (1961), Levine and P. White (1961), H. White (1961), Landsberger (1961), Litwak and Hylton (1962), Strauss (1962), Seiler (1963), and Strauss (1964).

Walton (16) distinguishes two opposite types of relationships, and refers to them as "distributive" and "integrative." (See Table 1.) The theory which underlies these constructs is concerned with lateral relationships in which the parties are required to enter into a joint decision-making process. Three components of such relationships are considered: (1) information exchange in the joint decision process; (2) the structure of interunit interactions and decision making; and (3) attitudes toward the

TABLE 1

COMPONENTS AND CHARACTERISTICS OF CONTRASTING TYPES OF LATERAL RELATIONSHIPS

Component of Relationship	TYPE OF LATERAL RELATIONSHIP:	
	Integrative	Distributive
1. Form of joint decision process between units	Problem solving: Free exchange of information. Conscientious accuracy of information transmitted.	Bargaining: Careful rationing of information. Deliberate distortion of information.
2. Structure of interaction and interunit decision framework	Flexible, informal, and open.	Rigid, formal, and circumscribed.
3. Attitudes toward other unit	Positive attitudes: trust, friendliness, inclusion of other unit.	Negative attitudes: suspicion, hostility, disassociation from other unit.

other unit. The theory consists of a set of propositions about how the modal process utilized by the participants for making joint decisions (i.e., bargaining versus problem solving) influences and, in turn, is influenced by various aspects of the interunit structure (e.g., frequency of interaction) and interunit attitudes (e.g., trust.)

The specific assumptions and rationale which underlie each of the propositions studied here are elaborated as we examine the field data. In the most general sense, however, the chain of assumptions which explains the tendency toward the "distributive" syndrome is as follows: (1) That goal competition between participants engaged in joint decision making induces the parties to practice concealment and distortion in their exchange of information with the effect that their joint decision making takes on the character of bargaining; (2) that in order to effectively and systematically ration, conceal, and distort information each party attempts to place limitations on his counterpart's interactions and other behavior in order to make the other more predictable and keep him within certain boundaries;

(3) that the sentiments which result from the way information is handled (concealment, distortion, etc.) and the way interactions are patterned (circumscribed, rigid, etc.) are suspicion, hostility, and so on; further, that these negative attitudes have a feedback effect which tends to reinforce the same interaction structure and information-handling pattern.

A review of the literature relevant to each of the elemental propositions (Walton, 16) indicated that for some individual propositions an abundance of supporting evidence exists, especially from the experimental literature on small groups. For other propositions (many of which were deduced from bargaining theory) few, or no, systematic findings exist. In any event, the greater majority of these propositions had not been studied in organizational settings, nor had any number of them been studied simultaneously in any setting.

We report here a study which provides one test of the theory. Standardized measures were applied to data gathered from six plants of an industrial organization. All six plants were similar in purpose, design, and function. We measure characteristics of the emergent lateral relationship between sales and production in each plant. The findings are correlated statistically and are analyzed for their theoretical implications.

THE ORGANIZATIONAL SETTING

The Peerless Company was a large decentralized manufacturer of fabricated metal door and window products.[2] Each of the company's more than one dozen fabricating plants, together with its corresponding sales district, was a geographically decentralized unit responsible for obtaining and producing customer orders in a profitable manner. Top management established detailed instructions for company plant personnel regarding plant organization, pricing of products, purchasing of materials, and methods of selling and producing. Production and sales personnel were evaluated, in part, on how well they accomplished their respective assigned tasks and, in part, on the overall performance of their district.

The general plan of organization, which was similar for all plants, established the principal positions, activities, and interactions for the sales and production groups. Responsibility for district operations was formally divided between two major departments, sales and production, each headed by a district manager. No general manager was responsible for both these activities at the district level. In fact, these two functions had separate lines of authority for the next two higher levels of the organization. The plant production group was expected to produce orders in an economical, timely and defect-free manner. The district sales group was

---

[2] Company data are disguised for protection of the firm and employees.

responsible for obtaining orders at profitable prices and for maintaining service contracts with customers.

The formal organizational plan included forces toward both cooperation and competition between sales and production. On the one hand, the activities of production and sales at the district level had to be coordinated to achieve maximum sales at the least cost. The success of the district as a whole could be furthered by a mutually cooperative approach to the critical problems, such as the scheduling of orders and quality control. Top management expected such an approach. On the other hand, production and sales personnel did not report to a common superior below the vice-president level. Thus, each unit could devote its entire attention to its own task, even at the cost of excluding the task of the other unit. Also, the several executives who supervised district sales and production managers could make differing interpretations of the general organizational plan— e.g., with respect to performance criteria, their emphasis on the routing of information to the district, or their leadership style. Even subtle differences in interpretation could have significant influence on the tendencies toward conflict or collaboration at the district level.

In many areas the task interdependence of the two departments was such that decisions or activities which improved the performance of one department did so at the expense of the performance of the other department. For example, one sequence of orders through a plant might best accommodate the sales department's operating objective of servicing customers in a certain way, whereas another schedule of orders would minimize plant costs (a factor on which production was measured). Four such areas of recurring decisions were:

1. The decision processes used to determine what orders to accept from customers and, also, what new designs to offer customers.

2. The decision process used to determine shipping dates and to schedule orders through the plant, including crisis scheduling.

3. The decisions and decision processes used in the prevention and detection of quality defects, in the disposition of defective material, in recording errors and losses and in following them up (including assigning responsibility and taking appropriate action).

4. The decision process used to determine in what way, if any, shift and overtime schedules will be altered to meet unusual incoming order requirements.

It was generally recognized throughout the company organization that there were differences between the emergent relationship patterns of the various districts. There was reason to believe that the patterns ranged along a continuum from close collaboration to serious conflict. In accordance with our theory we believed that significantly different modes of joint decision making would be central to these divergent patterns and that the other structural and attitudinal dimensions we identify in a lateral relationship would covary in a predictable way.

RESEARCH METHODS

Field Procedures.   The sample of plants investigated comprised six from more than a dozen similar company plants. The sample was selected in consultation with company officials as a representative group in terms of size, city-rural location, product-mix, age of plant, geographical location, and general performance of plant management.

The research strategy involved obtaining certain minimum quantifiable data on interunit relations which could be subjected to statistical analysis and also obtaining a complete case study on each plant to produce insights into the qualitative nature of the dynamics of the relationship.

The field research focused on how the two parties, production and sales at each of the plants, made and implemented decisions in the four areas of mutual concern listed above. The field data was produced by semistructured field interviews at each of the plants in the sample. The researchers employed a field interview guide which outlined the four decision areas to be investigated and suggested ways to probe these areas during the interview. The field interview guide also provided questions on procedural and attitudinal aspects of the relationship between sales and production at each plant. Interviews were conducted with 15 to 20 key personnel of the two departments, such as the sales manager, production manager, field sales manager, plant superintendent, field salesmen, foremen, shipping manager, sales service manager, production control manager, and office clerks.

The data produced by the field interviews were subjected to further analysis through the use of a structured plant relationship questionnaire. This instrument was designed to extract data from the field interviews in an organized and quantified form, by providing scaled responses to questions on each of the three major component areas of the relationship. Using this questionnaire the researchers coded the data according to the operational definitions used in the study. Each of the three researchers completed separate plant relationship questionnaires for each plant in the sample. One of the researchers was not involved with the collection of the field data and completed the standardized questionnaire on the basis of the extensive field notes of the other researchers.

The Form of the Data.   Each question in the structured questionnaire was designed to discriminate a particular dimension of process, structure or attitude. Raw data "scores" on this questionnaire were coded in a range from 0 to 4 as illustrated by the following sample question and response:

How channeled are the contacts between production and sales? That is, how many persons interact directly and significantly with persons from the other department in joint decision making?

		x				
0	1	2	3	4	x	

(Confined to minimum number who could physically carry the load)				(Involves all those who could contribute to decision)	(Inadequate knowledge)

This response was coded as 2. In the case of measures of process, a zero indicated an extremely competitive decision process (bargaining), while a 4 represented an extremely cooperative process (problem solving). In the case of attitude and structure variables, such as the one illustrated above, the end of the scale hypothesized to accompany an extremely competitive decision process was also valued as a zero, and vice versa.

Steps were taken in the research procedures to reduce the tendency for the researchers to perceive selectively and otherwise bias their ratings in the direction of consistency according to the model. First, in developing field notes on the semistructure interview they worked as nearly at the verbatim level as possible, permitting reanalysis of the original data. Secondly, in scoring structured questionnaires they imposed upon themselves the requirement that they cite the raw data on which they were scoring a particular item.

Each of the plant visits involved enough contact time with a sufficiently large number of persons that the researchers were confident of the validity of the findings. In their plant visits each researcher interviewed plant and office as well as management personnel in both production and sales. Interviews were concentrated within a two- or three-day period to minimize information exchange between the subjects. The interviewers concentrated on collection of recent anecdotal data which could be cross-checked across interviews. In this the researchers were assisted by the high degree of interdependence and the consequent frequency of joint decisions in the four areas selected for the study.

Statistical Methods. Nonparametric statistics were employed to analyze the resultant rated and coded data for several reasons. The study was exploratory with a small N of 6. The assumptions underlying most nonparametric statistical tests are less stringent than the assumptions for equivalent parametric tests. Nonparametric tests assume the research has only achieved ordinal as against interval or ratio measurement. And the power of the principal test used, the Spearman Rank Order Correlation, approximates the power and usefulness of parametric tests for the same sample size (**12**).

Rater Reliability. To what extent did the three raters independently agree that they saw the same thing in each plant? Refer to Table 2. Each column contains means across all questions pertaining to one of the three aspects of working relationships. Inspection of the figures shows a close association among the mean scores assigned to each of these areas within

TABLE 2

SUMMARY OF MEANS FOR ALL PLANTS, ALL COMPONENTS, ALL RATERS

| | COMPONENTS OF THE WORKING RELATIONSHIP: | | | | | | | |
| | Decision-Making Process (8 Questions) | | Decision-Making Structure (9 Questions) | | Attitudes (8 Questions) | | | |
Plants	Question Means	Raters and Question Means	Question Means	Raters and Question Means	Question Means	Raters and Question Means	Rater Means	Over-all Plant Means
Buckland								
Rater A	2.2		2.3		2.3		2.3	
Rater B	2.3	2.2	1.9	1.9	1.9	1.9	2.0	2.0
Rater C	2.3		1.4		1.4		1.7	
Laketown								
Rater A	1.2		2.7		0.1		1.4	
Rater B	1.3	1.2	1.1	1.8	0.5	0.5	1.0	1.2
Rater C	1.2		1.7		0.9		1.3	
Valleydale								
Rater A	1.8		2.4		2.0		2.1	
Rater B	2.3	2.2	2.0	2.4	1.9	2.3	2.1	2.3
Rater C	2.6		2.8		2.9		2.8	
Bowie								
Rater A	3.6		3.0		3.4		3.3	
Rater B	3.9	3.5	3.2	3.1	3.4	3.4	3.5	3.3
Rater C	3.2		2.9		3.3		3.1	
Elgin								
Rater A	0.9		1.2		0.1		0.8	
Rater B	1.6	1.3	1.2	1.1	1.4	0.9	1.4	1.1
Rater C	1.4		0.8		1.2		1.1	
Pine City								
Rater A	3.1		3.5		3.1		3.2	
Rater B	2.8	3.1	3.0	3.3	3.0	3.3	2.9	3.2
Rater C	3.4		3.2		3.9		3.5	
Means		2.3		2.3		2.0		2.2 Grand Means

each plant by each of the three raters. A nonparametric statistical test of the similarity of the three rater's ratings of these plants (Friedman Two Way Analysis of Variance) was computed. This test showed similarity at the .05 level of significance.

THE FINDINGS

A model showing the theoretical relationships which exist among different broad aspects of the working relationships between the two units is presented in Figure 1. Each of the boxes—Process, Structure, and Attitude—represents a panel of variables. The arrows connecting them imply a causal sequence, with solid lines for primary influences and dotted lines for feedback effects.

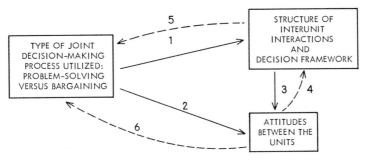

FIG. 1. Model of Factors in the Lateral Relationships

The propositions which comprise the theory take the following illustrated general form:

"Conflict in the decision process will tend to result in a joint decision structure which involves relatively few participants from each unit."

The theory indicates how two variables are expected to covary in a given relationship and also which variable tends to produce a change in the other. In many instances the influence is mutual. However, the limited hypotheses that are tested by our statistical analysis do not indicate the causal sequence. The statistical analysis tests only covariance of measures. Thus, the findings of this study test the question of internal characteristics of working relationships but not internal dynamics. We now take up, in turn, the relationship between process and structure (arrows 1 and 5); process and attitudes (2 and 6); and structure and attitudes (3 and 4).

Generalized Nature of Conflict in Joint Decision Making. The type of joint decision process employed by the two parties is of primary importance. We distinguish between a bargaining type and a problem-solving type of joint decision process. In bargaining, the orientation of the parties is, "How much will I gain or lose, and how much will the other party gain or lose?" The problem-solving process occurs when the parties explore problems for solutions which will yield maximum gain to both parties considered together.

At the heart of these two opposite concepts of decision making is information-processing activity. How much information do the departments share with each other at every stage in arriving at decisions, and how much consideration do they give to information about the other's problems? In the problem-solving process maximum use is made of voluntary, open, accurate discussion of an area which affects both groups, and both participants attempt to avoid consequences that would present new difficulties for either person. Just the opposite is involved in the bargaining process. Each participant attempts to gain maximum information from the other but to make minimum disclosures himself, often trying to manipulate and persuade the other. Each examines the implications of actions for possible unfavorable consequences for himself, but does not concern himself with the consequences for the other. Thus, the problem-solving process is exploratory and problem-centered while the bargaining process is defensive and issue-centered. The problem-solving process is a form of collaboration and the bargaining process one of conflict. It follows from this that the first aspect of conflict in a working relationship which we may examine is the amount of information sharing in the joint decision-making process.

The theory includes the hypothesis (not shown explicitly in Figure 1) that *there will tend to be a similar type of decision process in each of the substantive areas of joint decision making.* We predicted that there would be similar degrees of conflict in each of four critical areas of joint decision making in Peerless plants: (1) order acceptance and innovation, (2) normal and crisis scheduling, (3) quality control and error follow-up, and (4) hours scheduling and volume. Each question on a decision-making process was in two parts: Part A related to the amount of accurate information exchanged, and Part B related to the amount of consideration given by one unit to the preferences of the other unit.

In each of these areas there was some incentive for the two parties to enter into decision making competitively and some incentive to take a cooperative approach. However, for a given plant there was not necessarily the same mixture or balance between these two motivations in all four areas. Why should the parties tend to adopt the same type of decision process in the several areas, rather than differentiate the approach according to the amount of conflict potential? The answer is derived from the total theory presented here, namely, that given an average amount of conflict in decision making, certain structural forms and attitudes develop, and these tend to feed back and affect all interunit decision areas, at least those involving the same liaison personnel.

Evidence bearing on the question of the unitary nature of the decision process is contained in Table 3, which contains a standard deviation of means analysis. While all of the standard deviations in Table 3 are small, the standard deviations for the decision process column appear to be appreciably smaller than those for either decision-making structure or attitudes. This conclusion is supported by the data in the last three rows of Table 3, with decision process showing the smallest range of standard deviations.

In addition to supporting the above hypothesis, this conclusion justifies treating decision process measures as a single variable. The mean of all decision process question ratings for each plant was used to obtain correlations between decision process on the one hand and attitudinal and structural variables on the other.

TABLE 3

STANDARD DEVIATIONS OF QUESTION MEANS

| | STANDARD DEVIATIONS: | | |
Plant	Decision-Making Process	Decision-Making Structure	Attitudes
Buckland	.28	.91	.46
Laketown	.24	.80	.49
Valleydale	.29	.68	.46
Bowie	.19	.56	.47
Elgin	.26	.91	.19
Pine City	.35	.42	.42
Means of standard deviations of means	.27	.71	.42
Range of means	.16	.499	.30
Standard deviation of standard deviations	.049	.180	.103

Joint Decision Process and Structure Variables: Hypotheses and Findings

Arrows 1 and 5 in Figure 1 indicate a reciprocal influence between the joint decision process which is employed by the two groups and the structural characteristics of the relationship which develops between the parties. Specifically, we expect problem solving to be accompanied by: a high rate of interdepartmental interactions, many persons entering into these interactions; few limitations regarding the type of contact a person may have with the other department; infrequent appeals to higher officials; decision rules which are informal, loosely interpreted, and constantly changing; and considerable experimentation in decision procedures and organization. In contrast, a decision-making process which is bargaining in nature would be accompanied by an interaction and decision-making structure with opposite characteristics.

These hypotheses are based on the assumption that the interaction structures and decision frameworks are adopted because they facilitate a particular decision process being utilized by one or both of the parties. The influence is reciprocal between the decision process, as we define it, and most of the above structure variables. The reasoning underlying this statement will be supplied as we discuss each of these structure variables and its relationship to the decision-making process.

1.1. The first structure variable concerned the amount of work-related interaction between representatives of the two subunits. Because the problem-solving process involves more complete information exchange, and because interpersonal interaction is a vehicle for these exchanges, we expected a problem-solving decision process to lead to more task interactions than a bargaining process. Conversely, minimum contact between

TABLE 4

Hypotheses and Correlations between Decision Process and Structure Variables

Hypothesis	Predictions about Structure— The More Competitive the Process:	Correlation
1.1a	The less frequent the task interaction: PM–SM	.77
1.1b	The less frequent the task interaction: PCM–SSM	.65
1.2	The fewer persons interacting	.88*
1.3	The more limitations on activities in the other's work space	.54
1.4	The more use of extraplant relationships	.94†
1.5a	The more formalized the decision rules	.88*
1.5b	The more strictly are decision rules followed	.65
1.5c	The more static are the decision rules	.54
1.6	The less experimentation with procedures	.65

Based on the Spearman Rank Order Correlation coefficient.
* Significant at the .05 level.
† Significant at the .01 level.

departments would prevent problem solving from occurring, even if it were otherwise preferred. The hypothesis, generally stated, was that *the more competitive the decision process, the less frequent the task interaction*. The hypothesis was applied to predict the relative interaction frequency between the two departments in each plant. Our measures were applied to two specific sets of role relationships between production and sales personnel: the production manager–sales manager interaction; and the production planning manager–sales service manager interaction. These two pairs of positions comprised the main joint decision-making and implementing channels. The process measure and this structure variable were positively correlated for both pairs of managers (see Table 4), with values of .77 and .65 respectively.

The correlations in Table 4 were obtained by ranking the six plants according to (*a*) decision process and (*b*) frequency of task interaction, and then comparing the two rank orderings. Although, given the N of 6, a correlation of .77 does not achieve statistical significance at the .05 level, it does indicate that the rank orderings differed only by the reversal of two pairs of plants (see Table 5). The trend of the findings supports the hypothesis.

1.2. *The more competitive the decision process, the fewer persons interacting in the joint decision structure.* Less extensive contact is assumed to be deliberate and tactical to the competitive process—channeling communications to the other unit through one person from one's own unit is a way of increasing control of the information which reaches members of the other unit. Control may be exercised either to minimize the amount of information sent or to systematically bias the information. If too many persons are allowed to participate it is more difficult to keep their stories straight or consistent. This point is consistent with bargaining theory, but has not been tested experimentally. If one considers the

TABLE 5

COMPARATIVE RANK ORDERING OF PLANTS ON CONFLICT IN
DECISION-MAKING PROCESS AND FREQUENCY OF INTERACTION*

Plants	Rank Ordering for Decision Process	Rank Ordering for Frequency of Interaction
Bowie	1	2
Pine City	2	1
Buckland	3	3
Valleydale	4	4
Elgin	5	6
Laketown	6	5

* Spearman Rank Order Correlation of .77.

other direction of influence, a less extensive interaction structure allows less of the information required for effective problem solving.

The potential for decision-making contacts between members of the two units in each Peerless plant was considerable. For instance, in considering new designs, salesmen, designers, plant superintendents, foremen, estimating and specifications personnel possessed information of potential value of achieving commercially attractive and economical new designs. Therefore, we predicted that the number of such persons involved in interunit decision making would vary depending upon the type of process used.

The hypothesis was supported by one of the three highest correlations involving structure and process (.88). The contrasting interaction modes of the two plants with the most cooperative decision process and the two with the most competitive process are shown in Figure 2.

1.3. The third structure hypothesis is that *more competitive decision processes tend to be accompanied by more rigid prescriptions and pro-*

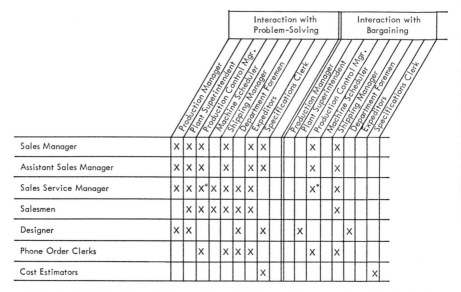

	Interaction with Problem-Solving								Interaction with Bargaining							
	Production Manager	Plant Superintendent	Production Control Mgr.	Machine Scheduler	Shipping Manager	Department Foremen	Expeditors	Specifications Clerk	Production Manager	Plant Superintendent	Production Control Mgr.	Machine Scheduler	Shipping Manager	Department Foremen	Expeditors	Specifications Clerk
Sales Manager	X	X	X		X		X	X			X	X				
Assistant Sales Manager	X	X	X		X		X	X			X	X				
Sales Service Manager	X	X	X*	X	X	X	X				X*	X				
Salesmen		X	X	X	X	X	X					X				
Designer	X	X			X		X			X					X	
Phone Order Clerks			X		X	X	X				X	X				
Cost Estimators							X									X

FIG. 2. Contrasting Interunit Contacts Where Problem Solving versus Bargaining Is Used

In all plants the greatest number of contacts involved interaction between the sales service manager and the production control manager.

scriptions about interunit contacts. We assumed that a unit involved in a competitive decision process will attempt to limit the contacts which can be initiated by the other unit, controlling who may contact, what types of contacts are allowed, and what procedures must be followed. Again, these would be deliberate and tactical for the control of information which reaches the other unit. There would be less reason for such control in a cooperative decision process.

Some of the prescribed limitations on movement reported in the six plants were: (1) All personnel must go through the sales service manager and production control manager on all matters relating to scheduling. (2) Salesmen must not go into the plant. (3) Sales clerks must not call the production control manager. (4) Salesmen must not try to influence shipment by calling foremen. (5) Production personnel must not show errors in quality to sales personnel, except under prescribed conditions. (6) Production people must not call customers.

Although the field research revealed a positive correlation between the degree of competitiveness of the decision process and the number of limitations placed on the activities of personnel within the plant or office space of the other department, the correlation was one of the lowest in this section and failed to give statistically significant support to the hypotheses.

This lower correlation was due to the fact that such limitations are sometimes used in an effort to prevent or reduce a source of conflict and not solely as a tactic in playing out existing conflict. These contacts are often a source of irritation between personnel and, if the top officials in the two departments want to control the hostilities, they may impose limitations on movement—at least for a period of time.

1.4. The fourth structure variable refers to how self-contained is the two-unit decision structure in terms of how little or how much the two units invoke influence from outside the system. The hypothesis is that *the more competitive the decision process between units, the greater the use of outside sources*. A competitive decision process makes relatively greater use of coercion (versus persuasion) than does a cooperative process. Assuming the outside authorities are agents with coercive capacities, we would expect competitive units to make more frequent attempts to utilize this source of power. This pattern could be complicated or obscured if the outside authorities are also contacted because they possess information relevant to the decision process not otherwise available to the unit.

We predicted that the more competitive the decision process, the more frequently will officials use hierarchical relationships, such as referring their question to their respective superiors in an attempt to invoke their influences. (See Hypothesis 1.4, Table 4.) This correlation is the highest (.94) and supports the hypothesis at the .01 level of significance.

1.5. The fifth hypothesis is concerned with the flexibility of the decision rules used to make decisions affecting both subunits: *decision rules which are developed to handle mutual problems in a competitive, as contrasted with a cooperative, decision process will tend to be more formal, more strictly applied, and less frequently changed*. This proposition is based on the assumption that in a competitive situation (where one might be taken advantage of) he will attempt to gain certainty and security through more rigid procedures.

The departments in Peerless tended to develop decision rules governing such matters as the minimum lead time on orders accepted by production, the conditions under which sales could make a request which interrupted a production schedule, the types of speciality items which sales could accept from customers and expect production to run, etc. These emergent rules ranged from guidelines to hard and fast agreements with a virtually contractual status.

The hypothesis contains three parts as reflected in the predictions for the Peerless plants. "The more competitive the decision process: (1.5*a*) the more formal will be the rules which govern decisions of mutual interest; (1.5*b*) the more strictly will the decision rules be applied; and (1.5*c*) the more static will be the decision rules." (See the relevent correlations in Table 4.) They reveal that part *a* of this hypothesis, formalization of decision rules, was supported by a particularly high statistical correlation, and the other two measures were correlated in the direction predicted.

1.6. A sixth hypothesis was that *the more competitive the decision process, the less experimentation there will be in decision practices, procedures, and organization*. This proposition is similar to the one above.

The status quo is more familiar, and a departure contains uncertainty from which a disadvantaged unit might not be able to retreat in a competitive situation.[3] Some instances of experimentation in procedures in the Peerless districts included: (1) consolidating the office staffs of the two departments or reallocating office duties; (2) developing or adopting new techniques for keeping track of the progress of orders through the plant; (3) creating a quality control position; etc. Our prediction for the plants was that our measures of this type of experimentation and decision process would vary together. (See Table 4.) The correlation here is .65.

Decision Process and Attitudes: Hypotheses and Findings

2.0. Referring again to Figure 1, Arrow 2 indicates that the cognitive decision process also influences the affective character of the relationship. The general proposition is that the conflictful decision process, bargaining, leads to negative affect; and the collaborative problem-solving process leads to positive affect. There are two aspects of bargaining that contribute to the development of negative affect. The first aspect is the very presumption of differentiated interests which underlies the competitive process. The second aspect is the activities required by the process, such as withholding or distortion of information and persistent disagreement over decision criteria.

The feedback effect represented by Arrow 6 indicates that intergroup attitudes directly affect the orientation the parties have toward the decision process, apart from the structure in which it occurs. If a person feels friendly toward another person, he is more likely to behave cooperatively in the decision process. Under conditions of hostility and low trust, persons will adopt competitive behavioral strategies in the decision process. For example, one adopts decision patterns which involve furnishing another less information and less accurate information when one dislikes or distrusts the other. In addition to the logic inherent in not sharing vital information with a person one doesn't trust, there are two other reasons for the tendency cited here.

The first reason is that negative attitudes lead to perceptual distortions which in turn lead to competitive decision making. Recall that the decision process involves identifying problems, searching for solutions and their consequences, and choosing among solutions. The decision process tends to move through these phases. If at any point in the process one or both of the units perceive substantial disagreement between them, they will tend to shift the decision process toward its more competitive form; hence

---

[3] This hypothesis appears at first to contradict the conclusion of H. White (17) that recurrent revisions of formal structure and reallocation of responsibilities for programs seemed to be distinctive concomitants of chronic conflict. Considering the two findings together, one might conclude that conflict will be accompanied by relatively fewer changes initiated by the participants themselves and relatively more changes initiated by organizational superiors to those in conflict.

perception is important as a mediating psychological process between attitudes and behavior in the joint decision process.

Negative attitudes result in more competitive behaviors in the decision process for a second basic reason. Strong negative affect often leads one unit to interfere with the other unit's activities, just to frustrate the latter's goal achievement. The parties tend to lose sight of their own positive goals and assume "whatever hurts them must be good for us." Thus, if negative attitudes originate apart from the decision process, they can nevertheless be expected to impinge upon it.

The relationship between orientation to the decision process and interpersonal or intergroup attitudes is a close one. There is persuasive reasoning that the influence between the joint decision process and interunit attitudes is both strong and mutual. Moreover the review of empirical literature revealed many laboratory studies of behavior in small groups that generally supported these ideas.

In summary, the hypotheses were that *more competitive decision process will be accompanied by intergroup relations with less cohesiveness, more prejudice, less trust, and less personal friendliness.* Our operations for these admittedly interrelated hypotheses are indicated, respectively, by the four questions below, each rated by the researchers on the basis of the interviews and interview notes.

2.1. How frequently did the persons interviewed use "we" and "they" as a way of distinguishing between "good motives" and "bad motives" or "their side" and "our side," rather than as a form of convenience?

2.2. How did a representative from one group talk about the other group, or a member of the other group? Specifically, how frequently was the other group labeled with an unflattering stereotype or characterization?

2.3. Did the anecdotes related to the interviewer portray behavior that was consciously helpful or deliberately detrimental?

2.4. How frequently did key representatives of the groups initiate nonwork-related interaction with their counterparts? (This included nonwork-related chit chat during work-related contacts.)

Each of these four questions was applied to two pairs of positions: first, the production manager (PM) and his counterpart from sales (SM); second, the production control manager (PCM) and the sales service manager (SSM). The results of the statistical analysis are presented in Table 6. The correlations in the direction predicted are all significant at the .05 level or better. The uniformly strong confirmation of these hypotheses is not surprising in view of the number of the different psychological mechanisms which we have cited above as tending in the same direction.

Although all four measures (each intended to get at different component attitudes) were sensitive to the degree of competitiveness in the plants, the absolute magnitude of one measure, in particular, needs to be placed in perspective. Actually, nonwork-related interactions between PM–SM and PCM–SSM were not prominent at plants with either competi-

TABLE 6

HYPOTHESES AND CORRELATION BETWEEN DECISION PROCESS
AND ATTITUDE VARIABLES*

Hypothesis	Predictions about Attitudes— The More Competitive the Process:	Correlation
2.1a	The stronger the differentiation of "we" and "they": PM–SM	.94†
2.1b	The stronger the differentiation of "we" and "they": PCM–SSM	.88‡
2.2a	The more unflattering stereotypes of the others: PM–SM	.88‡
2.2b	The more unflattering stereotypes of the others: PCM–SSM	.88‡
2.3a	The more telling of detrimental anecdotes about the others: PM–SM	.94†
2.3b	The more telling of detrimental anecdotes about the others: PCM–SSM	.94†
2.4a	The fewer the nonwork-related interactions with the others: PM–SM	.88‡
2.4b	The fewer the nonwork-related interactions with the others: PCM–SSM	.88‡

* Based on the Spearman Rank Order Correlation coefficient.
† Significant at .01 level.
‡ Significant at .05 level.

tive or cooperative decision making. The two parties did not have a great deal in common, socially, a fact of some importance to the orientation of the parties.

In addition to an absence of factors which might lead to social interaction, the pressures arising out of task interaction seemed to have an effect. The members of the sales and production groups at all plants indicated an unrelenting daily pressure on their relationship and generally did not evidence any interest in additional nonwork-related interaction.

Structure and Attitudes: Hypotheses and Findings

3.0. Arrow 3 in Figure 1 indicates that interunit attitudes are affected by certain variables regarding the structure of interactions and the framework for making decisions. Briefly, more frequent and more extensive interaction patterns, more freedom regarding intergroup contacts, more flexible and informal decision rules, more flexibility in organizational procedures, and less resort to use of outside influences—all these tend to result in more favorable attitudes in the working relationship. A reciprocal effect is postulated by Arrow 4—in other words, if one starts with favorable attitudes, one can expect an interunit structure with the features given above to develop.

The reasoning which underlies each of these specific propositions will be set forth below together with the findings of the field research. Because the several attitude measures produced such similar results, we use the mean as a single attitude score for the rank order correlation with the six structure variables.

3.1. The first proposition that *frequent interaction leads to positive sentiments and vice versa* is one that has been advanced frequently. However, the relationship probably does not hold if the parties do not have some preferences—likes, dislikes, values—in common. The more salient differences are in preferences (such as undeniable goal conflict in the joint decision process), the more likely frequently required interactions are to lead to great negative affect. Moreover, under certain conditions of task and goal interdependence, negative affect may well lead to more frequent contacts. For example, in labor-management relations, hostile institutional relations may require more frequent meetings to present grievances, to monitor the activities of the other, to place demands for changes in the terms of the relationship, and to express personal hostility. We acknowledged that a similar phenomenon could emerge in production-sales relations where the parties are interdependent not only for decision making but also for implementation activities. However, because of the high correlation between competitiveness of process and interaction (Table 4), we also obtained high correlation in our measures of interactions and attitudes. The correlations are shown in 3.1*a* and 3.1*b* in Table 7.

3.2. The second proposition in this section is that *a structure which involves more extensive contacts between the units will be accompanied by positive attitudes.* More points of contact between the two units lead to less differentiation in the joint structure. Also more points in the other's organization through which one unit may gain information lead to a more

TABLE 7

Hʏᴘᴏᴛʜᴇsᴇs ᴀɴᴅ Cᴏʀʀᴇʟᴀᴛɪᴏɴ ʙᴇᴛᴡᴇᴇɴ Aᴛᴛɪᴛᴜᴅᴇ ᴀɴᴅ Sᴛʀᴜᴄᴛᴜʀᴇ Vᴀʀɪᴀʙʟᴇs*

Hypothesis	Predictions about Structure— The More Negative the Attitudes:	Correlation
3.1*a*	The less frequent the work-related interaction PM–SM	.82†
3.1*b*	The less frequent the work-related interaction PCM–SSM	.77
3.2	The fewer persons interacting	.94‡
3.3	The more limitations on activities in the other's work space	.60
3.4	The more use of extraplant relationships	1.00‡
3.5*a*	The more formalized the decision rules	.77
3.5*b*	The more strictly are decision rules followed	.77
3.5*c*	The more static are the decision rules	.60
3.6	The less experimentation with procedures	.77

* Based on the Spearman Rank Order Correlation coefficient.
† Significant at .05 level.
‡ Significant at .01 level.

reality-based perception of the other, presumably resulting in fewer negative stereotypes and more trust. The influence is probably mutual because where there is hostility in the relationship, those members of a unit not absolutely required to interact will prefer to avoid contact with the other unit.

This structure variable did correlate significantly with the mean attitude score (rank order). The correlation was .94 and significant at the .01 level.

3.3. A *relatively greater number of norms or rules governing the interunit contacts will be accompanied by negative attitudes.* This structure dimension is not a measure of how frequent or extensive is the interaction pattern, but rather of how rigidly it is prescribed in terms of who may be contacted and for what purposes. High degree of freedom in this respect tends to result in more favorable attitudes. We assume that a person from one unit will tend to contact a member of the other unit when that interaction will yield the initiator some benefit and not to make contacts which yield him no benefit. Thus, in our third proposition relating structure and attitudes, we reason that the person with freedom to initiate contacts at his discretion tends to engage in rewarding interactions and thus tends to develop favorable attitudes toward the other.

The hypothesis is based on other assumptions or reasoning. If one is prevented from interacting with another unit at his own discretion, he can gain less relevant information about the other's motives or activities; as a further consequence he is denied a basis for building up his trust in the other and his stereotypic views of the other are less likely to be challenged. Also, if there is less spontaneity allowed in initiating the interaction, the interaction is less likely to lead to friendliness.

The positive correlation of attitudes and this structure variable was .60, the lowest of any structure variable. The explanation for this somewhat lower correlation is similar to that of process and the same structure variable (see 1.3).

3.4. The fourth proposition is represented by Arrow 3: *A decision structure which involves more frequent use of requests by one or the other unit for the intervention of persons outside the two-unit system will be accompanied by less favorable attitudes between the two units.* We expect these results because the pattern implies that the two units are less exclusively interdependent, and hence there are fewer reasons for identifying themselves with the two-unit system as a whole. Also this pattern is likely to lead to distrust on the part of the other, especially if he is not always warned in advance of the first's appeals. There was perfect rank order correlation (1.00) between these variables in the six-plant sample studied.

3.5. *More antagonistic attitudes between units will be associated with more formalized decision rules, stricter enforcement of the rules, and more static rules.* We assume that flexibility and informality in the structure of the situation facilitates the development of positive feelings. Also, if attitudes are antagonistic the participants who interact will tend to prefer the formality and certainty which can be built into the decision situation; where mutual trust and understanding are absent formal rules become more important in carrying on one's affairs.

Attitude and structure variables achieved the following positive correlations: (*a*) more negative attitudes and more formalized decision rules, .77; (*b*) more negative attitudes and stricter observance of decision rules, .77; (*c*) more negative attitudes and more static decision rules, .60.

3.6. *More antagonistic attitudes between units will be associated with less experimentation with procedures.* If there is low trust, there is likely to be a conservative attitude toward new arrangements which might have unforeseen disadvantages for one and advantages for the other. This reasoning is quite closely related to that regarding the influence of a competitive decision process on experimentation with procedures; and therefore the correlation of this structure variable and attitudes may result from their respective functional relationships with decision process. In any event, the experimentation and attitudes were positively correlated: .77.

SUMMARY AND CONCLUSIONS

The data yielded a comparative ranking of all six plants, combining all measures of process, structure and attitude. This result, given in Figure 3, shows two plants located near the distributive end of the continuum, two plants near the integrative end, and two plants in the middle range of values. This result came as somewhat of a surprise inasmuch as, prior to the field study, the authors had felt that relationships would tend rather strongly toward one or the other end of the continuum. There was some evidence that at least one of these midrange relationships was not stable. Nonetheless, at the time of the study they clearly fell in the indicated midrange on the majority of separate measures.

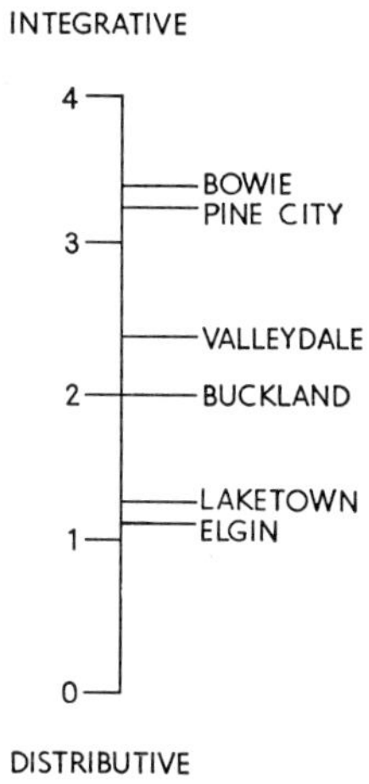

In general the data from the six plants supported the predictions of the study. We have seen that some combinations of variables were more sensitive to each other than others. The correlations of decision process and attitudes were the highest, indicating that decision process and attitude were more sensitive to one another than were either structure and process or structure and attitude. We have seen explanations for the lower correlation of structure and process, and similar reasons may explain the lower agreement in the case of structure and attitude.

Fig. 3. Overall Plant Ranks.

The findings produced quite high positive rank order correlations between the various dimensions of a lateral relationship which were hypothesized to relate to each other. They tended to range between .54 and .96 (and in the case of two particular variables a perfect 1.0 correlation occurred in the ranking of the six plants).

Because of the small N, only P scores above .88 are statistically significant at the .05 level of confidence. Roughly half of our individual findings achieved this level of confidence. However, considering that all of the hypotheses tested in this setting were supported by at least a P of .54, it seems reasonable to take seriously even these relatively lower individual correlations. Certainly, taken as a whole, we believe these findings present strong confirmation of the theory.

The positive correlations are not surprising when one considers the strong rationalistic basis of the individual hypotheses. It would be surprising if the findings were otherwise. Nevertheless, we are cautious in predicting as close a correlation in the same dimensions of lateral organizational relationships in other settings. We must acknowledge that the particular setting selected was an especially appropriate setting for the theory.

What was "appropriate" about the Peerless setting? First, the two departments were relatively equal in terms of power and status; they were highly interdependent with each other in the performance of their respective core activities; this interdependence was unusually mutual and symmetrical composed to intraorganizational relationships in general; in both cases their relationship with the other was more important than with any third organizational unit. Second, as a pair of departments at the district level, they were geographically isolated from other districts and from the home office; they did not report upward through the same chain of command; the nature of the districts' internal interaction and decision-making structure was not prescribed for them. The first set of conditions (relating to the type and importance of the interdependence) increased the magnitude of the forces toward a lateral relationship, in general, which is influenced by the requirements of their particular joint decision-making tasks. The second set of conditions (relating to automony at the district level) ensured that the parties were relatively free to respond to these forces and not constrained by unrelated organizational requirements. Where these conditions are weaker we would expect lower rank order correlations but trends in the same direction.

REFERENCES

1. BLAU, P. M. "Cooperation and Competition in a Bureaucracy," *American Journal of Sociology*, 59 (1954) pp. 530–35.
2. BURNS, T. "The Directions of Activity and Communicating in a Departmental Executive Group," *Human Relations*, 7 (1954), pp. 73–97.

3. CHAPPLE, E. D. AND SAYLES, L. R. *The Measure of Management: Designing Organizations for Human Effectiveness*. New York: Macmillan Co., 1961.
4. CROZIER, M. "Human Relations at the Management Level in a Bureaucratic System of Organization," *Human Organizations*, 20 (1961), pp. 51–64.
5. DALTON, M. *Men Who Manage*. New York: John Wiley & Son, 1959.
6. GREGSON, R. A. M. "Interrelation of Attitudes and Communications in a Sub-divided Working Group," *Occupational Psychology*, 31 (1957), pp. 104–12.
7. LANDSBERGER, H. A. "The Horizontal Dimension in a Bureaucracy," *Administrative Science Quarterly*, 6 (1961), pp. 298–332.
8. LEVINE, S. AND WHITE, P. E. "Exchange as a Conceptual Framework for the Study of Interorganizational Relationships," *Administrative Science Quarterly*, 5 (1961), pp. 583–601.
9. LITWAK, E. AND HYLTON, L. F. "Interorganizational Analysis: A Hypothesis on Co-ordinating Agencies," *Administrative Science Quarterly*, 6 (1962), pp. 395–420.
10. SEILER, J. A. "Diagnosing Interdepartmental Conflict," *Harvard Business Review*, 5 (1963), pp. 121–32.
11. SHEPHERD, C. AND WESCHLER, I. R. "The Relation between Three Interpersonal Variables and Communication Effectiveness," *Sociometry*, 18 (1955), pp. 103–110.
12. SIEGEL, S. *Non-Parametric Statistics for the Behavioral Sciences*. New York: McGraw-Hill Book Co., 1956.
13. SIMPSON, R. L. "Vertical and Horizontal Communication in Organization," *Administrative Science Quarterly*, Vol. 4 (1959), pp. 188–96.
14. STRAUSS, G. "Tactics of Lateral Relationship," *Administrative Science Quarterly*, 7 (1962), pp. 161–86.
15. ———"Work-Flow Frictions, Interfunctional Rivalry, and Professionalism: A Case Study of Purchasing Agents," *Human Organizations*, 23 (1964), pp. 137–49.
16. WALTON, R. E. "Theory of Conflict in Lateral Organizational Relationships," paper presented to the Conference on Operational Research and Social Sciences, Cambridge, England, September 14–18, 1964.
17. WHITE, H. "Management Conflict and Social Structure," *American Journal of Sociology*, 67 (1961), pp. 185–91.

29. WORKFLOW FRICTIONS, INTERFUNCTIONAL RIVALRY, AND PROFESSIONALISM: A CASE STUDY OF PURCHASING AGENTS*

GEORGE STRAUSS[0]

THE LARGE corporation has been traditionally viewed as a unified organization of employees working together in close coordination toward a common objective. An alternative conception is that of the corporation as a mass of competing power groups, each seeking to influence company policy in terms of its own interests, or, at least, in terms of its own distorted image of the company's interest.[1] This article uses the Purchasing Agent as a case example to illustrate the forms which rivalry among functional groups can take and to show how this rivalry, among other factors, encourages PA's (as they are commonly known) to seek to become "professionals."[2] Specifically the following processes seem to be involved, as I shall discuss in order:

1. The PA seeks to increase his status and power in the organization; particularly he seeks to influence the terms in which requisitions are given him.

2. This leads him into conflict with functional groups which are adjacent to him in terms of workflow.

3. In this conflict the PA looks instinctively for help from higher management, but higher management gives him less attention than he would like.

4. For this reason (among others) he turns to professionalism, which helps bolster his self-image and which, hopefully, strengthens his position in interdepartmental conflict.

The first of the final two sections points out that the PA is not alone in

* Reprinted from *Human Organization*, Vol. 23, No. 2 (Summer, 1964), pp. 137–149.

[0] George Strauss is in the Institute of Industrial Relations, University of California, Berkeley.

[1] De Witt C. Dearborn and Herbert A. Simon, "A Note on the Departmental Identification of Executives," *Sociometry*, XXI (June, 1958); Henry A. Landsberger, "The Horizontal Dimension in Bureaucracy," *Administrative Science Quarterly*, Vol. VI, No. 3 (December, 1961), pp. 299–332.

[2] The research methodology, which emphasized on-the-job observation and intensive interviews (supplemented by a questionnaire, $N = 144$), is reported in George Strauss, "Tactics of Lateral Relationship: The Purchasing Agent," *Administrative Science Quarterly*, Vol. VII, No. 3 (September, 1962), pp. 161–86. This previous article dealt with the PA's day-to-day tactics in dealing with other departments; here I shall be more concerned with overall strategy.

his quest for status and his turn toward professionalism; the second deals with the implications of interfunctional rivalry and organizational efficiency.

A word of warning: the discussion which follows by no means presents a balanced picture of the PA and his relations with other departments. I intend to paint with a broad brush and to emphasize areas of conflict rather than of harmony. The typical PA has learned to work well with other departments. Differences of opinion are healthy for the organization, particularly where (as in most cases I observed) they are resolved in a constructive fashion.

ASPIRATION AND ANXIETY

The PA's concern with status ran as a constant theme through my interviews. Comments such as the following were common:

> We are pretty proud of purchasing and we want to show off what purchasing can do . . . [Yet] most people look upon the PA as a freeloader with a basement full of liquor. Others see him as just an order writer. And everybody is encroaching on his responsibilities.

Many purchasing people feel that their capabilities are not sufficiently recognized either by management or other functional departments. They frequently make allusions to the higher pay,[3] better parking lots, and fancier offices enjoyed by others, particularly engineers, accountants, and personnel men. They often feel frustrated in dealing with college-trained[4] engineers and aspire to professional status equivalent to theirs.

The PA badly wants to persuade other people that he is an expert; yet he finds this hard to do. The average executive may be awed by the arcane mysteries of accounting, law, and engineering. But purchasing men claim that this same executive looks upon purchasing as something pretty simple, something which even his wife can do:

> People who trust the engineer's word without question, never look at the PA that way.

In moments of discouragement the PA feels that his job is "at the end of the line," too often filled by people who fail elsewhere. Engineers become purchasing agents, but purchasing agents rarely become engineers. Fur-

---

[3] An informal survey suggests that, as of 1961, the salary of the top purchasing agent in a company of 5,000 employees would probably fall in the $14,000–$18,000 bracket. Another survey indicated that, as of 1958, the average salary of top purchasing agents in metal working companies was $9,250, but some of these companies might have been quite small. *Purchasing News*, March 23, 1959.

[4] Of the questionnaire sample in this study, 45 per cent reported graduating from college, 36 per cent "some college," and 19 per cent grade or high school. Another study indicates 41 per cent of PA's in the metal trades have college degrees. *Purchasing News*, March 23, 1959.

ther, the PA, like most staff specialists, has a dead-end job; few PA's ever get promoted into higher management.

In addition, most PA's are quite sensitive to the charge of accepting gifts from salesmen, although they claim this practice is less common than it once was. As one man put it:

We'll never get accepted on a management or professional level as long as some of our group act like two-bit shysters.

All this leads to a certain amount of insecurity. A popular article, summarizing psychological data, concluded that

[The PA] is apt to be hypersensitive about anything which affects his status. He may be overconcerned with being "in" on everything. He might take minor lapses in communications as definite indications that he is not being used properly.[5]

The PA's frustration was colorfully stated by the Public Relations Committee of the National Association of Purchasing Agents.[6]

We examine the PA objectively, and from our viewpoint, he falls roughly into two classes or groups: (1) The quiet, steady plugger who feels that right will win out in time and that just and fitting rewards will eventually be bestowed upon him . . . and (2) . . . the fellow who shouts, "There should be a law!" He wants more recognition than he is getting and he wants it *now*. . . .

Both groups have a lot in common. Both have a God-given love and respect for people. Both believe in their chosen work. Both have confidence in their ability. They have seen their position in the business family improve. Both desire greater recognition, and sincerely and honestly believe they are entitled to it. Mixed in is just a bit of resentment toward the public for not reacting more rapidly and more favorably to the obvious. . . .

Of course, purchasing's problem is really not much different from that faced by most of the newer speciality groups: status systems are slow to adjust, and recognition frequently lags behind capabilities. Newer specialities are often more expansionist than older ones, since they have not been accepted and are still trying to prove themselves.[7] Although the PAs have special problems of their own their efforts to win greater recognition are probably fairly typical of similar efforts by other groups.

RELATIONS WITH OTHER FUNCTIONAL GROUPS

The causes of the PA's present discontent and for his desire for a more prestigeful position in the corporate hierarchy are rooted deep in technol-

---

[5] J. H. McPherson, "What Makes the PA Tick" *Purchasing*, December 8, 1959, p. 60. See also "Are PAs Neurotic?" *Purchasing*, May 26, 1958 and "Purchasing Opinion," *Purchasing*, June 6, 1959, p. 6. The conclusions of these articles, although perhaps overlurid, are generally supported by my interviews.

[6] *The Bulletin of the NAPA*, July 1, 1959, p. 13.

[7] See Victor A. Thompson, "Hierarchy, Specialization and Organizational Conflict," *Administrative Science Quarterly*, Vol. V, No. 4 (March, 1961), p. 513.

ogy and workflow. The PA originally had but two functions: (1) to negotiate prices and place orders on the best possible terms, but only in accordance with requisitions placed by others, and (2) to expedite orders, that is, to check with suppliers to make sure that deliveries are made on time. This kind of arrangement seemingly gives the PA broad powers in dealing with salesmen, yet within the company his power and status are often limited. As one PA put it:

> I spend half the day getting my ego blown up by salesmen and the other half getting it torn down by the rest of management.[8]

Many PA's feel that placing orders and expediting deliveries are but the bare bones of their responsibilities. In most circumstances they have become far more than just "order clerks."

1. They seek greater discretion in determining what the company will buy.

> The difference between a successful and an unsuccessful PA [one commented] is the difference between the man who is authorized to procure an adequate amount of protective coating, and the man who is told to buy ten gallons of Sherwin-Williams paint.

2. They seek to be consulted by other departments in regard to any question dealing with components (this is called "value analysis").[9]

3. They seek, in many instances, to win control over allied functions such as receiving, inventory control, stores, and production control (this is called "materials management").

These objectives naturally involve sensitive interdepartmental relations. In fact, most PA's reported that such relations were at least as important to them as relations with salesmen. In larger companies, where there is a PA in charge of the office, with a number of buyers and expediters reporting to him, the PA himself does little or no buying and spends only a small portion of the day with salesmen. Instead he devotes most of his time to internal problems—primarily with lateral relations. Many of these internal problems arise out of the PA's attempts to change the terms in which requisitions are drawn.

---

[8] "The PA, although he usually has the power of 'business or no business' with 90% of the company's suppliers, has yet to earn the confidence and respect of management. In pay and prestige he's a cut above the foremen in the shop. But rarely does he belong to the same country club as the heads of manufacturing, sales, and finance." Dean Ammer, "The Push toward Materials Management," *Purchasing*, January 5, 1959 p. 65. Whether this is true or not is perhaps not as important as the fact that many PA's think it is true.

[9] Understandably PA's object when Engineering Departments establish departments of "Value Engineering" and point out that PA's are far better qualified to perform this function. See Stuart F. Heinritz, "The Claim Jumpers," *Purchasing*, August 18, 1958, p. 57.

Requisitions

One of purchasing's primary functions is to place orders in response to *requisitions*. The normal requisition is concerned with three questions: quality, quantity, and time. It includes a *specification* as to the characteristics of the good to be purchased (quality), the *lot size* (quantity), and the *delivery date* (time). Setting of specifications is normally the responsibility of engineers; lot size and delivery dates are usually determined by production scheduling.[10] The ambitious PA is anxious to expand his discretion in regard to all three areas. He feels that he should be allowed to do more than merely buy a specified component at the lowest price and that his technical knowledge should be accorded recognition equal to the technical knowledge of the engineer and the accountant. He looks upon his most important function as that of keeping management posted about new developments in the market: new materials, new sources of supply, price trends, and so forth. To make this information more useful, he seeks to be consulted before the requisition is drawn up, while the product is still in the planning stage. The vice-president of purchasing at Westinghouse stated the PA's aspirations and problems as follows:[11]

> Under ideal conditions, the purchasing officer participates in a project from its inceptions. He sits with engineering, manufacturing, and marketing on the first decisions, beginning with design, choice of materials, and level of quality. He contributes his own experience, knowledge, and imagination; and he brings to the problem the rich technical experience of the company's suppliers. As a professional, he knows where the talent lies and which supplier is equipped to make the greatest contribution. He brings this supplier talent to bear early enough to really do some good, to conserve his own engineers' time, to get specialized knowledge working to supplement his company's efforts, to cost-reduce the product before it ever goes into production.
>
> The situation is far less than ideal when the purchasing officer receives only a piece of paper containing specifications, scheduling and amount. The higher decisions have already been made; only the price and the supplier remain undetermined.

One way of looking at purchasing's expansionist desires is in interaction terms. Normally, orders flow in one direction, from engineering, through scheduling, to purchasing. But purchasing is dissatisfied with being at the tail end of the process and seeks to reverse the flow and to initiate for others. Such man-bite-dog behavior naturally results in ill feeling—

---

[10] Although other departments are often involved, throughout this discussion we shall use the term "engineering" to refer to the department which sets specifications and "production scheduling" to refer to the department which sets lot sizes and delivery dates. Actually, for example, the office manager may set specifications for clerical supplies and the maintenance foreman may set them for maintenance supplies. And many companies have a separate inventory control department.

[11] Andrew M. Kennedy, Jr., "Does Management Get Its Best From Purchasing?" *New York State Purchasor*, August, 1959, pp. 49–50.

primarily with engineering and production scheduling. Of my question-naire sample of manufacturing PA's, 39 per cent said their biggest problem was with engineering and 37 per cent with production scheduling (while the remaining 24 per cent scattered their votes among other departments such as stores, manufacturing, quality control, and even accounting and sales.) Our attention here will be concentrated on conflicts with engineer-ing and production scheduling.

Conflicts with Engineering

In many plants PA's are engaged in a running battle with engineers. Most of these disputes revolve around purchasing's never-ending effort to gain greater control over deciding what to buy, particularly in relation to specifications. One PA said:

> The situation is so bad in our company that I could buy XXXX for $60,000 less if we could get Engineering to revise their specifications. But it is all tied up in power politics. Engineering won't admit they are wrong.

Purchasing's power and, in a sense, purchasing's status depends on how tightly specifications are worded.

Specification by Brand Name. PA's are anxious to avoid being given specifications which call for particular brands. If the specification calls for a particular brand, such as Sherwin-Williams paint, the PA has not much discretion; normally, he can deal with but one salesman and often must accept the set price. Thus he has little social status internally, or economic bargaining power externally. Instead PA's want *functional* specifications which permit them to buy any product which meets certain minimum requirements. In this way PA's feel they can find the product which best meets the company's needs (this may not be the cheapest product—it can be the one with the highest quality or the best delivery record).

Why do engineers specify by brand names? One reason is that it is much easier to write down a well-known brand name than to draw up a lengthy functional specification. Some PA's try to overcome this problem (1) by encouraging engineers to add to the brand name specification the two words "or equivalent," which then permits purchasing to shop around, or (2) by working for the establishment of standardized specifica-tions (e.g., standard size bricks, standard strength cartons). These "stand-ards" save the company money and, incidentally, reduce engineering's discretion.[12] But even if the engineer accepts one of these alternatives, he still must test proffered products to see if they actually are equivalents or

---

[12] But it has been suggested that excessive standardization can make purchasing's job too simple and thus threaten its "professional integrity. . . . Every reduction in the negotiation task is a reduction in the status and importance of the purchasing agent. . . . What differentiates the clerk and the PA is the ability to negotiate." Nor-man P. Levine, "The Hidden Threat of Standardization," *Purchasing*, March 2, 1959, p. 69.

up to specifications or standard—and engineers often prefer not to do such menial tasks.

Overspecification. The PA charges the engineer with being a perfectionist and with making specifications so restrictive as to give the PA little freedom in choosing the best value.

The typical engineer is more interested in quality than in price. And thus a conflict may arise between the "engineering approach based on idealistic concepts and the purchasing value analysis based on the realistic approach of the right thing for the right job.[13] PA's sometimes charge the engineer with being an impractical perfectionist, who

> . . . rarely sees the price and cares less . . . The chief trouble is his lack of cost consciousness . . . tendency to gold plate, to order a Cadillac where a Chevy would do.

The engineer may insist on a part which has a life of ten years when the product as a whole may have a life of only three years.

> The typical young engineer often creates something of such superior quality that it represents something of a monument.[14]

He insists on getting parts with extremely fine tolerances, although looser tolerances would be satisfactory. In addition, various PA's commented, the engineer

> . . . doesn't recognize that something may work out well in the laboratory, but not on the production line. Engineers sometimes order things which just can't be gotten. . . . The problem is to train them to ask for things which can be produced.

As a consequence, purchasing spends a great deal of energy trying to get engineers to accept looser, more realistic specifications.

Inadequate specifications. According to purchasing, engineers often provide insufficient information in their specifications or phrase them in technical terms which the PA cannot understand. Both situations lead to antagonism, and the second leads to the PA feeling inadequate before professionally trained engineers.

New sources. The PA claims that through his contacts with "sources" (that is, salesmen) he is in a position to learn about new products and techniques which will save the company substantial sums of money. He complains that the engineer rarely listens to his ideas and even less frequently asks his advice.

The completion barrier. All these problems are made more difficult by the "completion barrier": usually purchasing seeks to change specifications

---

[13] G. C. Fordyce, "The Job of the Buyer," *Central New York Purchasor,* December, 1958, p. 6.

[14] Andrew M. Kennedy, "Buying at Westinghouse Corporation," *Purchasing News,* June 15, 1959, p. 26.

only after the engineer has already committed his plans to blueprints, feels he has completed his work, and may in fact have started another project. Inevitably, purchasing's "interference" threatens the engineer's feeling of accomplishment and completion.

Professionalism. In addition, purchasing seeks to intervene in areas where the engineers feel that they are uniquely competent. One PA complained of

. . . the conservatism and professional jealousy of the engineer, his unwillingness to be told by anybody not an engineer.

Part of this is a status problem. Engineering is an accepted profession; purchasing, if a profession at all, is still fighting for recognition. All this leads to the PA having something of an inferiority complex, particularly if he does not have a college degree.

Engineers are a special breed of cat that think they know everything, including purchasing [one PA complained bitterly]. They feel the PA is just a clerk.

In a nutshell, the PA envies and resents the engineer because the engineer initiates for him and he cannot initiate in return. The PA does not like being dependent on the engineer. As one PA put it:

If the engineer won't play ball, you are dead. They can just sit there and say NO, NO, NO.

Back door selling. The PA's antagonism is accentuated when the engineer permits "back door selling," the worst sin in the PA's book. This type of selling occurs when a salesman bypasses the PA, sees someone else in the organization (usually an engineer), and seeks to influence this other person to requisition the salesman's product by name, or—more subtly—to list specifications which only the salesman's product can meet. Engineers sometimes claim that the salesmen provide them valuable information which they cannot get from purchasing. Purchasing, on the other hand, charges that engineers are overinfluenced by free lunches and the fawning attention that salesmen give them. (Engineers, of course, counterclaim that purchasing people are the ones who are really most influenced by free lunches.)

Back door selling threatens purchasing's status in two ways: (1) it encourages specifying by brands, and (2) it makes both salesmen and engineers less dependent on the PA. Where back door selling becomes widespread, the PA is reduced to little more than a cipher.

PA's try to make it clear to salesmen that they must clear through the purchasing office before seeing other individuals in the plant, and they imply strongly that salesmen who violate this rule will find it hard to get orders. A few companies require that engineers requisition catalogs and manuals through the purchasing department, even though manufacturers often distribute these free to engineers. One PA justified this rule on the grounds that "this is the only way we have to control this most insidious form of back door selling."

Control over salesmen has been an effective tool in the hands of a resourceful PA. By choosing which salesman he permits to see engineers, he can indirectly influence the specification process. In fact, once a PA decides that a product should be introduced, he and the salesman will often coordinate their strategies closely in order to get this product accepted by higher management.[15]

Conflicts with Production Scheduling

The size of the order and the date on which it is to be delivered is typically determined by production scheduling. Purchasing must seek to place the order on these terms and expedite suppliers to make sure that delivery is made on time.

PAs often feel more friendly towards production schedulers than they do towards engineers. In the first place there is less of a status barrier. Schedulers are less likely to be college men and they have little claim to being professionals. Secondly, PAs are in a stronger position to turn down scheduling's requests than they are those of engineers. As we shall see, the purchasing-production scheduling relation involves certain elements of bargaining between equals.

Conflict over lead time. Still there are some points of conflict. Purchasing's chief complaint against scheduling is that delivery is often requested on much too short notice. There may be a number of reasons for the short lead time. Production schedulers sometimes cry wolf; they claim to need deliveries earlier than they really do, on the assumption that it is better to play it safe. Sometimes scheduling engages in sloppy planning and delays placing requisitions until the last minute. On occasion engineering completes blueprints too late. Or the sales department may underestimate sales and so cause inventory to be exhausted. Or, where the product is custom-made the salesmen may make a commitment on a delivery date without consulting other departments. In addition, there are genuinely unexpected events such as equipment break-down and the like.

Regardless of the cause, scheduling puts pressure on purchasing and purchasing must make the commitment good by scurrying around to find the components in a hurry. Since purchasing is at the end of the line, it must make up for all the accumulated delays.

Cost of short lead times. In any case, requests for quick delivery cause purchasing much trouble. Many items require considerable lead time. If

---

[15] Significantly, PA's expressed quite friendly feelings towards salesmen as a group (even though they were antagonistic to individual salesmen whom they felt were incompetent or overinsistent). Typical comments were: "The vendor helps me, management doesn't"; "They are our allies in dealing with engineering"; "All I know, I've learned from salesmen"; "They are the PA's biggest support."

the requisition comes in too late, sometimes it is totally impossible to meet the deadline, or quick delivery may be obtained, but at a cost. The cost may be a premium price to reimburse the vendor for overtime work or premium transportation costs, such as air freight. Or the cost may be in terms of accepting a high-priced producer who can get things out in a hurry rather that a lower-priced producer who will not allow a special order to get in the way of his production scheduling.

Limited supply of "pressure." The cost may also be in terms of "pressure." If the PA exerts enough "pressure" on a vendor he can often persuade the vendor to rearrange his own production schedules or to "put on a big drive" to get a product out with special speed.[16] PA's, however, are quite reluctant to go all out in exerting pressure, in part because every time a vendor does him a "favor" the PA is in effect obligated to return this favor in placing an order. If a PA asks for too many favors of this sort, he ties his hands so that he can no longer buy from the lowest bidder.

In any case, every PA recognizes that he has only a limited number of "silver bullets"; he cannot exert maximum pressure all the time. Yet, as one PA put it:

> Scheduling and production men forget that you must develop a permanent relationship with the supplier. They are always saying "Call those bastards up and give them hell. They've got to get it here."

Requisitioning departments recognize that the PA does not exert all his pressure all the time. Many believe (often correctly) that if the PA really wanted to, he could get early delivery. So they place pressure on him in turn. Production schedulers "go up the ladder." If the expediter or buyer cannot get action, they see the PA himself—or even threaten to see the PA's boss. Exchange of favors and other influence tactics are also used extensively. Indeed, pressure of this sort gets to be expected. A somewhat perplexed PA explained to me why he had not expedited a badly needed component.

> Yes, the requisition gave the date and it was labeled "rush." But any time something is that rush, production brings it over by hand and they hound me on it every day. Since I hadn't heard anything from them, I assumed it was really routine.

Thus the purchasing-production scheduling relationships involve large elements of bargaining and bluff. This is particularly true since more than

---

[16] The use of pressure is an art in itself. To a considerable extent it involves persuading the vendor that you do need the product and are not crying wolf. To a lesser extent there is an implication that if the vendor will not meet the request, the PA will take his business elsewhere in the future. One technique, for example, is to "go up the ladder." If the salesman will not help, the PA can talk to the sales manager. If the sales manager will not help, he can talk to the plant manager or even the president. Actually, the salesman might be able to provide as much help as the higher-ups, but by going up the ladder the PA shows how anxious he really is. (At times, the salesman may even encourage the PA to do this.)

one scheduling department may be involved (and other departments place requisitions besides production scheduling). The PA must decide how much a given scheduler is crying wolf and try to discover the real order of relative priorities.

Better relations than with engineering. All this tends to make purchasing's relationship with scheduling considerably different from its relationship with engineering. Suppose scheduling requests delivery by a certain date and purchasing reports that it cannot find a vendor who can meet this date. Even if this is only a half truth, according to the record the PA has done his job. Now scheduling must use other informal or semiformal pressures if it is to induce purchasing to make use of its "silver bullets." Naturally, this sets the stage for bargaining.

The situation with engineering is very different. It is rare indeed for an engineer to submit a specification which some vendor cannot meet. True, the cost may be much too high, but this extra cost is not clearly isolated (as it is in the case of premium rates for air freight, for example). As a consequence, purchasing is rarely in a position to go back to engineering and say, "We can't find anybody who can meet your specifications." Thus purchasing has no natural lever to use to get engineers to loosen their specifications.

Inventory policy. Inventory policy is another cause of conflict between purchasing and scheduling. Purchasing complains that since scheduling determines lot sizes and delivery dates—and frequently at the last minute—it is difficult to take advantage of market fluctuations or quantity discounts. In many companies scheduling knows only the demand side of the picture and purchasing knows only the supply side. Just because scheduling does not know how long it will take purchasing to get delivery on vital parts, scheduling has a tendency to play it safe and maintain extra-large inventories.[17]

Materials management. Purchasing has persuaded top management in a number of companies that the best way to handle these problems of lead time and inventory policy is through combining purchasing, inventory control, and sometimes production scheduling in one "materials management" department which has the overall authority for insuring that materials are available when production needs them. In most instances, materials management also takes over receiving, the storerooms, and even traffic. Hopefully, problems of coordination will be vastly reduced if one buyer is given overall responsibility for purchasing a given commodity and

---

[17] Purchasing, of course, is interested in quantity discounts, so it, too, exerts pressure to build up inventory. In many companies there is no *systematic* pressure to lower inventories, although top management, at accounting's instigation, from time to time, will institute drives to cut them down. Thus inventory levels may normally tend to be larger than optimal. (This tendency may provide a partial explanation for the substantial savings many companies have made through substituting operations research techniques for power politics in determining inventory levels.)

making sure that an adequate inventory is maintained to meet manufacturing's needs.

The PA hopes, of course, that he will be the man appointed to head this new department—and in most cases his hopes are realized.[18] In many instances, the PA-now-materials-manager can report dramatic savings. There are fewer "stockouts" (occasions when inventory is exhausted and not replaced in time). Inventory is lower. The average cost of goods purchased is lower, and a substantial number of duplicating records are eliminated.

Thus materials management takes its place alongside of value analysis as a means by which the PA seeks to expand his area of influence. As one journal put it:[19]

Purchasing is at a dramatic crossroads. It is faced with the prospect (1) of being absorbed into the broader scope of the materials management structure, or (2) expanding its vision to include the entire material system. . . . Materials management logically and inevitably will be a major function in industry. You are in a better position than almost anyone in your company to understand it. Prepare yourself to lead it, or you'll be absorbed in it.

INADEQUATE RECOGNITION FROM HIGHER MANAGEMENT

The PA tends to look to higher management for support in his interdepartmental disputes. But management tends to give purchasing less attention that purchasing feels it deserves. At times management treats purchasing almost as a routine, clerical operation—and when this happens purchasing men are naturally resentful. This section will consider the nature of purchasing's contacts with higher management, why management apparently pays so little attention to purchasing, and the means which PAs have adopted to "sell" themselves to management and thus overcome this apparent neglect.

Contacts with the boss. Who is the PA's boss varies greatly from one organization to another. Most PA's feel that they should report directly to the company president.[20] But, in fact, many report to the general manufacturing manager, factory manager, controller, or director of supply. Only in the last case does the PA receive much attention from his boss.

The typical PA reported that he sees his boss only two or three times a

---

[18] One PA, who had strongly supported the concept of materials management, reversed his position sharply when the former head of production scheduling was appointed department manager. After considerable lobbying, the PA was finally able to win independent status for his department again.

[19] *Purchasing,* January 5, 1959, p. 63.

[20] Various studies seem to agree that about 70 per cent of PA's do report to "top management" although this term is variously interpreted. See, for example, *Purchasing News,* March 23, 1959, p. 37.

week and for not more than half an hour.[21] This relatively low level of interaction casts some doubt upon the commonly held belief by management students that staff men have much closer contact with top management than do line.

About what kinds of topics do PA's and bosses talk? PA's report that they are most likely to contact their bosses in regards to (1) personnel problems, such as getting a promotion or pay raise for one of their subordinates, and (2) "policy" or procedural changes in interdepartmental relationships (as contrasted to day-to-day operating problems). For example, PA's contacted their bosses in regard to the following types of problems:

> . . . to take the inventory control section from production control and place it under purchasing;
> . . . to win approval of standard company-wide stationery styles, thus preventing each department from picking its own letterheads and stationery styles;
> . . . to change the relationship with small branch managers, who had limited authority to purchase on their own;
> . . . to win authority to purchase certain maintenance supplies which in the past had been bought by the maintenance supervisor.

The PA is generally quite reluctant to appeal to his boss when he is at loggerheads with other departments regarding *day-to-day* questions of delivery or specification. Although each party to a dispute may threaten to bring in top management, in most cases the parties are bluffing.[22] The boss takes the initiative himself when he wants to make sure that goods arrive on time. Rarely does he concern himself with price or the selection of vendor, certainly not in any systematic manner (the prime exceptions being a small minority of more rule-oriented companies where the PA would check with the boss in regard to an unusually large order or even in regard to a moderately large order if it were not placed with the lowest bidder). As we have seen, purchasing's freedom to select vendors was severely restricted by other departments, but rarely by higher management.

Difficulties in measuring efficiency. One reason for higher management's apparent lack of interest in purchasing decisions[23] is the fact that

---

[21] The range of contacts reported was from "usually once or twice a day" to "perhaps once a month," while the reported average time per week devoted to seeing the boss ranged from ten minutes to one and one-half hours. Estimates of this sort are subject to considerable error. See Tom Burns, "The Direction of Activity and Communications in a Departmental Executive Group," *Human Relations,* VII, No. 1 (February, 1954), pp. 73–97. However, respondents were also asked, "How many times did you talk to your boss during the last week?" and "What did you discuss each time?" The answers to these much more specific questions were consistent with those reported above.

[22] This point is discussed at greater length in Strauss, *op. cit.,* pp. 167–69.

[23] We are talking about the ordinary operations of the purchasing department. Many companies provide special procedures for the purchase of the key raw mate-

purchasing's efficiency is difficult to measure. When a key boiler breaks down, management learns about it immediately. If labor efficiency in a manufacturing department declines or if sales fall off, statistical measures usually bring this to management's attention quickly. But management normally pays attention to purchasing only when deliveries are not maintained. Otherwise, it leaves purchasing pretty much alone. One study, financed by the National Association of Purchasing Agents, concluded:

> Most top managers make no attempt to measure the performance of the purchasing function, and many believe that measurement is not possible. Most assume that the purchasing function is being performed satisfactorily as long as there are no work stoppages because of a shortage of purchased materials or other evidence of purchasing failure. Thus, the principal measure of the basic purchasing function—getting the proper materials at the right time and price— is a negative one. The purchasing agent is criticized for failure to perform, but gets little or no credit for performing more economically or effectively.[24]

The PA resents being ignored. Now it might seem that the PA should welcome his relative freedom, but the evidence suggests that he does not. In contrast to many executives, the typical PA would like to see more of his boss. One man said explicitly what a number of others implied,

> I have too much autonomy and too much work. My boss doesn't know what I am doing and I'm not sure he cares. . . . I don't get any support from [him] so I've got to plug away on my own.

The sporadic nature of top management intervention makes many PA's insecure; they do not know where they stand. And management's lack of interest in them does not help them in their status struggles with other departments—or in getting larger budgets.

Perhaps expectations and even personality makeup enter into this. Purchasing agents expect the primary source of control and support to be their boss; they are confused when this control and support is not forthcoming. In discussing case problems in the author's classes, PA's showed a strong tendency to seek formalistic, bureaucratic solutions ("following the book") rather than informal, "human relations" approaches. The typical solution suggested was that the PA should bring his problem to his boss and, if the PA was right, the boss would "naturally" back him up.[25] Yet many of the PA's who advocated a formal go-see-the-

---

rials. Since fluctuations in raw materials prices may wipe out an entire year's profits in a vegetable oil, flour milling, or tire company, these companies' very survival may depend on successful hedging and speculation. Operations of this sort are often under the close control of the financial vice-president or even the board of directors. Organizationally, they are frequently quite distinct from the run-of-the-mill purchases handled by the purchasing department.

[24] G. W. Aljian, "What Does the Harbridge House Report Tell Us," *The Midwest Purchasing Agent*, July, 1958, p. 46.

[25] For a typical case, see George Strauss and Leonard R. Sayles, *Personnel*, (Englewood Cliffs, N.J.: Prentice-Hall, 1960), p. 376. In handling these same cases,

boss approach in class, in fact used informal tactics on the job. When confronted with this contrast, each said his own situation was unique.

Thus, there is reason to believe that the PA would welcome a stronger boss who would provide support and guidance. One study, based on psychological evidence, seems to confirm this point of view.[26]

. . . Although the purchasing agent wishes to get ahead, he wishes to do so within the secure structure of a large enterprise headed by a strong man. He apparently does not wish to "pioneer" or be on his own.

Yet the PA apparently rarely receives such support from his boss. As a consequence he often feels frustrated.

"Selling" management. Thus the PA feels he is forced to take the initiative in seeking to increase the degree of communication with top management—and in a sense top management's ability to control him. The typical PA shows great interest in "selling" top management on purchasing's value to the organization, particularly through measuring purchasing performance.

Almost every PA is interested in measuring performance. If there were objective tools to do it, purchasing's prestige would be greatly enhanced since management would be more aware of the many benefits of good purchasing.[27]

Other staff men, such as engineers, personnel men, quality control men, and the like are also anxious to develop objective measures to justify their paychecks. As a training director put it,

For me evaluation is a form of job insurance—to prove the value of training and to make sure our department is not eliminated by the next economy wave.

Purchasing men have developed numerous forms of statistical performance ratings, but for various reasons none provide a completely satisfactory means of measuring purchasing efficiency. For instance, cost per purchase is a measure of economy but not of effectiveness in investigating alternatives thoroughly and getting the best buy. Many PA's set goals or standards as to what they expect to spend—and then try to beat these goals and turn in a "savings" or "positive variance."[28] Standards of this sort

---

industrial relations students almost universally felt that the PA should try to convince the other departments first. They felt the PA's solution unwise because (1) it would antagonize the other departments, and (2) the boss might see the problem in a different light than the PA, he might not agree the PA was right, and even if he agreed, he might not back the PA in terms of action.

[26] McPherson, *op. cit.*, p. 92.

[27] "How Does Management Measure Purchasing Performance?" *Purchasing*, October 27, 1958, p. 15. When asked the question, "Do you think that top management's inability to measure purchasing performance has hindered recognition of the purchasing function?" 72 per cent of those polled by *Purchasing* answered "yes." *Ibid.*

[28] These standards are set at times by cost accounting. But since cost accounting must rely largely on purchasing's estimate on price trends, in practice, purchasing sets its own goals.

apparently provide an important form of self-motivation for PA's, as well as a means of internal control over buyers and a form of "success" to report to management. There is little evidence, however, that management uses these purchasing-set standards as a means of evaluating purchasing.

Some PA's seem to be obsessed with making elaborate reports to their bosses. The purchasing journals discuss this endlessly.[29] Note that the PA issues these reports on his own hook, not as a result of top management's request.

> Top management, in general, is not too specific about the manner in which the report is rendered—oral, written, or both. In fact, some feel that meetings and discussions are sufficient. That such a condition exists, particularly with relation to a department which ordinarily handles from forty to sixty per cent of the sales dollar, *clearly* shows that those responsible for purchasing are *failing* to use reports as a means of adequately presenting the activities of their department.[30]

One PA mentioned, "Whenever I do something which is pretty good I write a report on it and distribute lots of copies around. It doesn't hurt to blow your own horn." Two others said they timed their reports to coincide with cost-reduction drives. Value analysis programs also provide an opportunity for the PA to report to top management the savings he has induced.

In spite of all these efforts to publicize their achievements, most PA's agree that top management still pays too little attention to the purchasing function. As a consequence, PA's look to other means of bolstering their status—such as professionalism.

PROFESSIONALISM

Purchasing people look upon professionalism as a means of equating their status with engineers.[31] Once purchasing becomes a profession, "nonprofessionals" can be kept off the job. And professionalism may counteract the stereotype of being "gift takers." Among other means which purchasing agents utilize to win professional status are (1) the

---

[29] See, for example, C. D. Francisco, "A Sure Way to Win Management Recognition," *Purchasing*, February 16, 1959, p. 88. This article describes "fourteen charts, which can be read in less than one minute . . . to present purchasing's organizational structure, its strengths, its accomplishments, its goals and its objectives."

[30] J. E. Porier, "Improving Reports to Management," *Purchasor*, June 1960, p. 16.

[31] Interestingly, "professionalism" has become an important issue only in recent years. In 1958, Harbridge House, Inc., a management consultant service, was hired to make a thorough study of the association's program. Harbridge House recommended, among other things, that greater emphasis be given to education and professional development. Not too long after purchasing journals began discussing the matter of professionalism—and it has been a major issue since then. See, for example, "N.A.P.A. Organization Planning Committee," *Bulletin of the NAPA*, February 5, 1958, p. 1; Aljian, *op. cit.*, pp. 45–47.

activities of the National Association of Purchasing Agents (NAPA), (2) "professional education" programs, (3) efforts to win "certification," and (4) the Code of Standards (on ethics).

The National Association of Purchasing Agents

Most successful professional men (and women)—be they doctors, lawyers, Indian Chiefs, or purchasing agents—belong to professional associations. The professional association for purchasing agents and buyers is the National Association of Purchasing Agents.[32]

Without question, NAPA and its constituent local affiliates represent a potent force towards professionalization. NAPA is an active, aggressive organization.[33] In the two situations observed, attendance at monthly meetings averages 25 percent of membership, probably well above that of many similar organizations. In addition, becoming an association officer is a much sought-after prize, even though the incumbent must put in several unpaid nights a week on committee work. Why do PA's show so much interest in their organization?

1. First of all, as a "professional" organization the association provides purchasing agents with a sense of identity and solidarity, with their growing to be "cosmopolitans" rather than "locals."[34] Certainly some purchasing agents seem to develop as close friendships with purchasing agents in other companies as they do with nonpurchasing agents in their own company.

2. Since most PA's have dead-end jobs, being elected to association office provides a means of "getting ahead" which is absent within the company. (Further, association membership provides contacts that make it easier to find a job elsewhere.)

3. The Association meets real educational needs. Formal programs provide training for younger members. Officers and committee members learn human relations, public speaking, and organizational skills. And many PA's exchange information and learn the tricks of the trade in informal conversation around the bar before and after meetings.

4. The informal conversation at association meetings also gives members a chance to exchange woes in brotherhood with those who have similar problems—to let off steam in a safe environment. Thus they have a "free constituency"[35] in which their ideas, which may have been vetoed on the

---

[32] *Niagara Frontier Purchaser*, October, 1960, p. 50.

[33] Interestingly, NAPA's British counterpart, the Purchasing Officers' Association, is apparently also exceptionally aggressive in protecting its members' interests.

[34] See Alvin W. Gouldner, "Cosmopolitans and Locals: Towards an Analysis of Latent Local Roles," *Administrative Science Quarterly*, Vol. II, No. 3 (December, 1957), pp. 281–306.

[35] Thompson, *op. cit.*, p. 520.

job, may be reevaluated according to "professional" rather than nonprofessional standards.[36]

5. Finally, through its activities the NAPA promotes the occupational (and economic) interests of its members in the same fashion as do similar organizations such as the American Bar Association and the American Medical Association. Thus it functions as a quasi-union.[37]

Programs of Professional Education

One means of obtaining professionalism, as PA's see it, is to persuade universities to establish separate courses in "purchasing science." Eventually, many PA's hope a college degree will be an accepted requirement for doing purchasing work. Then and only then will they be successful in keeping unqualified people (such as engineers) from doing purchasing. "As purchasing goes in our colleges and universities," one publication puts it, "so will it go in the business world of tomorrow."[38] Significantly, the Education Committee of the NAPA has changed its name to the Committee for Professional Development. It seeks to "improve our relationships with colleges and universities to the end that Purchasing will be a Profession in fact."[39] Its mission, among others, is to lobby for college courses, majors, and even departments of purchasing as well as the establishment of scholarships and professorships in this area.

In addition, the local, regional, and national professional development committees of the NAPA offer training programs of their own. Whether led by PA's themselves or by outside instructors, these classes and conferences are generally very well attended.

Professional Certification

Some PA's seem to feel that the best way to achieve professional recognition is through a professional certification or licensing program. Presumably all potential PA's would be required to pass an examination and/or be a college graduate before they could be permitted to engage in purchasing (although a grandfather clause would perhaps exempt those who are doing purchasing now). This proposal still is quite controversial, but those who support it say that with a certification requirement:

[36] "The profession sets up institutions which make clients' judgments of secondary importance and colleagues' judgments predominate," Everett C. Hughes, *Men and Their Work*, The Free Press, Glencoe, Ill., 1958, p. 142. "Professional associations . . . severely limit managerial control by specifying just how their members may be employed in organizations. In short, they are devices for protecting specialist status and functions. . . ." Thompson, *op. cit.*, pp. 300–01.

[37] This point is elaborated in George Strauss, "Professionalism and Occupational Associations," *Industrial Relations*, Vol. II, No. 3 (May, 1963), pp. 7–31.

[38] *Purchasing News*, July 27, 1959, p. 28. The same point is made in "Education, Key to Purchasing Maturity," *Purchasing News*, July 13, 1959, p. 28 and in *Guide to the Selection of Competent Buyers*, NAPA, New York, 1956.

[39] *Bulletin of the NAPA*, July 1, 1960.

A company, in hiring a PA would know that he was hiring a man of capability and integrity . . . the PA would not have to start at the bottom.

If doctors, lawyers, engineers, and accountants all have their licensing requirements, it is asked, why should not PA's, as professionals, have the same thing? (And, in California, governmental purchasing agents have begun an elaborate program of testing and certification with the hopes that eventually no one but a certified purchasing agent would be permitted to engage in government purchasing. This program does not provide a grandfather clause. Similar efforts on a national scale are still in the discussion stage.)

Ethics

Although the NAPA Code of Standards covers a number of matters,[40] to the average PA the word ethics relates to only one thing—gift taking (which includes the acceptance of free meals or entertainment). The question of gift taking is the subject of frequent editorial comment in purchasing journals and much informal discussion among purchasing agents. It is generally agreed that the PA degrades the profession when he solicits gifts or permits these to influence his decisions. Borderline questions, however, are more difficult.

Should the PA permit a salesman to pick up a check when they go out for lunch? Many PAs feel that professional standards can be maintained only when they have expense accounts which will permit them to entertain salesmen in return. Many companies send letters to suppliers asking them not to send Christmas gifts. If—in spite of these letters—a PA receives a small gift, like a ham or a bottle of liquor, what should he do? Return it, give it to charity, or keep it himself?

Policies and their enforcement vary from company to company. PA's or buyers are at times disciplined by higher management for violation of rules, but there is no effective "professional" enforcement committee. Most PA's seem to feel that the practice of giving or accepting gifts has declined considerably in recent years, still they are anxious to do something about the small minority who give the profession a bad name. So far, however, the profession has not progressed sufficiently to engage in self-policing.

A Profession in Transition

Thus purchasing has many of the characteristics listed by Hughes of a profession in transition.[41] It already has a professional organization, a program of self-training, and a code of ethics. Universities are being encouraged to establish separate courses in purchasing and steps are being

---

[40] See "NAPA Standards of Conduct," *Bulletin of the NAPA,* July 22, 1959, pp. 5–8.

[41] Hughes, *op. cit.,* chap. 10.

taken (although with great hesitation) to require certification to "practice" purchasing.

PA's are beginning to slough off nonprofessional aspects of the job (such as routine buying and expediting) to subordinates (as nurses do to nurses' aides, and engineers do to technicians).[42] And PA's often object to being asked to utilize their purchasing skills buying items such as radios, antifreeze, tires, or washing machines for the personal use of individuals in the company. They feel this requires lots of work, results in lots of gripes, and, above all, lowers their professional status. (If anyone does this kind of work, they say, it should be the personnel department.)

Already there is a feeling developing among PA's that their professional judgment should not be questioned by management.[43] A leading handbook argues,[44]

> It is incumbent on the purchasing agent to keep his management informed [of proper purchasing procedure] and to insist that such procedures be followed in the absence of overriding contrary considerations.

One PA commented:

> Management at Chrysler was able to tell purchasing from whom to buy, and look at the scandal. I bet they couldn't get away with telling a professional accountant to falsify the books—or, if he did, he'd go to jail. With professional standards we could put out unethical practices.

Not all PA's, however, agree with this heavy emphasis on professionalism. The dissenters argue that PA's owe their primary loyalty to management, not to a profession. They oppose drawing a sharp line between purchasing and other aspects of management. For example, quite a number are opposed to requiring a certification or a college diploma. Still the trend is in the direction of greater professionalism.

CONFLICTING FUNCTIONAL GROUPS

This report has dealt primarily with the purchasing agent, but he is not alone in his quest for status. Quite the contrary. I have a hunch that every

---

[42] *Ibid.*, p. 135.

[43] Herbert Simon and Donald W. Smithburg make the point that the judgments of nonprofessional groups are much more often questioned in the organization than are the judgments of professional groups. "The specializations represented in overhead units are frequently of a kind that is not fully accepted as valid and scientific. Few of these specializations correspond to established bodies of scientific knowledge. Consequently, standards and controls imposed by overhead units are not as acceptable to most persons as are the standards on controls of a generally accepted scientific discipline. Personnel management and budgeting [the authors might have added purchasing] are less well established sciences—if, indeed, they are sciences at all—than engineering or medicine," *Public Administration* (New York: Knopf, 1950), pp. 302–303.

[44] George Aljian (ed.), *Purchasing Handbook*, (New York: McGraw-Hill Book Co., 1958), Part I, p. 5.

staff or functional group in industry feels its true worth to be underrecognized. Engineers, personnel men, accountants, quality control men, all claim to be underdogs (and in the same breath, to be in a unique, middle-of-the-road position, ground down by opposing forces).

Since status is a relative matter and obviously all groups cannot be top dog at once, interdepartmental conflict is inevitable. Even were status not an issue, one should expect friction from the very nature of the staff or functional specialist's job. Production men make *things,* and their accomplishments are visible to the eye. Staff men make *ideas* and can feel success and demonstrate accomplishment only to the extent other departments accept these ideas (willingly or otherwise).

In addition, different departments bring very different views to the situation. But, as Landsberger has pointed out, more than a conflict of perception is involved.[45] There are very real differences in the objectives of various functional groups, and one objective can be achieved only at the partial expense of another. Thus engineers' objectives of high quality can be obtained only at the expense of sales' objectives of low cost.

These problems may be accentuated by unrealistic managerial ideology. According to traditional theory, staff's primary function is to advise higher management. But staff groups perform such important functions today that the lines of communication would be hopelessly blocked were activities, in fact, cleared through the common boss. Staff men must work directly through other departments if they want to get things done. Similarly, as "experts" they are trained to deal with problems in rational, this-is-the-right-answer terms and expect that their proposals will be evaluated on their own merits, not in terms of power bargaining. Yet staff men must not only develop the right answers but must be able to win their acceptance by others. To a considerable extent staff men are left to devise their own means of survival, making use of whatever bargaining weapons they can muster.[46] Understandably, many feel that higher management has abandoned them. (When the emphasis is on hierarchical relations, it is clear who is boss! When it is on lateral relations, status distributions are much less clear and there is more chance for uncertainty, competition, and frustration.)

The trend towards professionalism can be explained, in part, in terms of the staff groups' acceptance of the fact that they must sink or swim on their own. The debate which runs in many staff groups, "Are we professional or are we management?" involves questions of identification and loyalty as well as self-interest. Many staff men, convinced that their jobs are dead-end and that management gives them too little recognition, turn to professionalism both as a means of bolstering their self-concept and

---

[45] Landsberger, *op. cit.,* p. 327.

[46] See Edward Gross, "Sources of Authority for the Personnel Department," *Industrial Relations,* Vol. III, No. 3 (May, 1964).

as an ideological weapon to use against other departments. Hopefully their "professional judgment" will be accepted without question; the necessity for bargaining and compromise will be eliminated.

But as one group dons the cloak of professionalism, other groups seek to do likewise in self-defense. Thus, to take an extreme case, in the hospital, where the status and power of top management is relatively weak, we see a vast proliferation of professional and semiprofessional occupational associations, covering groups ranging from housekeepers through medical librarians and lab technicians.[47] Each organization fights for the economic and social welfare of its members, and many seek the full accouterments of professionalism, such as certification, professional training, a code of ethics, and the right to exclude nonprofessionals from their special work. In this sense, the hospital may possibly provide a model for the industrial firm of the future.

THE VALUE OF INTERFUNCTIONAL CONFLICT

Further research is needed to see if the PA's experience is duplicated by other functional departments. However, the picture of the company we get from the PA's frame of reference is very different from that presented by many organizational theorists. It is not that of a highly coordinated organization, tightly controlled by top management. Rather it is one of a number of semiautonomous departments which keep each other in line through a series of checks and balances.

On the surface, at least, this seems to be a highly inefficient way of doing things. Even routine decisions regarding inventory level, make-or-buy, the acceptance of new products, or quality standards seem to involve a number of departments, each with its special point of view. Decisions seem to be made as much on the basis of pressure politics and implicit bargaining as of rational analysis, and there is no one department to bear the final responsibility. Certainly a case can be made for a unified systems approach which would take all variables into account.

Inefficient as it may seem, perhaps the system of checks and balances has its virtues in the industrial scene just as it does in the national state. Special interests do require lobbyists if a balanced point of view is to prevail. The restricted "professional" viewpoint tends to counterbalance the excessive conformity and rigidity of "organization man."[48]

---

[47] David Kochery and George Strauss, "The Non-Profit Hospital and the Union," *Buffalo Law Review*, Vol. VII, No. 9 (Winter, 1950-60), pp. 255–82.

[48] This point is elaborated in George Strauss, "Organization Man: Prospect for the Future," *California Management Review*, Vol. VI, No. 3 (Spring, 1964), pp. 5–16. In addition, it can be argued that the functional professional in industry has what Andrew G. Frank calls an "under-defined administrative role" which permits him opportunity for innovation. "Administrative Role Definition and Social Change," *Human Organization*, Vol. XXII, No. 4 (Winter, 1963–64), pp. 238–42.

Interdepartmental conflicts encourage the free competition of new ideas (as well as giving top management a chance to evaluate subordinates' behavior). Since each department has only a partial picture of the entire organization, competition improves the quality of each department's thinking and forces it to take the other department's point of view into consideration. In large organizations such internal competition tends to substitute for the external competition of the marketplace. And

> . . . jurisdictional disputes are an important means of bringing to the top administrator significant issues of policy, and of preventing these from being decided at lower levels without his knowledge.[49]

A centralized, "programed" decision-making procedure may give apparently optimum solutions, but suppose the original program is wrong? Mechanical decision-making programs may be useful when the relevant dimensions can be stated in measurable, numerical terms. But the optimum is less immediately apparent when intangibles, such as morale or consumer goodwill, are involved.

Interestingly, in many companies purchasing departments have been given the responsibility of handling internal purchasing—when one division buys from another—on the grounds that purchasing's skills are needed (1) to expedite the division from which the component is being purchased and (2) to counteract any tendency on the part of the buying division's engineering department to raise quality standards too high. Similar forms of built-in checks and balances exist in other organizations, for example, the consumer's counsel in some government agencies and the devil's advocate in the Catholic church. Theoretically, these divide responsibility, but they also insure that "the organization may benefit from having all sides of a problem clearly argued by some group within it."[50] In addition, it can be argued that, with proper safeguards, the checks-and-balances system permits problems to be safely resolved at lower levels, thus saving top management's time as well as giving subordinates a greater feeling of participation.

This approach is not without dangers. (1) Interdepartmental friction may cut down on operating efficiency; in particular, status rivalries between professional groups may become more intense. (2) One functional group may become extremely powerful and induce the organization to pursue professional rather than economic objectives.[51] (3) Compromises

---

[49] Herbert Simon, *Administrative Behavior*, (New York: Macmillan Co., 1947), p. 145. The same point is made by Wilfred Brown, *Explorations in Management*, (London, Tavistock Publications, 1960).

[50] Landsberger, *op. cit.*, p. 300.

[51] Amitai Etzioni points out that in industry the line organization is the custodian of the organization's goals—"Commitment to professional values runs counter to the economic values of the organization." "Authority Structure and Organizational Effectiveness," *Administrative Science Quarterly*, Vol. IV, No. 1 (June, 1959), p. 50.

based on relative power position may not be in the best interests of the organization as a whole: such compromises often involve "collusion" to violate company policy.[52] However, if too few problems are resolved at lower levels, higher management will be overburdened.

The task of higher management, then (and it is not an easy one), is to devise means which, on the one hand, facilitate the harmonious disposition of such differences as may be best resolved at lower levels, and, on the other hand, insure that top management makes those decisions which are appropriately its own.

---

[52] This point is discussed at length in Brown, *op. cit.*

30. RUMORS IN WAR*

Theodore Caplow

Methodological Note

It was one of the routine duties of the regimental S-2 section to which the writer belonged to prepare a monthly intelligence report, which included a section on rumors. The five members of the section ranged in rank from private to captain and were unanimously enthusiastic about gathering rumors. Since they were in contact with every company in the unit at frequent intervals and their several ranks allowed association with every individual in the organization, rather wide coverage was usually obtained. Most rumors were transmitted to the writer within a few hours of being heard and set down in writing immediately, both for official purposes and in the interest of this study. Each report of a rumor was noted on a separate sheet together with the immediate source, the ostensible original source, the estimated diffusion, the date and circumstances, and an estimate of validity from both the reporter and the source. All five men became familiar with the mechanisms of the rumor process and appeared to acquire some expertness in estimating diffusion and validity. In addition to these regular "interviewers," there were about 20 other individuals scattered through the organization who were familiar with the project in either its official or its private aspect, and made it their business to accumulate rumors and pass them on to the writer. Information obtained from them was recorded in the same way.

At the end of each month, a count was made of rumors in circulation during the period, classified as to subject-matter and diffusion. The number of reports of each rumor furnished a rough check on the observers' estimates of degree of diffusion. Needless to say, no mention of persons was ever made in the official reports.

The original notes, together with a prepared summary which included considerable numerical data, were confiscated during demobilization by a unit censor who took a broad view of his prerogatives, and the present report has been written from memory.

Studying the Rumors

Classroom experiments show a very high degree of distortion in the chainwise transmission of rumors. The usual method is to prepare statements in a field of interest to the student-subjects, to convey them to one

---

* Taken from *Social Forces*, Vol. XXV (October, 1946–May, 1947).

student either orally or in writing and to analyze the changes either step by step or in the final process. The most striking finding in such a study is typically the fantastic variation in content. Other findings are expansion and contraction dictated by interest motives, a tendency to simplify categories, increase amounts, and amalgamate logically connected events. From these findings—and from related experiments on the validity of eye-witness reports—social psychologists have tended to classify the rumor process as a rather aberrant form of communication and to focus attention only upon its sweeping unreliability.[1]

In security training of both the armed forces and the civilian population, great emphasis was placed upon the danger of rumor-mongering because of distortion, elaboration, and panic effects. Rumors do undoubtedly threaten military secrecy insofar as they may contain the gist of military secrets. But there is little evidence to show how the rumor process actually works and whether the generalizations derived from classroom experiments can be applied without hesitation to all situations in which rumors circulate.

During two years' service in the Pacific Theatre the writer had the opportunity to check the frequency of rumors in about a dozen company-size units of one regiment, and their transmission from unit to unit. Something more than the significance of casual observation is claimed for these findings, since definite hypotheses were held in view during the period and rather extensive notes were kept. On the other hand, it was not possible to estimate the completeness of so informal a survey with any confidence, and coverage is known to have varied during the period. Consequently, the material is at best descriptive and at worst unverifiable. It is presented here in the hope that it will invite discussion in terms of related observations of the rumor process in well-integrated functioning social groups.

The word "rumor" as used here, is defined as an item of information with definite interest connotations transmitted *only* by informal person-to-person communication within a group. Rumors are thus by definition "Unconfirmed." Also, there is sound perception in the colloquial usage which almost invariably exludes items not linked to group interests (e.g. these natives used to be cannibals) from the category of rumors.

The frequency of rumors in the group studied was surprisingly low in view of a great deal of concern with the rumor process and with the prevalence of rumors. The greatest number discovered in one month was seventeen, less than one per hundred men. During one period of two weeks, not a single new rumor could be discovered.

The rate of diffusion was invariably rapid. It is sometimes hard to ac-

---

[1] See, for example, Clifford Kirkpatrick, "A Tentative Study in Experimental Social Psychology," *American Journal of Sociology*, 38, 2, p. 194.

count reasonably for the speed with which a rumor can leap a 300 mile gap in the course of an afternoon. In one case, the rumor of an impending operation appeared in a detachment isolated on a tiny island without radio communication approximately one day after it was introduced to the main body of the regiment. Similar "grapevine" effects are noted in all groups in whose activities the rumor process plays an important part. A partial explanation will be suggested later.

The extent of diffusion was rather great, ranging from 100 per cent in several cases to perhaps as low as 1 per cent in cases where value was attached to possession of the information—but seldom that low, since the suitability of the item for transmission is what creates a rumor in the first place.

The majority of rumors contained three associated statements.[2] A considerable number contained one statement or two statements, and only a negligible proportion more than three statements. The tendency toward tripartite form was so great that even narratives tended to conform to it.

During a given period, there appear to be certain centers from which most rumors emanate. Headquarters is always such a center and so is the front line during actual battle. Individuals may assume the function of starting rumors, even in the absence of special information.[3]

The rate of diffusion appeared to decrease in some rough ratio to the distance from the center of emanation, though no very regular ratio could be discovered. In general, too, the extent of diffusion decreased as the distance from the center of emanation increased. The distance referred to here is a composite of physical distance and social distance. Diffusion of rumors was greater when the entire organization was collected in one or two ships but appeared to take place through the same channels established in the more normal situation on land.

The "channels" through which Army rumors diffuse are particularly important for an understanding of the whole process. Most of the diffusion of rumors actually took place through a relatively small number of rather well-defined paths. In two instances known to the writer, a rumor was planted at a fairly remote point in the channel with the intention of influencing a superior. In both cases, the information reached its destination, and in one case, had the predicted effect. Several factors combine to produce the channel system. Some of them, such as the limited number of contacts available to a single individual, the tendency to communicate

---

[2] For example (June 28, 1945): We are going to be in the Kyushu invasion . . . Already attached to the __ Division for it . . . High point men will be left behind . . .

[3] During one three-month period, Pvt. B— originated more rumors than the rest of the officers and men in his Battalion combined. B— was an elderly man, who had been an amateur of military history in civilian life, had considerable knowledge of strategy, and made it his chief business in the Army to extract reliable information from various sources.

new rumors where old ones have been received with appreciation, the dependence upon recognized centers of emanation, and the value attached to the possession of information are rather obvious. A particularly important one is the division of a military organization into sub-groups, both formal and informal, between which communication is limited. The most conspicuous of these divisions is that between officers and enlisted men. Only a few of the members of each group habitually communicated the rumors originating in their own group to members of the other, and these few habitual contacts—their number further reduced by considerations of confidence and of military secrecy—were the only bridges by which most rumors passed from one group to the other. The same was true of other divisions in terms of congeniality groups, sub-groupings of rank, company and battalion units, geographically separated groups linked only by radio operators, or by truck drivers and boat crews.

These tended to be two-way channels, since the communication of rumors is more often than not, marked by an exchange. The customary *quid pro quo* for a rumor is either another rumor or a validity judgment upon the one received. But the tendency was strictly limited by the rather small amount of valued information available at points in the channel distant from the center of emanation. It might be hypothesized that this would lead to greater stringency of validity judgments farthest from the center of emanation, and in fact this effect was often observed, though counterbalanced by the lack of background information with which to form a critical judgment; for example, among rear echelon personnel hearing of casualties on another island.

Several factors are related to the frequency and the extent of diffusion in a given period. The most important is the amount of nonrumored information in circulation. However, the curiosity of individuals may vary, the demand for information by a group—upon which the rumor process depends—appears to be easily saturated. The total amount of current information rather than the subject-matter of the information items is what seems to determine the state of demand. Before the invasion of the Philippines, the organization was elaborately briefed on the geography, ethnology, architecture, mores, and terrain of the new territory. Compulsory formations were held once or twice a week for instruction of this kind, and brochures were posted on bulletin boards, copied in unit newspapers, and often embodied in general orders. As this program continued, the number of rumors diminished sharply, despite sustained discussion of subjects like local enemy opposition and the accessibility of Filipinas, upon which the information program was reticent. The rumorless period previously mentioned occurred upon a ship in one of the invasion convoys in which the ship's captain made a practice of announcing over the public address system anything of interest that came to the bridge and would not be known on deck—such as a submarine search by escort vessels over the horizon. In this situation again, there were areas of immediate interest in which information was scant, and about which rumors would ordinarily have been expected, but the hourly bombardment of announcements on the convoy's progress seemed to satisfy the total demand for information.

Scores of similar incidents created the impression, presented here as an hypothesis, that the demand for particular information in a group of this kind can be satisfied by any other information not totally irrelevant, if presented in sufficient amount.

Anything which disrupted the arrangement of "channels" appeared to increase the frequency and decrease the diffusion of rumors. Very thorough scattering of the organization occasionally took place and had this effect. Occasional official campaigns directed against rumor-mongering invariably increased the number of rumors and decreased the average diffusion. In this case, another factor may have been the enhanced value placed on the forbidden information. Rapid changes of plan effected by higher headquarters at certain periods placed variant rumors in the same channels at the same time and for short periods led to increases in both frequency and diffusion. Periods of organizational inactivity were usually marked by increases in frequency of rumors, and decreases in average diffusion.

When the group structure—and most of the channels—is destroyed, the same pattern of increasing frequency and decreasing diffusion is noted in intensified form. About a third of the regiment left together in the first large group to be returned for demobilization after V–J day. During a two week period at a camp near port, as many rumors were heard daily as had been heard in a typical month of the preceding two years. However, diffusion was slight even within the same barracks, and different patterns of rumor prevailed in each of some twenty barracks despite almost frenzied interchange of items at all levels.

Turning from the form to the content of rumors, we find configurations equally alien to the classroom experiment.

The most frequent subject of rumors were impending operations, and the travels connected with them. These alone accounted for slightly more than half of the total number in the first twelve months, and slightly less than half in the remainder of the period. Next in frequency were rumors relating to rotation, repatriation, and demobilization, followed by administrative changes, such as anticipated regulations, secret orders, promotions, shifts in personnel functions, and in command. Other recurrent categories were casualties (particularly those in related regiments and divisions), disease, domestic politics, atrocities (about equally divided between those referred to the enemy and those referred to United States or allied troops), vice and corruption (either as prevailing in a particular unit, or attributed to high-ranking officers), and progress of the war (including peace rumors). These categories are admittedly very broad. The rumor of an impending movement might include not only the geographical objective, but also any of the related topics that might be found in a field order —from the calibre of emplaced artillery to the disposition of crocodiles in the creeks.

Then, too, many rumors took the form of an authoritative quotation, with the actual content left to the determination of private inference. A well-known general was quoted as saying that the organization would be home by Christmas, and the rumor remained in that form, leaving room for argument as to whether the statement implied the end of the war or return to the States in connection with training activities. Often, rumors in quotation form embodied no more than an attitude, as when a new commanding officer was reported to have promised to "make it tough" for headquarters troops. What is significant about these categories is the close correspondence to prevailing values. Information not linked to the major group interests simply failed to move along the rumor channels, though much of it was available at all points.

The veracity of rumors was high. With only two doubtful exceptions (doubtful because the appropriate rumor may have circulated without being observed by the writer), every major operation, change of station, and important administrative change was accurately reported by rumor before any official announcement had been made. In the category "progress of the war"—perhaps the most important category from the standpoint of morale—only one completely false rumor ever attained wide diffusion— the rumor that Germany had surrendered in November, 1944. The writer is not sufficiently informed to describe the apparently world-wide spread of this story. As circulated in the organization observed, it was based on a quasi-official announcement, which though vehemently denied later, seems actually to have been made. What is striking is that the reception of this peace story was marked by hesitation and reservation of judgment, as was the authentic peace news of 1945. Many of the "impending movement" rumors were based on plans which were later changed. Many of them contained half-truths, approximations, and inaccuracies of detail. But the selective process tended to favor the accurate items. Since military secrecy did not ordinarily forbid the informal denial or refutation of false information, a long period of planning invariably was accompanied by a progressively more accurate body of surmises.

The veracity of rumors did not decline noticeably during transmittal. Errors in transmission were apparently well-compensated by selection. Commanders were known to remark that their line companies (usually distant from centers of emanation) "knew" more than they did about the probability of impending movements. Quite often, this was literally true.

Exaggeration and distortion took place in the course of transmission along a channel, and were most readily observable where numerical statements were involved. But, in general, the final form of a rumor was more condensed than its early forms, and the three-statement form tended to maintain itself. Most changes were toward simplification of statements rather than addition or subtraction. The rapidity of ordinary transmission is itself selective. A rumor is usually heard more than once, and usually transmitted more than once by each individual in the channel. This re-circulation tends to eliminate variation and if circumstances allow sufficient time, the final form of a rumor for a sizeable percentage of the group may be a statement in prescribed form with a high degree of consensus on every word.

Distortion in terms of wishes and avoidances seems to be an individual rather than a group characteristic. As channels solidified, this phenomenon became comparatively rare, because of the exclusion of persons associated with previous invalidity. When the channels were broken up, wish-fulfillment again became conspicuous in the pattern.

There was a positive and unmistakable relation between the survival of a rumor, in terms of both time and diffusion, and its veracity. No relation between the survival of a rumor, and its favorableness, was observed. The absence of this phenomenon may be related to the conventional and defensive pessimism of an army in the field.

The question of veracity can be seen more clearly as a part of a total situation than by considering rumors separately. Typically, an interest-situation was created by circumstances (e.g., the conclusion of one operation focussed interest on the next), a number of rumors then appeared and began to circulate, the number progressively decreasing and the average diffusion increasing, until the interest-situation was terminated either by an official announcement or by the occurrence or nonoccurrence of the rumored event. This sequence was relatively invariable for the category of greatest frequency (impending movements and operations) and tended to occur—with greater or lesser time periods—in many of the other categories.

There were long-range trends as well during the two-year period. The decreasing number and greater average diffusion toward the end of the period points both to a solidification of channels and a greater expertness in evaluating information. Increasing negative prestige was attached to the transmission of false rumors, and this was accompanied by a tendency to attach sources to doubtful statements. At least one rumor circulated among hundreds of men with the name of the original source attached. A validity estimate was almost always attached to a rumor, and many of them were communicated with a warning, such as, "I don't believe a word of this, but. . . ." Increasing scepticism and objectivity led to the drawing of a sharp line between rumors and other information, so that rumors were usually labelled as such in the telling, and interestingly enough, official announcements were often doubted by men who had not seen them in written form. Neither the German surrender, nor the announcement of the point system, won general acceptance until a considerable time after the first radio announcement.

Conclusions

The rumor process in the group observed was a fairly successful group device for circulating desired information. Rumors tended to diffuse along definite channels of person-to-person communication. The formation of channels decreased the number of rumors and increased their diffusion. The effect of transmission was to increase rather than decrease the validity of the statements.

The wide variation between these findings and the results of classroom experiments, implies no criticism of the latter. The rumor process described here was a rather complicated group activity extended over a considerable period of time, and accompanied by group interests stronger than any of those found in a classroom. The modes of communication involved were vastly more complicated than the simple chainwise transmission of the experimental situation. It should be noted that most of the tendencies toward distortion which were discovered in the classroom did exist in the theatre of operations, but that definite group devices developed to diminish their effect. The findings do illustrate, however, the difficulty of projecting generalizations about an interaction process from the laboratory to the field.

31. CONTROL TOWER LANGUAGE*

F. C. Frick and W. H. Sumby

Shannon and others have estimated that written English is about 60 per cent redundant. These estimates are arrived at by considering linguistic constraints on our use of speech symbols; they do not consider additional restrictions imposed by the audience and the situation in which the speaker finds himself. In order to estimate the effects of such nonlinguistic constraints, an informational analysis has been made of the "sublanguage" used in the control of aircraft by Air Force control tower operators. When the situational, as well as linguistic, contexts are taken into account, the estimated redundancy is raised to 96 per cent.

How informative a given speech sample is—how much we say—depends to a large extent on how much we might have said.

"Speaking English" imposes certain constraints on our use of linguistic symbols. The individual elements—phonemes, letters, words—which make up our vocabulary are not used equally often and they are not combined at random. In addition, the rules of grammar and the desire to make sense impose restrictions on the order in which groups of these symbols are strung together. In short, knowing the language of the speaker implies that we know quite a lot about the rules which govern his selection of speech symbols. It means that we are less uncertain about what will be said than we would be if the speaker did not operate under these known restrictions.

If we define information transmission as the rate of change in our *a priori* uncertainty, then we must say that the English language conveys less information than it could convey. This reduction in information that occurs when we pass from what might have been said (given the same vocabulary) to what actually is said is called "redundancy."

Special languages—cant, patois, technical talk—all involve additional restrictions and, for the listener familiar with them, entail increased redundancy. What we wish to do here is to consider one particular sublanguage of English and estimate the reduction in information transmission from what could be transmitted using alphabetical sequences. The language considered is that used in the control of aircraft by the operator of a control tower at a military airbase. It is made up of sentences like: "Air Force 5264. Ready number one in take-off position. Over." Or: "Extend your base. We have a C-54 on final."

---

*Reproduced by permission from *The Journal of the Acoustical Society of America,* Vol. 24, No. 6, 595–96, November, 1952.

These messages form a subset of the set of all possible English sentences —which in turn is a subset of all possible English letter sequences.

What this means can be illustrated fairly simply. All that is required is for you to imagine the set of all possible permutations of the English alphabet and a space symbol. Each point in this set represents a possible sequence of letters.

We could now, in principle, go through this set of letter sequences and select out those sequences that are acceptable as English sentences. This will clearly cut down the size of our original set. The knowledge that we are operating within this subset of English sentences reduces our initial uncertainty. And Shannon[1] has developed a technique that permits us to estimate how much this reduction amounts to. Essentially, we ask our subjects to guess at successive letters of English text. When we do this, we find that the subject can exploit his implicit knowledge of the statistical structure of the language and predict the English sequence considerably better than he can predict sequences of letters chosen at random.

If we now ask the same subjects to guess at the text of control tower messages, we find that prediction is still further improved. The uncertainty of our subjects was, on the average, about 28 per cent of their uncertainty regarding random sequences of letters and spaces—that is, of course, subjects who are familiar with control tower language. They were, in fact, control tower operators. (Actually, people who are not practiced in this strange sublanguage do just about as well. The airplane and its control has apparently been absorbed into our linguistic culture.)

However, this is still an overestimate of the uncertainty, or unpredictability, of messages in the actual situation. The figure above is arrived at when we select letter sequences at random from the set of admissible tower messages. In any given instance, the message is, of course, not generated at random. The pilot, for example, knows whether he is landing or taking off and this (the situational context) further restricts the set of possible messages.

In order to estimate these situational constraints we described a group of hypothetical situations to 100 Air Force pilots and asked them to predict the tower message. For practical reasons we could not use Shannon's guessing game technique, so we adopted another device.

The messages the pilots predicted for us are rather easily split up into content units—phases that have the same meaning—e.g., gear down and locked, gear in the green—or that differ only with respect to the numbers or place names involved:—runway zero nine, runway two zero. A message is made up of a sequence of these message units. And it is at this level that the immediate situation seems to operate by determining what message units will be selected and in what order they will occur. These units, thought of as letter sequences, are subject to the linguistic con-

[1] C. E. Shannon, *Bell System Tech. Jour.*, Vol. 30, 1951, pp. 50–64.

straints that we have already estimated. In effect, we have the physical situation determining the gross uncertainty of the message (in terms of content units) and the linguistic constraints determining the uncertainty of the units (as sequences of letters and spaces).

To illustrate, let us consider a specific case. The pilot is told: *You are coming in to land. Ceiling and visibility unlimited. You have just called in: "Andrews Tower. This is Air Force 1234. Eight miles south of your station. Landing instructions please."* Each statement sets up additional restrictions on the set of possible tower messages.

If we now look at the actual distribution of predicted messages which we obtained in this case, we find that they are sequences of selections from only 13 message units. Furthermore, these elements do not appear with equal frequency, nor does any single message include all 13 elements. A large number of possible messages thus turn out to be impossible—or at any rate highly improbable. The message set is thus further reduced.

Lastly, this language has, at the level of content units, its own peculiar

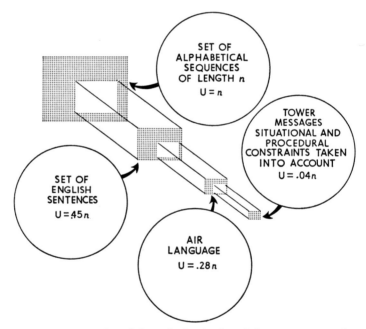

FIG. 1. Schematic representation of the reduction in size of the message set and consequent reduction in uncertainty (U) as additional message restrictions are taken into account.

grammar, known as *RT procedure*. The pilot knows this procedure (though ours didn't know it very well) and this procedure fixes the order in which particular units are selected to make up the predicted message.

With such a small sample we cannot determine the total effect of these sequential dependencies in restricting the message class. But we can estimate these constraints over two or three units. When we do this for this particular case, we find that the pilot's uncertainty of the message (in terms of content units) is about 80 per cent less than it would have been if the units were equally likely and messages were generated by a random selection of content units (with no repeats).

This figure of 80 per cent varies somewhat with the particular situation. For the 15 different situations that we chose, it averages 86 per cent.

In other words, the situational context, including the pilot's knowledge of procedures, reduces the gross uncertainty of the message about 86 per cent. Linguistic constraints reduce the residual uncertainty, in terms of letter sequences, another 72 per cent—giving us an estimated redundancy, with respect to what could have been conveyed using letter and space sequences, of approximately 96 per cent. The entire process is illustrated in Figure 1.

This is a large figure and any communication system which tolerates so much redundancy is in some sense inefficient. The situation is not as bad, however, as might at first be imagined. This is a noisy system. In part, at least, it is unavoidably noisy. It is also a system with a low tolerance for error—planes are more expensive than transmission time or band width—and redundancy is an effective means of combating noise and error. In other words, we may not transmit much information, but what is transmitted is important and the high degree of redundancy is a form of insurance—a sort of running check on our transmission.

Control and Evaluation

THE PROBLEM of control is that of obtaining a desired result in the face of conditions that might oppose or interfere. Evaluation, on the other hand, implies a more reflective and analytical approach to a way of controlling based on longer-term experience and resulting in less frequent intervention, which yields improved control for the future.

Much attention has been given to these two topics. They have been explored intensively in specific contexts, such as the management of organizations, and as an abstract mathematical problem. Theory at the mathematical level has become so highly developed that it can greatly assist the comprehension of specific applications. In fact, such concepts as *systems analysis* and *cybernetics* have come to denote the common elements that run through many control problems arising in different fields: engineering, physiology, ecology, and social science. A professional society, the Society for General Systems Research, has been formed to focus on the general similarities of system logic across all fields of application. Its Yearbook (12) publishes research in this vein.

A full statement of the theory that has been developed to unify these diverse fields requires preparation in the mathematics of Fourier and Laplace transforms, calculus of variations, and stochastic processes. The articles in this section by Haberstroh and by Fey include fairly elementary mathematical models (first-order differential and difference equations) that will provide some understanding for those with at least this much mathematical preparation. There are a number of textbooks which can be consulted, ranging in the level of preparation required from high school algebra (1) to quite advanced mathematics (7, 10, 17).

The major concepts in systems logic do not require the advanced mathematical treatment that is often accorded them. The ability to read flow charts and an intuitive grasp of the meaning of the symbols included in them are enough to permit the student to follow the arguments

503

presented in this section. The general structure of a control problem is presented in Figure 1. The most important elements of a system diagram (boxes and arrows) are present. The boxes represent *operators* of any degree of complexity. These are active elements, whose behavior may or may not be entirely determined by their *inputs* (arrows leading toward the box). Nevertheless, the input arrows denote causal variables that influence the behavior of the operators. The *outputs* from any box represent whatever behavior of that operator may be of interest to the systems analyst. The presence of an arrow implies some sort of measurement process that can be applied to the operator's behavior at any given time to determine a specific value for the output. The arrows, thus, represent communication channels from one operator to another. The message sent may be regarded as a mathematical function of time, the values of which are chosen from a particular range (alphabet) of values. Where advanced mathematics is used, it is generally to build models of the operators and derive the resulting system behavior.

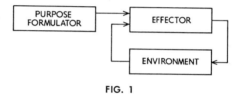

FIG. 1

The *system* is the configuration of elements that is completely specified by the flow chart. In Figure 1, the system is composed of three operators linked so that the first (purpose formulator) influences the behavior of the second (effector) which, in turn, both influences and is influenced by the third (environment).

A simple example may be helpful. Consider the operation of an ordinary household thermostat. The purpose formulator is the behavior of the householder, perhaps involving a great deal of interaction with his wife and children, that results in a setting of the thermostat. This setting is the arrow that leads from purpose formulator to effector. The value of this setting at any time may take any value within the range of normal household temperatures: say, from 55° F. to 90° F. The effector is the heating system itself, composed of a thermometer, control circuitry, switches, fuel valves, furnace, heat conduits, etc. The effector influences the environment by spilling forth large quantities of heat or by refraining from doing so. The environment, in turn, influences the furnace by communicating a temperature value to its thermometer. The control circuitry of the furnace compares the temperature with the thermostat setting and turns the furnace on or off according to whether the temperature is lower or higher than the setting. The resulting system behavior is a fairly even temperature inside the house during cold weather. Notice how the use of a system diagram simplifies the heating control problem and isolates the complexities of the design of heating systems (behavior of the householder, construction of the furnace, environmental heat flow) in three separate operators with the relevant relationships among them completely specified.

Much of systems theory has been concerned with defects that are commonly found in control systems. In our example, suppose that the operation of the heating system is blocked by furnace failure. Then the environment of the furnace would approach the outside temperature, fluctuating with it in an uncontrolled manner. Alternatively, suppose the system is blocked by jamming the furnace in the "on" position. Then the temperature of the environment of the furnace increases steadily until some element of the furnace fails or until heat from the furnace is balanced by heat flow from the house, the final result again being fluctuation in an uncontrolled manner. A more interesting example is the phenomenon of *overcontrol*. Suppose because of stickiness in the control circuit, the turning on or off of the furnace is delayed for one hour past the time when the temperature passes the thermostat setting. Then the temperature will show wide swings, building up far past normal room temperature and then cooling down well below. This is known as *oscillation* or *hunting*. It can also result from systematic changes in the thermostat setting by the householder in response to temperature changes.

Effects of this kind are common in feedback systems. They result from the use of weak forces (like the pressure of a finger on the thermostat or the movement of a thermocouple in the furnace control) to influence strong forces (like the heat output of a furnace). If interference then develops in the feedback, with the weak forces being buffeted by the strong ones, highly unstable behavior such as oscillation or explosion can occur. These failures include such phenomena as the gyrations of a missile after launching, a neurological disease (purpose tremor), migratory behavior of lemmings, and some of the organizational pathology reported in the articles reprinted below by Fey and Ridgway.

At this point, it is well to caution the reader against one misconception that he may have developed from our discussion of the thermostat. Operators are not necessarily to be regarded as concrete entities (householder, furnace, house) that are easily identified. An operator is that which operates on information inputs and generates observable outputs. Only in engineering systems are these operators designed one apart from the other and installed in separate boxes that can be physically handled independently of one another. In natural systems, and especially in organizational systems, one physical entity may take part in the activity of many different system operators. A single executive in an organization may have many problems on his mind that will result in information outputs to different parts of the organization. These may play a part in several very different control efforts. Even in automated systems, a large digital computer may, on a time-sharing basis, perform a part of the information processing of many different system operators. In the nervous system, blood and neurons may convey messages concurrently that are part of different bodily control functions. The "operator," thus, is an abstraction conceived by a theorist or a designer to explain or implement a controlled process. In social systems, control activities are frequently a part of social functions as described in Sections 1 and 2. It is the coherence in behavior patterns, rather than physical makeup, that is sought after in this kind of logical analysis.

In complex systems such as organizational controls or automated plants, the above is only a part, although an important one, of the total picture. The development of theory has turned recently (since 1950) to a different class of problems referred to variously as *second-order control, nonlinear systems,* and *adaptive control* (**10, 17, 18**). In Figure 1, this kind of problem could be introduced by a detailed exploration of the purpose formulator. Likewise, the occasional contribution of a heating engineer (as in remodeling) is an adaptive control function that occurs in real systems, although no provision for it has been included in Figure 1. Broadly speaking, the role of the second-order elements is to adapt the first-order control to a broader context, to see that it subserves more global and, perhaps, less explicitly formulated purposes. This reflects an *evaluation* function in respect to the first-order controls.

The expansion of systems theory to include operators that perform an evaluation or adaptive function has been a major advance comparable in scope to the original development of feedback models. It provides, in principle, a solution to any formulable problem in control. In specific applications to the control of organizations, it supplies the underlying rationale for many practices that have been recognized as effective. It also provides the kind of understanding that enables refinement and innovation in these practices.

The nature of adaptive or second-order elements is quite different from first-order feedback loops. The inputs are more numerous and more diffuse. The homeowner in setting a thermostat takes account of whether he is setting for daytime or nighttime use, who in the family will be occupying the house, what season it is, and whether the furnace has been functioning adequately recently. The heating engineer might need to know the structure of the house, the quality of insulation, the average number of days of sunshine, the average quality of fuel which is supplied to the furnace, the age of existing equipment, the expected useful life of various components as determined from industry experience, etc. The operations that are performed on these inputs are diverse and complicated. The determination of long-run averages and extreme limits of variation are important. Calculation of trends and other parameters is also common. These are the same operations that have long been used in statistical analysis for business and industrial decisions. The outputs, too, are different. They change in value relatively infrequently; but, when they do, it is by discrete jumps, such as changing a thermostat setting from day temperature to desired night temperature. These outputs are always inputs to lower-level elements in the control system. They change the mode of behavior of these lower-level elements.

Note the complexity of data processing implicit in the industrial dynamics simulation of the Sprague Electric production-inventory-sales system as described by Fey. The result of this processing was a prescription for certain changes in the mode of response of lower-order control functions. Likewise, the analysis of bombing scores contained in the Hemphill and Sechrest article has certain implications for the use of performance data in determining lead crew assignments. These studies are themselves sophisticated evaluations of system performance, and both have had direct impact upon the behavior of the respective organizational control systems. These evaluation activities were performed by outsiders acting essentially as consultants. Haberstroh's article, in reporting the nonroutine control activities of Integrated Steel, and the article by Williams and Wilson on project cost control at Raytheon's Wayland Laboratory illustrate a more usual kind of evaluation—within executive groups.

The preceding discussion has created a theoretical setting for the discussion of control problems that are peculiarly organizational in nature. When dealing with particular organizational phenomena or with the functioning of particular elements, their place in the system of control and evaluation is a matter of central concern. Systems logic provides a usable tool to establish that place and to consider its relationship to the functioning of the total system. Problems of control and evaluation thus require a conjoining of theories of social behavior with the more abstract ideas of systems theory (3, 6, 13).

Formulation of Purpose

As we have seen in Section 2, organizations are rationally designed instruments of social purpose. The formal goals of an organization typically subserve some more general social goal. Formal goals, in turn, are elaborated into a complex set of subgoals and means activities. Chester Barnard (2) has identified this function—the elaboration of purpose—as one of the key functions of the executive. This is one respect in which executives perform higher-order control functions. The problem of adapting the formal goals and the elaborated structure of subgoals to more global and more diffuse criteria of social value is indeed the highest concept of executive responsibility. Barnard clearly grasped the system significance of this function in his discussion of executive responsibility, which he related to feedbacks of information on the consequences of organized action interpreted according to relevant moral codes. A similar definition of executive responsibility is implicit in the work of Elliott Jaques (9) who measures responsibility (for pay purposes) as the time span between the executive's initiation of action and the feedback of the results thereof. Situations that can be corrected immediately are unlikely to be detrimental to overall system goals and, thus, involve less exercise of responsibility.

The formal, rationally planned structure is not, however, the only manifestation of purpose in organization functioning. Unlike components in an engineered system, human beings invariably play multiple roles in different social systems. The identity of the actor as an individual person requires him to harmonize these roles and permits him to exploit some in the service of others. Barnard's concept of *efficiency* captures the essence of this need to relate organizational systems to individual purposes. The negotiation of participation is another major executive function in his schema. Many examples of this, found in earlier articles, are relevant to control activities. In Horsfall and Arensberg's shoe factory work teams, the accommodation of the worker's allocation technique to management pressure for rush orders is a good example of the attainment of organization purposes under efficiency constraints. Similarly the inspection procedure in Dalton's industrial plant represented an accommodation between the social system and managerial demands for a control procedure. In Section 3, Chowdhry and Pal's textile mill A had not found an accommodation between individual needs and task requirements. In contrast to the instability of textile mill A, Crozier's tobacco factories are so rigidly structured that adaptation and change are almost nonexistent, although the system seems stable and productive in terms of its formal goals.

Power Elements

The question of social power, although an important and obvious one, remains difficult to formulate theoretically. In the case studies we have examined, the loci of power have been obvious enough: the agriculturists in TVA, the workers' clique in the shoe factory, the Swain clique, the managing agent of textile mill A. Perhaps the most important characteristic of power is the ability to choose one course of action rather than another for oneself, a group, an organization, or a society. Power is exercised within a range that is constrained by other power. Crozier's tobacco factories offer a very good illustration. The technical engineer was powerful because of his leadership of the interests of the maintenance workers together with their joint mastery of the plant technology. This gave them the power of choice in the only situation of uncertainty (machine breakdown) left in a rigidly structured system. By this ability to threaten or implement the common concerns of all, the maintenance department was able to control its own individual and collective satisfactions. In a few cases of major reorganization, however, power passed to the directors, as the area of uncertainty switched from routine, mechanical operations to longer-range planning. Here the talents and legitimate authority of the directors gave them significant choices.

If power implies choice, then the realization of system control implies a reduction of choice of action other than in support of organization purposes. Weber points out how the structure of rules in bureaucracy assures that the individual bureaucrat "is chained to his activity" and "forged to the community of all the functionaries . . . in seeing that the mechanism continues its functions." The programming of effector responses to information inputs in a way that supports organization purposes is achieved by designing and enforcing decision rules that guide the behavior of the various functionaries. The safety programs at Integrated Steel and the inventory and production policies of Sprague Electric are collections of such decision rules. In general the rules specify exactly what the effector is to do and on what occasions. All roles in the tobacco plant were thus constrained, with the exception of the maintenance department. At the same time that the power of individuals or groups is limited, the power behind the ideal interests represented by formal purposes is increased. The entire collection of programs and activities that can be mobilized in the effectors works directly in the service of these interests. The integration of effectors into the overall system assures this.

Although social power is linked closely with the ability to choose and is transformable from one sphere of action into another, this does not imply the existence or meaningfulness of a calculus of power comparable to that which exists for physical systems. The dimensionality of physical power is formulated in terms of *energy*, which can be measured by physical techniques. The dimensionality of social power is that of human values, the measurement of which poses certain apparently insuperable difficulties which will be dealt with in the section on decision making.

System Configuration

As formulated in system theory, the relationships among elements are the communication channels that serve as input and output. Communications of purpose and of performance feedbacks are typically part of formal communication. The maintenance of such communications is Barnard's third major executive function. As we have seen in Section 5, maintaining valid communication among people of different and often conflicting interests is difficult. Where corrective actions take the form of discipline, punishment, or other actions contrary to individual needs, resistance may take the form of manipulation of communications. The discussion of "surprise overruns" in project cost control by Williams and Wilson is an example. Research by Dalton, additional to that included in this volume, turned up case material illustrating a rich variety of ways in which performance information was falsified to protect matters of individual or group concern (5). Some of the examples cited by Ridgway (e.g., sacrificing maintenance for production records) also illustrate ways of manipulating performance reports.

The operation of second-order elements may also result in system difficulties. In management literature and in operations research, the operating parameters that result from evaluation activity are usually conceived as optima of some sort. In business, for example, production levels are thought to be set so as to maximize profits. In a classic operations research study during World War II, convoy size was set to minimize shipping losses due to enemy action. Such design features may be intended as optima, but they are rarely demonstrable as such. The existence of optima can be affirmed only within the framework of some model of the organization's functioning that admits of analytic methods (like the infinitesimal calculus) for defining the optima. An optimum value is a property of a model used by or recommended to an organization. A model in use is a design characteristic of the organization, a part of the formal organization usually, and may itself be subjected to an evaluation procedure.

Frequently a model is used because it is the best available choice even though optimum parameters derived from it are only remotely related to the overall goals of the organization. In such instances, the act of constraining organizational behavior in ways suggested by the optimality criteria of the model is referred to as *suboptimization* (8). An example of this is the use of measurements of performance that are compared with standards derived from a model. In this situation, the resources of the organization may be diverted to achieve the performance standards demanded even at the expense of the real goals. Thus in actual functioning the suboptima are likely to displace original goals. This is essentially the main thesis of the article by Ridgway.

In terms of the gross behavior of organizations as control systems, a number of interesting hypotheses exist in the literature. Cyert and March developed the term *organizational slack* to denote surplus resources, under the control of an organization, which are being converted to individual purposes (4). This surplus could be drawn upon in times of crisis to insure realization of organization purposes. Anecdotal evidence supporting the idea (e.g., frequent use of across-the-board budget cuts as a way of economizing) lends support to this hypothesis. A similar idea is advanced by Likert as to the relationship between morale and organizational effectiveness (11, p. 190). High morale can be exploited in times of crisis to generate unusual contributions to organization purpose; however, if this is done excessively it destroys the fabric of the social system. Since surplus resources, in a sense, buy high morale, the similarity of these mechanisms is clear. They differ in the prediction of long-run consequences. Both explanations have high face validity and both mechanisms probably operate in organizations.

Similar concerns have developed out of a measurement of "control structure" associated most closely with the work of Arnold Tannenbaum (14, 15). This involves the use of an attitude survey to measure member perceptions of the degree of control held by various organization components or categories of members. By plotting the degree of control against hierarchical level, as in Figure 2, contrasting control structures are identified. The general height of the control curve is hypothesized to

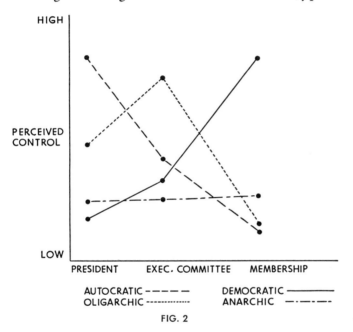

FIG. 2

differentiate active, highly-directed organizations from weak, inactive, uncoordinated organizations. This is supported by observed correlations between control structure and measures of effectiveness among local Leagues of Women Voters (15). A study of union locals suggests that the general degree of control may depend upon the degree to which the environment is perceived as threatening. Thus the power behind organization goals is, in part, a mobilization of the central interests of members.

BIBLIOGRAPHY

1. Ashby, W. R. *An Introduction to Cybernetics*. New York: John Wiley & Sons, Inc., 1956.

2. Barnard, Chester I. *The Functions of the Executive*. Cambridge, Mass.: Harvard University Press, 1938.

3. BONINI, CHARLES P.; JAEDICKE, ROBERT K.; WAGNER, HARVEY M. (eds.). *Management Controls: New Directions in Basic Research.* Seminar on Basic Research in Management Controls, Stanford University, 1963. New York: McGraw-Hill Book Co., 1964.

4. CYERT, RICHARD M. AND MARCH, JAMES G. *Behavioral Theory of the Firm.* Prentice-Hall, 1963.

5. DALTON, M. *Men Who Manage.* New York: John Wiley & Sons, Inc., 1959.

6. ECKMAN, D. P. (ed.). *Systems Research and Design.* First Systems Symposium, Case Institute of Technology, 1960. New York: John Wiley & Sons, Inc., 1961.

7. FLAGLE, C. D.; HUGGINS, W. H.; AND ROY, R. H. (eds.). *Operations Research and Systems Engineering.* Baltimore, Md.: The John Hopkins Press, 1960.

8. HITCH, C. J., AND R. McKEAN, "Suboptimization in Operations Problems," in J. F. McCLOSKEY AND F. N. TREFETHEN (eds.), *Operations Research for Management.* Baltimore, Md.: The John Hopkins Press, 1954.

9. JAQUES, ELLIOTT. *Measurement of Responsibility.* Cambridge, Mass.: Harvard University Press, 1956.

10. LEONDES, C. T. (ed.). *Advances in Control Systems: Theory and Applications.* New York: Academic Press, 1964.

11. LIKERT, R. *New Patterns of Management.* New York: McGraw-Hill Book Co., Inc., 1961.

12. SOCIETY FOR GENERAL SYSTEMS RESEARCH, *General Systems,* Yearbook, 1956 to date.

13. MALCOLM, D. G., AND ROWE, A. J. (eds.). *Management Control Systems.* Symposium on Management Information and Control Systems, Santa Monica, Calif., 1959. New York: John Wiley & Sons, Inc., 1960.

14. TANNENBAUM, ARNOLD S., AND KAHN, ROBERT L. "Organizational Control Structure," *Human Relations,* Vol. 10, No. 2, 1957.

15. TANNENBAUM, ARNOLD S. "Control and Effectiveness in a Voluntary Organization," *The American Journal of Sociology,* Vol. 67, No. 1, July, 1961.

16. WASSERMAN, P. *Measurement and Evaluation of Organizational Performance.* Ithaca, N.Y.: Cornell University, 1959.

17. WIENER, NORBERT. *Cybernetics.* 2nd edition. The M.I.T. Press and New York: John Wiley & Sons, Inc., 1961.

18. YOVITS, MARSHALL C.; JACOBI, GEORGE T. AND GOLDSTEIN, GORDON D. (eds.). *Self-Organizing Systems—1962.* Washington, D.C.: Spartan Books, 1962.

32. CONTROL AS AN ORGANIZATIONAL PROCESS*

Chadwick J. Haberstroh

The research reported is an attempt to discover to what extent the theory of self-regulating systems applies to human organizations in general and to one industrial plant in particular. Feedbacks of information on performance and objectives were found to have much influence on two types of executive decision processes: programming of routine work and innovation in the organization of executive functions. The control pattern included multiple, decentralized control loops. This combination worked adequately in an area—safety—where the results of decisions could not be forecasted with any accuracy.

THE STUDY of self-regulating systems, now generally known as cybernetics, explores the ways in which some output of a dynamic system can be maintained in a more-or-less invariant equilibrium, or steady state, in the face of disrupting external forces.[1] The most general answer to this question is that the system must somehow be supplied with information about the disrupting forces that is used to offset their effect. A common way of supplying this is by means of a feedback of information on the deviations of the output from equilibrium. This information flow causes the equilibrium to be restored in some appropriate manner.

Even assuming that one does know the feedback channel used and understands the laws through which the feedback restores equilibrium, he still has a right to ask how it is that the system exists at all, and why it tends to an equilibrium at that particular value and not some other. In the case of engineering control systems the answer to this question is simple and direct: the designer intended them to perform in the way they do. Thus, there is a purposive element in these control systems resulting from an *a priori* selection of the equilibrium to be obtained. If one asks the same question, however, about naturally self-regulating systems, such as homeostatic mechanisms in the living organism or ecological balances in a community of organisms, the answer is neither simple nor direct. The equilibria found and the mechanisms for attaining them have come about by the process of natural selection in the context of a particular environment. If we put the same question in the case of organizational systems, the answer is even less direct and more complicated, involving as it does a multitude of designers each consciously striving to realize his own ob-

---

* Reproduced from *Management Science*, Vol. 6, No. 2, January, 1960.
[1] N. Wiener, *Cybernetics* (New York: Wiley, 1948); W. R. Ashby, *An Introduction to Cybernetics* (New York: Wiley, 1956).

jectives, in the context of an environment and of selection pressure arising from the limitation of resources as well.

In organizations the conscious intentions of the participants are an important factor. In order to explain the gross behavior of an organization, these intentions must be measured and brought into relation with the other aspects of the organization's functioning. The existence of stable organization implies a degree of harmony and co-ordination among the participants, a sharing of intention. In order to secure this, participants communicate with each other and in doing so construct a common symbolic picture of the goals they have set for the organization and the means by which they intend to attain the goals. This picture, or representation, of the means and ends of organization (the "task model") is implicit in the verbal communication inside the organization. It can be measured by the use of content-analysis techniques. I have attempted to apply these techniques to a sample of communication from an integrated steel plant operated by one of the American companies.[2] This case will be used as an example in exploring organization purposes and other organizational characteristics affecting control processes.

Goal formation is influenced by the intentions of the individual participants and by the environmental constraints under which they operate. Both can be sources of conflict. The emergence of stable, enduring patterns of organization is in part a process of conflict resolution. The necessity of reducing conflict to manageable bounds tends to direct the organization's efforts toward a small number of goals and a small number of means activities for achieving them, relative to the number of alternatives that might be conceivable. It is to be expected, therefore, that the number of independent goals turned up in the task model will be rather small. Conflict reduction is facilitated if these goals are formulated in terms of acceptable levels, rather than in terms of optima,[3] and if the criterion of goal achievement is external and objective, rather than subjective and open to dispute. If members measure goal achievement objectively and perceive means to attain them, the goals are termed "operative."

In the case of Integrated Steel, four goals were discovered. These relate to cost reduction, production level, safety, and medical care. The safety and production goals are formulated in terms of acceptable levels set by an external office. Performance is measured in terms of tonnage

---

[2] This research was carried out at the Graduate School of Industrial Administration, Carnegie Institute of Technology, under a grant from the Ford Foundation for research on human behavior in organization. A full report of the methods and the results of this investigation, as well as a more thorough discussion of the topic of the present paper, is contained in my doctoral dissertation, *Processes of Internal Control in Firms*, University Microfilms, Inc. (Ann Arbor, Michigan, 1958).

[3] H. A. Simon, *Models of Man* (New York: Wiley, 1957), p. 241.

produced and frequency of injuries, and an elaborate technology exists for goal achievement. In the case of safety, this task model was measured in detail. The goal of providing adequate medical care was departmentalized in a plant hospital; and a standard cost system and various cost reduction programs were in operation. Neither the hospital nor the cost system was investigated, however.

If the process of goal formation results in a small number of operative goals, as it did at Integrated Steel, the basis for a feedback of information on deviations of performance from the established goals is already apparent. To affirm the existence of a control system we need only verify that this information is reported to executive centers and that the executives respond so as to achieve the goals. The task model comprises a program of means activities understood by the participants to lead to goal achievement. One way of responding would be to adjust the level of resource use in these means activities. Let us refer to this as "routine control." Another way of responding would be to look for a better way of achieving goals. This type of activity could take the form of inventing new means activities or of altering the system of executive organization (i.e., changes in personnel or in allocation of functions). It might be expected that this type of activity would occur only in a case of extreme or repeated failure. Let us call this "non-routine control." Sufficient pressure might even lead to modification of goals in order to assure survival of the organization. Normally, however, the evolved structure of goals and means activities determines what the participants do; communication channels carrying information on performance influence when and how much they do.

In the case of Integrated Steel's safety program the type of means activities which have been developed to implement the safety objective are accident investigations, safety conferences with workmen, implementation of safety work-orders, special inspections, clean-up work, etc. The execution of each of these activities is in some way conditional on the occurrence of injuries in the plant. Other activities are also carried on which are independent of the occurrence of accidents. These include routine inspections, training and screening procedures for new employees, safety clearance of engineering proposals, job analysis, publicity campaigns, etc.

The formal communication channels on safety performance begin with injury reports made by the plant hospital. This information is collated and distributed daily throughout the plant's executive organization in detail and in statistical summary. This information cues the line supervision to investigate injuries; alerts the plant safety staff to inspect for similar hazards and to assist in accident investigations; and, in summary figures, provides the basis for broader types of corrective action such as the study of classes of jobs for hazards, the issuance of special instructions to employees, and evaluation of supervisors. The same reports when aggregated into divisional and plant injury frequencies serve as an indicator of the plant's over-all performance relative to its safety goals.

The routine control processes discussed above are not the only, or even the most important, means of control used at Integrated Steel. The non-routine control processes, changes in personnel and in the institutional structure within which the participants operate, take precedence. The very nature of the accident process (i.e., the importance of human failure, rare events, conjunction of circumstances, and the randomness of occurrence of injuries) make for a different degree of reliability on the technological side from that encountered in connection with, for instance, production matters. Because the coupling between the program of means activities and the degree of safety performance is not fully determined, there is a need for relatively tight control over the programs themselves. This is achieved by response of the top plant management to deviations of the plant and departmental injury frequencies from the objectives set for them at the beginning of the year. These yearly objectives are set by company officers above the plant level, although the plant management has discretion to aim at a more difficult target if it chooses.

Figure 1 is a block diagram of the control structure discussed above.

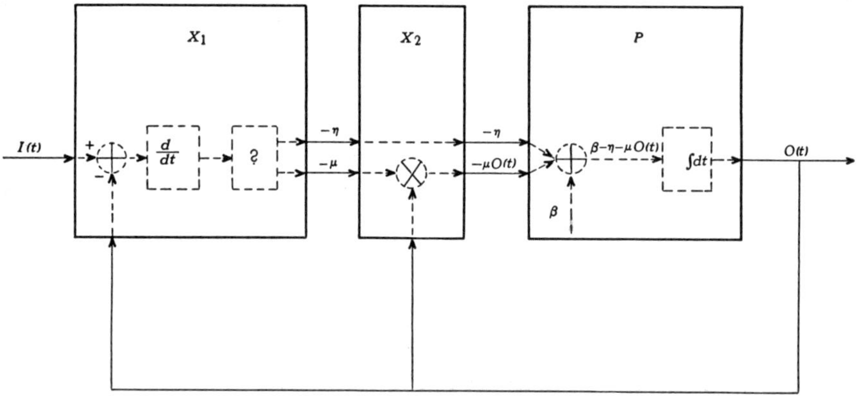

FIG. 1. Control Flow Chart of Safety Functions at Integrated Steel

The input (I) is the annual safety objective which is compared with the performance of the plant (O) by top management. The result of the nonroutine control functions of the top executive organization (X_1) may be expressed as the two parameters of the routine control system: the intensity of response to injuries (μ) and the level of independent safety activity (η). A complete model of the top executive function was not constructed, although there seems to be evidence[4] that it responds to

---

[4] Compare columns 4 and 11 in Table 1.

changes in the degree of error (a differentiating operator). Other than that it appears possible to say only that its effects are intermittent, rather than continuous, and respond only to error in excess of a certain threshold. It is therefore a nonlinear operator. In the case of the routine control function (X_2), however, a linear model seems appropriate. Executives appear to proportion their influence on the injury rate to the magnitude of that rate plus a constant. The "program" operator (P) relates the control activities to the actual performance of the plant, adding and integrating the safety efforts $(\mu O + \eta)$ and the exogenous load of new hazards (β).

Table 1 contains data on injury rates, safety objectives, and innovations in the safety program for a 10 year period. The changes in organization

TABLE 1

INNOVATION* AND PERFORMANCE AT INTEGRATED STEEL

		DISABLING INJURIES					TOTAL INJURIES			
Year	Aver- age All Plants	Error	Δ Error	Plant Per- formance	Error	Tar- get	Plant Perform- ance	Error	Tar- get	Innova- tion*
1	5.29	.98	.98	6.17			357			moderate
2	4.95	.13	−.85	5.08			422			none
3	5.41	1.77	1.64	7.18			407			heavy
4	4.66	1.24	−.53	5.90			302			none
5	3.66	.67	−.57	4.33			244			none
6	3.55	.65	−.02	4.20	.46	3.74	210	0	238	light
7	3.00	.83	.18	3.83	.50	3.33	196	0	210	moderate
8	2.38	.81	−.02	3.19	.72	2.47	183	11	172	light
9	2.07	.63	−.18	2.70	.54	2.16	133	0	168	none
10a	1.93	.91	.28	2.84	.80	2.04	128	0	133	heavy

a At time major decisions were taken.

* Level of innovation in the plant-wide safety program was rated by the author on the basis of a survey of plant safety files. The information found consisted of a description of the innovations made. This information is briefly summarized below.

In the first year studied the safety staff recommended and received management approval of a job analysis program which was to provide the basis for strict enforcement of safe working procedures. They also requested regular physical examinations for all employees.

In year 2, no safety innovations were discovered.

In year 3, one of the plant manager's top staff assistants announced to division managers the inauguration of an extensive program of job analysis and indoctrination of workmen in safe procedures. He also urged the division managers to inaugurate the practice of having foremen make thorough investigations of all minor injuries as a basis for corrective action. This was to be coupled with a program of training foremen in the responsibilities which would be placed upon them in these two programs, and also the formation of division safety committees at top division management level to expedite safety recommendations. He also announced inauguration of a plant-wide safety committee.

In years 4 and 5 no new activity was discovered.

In year 6 a proposal was made by the safety staff for transfer of some functions so as to improve the coordinating service of the safety staff and shift more executive responsibility on to the line organization. There was a new program of statistical reporting of injuries classified by types of accident.

In year 7 management inaugurated a revised system of job analysis, appointed a new plant-wide advisory committee, inaugurated an annual conference of all division managers for the purpose of setting objectives and reviewing the safety program, and also ordered the universal replacement of a hazardous type of crane controller in use through most of the plant.

In year 8 a new statistical basis for the reporting of injuries was inaugurated.

In year 9 no innovations were discovered.

In year 10 a revised and greatly expanded program of job analysis was instituted, with a number of executives re-assigned to safety responsibilities exclusively. Procedures for top level reporting and evaluation of safety performance were revised to place greater emphasis upon safety.

made by top management in year 7 did not take effect until year 9. Thus, during the period beginning with year 3 and ending with year 8, the routine control system operated with constant parameters μ and η. Under this assumption, the injury rate $(O(t))$ is given by

(1) $$O(t) = \int [\beta - \eta - \mu O(t)] \, dt$$

or equivalently

(2) $$O'(t) = \beta - \eta - \mu O(t) .$$

Solving this differential equation,

(3) $$O(t) = \frac{\lambda}{\mu} + \left[\hat{O} - \frac{\lambda}{\mu} \right] e^{-\mu t}$$

where $\lambda = \beta - \eta$ and $\hat{O}$ is the initial level of the injury rate.

This equation implies that first differences in injury rates tend to decrease by a constant ratio from year to year. The performance data for years 3 to 8 in Table 1 is fairly consistent with this.

Another principle of control, important in the case of organization, is that of factorization. Ashby has shown[5] that if trial-and-error changes are relied upon for control (compare the operator X_1 at Integrated Steel), a large system cannot practicably be stabilized unless its output can be factored into a number of independently controlled information sources. At Integrated Steel, the safety objective was broken down by divisions and injury rates were reported on that same basis. Part of the nonroutine control activity occurred at the division level. Innovation in divisional programs initiated by division management was correlated with the division's performance error.

This, of course, bears on the subject of decentralization in organizations. Meaningful decentralization is probably impossible without a resolution of the goals into nonconflicting, operative subgoals so that these can be placed under independent control. On the other hand, there is probably a size for organizations at which goal attainment becomes impossible without factorization, even though the method used may not resemble current definitions of "decentralized authority." The plant production, cost, and safety goals at Integrated Steel appear to represent just such a factorization of the company goals.

In summary, the characteristics postulated by cybernetic theory for self-regulating systems have their correlates in human organizations. In the case of Integrated Steel, the theory points up the influence of information feedbacks upon the actions of the executives in attempting to realize the organization objectives. Of particular importance are the role of the higher echelons of executives in controlling the mode of response of the lower echelons and the use of multiple feedbacks in the design of the executive system.

[5] W. R. Ashby, *Design for a Brain* (New York: Wiley, 1952).

33. AN INDUSTRIAL DYNAMICS CASE STUDY*

WILLARD R. FEY[1]

I. INTRODUCTION

Several years ago an Industrial Dynamics project was started at M.I.T.'s School of Industrial Management to study and improve one product line manufactured by the Sprague Electric Company. This study progressed through the stages of system study, problem definition, model formulation, model analysis, policy improvement, and new policy implementation. It is now in a period of evaluation both of the changes produced in the system by the new policies and of the lessons learned about carrying out a successful Industrial Dynamics study. This paper describes some of the problems that arose, the mistakes that were made, and the lessons that were learned at each stage of the analysis.

The objective of the Sprague Project was to understand the forces that influenced dynamic behavior in one product line and to find means of changing the system to improve profits and employment stability. The project began at a time prior to the development of much of the philosophy and methodology of Industrial Dynamics.[2] It proceeded through a series of steps which included study of the physical systems, definition of the company's objectives, selection of the major problems, development of hypotheses relating to the causes of the problems, model formulation, model analysis, development of better policies, introduction of the proposed policies into the operating system, and evaluation of the results. Findings at each stage influenced the development of the Industrial Dynamics approach.

* Reprinted from *Industrial Management Review*, Vol. 4, No. 1 (Fall, 1962), with revisions by the author, January, 1965. This project was directed by Professor Jay W. Forrester and sponsored by the Sprague Electric Company. The encouragement and participation of Robert C. Sprague, Ernest L. Ward, Bruce R. Carlson, and others in the company and the contribution of M.I.T. staff members Wendyl A. Reis, Jr. (now with the Sprague Electric Company), Carl V. Swanson, Jack A. Arnow, and Joseph V. Yance have made this work possible.

[1] Assistant Professor of Industrial Management, M.I.T.

[2] Industrial Dynamics is both a philosophy of the nature of industrial and other human-controlled systems and a methodology designed to enable the quantitative study of such systems. These systems can be studied through simulation on a large-scale digital computer. The models contain the same physical variables that are found in the real system. Therefore they are easily understood and can readily deal with large-scale top management, government, or military problems. No formal rules for obtaining optimum decision policies are known for such systems, but experimentation with the model based on a general understanding of the behavior of feedback systems will usually lead to major improvements.

The analysis was based upon an Industrial Dynamics model of the product line which contained representations of the firm's structure, its labor market, and its customers. Simulations on a large-scale digital computer[3] were run to produce the time response of the variables in the model for various input conditions and policy and parameter changes.

II. INITIAL STUDY

The Sprague Project began early in 1957 with the study of plant operations. The product line of high-quality electronic components had been active for over ten years. It was in the mature phase of its life cycle, that is, the period after research and development and intensive market expansion when the company's operating structure had become relatively fixed and the extent of the market had been well defined.

The product line contained several thousand active catalog items used in large military and industrial systems in which reliability and accuracy were required. Inventories were carried for about 10 per cent of the catalog items. Although some of the manufacturing operations required machines, the majority of the work was done by hand.

There were many customers, whose total weekly order volume fluctuated widely. The individual order size also varied substantially, and requested delivery time ran from two weeks ago to a year in the future. The company had several competitors in this field.

Much detailed data on individual catalog items and the total line accompanied the observations which led to the above description. Opinions and information were obtained from everyone associated with the line, and technical data on the production process and the characteristics of the product were studied. This added up to a considerable volume of unorganized information which presented many seemingly unrelated problems.

A substantial part of the first year was spent building a model of the company's production-inventory operations based on traditional order-by-order, item-by-item statistical simulation. The model was massive, difficult to understand, and oriented not at all toward the company's aggregate managerial decisions of employment, inventory, and delivery delay control and their interaction with the market. It attempted to represent every operation and transaction that occurred in the company in the hope that the important problems and their solutions would become clear when the model was analyzed. No progress was made, however, until it became evident that (a) the study should develop an understanding of the company's objectives and the major dynamic problems and their causes, rather than be a general fact-finding expedition, (b) the system

---

[3] Computations were performed on the IBM 704 and 709 computers at the M.I.T. Computation Center.

should be visualized as a whole, and (*c*) recognition should be given to the relationship between the aggregate decisions (like employment policy), system behavior as a whole, and individual item decisions which are made within the limits set by the aggregate policies.

III. DEFINITION OF PROBLEMS

The worth of a research project in large part is determined by the problems that are selected for study. The study of small or meaningless problems will produce corresponding results. A study of major problems, although it sometimes may fail to produce quantitative solutions, can still provide extremely useful understanding. The search in this case was for the dynamic problems which were most important relative to the company's objectives. No attempt was made to restrict the problems to those produced by linear systems or to those that would yield optimum solutions. There was, therefore, no formal way of finding the major problems; they instead had to emerge from an understanding of the company's objectives and the overall nature of the system.

The company's objectives considered in this study were profits and employment stability for its own sake. The major problems relative to these objectives were the long-term cyclic nature of the product's industry and the tendency for wider fluctuations to occur in production than in sales.

1. Long-term Fluctuations in the Industry

A long-term cycle, about two years in duration, appeared in all system variables. This problem arose in large part because the customers tended to follow a policy of ordering ahead as the company's service delay became long and of holding orders back when the delay was short. The company's employment decisions which directly affected the delay time were thus reflected in the customer's ordering rate. This problem forced a study of the interaction between the customers, the company, and the company's labor market. The labor market was the only factor market involved because this was a product line of predominantly handmade items. Therefore, production output was directly controlled by the size of the work force.

2. Wider Variation of Production than of Sales

The second major problem was the greater variation of production and employment than of sales. This was created when management followed a policy of trying to maintain inventory at its desired level and of quickly correcting deviations from the ideal. Thus, when sales were rising and inventory was falling, production was scheduled at a rate equal to the sales rate plus an additional amount needed to replace the units that had already been depleted. The depletion occurred in a rising sales situation even when production *orders* equaled sales because it took time to get the orders through the factory. During that manufacturing time, sales rose above the receipts of finished inventory units, and inventory fell. The added replacements orders placed an extra burden on the factory in busy periods, and the production rate exceeded the sales rate. In addition, the desired inventory level rose as sales did. Therefore, still more inventory orders were written to raise inventory to a level above the previous normal.

IV. STUDY OF THE SYSTEM

A review of data already collected and a second study of the system clarified the importance of the structure described below.

A customer, private or military, ordered a group of high-quality systems from a system manufacturer (i.e., component customer). This manufacturer, who did not have an inventory of finished systems, had to design the system (if it had not been ordered before), make a parts list, check this against parts inventories, schedule production, obtain necessary parts, employees, and capital equipment, manufacture the system, and ship the product to the buyer. The manufacturer tried to make employees, parts, and capital equipment come together at the proper time, so that production time was not wasted. If employees, capital equipment, or parts were needed, they were ordered. Seeing that the proper resources were on hand, and the desire to establish an inventory for quick access on rush orders, caused the prime contractor to place orders for electronic components with the subject company or one of its competitors.

The selection of the components supplier was influenced by quality, speed, and reliability of delivery; price; habit (convenience); and contractual conditions, as well as less rational forces. The timing of an order depended upon the expected delivery time and the time at which the customer needed the units.

The above was a description of one customer's operations with respect to one order. In fact, there were many customers, each continually receiving orders. Each operated differently in terms of quantities and timing, although each had to perform all the functions described in roughly the same sequence in order to produce the necessary systems.

At the components manufacturer, the sales department received the order and sent it to the engineering department. There, units were designed or specifications verified, and manufacturing orders were written. The orders proceeded to manufacturing, where an inventory search was performed if the order was for an inventory item. Orders that could be filled from inventory were sent through a short final process, packaged and shipped. Orders that could not be filled because they were not for stock items went to production to be made to order. Each such order was scheduled, manufactured and shipped to the customer.

Several actions were necessary to support the manufacturing process. (a) Inventory replenishment orders: these inventory orders went through the same manufacturing process that made-to-order customer orders used. (b) Factory priority decisions: these decided the sequence in which customer and inventory orders are produced. (c) Employment decisions: decisions to hire or lay off production workers were made based on the average sales level and the factory backlog of work. A decision to hire increased the productive work force only after delays in obtaining the people and training them. A decision to reduce workers decreased the work force only after the required notice delays. (d) Raw material

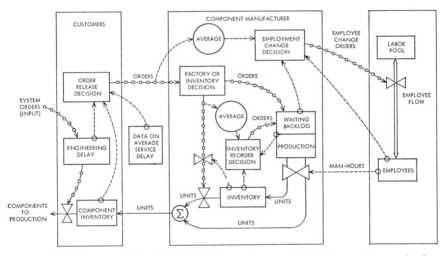

FIG. 1. Detailed View Showing the Principal System Components of Customers, Firm, and Labor Market. Delays in the Flow Channels are not Indicated.

ordering and capital equipment purchasing decisions: these led to the acquisition of the required items after appropriate delays.

The chain of events and decisions which resulted from a prime customer's order for a large electronic system can be displayed graphically by means of the flow diagram shown in Figure 1. This diagram represented the structure of the socioeconomic system of interest, and it was used as the basic outline for the simulation model which ultimately formed the heart of this study.

V. MODEL DESCRIPTION

The purpose of the following model was to represent the physical system in such a way that the previously defined problems could be meaningfully studied and understood and new policies and parameters could be tested before their use in actual operations. The following steps were taken, based on the problems and the system study:

a) The major sectors of the system to be included were selected.

b) The level of aggregation of the variables was determined.

c) The physical flows (decisions) and levels (inventories, backlogs, etc.) necessary in each sector were chosen.

d) The information to be used in each decision was defined.

e) The mathematical form of the equation for each variable was stated.

f) The values of the physical constants used in the equations were determined.

All variables and constants had to have physical meaning so that anyone in the company could clearly understand the model and any new policy that could be tested in the model would work in the operating system.

The model incorporated only those parts of the system that related to the defined problems. Included were the customers and their ordering and production-planning operations, the company with its inventory and production system, and the one factor of production (labor) which controlled the output. It was found that raw materials, capital equipment, costs, and prices did not have a significant influence on the decisions and actions in the system within the normal range of operations. Since the problems were of a highly aggregated nature involving all catalog items and operations and since changes in the mix of the incoming orders and inventory were small relative to other variations, the model dealt with the total flows of units ordered, units produced and employees. Distinctions were not made between catalog items, different customers' orders or employees in different production departments. Some of these considerations are currently under study to produce further improvements, but they were not necessary for studying the problems treated here. The sectors to be included, the level of aggregation, and the physical flows were based on the problems under study. Had other problems been chosen, a different model would have been necessary. For example, this model will not answer the question: What is the most efficient lot size for catalog item XYZ?

Equations were written to describe the system's actions. These were in the form of first-order, nonlinear, difference equations designed for simulation of the model's time behavior on an IBM 704 computer.[4] The

---

[4] The DYNAMO compiler program which was designed to carry out this simulation has been modified for use on the IBM 705, 709, 7090 and the 7094 with an M.I.T.-type time-sharing system.

time delays inherent in the flows of material, men, information, and orders were not explicitly shown in Figure 1, but were included in the equation set.

1. Demand for Electronic Components

The customers were represented by three functions: Component inventory, backlog of components to be ordered, and the component-ordering decision. Equation 1L, representing the component inventory, was an example of a representative equation. Only a few more important equations are included here as examples. A complete list of the equations can be found in Chapter 17 of *Industrial Dynamics* by Professor Jay W. Forrester.

$$IFAC.K = IFAC.J + (DT)(UAIC.JK - URMC.JK) \qquad (1L)[5]$$

IFAC	Inventory, Finished, Actual, at Customer (units)
DT	Delta Time (weeks)
UAIC	Units Arriving at Inventory at Customer (units/week)
URMC	Units Received in Manufacturing Customer (units/week)

In Equation 1L, *IFAC.K* was the inventory level at the present solution time. It was equal to the inventory at the previous solution time (*IFAC.J*) plus the difference between what was added (*DT*) (*UAIC.JK*) and what was depleted (*DT*) (*URMC.JK*) during the *DT* interval. *UAIC* and *URMC* are the rates of flow into and out of the inventory, respectively.

The critical customer characteristic was the rate of release of orders to suppliers. The customer controlled this rate by varying the length of time component orders are held in engineering before being released to the supplier. This engineering holding delay was set so that the total expected component acquisition delay (engineering holding delay plus expected supplier lead time plus desired buffer time in the customers' component inventory) would equal the production planning lead time. This assured that components arrived at the proper time for production. The customer order release rate, therefore, was equal to the backlog of orders to be released divided by the engineering holding delay. For a constant backlog, an increasing supplier delay resulted in a decreasing engineering holding delay and an increasing order release rate. A decreasing supplier delay caused an increasing holding delay and a decreasing order release rate.

---

[5] The four letters preceding the period represent the variable (*IFAC* means *Inventory, Finished, Actual, at Customer*), and the one or two letters following the period are a time "subscript". A single time letter indicates that the variable takes on its value at the specified instant of time (*K* is taken as the present instant; *J* is the instant preceding *K* with a time *DT* separating *J* and *K*). A double letter indicates that the variable takes on and holds its value during the time interval specified (*JK* or *KL*). These two variable types are referred to as levels and rates, respectively. Variables with no time notation are parameters that do not change.

2. The Company's Inventory-Production System

After delays in the customers' purchasing department, the mail, and the component suppliers' sales office, the orders encountered the first decision at the manufacturer: Should the order be made to order or sent from inventory? The policy was if the order could be filled from inventory, it should be; if not, it was made to order. Orders for inventory items underwent an inventory search. Orders found in stock were filled. Orders for inventory items not in stock or for noninventory items were made to order. The average fraction of orders filled from inventory was a function of inventory. As inventory increased, the portion taken from inventory increased. There were always some orders for special items, so the percentage filled could never be 100 per cent, even with infinite inventory.

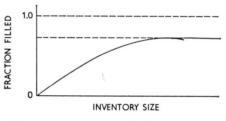

FIG. 2. Fraction of Orders Filled from Inventory.

Orders to be made to order went to production to be scheduled and produced. The production process was represented in two parts. First, there was a waiting delay caused by the excess of orders above the manufacturing capacity. Second, there was a manufacturing delay necessary because of the technology of the process itself. The second delay was constant, but the first was a function of the backlog and the output rate.

Output rate was equated to the average productivity per employee times the number of employees. Since there were inventory replenishment orders in the factory as well as customer orders, the output for customers was not the total output. It was a fraction of the total determined by the relation between the number of customer orders and inventory orders in the backlog. No priority was assumed in the model for either type, although some customer units were expedited in the real system. The inventory output was the difference between total production and customer production.

The inventory reorder decision was based on the average outflow of units from inventory, the desired and actual values of inventory, and the desired and actual values of inventory orders in production. Imbalances between the desired and actual values were adjusted over a period of time, *ASRS.*

$$UMSS.KL = AOIS.K + \left(\frac{1}{ASRS}\right) (IFIS.K - IFAS.K + IDPS.K - IAPS.K \text{ (2R)}$$

UMSS	Units to be Made for Stock at Supplier (units/week)
AOIS	Average Outflow from Inventory at Supplier (units/week)
ASRS	constAnt defining Speed of inventory Reorder at Supplier (weeks)
IFIS	Inventory, Finished, Ideal, at Supplier (units)
IFAS	Inventory, Finished, Actual, at Supplier (units)
IDPS	Inventory orders Desired in Production at Supplier (units)
IAPS	Inventory orders Actually in Production at Supplier (units)

A negative value of *UMSS* indicated cancellation of orders. This was reasonable as long as the cancellation did not exceed the backlog in the waiting delay. Further cancellations implied the dismantling of already started units and was unrealistic.

Desired inventory (*IFIS*) was a desired number of weeks of average sales. Desired orders in production (*IDPS*) was production lead time times average sales.

The employment decision (hiring and layoff rates) eventually led to changes in the number of productive employees by shifting people between the labor pool and the employee pool. A hiring decision was followed by an acquisition delay and a training delay. A layoff decision was followed by a notice delay. The decision itself was based on the difference between desired (*MDMS*) and actual (*MNES*) employees adjusted over a time period, *DLSS*.

$$MLHS.KL = \left(\frac{1}{DLSS}\right) (MDMS.K - MNES.K) \tag{3R}$$

MLHS	Men to be Laid off or Hired at Supplier (men/week)
DLSS	Delay in the change of Labor force Size at Supplier (weeks)
MDMS	Men Desired in Manufacturing at the Supplier (men)
MNES	Men, Net, Employed at Supplier (men)

The desired employee term (*MDMS*) had two components, the employees needed to sustain the production output at the average sales rate, and those needed to adjust the backlog toward its acceptable level. As backlog rose, hiring increased; and as sales increased hiring rose. As backlog and/or sales declined, layoff began. It was assumed that the labor pool was able to supply all employment requirements. Natural attrition of the work force was not included.

The last part of the model considered the calculation and transmission to the customer of the suppliers' average lead time. This delay was a variable depending on the state of the supplier's inventory and the backlog in manufacturing.

Figure 1 showed the two paths that an incoming order could take through the supplier's system. It could be filled from inventory or made to order. In the former instance, no manufacturing would be required, so the order could be filled quickly. If the order went through manufacturing, it would be delayed by the normal processing time plus the time necessary to pass through the waiting lines before each process stage. Therefore there were two paths, one with a more or less fixed delay of short duration and one of longer length which was variable and related to the size of the in-process backlog.

The delay information was the average delay associated with the units being shipped to the customers. The total output was the sum of the outputs from the two paths. To find the average delay associated with this total, a weighted average of the delays in the two paths was used (as shown in Equation 4A).

$$DBVS.K = \frac{(USIS.JK)\ (DICS)}{USIS.JK + USMS.JK} + \frac{(USMS.JK)\ (DCOS.K)}{USIS.JK + USMS.JK} \tag{4A}$$

DBVS   Delay, average, for total of Both paths, Variable at Supplier (weeks)
USIS   Units Sent from Inventory at Supplier (units/week)
DICS   Delay in Inventory-filling Channel at Supplier (weeks)
USMS   Units sent to Shipping from Manufacturing at Supplier (units/week)
DCOS   Delay of Customer Orders in manufacturing path at Supplier (units/week)

DBVS was the average total delay that units leaving the supplier experienced. The first term of Equation 4A was the fraction of the total output that came from inventory ($USIS.JK/USIS.JK + USMS.JK$) times the delay in filling from inventory ($DICS$). The second term represents the fraction of the total output that was made to order times the delay in the factory path ($DCOS$). The average service delay changed when the manufacturing time changed or when the proportion of units filled from inventory varied.

This information was necessary because customers used this information in making their order release decision. When the delay time rose, customers ordered ahead to insure receipt of the units at the time they need them. Information about the supplier delay was relayed to the customers through a delay which represented the time necessary for customers to become aware of and act upon changes experienced in the supplier's delay.

The model's structure and simulated behavior were studied, and it was decided by the investigators and company officials that the equations adequately represented the real-world situation in terms of decisions, operations, fluctuation amplitudes and periods, and relative phases and magnitudes of important variables. The model could not be completely accurate, but it was useful for understanding the two problems of interest.

The equations included parameters that required numerical values before simulations could be made. These parameters included, for example, the average delay times in all the flow channels and operating departments, the average sales rate of the product, and the average production lead time.

The methods used to obtain these parameters varied considerably depending on the type of parameter and the sector involved. The company parameters, where possible, were based on samples of orders that had passed through the systems, as opposed to regression-type methods that dealt with the aggregate variables. Occasionally it was necessary to estimate parameters based on the testimony of the decision maker and/or other people associated with the situation. The customer parameters were based on estimates by company personnel familiar with the customers' ordering patterns and on studies of similar functions in the company. Reasonable ranges were chosen and used to test the model's sensitivity. Only a few of the customer parameters turned out to be sensitive and thereby deserving of further study. The most important of these was the time the customer needed to become aware of and use the information about the delivery delay.

The last parameter was the computation interval (DT). This constant had to be made small enough so that the assumption that rates are constant during the solution interval did not introduce large errors. In the simulations, DT was one tenth of a week. The use of a one week interval made almost no difference in the values of the variables.

VI. MODEL ANALYSIS

The objectives of the model analysis were (a) to develop an understanding of the relationship between the structure of the model and the behavior it produced, particularly with respect to the important problems, and (b) to verify the adequacy of the model as a representation of the real system *relative to the problems under study* so that the understanding derived was meaningful and potentially useful.

1. System Dynamics

The problems under study in this case were the long-term cyclic pattern in all system variables and the tendency in the company for employment and production to vary more widely than sales. The model clearly exhibited these problems for a wide variety of input (system orders to the customer) patterns including instantaneous changes of various amounts, sinusoidal fluctuations, random disturbances, ramp type rises and declines, and data.

Different values of parameters and different decision policies were tried with these inputs in order to determine the sensitive parts of the model. Such changes produced variations in the magnitude of the fluctuations and the size of the production overshoot, but the existence and causes of the problems remained.

The following description of the system's behavior can be traced in Figure 1.

Suppose that system order rate to the customers (extreme left of Figure 1) began to increase. Then the customers' backlog of orders in engineering rose and forced their orders for components to increase. As the component supplier's sales rose, the unfilled order backlog in manufacturing increased because the labor force that produced the output had not yet been changed. In this period, input orders exceeded production output. As unfilled backlog grew, both the factory lead time and total service time increased.

The rising orders and backlog induced hiring. However, there were delays between the increase in sales and the desire to hire and between the desire to hire and the acquisition of fully productive employees. As a result, a sizable backlog accumulated before enough workers were hired and trained to raise the production rate to equal the order rate and thereby stabilize backlog. Further hiring drove production above orders, and backlog declined toward an acceptable level.

Meanwhile, assume that the orders for systems to the customers had returned to their average value and remained there. The customers began to order ahead on the basis of the expected suppliers' lead time in order to keep their production lines in operation. Then, even though the system orders returned to normal, the customers continued to increase their component orders because the service delay was increasing. They continued to order at a rate higher than normal until the delay fell to its usual value.

When the delay seen by the customers finally began to decline (sometimes ten weeks after the decline actually starts), the customers ordered less far ahead. They also reduced orders below normal, since their backlog of engineering orders had been depleted by excess ordering. This was the beginning of a period when the customers ordered less than normal because the lead time was short and there was not much to order. During this lower-than-normal order period, the component manufacturer reduced his work force below normal. When the customers built up their backlog again and the service time rose, the component orders were again increased to restart the cycle. The cycles were self-perpetuating and needed only a minor disturbance (i.e., the temporarily increased prime system orders) to start the process.

This cyclic shifting of orders from the customers' engineering department backlog to the component manufacturers' backlog and back again continued only as long as two conditions persisted. These were (a) the customers' practice of ordering ahead as service delay increased and holding back orders as the delay declined, and (b) the component manufacturers' inability to prevent their service delay from varying enough to be recognized by the customers. If customers were to stop basing order releases on expected service delay *or* if suppliers could maintain a constant service delay, the long-term oscillatory tendencies of this system would disappear. However, there might still be a small long-term cycle in the real system, if input orders had a cyclic component.

The second problem was that suppliers' production variations were wider than order changes. This was due to the short-term adjustment in inventory ordering. When sales rose, inventory declined. When this fall in inventory was quickly corrected by sending inventory orders to the factory, the load on the factory included the excess sales orders that could not be filled from inventory and these inventory orders. Since the inventory orders had to build the inventory back up to its original level as well as prevent a further decline due to the higher sales, total load on the factory was greater than just the added sales.

The target level of inventory also rose with sales, and an additional stress was placed on the factory by the orders necessary to raise inventory above its old level. When hiring was not done quickly, factory backlog rose, and the manufacturing delay increased. In response to longer factory delay, orders for inventory items were placed sooner, and the factory load was still heavier. Thus, policies associated with the company's inventory control caused greater changes in work force and production rate than originally occurred in sales.

This problem was present as long as inventory adjustment was rapid and the desired inventory level was based on short-term average sales. If peak inventory could be timed so that it occurred before the peak in sales, this would make a decline in inventory desirable at the peak of sales stress. Production rate would be less than the sales rate by the amount that inventory declined each week.

2. Validation of the Model

The model was accepted as an adequate (not perfect) representation of the real system *relative to the problems under study* for two reasons. The functions included in the model and the way in which the functions were interconnected conformed to our own and management's views of the system structure. Since the model represented the system in easily identifiable physical terms, the flows, decisions, inventories, etc., could be discussed and studied directly in factory and office by everyone. Secondly, the response of the model contained the short-term random factors, the long-term cyclic components, and the lag relationships between variables that were present in actual data. The amplitudes and periods of the fluctuations in individual variables and the time lags between variables were all close to the actual values for a range of reasonable inputs to the customer in the complete model and to the company in the partial, company-only, system. Simulations were also performed using the company sector with an independent input of total actual orders from customers to the company. The pattern of lags and amplitudes was again similar to the actual behavior.

VII. IMPROVED POLICIES

The problem of *improving* the behavior of this system was not a simple one. While there were methods for finding optimum decision policies relative to a single objective and a single input pattern in a simple, linear feedback system, there were no such methods for complex (100 or more dynamic interrelated variables), nonlinear models in which there were several objectives whose forms differed from those commonly used in traditional optimization techniques. Furthermore, any new policies suggested would not only have to perform well for the expected types of inputs (in this case fluctuations around a steady average value) but also would have to provide a certain level of protection in the event the input should develop a sizable trend either up or down.

With formal optimization ruled out, there were two possible approaches to improvement. One was the simulation of the model for all combinations of values of the parameters. The second was the modification of the system structure based on an understanding of the causes of the problems and of the general principles of information-feedback system behavior. The exhaustive parameter variation method would certainly have provided some improvement. However, system modification had a much greater potential. Thus the search for improvement concentrated on structure variation and led to the following changes.

1. Inventory Ordering and Production Priority Policies

The reservoirs which were of principal concern relative to management's objectives (profits and employment stability) were found to be inventory, unfilled order backlog (because it influenced the service delay), and employment level. The decisions which were supposed to control them were found to be the inventory reorder decision, which controlled inventory, and the employment decision, which controlled backlog and employment. The question was then asked: Can each decision actually control the variable intended without interfering with other decisions? The answer in the inventory reorder case was that it could not, because inventory was the aggregate accumulated difference between production and shipments. Since sending orders into production did not directly control the employment level which produced the production rate, inventory orders could only divert working time from customer orders.

The first change, then, was to shift the inventory adjustment process into the labor decision where all effective aggregate control resided. A new basis had to be selected for the generation of inventory orders. Since high productivity was desired, it seemed desirable to generate inventory orders only as they were needed to keep all production workers continuously busy. A priority list of inventory items needed was used as a guide to decide which type of unit to make for inventory.

2. Factory Priority

The long-term cyclic behavior of the industry to a large extent was due to the customers' reaction to variation in the delivery time. Variations in this delay were caused primarily by variations in the factory backlog relative to the work force. In times of high sales the backlog and delay rose. A sizable part of this backlog contained orders for inventory. Since there was no clear-cut and supervised priority for customer orders, these orders frequently waited while inventory orders were made. The establishment of a customer-first priority was necessary to reduce both the delay itself and its variability. This would tend to suppress the system's oscillatory tendencies and provide a competitively desirable short delay.

3. Employment Policies

The problem of production overshooting sales would be improved by building inventory at slack times rather than in high sales periods. An equation was designed to specify the desired factory work force in such a way that, when combined with the new inventory-ordering policy, it would maintain a stable work force and force inventory accumulation at the proper time (i.e., when sales were falling). It was to be calculated each week and was based on long-term average sales (to provide a stable basic work force), inventory adjustment over a long period of time (so inventory absorbed as much of the sales fluctuation as possible), and backlog adjustment (to keep service delay short and stable and thereby reduce the long-term cycle). The equation had the following form:

$$\text{Employment Desired} = \frac{\text{long term average sales}}{\text{average productivity per man per week}} + \frac{\text{Desired inventory} - \text{Actual inventory}}{(\text{Average Productivity})\,(\text{Inventory adjustment time})} \quad (5A)$$

The backlog term had the same form as the inventory term except the numerator was actual minus desired backlog. It was not included in (5A) because the changes in priority and loading in the factory had kept the delay in control, so the term was inoperative. By averaging sales over a long period (one year) and by taking a long time to adjust inventory, desired employment was relatively insensitive to short-term changes in sales. If employment changes were small and inventory orders were generated to keep workers uniformly busy, most inventory would be made in slack sales times.

The parameters in this new decision had to be numerical values. These values were determined by simulating the model using the new policies with different parameter values for a range of possible inputs to the customer sector. The selected parameters had to provide stable employment and service delay for any expected inputs having the form of variations around a nearly constant long-term average, while preventing major inventory changes if usage should suddenly change substantially. The parameter values could be no better than the assumptions that were made about the form of the system structure and the range in the values or in the form of the policies.

In the electronics industry, one characterized by rapid change, product obsolescence was always a major worry. Naturally, such a fear existed in this mature product line. Therefore, protection against a permanent decline in sales had to be included. This took the form of a variable adjustment time in the denominators of the inventory and backlog terms in equation (5A.) Adjustment time was to be long and constant when deviations of inventory and backlog from their respective desired values were within the normal range. When either deviation began to exceed its expected limit, the adjustment time was shortened.

An important part of the improvement process was the formulation of policies and procedures that had clear physical meaning. This was important (a) for one's own understanding of system behavior, (b) so that implementation would be possible given the existing system, and (c) so the people who had to use the policies could understand them and their limitations and could change them if necessary.

VIII. INTRODUCTION OF NEW POLICIES INTO THE SYSTEM

Changes were recommended in factory procedure (customer orders made first), inventory-ordering procedure (generated to maintain a constant, efficient factory work load from a priority list), and employment decision making (total authorized employment each week based on the calculation from an equation). The implementation of these new policies required making the changes work properly in the operating system, while resisting the temptation to make a great number of less important modifications which would involve a great deal more work. There seemed to be a general tendency to believe that large behavior changes could only arise from major physical dislocation and drastic changes in policies and/or people and/or paper work flows. While there was no reason to believe this in this study, the appeal of the fallacy was irresistible. Therefore, much planning and work was aimed at changes which were unnecessary to achieve the major revisions in system behavior. Actually, no changes in personnel, authority, location or production technique were necessary for these changes. All that was required was the regular generation of two or three easily obtainable pieces of information, fifteen minutes of secretarial time each week for these decisions to be calculated, and the slightly changed attitude of workers, foremen, and plant managers.

The procedure of the employment decision change included (a) establishment of several new information channels, (b) trial calculation for several months, and (c) gradual use of the new rule. The plant priority and inventory changes came about through encouragement over several months. There was no discontinuity in procedure or operations at any time. In fact, to some degree the customer-first production and the inventory ordering to maintain an efficient work load had always been in operation.

The implementation was introduced through the joint effort of the M.I.T. research group and several company people. The approach was to develop an understanding in the people concerned of the meaning of the changes and to motivate them to use the rules both to improve operations and to make more time available for other tasks. Therefore, the changes did not connote a loss in authority or individuality; rather they mechanized some time-consuming decision-making tasks, thereby freeing time for other considerations.

Attention was given to all minor practical details and problems so that incompatibility with the system's structure did not interfere with the use of the new policies. An attempt was made to consider the social, psychological, and physical realities in the overall information-feedback system to promote the fastest, best understood, and most lasting modifications.

IX. EVALUATION OF SYSTEM BEHAVIOR

By the time the new hiring decision had been in use for six months and the modified factory priority and inventory-ordering policies somewhat longer, there were characteristics of the system's behavior which indicated that improvements in labor and production stability, productivity, and sales were taking place. Most of the gains were attributed to the recommended modifications because no other changes capable of producing such major alterations in behavior could be found in the system, and the areas and magnitudes of the changes predicted agreed with the results.

1. Evaluation after Seven Months

Seven months after implementation of the new hiring decisions, data for the past 13-month period was analyzed, and the results showed that improvement was evident in several places. Average labor productivity had improved and was still rising. A comparable work force could sustain a production rate almost 12 per cent higher than was possible a year earlier. The sensitivity of employment and production to variations in sales had declined greatly because inventory was being forced to fall at peak sales (rather than rise as in the past), thereby relieving factory pressure at a time of crisis. Inventory could be built up during slack sales periods. Inventory level was lower in terms of both units and weeks of sales on hand. The average incoming orders were 16 per cent higher and more uniform than 13 months before.

Average productivity as measured by a 20-week exponential average of weekly productivity (productivity equals units produced divided by man-hours worked) had increased in the 13-month period by 11.8 per cent and was still rising. An 11.8 per cent increase in productivity will allow a 10.5 per cent decrease in employment, if production is to be held constant.

Improvement in employment stability (smaller variation in work force for a given change in sales) was also evident. The pattern of sales variation was shown as a 30-week exponential average. This average was at a peak at the beginning of the data period. A decline of 6.5 per cent occurred during the next six months. This was followed by a steady rise of 23 per cent, to 16 per cent above the previous peak, where it remained. Employment had a similar pattern of steady–decline–rise–steady, but the magnitudes of the changes were very different. During the 7 per cent decline in average sales, employment fell 38 per cent. During the 23 per cent sales rise, employment rose only 38 per cent back to its original value. Therefore, three times as large a sales variation failed to change the size of the employment adjustment.

Two factors caused this improvement. The first was the rise in productivity. The second was the use of inventory to ease factory pressure at peak sales by cutting back inventory production and allowing the stock to fall. At the first peak employment, inventory was *rising* at a rate (in units per week) of 10 per cent of the average sales rate. At peak employment after the changes, inventory was *falling* at a rate of over 11 per cent of the original average sales rate. This was a difference in factory stress of 21 per cent of sales. Had inventory been rising at its previous rate at the second employment peak, that peak would have been 16 per cent greater than it was. Had productivity been equal to the original value, employment would have been an additional 12 per cent higher, which would have increased the second employment peak by 28 per cent. Somewhat more than 57 per cent of this improvement in stability was due to better inventory control.

A third potential influence in the employment variation was the rate at which order backlog was changing. This was not considered here because the backlog was falling at about the same rate at both employment peaks.

At the beginning of the thirteen-month period, the thirty-week exponential average of incoming orders was at a peak. It declined slowly for about six months to a low of 6.5 per cent below the peak. A steady rise in the average followed for three months to a point 15 per cent above the previous peak. In the last four months of the data period, the average rose slowly and uniformly to 16.7 per cent above the beginning peak. In the last fifteen weeks of data, the average was contained in the +14.7 to +16.7 per cent range. At no other time during the period had the average stayed within a 2 per cent range for more than nine weeks. Although the causes were not clear, the sales level was less erratic and substantially higher than before. This was at least partially due to a shorter, less erratic, delivery delay.

At the beginning of the period, total inventory stood at about its normal level. The inventory was 13.4 per cent lower a year later. In terms of weeks of average sales on hand, the figures were 7.4 weeks and 5.5 weeks, respectively. The trend even at the low level was still downward. Since there had as yet been no inventory buildup phase using the new policies, the outcome was somewhat uncertain. However, there was good reason to believe that the average level of inventory over a complete cycle could be reduced by 10 to 20 per cent without impairing the ability to fill orders.

2. Evaluation after Two Years

In the second year, the company did not adhere as closely to the hiring decision formula as it had in the first year of its use. More rapid adjustments in employment were made in response to downward sales changes than were indicated by the rule. This was the declining phase of the cycle in this product line and in the electronics industry generally. The customer-first priority system and the creation of inventory orders as needed continued to operate fairly well. Labor productivity rose another 10 per cent during this second year. Employment, production and delivery delay became more volatile, but they did not return to their former excess overadjustment.

The gradual return to the old ways of making the employment decision continued in the third year. The trend probably will continue and, in the absence of strong pressures from the M.I.T. group, the use of the employment rule should disappear completely by the fourth or fifth year. The inventory ordering and production priority systems should persist. Productivity should continue to rise, but less rapidly.

3. Return to the Old Employment Policies

The new employment rule was used faithfully for the first year and a half for two reasons. The M.I.T. people were constantly in touch with the progress, giving encouragement, working out problems, and by their presence, putting pressure on company decision makers to use the rule. In addition no strong counterpressures were present from product line or overall company problems. Starting in the second year all of these conditions began to change.

It had been understood that M.I.T.'s participation would end after the policies had been implemented. Therefore, outside involvement (pressure) began to decline in the second year. After three and one-half years the company was receiving no M.I.T. assistance.

Also during the second year counterpressures began to build up. Sales in the line began to fall in response to the normal cyclic forces. Declining sales brought fears of obsolescence and increasing inventories. A fall in total industry sales occurred at about the same time, so to the product line problems was added a company-wide cost consciousness that focused on inventory reduction. It was also likely that the making of the employment decision served as a creative outlet for the decision makers. Having a secretary spend 15 minutes a week calculating the decision never was very satisfying.

The reduction in positive pressures and the emergence of counterpressures led to deviation from the rule. This was rationalized by the observation that the use of the decision for over a year had not smoothed out the cycle (though it had been reduced). It would have been necessary to adhere rather strictly to the rule for about a cycle and a half (three years) in order to suppress a large part of the cycle. Even then normal disturbances, military budgeting procedures, and the behavior of competitors would still have provided a measurable two-year cycle. The patience to wait for three years and endure some difficult times and strong pressures (even with a constantly rising productivity) is a rare commodity in today's world. It must also be fortified with courage, self-confidence, and great belief in systems dynamics principles.

While it is true that the new employment decision did not become a permanent part, in its quantitative form, of the product line, it is still partially influential and positive results were realized. From the company's point of view "the record of operations since the new policies were introduced clearly shows improvements."[6] The study stimulated a great deal of company introspection which led to new thinking and activities in several areas. The changes in inventory ordering and factory priority are still in operation and should remain so.

The Sprague Project in its successful aspects also played a major role in developing the techniques and procedures of Industrial Dynamics. Its shortcomings pointed the way for much of our research effort. This is particularly true now in the area of human factors in the managerial feedback system. Here the implementation problems forced an awareness of the importance of the human being in the business system and indicated fruitful quantitative approaches to such studies.

REFERENCES

1. CARLSON, BRUCE R. "An Industrialist Views Industrial Dynamics," *Industrial Management Review*, Vol. 6, No. 1 (Fall, 1964), p. 18.

---

[6] Bruce R. Carlson, "An Industrialist Views Industrial Dynamics," *Industrial Management Review*, Vol. 6, No. 1 (Fall, 1964), p. 18.

Mr. Carlson, a vice-president of the Sprague Electric Company, describes the company's view of this study.

2. FEY, WILLARD R. *An Industrial Dynamics Study of an Electronic Components Manufacturer.* Transactions of the Fifth Annual Conference of the American Production and Inventory Control Society, Boston, Mass., September 27–28, 1962.

A more detailed description of the changes in the system's behavior that occurred after the new policies went into operation can be found here.

3. FORRESTER, JAY W. *Industrial Dynamics.* M.I.T. Press and New York: John Wiley & Sons, Inc., 1961.

The background and equations for the model used in this study are presented in Chapters 17 and 18.

34. A COMPARISON OF THREE CRITERIA OF AIRCREW EFFECTIVENESS IN COMBAT OVER KOREA*

John K. Hemphill and Lee B. Sechrest

This paper reports a study of three criteria of the performance of 94 B-29 aircrews which flew combat missions over Korea during the period extending from March to September 1951. The three criteria to be considered are: (1) ratings by superiors of the performance of crews as units; (2) sociometric nominations from crew members; and (3) objective records of combat bombing accuracy. Following a brief description of each of these criteria, they will be compared in terms of their reliability and interrelationship. A general problem in the use of superiors' ratings as criteria is made evident by the apparently paradoxical finding of substantial and statistically significant relationships between (1) bombing data, which show no reliability, and (2) reliable superiors' ratings. This paradox is more apparent than real for it can be explained in terms of the contaminating effect of "unreliable" information shared in common by the raters.

Superiors' Ratings

The aircrews were rated as units by squadron or wing staff officers in terms of their performance in carrying out combat missions over Korea. The ratings were accomplished through the use of an eleven-item rating form. The eleven rating variables were:

(1) Skill as Technicians: The degree of basic knowledge crew members have of their specialties as indicated by their performance or the degree of skill they exhibit in handling various equipments.

(2) Successful Completion of Missions: The degree to which the crew reaches and bombs prescribed targets; including making necessary decisions in the absence of specific instructions and overcoming obstacles.

(3) Accuracy in Bombing Targets: The accuracy with which targets are identified and bombed.

(4) Effectiveness of Crew Leadership: The degree to which the aircraft commander organizes the crew to facilitate teamwork and cooperation among crew members.

* Reproduced from *Journal of Applied Psychology*, Vol. 36, No. 5, October, 1952.

(5) Consideration of Men on the Crew for One Another: The extent to which crew members look out for the welfare of the crew as a whole, are liked by other men on the crew, and turn to one another as friends.

(6) Effectiveness in Working with Other Crews: The degree to which the crew works as a part of a larger team and cooperates with other crews in carrying out a group effort.

(7) Effectiveness in Working with Superior Officers: The degree to which the crew accepts orders or suggestions from superior officers and achieves objectives without conflict with superiors.

(8) Care of the Aircraft: The degree to which the crew members insure proper maintenance of their aircraft and take personal interest in the plane and its equipment.

(9) Following SOP: The degree to which the crew members carry out their functions in the prescribed manner.

(10) Military Bearing of Crew Members: The degree to which members of the crew "conduct themselves in a military manner."

(11) Over-all Value to the Squadron (Wing): The degree of over-all effectiveness of the crew as a part of combat unit.

Ratings on the items or variables were expressed as numerical values along a nine-point scale. Each point on the scale was defined, *nine* being the rating given to "undoubtedly the best crew in the squadron" and *one* being the rating given to "undoubtedly the worst crew in the squadron." All ratings were obtained in interviews with the raters.

The original plan was to secure a minimum of five independent ratings for each crew. This plan proved to be impractical due to the difficulty of locating raters who knew the crews sufficiently well to rate all variables. A total of 24 wing and squadron officers were utilized as raters in securing the ratings of the 94 crews. The mean number of ratings per crew actually obtained was 2.7 and the mean number of crews rated by each rater was 10.5.

An examination of the means and standard deviations of the ratings obtained from each of the 24 raters showed marked differences in their rating habits or bias. Before the ratings given a single crew by different raters were combined to form the final rating of the crew's performance, an adjustment was made to compensate for the observed rater bias. The adjustment was computed in such a manner that each rater's mean rating was approximately 50 and his standard deviation approximately 10.

The reliabilities of these converted ratings were estimated by application of a method developed by Horst (1) that is designed for the case in which varying numbers of raters are available. Intercorrelations of the eleven crew performance variables were also calculated. These intercorrelations along with the reliabilities, means, and standard deviations of the eleven variables are presented in Table 1. The reliability of these ratings ranges from .61 to .95 and meets standards which are generally acceptable for rating data.

TABLE 1

THE RELIABILITY AND INTERRELATIONSHIPS OF ELEVEN VARIABLES OF AIRCREW
PERFORMANCE RATED BY SUPERIORS
Note: $N = 83$

Variable	Intercorrelation*											Mean	Standard Deviation
	1	2	3	4	5	6	7	8	9	10	11		
1 Technical Skill												49.6	8.21
2 Completion of Missions	84											51.3	7.64
3 Bombing Accuracy	74	68										47.7	9.65
4 Leadership	83	81	63									49.3	9.10
5 Consideration	62	66	56	70								50.3	7.30
6 W.W. Other Crews	69	69	63	74	73							49.6	7.72
7 W.W. Superiors	79	77	66	81	70	76						50.8	7.66
8 Care of Aircraft	66	64	47	63	61	67	56					50.1	6.93
9 Following SOP	80	73	62	78	59	68	75	66				50.2	7.74
10 Military Bearing	68	59	60	63	60	58	71	49	71			48.2	7.23
11 Over-all Value	85	78	73	82	67	78	78	61	82	62		47.4	10.25
Reliability	80	67	83	80	95	63	80	67	72	61	68		

* Decimal points have been omitted from these tables.

Sociometric Nominations

On a sociometric nomination form, crew members were asked the following question: "If you could make up a crew from among the crew members in your squadron, whom would you choose for each crew position?" There were three general possibilities of reaction to the nomination question: (1) nomination of a crew member who was a member of the same crew as the nominator; (2) nomination of an individual from some other crew in the squadron; and (3) no responses. An individual usually indicated an "on-crew" choice by responding "same," "my own crew," or by writing the name of a fellow crew member in the blank provided. "Off-crew" choices were indicated by responding with the name of a man not on the individual's crew, and by such remarks as "Captain Smith's radio operator." or "anyone except the one we have."

The sociometric nomination data for each crew were used to compute an index of "on-crew" choices. The index is the ratio between the number of "on-crew" choices made and the total number of choices made. These index values ranged from .30 to 1.00 and were approximately normally distributed about a mean of .75.

In order to test the reliability of the index of "on-crew" choice, index values derived from random halves of each crew total nominations were correlated with one another. This correlation was .83 which, when extended by the Spearman-Brown formula, gave an estimated reliability of .91.

Bombing Error Criteria

The accuracy with which an aircrew is able to bomb combat targets may be considered as a near ultimate criterion of its effectiveness. Despite the high relevance of bombing data to the problem of evaluation of aircrew effectiveness, many conditions exist which detract from its utility. Chief among these are: (1) extremely variable conditions under which bombing must be accomplished; (2) severe limitations on the possibility of determining exactly where bombs are dropped in combat; and (3) limits upon the number of crews for whom the opportunity to perform the complete bombing operations exists (only the lead crew in formation bombing performs the complete bombing operation). Nevertheless, all available data were collected concerning the bombing accuracy in combat of the 94 FEAF crews. No combat bombing data whatsoever were available for 50 of the crews (no lead experience). Each of the remaining 44 crews had had one or more opportunities to lead formations on which it had been possible to secure photographs of where the bombs actually dropped. The bombing accuracy data consisted of *circular errors* for each of these bombing missions. These errors were expressed as the linear distance between the mean point of impact of all the bombs identified in the strike photograph and the assigned target. The number of circular error measures available for each of the 44 crews ranged from 1 to 8 with a mean of 3.16.

Inspection of the distribution of the bombing error data disclosed a markedly skewed distribution. A log transformation of these data yielded data with essentially normal distribution. The reliability of the transformed data as estimated, again by utilizing Horst's procedure, was not significantly different from zero.

Table 2 presents an analysis of the variance of the bombing data into between-crew differences and within-crew differences. It can be seen readily that there is approximately as much variance between the errors made by the same crew on different missions as there is between the mean performance of different crews. The difference between the mean bombing accuracy scores of these crews appears to be wholly unrelated to crew differences.

Relationships Among the Criteria

In order to complete the comparison of the three criteria, each of the eleven superior rating variables was correlated with both the sociometric index of "on-crew" choice and with the mean bombing error of each

TABLE 2

An Analysis of the Variance of Transformed Bombing
Accuracy Data

Source of Variance	Sum of Squares	Df	Variance	F ratio
Between Crews	208.56	33	6.320	1.34
Within Crews	451.82	96	4.706	
Total	660.38	129	5.119	

crew for whom we had bombing data. Table 3 presents these correlations.

Attention is called to the correlations between the bombing data and the superiors' ratings. It is quite apparent that the raters utilized the official bombing data as a source of information in making their ratings. Mean differences in the official bombing records of the crews serve to "contaminate" the raters' judgments on all rating variables, although the contamination is more marked for certain variables than for others.

TABLE 3

Correlations Between Eleven Variables of Aircrew Performance Rated
by Superiors and (1) the Index of "On-Crew" Choice and (2) Bombing
Accuracy Data

Rating Variable	"On-Crew" Choice		Bombing Data		
	N	r	N	r	r corr.[1]
1 Technical Skill	90	.20	41	.58	.61
2 Completion of Missions	88	.10	41	.62	.70
3 Bombing Accuracy	80	.36†	41	.58	.58
4 Leadership	89	.13	41	.63	.67
5 Consideration	90	.10	41	.42	.48
6 W.W. Other Crews	90	.06	41	.47	.56
7 W.W. Superiors	90	.11	41	.57	.60
8 Care of Aircraft	90	.26*	41	.31	.38
9 Following SOP	90	.15	41	.40	.47
10 Military Bearing	90	.25*	41	.27	.30
11 Over-all Value	90	.18	41	.47	.54

[1] Corrected for restriction of the range of the rating variables (2)
* Significant at the .05 level.
† Significant at the .01 level.

The largest contamination is with the rating variable, Successful Completion of Missions. The original hunch responsible for the inclusion of this rating item was that it might identify variance in crew performance associated with low motivation and/or tendencies to abort missions. It appears, however, that information concerning the officially recorded performance of the crews determined much of this rating.

The sociometric index of "on-crew" choice does not appear to be related to any marked extent with the superiors' ratings. The sociometric data may provide a second and relatively independent estimate of the performance of the crew. The correlation between the index of "on-crew" choice and the objective bombing accuracy data was found to be .33. This suggests that the sociometric choices were also influenced by the unreliable bombing information but to a lesser degree than most of the superiors' ratings.

Discussion and Conclusion

The finding of substantial and significant correlations between the objective bombing accuracy data, for which we had estimated a reliability of zero, and the eleven superior rating variables has general methodological implications for the development of criteria. An explanation of these correlations can be found in a possibility of a "contamination" of the judgments of superiors. The results of each bombing mission are widely publicized among the personnel of the wings and squadrons. In fact, it is standard procedure to hold a critique of the mission on the morning of the day following the mission. In addition, mission results, expressed in terms of bombing errors, are made part of official records which are maintained and used in determining which crews will be given an opportunity to lead further missions. It can be expected, therefore, that each rater could have estimated the official bombing accuracy records of each crew with a relatively high degree of accuracy. The fact that these records represented little other than chance crew achievement was, of course, unknown to the raters. This commonly shared, but unreliable, information concerning the performance of the various crews tended to produce both spuriously high reliability of the superior ratings and the spurious correlations with the unreliable bombing data.

A general question is raised concerning the dependability of rating data as criteria. In situations where objective achievement information is available, we may expect that raters will utilize such information in the process of forming the judgments they express in their ratings. If these achievement data reflect reliable performance, they will, of course, add to the dependability of the ratings. However, should the achievement information be basically unrelated to differences in the performance of the individuals or units being rated, this fact is likely to be overlooked when a test of the agreement between raters proves the rating to have "adequate reliability." Raters may agree in their knowledge of the achievement records but be in error about the meaningfulness of such records.

REFERENCES

1. P. Horst. "A Generalized Expression for the Reliability of Measures," *Psychometrika*, 1949, 14, pp. 21–24.
2. Robert L. Thorndike. *Personnel Selection* (New York: Wiley, 1949), p. 173.

35. PROJECT COST CONTROL AT RAYTHEON'S WAYLAND LABORATORY*

E. L. WILLIAMS AND G. A. WILSON[0]

SUMMARY

This paper was written to assist those who wish to install a project cost control system in their own organization. It does not provide the detailed procedures or computer programs, but it does discuss in some detail: (1) the development and implementation of the system, (2) the definitions of responsibility and authority required to make the system work, (3) the roles and interrelationships of the controller, line management and project management, (4) the requirement for, and methods of, dividing projects into manageable pieces both in terms of size and of time, (5) the paper work required for documentation of both data inputs and data outputs (reports), and (6) the interpretation of reports in terms of project, organization, and individual performance.

The system described does not introduce any radically new approaches to management; it is clearly evident, however, that the application of the well-established principles discussed in the paper will produce worthwhile improvements in project cost control with an attendant improvement in management as a whole.

The cost control system is an excellent base for PERT/COST. The "work package" approach and the "manageable size task" approach are, in effect, synonymous. The changes required to produce data outputs in accordance with customer interpretations of the PERT/COST requirements are small. A major step toward PERT/COST, that of "fine-grained" cost control, is provided by the system.

RAYTHEON's Wayland Laboratory is the home of the Surface Radar and Navigation Operation (SURANO) Engineering function. The operation is engaged in the development and manufacturing of electronic equipment for a variety of military and nonmilitary government agencies. The size, type and duration of the projects handled by the engineering organization varies widely. Figure 1 illustrates the type of organization used by engineering. However, it should be understood initially that the cost control system can be adapted to any normal type of organization—vertical, horizontal, or any combination thereof.

---

* Reprinted from *IEEE Transactions on Engineering Management*, September, 1963, pp. 138–149. A shortened version was prepared for the Raytheon Company house organ, *Electronic Progress*.

[0] Equipment Division, Surface Radar and Navigation Operation, Raytheon Company, Wayland, Mass.

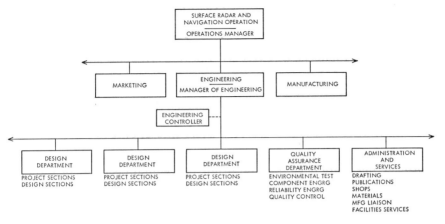

FIG. 1.   A Simplified Chart of the Engineering Organization

DEVELOPMENT OF THE SYSTEM

In the fall of 1960, a classical case of "surprise overrun" prompted the Operations Manager to call for better Engineering cost control. The Manager of Engineering responded by appointing a committee with directions to complete the following effort by early 1961:

1. Review and analyze various cost control systems and recommend a control system for use by SURANO Engineering.

2. Compare the recommended system with our present system to insure that the strengths of the present system are retained and the weaknesses are overcome.

3. Upon management approval of the recommended system, guide the development and implementation of procedures to put the system into effect.

The committee's cochairmen were the Engineering Controller and the Engineering Manager of Administration. The committee members were a Support Department Manager (representing Publications, Shops, Manufacturing Liaison, and Drafting), a Design Section Manager and a Project Section Manager. This group worked as a team and with the operating people—department managers, engineers, unit men, administrators, etc. By early 1961 the principles of a new system had been laid down. In February and March, 1961, indoctrination meetings were held with management and administrative personnel, and in April the first project went "on stream." During the next six months, almost all Engineering projects started to use the system. By mid-1962, all projects, including "small jobs" such as $100 shop efforts, were using the system. The milestones in the development of the system are shown in Figure 2.

To ensure effective implementation of the system, an experienced Administrative Engineer was assigned full time. Systems and Procedures, Controller, and Computer Programming personnel worked with the Administrative Engineer to revamp procedures and computer programs quickly whenever imperfections were detected. Many of the "bugs" were discovered during routine review meetings, and in most cases, corrections were made before the next set of reports was published.

The system has now been in use for nearly two years. It is still being improved, but there have been no major procedural changes for the past

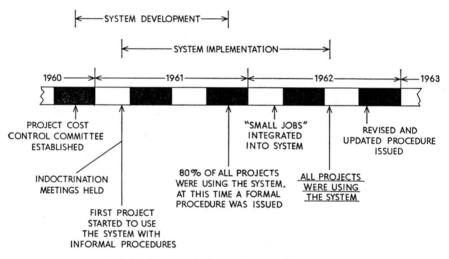

FIG. 2. Milestones in the Development of the System

year. The first project to use the system had a total product cost budget of $800,000 and was accomplished with a $48,000 underrun. Not all projects using the system have been performed with such startling results, but the trend has been toward improvement. This trend was synchronized with another trend—the shift from CPFF to fixed-price contracts.

PRINCIPLES AND POLICIES

It became apparent to the committee almost immediately that the real need was for better management at all levels, not just a new cost control procedure. Further, they concluded that better management did not necessarily require different managers; it could mean the improvement of the existing managers. This could be done by clearly defining the tasks they must manage and giving them the tools to measure their performance.

The fact that they could and would be measured was theorized as a compelling force to make them plan their work.

The responsibilities of all of the professional individuals in the Engineering organization must be clarified. Once and for all, the problem of equating responsibility and authority must be solved. The Wayland Laboratory handles many projects of widely differing sizes for a number of different customers: Air Force, Army, Navy, National Aeronautics and Space Agency, Federal Aviation Agency, and prime contractors to the government. For this reason, "horizontal" organization is used where project engineers coordinate and monitor projects without line authority to control the design and support functions. It is not the purpose of this paper to justify the choice of organization. Division, Operation and Laboratory management have been aware for over ten years that the present type of organization may be frustrating at times to project engineers, but it guarantees the most effective use of manpower and maximizes the Laboratory's flexibility.[1]

DEFINITIONS OF RESPONSIBILITY AND AUTHORITY

The cost system has been adapted to the horizontal organization used at the Wayland Laboratory. The system is applicable to vertical organization with little modification. The definitions which follow are for the horizontal case.

Design Department managers are responsible for all activity performed within their departments and for coordinating and monitoring the support activities performed in other departments. The project engineers who work for them are responsible for performing system tasks (interconnections, reporting, etc.) and for day-to-day follow-up of all project activities. Whenever possible, they solve coordination problems by working with the parties concerned. At all times, the project engineer must respect the fact that he is acting in this capacity for the department manager. He must, therefore, keep his department manager informed, thus ensuring the backing of line authority when necessary to solve coordination problems.

Only two types of authority are recognized: line authority and authority given through written orders. These orders are, in effect, internal subcontracts and may be used (1) by department managers to divide the units and activities of a project among his Design and Project sections and the Support departments; (2) by project or design engineers to buy services from other Design or Support departments; or (3) by Support departments to divide their effort among their subfunctions. Thus even the second type of authority reverts to line authority, since orders are

---
[1] Provisions for handling special projects on a "project organization" basis have been made. The existing systems and procedures will allow either approach.

given to line managers, who are responsible for getting the work accomplished. With this reversion, the problem of equating responsibility and authority, on the surface, is solved. An important element remains: how can efficiency be guaranteed to a department manager who subcontracts work to another department?

Clearly, overall efficiency must be the responsibility of the Manager of Engineering. The Project Cost Control System provides the tools for the Manager of Engineering to measure and control each of his departments, both Design and Support, by themselves. In reviewing cost performance, his first concern is the performance of each department; secondarily, he must follow the performance on each project. Similarly, Design Department managers have the dual responsibility of managing their departments and the projects assigned to them. Project engineers provide the assistance necessary to manage project details. Department administrators assist in managing the department.

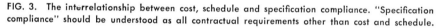

FIG. 3. The interrelationship between cost, schedule and specification compliance. "Specification compliance" should be understood as all contractual requirements other than cost and schedule.

COST, SCHEDULE AND SPECIFICATION COMPLIANCE RELATIONSHIPS

At this point, another factor was recognized. In addition to the effect the cost system has on management methods, the interrelationship of costs with schedules and specification compliance must be recognized. It is apparent to most everyone that "time is money" and that "gilding the lily" costs money. Stated most simply (and as shown in Figure 3), cost, schedule, and specification compliance are completely interdependent and, therefore, they must be controlled by a single manager. When an order is written, it must cover all three factors. Managers must realize that a task will cost more if a tighter specification is called for or if the schedule is shortened. For this reason orders written on other departments must be negotiated and must reflect a bilateral agreement between the issuer and accepter.

A final piece of basic policy that was necessary as a foundation for the system was that all projects must be managed on the basis of meeting contractual obligations at minimum cost. It should be apparent to management-oriented individuals that this is the only acceptable approach. Most engineers innately tend to do the best job possible without regard for cost or schedule. They must be convinced that they are part of the management team. Whereas the president of a company may be called upon to make a few large decisions each week or month, engineers are called upon each day to make many decisions that affect the cost, schedule and quality of the company's products. Engineers are important parts of the team which is shaping the company's reputation.

DATA HANDLING

To accomplish the principles outlined above, projects must be subdivided into tasks of manageable size. Records must be kept on many individual tasks in each of the many projects handled in the laboratory. Initially, the data was compiled and reports produced by simple tabulation equipment. When the quantity of data became great enough, it was necessary to use the computer to accomplish the work within the short time cycle allowed.

Previously, operating managers had been obtaining cost data from reports produced by the Controller for his own use and from an "Engineering Monthly Cost Report" that was usually weeks late and frequently not in agreement with the secondary records kept by the operating personnel. Concurrent with the development of the Project Cost Control System, the Controller was accomplishing a program of improved data handling. Presently, complete, accurate data is available to the operating personnel the sixth working day after the close of each fiscal month. Thus, the goal of getting accurate, timely cost data has been achieved entirely; secondary accounting has been essentially eliminated.

A most important aspect of the system's data handling is that the Project Cost Control Reports are produced strictly for Project Cost Control purposes; their content is tailored for and controlled by the operating personnel who use them.[2] By way of illustration, it may be pointed out that the reports include the cost of material on a commitment basis. When a requisition is submitted to the Materials Department (Purchasing Section), its total cost appears in the next cost control report as an actual expenditure. The company is not liable at this time or, perhaps, not until after actual delivery, but the individual who placed the requisition has, in effect, spent the amount shown in the requisition. This makes his planning task simpler, since the reported cumulative cost includes actual and committed cost—the difference between this and the budget may be committed for completion of the task. Note that this method of reporting makes the data easier to interpret, since the actual costs do not fluctuate as a result of partial payments and the relatively difficult process of forecasting the arrival of a partial billing and its payment are eliminated. Upon completion

---

[2] Note that the Project Cost Control Reports are produced by adapting basic accounting records, not by a separate accounting system.

of a material purchase, the material cost shown in the reports is adjusted by the Controller to account for all minor cost variations. Normally, these variations are small and do not cause the individual responsible for the task any appreciable trouble.

Another important aspect of the data-handling process is the use of "raw" data in the preparation of reports. Those responsible for each individual task submit their unreviewed actuals and forecasts to the data-processing section and, as a result, all levels of management receive reports based on inputs from those closest to the actual work. It has been argued that this method of preparing the reports builds in errors that would not occur if, typically, design engineers were allowed to review drafting and shop inputs and project engineers were allowed to review design and support function inputs. On the other hand, it has been found that reports prepared in this manner provide the working information required by those who argue that they should be able to review the inputs to insure the correction of errors. By the time that management reviews occur, the misunderstandings are well on their way toward correction; management asks only that action be taken to make the next report reflect an accurate picture.

In the past, reports to management had been "cleaned-up" by section and department managers and project engineers to avoid arousing higher management's "premature" interest in a problem. Perhaps these actions were justified in some cases—"they saved much concern by management over trivial points." Conversely, it is human nature to keep problems away from higher management as long as possible with the hope that these problems can be solved before management becomes aware of them. This process of "kicking problems under the rug" is a major reason for "surprise overruns." The Project Cost Control System calls for getting problems out where all can see them as soon as possible so that action can be taken in time to prevent financial embarrassment. Trivial problems will be solved with ease. The major problems will receive attention from functional and project management, and the sooner, the better.

BUDGETS AND EXPENDITURE LIMITS

The terms "budget" and "expenditure limit" are very carefully defined in the Project Cost Control System. These terms are applicable at the project, unit or activity, or task level, but in each case they mean:

Budget: The total amount of money that may be expected to fund a given task. Budgets do not change unless the scope of a task changes.

Expenditure limit: The amount of money that may be expended presently on a task.

Budgets are used to plan the overall job (task, unit, activity, or project) and as a basis for measuring cost performance at the completion of the job.

Management, Marketing, and the Controller have agreed to establish the budget for a project at its total value as soon as any reasonable agreement is made with the customer, and, if necessary, on a "management risk" basis. Backed with a total expected budget, the Project Engineer can plan the total project, and in turn, he must assign unit and activity budgets on a total basis and Task Orders written for specific tasks must again reflect the total task. This concept of budgeting allows total planning from the specific task level upward.

Expenditure limits are used for two main reasons. First, and most obvious, they limit expenditures in accordance with customer funding. If the customer has established a limit-of-liability below the amount equivalent to the total budget, the Project Engineer will be authorized (by the Controller) to expand only up to this amount to prevent the company from becoming "over-exposed." The Project Engineer may distribute expenditure limited funds to units and activities as is most expedient for the project. Typically, although support activities, such as Environmental Test, are fully budgeted for planning purposes, they may be limited to zero expenditure during the early stages of a project to allow all available funds to be used for design effort. A variation of this reason is the establishment of limits to prevent "accidental" expenditures; open charge numbers have innate abilities to collect charges even when no work is necessary against them.

The second use of the expenditure limit is in connection with the preservation of underruns. One of the most important goals of the system is the exposure of predicted overruns soon enough to allow effective action to be taken toward their reduction or elimination. Not so obvious, but almost as important, is the early exposure and preservation of predicted underruns. When underruns are forecast properly, persons responsible for units and activities and the Project Engineer have a clear picture of (1) how to cover overruns in other parts of the project, and (2) how to effectively use unspent funds to the best advantage of the company and the customer.

Management policy, as stated in the Project Cost Control procedure, requires that projects be accomplished on the basis of meeting contractual obligations at minimum cost. To do this, predicted underruns must be exposed quickly and must be preserved. Underruns' funds too frequently manage to get spent with little or nothing gained for the company or the customer.

If an underrun is forecast by a design section, the Project Engineer should first discuss the potential underrun with the Design Section Manager to assure that all of the potential underrun was exposed in the cost report. Secondly, he should reach a mutual agreement with the Section Manager concerning an expenditure limit. This limit should be reasonable—tight enough to insure realization of as much saving as possible, but not so tight that the Section Manager has no leeway at all. Future reviews of the limit may allow a lower value to be established.

It is important that the Project Engineer realize that he has "slack funds available to cover unforeseen overruns or funds available that can be used to expedite schedules or to give the customers a little better product (with management's full cognizance). If the Project Engineer talks the Section Manager out of budget, he is asking the Section Manager to accept a mediocre cost performance record; if he uses the budget obtained in this manner to fund another activity that is overrunning, he is improving the cost performance record of the group that does not deserve it. Once a Section Manager realizes that the Project Engineer will cut his budget if he exposes an underrun, he will be very reticent to make such exposures in the future. Thus, the Project Engineer is his own worst enemy if he cuts budgets to preserve underruns. By imposing an expenditure limit, he ensures that underrun funds will not be spent. His department manager and the Laboratory Manager check regularly to ensure that expenditure limits are not exceeded.

ORGANIZATION OF PROJECTS

As pointed out previously, an important aid to improved cost control is the division of the work into pieces which are small enough to clearly comprehend and manage. The system provides for breaking the effort down both with respect to the size and type of task and with respect to time through calendarization of plans. Dividing a project into a number of tasks, such as the design of a transmitter, receiver, antenna, indicator, etc., is usually the first step in the organization process. The next step is usually to peel off the drafting and shop fabrication efforts. It is important that a distinction be made between that drafting and shop effort which contributes directly to their assigned tasks and that effort which is supplied to assist the engineer in his design. To ensure that we are working with line authority in charge of all phases of the project, the main drafting tasks (detailing, assembly drawings, schematics, checking, etc.) must be defined in an order to Drafting. Layout effort performed by a draftsman under the immediate direction of an engineer, on the other hand, is part of the design task and should be included in the order for the design effort.

The cost control system provides for three levels of "orders": (1) a Development Order (DO), which describes the project as a whole and establishes project-wide ground rules, standards, etc.; (2) Development Suborders (DSO), which describe the units and activities necessary to complete the project; and (3) Task Orders (TO), which describe specific tasks. The DO is the Design Department Manager's total task definition; DSO's are normally assigned to Design Section and Support Department managers and the Project Engineer. Neither the DO nor its suborders are "chargeable" orders. Task Orders may be charged—they describe small manageable parts of the project that one responsible individual can plan and control. Figures 4 and 5 illustrate the method used to organize or "break" down a project into manageable tasks. Notice particularly that the breakdown is both by tasks and by responsible departments. This provides

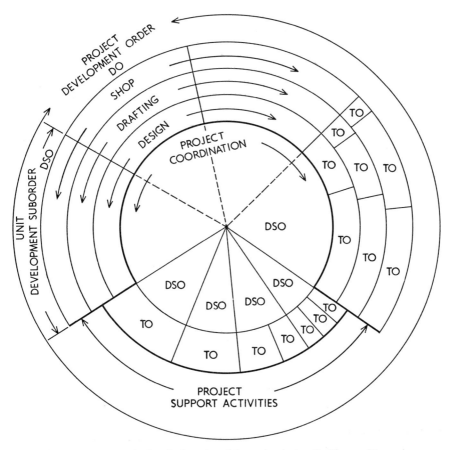

FIG. 4.   Project organization. Each section of the project is described by a written order.

the basis required to obtain reports both for projects and for departments.

The various types of orders are numbered with a nine-digit code. The project is identified by the first five numbers. 89-999-xxxx is a Development Order number; 89-999- identifies the project; the –xxxx identifies this number as a DO number, as these "numbers" are not used at the DO level. The unit or activity is identified by the sixth and seventh numbers, and the responsible functional department is identified by the eighth digit. 89-999-992x is a Development Suborder number; the -99 identifies the unit and the

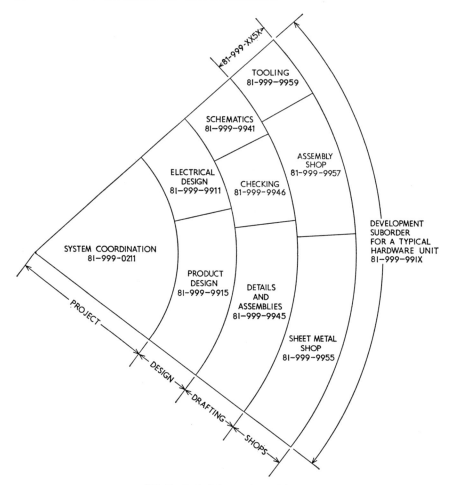

FIG. 5. Typical Unit Task Breakdown

2 shows that the Ordnance Radar Department is responsible for this particular unit. 89-999-9951 is a Task Order number; the 5, in this case, shows that the Shops Department is responsible for this specific task, which is identified by the last digit.

In the case of the Support departments the last digit is used to identify the particular subfunction that will perform the task. Typically, in the Shops Department the following coding is used: 5–Sheet Metal Shop, 6–Machine Shop, 7–Assembly Shop, and 8–Processing Shop. In the design department subfunction coding is not used. Initially, an elaborate subfunction coding system was established, but it was discarded because it seriously limited the flexibility of the numbering system.

The 0 and 9, as last digits of Task Order numbers, have been reserved for special purposes. A 0 indicates that the Task Order is a "funding order." Unlike other Task Orders, this type of order cannot be charged. It is used to transfer funds and task to an individual who will write one or more Task Orders under the funding order to get a specific task done. As a practical matter, each DSO automatically has a funding Task Order associated with it; the number is obtained by substituting a 0 for the final x in the DSO number. 89-999-9920 is the funding Task Order associated with DSO number 89-999-992x. When the shop is asked to build a model under this DSO, the design engineer may create a funding Task Order, 89-999-9950, to transfer funds and the model building task to the shop.

The 9, as the digit, is used for Tooling Task Orders and provides a systematic method of accumulating all tooling charges against a project. Tooling TO's are automatically opened when a tooling charge occurs; they do not require an official piece of paper. If the tooling charges are to be extensive, it is recommended that a tooling TO be written and a budget set up for the tooling charges.

CALENDARIZED BUDGETS AND FORECASTS

Each DO, DSO and Task Order covers three areas: task definition, financial information and schedule information. The problem of task definition is so serious that a separate paper would be required to cover it completely. Here, it will be pointed out only that a clearly defined task is essential to the functioning of the system; it is the basis for a well-negotiated Task Order.

Project, unit, and task schedules are normally handled by a procedure separate from, but related to, the Project Cost Control System. PERT is used on most projects. Because of the nature of some projects (such as the aids-to-production type) or because of customer demands, other schedule techniques are also used. The cost control system is compatible with all known scheduling systems.

Through calendarization of the Task Order's budget, a degree of schedule information is specifically included in the TO. The calendarized budget can be compared on a cumulative basis with the actual expenditures to provide some insight into the task's schedule performance. It also provides a basis for scheduling manpower for planning purposes in the various departments.

Calendarization of the budget is just one more way of dividing the job into controllable segments. Planning the expenditures on a monthly basis to completion permits an assessment of performance as the job progresses rather than waiting until most of the money is spent and finding that it is too late to correct an overrun situation.

As is the case with the total budget, the calendarized budget does not change unless the scope of the task changes. Retroactive recalendarization is allowed only in very special cases. For the most part, this practice is followed to make the records "look good"; it serves no useful purpose in this case. Occasionally, a task may have its scope changed in such a manner that retroactive recalendarization is justified; special permission is required.

Forecasts and calendarized budgets both involve prediction of expenditures on a monthly basis. Unlike calendarized budgets, forecasts (or reforecasts) are made whenever a significant change in spending plan occurs and at least every three months. Quarterly mandatory reforecasting is done on a schedule set up by the Controller to synchronize with the Quarterly Contract Financial Reviews held by the Operations Manager. A forecast can predict an overrun or an underrun; the total of the calendarized budget must be the same as the total budget.

Evaluation of the current month forecasts with respect to the current month actual is a good means of determining how well current planning is being done. Management uses this comparison, the current month variance, as a major review point. In order to minimize these variances, the individuals responsible for the Task Order must continuously plan their work.

Comparison of cumulative actual costs with the initial calendarization of the budget provides a measure of long-term planning ability; comparison of actual cost with up-to-date forecasts provides a measure of short-term planning ability. Comparison of forecasted cost-at-completion with the total budget provides a current forecast of task, unit, activity or project final performance.

OVERRUNS OF BUDGETS AND EXPENDITURE LIMITS

There are many aspects to the problem of handling overrun situations. The job must be completed; you just can't stop when you have spent the budget or reached an expenditure limit. This system allows actuals to exceed budgets and/or expenditure limits. It insists, however, that this situation be predicted and that permission from project and functional management be obtained before the overrun becomes actual. The system is guilty of having limits that can be exceeded. On the other hand, these variances are reviewed monthly and attract continuing attention from all those in a position to do something about them. Management has even gone to the extent of forbidding the existence of expenditure limits which exceed budgets. When an overrun situation is recognized as unavoidable, management wants this situation to look as bad as possible and in no way wants to condone the situation. If an expenditure limit was established that was greater than the budget, this limit would undoubtedly be reached. By not establishing such a limit, the hope is that at least some of the predicted overrun can be saved through action by all concerned.

THE CONTROLLER'S ROLE

From what one can read over the back fences, it seems that in many companies the role of the controller has varied from that of bookkeeper to that of being short of "all powerful." Not many years ago, most controllers in government-oriented engineering activities were much less influential than they are today. The reasons are many: Perhaps, the best is the growth of the industry itself and the consequent growth of governmental regulations. Another is the attraction to this profession of individuals more highly trained in the managerial services. During the period of growth, many lessons have been learned, and today we see an increasing attitude of partnership between controller and operating types of personnel.

In the past, operating personnel had no choice but to keep their own books; official cost information from the Controller was too late to be useful in the cost control process. As a result, the administrators in the various Design and Support departments, particularly those in project sections, spent a major part of their time keeping cost records. As the Controller's abilities improved and trust in his records was developed, the need for secondary accounts kept by the operating personnel has lessened to the point that it is all but eliminated.

The following data is published by the Controller each month for each task.

A. Concerning the current month
   1. Forecast expenditure
   2. Actual expenditure
   3. Variance (between the forecast and actual)
B. Concerning cumulative costs
   1. Cumulative budget
   2. Cumulative actual cost
C. Concerning expenditure limitations
   1. Expenditure limitation
   2. Available funds (differences between expenditure limit and cumulative actual cost)
D. Concerning cost-at-completion
   1. Forecast cost-at-completion (CAC)
   2. Budget
   3. Variance (between Budget and CAC)
E. Concerning changes from last report
   1. Change in expenditure limit
   2. Change in CAC
   3. Change in budget
   4. Change in variance
F. Other data
   1. Task title
   2. Task number
   3. Responsible individual's name
   4. Status, i.e., closed or open

At this point, a clear distinction must be made between the preparation of cost data and cost reports, and the use of this data and these reports to control costs. Since cost, schedule and quality of product are inseparably related, they must be managed by one person. To reduce cost, schedules and product quality are the immediate variables that can be manipulated. These variables are under the control of the persons responsible for projects, units, activities and tasks; these persons are operating-type people, not controller-type people. It is then incumbent upon the Controller to

	RESPONSIBLE ACTIVITY		
	CONTROLLER	CONTROLLER & PROJECT ENGRG.	PROJECT DESIGN & SUPPORT
AREAS OF RESPONSIBILITY →	Official Cost Records Billing Rate Calculations & Predictions (O.H., Labor & G&A) Preparation of Proj. Cost Control Reports Advice to Management & all Operating Personnel on Costs	Financial Reports for Customers	Project Cost Control
COST LEVEL →	Selling Price	Selling Price	Product Cost
COST BASIS →	Actual Incurred Costs	Actual Incurred Costs Plus Commitments	Commitment
COST BREAKDOWN →	Contract	Contract Items	Units, Activities & Specific Tasks
DATA USED →	Invoice Ledger Records Accounting Schedules Etc.	Commitment Reports Weekly/Monthly Labor Reports Etc.	Project Cost Control System Reports

FIG. 6.   Project Financial Responsibilities

provide accurate, timely data in a convenient form for use by operating people in controlling costs. It is further incumbent on the Controller to point out "danger areas" to the operating personnel. The Controller handles the data first and is equipped to analyze and interpret cost data. His inputs are most valuable to those charged with the responsibility of controlling project costs.

Figure 6 shows the division of financial responsibility between the controller and operating people. It points out the necessity of organizing projects in such a manner that both internal cost control requirements and customer financial reporting requirements can be most effectively combined. Experience has shown that relatively simple breakdowns can be made for even the most complex projects that will allow contract-line-item reporting to the customer and meaningful task reporting to operating personnel. It is fundamental to the process of organizing a project to consider all aspects of the reporting process. The requirements of systems such as PERT/COST further serve to emphasize this point.

Two important parts of the Controller's contribution to the system are that of reviewing all cost control documents (DO's, DSO's, TO's, etc.) to assure that they are in conformance with the procedures and that of producing reports for the operating personnel. Figure 7 summarizes in a very brief manner the Controller's role in preparing Project Cost Control

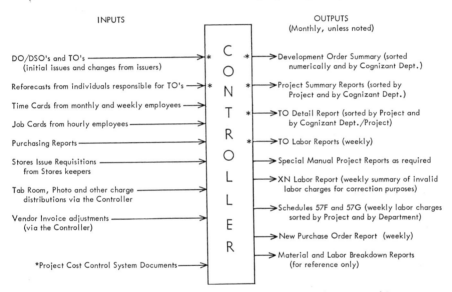

FIG. 7.   The Controller's Role in Preparing Project Cost Control Reports and Data

data. Once reviewed, the input data is machine tabulated to produce the various weekly and monthly reports.

The controller is most certainly responsible for generating or at least confirming all cost figures that are delivered to activities outside the Laboratory. These figures include financial reports to higher management and to customers.

SYSTEMS AND PROCEDURES CONSIDERATIONS

The procedure that satisfies the needs of the Project Cost Control System has to provide means for:

1. Subdividing projects into tasks of manageable size.
2. Assuring that these tasks are well defined.

3. Assuring that these tasks are well planned.
4. Measuring cost performance with respect to plans.
5. Controlling costs before financial problems become insoluble.

It must be easily understood and not burden its users with an unreasonable amount of paper work. Most important, it must establish line responsibility as the backbone for task, activity and project performance.

Apart from specific requirements, the procedures require two other elements. First, they must insure a uniform "cost language" which is common throughout engineering. Terminology must be the same and reports for all projects must be similar in order to allow functional department reports to be produced summarizing all effort on various projects within each department. Second, the system must be flexible enough to be applied to small and large projects, study projects and hardware development projects, projects organized vertically and projects organized horizontally, and Cost Plus Fixed Fee, Fixed Price, and other types of contracts.

Special "shortcut" procedures exist for small jobs, arbitrarily defined as jobs with budgets less than $5,000. These jobs are handled using Task Orders alone. There appears to be no gain in creating the paper work of Development Orders and Development Suborders. Calendarizing of the budgets and forecasting of these jobs are at the option of the person responsible for the job.

The system provides for the subdivision of projects necessary for application of systems such as PERT/COST. Calculation of cumulative budgets in the manner required by PERT/COST, viz.:

$$= \frac{\text{cumulative budget} = \text{actual cost} \times \text{total budget}}{\text{predicted cost-at-completion}}$$

can be added to the computer routing without any serious programing problems.

The relationship of the basic forms used in the system is illustrated in Figure 8. All of these forms are initiated and updated by the individuals responsible for the particular order except for Task Orders for small jobs which are initiated and updated by the Controller.

REPORTS

Each person responsible for a Task Order receives a copy of that part of the report applicable to his Task Order. This particular report, The Project Status Detail Report, is felt to be the most important, since it puts cost data into the hands of those who can take immediate action.

The data in the basic report is then summarized by project, by department, and by project totals for the Design Department and Engi-

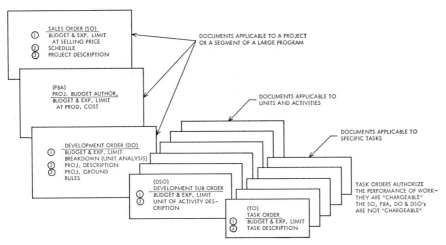

FIG. 8. A Summary of Basic Forms

neering Manager's use. Specifically, the following project reports are produced (see Figure 9):

1. Development Order (DO) Summary Report

   Distribution

   In total—distributed to only the Manager of Engineering.
   By department—distributed to the department cognizant of the various DO's (projects).

   Description

   One line entry for each DO.

2. Project Summary Report

   Distribution

   In total—distributed only to the Manager of Engineering.
   In part—distributed to cognizant department managers and project engineers.

   Description

   Line entries for each Development Suborder (DSO) with a total entry for the DO.

3. Project Status Detail Report

   Distribution

   To cognizant department managers and project engineers.
   To cognizant individuals responsible for DSO's.

   Description

   Line entries for each Task Order (TO) with totals for each DSO and the DO.

The following monthly departmental reports are produced:

4. Department Summary Report

Distribution

In total—distributed only to the Manager of Engineering.
By department—distributed to the functions responsible for the activities reported.

Description

One line entry per project (DO) showing the totals for all activity on the DO performed within the given department.

5. Department Status Detail Report

Distribution

In Project Order to cognizant department (Design and Manufacturing Liaison departments only).
In Department and Task Order to cognizant departments (Drafting, Shops, Manufacturing Liaison, Publications and Quality Assurance only).
This run is further distributed to the various sections within the departments.

Description

One line entry for each TO being performed by the given department. In the project order run totals for DO's are shown. This run is prepared for departments that have project responsibility. The run by department and Task Order is for support departments having a number of subfunctions. By sorting in this order, the run may be subdivided and sections of it given to the cognizant subfunctions.

In addition to the monthly reports described above, two weekly reports[3] are produced as follows:

6. Weekly Labor Report

Distribution

To persons responsible for TO's and to cognizant Department managers and project engineers.

Description

Labor charges in hours naming the individuals making the charges, with separate sheet for each TO.

7. Weekly New Purchase Order Report

Distribution[4]

To department offices for distribution to responsible individuals.

Description

Data, including cost, on all new purchase orders and change orders placed during the week, listed in project order.

---

[3] In addition to the weekly Labor Schedules, which are controller-type reports not specifically prepared for use by the operating personnel.

[4] This report is scheduled for improvement. When improved it will be distributed the same as the Weekly Labor Report.

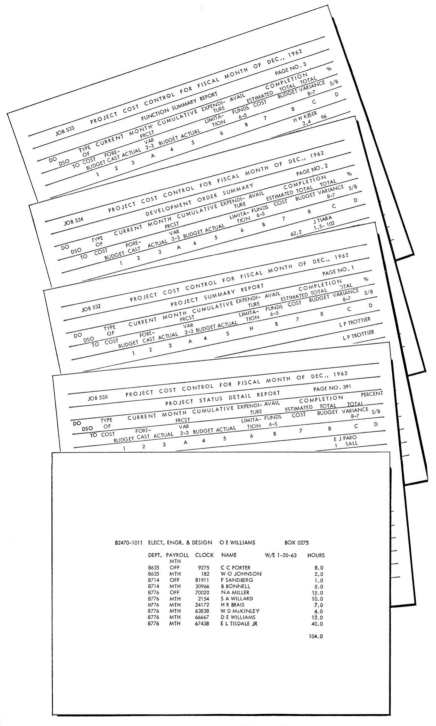

FIG. 9. Project Cost Control System Reports.

Note that the weekly labor and purchase order reports are intended to update the users between the monthly issues of the major reports. The weekly labor report also serves to inform responsible individuals who is or who is not charging his Task Order. Mischarging is often detected through these reports. The converse, someone *not* charging a particular order many times, is equally important to the man trying to get a job done.

PERFORMANCE EVALUATION

Section managers, department managers and the Laboratory Manager may use the cost control reports to evaluate organizations and individuals that work on projects. As pointed out previously, the current month variance between actual cost and forecast cost provides a running check on the planning being performed. Also mentioned previously, the comparison of cumulative actual cost with the cumulative budget provides a basis for questioning schedule performance.

In the normal case, the most important review points are the available funds and total variance. The available funds are the difference between the cumulative actual cost and the expenditure limit; a negative value here may mean that the company is overexposed, i.e., may have spent more than the contractual limit-of-liability. In the case of individual Task Orders, overrunning of the expenditure limit is important from a task management point of view; it becomes most important at the project level, where it invariably reflects on overrun of contractual findings.

The total variance is the difference between the forecasted cost-at-completion and the total budget; it differs from the available funds entry since it is a forecast of final results rather than a reflection of the present status. Negative available funds at the project level is correctable only by the customer's increasing of the contractual funding; this situation is not correctable by action within the company alone. The forecasted total variance frequently can be corrected by internal action if an overrun situation is predicted early enough.

The reports include entries for changes (from the previous month's report) in connection with expenditure limit, forecasted cost-at-completion, total budget and total variance. These entries provide the reviewer with a good starting point, since they reflect changes in scope and overall forecast performance.

Care must be taken in reviewing to assure that a proper forecasting job is being done. In certain cases where forecasts are not correct, the cumulative actual cost has been found to exceed the forecasted cost-at-completion. In this case, the total variance is stated incorrectly in the report, since it is calculated from the forecast cost-at-completion, which has already been exceeded. A good technique in reviewing a cost control report is to check for this condition first and to mark in the necessary changes. This situation always demands immediate attention.

The words above are directed toward the evaluation of *project performance on a running basis*. It is also desirable to evaluate project performance, organizational (functional) performance and individual performance on a cumulative basis. This must be done with great care since the analysis of any one report may not provide enough information on which to base a judgment. In fact, analysis of a single report may lead to false results. A complete discussion of this sort of performance evaluation is outside the scope of this paper. However, certain factors will be pointed out.

The only total variance figure that has lasting meaning is the one that exists when the project (unit, task, etc.) is completed. The forecasts of total variance that occur during the life of a project are working figures

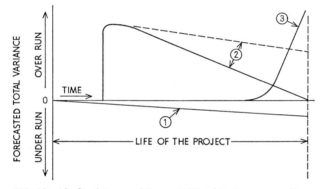

FIG. 10.   Idealized Curves of Forecasted Total Variance versus Time

that may change as the work progresses; these forecasts provide the inputs to the actual cost control mechanism. Through skillful management, forecasted overruns can be avoided or minimized and underruns preserved or increased.

Figure 10 illustrates three idealized histories of forecasted total variance. Curve 1 shows a variance condition that continuously improved during the life of the project. This could mean that the negotiated price of the contract was favorable and that with little effort all concerned performed their tasks within their budgets. In this case, performance was good, but it did not reflect any special management effort.

Curve 2, on the other hand, illustrates a large forecasted total variance occurring when the project is about one-third through its life. The solid line indicates that the necessary action was taken to reduce the total variance to zero at the time the task was complete. In this case, we can be fairly sure that all concerned worked hard and effectively to control the variance; performance was excellent. Even if the variance had followed the dashed curve, the performance may have been better than that illustrated in Curve 1, which was a "soft job."

The remaining curve shows the most serious situation. Here, no variance was forecasted until it was too late to do anything about it. It is possible that an unpredictable problem occurred at the last minute, but experience indicates that this is a rare case. The more common finding is to find that the potential overrun was covered up with the hope that a last-minute miracle would occur. It could also indicate lack of interest or ability to plan and forecast on the part of those performing the work. It almost certainly reflects inept management ability in those who were involved in the task.

The Project Cost Control System is a tool for controlling project cost; its usefulness appears to be improving continually. It may also serve in helping to evaluate the persons using the system, but it is foolish to think that a system and a machine can provide absolute judgment of human performance. With intelligent interpretation, the data provided by the system can certainly assist managers in their evaluation of their personnel.

ACKNOWLEDGMENT

This paper requires acknowledgment of both the creators of the system and those who have made it work. The original management requirements for a cost control system were delivered to a committee consisting of H. Frandsen, Engineering Controller; E. L. Williams, Engineering Manager of Administration; A. M. McCoy, Project Section Manager; D.L. McMurtrie, Design Section Manager; and J. Nye, Production Liaison and Technical Services Department Manager. These men set down the policies and parameters upon which the system is based. Detailed systems and procedures effort were supplied by W. J. Brown, A. E. Dubnow, and A. L. Porter. Direction of the actual implementation of the system was started by E. L. Williams and has continued by G. A. Wilson. Principal credit in making the system work belongs to J. R. Merrill, Manager of Engineering. It has often been said that no system is any better than its management backing. This system has had the best possible support from top engineering management. It is truly effective today because of the patient effort devoted to departmental cost control reviews and the continued urging toward improvement by the Manager of Engineering during the system's implementation stages.

36. DYSFUNCTIONAL CONSEQUENCES OF PERFORMANCE MEASUREMENTS*

V. F. RIDGWAY

THERE IS today a strong tendency to state numerically as many as possible of the variables with which management must deal. The mounting interest in and application of tools such as operations research, linear programming, and statistical decision making, all of which require quantifiable variables, foster the idea that if progress toward goals can be measured, efforts and resources can be more rationally managed. This has led to the development of quantitative performance measurements for all levels within organizations, up to and including measurements of the performance of a division manager with profit responsibility in a decentralized company. Measurements at lower levels in the organization may be in terms of amount of work, quality of work, time required, and so on.

Quantitative measures of performance are tools, and are undoubtedly useful. But research indicates that indiscriminate use and undue confidence and reliance in them result from insufficient knowledge of the full effects and consequences. Judicious use of a tool requires awareness of possible side effects and reactions. Otherwise, indiscriminate use may result in side effects and reactions outweighing the benefits, as was the case when penicillin was first hailed as a wonder drug. The cure is sometimes worse than the disease.

It seems worth while to review the current scattered knowledge of the dysfunctional consequences resulting from the imposition of a system of performance measurements. For the purpose of analyzing the impact of performance measurements upon job performance, we can consider separately single, multiple, and composite criteria. Single criteria occur when only one quantity is measured and observed, such as total output or profit. Multiple criteria occur when several quantities are measured simultaneously, such as output, quality, cost, safety, waste, and so forth. Composite criteria occur when the separate quantities are weighted in some fashion and then added or averaged.

Single Criteria

A single criterion of performance was in use in a public employment agency studied by Peter M. Blau.[1] The agency's responsibility was "to

---

* Reproduced from *Administrative Science Quarterly*, Vol. 1, No. 2 (September, 1956).

[1] Peter M. Blau, *The Dynamics of Bureaucracy* (Chicago, Ill., 1955).

serve workers seeking employment and employers seeking workers." Employment interviewers were appraised by the number of interviews they conducted. Thus the interviewer was motivated to complete as many interviews as he could, but not to spend adequate time in locating jobs for the clients. The organization's goal of placing clients in jobs was not given primary consideration because the measurement device applied to only one aspect of the activity.

Blau reports another case in a federal law enforcement agency which investigated business establishments. Here he found that work schedules were distorted by the imposition of a quota of eight cases per month for each investigator. Toward the end of the month an investigator who found himself short of the eight cases would pick easy, fast cases to finish that month and save the lengthier cases till the following month. Priority of the cases for investigation was based on length of the case rather than urgency, as standards of impartiality would require. This is one of many instances in which the existence of an "accounting period" adversely affects the over-all goal accomplishment of the organization.

Chris Argyris also reports this tendency to use easy jobs as fillers toward the end of a period in order to meet a quota.[2] In this case, a factory supervisor reported that they "feed the machines all the easy orders" toward the end of the month, rather than finish them in the sequence in which they were received. Such a practice may lead to undue delay of the delivery of some customers' orders, perhaps the most profitable orders.

David Granick's study of Soviet management reveals how the attention and glory that accrues to a plant manager when he can set a new monthly production record in one month leads to the neglect of repairs and maintenance, so that in ensuing months there will be a distinct drop in production.[3] Similarly, the output of an entire plant may be allowed to fall off in order to create conditions under which one worker can make a production record, when the importance of such a record is considered greater than over-all plant production.

Joseph S. Berliner's report on Soviet business administration points out sharply how the accounting period has an adverse effect upon management decisions.[4] The use of monthly production quotas causes "storming" at the end of the month to reach the quota. Repairs and maintenance are postponed until the following month, so that production lags in the early part of the month, and storming must again be resorted to in the following month. This has impact upon the rate of production for sup-

---

[2] Chris Argyris, *The Impact of Budgets on People* (New York, 1952).

[3] David Granick, *Management of the Industrial Firm in the U.S.S.R.* (New York, 1954).

[4] Joseph S. Berliner, "A Problem in Soviet Business Management," *Administrative Science Quarterly*, Vol. I (1956), pp. 86–101.

pliers and customers who are forced into a fluctuating rate of operations with its attendant losses and wastes.

Standard costs as a criterion of performance is a frequent source of dissatisfaction in manufacturing plants.[5] The "lumpiness" of indirect charges that are allocated to the plants or divisions (indirect charges being unequal from month to month), variations in quality and cost of raw materials, or other factors beyond the control of the operating manager, coupled with inaccuracies and errors in the apportionment of indirect charges, causes distrust of the standards. A typical reaction of operating executives in such cases seems to be to seek explanations and justifications. Consequently, considerable time and energy is expended in discussion and debate about the correctness of charges. Only "wooden money" savings accrue when charges are shifted to other accounts and there is no increase in company profits. It should be pointed out, however, that having charges applied to the proper departments may have the advantage of more correctly directing attention to problem areas.

Granick discusses two measures of the success of the Soviet firm which have been considered and rejected as over-all measures by Soviet industrial leaders and economists.[6] The first, cost-reduction per unit of product, is considered inadequate because it does not provide a basis for evaluating new products. Further, variations in amount of production affect the cost-reduction index because of the finer division of overhead costs, quality changes, and assortment. The second over-all measure of a firm's performance, profitability, has been rejected as the basic criterion on the grounds that it is affected in the short run by factors outside the control of management, such as shortages of supplies. Profitability as a measure of success led to a reduction in experimental work and de-emphasized the importance of production quantity, quality, and assortment. Neither cost-reduction nor profitability was acceptable alone; each was only a partial index. The Soviets had concluded by 1940 that no single measure of success of a firm is adequate in itself and that there is no substitute for genuine analysis of all the elements entering into a firm's work.

Difficulties with single criteria have been observed in operations research, where one of the principal sources of difficulty is considered to be the choice of proper criteria for performance measurement.[7] The difficulty of translating the several alternatives into their full effect upon the organization's goal forces the operations researcher to settle for a cri-

---

[5] H. A. Simon, H. Guetzkow, G. Kozmetsky, and G. Tyndall, *Centralization vs. Decentralization in Organizing the Controller's Department* (New York, 1954).

[6] Granick, *op. cit.*

[7] Charles Hitch and Roland McKean, "Suboptimization in Operations Problems," in J. F. McCloskey and Flora F. Trefethen (Eds.), *Operations Research for Management* (Baltimore, Md., 1954).

terion more manageable than profit maximization, but less appropriate. The efficiency of a subgroup of the organization may be improved in terms of some plausible test, yet the organization's efficiency in terms of its major goal may be decreased.

In all the studies mentioned above, the inadequacy of a single measure of performance is evident. Whether this is a measure of an employee at the working level, or a measure of management, attention is directed away from the over-all goal. The existence of a measure of performance motivates individuals to effort, but the effort may be wasted, as in seeking "wooden money" savings, or may be detrimental to the organization's goal, as in rushing through interviews, delaying repairs, and rejecting profitable opportunities.

Multiple Measurements

Recognition of the inadequacies of a single measure of success or performance leads organizations to develop several criteria. It is felt then that all aspects of the job will receive adequate attention and emphasis so that efforts of individuals will not be distorted.

A realization in the employment office studied by Blau that job referrals and placements were also important led eventually to their inclusion in measuring the performance of the interviewers.[8] Merely counting the number of referrals and placements had led to wholesale indiscriminate referrals, which did not accomplish the employment agency's screening function. Therefore, to stress the qualitative aspects of the interviewer's job, several ratios (of referrals to interviews, placements to interviews, and placements to referrals) were devised. Altogether there were eight quantities that were counted or calculated for each interviewer. This increase in quantity and complexity of performance measurements was felt necessary to give emphasis to all aspects of the interviewer's job.

Granick relates that no single criterion was universally adopted in appraising Soviet management.[9] Some managers were acclaimed for satisfying production quotas while violating labor laws. Others were removed from office for violating quality and assortment plans while fulfilling production quotas. Apparently there is a ranking of importance of these multiple criteria. In a typical interfirm competition the judges were provided with a long list of indexes. These included production of finished goods in the planned assortment, an even flow of production as between ten-day periods and as between months, planned mastery of new types of products, improvement in product quality and reduction in waste, economy of materials through improved design and changing of technological processes, fulfillment of labor productivity tasks and lowering of unit cost, keeping within the established wage fund, and increase in the number of worker suggestions for improvements in work methods

---

[8] Blau, *op. cit.*

[9] Granick, *op. cit.*

and conditions and their adoption into operation. But no indication of how these indexes should be weighted was given. The pre-eminence of such indexes as quantity, quality, assortment of production, and remaining within the firm's allotment of materials and fuels brought some order into the otherwise chaotic picture. The presence of "campaigns" and "priorities" stressing one or more factors also has aided Soviet management in deciding which elements of its work are at the moment most important.

Without a single over-all composite measure of success, however, there is no way of determining whether the temporarily increased effort on the "campaign" criteria of the month represents new effort or merely effort shifted from other criteria. And the intangibility of some of these indexes makes it impossible to judge whether there has been decreased effort on other aspects. Hence even in a campaign period the relative emphases may become so unbalanced as to mitigate or defeat the purpose of the campaign.

The Soviet manager is working then under several measurements, and the relative influence or emphasis attached to any one measurement varies from firm to firm and from month to month. Profits and production are used, among other measurements, and these two may lead to contradictory managerial decisions. Granick hypothesizes that some managers have refused complicated orders that were difficult to produce because it would mean failure to produce the planned quantities. Acceptance of these orders would have been very profitable, but of the two criteria, production quantity took precedence.

Numerous American writers in the field of management have stressed the importance of multiple criteria in evaluating performance of management. Peter Drucker, for example, lists market standing, innovation, productivity, physical and financial resources, profitability, manager performance and development, worker performance and attitude, and public responsibility.[10] This list includes many of the same items as the list used by Soviet management.

The consensus at a round-table discussion of business and professional men[11] was that although return on investment is important, additional criteria are essential for an adequate appraisal of operating departments. These other criteria are fairly well summed up in Drucker's list above.

Thus we see that the need for multiple criteria is recognized and that they are employed at different levels of the organization—lower levels as in the employment agency, higher levels as considered by Granick and Drucker. At all levels these multiple measurements or criteria are intended to focus attention on the many facets of a particular job.

---

[10] Peter M. Drucker, *The Practice of Management* (New York, 1954).

[11] William H. Newman and James P. Logan, *Management of Expanding Enterprises* (New York, 1955).

The use of multiple criteria assumes that the individual will commit his or the organization's efforts, attention, and resources in greater measure to those activities which promise to contribute the greatest improvement to over-all performance. There must then exist a theoretical condition under which an additional unit of effort or resources would yield equally desirable results in over-all performance, whether applied to production, quality, research, safety, public relations, or any of the other suggested areas. This would be the condition of "balanced stress on objectives" to which Drucker refers.

Without a single over-all composite measure of performance, the individual is forced to rely upon his judgment as to whether increased effort on one criterion improves over-all performance, or whether there may be a reduction in performance on some other criterion which will outweigh the increase in the first. This is quite possible, for in any immediate situation many of these objectives may be contradictory to each other.

Composites

To adequately balance the stress on the contradictory objectives or criteria by which performance of a particular individual or organization is appraised, there must be an implied or explicit weighting of these criteria. When such a weighting system is available, it is an easy task to combine the measures of the various subgoals into a composite score for over-all performance.

Such a composite is used by the American Institute of Management in evaluating and ranking the managements of corporations, hospitals, and other organizations.[12] These ratings are accomplished by attaching a numerical grade to each of several criteria such as economic function, corporate structure, production efficiency, and the like. Each criterion has an optimum rating and the score on each for any particular organization is added to obtain a total score. Although there may be disagreement on the validity of the weighting system employed, the rating given on any particular category, the categories themselves, or the methods of estimating scores in the A.I.M. management audit, this system is an example of the type of over-all performance measurement which might be developed. Were such a system of ratings employed by an organization and found acceptable by management, it presumably would serve as a guide to obtaining a balanced stress on objectives.

A composite measure of performance was employed in Air Force wings as reported by K. C. Wagner.[13] A complex rating scheme covering a wide

---

[12] *Manual of Excellent Managements* (New York, 1955).

[13] Kenneth C. Wagner, "Latent Functions of an Executive Control: A Sociological Analysis of a Social System under Stress," *Research Previews*, Vol. II (Chapel Hill, N.C.: Institute for Research in Social Science, March, 1954), mimeo.

range of activities was used. When the organizations were put under pressure to raise their composite score without proportionate increases in the organization's means of achieving them, there were observable unanticipated consequences in the squadrons. Under a system of multiple criteria, pressure to increase performance on one criterion might be relieved by a slackening of effort toward other criteria. But with a composite criterion this does not seem as likely to occur. In Wagner's report individuals were subjected to tension, role and value conflicts, and reduced morale; air crews suffered from intercrew antagonism, apathy, and reduced morale; organization and power structures underwent changes; communications distortions and blockages occurred; integration decreased; culture patterns changed; and norms were violated. Some of these consequences may be desirable, some undesirable. The net result, however, might easily be less effective over-all performance.

These consequences were observable in a situation where goals were increased without a corresponding increase in means, which seems to be a common situation. Berliner refers to the "ratchet principle" wherein an increase in performance becomes the new standard, and the standard is thus continually raised. Recognition of the operation of the "ratchet principle" by workers was documented by F. J. Roethlisberger and William J. Dickson.[14] There was a tacit agreement among the workers not to exceed the quota, for fear that the job would then be rerated. Deliberate restriction of output is not an uncommon occurrence.

Although the experiences reported with the use of composite measures of performance are rather skimpy, there is still a clear indication that their use may have adverse consequences for the over-all performance of the organization.

Conclusion

Quantitative performance measurements—whether single, multiple, or composite—are seen to have undesirable consequences for over-all organizational performance. The complexity of large organizations requires better knowledge of organizational behavior for managers to make best use of the personnel available to them. Even where performance measures are instituted purely for purposes of information, they are probably interpreted as definitions of the important aspects of that job or activity and hence have important implications for the motivation of behavior. The motivational and behavioral consequences of performance measurements are inadequately understood. Further research in this area is necessary for a better understanding of how behavior may be oriented toward optimum accomplishment of the organization's goals.

---

[14] F. J. Roethlisberger and William J. Dickson, *Management and the Worker* (Cambridge, Mass., 1939).

Decision Making

To SOME extent, the concept of "decision making" is an artifact imposed upon organizational behavior by observers and analysts. Although we can all agree that decision making must and does go on in organizations, the actual process and the individual acts of making decisions are frequently elusive. For example, we say that organizations "decide" on their annual budget, their hiring policies, their marketing strategy, and many other things. When we enter the organization to try to discover the exact locus and the exact time of a particular decision, we have difficulty. Our informants indicate that some of these decisions evolved naturally, that there was no particular point in time when they were "made," and that no individual or group actually made them—they "just seemed like the right thing to do."

Of course this difficulty is more characteristic of the "larger" and more significant decisions than of the many smaller and routine decisions that are made from day to day in an organization. The decisions to run machine X overtime, to hire Mr. Jones, or to reject a lot of merchandise for poor quality are readily identifiable in time and space. Foreman A, with the concurrence of his immediate superior, decided at 2:00 P.M. to run the machine overtime. The head of personnel decided to hire Mr. Jones, based on the specific request of a department head for Mr. Jones (alternatively, the department head decided, with the agreement of the head of personnel). The inspector, on his own authority but subject to later review by the production foreman, decided to reject the lot. The definition here is provided by the organization's own programming and delegation of formal authority.

The degree of specificity needed on who made what decisions when and why depends on why we are examining decision making in the organization. As in the discussion of communication (Section 5) the motives will vary between the organizational theorist, the management scientist, and the practicing manager.

In general, the organization theorist is interested in developing a better understanding of organizational decision making. He is intrigued by the possibility of a large collection of individuals, with diverse backgrounds and goals, continually reaching agreement, or at least giving the appearance of agreement on a wide variety of issues. He is also intrigued by the lack of agreement that is often evident in organizations and that frequently results in conflict. He asks: What is this process of decision making? Who are the decision makers and what are they like? And what do we really mean by a "decision"?

If we include in the category "organization theorists" all researchers who systematically study decision making in organizations, we can visualize the range of their interest with the aid of Figure 1. This figure

FIGURE 1

LEVELS AT WHICH DECISION MAKING HAS BEEN STUDIED,
WITH ILLUSTRATIVE RESEARCH QUESTIONS

	DESCRIPTIONS OF BEHAVIOR (What Is Happening or What Has Happened)	PRESCRIPTIVE OR NORMATIVE MODEL BUILDING (What Ought to Happen)
THE DECISION	What decisions are made in an organization? How do these decisions "turn out"?	What is an optimal decision? How can decisions be improved?
THE DECISION MAKER	What are the characteristics of the decision makers in the organization? What factors influence the behavior of decision makers?	How should a rational decision maker behave?
THE DECISION PROCESS	How are decisions actually made in the organization?	How should decisions be made in an organization?

illustrates the levels at which decision making has been studied and also differentiates between two viewpoints: *de*scriptive and *pre*scriptive or normative. These two viewpoints are discussed in more detail below.

THE DECISION

In recent years, a body of knowledge has developed which deals with the normative aspects of decision making. Contributors to this body of knowledge—mathematicians, statisticians, psychologists, economists, and operations researchers—are interested in developing models for organizations that will improve decision making. Much of the work in this new field has been concentrated in areas where there are clear measures of the "goodness" of decisions. Where monetary measures such as cost, profit, or return on investment are concerned, "optimizing" models are feasible, and many have been developed. Where only nonmonetary measures are available, such as in military operations, other measures are sought which can be used in a manner analogous to money. This results in the construction of some index of "utility." This unit, like the dollar units of *cost* and *return*, is used to summarize all of the costs and benefits involved in the decision. Some of these contributory factors in military decisions, for example, are: the costs of material and logistic support, the losses of equipment and personnel to "our" side and "their" side, the proportion of national productive effort devoted to the war or the battle, etc.

While this is a convenient way of combining unlike entities (equipment, lives, and military objectives), it is fraught with the dangers described by Ridgway (Article 36). One can lose sight of the intrinsic nature of the individual entities and make decisions that are really "nonoptimal" with respect to many of them.

While the normative literature about decisions is large and growing rapidly, the descriptive literature is small and not increasing very much. There are a number of reasons for this. One is the difficulty of identifying "decisions" in real organizations and finding out what their consequences were. Not only are most organizational members not anxious to reveal the consequences of their decisions to outsiders, but they are also reluctant to do post mortems for internal purposes. For example, in studies of research project selection over many years, we have found almost no organizations that routinely examine the consequences of the decisions made. In the few cases encountered where one or more decisions were actually traced to their ultimate outcome, many reasons were given for the nontypical nature of the decision. There is strong reluctance to perform this kind of analysis in most organizations. In addition, there is a belief on the part of many organization members that history is not really relevant to the future and that each new decision situation is unique.

Despite this state of affairs, some organization theorists are attempting to identify decisions in organizations and to study their consequences.

Most research on decisions in organizations, however, is of the normative variety—attempts to develop good or optimal decision rules, policies, and decisions. The basic factors used by normative theorists in analyzing a decision are generally these:

$S_1 \ldots S_n$	A set of alternative decisions that might be made or of strategies that might be followed.
$N_1 \ldots N_m$	A set of states of nature that could prevail, that are relevant to the decision or strategy.
$P_1 \ldots P_m$	The probability of each state of nature occurring.
$V_{11} \ldots V_{mn}$	The outcome or "payoff" to the decision maker for each combination of strategy he could choose and each state of nature that could prevail.

Where the outcome is known, we refer to a situation of "certainty." Where only a set of probabilities can be assigned to the set of possible outcomes, we refer to this as decision-making under "risk." Where we cannot even assign probabilities to the outcomes, we call the situation one of "uncertainty."

Edwards (7) discusses these distinctions in some detail, and indicates that there is disagreement among economists and statisticians on the exact definitions of "risk" and "uncertainty." He gives the example of coin-tossing, where (for an "honest" coin), almost everyone will agree that the probability of getting a head on any particular toss is .5. Many situations are not as clear as that of coin-tossing, but general agreement can often be achieved as to the probability associated with each possible outcome—e.g. a particular baseball team has only a one in ten chance of winning the pennant, but it has a fifty-fifty chance of ending up in the first division.

There are many situations, however, about which there is no set of probabilities that are generally agreed upon. For example, there may be no consensus (this year) on the probabilities associated with the possible outcomes of the baseball season three years hence.

For illustrative purposes, consider a situation where the decision maker is engaged in deciding on the price of a new product. His alternatives might be the specific prices he might charge for his product—e.g., $1.00, $1.25, $1.49, $1.98, $2.00, $2.25.

The states of nature might be the possible attitudes of his customers toward the price of a product such as the one he is offering. For example, these attitudes might be: indifference to the specific price; interest only in low prices for this product; interest in "round number" prices; interest in "bargainlike" prices. Based on his experience in the field or a consumer survey, the decision maker might assign a probability to each of the consumer attitudes (states of nature). He may think that the first is very unlikely, the second is very likely, and the others are about equal.

Finally, the model is complete when the set of values for each combination of alternatives and states of nature is constructed. For example, a high price (e.g., $2.25) encountering the second state of nature (interest only in low prices) would result in a very low value for the decision maker (no sales). The problem is usually presented in a payoff matrix such as that in Figure 2.

Among the interesting things that can be done with the payoff matrix, in addition to displaying the data for the analysis in a systematic fashion, is to compute expected values for any given strategy under condition of risk. For example, if we really do not know which state of nature will prevail and we want to examine the "average" outcome of Strategy 1 (as in situations such as insurance underwriting where the same decision will be made many times), we can compute the "expected" value of Alternative 1 over all possible states of nature that might prevail. This would be the value of the sum of the products of all V's in the first row with their cor-

FIGURE 2

THE PAYOFF MATRIX

Alternatives or Strategies	Possible States of Nature							
	N_1 N_2 N_3 N_4	$\cdot$	$\cdot$	$\cdot$	$\cdot$	N_m		
	Probability That It Will Occur							
	P_1 P_2 P_3 P_4	$\cdot$	$\cdot$	$\cdot$	P_m			
S_1	V_{11} V_{12} $\cdot$	$\cdot$	$\cdot$	$\cdot$	$\cdot$	$\cdot$	V_{1m}	
S_2	V_{21} $\cdot$	$\cdot$	$\cdot$	$\cdot$	$\cdot$	$\cdot$	$\cdot$	
S_3	$\cdot$ $\cdot$							
S_4	$\cdot$ $\cdot$							
$\cdot$	$\cdot$							
$\cdot$								
S_n	V_{n1} $\cdot$	$\cdot$	$\cdot$	$\cdot$	$\cdot$	$\cdot$	V_{nm}	

responding P's. Specifically, the formula for finding the expected value of Alternative 1 is:

$$\text{Expected value of } S_1 = P_1 V_{11} + P_2 V_{12} + \ldots P_m V_{1m}.$$

In reality, many organizational decisions are made only once, so that the use of expected values based on subjective probability distributions is highly questionable. Nevertheless, research in game theory and statistical decision theory, as well as in psychological probability, uses this schema.

As Shubik (Article 43) points out, formal models have not as yet really formed the basis for actual decision making in any significant number of instances, but they are useful in thinking about the decision problem and assembling the information required for good decisions. (9)

THE DECISION MAKER

When we examine the individual decision maker, we must be careful to state our terms of reference: Are we inquiring into the decisions he *should* make, if he were behaving "properly," or are we concerned with the decisions he actually *does* make? In other words, we can analyze the decision maker (individual, group, or organization) from a *de*scriptive (what *was* decided) or a *pre*scriptive (what *should* have been decided) point of view.

Let us consider the prescriptive or normative viewpoint first.

When we speak of "proper" behavior, we imply some standard of value against which we can compare alternative behaviors. The values may be those of the decision maker himself or of an observer. We further imply that this proper behavior is linked with consequences that are more or less desirable in terms of the standard. These consequences result, in part, from rewards or penalties dispensed by other individuals, groups, the organization, or society. For example, if an individual makes a decision that his immediate supervisor does not like, there is the possibility of some unpleasant consequences for the decision maker. This, of course, is modified by many surrounding circumstances, such as: the gravity of the situation; the prior (and anticipated future) relationship between the individuals concerned; the extent to which the decision maker had exceeded his authority or had exercised bad judgment; the general reward-penalty atmosphere in the organization, etc.

When an organization makes a bad marketing or pricing decision, the consequences may be determined by actions of the consumer or by competitors. Thus, value considerations, in the form of social facts, may enter into the relation between alternatives and consequences. When an individual or an organization makes a decision that runs counter to nature—e.g., drills for oil in a place where there is none—likewise, the adverse consequence is immediate and clear in terms of financial damage to the decision maker.

The choice of values (for the observer) or their measurement (for the decision maker) is a crucial problem and poses great difficulties. In the context of economic theory, a result by Arrow (1) demonstrates the impossibility of deriving an objective measure of social value, even if we were able to measure the values (utilities) of all the individual members of society. Although economists have generally assumed that the individual can uniquely order his preferences among alternatives (a scalar utility function), psychologists have found that people experience conflict and ambivalence in situations of choice. Studies of organizations also have shown the existence of *multiple* value criteria (vector utility) in action situations. Nevertheless, situations do arise, especially in commerce, where a financial or other quantifiable value standard is agreed upon.

In essence, then, once values are specified "proper," decisions help to accomplish or further desired goals and help the decision-maker to avoid unfavorable consequences. For many decision situations, even then, there are no specific decisions that will guarantee the best possible outcome. Too many other factors impinge.

Given this state of affairs, what can we say about how the decision maker *ought to* behave—that is, what decisions *should* he make? Most of the formal normative models for making decisions rest on certain assumptions about the characteristics and/or capacities of the (hypothetical) decision maker. Among the most familiar assumptions are those surrounding the economists' concept of "economic man" as a decision maker. (See Edwards (7) for a discussion of this concept.)

Economic man is endowed by the economist with three characteristics:

1. He has *complete information* about the decision situation. This means that he knows all the alternatives available to him, and that he knows the outcome associated with each of these alternatives. This assumption holds primarily for decisions under a condition of certainty—where the decision

maker knows not only the possible states of nature, but also the specific state of nature that will prevail. In models that involve risk, he may not know the specific state of nature to expect, but knowledge of the probabilities is sufficient to qualify as "complete information." The other possibility—uncertainty—appears to be incompatible with models of "economic man" although attempts have been made to deal with it.

2. He is *infinitely sensitive*, in the sense that he can discriminate minute differences along a continuum of alternatives. This assumption was initially made for mathematical convenience and is not strictly necessary in the general analysis of the behavior of economic man.

3. He is *rational*. This is the critical characteristic and the one that causes the most difficulty in applying the results of normative theory to the behavior of actual decision makers. The characteristic of rationality implies two things:

a. He can *weakly order* (indicate preference for) the different states he can be in. This means that, given a number of possible outcomes of his decision making, he can compare them and tell the difference in his preference for them (if he has one). Given outcomes A and B, the economic man can tell whether he:

Prefers A to B: $A > B$
Prefers B to A: $B > A$
Is indifferent between A and B: $A = B$

In addition, all preferences of a rational man must be *transitive*. That is, given three choices—A, B, and C:

If he prefers A to B: $A > B$, and
if he prefers B to C: $B > C$, then
he must prefer A to C: $A > C$.
$(A > B) \wedge (B > C) \Rightarrow (A > C)$

The same situation must hold true for indifference between his choices:

If he is indifferent between A and B: $A = B$, and
if he is indifferent between B and C: $B = C$, then
he must be indifferent between A and C: $A = C$.
$(A = B) \wedge (B = C) \Rightarrow (A = C)$

Some recent experimental work has explored the empirical question of whether, in fact, "real" people (as contrasted with economic man) do have perfectly transitive preferences for all situations, or whether there are some combinations of choices which contain stable *in*transitive preferences of this kind: A is preferred over B, B is preferred over C, but C is preferred over A. Davis (6) presents some experimental evidence that such apparent intransitivities can be explained by random choices among indifferent alternatives.

b. He makes his choices in such a way as to *maximize* (or minimize) something (dollars, utility). The specific way in which he computes this maximum or minimum varies according to the nature of the choice situation: certainty—maximize the value or minimize the penalty; risk—maximize the expected value. Under uncertainty, the best known equivalent is the minimax principle i.e., choosing the alternative that minimizes the maximum possible penalty.

This very strong assumption about the behavior of economic man—that he always attempts to choose the "best" alternative, from his point of view—is the one that causes the most difficulty in the attempts to use the results of normative theory in describing or predicting actual decision-making behavior.

Of course, the qualification—*from his point of view*—provides certain loopholes. If we take this qualification literally, and if we make a thorough attempt to understand the decision maker's point of view, we will be hard put to find any behavior that is not "rational." Normative theorists, in the tradition of economic theory, do not take this literally, however. Their definition of rationality requires maximization behavior that is reasonable and obvious. That is, a normal prudent person will attempt to maximize his choices in a nonsurprising and reasonable way. In summary, we can say that, given the ability to weakly order his alternatives, economic man will choose the best one.

If his ordering is in terms of probabilities—e.g., he prefers A to B 75% of the time—then he is "more likely" to choose A over B than he is to choose B over A. There are many elaborations on these assumptions, and many questions raised about them. For example, the very act of ordering his preference may cost him more than it is worth to have the weak ordering available.

In any discussion of maximization, one must clearly indicate whether a single scalar measure of "utility" is being used or whether multiple measures are in use (see the articles by Haberstroh, No. 32; Ridgway, No. 36; and Cyert *et al.*, No. 37). The mathematical treatment of multiple criteria (vector utility) is much more complex than that of single criteria (scalar utility). Multiple criteria are much more common in real organizations.

The issue of whether the model of economic man is of any use to the nonnormative theorist or the organization designer rests on whether these assumptions make a significant difference in the predictions about individual decision-making behavior.

Suppose the theorist or organization designer is interested in a general understanding of how decisions are made or wants to make a modest improvement in decisions in an actual organization. If the assumptions of rationality, etc., provide "good enough" predictions or descriptions—that is, if he is caused to make no bad errors in using them—then the question of whether the assumptions are "true" is not important. If, on the other hand, these assumptions cause him to construct a dream world with very little resemblance to one inhabited by real people, then he can make some very bad descriptions or design some very bad organizations.

An increasing number of organization theorists and many behavioral scientists (who are not necessarily interested in organizational behavior) are attempting to improve our descriptive models and theories about individual decision makers. They raise questions that pertain to the actual decisions made by people under various circumstances and the factors which affect these decisions.

If one broadens the definition of individual decision making to include some aspects of learning, problem solving, creativity, and interaction with others, then a great many researchers are contributing, directly or indirectly, to our understanding of decision making. The classical experiments of Asch (2) on the effects of group pressure on individual judgments have been followed by many other studies of how individual decisions and judgments are influenced by social factors.

Asch's general finding that there are distinct differences among individuals in their ability to withstand group pressure is not counter to intuition or common observation. However, his experimental results on the numbers of subjects who did, indeed, succumb to group pressure and deny their own sense and judgment, are quite sobering. Among the factors which he found to influence whether a person "held out" or succumbed against the consensus of his colleagues were: staunch confidence in his own judgment; a capacity to recover from doubt and to re-establish his equilibrium; a perceived obligation to call things as he saw them; a desire to hide self-perceived deficiencies.

Wallach, Kogan and Bem (Article No. 41) present experimental evidence about another aspect of individual decision-making in a group situation. They are concerned with the effects of group interaction on the individual's degree of risk or conservatism—"the extent to which the decision-maker is willing to expose himself to possible failure in the pursuit of a desirable goal."

There is great potential for application of the results of such research— that of Asch (2) and Wallach et al. (Article No. 41)—to organization theory and organization design. Some of the obvious areas of practical application are in design of a committee for decision making, selection of individual supervisors and executives, matching of closely linked executives and supervisors, and training of decision makers at all levels. One commonly used application is to arrange for junior members of a committee to express their opinions first, so as to reduce the pressure on them to conform to the opinions of the senior members.

Such application, however, must be preceded by extensive testing and further development of the theories that emerge from small-group experiments. It is always possible that some results are strongly influenced by the artificiality of the laboratory situation and that some are, in fact, artifacts of the experimental procedure itself. These questions can only be resolved by more "field testing" of the ideas and findings in real, operating organizations.

Several lines of investigation have the potential for providing some clues on how individuals view the real world and transform it into a personal world in which they make judgments and decisions. A clearer understanding of this transformation might enable us to better account for apparently "nonrational" or "irrational" behavior by organization members. We know that individual organization members—functional specialists, for example—view the world differently. We frequently ascribe a perennial optimism to the "salesman type" and a strong conservatism to the "accounting type". When a joint decision has to be made by these two types—such as a decision on whether a new product is ready for marketing—differences and conflicts frequently appear. One hypothesis is that each has his own set of subjective probabilities associated with the states of nature that might prevail relevant to the alternative decisions about introduction. That is, each has his own estimates of the chances of success and failure. This idea fits nicely with normative decision theory. Much more empirical work has to be done in this area, but it appears extremely promising for the future understanding of individual decision making.

Other areas of behavioral science research are also highly relevant to our attempts to understand the decision maker. They are theories of personality and theories of enculturation (or acculturation). These areas have traditionally been the province of, respectively, the clinical psychologist and the sociologist or anthropologist.

The former area might yield information of value to the organization theorist on the "natural" risk propensity of individuals. We certainly recognize different behavior patterns in individual risk takers—e.g., gamblers, sportsmen, investors. We know, from the kind of work reported by Wallach et. al. that some decisions are influenced by situational factors—e.g., group pressures. But we feel intuitively, based on experience and observation, that people do differ basically with respect to both their assessment of risk and their willingness to take action, based on that assessment. As better tests for risk propensity are developed, knowledge about the individual decision maker might be applied to the practical organization design problems mentioned above.

The other area—theories about enculturation—deals with how individuals, groups, and societies change or accommodate their values to those of other individuals, groups, or societies. Much of the interesting early work was done at the society level, where anthropologists were concerned, for example, with how a traditional society (often an isolated "nonadvanced" society) adjusted to and borrowed from a more advanced society, such as a colonial power. The general notions of this field have been adapted to analysis of intrasociety instances of value exchange and to the phenomenon of introducing new employees into an organization. In some of our studies of the organization of research and development, we have found the notion of an "enculturation process" very useful in explaining (1) how the new recruit gets to learn what kinds of decisions and other behaviors are expected of him, and (2) how his decision criteria change with his organizational age and his position in the organizational hierarchy (3). Specifically, the focus has been on the decision to submit for approval or otherwise communicate an idea for a new research project to his superiors or colleagues.

From the manager's viewpoint, such considerations can be handled in two ways: through proper indoctrination and training after the recruit enters the organization, and by preselection of organization members according to the values and criteria they already possess—e.g., the "right type" of bank employee described by Argyris in Article 13.

THE DECISION PROCESS

Most of the research discussed under the topics of the "decision" and the "decision maker" ignored the circumstances under which the decision was being made and the decision maker was acting. Neither the normative models of decision making nor the experiments in individual or small-group decision making attempt to deal with the complexities of the organizational environment in which decision making actually occurs. One receives the impression from much of the work in the field that the specific act of choosing among alternatives is the main part of the decision-making process and that preliminary or subsequent events are not very important or subject to analysis. This is far from the case on both scores.

In real organizations, the steps that lead up to and away from "the act of choice" are often the critical ones. The actual choice among alternatives is frequently anticlimactic or preprogrammed, and the really important parts of the decision process generally precede or follow this act of choice—if there was, indeed, a clear act of choice. Consider, for example, the following incident, related by a corporate vice-president to one of us while this essay was being written:

We had been considering several merger and diversification moves for the corporation. One diversification, involving acquisition of another company outside our field, was thoroughly investigated. We went through all of the kinds of economic analysis one uses in such cases and came to the firm conclusion that we would stay out of that business. A year later, with no aspects of the economic or technical picture changed, we found ourselves buying the company and going into that field. I still can't figure out how it happened.

This was an example of an apparently clear decision being reversed by some "mysterious" process—perhaps the introduction of unacknowledged considerations by one executive in a position of power in opposition to the expressed wishes of the others. There are many examples of another kind of mismatch between decision and final outcome—the failure to implement a decision properly, once made.

At the time of the first edition of this book, there was not much literature on actual studies of the decision process in real organizations. The article by Cyert, Simon, and Trow and the one by Weiss (retained in this revision as Articles 37 and 39) are the only ones included in both the first and second edition sections on decision making. Also at that time, the work in normative decision theory appeared to hold great promise for the understanding of organizational decision making; three of the six articles on decision making in the first edition were of that type. So far, this promise has not been fulfilled. It appears that much of the work in normative models of decision making is drawing further away from real organizational behavior rather than closer to it. It also appears that the kinds of simplifying assumptions that are required to make such models mathematically manageable and "interesting" to the model builders are resulting in an even lower chance of eventual application to the description and understanding of real organizational behavior. The cost of significantly altering some of the assumptions will be the loss of the results obtained from the simplified model.

For this reason, and because there has been a significant increase in research and published articles on the actual decision process in real organizations, half of the articles in this revised section report such studies.

It is clear from direct observation by organization members and from the evidence in the studies by Lefton et al., Dufty and Taylor, and Cyert et. al. (Articles 40, 38, 37) that there is a great deal more to organizational decision making than the mere act of choosing among alternatives. Figure 3 attempts to describe, for a given decision of the nonprogrammed or nonroutine type, the major steps in the process we call organizational decision making.

In some instances, the most critical aspect of the process may be the recognition of a problem or the need for a decision. Once this step has been taken, many decisions follow almost automatically from the nature of the situation and the relevant constraints. Whole classes of organizational decisions have been analyzed by managers and management scientists and preprogrammed. That is, once the problem is identified, routine procedures exist for finding and examining alternatives, choosing between them, and implementing them.

One of the promising areas of recent research on decision making has been the computer simulation of behavior in decision situations. Cyert and March (5) have developed and tested a model for decision making with respect to certain key activities of a department store buyer. Clarkson (4) presents a related model of decision-making in the trust investment activity of a bank. Other examples of the simulation of cognitive processes are given in the book by Feigenbaum and Feldman (8).

In other instances, the search for and analysis of alternative courses of action—decision choices—may constitute the major and critical phase. Much of the money spent on methods engineering, research and development, and management consulting in a firm is intended to uncover and evaluate decision alternatives. The principal task of operations researchers and other staff specialists is considered by many organization members and analysts to be this search for and analysis of alternatives. The results of their efforts are typically a set of analyzed alternatives (including their

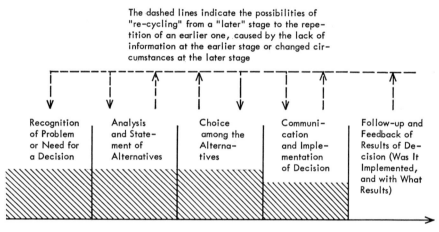

FIG. 3.   Steps in the Organizational Decision Process

probable consequences for the organization) and usually, but not always, a set of recommended choices among these alternatives.

The studies of the decision process reprinted in this section deal with all of the stages described in Figure 3. Cyert et al. present one of the first published studies of the anatomy of a major decision. Although most biographies and historical novels present descriptions of decisions that were made and the processes whereby they were made, few of these descriptions are systematically related to other aspects of organizational behavior.

Both Weiss and Lefton et al. concentrate on the role of different kinds of individuals in the decision process and deal with notions of power and influence. The brief study by Dufty and Taylor is one of the few in the literature that carry the study of decision through the implementation phase—the one that determines if the whole process was of any value to the organization.

REFERENCES

1. ARROW, KENNETH. *Social Choice and Individual Values.* John Wiley & Sons, Inc. New York. (1963 Revised edition). See also his "Alternative Approaches to the Theory of Choice in Risk-Taking Situations." Cowles Commission Discussion Paper: Economics No. 298. Nov. 30, 1950.

2. ASCH, SOLOMON S. "Opinions and Social Pressure." *Scientific American.* Vol. 193, No. 5, (November 1955) pp. 31–5.

3. AVERY, ROBERT W. "Enculturation in Industrial Research." *IRE Transactions on Engineering Management.* March, 1960. Vol. EM7, No. 1, p. 20.

4. CLARKSON, GEOFFREY P. E. "A Model of the Investment Trust Process." In *Computers and Thought,* edited by Edward A. Feigenbaum and Julian Feldman. McGraw-Hill. 1963. pp. 347–371.

5. CYERT, RICHARD M. AND MARCH, JAMES G. *A Behavioral Theory of the Firm.* Prentice Hall. (1963.) Chapter 7.

6. DAVIS, JOHN MARCELL. "The Transitivity of Preferences." *Behavioral Science.* Vol. 3, No. 1. (January, 1958), pp. 26–33.

7. EDWARDS, WARD. "The Theory of Decision-Making." *Psychological Bulletin.* Vol. 51, No. 4. (July, 1954).

8. FEIGENBAUM, EDWARD A. AND FELDMAN, JULIAN. *Computers and Thought,* McGraw-Hill. 1963.

9. HITCH, CHARLES. "Uncertainties in Operations Research." *Operations Research.* July-August 1960. p. 437.

37. OBSERVATION OF A BUSINESS DECISION*

RICHARD M. CYERT, HERBERT A. SIMON, AND DONALD B. TROW[1]

DECISION-MAKING—choosing one course of action rather than another, finding an appropriate solution to a new problem posed by a changing world—is commonly asserted to be the heart of executive activity in business. If this is so, a realistic description and theory of the decision-making process are of central importance to business administration and organization theory. Moreover, it is extremely doubtful whether the only considerable body of decision-making theory that has been available in the past—that provided by economics—does in fact provide a realistic account of decision-making in large organizations operating in a complex world.

In economics and statistics the rational choice process is described somewhat as follows:

(1) An individual is confronted with a number of different, specified alternative courses of action.

(2) To each of these alternatives is attached a set of consequences that will ensue if that alternative is chosen.

(3) The individual has a system of preferences or "utilities" that permit him to rank all sets of consequences according to preference and to choose that alternative that has the preferred consequences. In the case of business decisions the criterion for ranking is generally assumed to be profit.

If we try to use this framework to describe how real human beings go about making choices in a real world, we soon recognize that we need to incorporate in our description of the choice process several elements that are missing from the economic model:

(1) The alternatives are not usually "given" but must be sought, and hence it is necessary to include the search for alternatives as an important part of the process.

(2) The information as to what consequences are attached to which

* *Journal of Business, 29,* 1956.

[1] Graduate School of Industrial Administration, Carnegie Institute of Technology. This is a preliminary report on research carried out under a grant from the Ford Foundation for studies in organization and decision-making. The authors are grateful to the Foundation for its support, to the executives of the company that opened its doors to them, and to colleagues and graduate students who have assisted at various stages of data collection and analysis.

alternatives is seldom a "given," but, instead, the search for consequences is another important segment of the decision-making task.

(3) The comparisons among alternatives are not usually made in terms of simple, single criterion like profit. One reason is that there are often important consequences that are so intangible as to make an evaluation in terms of profit difficult or impossible. In place of searching for the "best" alternative, the decision-maker is usually concerned with finding a *satisfactory* alternative—one that will attain a specified goal and at the same time satisfy a number of auxiliary conditions.

(4) Often, in the real world, the problem itself is not a "given," but, instead, searching for significant problems to which organizational attention should be turned becomes an important organizational task.

Decisions in organizations vary widely with respect to the extent to which the decision-making process is *programmed*. At one extreme we have repetitive, well-defined problems (e.g., quality control or production lot-size problems) involving tangible considerations, to which the economic models that call for finding the best among a set of pre-established alternatives can be applied rather literally. In contrast to these highly programmed and usually rather detailed decisions are problems of a nonrepetitive sort, often involving basic long-range questions about the whole strategy of the firm or some part of it, arising initially in a highly unstructured form and requiring a great deal of the kinds of search processes listed above. In this whole continuum, from great specificity and repetition to extreme vagueness and uniqueness, we will call decisions that lie toward the former extreme *programmed*, and those lying toward the latter end *non-programmed*. This simple dichotomy is just a shorthand for the range of possibilities we have indicated.

It is our aim in the present paper to illustrate the distinctions we have introduced between the traditional theory of decision, which appears applicable only to highly programmed decision problems, and a revised theory, which will have to take account of the search processes and other information processes that are so prominent in and characteristic of nonprogrammed decision-making. We shall do this by recounting the stages through which an actual problem proceeded in an actual company and then commenting upon the significance of various items in this narrative for future decision-making theory.

The decision was captured and recorded by securing the company's permission to have a member of the research team present as an observer in the company's offices on substantially a full-time basis during the most active phases of the decision process. The observer spent most of his time with the executive who had been assigned the principal responsibility for handling this particular problem. In addition, he had full access to the files for information about events that preceded his period of observation and also interviewed all the participants who were involved to a major degree in the decision.

THE ELECTRONIC DATA-PROCESSING DECISION

The decision process to be described here concerns the feasibility of using electronic data-processing equipment in a medium size corporation that engages both in manufacturing and in selling through its own widely scattered outlets. In July, 1952, the company's controller assigned to Ronald Middleton, an assistant who was handling several special studies in the accounting department, the task of keeping abreast of electronic developments. The controller, and other accounting executives, thought that some of the current developments in electronic equipment might have application to the company's accounting processes. He gave Middleton the task of investigation, because the latter had a good background for understanding the technical aspects of computers.

Middleton used three procedures to obtain information: letters to persons in established computer firms, discussions with computer salesmen, and discussions with persons in other companies that were experimenting with the use of electronic equipment in accounting. He also read the current journal literature about computer developments. He informed the controller about these matters principally through memorandums that described the current status of equipment and some of the procedures that would be necessary for an applications study in the company. Memorandums were written in November, 1952, October, 1953, and January, 1954. In them, in addition to summarizing developments, he recommended that two computer companies be asked to propose possible installations in the company and that the company begin to adapt its accounting procedures to future electronic processing.

In the spring of 1954 a computer company representative took the initiative to propose and make a brief equipment application study. In August he submitted a report to the company recommending an installation, but this was not acted upon—doubt as to the adequacy of the computer company's experience and knowledge in application being a major factor in the decision. A similar approach was made by another computer company in September, 1954, but terminated at an early stage without positive action. These experiences convinced Middleton and other executives, including the controller, that outside help was needed to develop and evaluate possible applications of electronic equipment.

Middleton drew up a list of potential consultants and, by checking outside sources and using his own information, selected Alpha as the most suitable. After preliminary meetings in October and November, 1954, between representatives of Alpha and the company accounting executives, Alpha was asked to develop a plan for a study of the application of electronic data-processing to sales accounting. Additional meetings between Alpha and company personnel were held in February, 1955, and the proposal for the study was submitted to the controller in March.

Although the proposal seemed competent and the price reasonable, it was felt that proposals should be obtained from another consulting firm as a double check. The controller agreed to this and himself selected Beta from Middleton's list. Subsequently representatives of Beta met with Middleton and other department executives. Middleton, in a memorandum to the controller, listed criteria for choosing between the two consultants. On the assumption that the written report from Beta was similar to the oral proposal made, the comparison indicated several advantages for Beta over Alpha.

After the written report was received, on May 2, the company's management committee authorized a consulting agreement with Beta, and work began in July, 1955. The controller established a committee, headed by Middleton, to work on the project. Middleton was to devote full time to the assignment; the other two committee members, one from sales accounting and one from auditing, were to devote one-third time.

The consulting firm assigned two staff members, Drs. Able and Baker, to the study. Their initial meetings with Middleton served the purpose of outlining a general approach to the problem and planning the first few steps. Twenty-three information-gathering studies were defined, which Middleton agreed to carry out, and it was also decided that the consultants would spend some time in field observation of the actual activities that the computer might replace.

During July, Middleton devoted most of his time to the twenty-three studies on volume of transactions and information flow, obtaining data from the sales department and from the field staffs of the other two committee members. Simultaneously, steps were taken to secure the co-operation of the field personnel who would be visited by the consultants early in August.

On July 22 Middleton submitted a progress report to the controller, describing the data-gathering studies, estimating completion dates, and summarizing the program's objectives. On July 25 the consultants met with Middleton and discussed a method of approach to the design of the data-processing system. The field trip took place early in August. The consultants obtained from field personnel information as to how accounting tasks were actually handled and as to the use actually made of information generated by the existing system.

On August 8 Middleton submitted another progress report, giving the status of the data-gathering studies and recording some ideas originating in the field trip for possible changes in the existing information-processing system. On August 10 he arranged with the assistant controller to obtain clerical assistance on the data-gathering studies, so that the consultants would not be held up by lack of this information, and on August 17 this work was completed.

On the following day the consultants met with the company committee to review the results of the twenty-three studies. They then listed the outputs, files, and inputs required by any sales accounting system the company might adopt and drew a diagram showing the flow of the accounting information. The group also met with the assistant controller and with the controller. The latter took the opportunity to emphasize his basic decentralization philosophy.

Upon returning from his vacation early in September, Middleton discussed the flow diagram in greater detail with Able and Baker, and revisions were made on the basis of information Middleton supplied about the present accounting system. Baker pointed out that all the alternative systems available to the company could be defined by the location of seven principal functions and records. Further analysis reduced this number to three: stock records, pricing of orders, and accounts receivable. The possible combinations of locations of these gave eighteen basic alternative systems, of which eight that were obviously undesirable were eliminated. Middleton was to make a cost analysis of the existing system and the most decentralized of the proposed systems, while the consultants were to begin costing the most centralized system.

Middleton reviewed these tentative decisions with the other members of the company committee, and the group divided up the work of costing. Middleton also reported to the controller on the conference, and the latter expressed his attitudes about the location of the various functions and the resulting implications for the development of executive responsibility.

During the next week, in addition to working on his current assignments, Middleton gave an equipment salesman a preliminary overview of the probable requirements of a new system. Next, there was a two-day meeting of the consultants and the company's committee to discuss the form and implications of a centralized electronic system. The consultants presented a method of organizing the records for electronic processing and together with the committee calculated the requirements which this organization and company's volume of transactions would impose on a computer. The group then discussed several problems raised by the system, including the auditing problems, and then met with the assistant controller to review the areas they had discussed.

On the following day, Middleton summarized progress to date for the controller, emphasizing particularly the work that had been done on the centralized system. The controller expressed satisfaction with several new procedures that would be made possible by an electronic computer. During the next several days the committee members continued to gather the information necessary to determine the cost of the present system. Middleton also checked with the assistant controller on the proposed solutions for certain problems that the consultants had indicated could not be handled readily by a computer and relayed his reactions to the consultants.

A week later the consultants returned for another series of meetings. They discussed changes that might be necessary in current practices to make centralized electronic processing possible and the way in which they would compare the centralized and decentralized proposals. The comparison presented some difficulties, since the data provided by the two systems would not be identical. A general form for a preliminary report was cleared with the assistant controller, and a date was set for its submission. The processing, outputs, and costs for the two alternatives would be described, so that additional information required for a final report could be determined.

During the next week Middleton continued collecting cost data. He phoned to the consultants to provide them with important new figures and to inform them of the controller's favorable reaction to certain proposed changes in the system that had implications for the company's policies.

On October 17 Baker met with Middleton to review the content of the accounting reports that would be produced by the centralized system, to discuss plans for the preliminary report, and to discuss the relative advantages and disadvantages of the centralized and decentralized systems. On the next day, Middleton checked on their decisions relative to the report with the controller and assistant controller and raised the possibility of an outside expert being retained by the company to review the final report submitted by Beta. During the last days of this week, Middleton attended the national meeting of a management society, where he obtained information about the availability of computers and computer personnel and the existence of other installations comparable to that contemplated for the company.

Work continued on the planning and costing of the two systems— Middleton worked primarily on the decentralized plan, and the consultants on the centralized. On October 27 the two consultants met with Middleton and they informed each other of the status of their work. Baker discussed methods for evaluating system reliability. Plans for the preliminary report were discussed with the company committee and the assistant controller. Since the controller strongly favored decentralization of authority, the question was raised of the compatibility of this with electronic processing in general and with the centralized system in particular. The groups concluded, however, that centralization of purely clerical data-processing operations was compatible with decentralization of responsibility and authority.

After several meetings between the committee and the consultants to iron out details, the preliminary report was presented to the company committee, the controller, and the assistant controller on November 3.

The report was devoted primarily to the centralized system. The following points were made in the oral presentation: (1) that both the centralized and decentralized proposals would yield substantial and roughly equivalent savings but that the centralized system would provide more and better accounting data; (2) that the alternatives had been costed conservatively; (3) that the centralized system involved centralization of paper work, not of management; (4) that not all problems raised by the centralized system had been worked out in detail but that these did not appear insurmountable; (5) that the centralized system would facilitate improved inventory control; and (6) that its installation would require nine to twelve months at a specified cost. At this meeting the group decided that in the final report only the two systems already considered would be costed, that the final report would be submitted on December 1, and that investigation of other accounting applications of the system would be postponed.

In informal conversations after the meeting the controller told Middleton he had the impression that the consultants strongly favored the centralized system and that he believed the cost considerations were relatively minor compared with the impact the system would have on executives' operating philosophies. The assistant controller told Middleton he thought the preliminary report did not adequately support the conclusions. The committee then reviewed with the assistant controller the reasons for analyzing in detail only the two extreme systems: the others either produced less information or were more costly.

The next day the committee met with the controller and assistant controller to determine what additional information should be requested for the final report. The controller outlined certain questions of practicability that the final report should answer and expressed the view that the report should contain a section summarizing the specific changes that the system would bring about at various levels of the organization. He thought the comparison between systems in the preliminary report had emphasized equivalence of savings, without detailing other less tangible benefits of the centralized system.

Middleton reported these discussions to the consultants and with them developed flow charts and organization charts for inclusion in the final report, settled on some intermediate deadlines, and worked up an outline of the report. Within the company he discussed with the controller and assistant controller the personnel and organizational requirements for installation of an electronic system and for operation after installation. Discussion focused on the general character and organizational location of the eventual electronic-data-processing group, its relation to the sales accounting division, and long-term relations with manufacturing accounting and with a possible operations research group.

On November 14 the controller, on recommendation of Middleton, attended a conference on automation for company senior executives. There he expressed the view that three to five years would be required for full installation of a centralized electronic system but that the fear of obsolescence of equipment should not deter the company in making the investment. He also concluded that a computer installation would not reverse his long-range program for decentralizing information and responsibility.

Middleton, his suggestion being accepted, made tentative arrangements with an independent expert and with two large computer companies for the review of the consultants' report. Middleton presented to the controller and assistant controller a memorandum he had prepared at the latter's request, establishing a new comparison of the centralized and a modified decentralized system. The modification made the two systems more nearly comparable in data-processing capacity, hence clarified the cost comparison, which was now in favor of the centralized system. Consideration of the possibility of starting with a partially electronic decentralized system as a step toward a completely electronic system led to the decision that this procedure had no special advantages. The controller reported that conversations with the sales manager and the president had secured agreement with the concept of removal of stock record-keeping from field locations—an aspect of the plan to which it had been assumed there would be sales department opposition. The group discussed several other specific topics and reaffirmed that the final report should discuss more fully the relative advantages and disadvantages of centralized and decentralized systems.

Toward the end of November there was further consultation on the report, and final arrangements for its review were made with the two equipment companies and the independent expert. Each equipment company was expected to determine the method for setting up the proposed system on its computer and to check the consultants' estimates of computer capacity. During this week the controller informed the company's management committee that the report from the consultants would be submitted shortly and would recommend a rather radical change to electronic data-processing.

The final report, which recommended installation of the centralized system, was submitted on December 1. The report consisted of a summary of recommendations, general description of the centralized system, a discussion of the installation program, and six appendixes: (1) statistics on volume of transactions (the twenty-three studies); (2) costs of the present system; (3) the requirements of a fully centralized system; (4) changes in allocation of functions required by the system; (5) an outline of the alternative decentralized system; and (6) a description of the existing system in verbal and flow-chart form. When the report was received and reviewed initially, the company's committee members and the consultants made some further computations on installation costs.

At a meeting the following Monday the assistant controller proposed an action program: send copies of the report to equipment companies, send copies to the sales department, and await the report of the independent expert. The controller decided that the second and third steps should be taken before giving the report to the machine companies, and the assistant controller indicated to Middleton some points requiring further clarification and elaboration.

By January 7 Middleton had prepared an outline for a presentation of the report to the sales department. This was revised on the basis of a meeting with the other interested accounting executives. A final outline was agreed upon after two more revisions and three more meetings. The report was presented on January 28 to the president and to six of the top executives of the sales department. The presentation discussed large-scale computers briefly, described with flow charts the proposed system, emphasized the completeness and accuracy of the information produced, discussed costs and savings, and mentioned the current trend in other companies toward electronic data-processing.

At Middleton's recommendation the same presentation was made subsequently to top members of the accounting department and still later to a group from the manufacturing department. At the same time the preliminary report of the independent expert was received, agreeing that the electronic installation seemed justifiable and stating that there might not be any cost savings but that it would make possible numerous other profitable applications of the computer. The consultants' report was then distributed to the computer companies, and Middleton began more detailed planning of the installation.

Middleton, the assistant controller, and the controller now met with the independent expert, who reported his conclusions: the feasibility study was excellent, the estimates of processing time were probably optimistic, the installation program should provide for an early test run, and the two principal available computers were highly competitive. Independent comfirmation had been obtained on the last two points from another outside source. Middleton now proposed that the company proceed with its planning while awaiting the final written report from the independent expert and the proposals of the equipment companies. The assistant controller preferred to wait until these reports were actually in hand.

During the next week the equipment companies proceeded with their analysis, meeting several times with Middleton. Baker sent a memorandum on his estimates of processing time to meet the criticism of the independent expert. Middleton prepared two charts, one proposing a schedule and the staffing requirements for the installation phase, the other proposing organizational arrangements for the computer center. Middleton and the assistant controller presented these to the controller at the beginning of February, discussion centering responsibility for accuracy of input information.

Middleton and the assistant controller also had a meeting with sales executives who reported that on the basis of their own internal departmental discussions of the consultants' report they were in general agreement with the program. Middleton and one of the other committee members then spent two days inspecting computer installations in two other companies.

In the middle of February the two equipment companies presented their reports, each bringing a team of three or four men to present their recommendations orally. The two recommendations were substantially alike (except for the brand of the machine recommended!), but one report emphasized the availability of its personnel to give help during the installation planning stage.

Discussions were held in the accounting department and with consultant Baker about these reports and the next steps to be taken. The question was debated whether a commitment should be made to one equipment company or whether a small group should continue planning the system in detail, postponing the equipment decision until fall. Most of the group preferred the former alternative.

On February 15 the controller, in conference with the assistant controller and Middleton, dictated a letter to the company's president summarizing the conclusions and recommendations of the study and requesting that the accounting department be authorized to proceed with the electronics program.

On the following day the controller read the letter to the management committee. The letter reviewed briefly the history of the project and summarized the conclusions contained in the consultants' report: that there was ample justification for an electronic-data-processing installation; that the installation would warrant use of the largest computers; and that it would produce savings, many intangible benefits, and excess computer capacity for other applications. The letter quoted the consultants' estimate of the cost of the installation and their recommendation that the company proceed at once to make such a conversion and to acquire the necessary equipment. It then cited the various cross-checks that had been made of the consultants' report and concluded with a repetition of the conclusions of the report—but estimating more conservatively the operating and installation costs—and a request for favorable management committee action. Supplementary information presented included a comparison of consultant and equipment company cost estimates and a list of present and proposed computer installations in other companies. After a few questions and brief discussion, the management committee voted favorably on the recommendation, and the controller informed Middleton of the decision when the meeting ended.

THE ANATOMY OF THE DECISION

From this narrative, or more specifically from the actual data on which the narrative is based, one can list chronologically the various activities of which the decision process is composed. If we wish to describe a program for making a decision of this kind, each of these activities might be taken as one of the steps of the program. If the rules that determined when action would switch from one program step to another were specified, and if the program steps were described in enough detail, it would be possible to replicate the decision process.

The program steps taken together define in retrospect, then, a program for an originally unprogrammed decision. The program would be an inefficient one because it would contain all the false starts and blind alleys of the original process, and some of these could presumably be avoided if the process were repeated. However, describing the process that took place in terms of such a program is a useful way of organizing the data for purposes of analysis.

In order to make very specific what is meant here by a "program," Chart 1 has been prepared to show the broad outlines of the actual program for the first stages of the decision process (through the first seven paragraphs of the narrative).

CHART 1
Program Steps from Inception of the Problem to Selection of a Consultant

KEEPING-UP PROGRAM (paragraphs 1 and 2 of narrative):
Search for and correspond with experts;
Discuss with salesmen and with equipment users;
Search for and read journals;

PROCUREMENT PROGRAM (paragraph 3):
Discuss applications study with salesmen who propose it;
Choice: accept or reject proposed study;
(If accepted) transfer control to salesmen;
Choice: accept or reject applications proposal;
(If rejected) switch to consultant program;

CONSULTANT PROGRAM (paragraphs 4 through 7):
Search for consultants;
Choice: best consultant of several;
Transfer control to chosen consultant;
Choice: accept or reject proposal;
(If accepted): begin double-check routine;
Request expenditure of funds;
(If authorized) transfer control to consultants;
And so on.

Subprograms. The various program steps of the decision process fall into several subprograms, some of which have been indicated in Chart 1. These subprograms are ways of organizing the activities *post factum*, and in Chart 1 the organizing principle is the method of approach taken by the company to the total problem. It remains a question as to whether this organizing principle will be useful in all cases. As in the present example, these subprograms may sometimes be false starts, but these must be regarded as parts of the total program, for they may contribute information for later use, and their outcomes determine the switching of activity to new subprograms.

In this particular case the reasons for switching from one subprogram to another were either the proved inadequacy of the first one or a redefinition of the problem. Other reasons for switching can be imagined, and a complete theory of the decision process will have to specify the conditions under which the switch from one line of attack to another will occur.

Common Processes. In the whole decision-making program there are certain steps or "routines" that recur within several of the subprograms; they represent the basic activities of which the whole decision process is composed. For purposes of discussion we have classified these common processes in two categories: the first comprises processes relating to the communication requirements of the organization; the second comprises processes relating directly to the solution of the decisional problem.

Communication Processes. Organizational decision-making requires a variety of communication activities that are absent when a decision is made in a single human head. If we had written out the program steps in greater detail, many more instances of contacts among different members of the organization would be recorded than are now explicit in the narrative. The contacts may be oral or written. Oral contacts are used for such purposes as giving orders, transmitting information, obtaining approval or criticism of proposed action; written communications generally take the form of memorandums having the purpose of transmitting information or proposing action.

The information-transmitting function is crucial to organizational decision-making, for it almost always involves acts of selection or "filtering" by the informational source. In the present instance, which is rather typical in this respect, the consultants and subordinate executives are principal information sources; and the controller and other top executives must depend upon them for most of their technical information. Hence, the subordinate acts as an information filter and in this way secures a large influence over the decisions the superior can and does reach.

The influence of the information source over communications is partly controlled by checking processes—for example, retaining an independent expert to check consultants—which give the recipient an independent information source. This reduces, but by no means eliminates, filtering. The great differences in the amounts and kinds of information available to the various participants in the decision process described here emphasize the significance of filtering. It will be important to determine the relationship of the characteristics of the information to the resultant information change and to explore the effects of personal relations between people on the filtering process and hence upon the transmission of information.

Problem-Solving Processes.   Alongside the organizational communication processes, we find in the narrative a number of important processes directed toward the decision problem itself. One of the most prominent of these is the search for alternative courses of action. The first activities recounted in the narrative—writing letters, reading journals, and so on— were attempts to discover possible action alternatives. At subsequent points in the process searches were conducted to obtain lists of qualified consultants and experts. In addition to these, there were numerous searches—most of them only implicit in the condensed narrative—to find action alternatives that would overcome specific difficulties that emerged as detail was added to the broader alternatives.

The data support strongly the assertion made in the introduction that searches for alternative courses of action constitute a significant part of non-programmed decision-making—a part that is neglected by the classical theory of rational choice. In the present case the only alternatives that became available to the company without the expenditure of time and effort were the systems proposals made early in the process by representatives of two equipment companies, and these were both rejected. An important reason for the prominent role of search in the decision process is that the "problem" to be solved was in fact a whole series of "nested" problems, each alternative solution to a problem at one level leading to a new set of problems at the next level. In addition, the process of solving the substantive problems created many procedural problems for the organization: allocating time and work, planning agendas and report presentations, and so on.

Examination of the narrative shows that there is a rich variety of search processes. Many questions remain to be answered as to what determines the particular character of the search at a particular stage in the decision process: the possible differences between searches for procedural alternatives, on the one hand, and for substantive alternatives, on the other; the factors that determine how many alternatives will be sought before a choice is made; the conditions under which an alternative that has tentatively been chosen will be subjected to further check; the general types of search strategies.

The neglect of the search for alternatives in the classical theory of decision would be inconsequential if the search were so extensive that most of the alternatives available "in principle" were generally discovered and considered. In that case the search process would have no influence upon the alternative finally selected for action. The narrative suggests that this is very far from the truth—that, in fact, the search for alternatives terminates when a satisfactory solution has been discovered even though the field of possibilities has not been exhausted. Hence, we have reason to suppose that changes in the search process or its outcome will actually have major effects on the final decision.

A second class of common processes encompasses information-gathering and similar activity aimed at determining the consequences of each of several alternatives. In many decisions, certainly in the one we observed, these activities account for the largest share of man-hours, and it is through them that subproblems are discovered. The narrative suggests that there is an adverse relation between the cost or difficulty of this investigational task and the number of alternative courses of action that are examined carefully. Further work will be needed to determine if this relation holds up in a broader range of situations. The record also raises numerous questions about the *kinds* of consequences that are examined most closely or at all and about the conditions under which selection of criteria for choice is prior to, or subsequent to, the examination of consequences.

Another set of common processes are those concerned with the choices among alternatives. Such processes appear at many points in the narrative: the selection of a particular consulting firm from a list, the choice between centralized and decentralized electronic-data-processing systems, as well as numerous more detailed choices. These are the processes most closely allied to the classical theory of choice, but even here it is notable that traditional kinds of "maximizing" procedures appear only rarely.

In some situations the choice is between competing alternatives, but in many others it is one of acceptance or rejection of a single course of action—really a choice between doing *something* at this time and doing nothing. The first such occasion was the decision by the controller to assign Middleton to the task of watching developments in electronics, a decision that initiated the whole sequence of later choices. In decisions of this type the consequences of the single alternative are judged against some kind of explicit or implicit "level of aspiration"—perhaps expressed in terms of an amount of improvement over the existing situation—while in the multiple-alternative situations, the consequences of the several alternatives are compared with each other. This observation raises a host of new questions relating to the circumstances under which the decision will be formulated in terms of the one or the other of these frameworks and the personal and organizational factors that determine the aspiration levels that will be applied in the one-alternative case.

Another observation derivable from our data—though it is not obvious from the condensed narrative given here—is that comparability and non-comparability of the criteria of choice affects the decision processes in significant ways. For one thing, the criteria are not the same from one choice to another: one choice may be made on the basis of relative costs and savings, while the next may be based entirely on non-monetary criteria. Further, few, if any, of the choices were based on a single criterion. Middleton and the others recognized and struggled with this problem of comparing consequences that were sometimes measured in different, and incomparable, units, and even more often involved completely intangible considerations. The narrative raises, but does not answer, the question of how choices are made in the face of these incommensurabilities and the degree to which tangible considerations are overemphasized or underemphasized as compared with intangibles as a result.

CONCLUSION

We do not wish to try to transform one swallow into a summer by generalizing too far from a single example of a decision process. We have tried to illustrate, however, using a large relatively non-programmed decision in a business firm, some of the processes that are involved in business decision-making and to indicate the sort of theory of the choice mechanism that is needed to accommodate these processes. Our illustration suggests that search processes and information-gathering processes constitute significant parts of decision-making and must be incorporated in a theory of decision if it is to be adequate. While the framework employed here—and particularly the analysis of a decision in terms of a hierarchical structure of *programs*—is far from a complete or finished theory, it appears to provide a useful technique of analysis for researchers interested in the theory of decision as well as for business executives who may wish to review the decision-making procedures of their own companies.

38. THE IMPLEMENTATION OF A DECISION*

N. F. Dufty and P. M. Taylor°

Following their analysis of a business decision (Article No. 37), Cyert, Simon, and Trow concluded, "We do not wish to try to transform one swallow into a summer by generalizing too far from a single example of a decision process."[1] Our intention here is to add another swallow in the hope that eventually a sufficient number of them accumulate to justify calling it a summer.

March and Simon have substantially revised the traditional theory of decision making, and the decision described and discussed here will be analyzed in the framework they have suggested.[2] Unlike the decision studied by Cyert et al., which was analyzed by having a member of the research team present as an observer during the active phases of decision process, in the decision reported here one of the authors[3] played a prominent role in the implementation of the decision made—to transfer personnel from one part of an organization to another. The transfer process was of short duration (13 days) compared to the case discussed by Cyert, Simon, and Trow. It is not the decision to transfer the personnel that is analyzed here; we are concerned largely with the subsequent decisions.

THE PROBLEM OF TRANSFER OF PERSONNEL

The organization concerned was the Metropolitan Transport Trust (hereafter MTT) in the city of Perth, Western Australia. It had about 420 buses and 1,500 personnel in the early part of 1960. In July of that year it acquired another organization known as the Western Australian Government Tramways (hereafter WAGT), comprising one large depot, 206 buses, and over 800 employees. Soon after the merger, it was decided that the efficiency of the whole organization could be improved by transferring

---

* Reprinted from *Administrative Science Quarterly*, Vol. 7 (June, 1962).

° N. F. Dufty is Head, Department of Management Studies, Perth Technical College, Perth, Western Australia. P. M. Taylor is associated with Chamberlain Industries, Ltd., Welshpool, Western Australia.

[1] R. M. Cyert, H. A. Simon, and D. B. Trow, "Observation of a Business Decision," *Journal of Business*, 29 (1956), pp. 237–248.

[2] J. G. March and H. A. Simon, *Organizations* (New York: John Wiley & Sons, Inc., 1958), chap. vi.

[3] P. M. Taylor.

certain services from the former main depot of the WAGT to an MTT depot at Claremont, some miles away.

On Friday, September 2, 1960, the chief executive, the chairman of the MTT, informed the personnel superintendent that it had been decided to transfer certain services to the Claremont depot. This involved the movement of buses, which was no problem, and the more difficult question of transferring personnel. On Monday, September 5, at the suggestion of the chairman, a conference was held which was attended by the personnel superintendent, the traffic manager and the assistant traffic manager. It was decided that the new service should start on September 27 and that 11 bus drivers and 11 fare collectors would have to be transferred to the Claremont depot to maintain it. The task of obtaining the required number of people who would be willing to transfer from the former WAGT depot to Claremont was given to the personnel superintendent. He was to arrange with the assistant traffic manager for the training of new staff to operate the other routes already operating from the Claremont depot. As the arbitration court award (equivalent to the collective bargaining contract) required "reasonable" rotation through the rosters at any depot, the personnel transferred could not be confined to any one route.

Immediately following this conference, the personnel superintendent sent for the employment and training officer and the staff records officer to discuss the implementation of the decision. They agreed that it would not be easy to get the necessary volunteers to transfer to Claremont because when applications had been called in August to fill a driver's vacancy then existing at Claremont, only two licensed conductors (having driving licenses) applied, even though the transfer meant considerable financial gain. One of the applicants subsequently withdrew without giving any reason. In addition, the personnel at the former WAGT depot, who had been government employees for many years, tended to view with suspicion MTT personnel from other depots, all of whom had formerly worked for private employers. Their general belief was that working conditions were inferior in MTT depots, that discipline was stricter, and that there was a tendency for the MTT depot masters to "sweat" their drivers in order to maintain tight schedules. Another factor was that the Tramways Union had no members at MTT depots, most of the latter's employees being in the Transport and Motor Operator's Union. These anxieties had recently been expressed in the State Arbitration Court by witnesses for the Tramways Union in a hearing on the issue of a contract covering all MTT traffic employees.

In the August issue of the MTT staff newsletter the policy of interdepot transfers had been explained in detail for the benefit of former WAGT personnel. Briefly, those interested in transfers were to make written application to the personnel department, giving their reasons for requesting transfers. If the reasons were judged to be satisfactory, the application was filed in the transfer register. Whenever vacancies occurred the employment officer first consulted the transfer register before taking any other action to fill a vacancy. This policy had operated quite well for some time—ever since the responsibility for transfers had been passed to the personnel department. The employment officer reported that despite this publicity, he had received only one transfer application from the former WAGT depot, and this was not for a transfer to Claremont.

The personnel superintendent and his colleagues considered that the task of persuading 11 fare collectors to transfer to Claremont would be even more difficult. Very few of the former WAGT depot fare collectors lived within reasonable distance of the Claremont depot. This was important because the fare collectors, being women and on considerably lower rates of pay than the drivers, were picked up by the MTT when they were rostered on early shifts and taken home when they were on late finishing shifts. After some discussion it was agreed that the immediate program should be as follows:

1. The personnel superintendent was to issue a notice calling for applications from qualified drivers, conductors, and fare collectors who were prepared to transfer to Claremont.

2. The staff records officer was to produce a list showing all former WAGT personnel living within a four-mile radius of the Claremont depot.

3. The employment officer was to consider all applications on the transfer register to see if alternative transfers could be made, e.g., Perth to Claremont and the WAGT depot to Perth.

4. A further meeting to discuss progress was scheduled for September 8.

Immediately after the meeting the personnel superintendent discussed a tentative training program with the assistant traffic manager. It was thought that conductors not qualified as drivers would have to be considered for the driving positions and that this would throw a heavy burden on the instructional staff. It was felt that two instructors could handle the problem of training up to six men for their licenses as well as for route and fare instruction. The problem of training the fare collectors could be overcome by adding a competent and experienced fare collector to the training staff during the emergency.

The assistant traffic manager and the personnel superintendent then conferred with the traffic manager, who agreed to the following proposals:

1. Unlicensed conductors would be accepted for transfer and training, provided that an adequate response was not obtained from the notice that had been issued.

2. The most suitable fare collector should be added to full-time training duties and she should be trained in these duties by the chief instructor.

On September 6, applications were received from three fare collectors who shared an apartment and who were prepared to move to another apartment near Claremont. Despite the fact that two of these girls had high absentee records and the other had a history of cash shortages, their transfers were approved, and the training arrangements were completed. The next day an inquiry was made by a driver who had been reduced to a conductor because of a high accident record, but this application was rejected. On the same day two employees from the former WAGT depot gave notice that they were quitting. It was decided not to replace them but to engage two new men to be trained as drivers for the Claremont depot.

On September 8 the superintendent of another depot reported that an adjustment of the rosters had left him with a surplus driver. The addresses of the drivers at this depot were examined, and one was located living near Claremont. No difficulty was experienced in persuading him to transfer. That afternoon the employment officer, staff records officer, and personnel superintendent met to discuss progress, and it was decided to interview the 23 people located within four miles of the Claremont depot and attempt to persuade some of them to transfer. The employment officer reported that his examination of the transfer register had been unfruitful so far as drivers were concerned, but that two fare collectors from the Perth depot were willing to transfer. They were easily replaced by transfers from the former WAGT depot. Another meeting was scheduled for September 12.

Later that day the secretary of the Tramways Union saw the personnel superintendent about other matters and mentioned his concern about the notice and rumors that members would be compelled to transfer. He thought it most unlikely that volunteers would be obtained, and he was afraid that any members transferred would be lost to his union. The personnel superintendent pointed out that he could use any transferred members as ambassadors to help him in his struggle with the Transport and Motor Operator's Union. This idea appealed to the secretary, and he even suggested that he might help by persuading likely candidates to transfer. It seemed from this conversation that union opposition was not likely to continue, and this opposition may have been an important factor in hindering transfers.

On September 9 the employment officer began his interview program. By the end of the day seven drivers had been interviewed; two had agreed to transfer, one said that he would consider it, and the other four rejected the proposal completely. One fare collector was seen and agreed to consider the transfer, and the two licensed conductors interviewed were willing to move. One unlicensed conductor was interviewed but was considered to be unsuitable for training as a driver.

On Monday, September 12, the employment officer completed his interviewing program. This yielded the following: five bus drivers, two licensed conductors, two unlicensed conductors, and one fare collector. In addition, the superintendent of the former WAGT depot reported that one bus driver was giving up his job because of a medical disability.

That afternoon the scheduled meeting of the personnel superintendent, employment officer, and staff records officer took place to consider the situation. It was decided to submit the two unlicensed conductors to the standard driving test to ascertain their fitness for training as drivers, before making a final decision. The next day, when the test were given, one was found to be satisfactory, and the other was classed as unsuitable. This made the number of drivers and potential drivers for the Claremont depot ten; the eleventh was provided by the replacement of the medically unfit driver at the former WAGT depot by promotion and by engaging a new driver for Claremont. The driver requirements were now filled, subject to the training of the conductor who had passed the selection test. The quota of fare collectors was still four short of its target, and it was considered that all reasonable alternatives had been explored. The recommendation was made to the assistant traffic manager that four new fare collectors should be recruited in the Claremont area despite the fact that this would leave four surplus fare collectors at the former WAGT depot. It was felt, however, that changes in the leave program could be made to utilize one or more of the fare collectors temporarily and that labor turnover, normally high in this class of worker, would soon account for the rest. Discussions were held with the assistant traffic manager, who agreed with the recommendations. Arrangements were made to alter the leave program to absorb one fare collector temporarily, and the other three, pending their absorption through labor turnover, were scheduled to city queue fare collecting to improve the efficiency of one-man bus services during the peak periods.

On September 14 the personnel superintendent notified the chairman that the required personnel would be available at the Claremont depot in time to start the newly scheduled service on September 27.

ANALYSIS OF THE DECISIONS

As indicated, the analysis here is not an analysis of the decision to transfer the personnel, but rather an analysis of the several decisions made by the personnel superintendent in order to implement the transfer. As March and Simon point out, the programs of members of higher levels of an organization have as their main output the modification or initiation of programs for people at lower levels.[4]

---

[4] March and Simon, *op. cit.*, p. 150.

The organizational goals of efficiency and decentralization, which led to the original transfer decision, were not questioned by the personnel superintendent at any stage, nor were they questioned by any other person concerned with the implementation of the decision. It might have been thought that the acceptance of this "logic of efficiency" would also have implied an acceptance of the machine model of organization, in which the employee is an instrument. This thesis ignores many of the motivational aspects of modern organization theory, of which the personnel superintendent and his staff were well aware. No attempt was made to take the simplest course of action—to select 11 drivers and 11 fare collectors and transfer them arbitrarily, complying only with the legal requirement of giving them the appropriate notice. Indeed, there was no evidence that this course of action was even considered. So far as the personnel superintendent was concerned, he was not only fully aware of the probable dysfunctional consequences of such action, but he would also have found it to conflict with his personal value system.

In this case the step initiating the program was taken by the chief executive, but he specified only the outcome or ends, i.e., that 22 people be provided for certain jobs at a certain place at a certain time. It was left to the personnel superintendent to supply the means-ends connections; he was given wide discretionary powers to use both the standard programs in his repertory and to develop new programs or modify old ones through problem-solving and learning processes.

If the implementation of the transfer decision had involved only the movement of one or two drivers, the stimulus would have evoked a routine response, namely, consultation of the transfer register. In the circumstances, it was obvious to the personnel superintendent that this step alone would not be adequate, and the first action taken was to initiate problem-solving activity by calling a conference of those people whom he thought could help solve the problem. The aim of the conference was to define the situation and then develop a number of performance programs, including the routine program of consulting the transfer register. The programs developed were as follows:

1. The issue of a special notice calling for transfer applications.
2. The production of a list showing all WAGT staff living within a four-mile radius of Claremont.
3. An extension of the normal program of consulting the transfer register by examining the possibility of making complex transfers, e.g., Perth to Claremont, WAGT depot to Perth.

This initial planning may be classified as substantive—developing new programs or modifying old ones—rather than procedural—developing programs for problem solving. Much of the narrative emphasizes the importance of communication processes when the decision making involved more than one person in the organization. These procedures included conferences, face-to-face or telephone communication between those participating in the performance programs, written notices to employees, interview programs, and discussion with an external organization—the union. The following five types of communication mentioned by March and Simon were all represented.[5]

1. Communication for nonprogramed activity, e.g., discussion with the official of the union, which apparently resulted in a change in the union's attitude and a reduction in its opposition to the transfer of its members to Claremont.

2. Communication to establish programs, including their adjustment and coordination. Examples would be the conference between the personnel superintendent and his colleagues to establish the programs mentioned and that between the personnel superintendent and the assistant traffic manager leading to the widening of acceptance standards for drivers.

3. Communications to provide data required for the execution of programs, such as the interview program to find out who would be willing to transfer to Claremont.

4. Communications to initiate programs. The communication to the personnel superintendent of the chief executive's decision to transfer personnel to Claremont would be one example. Another would be that from the personnel superintendent to the chief instructor to give the standard driving test to the two unlicensed conductors.

5. Communications to provide information on the results of activities. Examples of this would be the communication of the result of the interviews to the personnel superintendent and the latter's final report to the chief executive.

In the model of March and Simon, the decision maker is concerned with the discovery of satisfactory rather than optimal alternatives.[6] In the case considered here, there was no attempt to define what was meant by optimal even though a less-than-optimal solution could have been attempted by treating the transfer as an assignment problem. This method, however, assumes that the effectiveness of the various personnel available for transfer can be measured.[7] Such a procedure was obviously impractical under the circumstances. A "satisfactory" level of performance in this

---

[5] *Ibid.*, p. 161.

[6] *Ibid.*, p. 141. Also see H. A. Simon, "A Behavioral Model of Rational Choice," *Quarterly Journal of Economics*, Vol. 69 (1955), pp. 99–118.

[7] C. W. Churchman, R. L. Ackoff, and E. L. Arnoff, *Introduction to Operations Research* (New York: John Wiley & Sons, Inc., 1957), chap. xii.

particular case was the transfer of 11 drivers and 11 fare collectors to the Claremont depot in time for the newly scheduled service to begin on September 27. Almost at the outset, however, this definition of what was satisfactory was reformulated in the light of what was known of the difficulty in persuading people to transfer to the Claremont depot. The relaxation took the form of accepting unlicensed conductors, who would require training. This alternative initiated routine subprograms, such as those for testing potential drivers and for training those who were suitable. A further adjustment to the desired level of satisfactoriness occurred when, because of the problems of transferring fare collectors, a surplus of four collectors at the former WAGT depot was considered a lesser evil than the inability to provide sufficient collectors at Claremont on the date set. The chief executive had specified the main task as the transfer of a particular bus service to the Claremont depot. An inferred subgoal was the elimination of the organizational slack[8] which would develop at the old WAGT depot if the surplus personnel were allowed to remain there. This subgoal was to some extent abandoned. Lack of optimization was also evidenced by the acceptance of two fare collectors with past records of high absenteeism.

In the former WAGT depot, the staff generally was strongly identified with its union. In the opinion of the personnel superintendent, they were more concerned with the goals of the union, an external organization, than those of the organization which presumed that it had purchased their allegiance by the payment of wages. The union's attitude was predominantly defensive. It perceived the MTT as a hard taskmaster whose primary goal was efficiency, probably because the chief executive had formerly held a similar position in a privately owned bus company. The union officials felt that working conditions had been easy for their organization and their members when the depot had been under the control of the WAGT; i.e., when there had been some organizational slack. They saw any action on the part of the MTT as a move to eliminate this organizational slack with a consequent tightening up of working conditions for their members. Their members saw it in this light too, and the ensuing feedback loops served to reinforce this impression. It was not surprising, therefore, that all communications from the MTT on the transfer issue were filtered, so that they fitted the established perceptions of this organization. This was almost entirely due to the fact that most of the communicators, both within the suborganization and the union, had similar frames of reference. All this was known to the personnel superintendent, who took two steps to remedy the situation. One was an attempt to change the union's attitude by discussing the situation with the union secretary—a step which seemed to have been quite successful, at least

---

[8] See March and Simon, *op. cit.*, p. 126.

superficially. The other step was an effort to change the attitudes of those union members who lived close to the Claremont depot by means of the interview program. This also was successful in some cases.

CONCLUSION

We have tried to analyze an organizational decision of a largely nonprogramed type within the framework laid down by March and Simon. This framework, similar to that developed by Simon, Cyert, and Trow, seems to be considerably more fruitful than the conventional one of classical rational choice, which leaves many questions unanswered. Even in such a relatively minor decision and short time span as this, the hierarchical structure of programs is apparent, and the importance of search programs, communications, perceptions, and value systems can be seen. It is our conviction that the deeper understanding of decision-making processes made possible by this type of analysis will lead to an improvement in those processes.

39. FACTORS DETERMINING THE ADOPTION OF DECISION MAKING AS A ROLE BEHAVIOR: A STUDY OF SCIENTISTS IN A GOVERNMENT ORGANIZATION*

ROBERT S. WEISS

IT'S FREQUENTLY recognized that different individuals will work, in a job, in different ways; that one individual tends to assimilate one set of activities to his job, while another individual tends to assimilate a slightly different set. Given the same job, one individual may tend to make his own decisions where another would rely on his supervisor. Or one individual might tend to see a great many clients where another would de-emphasize that aspect of the job.

This paper has to do with factors which determined the way scientists, working in a government organization, structured their jobs. These factors may be put under four headings: (1) job imperatives—absolute requirements of the job, things anyone in the job simply *has* to do; (2) authoritatively assigned activities—things required of the individual by his supervisor, or someone else higher than he is in the organization's hierarchy; (3) socially assigned activities—things which are expected of the individual by his coworkers because he seems to be the proper person to do them; and (4) things the individual decides to do on his own initiative.

Most frequently we've thought that individual preferences for certain activities over others was the crucial factor in determining the way an individual structured his job. Thus, if an individual introduced decision-making into his job, he was considered someone who enjoyed having influence, and this was accepted as describing the source of his role behaviors. The data we have obtained suggest that individual preferences are not nearly so important in determining what optional activities—activities not summed up by the job imperatives—the individual performs. We find that aside from the job imperatives, social pressures based on the individual's possession of what we call *legitimizing characteristics*, and the *attitude of the individual's supervisor*, are much more important.

A *legitimizing characteristic* is an objective attribute of an individual, such as age or length of service in an organization, which may become generally known to the group with whom the individual works, and which is considered by this group to be related to the propriety of the individual's performing certain activities. For example, if, in the study of

* Presented at the Meetings of the American Psychological Association at New York, September, 1954.

an industrial operation, someone in the plant said to us, "They made so-and-so the inspector. After all, he's been here the longest," then we would think that length of service was a legitimizing characteristic for, or legitimized, performance of this quasi-supervisory activity. We would be convinced of this if we found that someone else was considered an improper choice because he did not have sufficient service.

Legitimizing characteristics probably correlate with competence to perform an activity, but probably are not directly related. The reason for their use may be found in a tendency for a group of individuals to avoid ambiguity in areas of importance to the group wherever this is possible. In an office situation, or any other situation where individuals work closely together, the allocation of tasks is a matter of concern to the group, and what seems to happen is that informally, and without people being aware of the specificity of some of the formulations, criteria arise regarding who can do what. It's then in terms of these criteria that social reaction takes place. For example, if A starts to perform an activity that B has been performing right along it's possible for coworkers of A and B to say to each other, in complete agreement, that A has a lot of nerve. And if A says, well, B's been doing this, the response will come in concert, yes, but B's been here for twenty years, or B is much older than you, or B has twice as much education as you, or B's been in this field for a dozen years, whatever the criteria agreed upon by the group in respect to the activity.

In the organization we studied there were 63 jobs which, so far as we could tell, were identical in the nature of their job imperatives. The things people *had* to do in their jobs were the same. Only the optional activities varied. The organization is a research organization, built as a series of parallel units, with each unit being assigned responsibility for investigation in a particular specialty. The jobs we chose were those of the scientific member of a unit, without supervisory responsibility. These jobs were identical, or quite similar to each other, on a number of other criteria besides job imperatives, including title, salary range, and position of the job in relation to other jobs.

We interviewed each scientist who held one of these jobs for from one to three hours, and among the questions we asked them, was to describe in detail the things they did in the course of a day's work. Their responses were categorized in terms of the organizational function or functions they seemed to be performing. One of the categories used was that of decision-making, which included the activities of deciding major allocation of funds, or otherwise committing the organization to a certain line of action. The response of one of the 63 scientists could not be coded, but of the remaining 62, 20 reported activities which were coded as decision-making, and 42 did *not* report such activities.

We decided that for a characteristic to qualify, for us, as a legitimizing characteristic, it must meet two criteria:

(1) It must be used by members of the group as a basis for discussing the appropriateness of the activity being performed either by themselves or by other members of the organization, and

(2) It must relate to actual performance of the activity, that is, other things being equal, people who have it should perform the activity, and people who do not have it should not.

Characteristics which seemed to legitimize decision-making were: possession of an advanced degree, long service with the organization, and wide experience in the field. A number of individuals suggested that without advanced degrees they were limited in the work they could do, and the implication was strong that increased education might not increase their competence, but it would certainly better their position in the social system. Length of service was also mentioned frequently, for example, in relation to an individual who performed his job in an amazingly autonomous fashion. This was justified by his coworkers on the basis of his being a fixture in the organization. Experience was mentioned much less frequently than education and length of service, but a few individuals did refer to it, usually in regard to themselves. Education was by far the most important: so important, it seemed, that without some graduate training, nothing else counted: experience was sufficiently minor so that it came into the picture only when other things were indecisive.

After examining the sample, we put these three elements together into operational criteria for whether an individual possessed legitimizing characteristics for decision-making. An individual was considered to have legitimizing characteristics if he had:

(1) A Ph.D.

(2) Some graduate work, and a fair amount of service with the organization (operationally set at four years).

(3) Some graduate work, some service with the organization (set at two years), and a fair amount of experience in the field (set at ten years).

Earlier I mentioned that legitimization was only part of the story in regard to whether the individual adopted an activity. The other part had to do with the attitudes of the individual's supervisor in regard to performance of the activity by his subordinates. During their interview we had asked each supervisor about his practices in regard to decision-making, and we were able to categorize them by their responses, into those who *retained* decision-making power, those who *permitted* decision-making by subordinates, and, in the third category, a single supervisor who *required* his subordinates to perform decision-making activities.

Table 1 shows that decision-making is reported by only five out of the thirty-three scientists whose supervisors retain decision-making power, but by ten out of the twenty-four whose supervisors permit decision-

making by subordinates. The five subordinates of the supervisor who requires decision-making of his subordinates all report that they do, indeed,
make policy decisions.

Looking now to Table 2, which shows the relationship of legitimizing

TABLE 1

REPORT OF DECISION MAKING BY SCIENTISTS AND ATTITUDE OF SUPERVISOR
IN REGARD TO DECISION MAKING

		No. of Their Subordinates:		
			who do not	
	No. of	who report	report decision-	
Supervisor's Attitude	Supervisors	decision-making	making	Total
Retains decision-making	11	5	28	33
Permits decision-making by subor- dinates	9	10	14	24
Requires decision-making by subor- dinates	1	5	0	5
Total	21	20	42	62

characteristics and decision-making among scientists whose supervisors
permit decision-making by subordinates, we find that all scientists who
report decision-making have legitimizing characteristics, while all but
three of those who do not report decision-making do not have legitimizing characteristics. I should remind you, in connection with the significance level of this table, that the criteria of legitimizing characteristics

TABLE 2

DECISION MAKING AND LEGITIMIZING CHARACTERIS-
TICS AMONG SCIENTISTS WHOSE SUPERVISORS PERMIT
DECISION MAKING BY SUBORDINATES

| | Legitimizing Characteristics | | |
Decision-making	Have	Do not have	Total
Report	10	0	10
Do not report	3	11	14
Total	13	11	24

$p = .0001$, Fisher exact test, one-tailed

are based in part on a fitting operation, and the level of significance is as
much an indicator of how good a fit can be made as it is anything else.

Turning now to the scientists whose supervisors retain decision-making power (Table 3), we find that four of the five who report decision-
making activities have legitimizing characteristics. We were interested in
how *any* of these five could have decision-making activities, *particularly*
the individual who did not have legitimizing characteristics, when their
supervisors were definite about making all important decisions themselves.
We therefore returned to interview protocols of the five and did something like a deviant case analysis. We found first that the supervisor of the
scientist who did not have legitimizing characteristics vacillated between

retaining decision-making power himself, and *requiring* decision-making of his subordinates. He wanted to do things himself, and he also wanted his subordinates to stand on their own feet, and he swung between demanding the one or the other. The subordinate who is one of the paradoxical five had just not caught up with the latest swing. There was some indication on the subordinate's protocol, in the form of confusion over

TABLE 3
DECISION MAKING AND LEGITIMIZING CHARACTERIS-
TICS AMONG SCIENTISTS WHOSE SUPERVISORS RETAIN
DECISION MAKING POWER

Decision-making	Legitimizing Characteristics		
	Have	Do Not Have	Total
Report	4	1	5
Do not report	9	19	28
Total	13	20	33

$p = .07$, Fisher exact test, one-tailed

the extent to which his supervisor worked together with him, that the relationship was not smooth, and that the subordinate might drop decision-making. The other four, all of whom *had* legitimizing characteristics, had been able to parlay their legitimizing characteristics, persistence and, in some cases, ingenuity, into a restructuring of their jobs within their supervisor's definitions of the situation. One of these individuals was the "fixture" I mentioned. He had been with his group longer than anyone else, including the supervisor, and he went his own way, secure in his status as grand old man. Another of these individuals had managed to convince his supervisor that when he, the scientist, made policy decisions, he was following through on leads the supervisor had given him.

The five subordinates of the supervisor who required that they make those decisions which fell within their own area, all reported decision-making activities. The supervisor here is a man who is highly respected in his specialty, recognizes his own competence, and demands similar competence from his subordinates. All his subordinates but the individual who lacks legitimizing characteristics think the world of him. But the fellow without the legitimizing characteristics complains that when he came to the organization he accepted one sort of job, and now he has another. He feels uncomfortable in his present job. Oddly enough, he feels that he doesn't have much influence, in spite of his performing decision-making activities. His summary of the situation is: "I guess I'm developing an inferiority complex by being here."

To summarize: legitimizing characteristics are used in this situation as a basis for shared evaluations of the competence of the scientist to make policy decisions. With one exception, all scientists who are not required to perform decision-making activities, but who nevertheless do so, have legitimizing characteristics. Where the supervisor assumes decision-making himself, some of the scientists who have legitimizing characteristics seem able to compete with him successfully. The report of a scientist who does not have legitimizing characteristics, but is *required* to perform decision-making in spite of the lack suggests that legitimizing characteristics are important to the scientist in that they justify to him and to others his adoption of a particular role.

The conclusion we would draw from all this is that it is important to consider the factors which have to do with social sanction for the performance of a role whenever we consider either problems of filling particular roles, or problems of individual reaction to assigned roles.

40. DECISION MAKING IN A MENTAL HOSPITAL: REAL, PERCEIVED, AND IDEAL*

Mark Lefton, Simon Dinitz, and
Benjamin Pasamanick

This paper attempts to examine the decision-making process in a small, institute type of psychiatric hospital in terms of the differences in real, perceived, and ideal influence patterns of 53 mental health specialists. It was hypothesized that these decision-making patterns would reflect the influence of a dual criteria system with respect to the organization and functioning of the hospital. These criteria are, first, the traditional medical bureaucracy and, second, the currently emphasized "team" or equalitarian approach regarding the care and treatment of patients. Under investigation were the nature and implications of this organizational dualism for both the involvement of staff members in the ongoing decision-making process and their evaluations of this process.

THE SMALL psychiatric hospital is rapidly becoming the focus of a great deal of sociological and interdisciplinary research.[1] On the assumption that the psychiatric hospital is a microcosm of the larger social order, a variety of sociological interests have been pursued in this setting. In addition to studies of the structure of the hospital, the role behavior of staff personnel and patients, communications networks, and the ward as a "therapeutic community," increasing interest has been devoted to decision making and its association with status and power in the hospital organization.[2]

Although it is readily agreed that the degree of influence which different kinds of people have in making administrative and otherwise functional decisions is an important variable for organizational analysis, the conditions and circumstances which result in differential participation in the making of decisions have not as yet been made explicit. This study, therefore, represents an attempt to delineate empirically some of the factors which operate to affect influence and participation in the decision-

* Reprinted from *American Sociological Review*, Vol. 24, No. 6 (December, 1959), pp. 822–29. This research was undertaken by the Research Division of the Columbus Psychiatric Institute and Hospital and was supported by a grant (M–2940) from the National Institute of Mental Health.

[1] See, for example, A. H. Stanton and M. S. Schwartz, *The Mental Hospital* (New York: Basic Books, 1954); William Caudill, *The Psychiatric Hospital as a Small Society* (Cambridge, Mass.: Harvard University Press, 1958); and Maxwell Jones, *The Therapeutic Community* (New York: Basic Books, 1953).

[2] For a discussion of the decision-making process in the mental hospital, see Stanton and Schwartz, *op. cit.,* pp. 244–91. For discussions of decision making in general, see the several contributions in "Authority and Decision-Making," in R. K. Merton *et al.* (ed.) *Reader in Bureaucracy,* (Glencoe, Ill.: Free Press, 1952), pp. 179–240.

making process of several interacting specialty groups. In addition, it draws attention to some of the personal and organizational consequences of this process.

The small psychiatric hospital offers an especially valuable locus for this type of research since it exhibits a dual-value system with respect to the making of decisions concerning the care and treatment of patients. On the one hand, the psychiatric hospital, in common with the general hospital and with other more specialized institutions—such as hospitals serving tuberculosis patients—features a more or less rigidly bureaucratized structure in the classic sense of bureaucracy. There exists a hierarchy of authority in decision making (indeed, parallel hierarchies, one administrative and the other clinical), the specialization of personnel with certified competencies, formally recognized and routinized role distinctions, and a great preoccupation with the symbols and trappings of status and prestige. The mental hospital, however, possesses a strong, recent, and unique counterforce to bureaucracy. This is the emphasis on the hospital ward as a therapeutic community and on the healing effects of a warm, conflict-free environment. In pursuance of this type of climate, the attempt is usually made to subordinate the traditional medical structure to the presumed organizational requirements of the therapeutic community. These requirements include an emphasis on the "team" and on "teamwork." The roles, duties, and obligations of each specialty are regarded as being more or less equally vital in the functioning and objectives of the organization. In such a context, which admittedly is an ideal, status and power gradations would be minimal, and decisions should therefore be consensual rather than unilateral.[3]

In this study it was hypothesized that both the traditional bureaucratic medical organization and the more equalitarian organization would be reflected in the ongoing decision-making process as well as in the attitudes of professional personnel with respect to their actual and desired involvement in the process. Under investigation are the nature and implications of the discrepancies in the perceived, actual, and ideal decision-making influence of the various specialists in the mental hospital. It will be shown that actual decision-making practices and staff perceptions of involvement and influence in this process are affected, on the one hand, by professional status within the officially recognized authority system and, on the other, by differing psychiatric orientations and concomitant ward policies and practices.

METHOD

The study was conducted at the Columbus Psychiatric Institute and Hospital, which is an adjunct of the State Department of Mental Hygiene

---

[3] For a concise summary of this point of view, see M. Greenblatt, R. H. York, and E. L. Brown, *From Custodial to Therapeutic Patient Care in Mental Hospitals* (New York: Russell Sage Foundation, 1955), p. 421.

and Correction and the Department of Psychiatry of the College of Medicine of The Ohio State University. The hospital contains 126 beds, divided into five wards (three female and two male); it is an institution for research, training, and short-term treatment. The significance of the Institute for the present research lies in, first, its large complement of trained professional personnel, which includes, among the purely clinical staff of the five wards, five senior psychiatrists (that is, ward administrators), 15 resident psychiatrists, 18 registered nurses, and five each of clinical psychologists, social workers, and occupational therapists, as well as a large number of interns, externs, and trainees in the other specialities; second, its intensive therapy as opposed to "back ward" custodial-type treatment program; third, its emphasis on establishing an ideal "clinical team" on each of the wards; and, finally, its effort to provide an outpatient program.

All 53 professional clinical personnel, as enumerated above, served as subjects in the study. These persons, all of whom were interviewed individually, were asked to estimate their influence in each of six decision-making areas of vital concern for patient care and treatment. The decision areas include: (1) the working diagnosis, (2) medical treatment, (3) patient privileges, (4) occupational therapy, (5) special supervision, and (6) the time and type of release given patients. Each staff member rated the influence of his professional group in each of these areas in terms of two frames of reference: the amount of influence the respondent believed that his profession, first, *had* and, second, *should have* on his ward. In addition, each subject rated the general decision-making influence of each of the other professions on the ward and, again, according to how much influence each should have.[4]

These ratings were made on a novel type of magnetic board instrument which had been developed, tested, and used by another research team at the hospital.[5] In applying the magnetic board, the rater merely places a magnet or series of magnets to which the stimuli have been attached upon one or more rating scales ranging from 0–100. This technique permits quantitative comparisons, allows for modification of responses by the interviewee, and generally evokes the respondent's interest.

The entire schedule was pretested at another institution, and appropriate changes were made. In order to determine instrument and rater reliability, 25 staff members of the 53 originally tested were retested in three to 51 days after the initial interview. All 12 decision-making items were found to

---

[4] A number of other ratings were obtained including, for example, estimates of the competence of specialty groups, the effectiveness of treatment procedures, perceived status levels of all professional groups, and ratings concerning the effectiveness of information flow. For a complete description of these factors, see Mark Lefton, "Staff Participation in a Mental Hospital," Ph.D. thesis, The Ohio State University, 1958, microfilm.

[5] S. Rettig, F. N. Jacobson, and B. Pasamanick, "The Magnetic Board Rating Technique," *Journal of Psychology*, Vol. 45 (April, 1958), pp. 201–6.

be reliable (in only one instance was $P > .01$, and this item was significant at the .05 level). Similarly, the respondents were found to be consistent over time ($P < .01$).

In order to assess differences among professionals in perceptions of decision-making influence, the data were analyzed in two ways. Responses were first analyzed in terms of discrepancy scores, which were computed for each of the 53 respondents and were simply the differences between the estimates given for the amount of influence *desired* in each of the six decision-making categories and the amount *perceived* to be accorded them. A total discrepancy score was then computed for each respondent by combining the discrepancies between estimates of desired and perceived influence scores in all six decision-making areas.[6] These scores were interpreted as an index of the relative degree of the respondents' personal dissatisfaction with respect to the existing authority system and their participation in it.

The use of the total discrepancy score in the analysis seemed justifiable for the following reasons: First, the discrepancy scores in each of the six decision-making areas for all respondents were positively and significantly correlated with the total discrepancy scores. Second, respondents who scored high on the combined discrepancy scores also tended to show high discrepancies in each of the substantive decision categories; t tests computed between the high and low total discrepancy subjects for their discrepancy scores in each of the six decision-making areas revealed significant differences between the two groups in each of these functional areas. Finally, tests for concordance (Kendall's W) indicated that the respondents, whether analyzed by professional group membership or by ward assignment, revealed no consistency with respect to a rank ordering of the six decision-making areas when measured in terms of the discrepancy scores between desired and perceived influence (P values were all greater than .90).[7] These findings strongly suggest that the respondents

---

[6] A second discrepancy score was also computed. This measure was a total directional discrepancy score and differed from the former in that it took into consideration algebraic sign. This scoring revealed that 14 subjects were consistent in indicating that perceived actual influence was generally greater than such influence should be. However, both total discrepancy measures were positively and significantly correlated with each other (rho $= + .80$). This association suggests at least three conclusions: (1) An important degree of consistency existed between the size of the total discrepancy score and the direction of the score itself (i.e., those who viewed their actual influence as less than it should be tended to increase the size of the discrepancy, whereas those who reversed direction tended to minimize the discrepancy). (2) Most subjects thought that their perceived influence was less than it should be. (3) The 14 reversed-direction scores might have been a function of the type of rating instrument employed—a possibility that is supported by the fact that these 14 subjects consistently agreed with those who tended to minimize the discrepancy between ideal and actual amounts of influence.

[7] A comparable analysis was made using the total directional discrepancy scores, showing similar results.

tended to generalize the decision-making discrepancies across all six items and that the total discrepancy score was a reliable index of this tendency.

A second method of analysis involved the use of the actual estimates of *desired* and *perceived* decision-making influence without regard to the discrepancies between them. When these scores were assessed, using group means and by rank ordering the estimates for each respondent, two role profiles resulted. The first of these was interpreted as an index of desired role prerogatives and the second as an index of perceived role prerogatives.

Estimates of the generalized decision-making influence of professional groups were treated in the same fashion as those relevant to desired and perceived role profiles. Mean scores for each professional group, as well as the rank ordering of the judgments of each respondent, thus resulted in a third decision-making dimension. These scores were interpreted as an index of the desired as well as the perceived authority hierarchy in the hospital and, therefore, as an operational portrait of interprofessional relations.

As a means of gathering information about *actual* decision-making influence, two of the authors attended all morning ward staff conferences for a period of five months, during which they recorded information on the ward personnel present, their involvements in conference discussions, the types of decisions made, and by whom they were made. Insofar as possible, the contributions of each person were recorded.

In summary, then, four indices of decision-making influence were derived from the data: (1) a discrepancy score based on the differential between desired and perceived influence, which was interpreted as an index of *dissatisfaction;* (2) the raw scores relevant to desired and perceived decision-making influence, which were regarded as an index of *role conception;* (3) raw scores relevant to the general decision-making influence of professional groups, which became an index of the perceived *hospital power structure;* (4) attendance at ward staff conferences, which resulted in a measure of *actual* decision-making influence.

FINDINGS

Decision Making at Morning Ward Staff Conferences. The systematic recordings of actual decisions made, and by whom (requiring about 100 hours of attendance at ward conferences), revealed the fact that these meetings adhere procedurally to the requisites of medical tradition and practice. Particularly significant is the finding that senior or resident psychiatrists made 96 per cent of all the actual decisions on the five wards. On only two wards did nonmedical staff members make any decisions—two social workers accounted for 4 per cent of the decisions made. In addition, the data revealed that general discussions at these conferences were dominated by the medical staff and those specialists most closely related to them in ward operations, namely, the charge nurses. When ancillary personnel (social workers, psychologists, and occupational therapists) participated in these discussions, they usually did so in response to questions specifically pertinent to their areas of competency.

Perceived Hospital Power Structure. The ward observations reinforced the findings derived from the interview data. Estimates of each profession's general decision-making influence as desired and perceived by the participant professional groups tended to show that respondents recognized the formal power structure in the hospital (see Table 1). With only four exceptions, the personnel rated the five senior psychiatrists as actually having the most influence in the decision-making process; furthermore, they believed that this should be the case. Only slightly subordinate in these respects were the 15 resident psychiatrists. At the other extreme, respondents agreed that the occupational therapists do have and should have the least influence on decisions concerning patients. The intervening groups, although hardly separable in terms of actual ratings and often viewed differently as to rank, were generally ranked in the following order: nurses, clinical psychologists, and social workers.

Comparison of the mean estimates presented in the two parts of Table 1 also indicates that, with very few exceptions, the 53 mental health specialists generally agreed on both the perceived and desired influence indices. When differences did occur they almost always involved the middle three groups of nurses, psychologists, and social workers.

Role Conception Index. The findings relevant to the role conception index provide a second substantive dimension regarding decision making in the type of mental hospital studied. It should be recalled that this index was derived from the raw scores on influence desired and perceived in all six decision areas without regard to the discrepancy between them.

When mean scores of the professional groups for each of the decision areas were analyzed it was found that the groups differed in the resultant rank order distributions of these decision areas (see Table 2). Thus, for example, the nurses both desired and perceived their influence to be highest in the realm of "special supervision" (for example, suicidal precautions) and lowest in the area of "working diagnosis." Clinical psychologists, on the other hand, rated "working diagnosis" highest and "medical treatment" lowest among the six areas in which they desired and perceived their group's influence on decision making.

Such results indicate some of the specific criteria which the several groups differentially take into account in evaluating their own roles in the decision-making process. But they also direct attention to another and perhaps more universal set of operational standards by which roles are assessed. As shown in Table 2, the mean scores tend to be considerably greater for those groups at the top of the power structure (the ward chiefs and especially the residents); in addition, the scores are relatively high for all six decision-making areas. A reverse tendency is exhibited by the

TABLE 1
PROFESSIONALS' MEAN ESTIMATES OF THE GENERAL DECISION-MAKING INFLUENCE—DESIRED AND PERCEIVED—FOR OTHER PARTICIPATING PROFESSIONAL GROUPS

Rater	N	Mean Estimates of Decision-Making Influence Desired for: Psychiatrists:						Mean Estimates of Decision-Making Influence Perceived for: Psychiatrists:					
		Ward Administrators	Residents	Clinical Psychologists	Nurses	Social Workers	Occupational Therapists	Ward Administrators	Residents	Clinical Psychologists	Nurses	Social Workers	Occupational Therapists
Psychiatrists:													
Ward Administrators	5	—	73.0	37.0	49.2	39.0	30.2	—	69.0	33.0	41.0	39.0	18.0
Residents	15	93.3	—	58.9	54.0	46.9	38.4	92.9	—	52.0	54.7	44.6	35.0
Clinical Psychologists	5	63.2	60.2	—	36.8	44.6	25.6	74.2	54.8	—	37.2	35.4	18.2
Nurses	18	92.7	83.4	63.5	—	49.1	38.6	94.1	83.4	49.1	—	52.1	28.4
Social Workers	5	83.2	75.4	62.6	63.0	—	50.6	88.4	74.8	48.0	48.4	—	40.0
Occupational Therapists	5	73.8	76.6	75.0	68.6	65.4	—	90.4	75.2	49.4	67.0	70.6	—

TABLE 2

ESTIMATES OF INFLUENCE—DESIRED AND PERCEIVED—FOR OWN PROFESSION
IN SIX DECISION-MAKING AREAS, BY MEANS

Raters	N	Mean Estimates of Decision-Making Influence Desired for Own Profession Concerning:					
		Occupational Therapy	Working Diagnosis	Patient Privileges	Special Supervision	Medical Treatment	Time-Type Release
Psychiatrists:							
Ward Administrators...	5	51.8	70.6	65.8	73.8	81.8	79.8
Residents..............	15	79.1	87.0	81.3	83.5	81.3	80.2
Clinical Psychologists.....	5	42.0	61.0	40.8	44.6	12.2	44.6
Nurses................	18	60.5	34.3	64.8	77.6	41.4	46.6
Social Workers.........	5	39.0	61.0	59.8	48.2	31.8	84.0
Occupational Therapists..	5	88.0	67.8	62.0	81.8	48.8	67.6

Raters	N	Mean Estimates of Decision-Making Influence Perceived for Own Profession Concerning:					
		Occupational Therapy	Working Diagnosis	Patient Privileges	Special Supervision	Medical Treatment	Time Type Release
Psychiatrists:							
Ward Administrators...	5	50.8	65.8	64.8	59.8	71.8	80.8
Residents..............	15	71.5	79.5	81.8	82.3	80.3	69.5
Clinical Psychologists.....	5	23.6	43.8	23.0	27.4	12.4	19.2
Nurses................	18	47.8	26.8	58.1	71.0	36.4	32.7
Social Workers.........	5	25.0	54.8	44.6	43.4	22.0	65.4
Occupational Therapists..	5	83.4	37.4	36.2	54.8	27.2	39.2

ancillary groups: nurses, social workers, psychologists, and occupational therapists. The mean scores for these groups are generally lower, and the fluctuations from item to item are significantly greater, than those of the physicians.

Thus our findings suggest that one of the basic distinctions to be made between high- and low-echelon groups in a mental hospital ward lies in their perceptions regarding the nature of their roles and in the criteria by which the roles are evaluated. While groups of high standing in the authority hierarchy are much more strongly inclined to perceive their roles on the basis of a generalized power standard than specific prerogatives or requisites, groups of lower position in the hierarchy manifest the opposite tendencies.

The Dissatisfaction Index. It has often been suggested that one of the important concomitants of bureaucracy is the dissatisfaction of those persons who occupy low-echelon positions.[8] The findings based on the

[8] See, e.g., Peter M. Blau, *Bureaucracy in Modern Society* (New York: Random House, 1956), p. 80.

dissatisfaction index tend to corroborate this view. It was found that the discrepancy indicated by each professional group between the amount of influence it should have and the amount it actually does have is inversely related to the degree of influence exercised by that specialty, as observed and recorded at the ward conferences. Similarly, there is an inverse relationship between the size of the decision-making discrepancy score and the perceived position of the specialty in the hospital structure. As shown in Table 3, the discrepancy scores between actual and desired influence increase markedly from the senior psychiatrists to the occupational therapists.

The data presented thus far support the often enunciated proposition that professional mental health specialists are inclined to perceive and to act as members of specific professions who are more or less rigidly bound

TABLE 3
TOTAL MAGNITUDE DISCREPANCY SCORES FOR EACH OF THE
PARTICIPATING PROFESSIONAL GROUPS, BY MEANS

Profession	N	Mean Discrepancy Score*
Psychiatrists		
Ward Administrators	5	56.2
Resident Psychiatrists	15	67.4
Social Workers	5	79.4
Nurses	18	89.4
Clinical Psychologists	5	115.8
Occupational Therapists	5	162.2

* The Mean Discrepancy Score represents a summation of individual discrepancy scores by profession and by ward rather than the difference between group means for each of the two reference points.

by the traditional definitions of their roles and by their position in the power structure.[9] Our remaining data, however, reveal the existence of an additional and, for various reasons, heretofore slighted, correlate of staff evaluations of their participation in the decision-making process. This factor concerns the role of ward *therapeutic policies and practices* in accentuating or minimizing the discrepancies between desired and perceived influence in the decision-making process.

Two profiles resulted from the analysis of the wards. There are those wards, first, which may be characterized as eclectic in therapeutic policy,

---

[9] See H. L. Smith and D. J. Levinson, "The Major Aims and Organizational Characteristics of Mental Hospitals" (pp. 3–8), M. B. Loeb and H. L. Smith, "Relationships Among Organizational Groupings within the Mental Hospital" (pp. 9–13), and T. Parsons, "The Mental Hospital as a Type of Organization" (p. 127), in M. Greenblatt, D. J. Levinson, and R. H. Williams, (eds.), *The Patient and the Mental Hospital* (Glencoe, Ill.: Free Press, 1957); also A. Zander, A. R. Cohen, and E. Stotland, *Role Relations in the Mental Health Professions,* (Ann Arbor: University of Michigan Press, 1957).

in that both organic and nonorganic methods of treatment are employed to a considerable degree. The second general type refers to those wards characterized by an explicit commitment to, and almost exclusive use of, nonorganic treatment methods, especially individual psychotherapy.[10]

On those wards which show greater utilization of organic treatment, staff members, including the psychiatrists, tend to minimize the amount of influence which they should have in making decisions about patient care and treatment. It would seem that the more traditionally "medical" the ward, the less the discrepancy between the desired and perceived amounts of influence (see data for Wards 1, 4, and 5 in Table 4). As also shown in Table 4, the responses of those staff members assigned to the two

TABLE 4

PERCENTAGE OF PATIENTS* RECEIVING ORGANIC-TYPE
TREATMENTS AND TOTAL MAGNITUDE DISCREPANCY
SCORES FOR EACH OF THE FIVE HOSPITAL WARDS,
BY MEANS

Ward	N	Percentage of Patients	Mean Discrepancy Score†
1	10	45	86.4
2	11	17	101.5
3	11	12	113.5
4	10	44	47.8
5	11	36	93.0

* These percentages of patients receiving organic-type treatments were obtained from the medical records. While the percentages reported here are based on data collected during the study period, further examination of the hospital records in connection with another study indicates that they are representative of the usual treatment patterns for these wards.

† This score was derived from the individual discrepancy scores of all professional staff members, including the psychiatrists, on each of the wards.

psychotherapeutically oriented wards reveal an opposite trend. The personnel on these wards indicated the greatest discrepancy between the influence they perceived themselves to have and that which they thought they should have. While these specialists generally agreed with those assigned to the more medically oriented wards as to the actual extent of decision-making influence, they indicated a greater desire for increased involvement for their respective professional groups.[11] In short, whereas

[10] For a more detailed description of these types of wards, see S. Dinitz, M. Lefton, J. E. Simpson, B. Pasamanick, and R. M. Patterson, "The Ward Behavior of Psychiatric Patients," *Social Problems*, Vol. 6 (Fall, 1958), pp. 107–15.

[11] The *t* tests computed between the two extreme ward populations for their mean scores regarding perceived influence in each of the six areas were not significant. Thus differences in discrepancy scores were due primarily to differences in *desired* amounts of influence.

staff assigned to the medically oriented wards were apt to indicate minimal dissatisfaction with the officially promulgated authority system, those assigned to psychotherapeutically committed units, although equally cognizant of the existing structure, were inclined to view the official system in a highly critical manner.[12]

DISCUSSION

The findings presented clearly indicate that actual and perceived staff participation in the ongoing decision-making process of the mental hospital considered here reflects the influence of several distinct features of hospital organization and functioning. Most important is the fact that staff involvement adheres to the requisites of medical tradition and practice; the interview data and our first-hand observations are mutually supportive on this point. Thus the frequently stated thesis regarding the role of professional group membership as a determinant of both actual and perceived staff involvement in the decision-making process of the psychiatric hospital is corroborated. These findings would seem to add further evidence for the point of view that bureaucracy, in some measure, is dysfunctional for the attainment of the goals of the mental hospital. This thesis holds that incorporation of certain bureaucratic features (for example, hierarchies of authority and prestige) into the clinical milieu serves to create intrastaff stresses and tensions that are undesirable for what is regarded as the optimum condition for effective psychotherapy.[13]

While it was not the intention of this study to test explicitly the merits or the validity of this thesis, the design permits examination of its fundamental argument, namely, that dissatisfaction on the part of ancillary staff members is a necessary consequence of bureaucratic organization. Exploration of this particular claim resulted in the discernment of the influence of ward therapeutic orientations in modifying or accentuating the magnitude of the discrepancies between desired and perceived decision-making influence of the 53 mental health specialists who were interviewed. Such a finding strongly suggests that the "dissatisfaction" thesis regarding low-echelon personnel should be further examined. Additional research is especially important for, as far as the mental hospital is concerned, it seems that bureaucratic rigidities are viewed more negatively by precisely those personnel operating in wards (the psychotherapeutic wards) the orientation of which is specifically designed to minimize the presumed inadequacies of formal organization. The reverse situation

---

[12] These ward differences become more pronounced when it is recognized that personnel are assigned randomly to the five hospital wards. An analysis of relevant background factors (e.g., length of time in the profession, in the hospital, and on the ward) reveals no significant differences between the ward populations.

[13] See esp. Stanton and Schwartz, op. cit., chaps. 13, 14 , and 15.

occurs on those wards (the organically oriented wards) the structural aspects of which have been heretofore severely criticized as perpetrators of staff discontent. Thus it is clear that, although these mental health professionals operate within a formally structured setting and perceive this organization as the official and functional pattern for the hospital as a whole, their views regarding specific involvement of their own specialty groups are significantly influenced by the actual situational context—the wards—in which they work.

It is apparent that personnel assigned to the more psychotherapeutically oriented wards are led to believe that they are to exert greater initiative and responsibility in the ongoing decision-making process. But in reality they are also aware that they cannot circumvent the formally prescribed medical hierarchy. Accordingly, their degree of dissatisfaction is relatively high. However, personnel assigned to the more organically oriented wards work in a contrasting context which is in relative harmony with the official hospital structure. This situation serves to reduce the discrepancy between expectations and reality; consequently the degree of staff dissatisfaction is relatively low.

SUMMARY

This paper attempts to relate the actual influence of professional personnel on decisions concerning patient care and treatment to staff perceptions of the extent of this influence and of how much influence they should have. Actual decisions and participation in their formulation were observed and recorded at ward staff conferences. Perceptions of influence were obtained in lengthy structured interviews with all professional staff members.

The findings suggest that (1) staff personnel in the type of mental hospital herein considered tend to perceive their influence and participation in the decision-making process in terms of their professional group membership rather than as private operatives; (2) ward policy and particularly therapeutic practices are crucial in modifying or accentuating these professional and parochial perceptions; and (3) perceptions of influence and actually observed influence are only indistinctly related except at the highest professional levels where the two coalesce.

41. GROUP INFLUENCE ON INDIVIDUAL RISK TAKING*[1]

Michael A. Wallach, Nathan Kogan, and Daryl J. Bem[2]

What are the effects of group interaction on risk and conservatism in decision making? By risk and conservatism we mean the extent to which the decision maker is willing to expose himself to possible failure in the pursuit of a desirable goal. Consider the situation in which several individuals working separately arrive at a series of decisions and then are brought together to arrive at a group consensus regarding those decisions. What relationship should one expect to find between the individual decisions and the group consensus?

On the basis of prior experimental studies of individual and group judgment (e.g., Schachter, 17; see also the section on group pressures and group standards in Cartwright & Zander, 4, pp. 165–341), we should predict an averaging effect, i.e., group decisions randomly distributed around the average of the prediscussion individual decisions. Such an effect would seem to imply a process of minimizing individual losses or minimizing the maximum individual concession. The cited studies report that inducements toward compromise and concession seem to be exerted most strongly toward group members whose initial individual views are most deviant from the central tendency.

An equally if not more compelling alternative hypothesis is that the group discussion will lead to increased conservatism, relative to the average of the prior individual decisions. One may cite the observations of Whyte (27), among others, concerning the outcomes of conferences and meetings in bureaucratic organizations. Whyte argues that the use of committees and teams in the management of business and other kinds of enterprises leads inexorably to an inhibition of boldness and risk taking, a concentration on

* Reprinted from *Journal of Abnormal and Social Psychology*, Vol. 65, No. 2 (1962), pp. 75–86.

[1] This research was supported by a grant (G-17818) from the National Science Foundation. A master's thesis by J. A. F. Stoner at M.I.T.'s School of Industrial Management, with D. G. Marquis and M. A. Wallach as faculty advisers, was instrumental in inspiring the present investigation. We are greatly indebted to J. A. F. Stoner and D. G. Marquis for their aid and advice, and to V. Raimy and M. Wertheimer for facilities at the University of Colorado in Boulder. Thanks also are due S. Messick and A. Myers for comments.

[2] Michael A. Wallach, formerly of Massachusetts Institute of Technology, now at Duke University; Nathan Kogan, Educational Testing Service; Daryl J. Bem, Carnegie Institute of Technology.

the conservative course when a choice must be made between more and less risky courses of action. How are such effects to be explained? First, it may be that the very nature of the group process or atmosphere encourages such a trend: there may be a fear, for example, of appearing foolhardy to others. Alternatively, or in addition, it is possible that the mechanism underlying an increase in conservatism is one of greater influence being exerted within the group by members whose individual conservatism tendencies are stronger. These two interpretations are not incompatible, of course, since the group process, if encouraging of conservatism, will enhance the influence of the initially more conservative members.

Finally, consideration should be given to the remaining and least likely possibility—that group interaction will eventuate in increased risk taking relative to the average of the prior decisions of the group members working separately. In this regard, Osborn (15) has reported that group interaction may lead to quite radical, bold, problem solutions. While Osborn claims that special conditions must exist if such effects are to be observed, attempts to produce such conditions experimentally (Taylor, Berry, & Block, 21) have yielded no evidence whatever for the so-called "brainstorming" phenomenon. Thibaut and Kelley (22, pp. 267–68) discuss the conflicting evidence on this issue. We might, in passing, also mention mass or crowd phenomena, in which extreme actions taken by groups are well beyond the capacities of the members of such groups considered individually (Brown, 3; Turner & Killian, 23). The relevance of such mass phenomena to group decision making in a laboratory context, however, is probably quite remote. In sum, increased risk taking as a consequence of group interaction appeared to us to be the least feasible of the three possibilities discussed above.

An examination of the literature reveals little experimental research which addresses itself explicitly to the problem of the present investigation. Lonergan and McClintock (12) report that membership in an interdependent group led to no significant move toward greater conservatism or risk taking in a betting situation involving monetary gain or loss. Since the group situation was so structured that a consensus was not required, however, this experiment is not directly relevant to the aims of the present study. Hunt and Rowe (7) report no difference between three-person groups and individuals in riskiness of investment decisions. However, the brevity of the group interaction (15 minutes) and the disruptive influence of having the various groups meet within sight of each other in a large room render their results inconclusive. Atthowe (1), comparing individual and dyadic decisions in the choice of the better of two alternative wagers, found greater conservatism in the dyadic decisions. But the relevance of this result to the problem at hand is called into question when we learn that the alternative wagers were presented to the subjects as "problems taken from the mathematical reasoning section of an advanced intelligence test and arranged as wagers" (p. 115). This could well contribute to a conservative strategy.

We turn, finally, to a study by Stoner (19), which provides the starting point for the research to be reported. Using male graduate students of industrial management as subjects, Stoner observed that a group consensus regarding degree of risk to be taken in resolving a "life dilemma" situation deviated from the average of prediscussion decisions in the direction of greater risk taking. These results took us by surprise. We wondered whether the finding could be generalized to other subject populations, whether it was an enduring effect, and whether it might have anything to do with relationships between risk taking and perceived group influence.

One issue that arises in interpreting Stoner's study concerns the effect that expectations about one's role might have on the results. Thus, a group of male graduate students of industrial management might make more risky decisions qua group than would each such student individually—the result obtained by Stoner—because the presence of their peers reminds each that one of the positively sanctioned attributes of the business manager role which they occupy or aspire to occupy is a willingness to take risks in their decision making. Stoner's use of a male business school sample, therefore, leaves open the possibility that his results may be a function of this particular group's self-assigned professional role alone. It also is possible that a group of males, regardless of their professional role, might make more risky decisions when gathered together because the presence of other males serves as a reminder that one of the expected indications of manliness in our society is a willingness to be bold and daring in decision making. Conversely, a group of females might make more conservative decisions when gathered together, or at least might fail to shift in a risky direction, since risk-taking tendencies are not likely to be mutually reinforced in groups for whom risk is not a positive social value (see, e.g., Komarovsky, 10; Milner, 14; Wallach & Caron, 24).

In the present experiment, we shall employ samples of male and female undergraduates enrolled in a liberal arts curriculum at a large state university. If the effects observed by Stoner (19) are found to hold for both of the above samples, this would constitute strong evidence for the generality of the phenomenon and its independence of occupational and sex role considerations. Furthermore, the use of previously unacquainted subjects whose ascribed status is initially equal will insure that whatever effects are obtained cannot be attributed to an association between initially high or low status, on the one hand, and risk or conservatism, on the other. If initial status levels were unequal, low status individuals might simply adopt the standards of those whose status is high—an outcome which would tell us nothing about the effect of group interactional processes as such on individual risk taking.

One should distinguish initially ascribed status from status indices (e.g., perceived influence and popularity) derived from the group experience. Since such indices may bear some relation to initial risk-taking level, the necessary sociometric-type judgments will be obtained.

Finally, evidence will be presented with regard to the following two questions: Is the group-induced effect on risk taking limited only to the group member's overt compliance in the group setting, or does it also extend to his covert acceptance when he makes postgroup decisions as an individual (see Festinger, 5; Kelley & Thibaut, 8)? To what extent are group effects on individual decision making relatively enduring or short-lived?

METHOD

Assessment of Level of Conservatism or Risk Taking

The instrument used for assessing level of conservatism or risk taking, as developed in some of our prior research (Kogan & Wallach, 9; Wallach & Kogan, 25, 26), is called an "opinion questionnaire" and contains descriptions of 12 hypothetical situations. The central person in each situation must choose between two courses of action, one of which is more risky than the other but also more rewarding if successful. For each situation the subject must indicate the lowest probability of success he would accept before recommending that the potentially more rewarding alternative be chosen. The probabilities listed are 1, 3, 5, 7, and 9 chances of success in 10, plus a final category (scored as 10) in which the subject can refuse to recommend the risky alternative no matter how high its likelihood of success.

The situations were so designed as to cover a wide range of content, and may be summarized as follows:

1. An electrical engineer may stick with his present job at a modest but adequate salary, or may take a new job offering considerably more money but no long-term security.

2. A man with a severe heart ailment must seriously curtail his customary way of life if he does not undergo a delicate medical operation which might cure him completely or might prove fatal.

3. A man of moderate means may invest some money he recently inherited in secure "blue chip" low-return securities or in more risky securities that offer the possibility of large gains.

4. A captain of a college football team, in the final seconds of a game with the college's traditional rival, may choose a play that is almost certain to produce a tie score, or a more risky play that would lead to sure victory if successful, sure defeat if not.

5. The president of an American corporation which is about to expand may build a new plant in the United States where returns on the investment would be moderate, or may decide to build in a foreign country with an unstable political history, where, however, returns on the investment would be very high.

6. A college senior planning graduate work in chemistry may enter University X where, because of rigorous standards, only a fraction of the graduate students manage to receive the Ph.D., or may enter University Y, which has a poorer reputation but where almost every graduate student receives the Ph.D.

7. A low-ranked participant in a national chess tournament, playing an early match with the top-favored man, has the choice of attempting or not trying a deceptive but risky maneuver which might lead to quick victory if successful or almost certain defeat if it fails.

8. A college senior with considerable musical talent must choose between the secure course of going on to medical school and becoming a physician, or the risky course of embarking on the career of a concert pianist.

9. An American prisoner-of-war in World War II must choose between possible escape with the risk of execution if caught, or remaining in the camp where privations are severe.

10. A successful businessman with strong feelings of civic responsibility must decide whether or not to run for Congress on the ticket of a minority party whose campaign funds are limited.

11. A research physicist, just beginning a five-year appointment at a university, may spend the time working on a series of short-term problems which he would be sure to solve but which would be of lesser importance, or on a very important but very difficult problem with the risk of nothing to show for his five years of effort.

12. An engaged couple must decide, in the face of recent arguments suggesting some sharp differences of opinion, whether or not to get married. Discussions with a marriage counselor indicate that a happy marriage, while possible, would not be assured.

The response categories are arrayed from chances of 1 in 10 upward for the odd items and in the reverse order for the even items, thus counterbalancing for any possible order-preference effect in choice of probability levels. An overall conservatism-risk-taking score is derived by adding the scores for the separate items. The larger this score, the greater the subject's conservatism.

Our prior research, cited above, yielded split-half Spearman-Brown reliability coefficients ranging from .53 to .80 for various age and sex samples, suggesting that the instrument possesses satisfactory internal consistency. The results of the present experiment will provide evidence, furthermore, of high test-retest reliability.

Regarding the instrument's construct validity as a risk-taking measure, our earlier studies, cited above, have yielded findings consistent with a risk-taking interpretation. For example, degree of conservatism as measured with the present instrument increases with age from young adulthood to old age for both males and females and increases with degree of subjective probability of personal failure in a motor skill game with actual motor skill controlled.

Experimental Condition

Subjects. The subjects were invited to participate in an experiment which would take no longer than two hours and for which remuneration would be provided. Six subjects were scheduled for any one time, with every effort being made to insure that previously acquainted persons were not signed up for the same session. A total of 167 subjects participated in the experimental condition—14 all-male groups and 14 all-female groups.[3] The subjects were liberal arts students enrolled in summer session courses at the University of Colorado in Boulder.

Prediscussion Individual Decisions. The experiment was run in a seminar room around a very long table. For the initial administration of the questionnaire, subjects took alternate seats with the experimenter at one end. The six subjects were requested to read the instructions to the questionnaire and to look over the first item. The experimenter then emphasized two points in further standard instructions: that the more risky alternative is always assumed to be more desirable than the safer course, if the former should prove successful; that the odds which the subject marks indicate the lowest odds the subject would be willing to take and still advise the central figure to give the risky alternative a try. The subjects were told there was no time limit, that they should consider each of the 12 situations carefully, and that they could return to an earlier question if they wished to. The conservatism-risk instrument then was filled out individually by each of the six subjects in a group administration session that took about 20 minutes. To avoid giving any of the subjects the feeling that they were being rushed, the questionnaires were not collected until all had finished.

Group Discussion and Consensual Group Decisions. Without having had any prior expectation that they would be requested to discuss their decisions, the six subjects were then asked to move together into a discussion group at one end of the table. They now each were given another copy of the questionnaire, and a stand-up cardboard placard with the identification letter K, L, M, N, O, or P on it was placed before each subject. The experimenter then told them that the questionnaire now before them was the same one they just finished taking. They had taken it, he continued, to familarize them with all the situations and to give them some idea where they might stand on each. Now he wanted the group to discuss each question in turn and arrive at a unanimous decision on each. This time they could not return to a question, but rather had to discuss each one until the group decision was reached before going on to the next. When the group reached its decision on a question, all subjects were to mark it on their questionnaires in order to have a record. The group would

---

[3] Of the 14 male groups, 13 contained six subjects each, and one contained five subjects. A subject in one of the six-person male groups misunderstood instructions for the prediscussion individual decisions, so that his decision scores were removed prior to analysis. All 14 of the female groups contained six subjects each. A subject in each of two female groups misunderstood instructions for the prediscussion individual decisions, so that the decision scores of these two females were removed prior to analysis.

be completely on its own, the experimenter not participating in the discussion at all.

The experimenter then retired to the other end of the table in order to be as far from the group as possible. A question that often arose before discussion had started was what to do if a deadlock occurs. The experimenter's standard reply was:

Most groups are able to come to some decision if those who disagree will restate their reasons, and if the problem is reread carefully.

Most groups succeeded in reaching a unanimous decision on most items, although an occasional deadlock did occur on one or another item. The group discussions were of such a nature as to indicate that the participants were highly involved in the decision tasks.

Postdiscussion Individual Decisions. After the discussion was over, the experimenter proceeded to ask the group members to spread apart for some further individual work and to take their questionnaires and identification placards with them. In standard instructions, he requested them to go back over the situations and indicate their own present personal decisions with a "P." He noted that while in some cases the subjects may have agreed with the group decision, in other cases they may have disagreed with it. In the former cases the P would be placed on the same line as the check mark; in the latter cases, on a different line.

While the consensual decisions by the group would indicate the public effect of the discussion process, the private postdiscussion decisions made once again on an individual basis would indicate whether the discussion process had influenced covert acceptance as well as public compliance.

Rankings for Influence and Popularity. After the postdiscussion individual decisions had been made, a ranking sheet was passed out to each subject requesting that he rank everyone in the group (identified by their letter placards), including himself, in terms of how much each influenced the final group decision. Then each subject was requested to rank everyone in the group (except, of course, himself) in terms of how much he would like to become better acquainted with each.

The rankings for influence provided the information needed for examining possible relationships between strength of individual risk-taking or conservatism tendencies, on the one hand, and degree of influence in the group, on the other. If such relationships existed, it seemed to be of interest to determine whether they were specific to perceived influence or would prove to be dependent upon the subject's popularity; hence the second set of rankings.

Secrecy Instructions. After the ranking sheets were collected, the experimenter told the group that the research would be carried out in coming weeks, and that they could now appreciate why it would be important for the content of the experiment to be kept secret, since a person who even knew that the group would be discussing the same questions which he had filled out individually would have a tendency to mark logically defensible answers instead of his true opinion, etc. The subjects therefore all were sworn to secrecy. Various indications suggest that this pledge was faithfully kept.

Post-Postdiscussion Individual Decisions. A further session of individual decision making took place approximately two to six weeks later for some subjects. These subjects individually were given the conservatism-risk questionnaire a third time and were asked to reconsider the situations. The standard instructions emphasized that the experimenter was not interested in testing the subject's memory, but rather wanted the subject truly to *reconsider* each situation. The instructions thus oriented the subjects away from simply trying to recall their prior decisions. Each subject was paid for this further work.

Control Condition

Subjects. Control subjects were obtained in the same way as the experimental subjects, and likewise received remuneration for their work. The controls were signed up to participate in two sessions: the first to last about 20 minutes; the second, exactly one week later, to last about 15 minutes. A total of 51 subjects participated in the control condition—24 males and 27 females. Like the experimental subjects, the controls were liberal arts students enrolled in summer session courses at the University of Colorado in Boulder.

First Individual Decision Session. The first session was identical to the prediscussion individual decision part of the experimental condition. From six to eight subjects of the same sex, scheduled for the same time, filled out the conservatism-risk instrument while sitting together in physical conditions identical to those of the experimental subjects and at approximately the same time of day as the experimental subjects had worked. Exactly the same instructions were provided as had been given the experimental subjects.

After the first session, the control subjects were sworn to secrecy. They also were told that they would be taking a similar questionnaire the next week, and that it was extremely important that they not discuss it with one another nor with anyone else, since such discussion might affect the way they filled out next week's questionnaire.

Second Individual Decision Session. The same control subjects who had participated in a particular first individual decision session came back exactly one week later. After checking that no discussion had taken place in the intervening week among the controls, the experimenter handed out new copies of the questionnaire and explained that this questionnaire was identical to the one taken last week. Each subject was requested to go back over the situations and reconsider them, the experimenter emphasizing that he was not interested in testing the subject's memory but rather wanted the subject truly to *reconsider* each situation. The instructions were so designed, therefore, as to dissuade the subject from assuming that the most socially acceptable thing to do would be to try to make the same decisions that he had made a week ago. Change was encouraged rather than discouraged. Control subjects were sworn to secrecy again at the end of the second session.

RESULTS

Consensual Group Decisions Compared with Prediscussion Individual Decisions

Tables 1 and 2 examine, for male and female groups, respectively, the significance of the conservatism difference between the mean of the prediscussion individual decisions made by the members of each group and that group's consensual decisions. The basic test is carried out using the total conservatism score, which consists of all 12 item scores combined. Tests also are carried out for each item separately.

In the case of the total score, a group's difference score is the sum of the 12 unanimous group decision scores minus the average of the prediscussion total individual decision scores for the six members.[4] Since larger scores indicate greater conservatism, a negative difference (or score decrease) indicates a shift in the risky direction. A *t* test is used to determine whether the 14 difference scores for the groups of each sex are significantly different from zero (McNemar, 13, pp. 108–9).[5] These total score data indicate a move in the risky direction significant beyond the .001 level for the 14 male groups and a move in the risky direction significant beyond the .005 level for the 14 female groups. Furthermore, the degree of shift is not significantly different for the two sexes.

In the case of the scores for a single item, a group's difference score consists of the unanimous group decision on that item minus the average of the prediscussion individual decision scores on that item for the six members. Once again a negative difference or score decrease indicates a shift in the risky direction, and a *t* test is applied to determine whether the difference scores for all groups that reached a unanimous decision on the item in question are significantly different from zero. For both the male and female groups, we find that ten of the 12 items show shifts in the risky direction, seven of them significant in each case. Five of those seven are the same for both sexes. Only two items show any indication for either sex of not sharing in the general shift toward greater risk taking: Items 5 and 12. It should be noted that these two items exhibited, in our previous research,

---

[4] Any deadlocked item is, of course, not included in either term for the group in question.

[5] All significance levels cited in this study are based on two-tailed tests.

TABLE 1

SIGNIFICANCE OF CONSERVATISM DIFFERENCE BETWEEN MEAN OF
PREDISCUSSION INDIVIDUAL DECISIONS FOR A GROUP'S MEMBERS
AND GROUP'S CONSENSUAL DECISION: MALES

Item	Mean Difference*	Number of Groups†	t
All combined	−9.4	14	6.46¶
1	−1.0	14	4.34¶
2	−0.2	14	<1.00
3	−1.1	13	2.19‡
4	−1.8	13	6.18¶
5	+0.1	13	<1.00
6	−1.2	13	3.35§
7	−2.0	14	9.64¶
8	−1.1	14	1.97
9	−1.0	10	3.67§
10	−0.4	13	<1.00
11	−1.1	12	4.37‖
12	+0.8	11	2.34‡

* In Tables 1, 2, 3, 4, 6, and 7, a negative difference signifies a risky shift, a positive difference signifies a conservative shift.
† In Tables 1 and 2, number of groups for an item is less than 14 when one or more groups deadlocked on that item. Any deadlocked item is, of course, not included when calculating scores for all items combined.
‡ $p < .05$.
§ $p < .01$.
‖ $p < .005$.
¶ $p < .001$.

TABLE 2

SIGNIFICANCE OF CONSERVATISM DIFFERENCE BETWEEN MEAN OF
PREDISCUSSION INDIVIDUAL DECISIONS FOR A GROUP'S MEMBERS
AND GROUP'S CONSENSUAL DECISION: FEMALES

Item	Mean Difference	Number of Groups	t
All combined	−9.4	14	3.91‡
1	−1.0	13	4.17‡
2	−0.6	14	1.65
3	−0.4	14	1.12
4	−1.4	14	2.60§
5	+0.7	14	1.90
6	−0.8	13	2.63§
7	−2.0	12	3.21†
8	−1.7	14	5.26‖
9	−0.8	12	1.19
10	−1.5	13	3.18†
11	−0.9	13	2.28*
12	+0.6	6	2.00

* $p < .05$.
† $p < .01$.
‡ $p < .005$.
§ $p < .025$.
‖ $p < .001$.

the lowest correlations with the overall risk-conservatism score, suggesting that they are relatively impure measures of the psychological dimension being tapped by the other ten items.

In sum, the evidence from Tables 1 and 2 indicates a strong move toward greater risk taking when groups arrive at unanimous decisions, compared with the risk levels ventured by the same persons in prediscussion individual decisions. Furthermore, this move toward greater risk taking obtains for females as well as for males.

A further question concerns the extent to which the risky shift is consistent from one group to another. Consider one example of several consistency tests that have been conducted, all of which yield highly similar results. Suppose we define a group as showing a risky shift from prediscussion individual decisions to consensual group decisions if the difference score for its total score, as defined above, is a negative one. Fourteen out of 14 male groups and 12 out of 14 female groups are found to move in the risky direction, both results being very significant by a sign test. Such a finding demonstrates, therefore, that the risky shift phenomenon is quite consistent across groups.

Postdiscussion Individual Decisions Compared with Prediscussion Individual Decisions

In Tables 3 and 4 we present, once again for male and female groups, respectively, the significance of the difference between the mean of the prediscussion individual decisions and the mean of the postdiscussion individual decisions made by the members of each group. The basic test once again is provided by the total conservatism score, but tests also are presented for each item separately.

For the total score, a group's difference score consists of the average of the postdiscussion total individual decision scores for the members minus the average of the prediscussion total individual decision scores for the same members. Negative difference scores again indicate risky shifts, and a t test is applied to determine whether the 14 difference scores for the groups of each sex are significantly different from zero. We find, once again, a shift in the risky direction significant beyond the .001 level for the 14 male groups, and a risky shift significant beyond the .005 level for the 14 female groups. As before, the degree of shift is not significantly different for the two sexes.

Turning to the scores for each separate item, a group's difference score consists of the average of the postdiscussion individual decision scores on that item minus the average of the prediscussion individual decision scores on that item. With a negative difference score indicating a risky shift and a t test applied to indicate whether the 14 difference scores for each sex on an item are significantly different from zero, we find that nine of the 12 items show separate significant shifts in the risky direction for the male

TABLE 3

SIGNIFICANCE OF CONSERVATISM DIFFERENCE BETWEEN MEAN OF
PREDISCUSSION INDIVIDUAL DECISIONS FOR A GROUP'S MEMBERS
AND MEAN OF POSTDISCUSSION INDIVDIUAL DECISIONS FOR
A GROUP'S MEMBERS: MALES

Item	Mean Difference	Number of Groups	t
All combined.................	− 10.4	14	9.12§
1...........................	− 1.0	14	4.32§
2...........................	− 0.6	14	2.87*
3...........................	− 1.1	14	3.04†
4...........................	− 1.7	14	8.14§
5...........................	+ 0.1	14	<1.00
6...........................	− 1.1	14	3.79‡
7...........................	− 1.8	14	7.80§
8...........................	− 1.1	14	3.54‡
9...........................	− 1.1	14	3.99‡
10...........................	− 0.3	14	<1.00
11...........................	− 0.8	14	4.36§
12...........................	+ 0.1	14	<1.00

* $p < .02$.
† $p < .01$.
‡ $p < .005$.
§ $p < .001$.

groups (with one additional item shifting nonsignificantly in the same direction) and that eight of the 12 items show separate significant shifts toward greater risk taking for the female groups (with two additional items shifting nonsignificantly in that direction). The eight items showing significant risky shifts for the females are among the nine showing significant risky shifts for the males. Items five and 12 once again are the only ones for either sex showing any indication of not sharing in the general shift toward greater risk taking found in both sexes.

There is clear evidence, therefore, that postdiscussion individual decisions exhibit a strong move toward greater risk taking when compared with prediscussion individual decisions arrived at by the same persons, and do so for both sexes. The group discussion process, in other words, seems to have an effect on private attitudes (postdiscussion individual decisions) that is just as significant as its effect on publicly expressed views (unanimous group decisions).

Once again we may inquire about the extent to which the risky shift is consistent from group to group. Several consistency tests have been carried out, all yielding highly similar results. As an example, suppose we define a group as exhibiting a shift in the risky direction from prediscussion to postdiscussion individual decisions if the difference score for its total score, as defined in this section, is a negative one. Fourteen out of 14 male groups and 12 out of 14 female groups are found to shift in the risky direction, both results being quite significant by a sign test. Such a finding

TABLE 4
SIGNIFICANCE OF CONSERVATISM DIFFERENCE BETWEEN MEAN OF
PREDISCUSSION INDIVIDUAL DECISIONS FOR A GROUP'S MEMBERS
AND MEAN OF POSTDISCUSSION INDIVIDUAL DECISIONS FOR
A GROUP'S MEMBERS: FEMALES

Item	Mean Difference	Number of Groups	t
All combined	−8.2	14	3.67†
1	−0.9	14	5.09§
2	−0.7	14	2.67*
3	−0.6	14	2.58‡
4	−1.4	14	3.40†
5	+0.6	14	1.85
6	−0.8	14	2.90*
7	−1.7	14	3.56†
8	−1.2	14	4.44§
9	−0.5	14	<1.00
10	−0.7	14	1.95
11	−0.9	14	2.89*
12	+0.7	14	3.66†

* $p < .02$.
† $p < .005$.
‡ $p < .025$.
§ $p < .001$.

demonstrates, therefore, that the risky shift phenomenon is quite consistent across groups in regard to covert acceptance as well as overt compliance.

Control Subjects

To insure that the move toward greater risk taking just described actually is a result of the group discussion process, we must turn to the findings for the control subjects. The comparability of control and experimental subjects is indicated in Table 5. We note that, in the case both of males and females, the experimental and control subjects have approximately the same initial total conservatism scores and also are approximately

TABLE 5
COMPARABILITY OF EXPERIMENTAL AND CONTROL SUBJECTS
IN INITIAL CONSERVATISM AND AGE

| | MEAN INITIAL OVERALL CONSERVATISM | | | | MEAN AGE | | | |
| | Males | | Females | | Males | | Females | |
Subject	M	N	M	N	M	N	M	N
Experimental	66.9	82*	65.6	82*	20.7	82†	20.3	84
Control	68.3	24	64.6	27	21.0	24	20.7	27
t	0.41		0.34		0.41		0.67	

* Initial overall conservatism scores were available for 164 of the experimental subjects. See Footnote 2 in text.
† One subject forgot to list his age, and one group contained five rather than six subjects.

TABLE 6

SIGNIFICANCE OF CONSERVATISM DIFFERENCE BETWEEN FIRST AND
SECOND DECISIONS BY MALE CONTROL SUBJECTS

Item	Mean Difference	Number of Subjects	t^*
All combined...................	+1.5	24	<1.00
1............................	+0.4	24	<1.00
2............................	−0.3	24	<1.00
3............................	+0.3	24	<1.00
4............................	+0.8	24	2.00
5............................	−0.4	24	1.06
6............................	0.0	24	<1.00
7............................	+0.4	24	1.03
8............................	+0.5	24	1.63
9............................	−0.1	24	<1.00
10............................	+0.1	24	<1.00
11............................	+0.1	24	<1.00
12............................	−0.4	24	1.42

* All t values ns.

the same in age.[6] Item-by-item comparisons of experimental and control subjects of each sex on initial conservatism scores also were carried out and show that controls and experimentals within sex obtain highly similar scores.

In Tables 6 and 7 we present, for male and female control subjects, respectively, the significance of the difference between decisions made

TABLE 7

SIGNIFICANCE OF CONSERVATISM DIFFERENCE BETWEEN FIRST AND
SECOND DECISIONS BY FEMALE CONTROL SUBJECTS

Item	Mean Difference	Number of Subjects	t
All combined...................	−2.2	27	1.26
1............................	−0.4	27	<1.00
2............................	−0.2	27	<1.00
3............................	−1.0	27	2.61*
4............................	−0.4	27	1.12
5............................	−0.3	27	<1.00
6............................	−0.2	27	<1.00
7............................	0.0	27	<1.00
8............................	0.0	27	<1.00
9............................	+0.2	27	<1.00
10............................	+0.3	27	1.03
11............................	−0.3	27	<1.00
12............................	+0.1	27	<1.00

* $p < .02$.

[6] It might also be mentioned that, in confirmation of earlier findings (Wallach & Kogan, 25, 26), there is no sex difference in initial total conservatism scores for either the experimental or the control subjects.

during the first and the second sessions. It will be recalled that one week intervened between these two sessions, and that instructions for the second session requested the subjects not to try simply to remember what they had marked before, but to reconsider their decisions. It is evident that the total conservatism score shows no shift from first to second session for either sex. Turning to the separate tests carried out on each item, we find that none of the 12 items shows a significant shift for the males, and only one of the 12 items shows a significant shift for the females. When no group discussion and achievement of group consensus intervenes, then, there is no systematic shift toward greater risk taking or greater conservatism, and this despite instructions that encourage shifts by emphasizing that we are not interested in the subjects' memories.

The data for the control subjects also provide us with an opportunity for determining the test-retest reliability of the conservatism-risk instrument, with one week intervening and under instructions that encourage change rather than constancy. For the 24 male subjects, the product-moment correlation coefficient between total conservatism scores in the first and second sessions is .78. For the 27 female subjects, the same correlation coefficient is .82. Test-retest reliability of the instrument, therefore, is quite high.

Prediscussion Risk Taking and Influence in the Group

Our data concerning perceived influence within the group consisted in each individual's ranking of all group members, including himself, in terms of how much each influenced the group's decisions. A first question to ask of these influence rankings is: How consistent are they from member to member within a group? To determine the degree of agreement among a group's members in their rankings of one another for influence, Kendall's coefficient of concordance (Siegel, 18, pp. 229–38) was applied to each group's influence rankings. If the members of a group agree regarding who among themselves are more influential and who less so, then W will be significantly large. Table 8 presents the results of these tests for all 28 groups. It is evident that agreement in influence rankings is quite high: the degree of agreement is significant for all 14 of the male groups and for 11 of the 14 female groups.

Given this high agreement among group members in their rankings of one another for influence, an approximate overall estimate of degree of influence for a given group member was obtained by averaging the influence ranks that had been assigned to that person by all members of the group (including that person). The lower the average, the greater that subject's perceived influence (i.e., the higher the assigned influence ranks for that person). These average influence scores for the subjects of each sex were correlated with the initial total conservatism scores obtained by the same subjects. The resulting product-moment correlation coefficients

TABLE 8

DEGREE OF AGREEMENT AMONG GROUP MEMBERS IN
RANKINGS OF ONE ANOTHER FOR INFLUENCE*

Group	Males N	W	Group	Females N	W
1	6	.64‡	1	6	.85‡
2	6	.55‡	2	6	.61‡
3	6	.74‡	3	6	.31
4	6	.72‡	4	6	.79‡
5	6	.70‡	5	6	.47‡
6	6	.50‡	6	6	.67‡
7	5	.56†	7	6	.13
8	6	.50‡	8	6	.59‡
9	6	.62‡	9	6	.59‡
10	6	.66‡	10	6	.69‡
11	6	.66‡	11	6	.83‡
12	6	.55‡	12	6	.80‡
13	6	.54‡	13	6	.70‡
14	6	.73‡	14	6	.30‡

* Kendall's coefficient of concordance.
† $p < .05$.
‡ $p < .01$.

are shown in Table 9. They are significant beyond the .005 and .05 levels for the 82 males and the 82 females, respectively: persons higher in initial risk taking are rated as having more influence on the group decisions.

Average popularity scores for each group member were constructed by averaging the popularity rankings assigned by all the other members of the group. We note in Table 9 that there emerges a very strong relationship

TABLE 9

PRODUCT-MOMENT CORRELATIONS AMONG INITIAL CONSERVATISM,
INFLUENCE, AND POPULARITY*

	Males ($N = 82$)† r	Females ($N = 82$)† r
Initial overall risk taking and influence............32**		.22§
Initial overall risk taking and popularity...........15		−.04
Influence and popularity........................72††		.54††
Initial overall risk taking and influence, popularity held constant‡.....................30¶		.28‖

* Small score values signify greater risk taking, greater influence, and greater popularity.
† While all influence and popularity scores are based on the 167 subjects in the experimental condition, the correlations are based on the 164 of those subjects for whom initial overall risk taking scores were available.
‡ Partial correlation coefficients.
§ $p < .05$.
‖ $p < .02$.
¶ $p < .01$.
** $p < .005$.
†† $p < .001$.

between this average popularity score and the average influence score for both the male and the female group members: persons rated high in influence also tend to be rated high in popularity. This general relationship has, of course, been known for some time (see, e.g., Back, 2; Horowitz, Lyons, and Perlmutter, 6; Tagiuri and Kogan, 20), so that our obtaining it here increases our confidence in the respective measures being used to assess influence and popularity. It is further evident in Table 9, however, that degree of initial risk taking is *not* related to degree of popularity within the group for either sex.

Finally, we also find from Table 9 that risk taking and influence are significantly related for each sex when popularity ratings are held constant. The partial correlation coefficients are significant beyond the .01 and .02 levels for the males and females, respectively. It is evident, therefore, that the relationships obtained for both sexes between degree of initial risk taking and degree of influence on group decisions are not dependent upon members' popularity.

Maintenance of the Risky Shift over a Subsequent Period of Time

An interesting further question concerns the extent to which the shift toward greater risk taking, which we have found to result from group discussion, is maintained over a subsequent period of time. We were able to gather evidence on this point for males but not for females. In the case of the former, but not in the case of the latter, a random sample of subjects from the original groups could be obtained for further study. The 22 males who were available for further work were approximately evenly distributed among the 14 original male groups. After a time interval of roughly two to six weeks had elapsed since the group session, these subjects individually were given the conservatism-risk questionnaire a third time, as described in the section on procedure.

The comparability of the random male subsample of 22 to the original male experimental condition sample of 82 is evident from the following data on total conservatism scores. The mean prediscussion total conservatism score was 66.9 for the sample of 82, and also was 66.9 for the subsample of 22. The mean postdiscussion total conservatism score, in turn, was 56.6 for the whole sample and 56.2 for the subsample. The t test of the difference scores had yielded a t significant beyond the .001 level ($t = 9.12$) for the whole sample, and it also yielded a t significant beyond the .001 level ($t = 4.70$) for the subsample.

Turning now to the total conservatism scores obtained by this subsample when they took the questionnaire again two to six weeks after the group discussion (call these scores the "post-postdiscussion" individual decisions), the mean score is 54.6. The mean of the difference scores obtained by subtracting each subject's prediscussion total conservatism score from his post-postdiscussion total conservatism score is -12.3, with a

t test of these difference scores yielding a t value of 4.92 ($p < .001$), hence indicating a risky shift from the prediscussion individual decisions to the post-postdiscussion individual decisions. The mean of the difference scores obtained, in turn, by subtracting each subject's postdiscussion total conservatism score from his post-postdiscussion total conservatism score is only -1.6, and a t test of these difference scores is not significant, hence indicating no further change from the postdiscussion individual decisions to the post-postdiscussion individual decisions. Item-by-item analyses tell the same story: the only significant item shifts are risky ones, and they are as strong from prediscussion to post-postdiscussion sessions as they are from prediscussion to postdiscussion sessions.

In sum, the data available on the point indicate that the shift in the risky direction found to occur as a result of the group discussion process is maintained over a subsequent period of time.

DISCUSSION AND CONCLUSIONS

The following conclusions may be drawn from the preceding evidence:

1. Unanimous group decisions concerning matters of risk show a shift toward greater risk taking when compared with prediscussion individual decisions made by the same persons and concerning the same matters. This holds for both sexes.

2. Postdiscussion individual decisions that follow unanimous group decisions exhibit the same kind of shift toward greater risk taking as appears in the group decisions. This is the case for both sexes. Covert acceptance as well as overt compliance, thus, are affected in the same manner by the discussion process.

3. This shift toward greater risk taking as a result of the discussion process is still maintained when 2–6 weeks have elapsed since the discussion occurred. Evidence on this point was available only for males.

4. No shift in risk-taking level of individual decisions occurs over time in the absence of the discussion process. This holds for both sexes.

5. There is a positive relationship between degree of risk taking in prediscussion individual decisions and the extent to which group members are perceived by one another as influencing group decisions. This relationship is specific to judgments of influence, in that it obtains when judgments of popularity are held constant, and also no relationship is found between prediscussion individual risk taking and the extent to which group members are judged to be popular. These statements all hold for both sexes.

The present study indicates, then, that group interaction and achievement of consensus concerning decisions on matters of risk eventuate in a willingness to make decisions that are more risky than those that would be made in the absence of such interaction. Furthermore, although initial ascribed status levels of the group members are equal, it is found that persons with stronger individual risk-taking proclivities tend to become more influential in the group than persons who are more conservative. Two alternative interpretations of these findings can be suggested; one more group centered, the other more person centered: It is possible that there is at work in these groups a process of diffusion or spreading of responsibility as a result of knowing that one's decisions are being made jointly with others rather than alone. Increased willingness to take risk would eventuate from this decreased feeling of personal responsibility. That initial risk taking and judged influence within the group are positively related could well occur as a consequence of this process, since one of its effects would be for the views of high risk takers to be given more weight by the rest of the group. Alternatively, the fact that high risk takers exert more influence may be a cause of the group's movement toward greater risk taking. It is possible that high risk takers are also more likely to take the initiative in social situations. Of course, these two interpretations are not necessarily mutually exclusive. Both of them may contribute to the group effect.

That females as well as males show the same change toward greater risk taking as a result of the group interaction condition, and that the samples of both sexes were liberal arts university students, renders it unlikely that the results can be explained on the basis of reinforcement by others of one's expectation as to whether one's appropriate role is to be more or less of a risk taker. We noted earlier that Stoner (1961) found a move toward greater risk taking in group as compared to individual decision making by male graduate students of industrial management, and we pointed out that this result might be accounted for in terms of the professional role that they had assigned themselves by becoming graduate students in a business school. Presence of peers might be expected to increase the salience of their business manager role, and a greater willingness to take risks in decision making might well be perceived as one of the attributes of that role. Such a role expectation interpretation is ruled out for the present study, however, through our use of liberal arts students as subjects. In addition, the possibility of explaining the results in terms of males' perceiving their appropriate role as one of willingness to be bold and daring, and being reinforced in this view by interaction with other like-minded males, is ruled out by the present study's obtaining the same results for females as for males. This outcome would not be expected if the findings depended on sex-linked role expectations as to whether one should be more risky or more conservative. This outcome also, of course, rules out interpretation in terms of any possible sex-linked differences in major fields of study.

That the group-induced move toward greater risk taking in individual decisions is still maintained two to six weeks after the discussion provides evidence, incidentally, which supports Lewin's (77) view that "group carried" attitudinal changes maintain themselves (see also 16, 1958).

REFERENCES

1. ATTHOWE, JR. J. M. "Interpersonal Decision Making: The Resolution of a Dyadic Conflict," *Journal of Abnormal and Social Psychology*, Vol. 62 (1961), pp. 114–119.

2. BACK, K. W. "Influence through Social Communication," *Journal of Abnormal and Social Psychology*, Vol. 46 (1951), pp. 9–23.

3. BROWN, R. W. "Mass Phenomena," in G. LINDZEY (ed.), *Handbook of Social Psychology*, Vol. 2. *Special Fields and Applications*, pp. 833–76. Cambridge, Mass.: Addison-Wesley, 1954.

4. CARTWRIGHT, D., AND ZANDER, A. (eds.) *Group Dynamics*. 2nd ed. Evanston, Ill.: Row, Peterson, 1960.

5. FESTINGER, L. "An Analysis of Compliant Behavior," in M. SHERIF AND M. O. WILSON (eds.), *Group Relations at the Crossroads*, pp. 232–55. New York: Harper, 1953.

6. HOROWITZ, M. W., LYONS, J., AND PERLMUTTER, H. V. "Induction of Forces in Discussion Groups," *Human Relations*, Vol. 4 (1951), pp. 57–76.

7. HUNT, E. B., AND ROWE, R. R. "Group and Individual Economic Decision Making in Risk Conditions," in D. W. TAYLOR (ed.), *Experiments on Decision Making and Other Studies*. Technical Report No. 6, AD 253952, pp. 21–25. Arlington, Va.: Armed Services Technical Information Agency, 1960.

8. KELLEY, H. H., AND THIBAUT, J. W. "Experimental Studies of Group Problem Solving and Process," in G. LINDZEY (ed.), *Handbook of Social Psychology*, Vol. 2, *Special Fields and Applications*, pp. 735–85. Cambridge, Mass.: Addison-Wesley, 1954.

9. KOGAN, N., AND WALLACH, M. A. "The Effect of Anxiety on Relations between Subjective Age and Caution in an Older Sample," in P. H. HOCH AND J. ZUBIN (eds.), *Psychopathology of Aging*, pp. 123–35. New York: Grune & Stratton, 1961.

10. KOMAROVSKY, MIRRA. "Functional Analysis of Sex Roles," *American Sociological Review*, Vol. 15 (1960), pp. 508–16.

11. LEWIN, K. "Frontiers in Group Dynamics," *Human Relations*, Vol. 1 (1947), pp. 2–38.

12. LONERGAN, B. G., AND McCLINTOCK, C. G. "Effects of Group Membership on Risk-Taking Behavior," *Psychological Reports*, Vol. 8 (1961), pp. 447–55.

13. McNEMAR, Q. *Psychological Statistics*. Rev. ed. New York: John Wiley & Sons, 1955.

14. MILNER, ESTHER. "Effects of Sex Role and Social Status on the Early Adolescent Personality," *Genetic Psychology Monographs*, Vol. 40 (1949), pp. 231–325.

15. OSBORN, A. F. *Applied Imagination*. New York: Scribner, 1957.

16. PELZ, EDITH B. Some Factors in "Group Decision," in ELEANOR E. MACCOBY, T. M. NEWCOMB, AND E. L. HARTLEY (eds.), *Readings in Social Psychology*, 3rd ed., pp. 212–219. New York: Henry Holt & Co., Inc., 1958.

17. SCHACHTER, S. "Deviation, Rejection, and Communication," *Journal of Abnormal and Social Psychology*, Vol. 46 (1951), pp. 190–207.

18. SIEGEL, S. *Nonparametric Statistics for the Behavioral Sciences*. New York: McGraw-Hill Book Co., 1956.

19. STONER, J. A. F. "A Comparison of Individual and Group Decisions Involving Risk." Unpublished Master's thesis, Massachusetts Institute of Technology, School of Industrial Management, 1961.

20. TAGIURI, R., AND KOGAN, N. "Personal Preference and the Attribution of Influence in Small Groups," *Journal of Personality*, Vol. 28 (1960), pp. 257–65.

21. TAYLOR, D. W., BERRY, P. C., AND BLOCK, C. H. "Does Group Participation When Using Brainstorming Facilitate or Inhibit Creative Thinking?" *Administrative Science Quarterly*, Vol. 3 (1958), pp. 23–47.

22. THIBAUT, J. W., AND KELLEY, H. H. *The Social Psychology of Groups*. New York: John Wiley & Sons, 1959.

23. TURNER, R. H., AND KILLIAN, L. M. (eds.) *Collective Behavior*. Englewood Cliffs, N. J.: Prentice-Hall, 1957.

24. WALLACH, M. A., AND CARON, A. J. "Attribute Criteriality and Sex-Linked Conservatism as Determinants of Psychological Similarity," *Journal of Abnormal and Social Psychology*, Vol. 59 (1959), pp. 43–50.

25. WALLACH, M. A., AND KOGAN, N. "Sex Differences and Judgment Processes," *Journal of Personality*, Vol. 27 (1959), pp. 555–64.

26. WALLACH, M. A., AND KOGAN, N. "Aspects of Judgment and Decision Making: Interrelationships and Changes with Age," *Behavioral Science*, Vol. 6 (1961), pp. 23–36.

27. WHYTE, JR., W. H., *The Organization Man*. New York: Simon & Schuster, 1956.

42. A NOTE ON THE APPEARANCE OF WISDOM IN LARGE BUREAUCRATIC ORGANIZATIONS*

Karl W. Deutsch and William G. Madow[1]

Modern life is characterized by the existence of many bureaucratic organizations, such as government agencies, the military services, political parties, educational institutions, and business corporations. In such organizations, officials sometimes are called upon to make decisions which are considered important and which are recognized later as having been clearly right or clearly wrong. It is often customary to single out for praise or promotion those officials whose decisions in important matters have frequently or always turned out to be right. The presence of such tested and proven wise men on its decision-making staff may then strengthen confidence in the wisdom of the organization that employs them, since it may be thought likely that these wise men and their organization will continue to make correct decisions in the future.

Such expectations sometimes may be justified and sometimes not. The correct answers may have been arrived at with the help of some manifest or hidden resources or procedures which in fact are likely to continue to yield correct results when new decisions must be made; or else they may be the product of a blind statistical process which may leave the apparent wise men and their employers helpless at the next juncture.

It seems desirable, therefore, to try to separate these two phenomena: (1) the instances of presumably genuine wisdom, which we may define for the purposes of this argument as the likelihood of an individual or small group to make correct decisions, for reasons inherent in the actor; and (2) the statistical appearance of pseudowisdom, defined here as the accidental making of correct decisions in the past (e.g., for reasons external to the actor), and unlikely to lead him to further correct decisions any more often than his previously less successful peers. If we can say something about the probable extent of the appearance of such pseudowisdom in large organizations under various conditions, it should be easier to say whether the decision makers in the organization have performed about equal to statistical expectation, or whether they have done significantly worse or better.

* Reprinted from *Behavioral Science* (January, 1961), pp. 72–78.

[1] The authors are indebted to the Center for Advanced Study in the Behavioral Sciences where they spent the year 1956–57 as Fellows and where most of the work on this paper was done, and to Dean W. Allen Wallis and Walter Pitts for helpful suggestions. The responsibility for the present paper remains, of course, their own.

For purposes of exposition of the argument that follows we make the following assumptions: (1) There is a number of clearly identifiable bureaucrats in the organization who are charged with the making of decisions and whose decision-making records can be compared. Let the number of such bureaucrats be m. (2) There is a number n of important decisions to be made which can be clearly distinguished from trivial decisions. (3) It is further assumed that these important decisions are independent of each other. (4) It is assumed that the organization has a clear criterion for distinguishing "correct" from "incorrect" decisions within a reasonable time after the decisions have been made, so that the past decision-making performance of each bureaucrat can be clearly established.

Assuming that a reputation for wisdom will be established by a bureaucrat who makes correct decisions in a limited number of important cases, it should follow that in a large bureaucratic organization a number of bureaucrats will establish such reputations, even if their probability of finding the correct answer in each case were no better than pure chance, such as .5 or the fall of a true coin. If we call the probability p of a bureaucrat making a correct decision his "competence," and if we assume for the sake of argument that this level of competence is the same for all bureaucrats in the organization, we may ask the question: How many apparently wise men will be produced by pure chance for a given number of bureaucrats and of important decisions, and for a given level of bureaucratic competence?

A SIMPLE EXERCISE IN PROBABILITY

Let p be the average probability of making the "correct" decision in a single instance. Let n be the number of independent decisions to be made, and suppose that correctness in all n decisions is required of an individual bureaucrat in order to give him a reputation for great competence. (Thus, if $n = 8$, there are eight independent decisions to be made and a record of eight correct independent decisions would be considered, at face value, to be evidence of high ability.) Then let there be m bureaucrats on the same initial level and suppose we want to determine m such that one bureaucrat is expected to emerge after n decisions with a perfect record of correct independent decisions.

Example 1:
Let $p = \frac{1}{2}$
  $n = 8$
  m = number of bureaucrats at start of testing period
  y = expected number of bureaucrats with perfect records at its end.

Taking $y = 1$, it follows that $m = 2^8 = 256$, or generally, $m = y(1/p)^n$. (Other conditions for determining m are discussed below.)

Thus, among 256 bureaucrats each having to make eight major decisions, there should be on the average one with a perfect record of correct decisions, even if his actual probability of deciding correctly was only 50:50 in each case, and even if nobody learned anything from any previous decisions.

Furthermore, the probability that at least one of the 256 bureaucrats would make all eight decisions correctly on this random basis is about $\frac{2}{3}$, and even the probability that four or more of the 256 would make all eight decisions correctly would be about .05.

If the level of competence is less than .5, or if in each decision a choice between more than two alternatives must be made, a larger number of bureaucrats, m, will be required to produce the expected appearance of one spurious wise man.

Example 2:
Let $p = \frac{1}{3}$
$\quad n = 4 \qquad m = 3^4 = 81$
$\quad y = 1$

In actual situations, bureaucrats usually are more competent than tossed coins. If so, p will be larger than $\frac{1}{2}$ and the ratio of m to p will be much less. (Also, there usually is some learning; but the learning effects and the probability effects should be disentangled.) The case of somewhat more competent bureaucrats, with a 2:1 probability of making correct decisions, is illustrated in Examples 3 and 4:

Example 3:
Let $p = \frac{2}{3}$
$\quad n = 4 \qquad m = \left(\frac{3}{2}\right)^4 = \frac{81}{16} = 5.06$
$\quad y = 1$

Example 4:
$p = \frac{2}{3}$
$n = 8 \qquad m = 2\left(\frac{3^8}{2^8}\right) = \frac{6561}{2^7} = \frac{6561}{128} = 51.26$
$y = 2$

Thus, even a half-dozen bureaucrats may produce one "wise man," if only four decisions are considered relevant; and if we are looking for two bureaucrats with a perfect record on eight major decisions, we may expect to find them in the majority of organizations large enough to employ at the appropriate bureaucratic level more than 52 decision makers of average ability.

Following a similar line of reasoning for the field of private business enterprise, Professor Harold Guetzkow has suggested that out of a large number of new business firms, there should emerge an appreciable number of survivors y with a perfect record of correct major decisions per year or even per decade, so long as the number of "major" decisions, that is, n, remains small relative to m, the number of new firms.

This situation may occur not infrequently in real life, when the standards for the routine conduct of small businesses have become fairly uniformly accepted, and the success or failure of competitors may depend largely on a very few major decisions such as the choice of location, the choice of lines of goods to be carried, and the decision whether or not to seek substantial credit for expansion. If half a dozen major decisions of this kind should be sufficient to decide about success or failure among hundreds or thousands of competing small businessmen, statistical chance might contribute a substantial contingent to the ranks of those successful men who may be tempted to congratulate themselves upon their prudence and foresight in making the right decisions for business survival.[2]

Our model could be further refined by introducing z as a "coefficient of wisdom," that is, the smallest acceptable ratio of correct to total relevant decisions. In the preceding discussion, z was held equal to one; but if a "batting average" of 0.8 or 0.4 should be acceptable, the number of bureaucrats or businessmen with acceptable records should increase in accordance with some formula connecting z with the other variables.

At the present stage it should be more useful, however, to make explicit the effects on the size of m of taking account of statistical variability in the case of the simple models discussed above.

A FEW MATHEMATICAL NOTES

Let us recall and elaborate our simplifying assumptions. We shall suppose that every decision of each decision maker is independently made of all others that he makes, and that each decision maker is independent of all other decision makers. Furthermore, we shall suppose that there is a fairly uniform probability p of being correct in a single decision, which holds for all decisions and all decision makers. Clearly, this assumes an excessive amount of uniformity and mediocrity. Yet these conditions have been chosen to highlight the process by which appearances of singularly high performance are produced. The same tendency will occur when the

---

[2] Dean W. Allen Wallis has drawn our attention to a related example from the practice of stock market fraud. According to Mr. Wallis, the practice consists in sending letters about some highly speculative stock to, say, 4,000 prospective investors, advising half of them that the stock is certain to rise, while telling the other half that it is certain to go down. After some weeks, to those 2,000 investors to whom "correct" advice was given as proved by subsequent events, a new letter is sent about another speculative stock telling again one half of the addressees that the stock will rise, and asserting the opposite to the rest. This practice is then repeated for the thousand who have now received two "correct" predictions in a row, and to the 500 who received three correct predictions and to the 125 who received four correct predictions. At this stage the authority of the forecasting service may be so thoroughly established with this last group that they may be willing to part with substantial amounts of money to buy some worthless stock which is now offered them at the fifth stage, by the same source whose authority has been so impressively demonstrated to them.

probabilities of being right vary among decision makers and decisions.

The probability that a specified decision maker is correct in j of n decisions is then

$$P(j, n) = C^n p^i q^{n-i};$$

and the probability that all n decisions are correct is

$$P(n, n) = p^n,$$

which we shall denote by P.

If there are m decision makers, then the probability R that at least one of them makes all decisions correctly is

$$R = 1 - (1 - P)^m = 1 - (1 - p^n)^m$$

since $1 - P$ is the probability that any specific decision maker makes at least one error.

Now suppose we want to fix n at eight and to determine m so that R has some specified value, say, .95.

Then, the number of decision makers m_n such that the probability is R that at least one of the decision makers makes all n decisions correctly, is

$$m_n = \frac{\log (1 - R)}{\log (1 - p)}$$

and the necessary values of m_n for specified values of p are given below.

Similarly the probability that at least $n - 1$ of the n decisions are correctly made by a single decision maker is

$$np^{n-1}q + p^n = p^{n-1}(p + nq)$$

and hence the probability that at least one decision maker is correct in at least $n - 1$ decisions is

$$C = 1 - [1 - p^{n-1}(p + nq)]^m$$

and, the number of decision makers $m_n - 1$ such that the probability is C that at least one of the decision makers makes at least $n - 1$ decisions correctly is

$$m_n - 1 = \frac{\log (1 - C)}{\log [1 - p^{n-1}(p + nq)]}$$

Many extensions of these results may be obtained.

Furthermore among m decision makers the expected number y of decision makers who make all n decisions correctly is

$$mp^n$$

and the variance of the number of decision makers who make all n decisions correctly is

$$mp^n(1 - p^n).$$

It is worth remarking that the Poisson approximation to the binomial will be good if m is fairly large, since even $(\frac{1}{2})^8$ is fairly small, i.e., $\frac{1}{256}$. Also, if one wishes m to be large enough so that the expected number of decision makers who make all decisions correctly is an integer K, e.g., 1, then one determines m by the equation

$$m = \frac{K}{p^n}$$

and hence m will often be large enough for the Poisson approximation to be used, unless n is very small.

Let us finally consider a related problem. Suppose that a decision maker has a probability P of succeeding (e.g., success may mean that he makes eight decisions correctly), and that we test successive decision makers until K are successful. (This might be done, for example, to choose a team of K "successful" decision makers.)

Then, the probability that the Mth decision maker is the Kth successful decision maker is

$$C_{K-1}^{M-1} P^K Q^{M-K}, \; M = K, K+1, \ldots$$

Also the expected number of decision makers that must be considered until K are successful is

$$\frac{K}{P}$$

and the variance of the number of decision makers that must be considered until K are successful is

$$\frac{KQ}{P^2}$$

where

$$Q = 1 - P.$$

SOME IMPLICATIONS FOR POLITICAL AND ORGANIZATIONAL BEHAVIOR

Some Effects of Size of Organization

The general shape of these probability functions shows that selection and promotion of high-level personnel in large organizations may be seriously affected by the contaminating effect of the appearance of spurious "wise men," if the number of competing bureaucratic decision makers is large, while the number of important decisions is small. Thus, every major country has several hundred generals in its armed forces, yet each of them might have to make no more than half a dozen really crucial decisions in the course of his career. If so, several "military geniuses" might be produced by chance, and these men might be put into important positions without being in any way more competent than those other men over whom they are preferred.

Some Effects of the Steepness of Personnel Selection

This contamination effect itself depends only on the number of crucial decisions and on the number and competence of bureaucrats at the lower level of promotion. Thus, in our first example, 52 bureaucrats facing eight crucial decisions with indifferent or 50:50 competence would produce an expected number of two spurious "wise men," regardless of the number of higher-level positions to be filled. The possible impact of this spurious effect on the organization may vary, however, with the proportion of personnel selected for promotion. If 10 of the 50 were to be promoted, the spurious "wise men" could be expected to fill no more than two of these 10 positions, or one-fifth of the total at the higher level. The contamination effect at this higher level would thus remain relatively limited.

If, on the other hand, only one or two of the original 50 were to be promoted, then the situation might become more hazardous for the organization involved: sometimes the spurious "wise men" might happen to fill one-half or even all of the positions on the next higher level. The situation would be similar to the taking of small samples from a large universe: some of them would represent the results of variance and not the average composition of the system as a whole. In this way a few small samples may be unrepresentative of the total; and gamblers with limited funds risk being wiped out by fluctuations of the game even if the long-run odds were in their favor. The same may hold true for the problem of high-level personnel selection in large organizations. Analogous to the gambler's ruin, the possible impact of the contamination effect at higher levels will thus increase with the steepness of selection, while the long-run probability of spurious "wise men" being picked instead of real ones will continue to vary with the relative proportions of the former to the latter.

A bureaucratic organization thus should become more vulnerable to the contamination effect on its higher levels in proportion to the steepness of its organizational pyramid. The smaller the proportion—let us call it s—of higher bureaucrats at each level to those immediately below them, the greater—other things being equal—would be the effect of variations from the average, and thus the greater could be in some instances the actual proportion of spurious "wise men" in the higher echelons. This risk becomes more significant as s, the proportion of bureaucrats to be promoted, approaches or falls below y/m, the proportion of bureaucrats likely to appear wise by chance.

In such cases, what could a large organization do? At best, it could insist on evaluating a large number of candidates for each high-level position, even where a few apparently well-qualified ones are already in appearance. This would require a greater expenditure of time and resources on the evaluation of candidates from outside the "inner circle," and it could reduce the expected contamination effect to its original proportion on the lower bureaucratic level, but it could not make it any smaller than that.

Some Effects of the Difference Between Trivial and Crucial Decisions

Are there more general ways in which the statistical contamination effect in large organizations could be reduced?

One remedy would consist in increasing the number of crucial decisions. One way of doing this is to wait longer, until more crucial decision situations had occurred, but this may often not be practical. Another solution would be to treat trivial decisions as if they were samples of important ones. Thus, big business organizations have at times been satirized as being inclined to take the good judgment which a junior executive has shown in the choice of his neckties as an indication of his presumable judgment in the making of major business decisions. The satirical description of this practice may be much exaggerated, but our previous remarks may have suggested that the practice itself may not be wholly without reason. Nevertheless, trivial decisions cannot be always presumed to be samples of critical ones: Ulysses Grant seems to have made an undistinguished record in regard to the routine that marked the career of an ordinary Army officer but showed remarkable skill in making some of the crucial decisions that led to the winning of the Civil War.

From this we may derive a general proposition: *the greater the difference between routine decisions and crucial decisions in an organization, the more vulnerable this organization is likely to be to the contamination effect* that we have been discussing. The relative distribution of crucial versus routine decisions in any organization is to a large extent determined by the kind of work which it does. Thus, doctors in a hospital, or field commanders in wartime, may be called upon more often to make crucial decisions than are file clerks in a bank or post office. This does not mean, however, that the Army or a large hospital will always have a better chance of distinguishing the reality of talent from its spurious appearance. What counts will be rather this: how large will be the number of decisions that will be relevant for the reputation or promotion of a bank manager or post office superintendent, as against the number of decisions relevant for the career of a chief surgeon or a colonel? The larger the number of relevant decisions which the candidate has to make in establishing his record, and the more similar the nature of these decisions to the crucial decisions which he will have to make in behalf of the organization in the future, the safer the personnel policies of the organization will be from the effects of statistical contamination. Up to a point, organizations can deliberately increase the number of crucial or at least nontrivial decisions with which they are confronting a candidate for promotion before they decide about his career.

On the other hand, organizations, wittingly or unwittingly, can do the exact opposite. They can reduce the effective number of decisions that are crucial for a man's career, and thus they may make their own task of selection of able personnel more difficult and the promotion of incompetents more likely.

Some Effects of Ideological Tests and Political Purges

A powerful way of increasing these undesirable effects consists in the introduction of political, religious, or ideological tests, and of political purges. Such tests, if taken seriously, usually will tend to override in importance any criteria of technical performance. The number of such independent political tests will be few, corresponding to major changes in the governing personnel or in the ruling ideology or party line—changes which in the nature of things must be relatively infrequent, occurring on the average less than once a year. During the ten or fifteen years decisive for their careers, bureaucrats under a totalitarian system of government are not likely to go through more than perhaps six or eight major purges or changes in the party line. Yet the decision of the bureaucrat as to which side to choose at each such juncture, and how to forecast correctly the winning side, may be of much greater importance for his fortunes and his reputation within the totalitarian context than any decisions on merely technical matters.

Out of the several hundreds and thousands of middle-level bureaucrats, a totalitarian system may thus tend to promote a number of persons who are genuine artists in well-timed conformity, and a number of others who have demonstrated genuine high competence in their technical fields, and even a small number of persons who rank high in both opportunism and competence. But on the showing of our argument, they will also tend to promote an appreciable number of persons of indifferent competence and loyalty to the currently ruling party line or faction. These will be the persons who chose sides with indifferent skill in each of the crucial political purges but survived them in accordance with the laws of probability.

Totalitarian or quasi-totalitarian personnel practices may thus be less selective than they seem, and the introduction of ideological tests or purges in the large bureaucratic organizations of free countries might make their personnel policies rather more erratic and unreliable than their proponents would intend.

Some Possible Effects of "Emergency Thinking" on Public Confidence in Large Organizations

More broadly speaking, whenever personnel selection is carried out against a background of "emergency thinking," it is part of the concept of an emergency that decisions made to meet it are considered much more important than the routine decisions that are being made at other times. If the workings of a government or of a large private organization should come to be characterized by a succession of spectacular emergencies, and if their bureaucrats should come to be judged mainly in terms of their performance in meeting them, the effects might be somewhat similar to those of a succession of major political purges. In both cases, a small sequence of spectacular decisions will become decisive for personnel selection and promotion while most other decisions made by the same bureaucrats would be relegated to comparative insignificance.

A related consideration should hold true for the reputation of large bureaucratic organizations with the general public. The larger the number of decision-making bureaucrats in such an organization and the fewer the number of decisions to which the public pays attention, the easier it should be for the organization or agency to impress the public with the appearance of time-tested wisdom among its high-ranking personnel.

43. GAMES DECISIONS AND INDUSTRIAL ORGANIZATION*

M. Shubik[0]

ABSTRACT

A survey of the current relationship between the many different problem areas investigated by means of game theory and the study of industrial organization is presented. Several examples are provided to illustrate the nature and relevance of work on (1) two-person constant-sum games; (2) the extensive form of a game; (3) theories of solution for n-person games; (4) theories of solutions for games against nature; and (5) theories of solution for dynamic games. The nature and state of the current applications of game theory to organizational problems and to parts of the behavorial sciences are summarized.

INTRODUCTION

Approximately 15 years ago, with the publication of the book by von Neumann and Morgenstern[1], the theory of games came into being. There had been previous publications which indicated that both von Neumann and Morgenstern considered problems which eventually led to this theory many years before. There are also historical references as far back as the early eighteenth century;[2] nevertheless, it was not until 1944 that the theory of games emerged as a formal discipline.

Since that time over a thousand papers and articles have appeared under the general classification of the theory of games. The latter part of the title of the first book, *The Theory of Games and Economic Behavior*, indicates that game theory was conceived of as an applied mathematics with economics and possibly other behavioral sciences as the substantive fields for application. How well has it lived up to this? The work by von Neumann and Morgenstern contains disappointingly little economics. Among the articles, papers and other books which have been written, most are strictly mathematical, a number are applied to military problems, and a few deal with other areas of application. There have been almost no direct applications of game theory to problems in the behavioral sciences or in

---

* Reprinted from *Management Science*. Vol. 6, No. 4 (July, 1960), pp. 455–74.

[0] The author is indebted to W. W. Cooper and to R. Vaswani for valuable comments and criticisms.

[1] J. von Neumann and O. Morgenstern, *Theory of Games and Economic Behavior*, (3rd ed.; Princeton, N.J.: Princeton University Press, 1953).

[2] Harold Kuhn has noted that in a letter between Montmort and Nicholas Bernouilli appearing in *Essay d'Analyse sur les Jeux d'Hazard* (1713) mention is made of the concept of a mixed strategy by the English mathematician Waldgrove.

business in the same way as there have been applications of linear programming to refining, mixing, and scheduling problems.

In spite of the lack of direct applications, the influence of game theory has been considerable. In this paper problems concerning the application and the nature of the influence of game theory are examined.

2. METHODOLOGIES AND THEORIES OF THE SOLUTION OF GAMES

Before one is in a position to understand fully the possibilities for the application of game theory it is desirable to distinguish among five very different developments. They are, respectively:

1. The theory of solution for two-person constant-sum games,
2. The description of the extensive form of a game,
3. The theories of solution for n person games (where $n \geqq 2$ for non-constant-sum games; $n \geqq 3$ for constant-sum games),
4. The theories of solution for games against nature (games in which the rules are not completely specified), and
5. The theories of solution for dynamic games.

3. TWO-PERSON CONSTANT-SUM-GAMES

Perhaps owing to a formal relationship between the mathematics required for the solution of a two-person zero-sum game and that required for the solution of a linear program, this part of game theory has been the most familiar to those not working directly in the field.

The class of two-person constant-sum games is naturally divided into those games where both players have a finite set of *pure strategies* and those where at least one player has an infinite set of pure strategies. Board games, such as Chess, Checkers, and Go, as well as two-person card games, belong to the first class. Most "dueling" problems give rise to games of the second type.

The first are referred to as matrix games. All their relevant features can be represented by a payoff matrix. Let S_1 and S_2 be the set of pure strategies for players 1 and 2 respectively. Let $s_1 \epsilon S_1$ and $s_2 \epsilon S_2$ represent specific strategies chosen by players 1 and 2 from the sets of strategies they have available. We define a payoff function $P_1(s_1, s_2)$ for player 1. This function assigns a value to the outcome of the game for the first player if the strategies s_1 and s_2 are played.

Suppose that the first player has n_1 and the second player has n_2 pure strategies. The payoff matrix in Table 1 completely describes the values of the outcomes to the first player for all possibilities where $s_1 = 1, 2, \ldots, n_1$ and $s_2 = 1, 2, \ldots, n_2$.

By definition, as the game is two-person and constant-sum, the payoff

TABLE 1

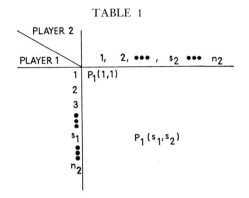

for the second player is the negative of that for the first, except for a constant.

$$P_2(s_1, s_2) = -P_1(s_1, s_2) + K.$$

There is one commonly agreed-upon concept of solution for two-person constant-sum matrix games and a complete theory for their solution.[3]

The behavioristic assumption for the play of two-person constant-sum matrix games is that of *minimax*. The game in Table 2 illustrates this. For simplicity, in our examples we set the constant $K = O$.

The worst that can happen to Player 1 if he uses his first strategy is that he obtains 4 if Player 2 uses his second strategy. The worst that can happen if he uses his second strategy is that he obtains 6. The best that he can obtain is 8 if Player 2 uses his first strategy and 6 if he uses the second strategy.

By utilizing his second strategy, the first player can guarantee that he obtains at least 6. Similarly, by utilizing his second strategy the second player can guarantee that he will lose at most 6. We note that the

TABLE 2

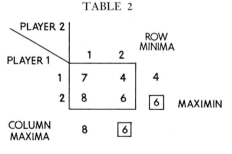

_____

[3] For a detailed exposition of the concept and method of solution for a two-person constant-sum game, the reader is referred to J. C. C. McKinsey, *Introduction to the Theory of Games,* chap. 2, (New York: McGraw-Hill Book Co., 1952).

maximum of the minima that the first player can win is 6. Furthermore, the minimum of the maxima of the second player's losses is 6. For this matrix we can state:

$$\text{min. max. } P_1(s_1, s_2) = \text{max. min. } P_1(s_1, s_2)$$
$$\quad s_1 \quad s_1 \qquad\qquad\qquad s_1 \quad s_1$$

The game in Table 3 does not have the *saddlepoint* property that the minimax equals the maximin. However, if, instead of limiting a player to pick a *pure strategy* we allow him to utilize a probability mix over his alternative plans for action, this property is restored. Suppose Player 1 uses his first strategy with a probability of 5/8 and the second with a

TABLE 3

PLAYER 1 \ PLAYER 2	1	2	ROW MINIMA
1	10	−5	−5
2	−15	10	−15
COLUMN MAXIMA	10	10	

probability of 3/8. If the second player uses his first strategy, the first will expect to win

$$\tfrac{5}{8}(10) + \tfrac{3}{8}(-15) = \tfrac{5}{8}.$$

If the second plays his second strategy, the first player will win

$$\tfrac{5}{8}(-5) + \tfrac{3}{8}(10) = \tfrac{5}{8}.$$

By utilizing the *mixed strategy* characterized by (5/8, 3/8) the first player can guarantee a win of 5/8 for himself. Similarly, by using the mixed strategy of (3/8, 5/8) the second player can guarantee that he will not lose more than 5/8.

The fundamental theorem[4] of two-person constant-sum games establishes that for all games of this type there will be a saddlepoint at which the first player can guarantee a minimum gain for himself. The second player can simultaneously guarantee that the maximum the first player will win is precisely that minimum.

The assumption that the behavior of the players can be described by the conscious application of the minimax rule is based on possibly a peculiarly "rationalistic utilitarian" view of the players. It can be interpreted as a normative assumption telling individuals how they should behave in such a situation.

There are a few situations or organizations which can be characterized successfully by means of two-person constant-sum games. Several attempts

[4] *Ibid.*, chap. 2.

have been made to draw the analogy between situations involving competition in advertising,[5] however, although they are of value, the problems of formulation are great. Several applications have been made to problems in the oil industry.[6]

The second type of constant-sum game, involving at least one player with an infinite set of strategies, includes games of search and duels. The concept of solution is the same for these as for the matrix games, however, the mathematical difficulties are much greater, and in some cases solutions may not exist. These games have considerable value to military work. The games of search have direct applications to defense systems and the dueling games are of use in the evaluation of new weapon systems.

In summary, to date there appears to be direct application of two-person constant-sum games to problems of the military but little direct application to economic, social, or industrial organization.

4. THE DESCRIPTION OF THE EXTENSIVE FORM OF A GAME

The first part of the work of von Neumann and Morgenstern[7] was devoted to a detailed description of the anatomy of a game, or the *extensive form* of a game. This framework has provided a language for modern decision theory and a basis for investigations of organization theory.

In the context of the description of a game, the words *move, play, information set, strategy, payoff, rules of the game* and *perfect information* are defined.

The matrix game portrayed in Table 3 can be represented by a *game tree*. This is done in Figure 1.

The vertices in this game tree represent choice points. The branches

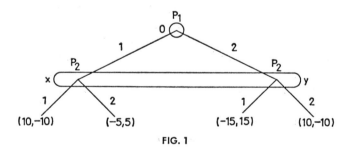

FIG. 1

[5] A. Charnes, and W. W. Cooper, "A Constrained Game Formulation of Advertising Strategies," *Econometrica*, October, 1954. See also L. Friedman, "Game-Theory Models in the Allocation of Advertising Expenditures," *Operations Research*, 6: 5, September–October, 1958.

[6] G. H. Symonds, *Linear Programming: The Solution of Refinery Problems,* chap. 5, (New York: Esso Standard Oil Company, 1955), and E. G. Bennion, "Capital Budgeting and Game Theory," *Harvard Business Review*, 34, (1956).

[7] von Neumann and Morgenstern, *op. cit.,* chap. II.

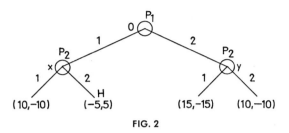

FIG. 2

indicate alternatives. The vertices are labeled with the names of the players to whom they belong. Thus, at the vertex 0, which is also labelled with P_1, the first player is called upon to make a choice between two alternatives. These are the branches originating from the vertex and labeled 1 and 2.

At the two vertices labeled P_2 the second player is called upon to make his move by choosing between two alternatives. After each player has made his move the game reaches a terminal point of the game tree and each player obtains his payoff. For example, if both players select their first alternative, the game terminates with payoff $(10, -10)$.

The two vertices labelled with P_2 are enclosed by single curve. This indicates that these choice points belong to the same *information set*. The matrix game in Table 3 is a simultaneous move game. The two players select their strategies without knowledge of each other's actions. Thus, in the game tree, although the first player selects between his two alternatives first, in effect the second player is not aware of the choice, hence he cannot tell if he is making a choice at the vertex x or y.

The game illustrated in Figure 2 is a different game inasmuch as the *information* conditions have been changed. The vertices x and y no longer belong to the same information set. The first player's move is disclosed to the second player prior to his own move. This game does not give rise to the same matrix game as the other. The equivalent matrix game still has two strategies for the first player but has four strategies for the second. These are illustrated in Table 4.

These two examples illustrate the use of a precise language for decision making in games.

The *rules of the game* specify the complete structure of the game. They

TABLE 4

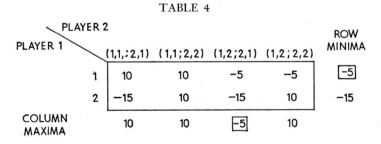

PLAYER 1 \ PLAYER 2	(1,1,:2,1)	(1,1;2,2)	(1,2;2,1)	(1,2;2,2)	ROW MINIMA
1	10	10	−5	−5	−5
2	−15	10	−15	10	−15
COLUMN MAXIMA	10	10	−5	10	

indicate the span of the alternatives faced by a player at any point during the play, his information state and the payoffs resulting from any play.

A *play* of a game is a path followed down the game tree. In Figure 2 such a path is denoted by $0 \times H$. This results when the first and second players make their moves by selecting their first and second alternatives, respectively.

The *payoff* is the resultant allocation from the play of a game. In chess this is the value attached to a win, loss, or draw; in poker it is money.

A *strategy* is a complete plan of action for a player. It contains instructions to handle all contingencies. For example, the third strategy of the second player indicated in Table 4 is $(1, 2; 2, 1)$. This states: "If Player 1 uses his first alternative my move will be to select my second; if he uses his second my move will be to select my first."

A *move* is the selection of one among a set of alternatives at a choice point in a game. In a game in which each player has a single move and these are made simultaneously, a strategy and a move are equivalent. The players have no contingencies to plan for.

The game illustrated in Figure 2 has *perfect information*. Each *information set* is a one-element set. This implies that at any point in the game any player is perfectly informed about all moves made up to the time of his move.

Possibly one of the most important contributions of the Theory of Games to date has been this language to aid in the study of decision making.

Paradoxically, the power of this notation has enabled those working in the behavioral sciences to isolate and specify some of the major weaknesses in the theories of solutions to games and in the other economic theories invoking "rational behavior."

Once an attempt is made to study a game of moderate complexity in the extensive form, such as chess, the difficulties concerning theories of "rational choice" are highlighted. The first two moves in the game of chess can occur in 400 ways. By the tenth move there are many billions of alternatives!

It is evident that humans do not search through millions of alternatives, but they have various methods to limit their search in a relatively successful manner. Consideration of this has led Shannon, Simon, Newell, Samuel and others[8] to construct chess and checker-playing computer

---

[8] R. M. Friedberg, "A Learning Machine: Part I," *IBM Journal of Research and Development*, 2: 1 (January, 1958).

———, B. Dunham and J. H. North, "A Learning Machine: Part II," *IBM Journal of Research and Development*, 3: 3 (July, 1959).

Allen Newell, J. C. Shaw and H. A. Simon, "Chess-Playing Programs and the Problem of Complexity," *IBM Journal of Research and Development*, 2: 4 (October, 1958).

A. L. Samuel, "Some Studies in Machine Learning Using the Game of Checkers," *IBM Journal of Research and Development*, 3: 3 (July, 1959).

programs based on "heuristics," which are general rules or principles that serve to cut down the alternatives to be examined to a manageable number.

Closely tied to the work on chess playing is work on other "search processes" and on learning. M. M. Flood and others[9] have experimented directly with game learning situations.

Of more direct influence upon industry has been the direct effect of the terminology of Game Theory on operations research and planning work. The Payoff Matrix is now common terminology in many parts of U.S. industry. And with it are the concepts of contingent forecasting, strategic planning and sensitivity analysis. Obviously, the growth of linear programming, sequential decision theory and other mathematical techniques have also had influence. They, too, apart from specific applications, have played their cultural role of preparing the "climate" in industry for the scientific study of decision processes.

5. THEORIES OF SOLUTION FOR *N*-PERSON GAMES

To those only slightly acquainted with the Theory of Games the title of the book by von Neumann and Morgenstern is misleading in several ways. The authors wrote, in effect, three books under one cover. The first book deals with the description of a game in extensive form. The second offers a theory for the solution to two-person constant-sum games. It has been argued with considerable effect that the mode of behavior suggested by von Neumann and Morgenstern is very reasonable and that people "should" play in the manner suggested by their theory.[10] This, to some extent depends upon the acceptance of the von Neumann and Morgenstern concept of utility which can be regarded as a major contribution by itself.

The third book presents a theory of behavior for players in a variable sum *n*-person game ($n \geq 2$). This theory has not been found to be satisfactory to most behavioral scientists. It does not appear to provide solutions that match even casual observations. Furthermore, the concept of solution only provides for a very weak type of prediction for the outcome of a game.

At this time there are about twenty different theories for the solution of a variable sum *n*-person game. Most of them are described by Luce and Raiffa.[11]

---

[9] M. M. Flood, "On Game-Learning Theory and Some Decision-Making Experiments," chap. X of *Decision Processes*, Thrall, Coombs and Davis (eds.), (New York: John Wiley & Sons, Inc., 1954). See also Wm. K. Estes, "Individual Behavior in Uncertain Situations: An Interpretation in Terms of Statistical Association Theory," *Ibid.*, chap. IX.

[10] There are some who disagree. See for example D. Ellsberg, "The Theory of the Reluctant Duelist," *American Economic Review*, 46 (1956).

[11] R. Duncan Luce and Howard Raiffa, *Games and Decisions* (New York: John Wiley & Sons, 1957).

The multiplicity of solution concepts indicates how little we know about behavior in different situations involving group conflict. Perhaps it would be wise at this time to consider several solution concepts, each applying to a specialized area such as

a) Behavior within the firm
b) Small group behavior
c) Conflict situations involving two individuals
d) Markets

and so forth. In this manner some of the groundwork necessary to the eventual construction of a general theory of organization could be done.

At this point a fundamental analogy between two aspects of the theory of games and two aspects of industrial organization can be made. The description of a game, its extensive form, for example, is equivalent to a description of *market structure* in an industry or organizational structure in a firm. The specification of a solution concept is equivalent to the description of *market behavior* or behavior within a firm.

TABLE 5

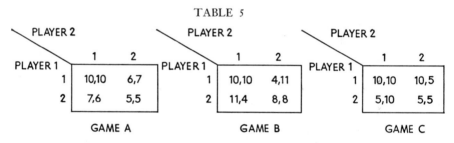

It is highly desirable to distinguish clearly between structure and behavior, especially when investigating the meaning of several concepts which are crucial to an understanding of socioeconomic organization. These include the concepts of competition, collusion, power, centralization, and decentralization.

Three simple 2 × 2 nonconstant-sum games and three different concepts of solution, shown in Table 5, serve to illustrate the interplay between structure and behavior.

In the payoff matrices in Table 5 the double entries stand, respectively, for the payoff to the first player and then to the second. Thus, for example, in Game B the result of the play in which Player 1 uses his first strategy and Player 2 his second is 4 to Player 1 and 11 to Player 2.

Although highly simplified, the matrices can be regarded as representing *market structure*. Thus, Game A may portray a rationalized industry where the first strategy for each player is a commitment to a high price *provided* his competitor maintains the high price, together with an intent to meet any cut if the price is not maintained. The second strategy for each is a price cut.

This particular payoff matrix reflects a hypothetical situation in which, if both maintain a high price, they both profit considerably. If one leads off with a cut he may obtain a temporary advantage but eventually both do not do as well as previously. If both begin with price cuts neither does very well. Such might be the case in a dying industry.

The strategies in Game B can be interpreted as decisions concerning advertising and distribution. The first strategy is a decision to spend little on advertising and distribution. The second calls for a large expenditure. Here the matrix reflects the market properties to be expected in a situation where the total sales cannot be heavily changed by advertising or distribution but shares may be radically effected. Furthermore, if one firm establishes a market lead there is little hope for the competitor to retaliate effectively by a "me-too" strategy.

The third game represents, in the terminology of economics, a purely competitive market. This will be discussed after some solutions are examined.

The von Neumann and Morgenstern solution to the general n-person game calls for the players to *jointly maximize* and then work out some manner to share the proceeds between themselves. There are other cooperative solutions which suggest joint maximization.[12]

Using the notation of section 3, joint maximization calls for the players to select strategies s_1 and s_2 such that

$$\underset{s_1 \in S_1}{\text{Max}} \underset{s_2 \in S_2}{\text{Max}} \ (P_1[s_1, s_2] + P_2[s_1, s_2]).$$

Another concept of behavior postulated in order to obtain a solution to a game is so-called noncooperative behavior. John Nash has developed the theory which gives noncooperative equilibrium points as the solutions to games. The type of equilibrium proposed is one familiar to all economists and is directly related to the equilibrium solutions put forward by Cournot, Chamberlin, and many others.

Expressed mathematically, a pair of strategies $(\bar{s}_1, \bar{s}_2)$ gives rise to an equilibrium point if the following conditions are simultaneously satisfied:

$$\underset{s_1 \in S_1}{\text{Max}} \ P_1(s_1, \bar{s}_2) \rightarrow s_1 = \bar{s}_1$$

$$\underset{s_2 \in S_2}{\text{Max}} \ P_2(\bar{s}_1, s_2) \rightarrow s_2 = \bar{s}_2$$

In words, if Player 1 attempts to maximize his payoff on the assumption that Player 2 will use his strategy $\bar{s}_2$, then Player 1 will use his strategy $\bar{s}_1$ and vice versa.

A third theory of behavior giving rise to another solution concept

---

[12] For example: John Nash, "Two-Person Cooperative Games," *Econometrica*, 21 (1953).

would be that the players each assume that their opponents are "out to get them." This is a paranoid world in which it is necessary (as the French view it) that *"on se defend."* Such behavior calls for a maxmin strategy regardless of the type of game. It is the behavior of the highly cautious and pessimistic individual. If both players follow this behavior their actions will be characterized by

$$\underset{s_1 \in S_1}{\text{Max}} \ \underset{s_2 \in S_2}{\text{Min}} \ P_1(s_1, s_2)$$

$$\underset{s_2 \in S_2}{\text{Max}} \ \underset{s_1 \in S_1}{\text{Min}} \ P_2(s_1, s_2)$$

We now apply the three different behavior concepts to each of the three games.

The entries in Table 6 are the strategy pairs which are the solutions to the games. For example, the equilibrium solution to Game B is obtained when both players use their second strategies and the payoff to each is 8.

An inspection of the three games yields the joint maximization solutions

TABLE 6

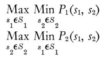

BEHAVIOR	GAME A	GAME B	GAME C
JOINT MAXIMUM SOLUTION	(1,1)	(1,1)	(1,1)
EQUILIBRIUM SOLUTION	(1,1)	(2,2)	(1,1)
MAXMIN SOLUTION	(1,1)	(2,2)	(1,1)

immediately. For all the games the strategy pair of (1, 1) produces the joint maximum of 20.

The equilibrium solution to Game A is obtained by the following argument. Player 1 observes that if Player 2 uses his first strategy Player 1 will be likewise motivated. Furthermore, placing himself in the position of his competitor he can carry out a similar argument. The solution can be tested in the formal equations given previously in this section.

In Game B if Player 1 presumes that his opponent will use his first strategy he will switch to his second. Carrying this type of argument further, the pair of strategies (2, 2) is the equilibrium solution.

It was noted that Game C represents a purely competitive market (following the terminology of economists). An inspection of the matrix shows that the strategy sets of the players are not interlinked in the sense that the actions of one player have no influence on the payoff for the other. For example, a change in the price of hamburgers by a diner near Philadelphia will have no effect on the trade of another independent diner near Boston.

Because there is no interlinkage between the fates of the players it is not surprising that in a game of this structure all the forms of behavior postulated lead to the same solution. In other words, given the structure in Game C, it is not possible to *identify* the behavior of the players by observing the solution.

In Game A, even though the payoff to each player depends strongly on the actions of both, the structure is such that most forms of behavior lead to the same result. The maxmin behavior produces possibly the most paradoxical result. The extreme caution and pessimism of each player brings them a jointly optimal result.

In Game B, it is possible to distinguish different outcomes resulting from jointly maximizing or noncooperating behavior. Other structures can be portrayed easily in which it becomes possible to distinguish different outcomes resulting from noncooperative and maxmin or other forms of behavior.

In Games A and C it is not possible to distinguish between competition, collusion, or cooperation.

Suppose both players belong to the same organization, and the structure of the joint enterprise were reflected by the matrices of Games A or C. Such an organization would be naturally fully *decentralized*. The structure of the organization is such that under the very weakest of assumptions concerning the motivations of the players, the joint maximum will be obtained. No communication or messages are needed. The subsystems will be independently controlled in a manner that benefits the organization as a whole.

In Game A decentralization is achieved because both players have considerable incentives to seek a joint optimum and have no incentives to do anything else. In Game C decentralization is actually isolation. The fates of the players are not intertwined.

For the joint maximum to be achieved in Game B the players must exhibit cooperative behavior. This may entail an elaborate system of communication, coordination, and policing. A slight deviation in behavior in Game B would destroy the joint maximization. This is not so in the other games.

A system is successfully decentralized with respect to a set of decisions if the independent actions of individuals in control of the actions of subsystems achieves the same outcome as a single decision maker making all the decisions.

Decentralization will depend upon both structure and behavior. The less cooperative the individuals are and the more they commit mistakes or change their behavior, the more difficult it will be to design a system that is successfully decentralized.

The more highly the payoffs of the players are correlated, the easier it is to decentralize decision making.

Possibly the most fundamental concept to political science is that of *power.* The study of political science can be defined as the study of power. Yet from Sun Tzu[13] to Machiavelli to the present day this concept has been elusive to the best of minds. In an elementary and highly limited way game theory analysis serves as a means to clarify, examine and extend some of the concepts of power.

To date even the concept of power in a chess game is not fully understood. However, the formalization of the analyses of games permits an isolation of problems for study. An example of such a formalization is provided in the construction of an index of power in voting systems.[14]

The political problems of power merge directly into economic and industrial ones. The measurement of the power or control of a firm over its market is of prime socioeconomic importance. The delegation of authority in decision-making systems presents measurement problems concerned with power.

The direct applications of theories of solution to n-person nonconstant-sum games to operating problems of industry have been few. Apart from the investigation of several different aspects of bidding[15] and the allocation of joint costs, few others have been utilized. An interesting use of an n-person game model with Nash equilibria has been made by Charnes and Cooper[16] in association with the Chicago Area Transportation Study to simulate patterns of traffic flow when the huge size of the problem made ordinary cut-and-dried simulations prohibitive for electronic computer runs.

6. THEORIES OF SOLUTION FOR GAMES AGAINST NATURE

In Section 4 the description of the extensive form of a game was given. The formalization made use of an implicit assumption that all the *rules of the game* were known. This means that (at least theoretically) it is possible to enumerate every alternative available to the players. All physically and legally possible events are comprehended.

---

[13] Sun Tzu, "The Art of War," in *Roots of Strategy*, Brig. Gen. Thomas R. Phillips, (ed.) (Harrisburg, Pa.: The Military Service Publishing Co.

[14] Martin Shubik, "The Uses of Game Theory in Management Science," *Management Science*, 2 (1955); Shubik and L. S. Shapely, "Method for Evaluating the Distribution of Power in a Committee System," *American Political Science Review*, 48 (1954); and L. S. Shapley, "A Value for n-Person Games," *Contributions to the Theory of Games*, Vol. II, *Annals of Mathematics*, No. 28 (Princeton, N.J.: Princeton University Press, 1953).

[15] Wm. Vickrey, "Counterspeculation, Auctions, and Competitive Sealed Tenders," mimeographed, 1959. See also Martin Shubik, "Economics, Management Science, and Operations Research," *The Review of Economics and Statistics*, XL: 3 (August, 1958).

[16] See A. Charnes and W. W. Cooper, "External Principles for Simulating Traffic Flows over a Network of City Streets," *Proceedings of the National Academy of Sciences*, 44: 2, (February, 1958).

Even in certain board games, such as the Japanese game of Go (and its Chinese predecessor)[17] there have been difficulties in defining rules to describe the outcome from every eventuality! How much more difficult is the definition of rules concerning industrial or social organization.

The normalized form of the game serves to illustrate the difficulties faced when an attempt is made to construct a model of a market, firm, or other institution.

"Game" D in Table 7 portrays a situation in which the first player knows all the strategies available to both sides, he knows his own payoffs,

TABLE 7

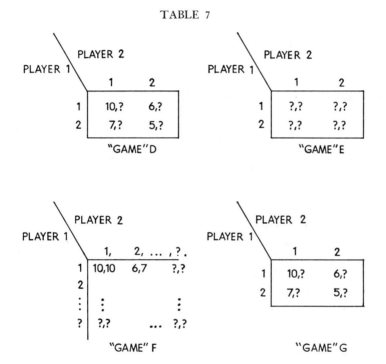

but he does not know the payoffs to his competitor. This is often the case in bargaining and haggling.

In these examples, the word "game" has been placed in quotes to indicate that in the strict sense of game theory these examples are *not* fully defined games. However, from the viewpoint of the behavioral scientist these situations involving almost- or pseudo-games must be investigated. The quotes subsequently will not be shown, although the text may imply them.

Experiments have been carried out to study bargaining under varying

---

[17] H. J. R. Murray, *A History of Board Games other Than Chess*, chap. 4 (Oxford, England: Clarendon Press, 1952).

conditions of information.[18] Even the mathematical analysis of simple and familiar bargaining structures is far from complete, assuming the behavior of the players is known. Vickrey[19] has investigated the properties of the usual high-bid auction as compared with the Dutch auction.

Many theories of equilibrium in an economic system appear to have the type of game illustrated by Game D as their model. Specific information about one's own payoffs is known, but little is know about the others. An example of an institutional attempt to cope with some of the aspects of ignorance in bidding behavior is to be found in some of the Danish building and crafts trades. After closed bids are submitted, the contract is awarded to the bidder whose tender is closest to a fixed percentage below the *average bid!* In this manner it is hoped that the incompetents whose low bids may be based on misestimates and who might be driven bankrupt while executing the contract will be eliminated. The analysis of this procedure presents several logical difficulties.

Game E illustrates a level of ignorance that is deeper than Game D. Here not only are the payoffs of the competitor unknown, but the player is not aware of the worth of some of his own payoffs. This corresponds to situations that often exist in multiproduct firms with complicated manufacturing processes. The firm may not know the true contribution to profits made by some of its products. Individuals operating in new markets and with unfamiliar products are faced with this type of ignorance. Thus the art, antique, and jewelry markets display great imperfections. This is so to such an extent that the ignorant may easily pay more for Japanese prints in Japan, English silver in England, or period pieces in France than if they purchased the same items in New York.

The type of matrix in Game E brings up problems concerning the value of information. How much should a player be willing to spend to find out the worth of his and his competitors' payoffs? Feeney and Shubik have constructed an example[20] to illustrate that even if the players knew that the payoffs were fixed but determined by numbers drawn from known random distributions, it would not necessarily be rational to "explore the complete environment."

There is a further difficulty which is not illustrated in Game E but might also be present. Even though the players are aware of the strategies available to each, they may not know which strategy has in fact been utilized by the competitor. As the payoffs are not known, suppose, for example, initially the first player uses his first strategy in Game E. He finds out that there is a resultant payoff of, say, $+3$ to him and -3 to his

---

[18] Sidney Siegel and L. E. Fouraker, *Bargaining and Group Decision Making: Experiments in Bilateral Monopoly,* New York: McGraw-Hill Book Co., 1960.

[19] Wm. Vickrey, *op. cit.*

[20] George J. Feeney and Martin Shubik, "A Multi-State Game with Uncertain Payoffs," mimeographed note, February 16, 1960.

competitor. He may not necessarily be able to tell if this is the result of the strategy pair (1, 1) or (1, 2).

In Game F the players do not know the range of their strategies. It is possible for them to explore for new alternatives. This model confronts the behavioral scientist with the necessity for empirical work on search processes and the need for the development of a theory of search.

Game G illustrates a situation in which the nature of the opponent is not known. He may be "nature," the weather, the tide, a mechanism, a nonhuman animal, a rat, a psychologist, a sociologist, a Trobriand islander or an ordinary businessman.

In order to "solve" this type of game, i.e., to be able to predict the outcome of a play or to recommend a form of behavior to Player 1, it is necessary to add some postulates concerning the type and behavior of the opponent. Luce and Raiffa[21] present a comprehensive survey of the many different methods for playing against "nature" which have been suggested.

Many problems dealing with quality control and involving sequential decisions based on statistical sampling are formally equivalent to one-person games against nature. In this sense, it may be said that there has been considerable direct application of this type of game theory.

7. THEORIES OF SOLUTION FOR DYNAMIC GAMES

Throughout this article the discussion has proceeded and the examples have been presented as though all game models could be represented by the matrix form. In many instances, especially in the examination of Games A, B and C in Section 5, the discourse had an "almost dynamic" flavor. The dynamics, however, was not made explicit.

The dynamic features of interest can be illustrated by simple examples closely related to the gambler's ruin problems studies in probability theory.[22]

In Section 4, the extensive form of a game was described. It was implied that any game could be represented by a finite (oriented) game tree. The payoffs from a play of the game in this representation are to be found at the terminal branches of such a diagram. Even though the diagram would be of immense size, such a portrayal of the game of chess is conceivable. Every path from the vertex of the game tree down to a terminal for win, lose, or draw will occur there.

The chess analogy does not serve too well for a model of the firm. There are two features which are lacking. Chess, poker and most other games are of *finite* length with a single payoff at the termination of the game. Theoretically (if not practically) a corporation is immortal. There

---

[21] Luce and Raiffa, *op. cit.*

[22] Wm. Feller, *An Introduction to Probability Theory and Its Applications*, chap. 14 (New York: John Wiley & Sons, 1950).

is no foreseen finite end to the game it plays. Furthermore, it receives payoffs at many times during the game. Sometimes it pays them out as dividends, sometimes it ploughs them back.

If an analogy between a game and the activities of a corporation is to be drawn, corporate activity might be viewed as a nonterminating poker game in which players occasionally die or are born and furthermore in which there is an inflow of edible poker chips which provide the only food![23]

Games which have no definite termination cannot be portrayed by a game tree of finite length. The situation of the fanatic gambler playing roulette until he is ruined provides an example of this type of game. Even though the probability may become fantastically small, there is always a small chance that the length of the game will exceed any specific number.

An example of the differences that may be observed between a game of finite length and of indefinite length is illustrated by two closely related games, shown in Table 8. Consider the simple 2×2 matrix game that is

TABLE 8

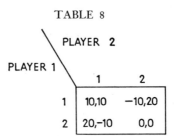

played for 100 periods. An analysis of the one-period game shows that there is an equilibrium point which yields the players (0, 0) and which occurs when they both use their second strategies. Initially we might suspect that if the players were to play for 100 periods they would persist in playing in a manner that yielded zero to each on every trial when they have the possibility of obtaining 1,000 each. Yet it can be shown that the equilibrium strategies in the overall game call for the players to always use their second strategies in the subgames (i.e., in the single-period games).

An inspection of the matrix shows that if the game lasts for only one period the players will use their second strategies. Suppose that the game is to be played for 100 periods and that the players have decided each to use their first strategies, thus obtaining ten each. In the last subgame of the series it will pay each player to "double-cross" his competitor. Both can calculate that they will be forced to the strategy pair (2, 2) on the last game. Each can then reason one stage further back and double-cross each other at stage 99. By continuing the backwards induction it is shown that (2, 2) is always played.

---

[23] I am indebted to Max Woodbury in the formulation of this analogy.

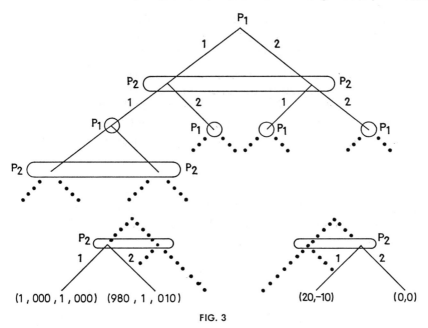

FIG. 3

The game tree of the 100-stage game is as indicated in Figure 3. Experiments with this type of game have been run and the evidence to date points towards the type of behavior where the joint minimum is obtained.[24]

The closely allied game that is now examined is one in which the period-by-period subgame is precisely the same; however, at every period there is a probability of p that the game will terminate at the end of that play. The expected duration of the game will be:

$$p + 2(1 - p)p + 3(1 - p)^2p + \ldots + n(1 - p)^{n-1}p + \ldots$$

which represents the probabilities that it lasts exactly one, two, three, . . . periods multiplied by the length of the period. This sums to:

$$1/p$$

hence if this game is to have an *expected* length of 100, p can be obtained by setting

$$1/p = 100$$

giving $p = 0.01$ to three figures of accuracy. This game now only differs from the first inasmuch as its expected duration rather than fixed duration is the same as the finite game. All else is identical. Yet now there will exist

[24] A. Scodel, J. S. Minas, P. Ratoosh and M. Lipetz, "Some Descriptive Aspects of Two-Person, Non-Zero-Sum Games," *Conflict Resolution*, II: 2 (June, 1959).

strategies in the overall game which cause the players to utilize their first (sub) strategies in the period-by-period subgames.

Suppose the first player were to adopt the following policy:

In every subgame I will use my first strategy as long as I observe that Player 2 has utilized his first strategy. As soon as my information tells me otherwise, I will switch to and maintain my second strategy in every subsequent subgame.

If the second player knew of this strategy and tried to maximize his payoff, given this information his overall expected payoff would be at most

$$10p \sum_{t-0}^{r-2} (1 - p)^t + 20p(1 - p)^{r-1} + (0)p \sum_{t-r}^{\infty} (1 - p)^t.$$

This is obtained on the assumption that at any time, say at period r, he utilized his second strategy in a subgame. If he only utilized his first strategy his expected payoff is:

$$10p \sum_{t-0}^{\infty} (1 - p)^t.$$

The difference between following the latter policy or the former is always positive for $p = 0.01$; hence the policy of adhering to the first strategy will always be preferred, rather than the second. Similarly, if Player 2 "threatens" Player 1 with the same type of reprisal if he deviates from his first strategy in any subgame, Player 1 will be motivated to play only his first strategy in every subgame.

In the finite game neither side had an effective threat, as was shown by their inability to carry out a reprisal against a double cross at the play of the last of the subgames. In the infinite game, at any play of a subgame, the length the game is still expected to last remains constant and is always long enough to make some reprisals effective.

Referring back to Games A, B, and C in Section 5, they can be rephrased in fully dynamic terms and studied accordingly. The details of market structure such as time lags, degree of fixed investment, flexibility in advertising, research, or pricing policy all will effect the maneuverability of the firms and their ability to enforce stability in a market.

A further modification to a game of indefinite length can be obtained in the construction of a game of economic survival[25] as a model of the corporation. A simple example illustrates the construction of this type of game and provides the analogy between it and the corporation. In the ordinary gambler's ruin game, the gambler commences with an amount x and plays until he has won a specified amount or the game terminates with his ruin.

---

[25] Martin Shubik, *Strategy and Market Structure*, chap. X, (New York: John Wiley & Sons, 1959). See also Shubik and G. L. Thompson, "Games on Economic Survival," *Naval Research Logistics Quarterly*, 6: 2 (June, 1959).

In a game of economic survival the player has two accounts, a *corporate account* and a *withdrawal account*. If the assets in the corporate account fall below a specific amount the game terminates and the player is bankrupt. There is a discount rate ρ where $0 < \rho < 1$, which must be used when evaluating income paid into the player's withdrawal account. Every period the player plays is a subgame. This subgame may represent the current market. He received a payment as a result of having played the subgame. This enters his corporate account. He then has a financial move which is to rearrange his assets by shifting money between his corporate and his withdrawal accounts.

By means of this type of model, entry and exit or the birth and death processes of the firm can be portrayed explicitly. Furthermore, different goals or objectives of the firm can also be displayed and studied. Formal models giving emphasis on paying out dividends to stockholders, speeding the growth of the firm, or minimizing the risks of being driven out of business may be examined.

The complete portrayal of a simple, one-person game of economic survival is given below:

$$W(0), \; C(0), \; \rho, \; B, \; L, \; \begin{pmatrix} -1 & 1 \\ 1 & -1 \end{pmatrix}, \qquad (p, \, 1-p).$$

$W(O)$ is the initial value of the withdrawal account.
$C(O)$ is the initial value of the corporate account.
ρ is the discount rate.
B is the bankruptcy level which has effect as soon as $C(t) \leq B$.
L is the liquidation value or worth of the corporate account of the firm if it is forced to liquidate.
(a_{ij}) The matrix of the subgame represents the payoffs obtained for the corporate account after each play of the subgame. Here the matrix is specialized to a very simple form.

As this is a one-person game, we assume that the opponent or competitor is "Nature" which is employing a known strategy. This is indicated by $(p, 1-p)$ where $0 \leq p \leq 1$.

The player could attempt to maximize the discounted expected value of his withdrawal account. Alternatively he may wish to maximize the probability of survival for his firm subject to fixed requirements on the dividend policy. The optimal policies under both of these circumstances have been obtained.[26, 27] In the first instance, the optimal policy is such that the firm will eventually be ruined with a probability of 1. This is not surprising when finances are viewed in terms of inventories. Under an optimal inventory policy, unless out-of-stock costs are infinite, the firm will run out of stock sooner or later.

---

[26] *Ibid.*
[27] M. Shubik, *op. cit.*, pp. 260–64.

The type of game described here is closely related to processes that are dealt with by dynamic programing.[28]

As it is for most of game theory, little claim can be made for direct application of dynamic games. They appear, however, to provide a framework in which many concepts of importance to an understanding of markets, firms, and other organizations can be studied. Viability, flexibility, maneuverability, ability to survive, power of threat, ability to retaliate, and sensitivity to information are all examples of concepts which lie in the penumbra between the vague and ill defined and the clear and well defined. An understanding of these aspects of the study of strategy is as important to the knowledge of industry and bureaucracy as it is to the knowledge of international affairs, politics or war.

---

[28] Richard Bellman, *Dynamic Programming* (Princeton, N.J.: Princeton University Press, 1957).

SECTION EIGHT

Field Study Techniques[1]

MANY PEOPLE have an image of the basic or pure researcher in science as the lone wolf who operates in the solitude of his one-man laboratory or at his desk, with paper and pencil or chalk as his main weapons against the unknown, in addition to his knowledge and reasoning power.

We have often tended to regard the equipment-filled large laboratory or the team of researchers milling around as characteristic of the more applied or less basic research effort.

While this image has never been completely accurate in the modern scientific era, it is becoming less and less accurate today in most fields of scientific research—physical, life, and behavioral. For while it is true that most of the important breakthroughs in scientific theory have been the result of the reasoning power or sudden insight of individuals, it is also true that many of these individuals have worked up to the point of break-through or insight as well as after that point in environments character-ized by groups of people and complexes of equipment.

There is hardly an area of basic research today that has not benefited, and in many cases depended on, the development and availability of new equipment and techniques for observing, measuring, analyzing, or simulat-ing the phenomena under study. Some examples are the cyclotron, the reactor, the high-altitude balloon, the arctic airlift, the high-speed com-puter, the ultracentrifuge, the electron microscope, and the earth satellite.

This is a prelude to saying that if the field of organization theory is to progress, it too must utilize new tools and equipment for research. Some of these techniques and tools are already in use, although on a very limited scale. Most of them are not as dramatic as high-altitude balloons, satellites, or nuclear reactors. For the purposes of building organization theories, however, they may be equally powerful.

---

[1] The initial part of this essay is based upon a paper presented at the Academy of Management, St. Louis, December 28, 1960, by Albert H. Rubenstein.

We will discuss four such tools or techniques, some of which have been in use for as long as 30 years, some for only ten. Some of them have not as yet been fully exploited as research tools to develop organizational theories which can help us to explain, predict, and eventually to systematically influence organizational behavior. These four tools are:

1. The small-group experimental laboratory.
2. Simulation of behavior on computers and in "almost-real-life" situations.
3. Mathematical models.
4. Field study methods.

The first of these research tools is perhaps the best known of the four. It is also the only one that is truly a piece of equipment or hardware analogous to some used in the natural sciences. In its pure form the small-group laboratory is a complex instrument for establishing experimental conditions and providing observations of the experiment in progress. One of the earliest such laboratories, perhaps the first, was the one at Harvard in the Department of Social Relations, designed and built under the direction of R. F. Bales in the 1940's. Its principal feature was a one-way mirror for observing the members of small groups without, in turn, being observed.

Certainly this was not the first time that anyone had observed small groups in action. But with the development and refinement of the laboratory, a degree of control began to be achieved which was a distinct advance in the art of experimentation. Other rooms were designed and built, some based directly on the Harvard one, others incorporating innovations.

At the same time that such experimental rooms—and there are now dozens of them in the U.S. and abroad—helped in the attempt to achieve the experimenter's dream of a behavioral experiment not influenced by the presence of the experimenter, it has raised certain ethical and practical questions associated with secret observation. Such questions are not unique to this research method; they also apply to the participant-observer in field studies and the role of the experimenter in simulation studies. They do come closest, however, to our cultural image of white mice or guinea pigs being manipulated in a cage.

Despite such possible drawbacks, the small-group experimental room has been the first real experimental tool or piece of equipment for studying organized human behavior. As one might expect, when researchers at M.I.T. became interested in small-group research—notably the famous Bavelas experiments (4)—they added technological refinements in the form of electronic controls and analytical tools, i.e., a computer.

The question of what researchers do with these experimental rooms is another matter. One of the major drawbacks that has been recognized in some fields of physical science research is the tendency to become equipment-centered and to carry out studies which are adaptable to the tools available, whether they are significant or of prime interest to the researcher or not. This tendency is noticeable in the behavior of many engineers who rush into the laboratory and begin manipulating equipment instead of sitting and developing adequate theory and hypotheses.

Some of the small-group experimenters, with or without the aid of the experimental lab, are primarily interested in small-group phenomena as such. They may see possible direct applications of findings to committees, problem-solving groups, or play and work groups; or they may be fascinated by the esthetics of the experimental group itself as a phenomenon worth studying.

Other small-group experimenters are interested in the possibilities of generalizing from the results of small-group experiments to the organization of society as a whole. This latter procedure—the interaction between field observation and laboratory experiments—holds great promise for advancing the field. This has been one of the major research strategies of the Institute for Social Research at the University of Michigan and has been used by the organizational behavior group at Carnegie Institute of Technology.

The second research tool or method is partly hardware and partly experimental design. It is the simulation of organizational behavior. This simulation is being performed in two ways—on high-speed computers and in organizational laboratories. Simulation of organizational behavior by computer is relatively new, with only a few actual studies in the literature. One of the earliest of these was the simulation of small-group decision making done in the summer of 1951 at the RAND Corporation. The start of this exercise was a series of memoranda setting forth the essential features of the small group interaction process as observed by Bales in his small-group laboratory. A. S. Householder rewrote some parts of these interaction models in mathematical form and prepared flow diagrams to guide a Monte Carlo computation of the models. (3) Severe mathematical and computational difficulties were encountered in this work, including the estimation of parameter values from experimental data. More recent computer simulation includes Article No. 33 and the decision simulations discussed on pages 588–89.

With the increased availability of high-speed computer facilities all over the country, and increased access to them for behavioral research, this method holds tremendous promise for breakthroughs in the field. The major obstacles encountered by the RAND experimenters, however, still persist. The computer can approach reality only in relation to our systematic knowledge of reality. That is, nonsense instructions on human behavior, fed into a computer, will produce nonsense results. Computer simulation, despite its great promise, cannot stand alone without adequate formal—that is, mathematical—theory and good empirical or experimental data. The beauty of simulation experimentation, of course, is its economy of time and money (depending on the cost of computer time). Organizational parameters such as growth rates, size, status relationships, decision rules, etc., can readily be changed to see what *would* happen, or what *might* happen. One can start with very simple models and gradually increase their complexity so as to approach real life.

The other major method of simulation involves controlled experiments on organizations in an almost-real-life situation. This is about the closest we can come to "real, real life," because in "real, real life" there are no experimenters, at least none that we are aware of.

Again, refer to the work discussed in section 2—the earliest and still the largest scale simulation of this type that was done at the RAND Corporation. The salient feature of this kind of simulation is that actual people are involved with all of the richness of perception and behavioral potential that is human. The control is achieved through control over the inputs to the system (i.e., information, assigned tasks, etc.) the reward and penalty system, and the ability to manipulate certain other environmental constraints and interpersonal relations. For example, communication patterns can be systematically varied, alternative decision rules can be tried, and so on.

This method of experimentation, used extensively by the military under the heading of war gaming, is a very powerful tool, but very expensive and much less neat (in an experimental sense) than group laboratory experimenting or computer simulation. Control is difficult to achieve, observation is difficult, and the degree of complexity is very high.

Two other examples of such simulation may be mentioned. One is the ill-fated but extremely interesting work at the Air Force Survival Training School (6) where the degree of reality achieved aroused the public and led to modification of the program. Another is the work currently being done by Guetzkow at Northwestern in simulating international relations (5).

The third and perhaps most powerful research method in organizational theory has been in general use less than 15 years. It is the use of mathematical models for describing and representing organizational behavior. It is also, perhaps, the most controversial method.

This controversy is well exemplified in a paper by Abraham Kaplan, called "Sociology Learns the Language of Mathematics" (8). In it he criticizes the vast amount of pseudomathematics and nonapplicable mathematics that has entered the literature. There have been attempts prior to the recent upsurge in mathematical modeling to apply directly the mathematical methods and specific mathematical models from various fields of science and engineering to the study of organizational behavior. Most of them have not been very useful so far in advancing the field. The major result has been stimulation of new activity, although in some cases a valid abstraction from real life has been produced. It is possible that as simulation techniques and data collection and experimental methods advance, some of the models and analytical tools provided by servomechanism theory, information theory, game theory, etc., may produce important insights or breakthroughs.

Certainly much has already been gained in making certain concepts and data more precise by the introduction of mathematical rigor and, in some cases, mathematical models. One of the most striking examples was the paper by Simon in which he expressed a number of the basic relationships in Homan's book, *The Human Group*, in a set of three differential equations (**11**). Among the most exciting possibilities has been the work in stochastic learning theory, decision theory, and other frameworks which can account for the complex and dynamic nature of human behavior.

The fourth tool—the field study approach of the anthropologist—is the one of most direct interest to us in our teaching and research on organization theory. In many of the courses in organization theory which we have taught over the past 15 years, field studies have been an integral part. With the increase in volume of required reading, however, it has been necessary to institute a separate course in organizational field studies.

The field study method permits flexibility of research design and the opportunity to modify data-collection methods and the nature of the specific data required as the study progresses. This permits the researcher to capitalize on what he is learning about the organization. This is a critical part of the field researcher's strategy, but does not eliminate the possibility of a rigorous field study design. The overall design can be constructed in advance of actual entry into the field site, but it must be subject to modification if the advantage cited above is to be achieved.

With proper interplay between the other research methods and this one, we believe that field *experiments*—not mere data collection exercises or case studies of current practice—provide the greatest hope for increasing our understanding of organizational behavior. The Hawthorne studies (**9**) were an early example of this.

There has been some discussion among organization theorists about the possibility of field experimentation with organizations on a scale similar to the simulation experiments conducted by RAND (Articles 11 and 12). Seashore (**10**) describes such an approach. Except for the Hawthorne studies and other studies involving small groups in their natural organization setting, not much actual progress has been made in this direction. If we are willing to give up our model, borrowed from the natural sciences, of a rigorously controlled experiment, however, we may find that some of the studies of planned change and other "before-and-after" studies might qualify as field experiments.

Unfortunately, field studies have not been easily worked into the curricula of most of the social sciences as yet—many prefer the laboratory or the library—and so the total amount of such activity is not very high.

There is increasing interest in it, however, and we believe we will see some dramatic results from its use in the next few years.

There are two common categories of such field studies, each with its own advantages and procedural difficulties. The traditional method, borrowed directly from social anthropology, uses an observer who is clearly a researcher—an outsider to the group or organization being studied. The second kind, which is rather hazardous both methodologically and physically at times, is the participant-observer method in which the researcher is actually part of the organization being studied, either through design or by chance.

Aside from the high potential for contributions to organization theory, we have found limited field experiments—designed and conducted as rigorously as a simulation or laboratory experiment, but adapted to field circumstances—to be a very valuable teaching device when proper professional supervision is used.

Although there now exists a substantial literature on research methods in the social sciences, there is still no standard or "best" way of conducting an organizational field study. The procedures and specific measuring instruments used depend very heavily on: the research questions being asked; the background and experience of the investigators; the characteristics of the specific organization(s) being studied; and the environmental conditions which may affect the use of particular procedures.

Despite this lack of uniformity, however, certain general approaches and specific data gathering procedures have become fairly common among people who conduct field studies in organizations. The discussion which follows is an attempt to point out some of these common features and to present a set of research questions which may be applicable to a wide range of field study investigations. For more detail on specific techniques—e.g., interviews or questionnaires—the reader is referred to the references at the end of this section (1).

The discussion of field research techniques given below covers the following general areas: (1) Obtaining background information on the organization being studied; (2) making field notes and keeping the notebook; (3) gaining rapport with the people to be studied; (4) questionnaire and interview construction and administration; and, (5) direct observation of organizational behavior.

1. Obtaining Background Information. One of the major reasons for conducting a field study, in preference to using other techniques such as simulation or small-group experimentation, is to get as close as possible to the "real" organizational phenomena we are studying. For this reason it is important for the field researcher to know a lot about the organization, especially about those aspects that relate to the phenomenon being studied. If, for example, the focus of the research is communication, one should know as much as possible about the modes of communication that are available to the organization and the aspects of physical layout that might significantly affect communication. In general, these questions can guide the search for background information on the organization:

What kind of organization is it? What does it do?

Who runs the organization? Who are the important people in it?

How are duties divided in the organization? Who is who and who does what?

What is the history of the organization? How did it get to its present stage of development?

What significant organizational events have occurred?

Apart from its formal function, what kind of organization is it in comparison with other, similar organizations?

These questions can be raised at different levels in the organization, depending on the focus of the field investigation. The question of the place of the organization in society at large may be quite relevant for some levels of investigation—e.g., goal formation, growth, relations with other organizations. Comparison of this organization with others in its field is generally relevant for a study of the organization as a whole. If only a part of the organization is being studied (a functional department, a certain level in the hierarchy, or a particular group of individuals), analogous questions can be raised relating the unit being studied to other units in the organization.

An excellent starting place for background description at any organization level is the "workflow process." Assume that any organization one might study has some sort of mission or function. One should attempt to determine the general organization of work and the step-by-step process by which that work is accomplished. This is not always easy in some kinds of organizations which do not have a clearly defined work process, e.g., a social club or an honorary society. However, it is generally possible to obtain some sort of description of who does what, when, and how.

The crucial thing about obtaining background information is the need to avoid missing the obvious or the basic things about the organization. For example, consider the effects these circumstances might have on a study of decision making, labor relations, communication, or control.

There have been a series of serious strikes in recent years in the company, some violent.

The organization is owned by a family group, all but one of whose members are inactive in the affairs of the organization, but who depend on its profits for their income.

This organization has become the leader in its field only recently and has been in a seesaw battle for first place for many years.

Until recently, the organization was dominated by one individual—the founder, who did not allow anyone else to exercise much authority.

The reputation of the organization in its environment is that of a keen competitor, who sometimes straddles the line between legality and ethical considerations.

There is currently under way a major reorganization in the parent organization of which the organization being studied is a branch, chapter, or subsidiary.

It may appear obvious that such information as the kind illustrated above is necessary. However, the field investigator cannot be sure that such information will be given to him unsolicited. Sometimes, situations and events such as these are so well known and taken for granted by members of the organization that no one bothers to mention them. In other cases, the information may be considered proprietary or confidential.

The point of the discussion so far is that there are certain facts of life about an organization that are critical to an understanding of it. Missing some of these points can make the difference between a good field investigation and one that is merely fair or that actually fails to achieve its purpose.

The sources of data for this background information depend on the kind of organization and the specific circumstances. Some kinds of organizations (e.g., publicly held business firms and government agencies) receive substantial press coverage and issue a considerable volume of information about their operations. Others keep their activities very quiet and neither issue information nor allow the press to find out much. Where such published information is available, it provides an excellent starting point. The back files of annual reports, local and national newspapers and magazines, directories, and catalogs and brochures can provide a great deal of background information. Apart from certain information such as size, location, and general operations, one should attempt to seek confirmation of published information. Certain events and situations are described in published form for purposes other than background information for research purposes. Some of it is for sales purposes or general public relations.

An indispensable source of background information is an informant who has been in the organization for some time and is familiar with it. Such an individual (or individuals) can provide much insight into the way the organization actually works, who does what, and how things arrived at their present state. Complete dependence on the information from one informant can be dangerous, however. Such data is subject to all the biases discussed below under "interviewing" and some additional ones.

Frequently an organization member who places himself at the disposal of an outside researcher has a point of view or an "axe to grind" that might color the description he provides. In addition, he may not be the best source of such information, merely the most willing. One frequently encounters new members of organizations who are eager to talk about the history of the organization as though they had participated in it. Sometimes these historical accounts consist of second- or third-hand impressions, rumors, and folklore. The attractions of an eager, valuable informant are high for the field researcher, but extreme care must be used in selecting (or being selected by) such a person and in using the information he provides.

In addition to external published sources and informants, there are a myriad of other information sources available to the field researcher. These include internal documents (if made available by the organization), organization charts, organization manuals, internal house organs, bulletin boards, general memoranda circulated in the organization, and special reports. The alert researcher can also pick up odd bits of gossip to be later verified and followed up, *if relevant to the investigation.* This latter point is important. Organizations are complex entities and there are innumerable events occurring which may be of casual interest to the researcher as a researcher or merely as a person (and a member of some organization himself). Aimless information gathering and chasing intriguing leads can easily divert the researcher from his main focus. It is a temptation to even highly experienced field investigators and can be very costly in terms of the main research objectives.

2. Field Notes and the Notebook.   Many field investigations fail as the result of poor data recording. Even when the field study is sharply focused around a simple research question, other information may bear on that question. Such information may be critical in interpreting the main body of data collected by systematic means such as structured interviews and questionnaires. Care must be taken that this data is properly recorded and identified as to source, time of collection, and surrounding circumstances. Frequently, a half-remembered casual conversation with an organization member may hold the clue to interpretation of a vital set of data after the field phase has been completed. If there is no record of that conversation, the researcher is running the risk of misremembering the details, attributing it to the wrong source, or otherwise distorting the data.

Even with respect to systematically collected bodies of data from such instruments as questionnaires, it is important to have a record of the circumstances surrounding the construction, modification, administration, and analysis of the data from the instrument. It is frustrating to encounter a situation where several modifications have been made to an instrument (e.g., an interview) during the course of a study and there is no record of which subjects received which versions, which versions were pilot-tested, and what specific things were happening in the organization at the time of administration that might have affected the responses.

There is no absolute guarantee against problems of lost data and incomplete or incorrect interpretation due to failure to record enough information. However, the making of careful and complete field notes and the conscientious maintenance of a notebook can help considerably.

The mechanical form of the notebook varies according to the type of study, the magnitude of data, the number of investigators, and individual preferences of investigators. The "notebook" may not necessarily be a notebook. It may be a card file, a set of carefully coded file folders, or a notebook, looseleaf or bound. Strict measures must be taken to avoid loss of data.

What should the notebook contain? Again, this depends on the particular circumstances of the study. In general, the following information should be included in the notebook (or other project record):

1. The originals or duplicate copies of all field notes. These notes have mysterious ways of becoming misplaced or lost. They are the chief sources of interview and observational data, as well as background information on the organization. Safeguarding them and keeping them in proper order is essential. Each page of field notes should be numbered serially, and a running chronological record of them should be kept. The name of the field investigator, the date the notes were made, and surrounding circumstances are all important. Since the handwriting of many field researchers is not very intelligible to others (particularly when notes are made under adverse conditions), every effort should be made to transcribe them as soon as possible into typewritten form. This may be expensive, but it is well worth the cost when the investment in the data collection itself is jeopardized by illegible handwriting, illegible even to the writer after some time has elapsed.

2. Copies of all research instruments—questionnaires, interview schedules, observation guides, etc. All versions of a given instrument should be placed in the notebook and all changes in methods of administration should be recorded. The designers, testers, administrators, and analysts of the data from the instruments should be identified.

3. Copies of all data—originals or duplicates should be in the notebook or project file. The loss of a key set of data (even temporarily, while someone is on a trip) can be costly.

4. Minutes of all meetings between project members. In particular, there should be a clear record of problems and their solutions, decisions, and changes in design. This is vital when a number of field investigators are involved.

5. Copies of all background documents and internal documents. With the increased availability and the decreased cost of duplicating printed and written materials, this is generally a good investment.

The method of organizing material in the notebook or file is important. In some cases, a purely chronological arrangement will suffice. In others, a system of categories with cross-classification is needed. The more initial indexing and systematizing that is done in construction of the notebook or file, the easier will be the retrieval of information and the analysis of data.

Many study schedules fail to allow enough time for data reduction, analysis, and write-up. A well-organized notebook or file can help in the hectic period when the study is drawing to a close.

Notebooks, field notes, and files tend to become disorganized during the course of the study; care should be taken to keep them organized and up to date. Some sections of the data can be analyzed immediately, or during slack periods in field activity. This should be done whenever possible, to avoid the last minute scramble to get the study finished and written up. Field notes should be continually examined, analyzed, and interrelated. Clues to gaps in the information being collected can be discovered by this process and a well-organized notebook or file system can help tremendously.

Some investigators integrate their literature search with the data continuously. Others do the literature search at one time and then relate it to the data later. In either event, ideas from and references to the literature should also be integrated into the notebook system.

3. Gaining Rapport. Field research is an imposition on the time and an intrusion into the privacy of organization members. Even though permission has been received for the investigation from their superiors, many organization members are reluctant to participate. There is seldom any direct advantage to them in supplying information to a stranger, despite his credentials, and there is always the chance that it may do them harm. It is, therefore, crucial to try to obtain the cooperation of the people in the organization being studied. This is not always possible, but is worth a great deal of effort. In some instances, subjects may be "too" cooperative. They may try to use the researchers to their own advantage. The researcher must be alert to this possibility.

Two general categories of people are involved in this attempt to establish rapport. The first group consists of "gatekeepers," who may or may not supply information directly. But they are the means of access to those who do. Often these people are in top management and must give their overall consent to the study, in addition to arranging for the investigators to be introduced in the organization. The second group are the subjects themselves, whose behavior and/or attitudes form the basis of the study.

Two extreme views are held by field researchers in organization theory, and there are many gradations of opinion between the extremes. One group advocates keeping as much personal distance as possible between investigator and subject or informant, emphasizing objectivity and detachment. This view reflects the traditions of natural science, where there is a sharp dividing line between the researcher and the object of his research. The other viewpoint frankly admits that complete objectivity is not possible in studying human organizations and advocates taking advantage of the fact that the investigator is, himself, a person. This leads to a deliberate attempt to become involved with the subjects for purposes of increased understanding of the situation by the researcher, closer rapport between him and the subjects, and—in some cases—bringing about changes in the organization being studied. This latter objective was dominant in several of the studies of planned change described in Section 4. Bringing about organizational change is an avowed objective of members of the Society for Applied Anthropology who broke away from the American Anthropological Association in the early 1940's in order to concentrate on that objective. In general, the discussion of research techniques in this section tends toward the natural science model, where every effort is made to reduce the impact of the investigation on the people being studied.

Gaining and maintaining rapport with subjects in a field investigation is an art, and we cannot lay down firm rules for procedure. We can, however, make a few potentially helpful observations on pitfalls to avoid. These observations are based on more than 30 research programs involving field investigations in which we have participated and another 50 or more that our students have conducted under our direction.

Do not deliberately mislead the members of the organization as to the purpose of the study. A careful, well-thought-out briefing of all participants is necessary to avoid misunderstandings. This briefing should not provide any more detail than is necessary for the participants to know what is expected of them and why they are being asked to participate. Too much technical detail or too much exposure to the theory underlying the study may tend to confuse people, lead to attempts on their part to help the investigators reformulate the theory, or produce spurious data. The briefing should be consistent for all people concerned, so that the rumor system will have less chance of producing boomerangs for the investigators.

Assure the respondents that their answers will not be fed back to anyone in the organization and that no data will be associated with them by name or in any way that can identify them (if those are the agreements). *Keep the promises* of anonymity.

Try to avoid personal involvement in the affairs of the organization and identification with one faction or another. This may be difficult when several levels or groups of an organization are involved in the study and the "gatekeeper" is in one of them.

Avoid showing off your knowledge of the organization by feeding back information received from other organization members to a person being interviewed. This may not always be possible, since many field study designs involve the following up of leads from interview to interview.

Try to avoid acting the role of expert or consultant or confidant. This can both reduce the objectivity of your approach and the willingness of other people to give you the data you request. Try to avoid becoming a tool of the organization members with whom you are engaged—that is, a status tool or an information source.

Respect the time schedule and major preoccupations of your subjects. The field research participation may be an assignment for them or it may be an enjoyable interlude, but do not abuse the privileges extended to you by making an extended social event out of it. If the subject does not complain, his supervisor or subordinates might, especially if the latter are queued up waiting to see their boss.

Don't promise anything you cannot or should not deliver—advice, feedback, etc.

Dress appropriately and behave appropriately for the organization and the specific circumstances of the field contact.

There are many other hints and cautionary constraints that one picks up in field research, such as attempting to avoid being a threat to the people being studied. But these are part of the art of field research mentioned above and can best be learned through experience.

4. Questionnaire and Interview Construction and Administration. Like field research itself, the construction and administration of questionnaires and interviews in research on organizational behavior are matters of art. This is not necessarily true for all kinds of questionnaires and interviews, however. There are some useful general principles that have been developed in connection with census taking, opinion polling, and consumer surveys, for example, that can serve as guides for design and administration of such instruments. Where the subject of the research is individual behavior, opinion, or factual data such as the census taker seeks, long years of experience and thousands of responses have resulted in rules for reducing errors and increasing responses. In general, this stage has not yet been reached in field research in organizations.

Part of the reason is the lack of replication and the typically small sample sizes. The usual organizational field study is conducted in one organization or a small sample of them. It is seldom replicated by its author and almost never by other investigators. Even where similar studies are attempted, the field methods are generally changed and the original instruments are seldom used again in the same form. An additional complication is that most organization theorists are not specialists in questionnaire or interview techniques. There are such people in advertising agencies, government bureaus, and professional survey organizations, but such professionals are seldom used by organization researchers. This is not to say that professional survey people would or would not do a better job than an individual organization theorist, but merely to indicate that current practice is such that the instruments used in organizational field studies are typically not developed by specialists. The major exception to this is, of course, the survey research done by the Survey Research Center at the University of Michigan and the various University Bureaus of Social Research which have entered the organization theory field.

A few of the articles in this book report the results of survey research through mass questionnaire administration. The majority of empirical studies included, however, involve the use of multiple data-gathering techniques and an extended period of investigation *at the field site*. Survey research, employing lengthy questionnaires and very large samples, has contributed greatly to our understanding of some aspects of organizational behavior. It is our conviction, however, that this approach alone is not adequate in developing organization theories. The survey method used alone and generally employing self-administered questionnaires does not provide the opportunity for a thorough analysis of the organization and consideration of the important interrelationships discussed above under "background information." As an adjunct to a comprehensive field study which employs a whole battery of techniques, it can be very valuable. Data on specific aspects of organizational behavior can be collected quickly, uniformly, and relatively cheaply, compared to other field techniques. The essential point here is that "field research" on organizational behavior implies multiple techniques and, above all, *direct, continuing contact* with the subject organization.

Due to the artful nature of questionnaire and interview construction, discussed above, it is not possible to present a full discussion of "how to do it." There are several good references on this subject (1), and we will confine our comments here to a few major issues.

Questionnaires vs. Interviews: The content and format of questionnaire and interview schedules (the list of questions or the line of questioning to be pursued) can be very similar. We might consider a continuum from a highly structured, self-administered questionnaire where the respondent merely checks off the appropriate answer, to a completely open-ended interview where the interviewer merely mentions the purpose of the interview and sits back to listen.

Structured questionnaires are easier to administer and analyze than interviews, but are typically more costly to prepare. Interviews require more skill in administration and analysis. Aside from the extremes cited above, there are all manner of combined formats. Administered questionnaires (or highly structured interviews) require that a researcher read the questions to the subject and record the answers. Some field procedures combine questionnaires and interviews in one administration. For example, a field researcher may begin an "interview" with some open-ended questions and end by leaving or administering a highly structured questionnaire. In one of our studies of research scientists at Northwestern, we are experimenting with a new type of "self-administered interview." This requires that the respondent, at a given time or after a given stimulus (e.g., a telephone call from the investigator), respond to several standard questions about his information-seeking activities by reporting over a remote telephone–tape recorder system.

Measurement and Scaling: In all aspects of data collection in organizations (as in all attempts at scientific investigation) problems of measurement and scaling arise. The difficulties of finding adequate units of measure or scales for human behavior, attitudes, and perceptions are well known to organization researchers. Many studies with careful, well-constructed research designs fail because of measurement and scaling problems. Some progress has been made in constructing scales specifically for the kinds of variables encountered in organization research, but the situation is still not encouraging. The kinds of scales used by the physicist and the engineer—arithmetic or extensive scales—are generally not feasible for describing human behavior at the level of interest to the organization theorist. As indicated in the introduction to the section on decision making, we are frequently at a loss in saying whether a person merely *prefers* object or situation A to B. We are not able to make simple quantitative statements about *how much* he prefers A to B—e.g., "twice as much."

We are unable, for example, to compare people or organizational units with respect to variables like "morale," "power," or "motivation," in any rigorous manner. We rely heavily on ordinal scales (A is less than B, which is less than C, etc.) and on categories that do not even imply order. Some progress has been made in constructing scales especially for the variables of human behavior and cognition, but more work is desperately needed.

Reliability of Data from Respondents: Much of the work that has been done in describing or measuring organizational behavior has rested on the implicit assumption that reports of events by informants or subjects correspond closely or exactly with the actual way in which the events occurred. If such reports are the only source of data for determining what "really happened," there may be several uncontrolled and even unacknowledged sources of error:

1. One general source of error is the informant's perceptual slant—his *einstellung* or perceptual set. The effect of perceptual set or slant has been investigated by many students of intergroup prejudice by such means as attitude tests. Perceptual ability is also known to vary and much has been said about it. Reports of a given event from several witnesses without training in careful observation have often been found to bear little resemblance to each other.

2. A second general source of error is the informant's failure to remember just what did happen. Assuming that he received a fairly reliable impression of an event at the time that it happened, it has been indicated by experiments in recall and by the experience of all of us that it generally becomes more difficult with passage of time to describe the details of an event as we originally perceived it. A great deal has been said on this

matter in relation to the reliability of witness reports weeks or months after the occurrence of the event.

3. A third general source of error may be the reluctance of the subject, for whatever reason, to report his "true" impression of what occurred. This condition has been encountered often in organizational studies where subjects may distort descriptions of events or interpersonal relationships for fear of retaliation, desire not to upset others, or a general reluctance to verbalize a particular type of situation or event.

4. Assuming that all of these sources of error have been acknowledged and accounted for, there is a fourth and overriding source of error which is usually explicit in rigorously designed and executed investigations—the inability of the subject to communicate his report; or conversely, the inability of the investigator to get from the subject through whatever techniques (interview, questionnaire, observation) the information that the subject is willing and able to give.

Pilot Testing: Heavy investments of time and energy go into the construction and administration of questionnaires, interview schedules, and other field study instruments. The most important resource is the time of the respondents or subjects in the organization being studied. Where an instrument is administered to the entire set of subjects at one time, there is no opportunity to correct its design or administration technique unless there is a rigorous pilot test in advance of full administration. Careful pilot testing, as many times as are necessary, is one of the best investments the field researcher can make of his time and resources.

A questionnaire item or a line of questioning in an interview schedule may seem perfectly reasonable and clear back at the university, but may fail miserably in the field. Simulated testing on colleagues, students, or other nonsubjects can help, but it is not adequate for many situations. In view of the possible sources of error described above, the researcher must try his instruments in a situation as close to the real one as possible—the real one, if possible. Most organizations in which we have conducted field studies have been agreeable to an exploratory period and a pilot test of some of our instruments. In some cases a full pilot-testing procedure was not feasible, due to time pressures or small sample sizes; therefore, efforts were made to administer the instruments in some sequential order that would allow at least a few days or hours for slight modifications in administration procedure or in the content of the instrument itself. Some researchers are reluctant to make any substantial changes, such as dropping or adding items, because this can reduce the sample size for purposes of statistical analysis. However, a small sample of good data is superior to a large sample of bad (irrelevant or unreliable) data. Pilot testing of critical instruments is usually possible if the early stages of the field investigation are concerned with the less structured exploratory aspects of data collection—background information and general orientation. This permits modifications and testing of the instruments in a casual or leisurely fashion with a small sample of the respondents.

Once a mass data collection effort has been conducted—e.g., interviews or questionnaires administered to all members of the organization—the organization needs time to recover and therefore the field investigators are often asked to withdraw for a limited period or permanently.

Among the specific things the pilot study can accomplish are these: (1) Descriptions of the behavior of the respondents during the administration of the instrument. This is particularly important when remote administration is used—e.g., a self-administered questionnaire. It is important for the researcher to know what kinds of questions and what kinds of interpretations and decisions he is making. There should be an opportunity for the respondent to "think aloud" in the presence of the researcher while he is attempting to formulate answers. (2) Uncovering the possible reasons for nonresponse in advance of the administration. This can save the whole program from disaster, if properly done. (3) Testing of alternative order or format of the items in the instrument. We know, intuitively, that these features of an instrument can affect the responses. Sometimes these effects can be highly significant.

Categories for Data Collection: This is a perennial problem for all aspects of field research in organizations. It is a little easier for field research than it is for remote data-collection methods such as mail surveys. The advantage comes from being able to formulate the categories from a combination of the theory behind the study, the preconceived design, and the realities of the field situation. Many category schemes are theoretically fine but fail in the field due to particular circumstances in the subject organization. These can include proprietary considerations, special languages used in the organization, conditions which are not obvious from "outside," and many others. Balanced against this flexible stance are strong arguments for preselection of categories for data collection.

Many field investigators have found it easy to collect data according to *ad hoc* categories, based on what they were able to obtain in the field and modified as the research progressed. Some of them have encountered severe difficulties, however, when the time came to reduce and analyze the data. The picture of researchers struggling to extract meaningful categories from a mass of data collected without benefits of a systematic framework is a familiar one in organization research. The data from open-ended interviews, casual observation, and piles of unclassified documents can pose tremendous problems of data reduction and analysis after the field phase is over and no more data can be collected to fill in gaps or reconcile conflicting information.

Some category sets are implied by the research questions being asked. If one is interested in the number of events that have occurred over a certain time period, the major precaution in categorization is to be sure that the analysis planned for that data is compatible with the categories made available to the respondent. For example, if the respondent can only answer "very often," "not so often," or "rarely," the investigator is stretching the limits of credibility when he assigns numerical values to these frequencies, based on an arbitrary *post hoc* scaling procedure. In many cases, the theory or the research question will generate the categories for interviews and questionnaires. In other cases, measurement problems will dictate them. In measuring "competence" for example, it may not be possible to validly distinguish more than 2 or 3 gradations among the subjects being rated as to competence. In any case, care must be taken to assure the logical consistency of category sets in advance of serious data collection. Failure to do this can lead to much cutting and slicing of the data in an attempt to extract useful categories.

   5. Direct Observation: This is the most difficult of all the usual techniques used by field researchers. It requires the most intrusion into the field study site and can cause extreme reaction by organization members if not handled properly. Some form of casual observation is used by every field researcher. He notices aspects of the physical layout of the organization, the location and movement of people, and the overt aspects of the workflow process. He is also alert to the outward behavior of the people he is interviewing and other people his subjects come into contact with in the presence of the researcher. The changes in behavior of a respondent in the presence of subordinates, superiors, and colleagues can provide the experienced field researcher with clues that can help him put the respondent's interview behavior in perspective.

   Apart from this casual, routine sort of observation, many field study designs incorporate systematic observation techniques as a major source of data (e.g., Article 9 by Horsfall and Arensberg). In societies where there is a language barrier, the cultural anthropologist may have to depend heavily on direct observation for much of his data about the way the subject society operates. This tradition, carried over into Applied Anthropology by Chapple, Arensberg, Richardson and others (7), has led to the kind of interaction studies used by a number of investigators. Another tradition of observation comes from the small-group laboratory, using the procedures and categories of interaction process analysis developed by Bales (2). Other investigators developed their own techniques and categories. For example, Marquis, Guetzkow, and Heyns (6) developed categories and techniques for observing decision-making conferences in real organizations, as compared to laboratory groups.

   Among the questions that should precede a decision to use observation techniques are these: what behavior can be observed that cannot be described in other ways; what data can be obtained more easily or more reliably by observation than by other means; what assurances can be given that the observation process is not seriously affecting the behavior being observed; what interpretation needs to be performed on observational data to avoid being misled by the obvious; and how much skill is required and available for the actual observation itself? If direct observation is to be done properly in a complex situation, it can be very time consuming. Proper sampling procedures must be used to ascertain the degree of stability in the behavior being observed. Without knowledge of stability, inferences drawn from small samples of behavior (small time slices) can be very inaccurate. For example, sampling communication or decision making during a very limited time period (e.g., several hours on one particular day) may be a very poor basis for drawing inferences about the usual day-to-day behavior in the organization and vice versa.

Some Examples of Field Study Exercises: As an illustration of the possibilities of field studies as part of a course or courses in organization theory, we present below, in capsule form, a number of the studies that have been carried out as part of such course work at M.I.T., University of Denver, and Northwestern University. The length of time devoted to field studies has varied between schools and between levels (graduate or undergraduate courses). Some of the studies were designed, conducted, and written up in a period of five to six weeks, as part of semester-long courses; the others were conducted over a nine- to ten-week period, as part of a quarter-long field study course.

These studies were primarily class exercises designed to introduce the student to the realities of studying organization life and to illustrate some of the problems of conducting investigations in operating organizations. In addition, however, some of them achieved interesting research results and led to a number of theses and dissertations in organization theory, business administration, and educational administration. Each study is described in terms of: 1) Setting—the place where the study was conducted; 2) Variables—the major factors studied, including principal variables and parameters, and other "interesting" factors on which data was gathered; 3) Relationships—The hypotheses or propositions that the study was designed to explore or test. In some cases, the investigators were not able to test these prior hypotheses due to lack of data, lack of access, or other factors. In the case of Number 8, the study was not structured around an *a priori* hypothesis; 4) Findings—the results of the study including, where possible, tests of the relationships or hypotheses and other "interesting" findings.

1. AN EXPLORATORY STUDY OF COMMUNICATION AS A FUNCTION OF LEVEL IN AN ORGANIZATIONAL HIERARCHY
Setting: A men's clothing factory.
Variables: Organizational level, individual propensity to communicate, group effect, nature of the task, task-oriented communications.
Relationships: The time spent in task-oriented communication—oral and written combined—for the personnel in a structured organization increases

from the lowest level in the organization to some level where it ceases to increase, and finally decreases at the highest level.

Research Methods: Half a day of observation at each level of the organization. Interview follow-up. Sample consisted of 16 men at six different formally designated levels in the organization.

Findings: Oral communication is the most important means of communication in this company. It increases with level up to the fourth level. After that, for the remaining levels, it declines.

2. A STUDY OF THE IMAGE OF THE FOREMAN AND COMPANY AS PERCEIVED BY THE WORKER

Setting: A company which manufactures precision parts and machinery—400 workers.

Variables: Workers' personality, personality of the foreman, type of company.

Relationships: The image of the foreman and the image of the company are alike in the mind of the employee.

Research Methods: A questionnaire was designed to measure, in a relative sense, how the worker feels toward his foreman and how he feels toward the company for which he works. Administered to 40 skilled workers.

Findings: The t test indicated to a high degree of statistical significance that there was a difference between a worker's perception of the company and his perception of his foreman. The image of the company differed across the work groups, but the image of the foreman did not do so to a substantial degree.

3. THE USE OF INTERACTION MATRICES IN ASSESSING THE EFFECTIVENESS OF A COMMITTEE

Setting: Trust Investment Committee of a bank.

Variables: Behavior of members of the group; size of the committee, composition of the committee; participation of the members; leadership of the committee.

Relationships: The effectiveness of a committee can be assessed by recording and analyzing the contributions made by its members. Since contributions may be task oriented or personality oriented, account must be taken of the interaction pattern of the group and within the group.

Research Methods: The contributions of the members were logged on a matrix. Three criteria of success were established: (*a*) large range of judgment; (*b*) large amount of task-oriented disagreement; and (*c*) small amount of personality-oriented disagreement.

Findings: It is possible for one observer to record the interactions in a committee of up to ten persons. The use of an interaction matrix such as the one utilized yields significant information. A comparison of the histograms produced from the matrices showed that the method was an objective one.

4. A STUDY OF PERCEPTION: SUPERIOR VS. SUBORDINATE

Setting: Account manager level of an advertising agency.

Variables: The ways in which a superior and a subordinate perceive the subordinate's job; the perceptive differences of a "real-life" situation; level of people in the organization; complexity of the organization; tenure of the encumbent; critical function of the individual; degree of control, i.e., the closeness of supervision.

Relationships: The perception which people have of a job will be significantly different from the perception other people have of the same job, depending upon their respective relationship to the job.

Research Methods: Perceptual differences were sought by interviews of both superiors and subordinates.

Findings: The job descriptions offered by the superiors and subordinates did not coincide exactly. In certain cases, the procedures the supervisor would use did not correspond to the procedures that the subordinates stated they would use.

5. FIELD STUDY OF GROWTH OF AN INDUSTRIAL ORGANIZATION RELATED TO CHANGING PATTERNS OF STRUCTURE

Setting: A rapidly growing manufacturing company.

Variables: Persons dealing with internal and external activities; varying functions; varying size of the organization.

Relationships: As an organization grows, the number of people within the internal administration function grows at a more rapid rate than does the total number of people in the whole organization.

Research Methods: Literature survey of theory of growth; research of all available documents concerning the growth rate of the organization.

Findings: Unable to demonstrate that nonproductive costs grow more rapidly than total costs. After several weeks of preliminary study and negotiation, researchers were unable to obtain enough information due to the unusual circumstances in the company and the deadline of the end of the semester.

6. ABSENTEEISM IN A PUBLIC UTILITY

Setting: Two major departments in a public utility.

Variables: Information shortage; difference in work situations; personal differences.

Relationships: A difference in work situations is related to the rate of absenteeism. Absences due to illness occur more frequently in firms with liberal benefit programs and lenient absentee policies. Incidental absence (first seven consecutive days of employment), if controlled, causes a reduction in the overall rate of absenteeism. The attitudes of policy makers affect absenteeism. There is a direct relationship between the hours of work and the absenteeism rates.

Research Methods: Interviews—personal or over the telephone.

Findings: Human factors are strategic factors to be considered in the problem of absenteeism. There are different conceptualizations of the problem on different levels in the organization. The feedback of accurate information would permit top management to develop better programs for coping with absenteeism.

7. THE RELATIONSHIP BETWEEN CRITERIA AND FEEDBACK

Setting: Home Economics Department of a small college.

Variables: Information available; personality differences.

Relationships: The criteria used to judge a teacher and her performance are determined by the nature of the feedback.

Research Methods: Interviews were held with the Dean and with teachers. The information gained was analyzed statistically.

Findings: Feedback is a function of criteria. A teacher would not recognize performance feedback channels and would not have an interest in the information itself unless she, even subjectively, compared this performance data to some standard.

8. A TRAINING PROBLEM AT A LARGE PUBLIC UTILITY
Setting: A large public utility.
Variables: The training programs and their implementation; personality differences.
Research Methods: Discussions with men on each level of the organization and analysis of programs.
Findings: An imposed training program to disclose which mismatch (discrepancies between training required and training received) exists and fails of implementation because of no supervisor and worker motivation to increase the overall knowledge level.

9. A MORALE AND LEADERSHIP STUDY
Setting: A government research laboratory.
Variables: Different composition of the groups; personality differences of members and leaders; goals of the groups.
Relationships: Good, average, and poor leadership does not necessarily correspond to high, average, and low morale in small scientific groups.
Research Methods: Questionnaire.
Findings: Although poor leadership is associated with low morale, good leadership does not appear to be as significant in determining the level of morale.

10. A STUDY OF COMMUNICATION CHANNELS IN ORGANIZATION CHANGE
Setting: Mechanical assembly group of a small firm in a period of rapid growth and expansion.
Variables: Amount of interest employee had in obtaining information; amount of information employee already had; personality differences.
Relationships: Workers accept organizational change willingly only when no threat to their "certainty pattern" is posed by the change. (This holds true only when the existing organizationl structure has been satisfactory for the achievement of worker goals.) If information is not forthcoming to relieve the uncertainty, employees will initiate their own efforts to answer their questions. Both formal and informal channels will be used.
Research Methods: A questionnaire was administered to employees.
Findings: Inconclusive findings. The figures tended to confirm the premise that there was a difference between actual communication and that desired by workers, but the assumption that workers will be motivated to obtain the information they desire did not stand up conclusively.

11. A STUDY OF INFORMAL MANAGEMENT COMMUNICATIONS
Setting: Local division of a large automotive manufacturing company.
Variables: Line or staff man; frequency of task contacts; frequency of general business contacts; frequency of social contacts; frequency of external and internal contacts; variations in level of contact.
Relationships: The staff man receives and transmits communications more actively than does the line man on the same organizational level.
Research Methods: Observations of one hour per person at the same time of day. A statistical test was applied for differences in frequencies.
Findings: There were no statistically significant results: the sample size was too small and time did not permit the use of a larger group. The results did tend to agree with the hypothesis.

12. A STUDY IN COMMUNICATION

Setting: A group leader of 10 mechanical engineers in a large manufacturing company.

Variables: Personal and environmental factors.

Relationships: The communication channels utilized for task-oriented communications in a modern business organization are markedly different than the channels indicated by the firm's organization chart.

Research Methods: A formal organization chart was obtained and the formal lines of organization were studied. The group leader kept a chart of his communications. The group leader was interviewed at length twice.

Findings: There were five times as many substitutes as "normal communication channels" communications.

13. STUDY OF STATUS SYMBOLS AND THEIR RELATION TO, OR MEASURE OF, POSITION IN THIS ORGANIZATION

Setting: One of the largest departments of a medium-sized insurance company.

Variables: Office items considered to be status symbols.

Relationships: An individual's responsibility or position can be determined in relation to others in the organization by evaluating those status symbols associated with one individual against those associated with others.

Research Methods: Organization charts were drawn up. The offices were observed and lists were made of the contents, location, etc. The items on the list were ranked subjectively.

Findings: Company policy tends to give more status through the allocation of status symbols to people of higher position in the organization. Individuals tend to circumvent that policy by personal acquisition of status symbols.

14. A STUDY OF THE FEELINGS OF ADVANCEMENT AND SE-CURITY AS A FUNCTION OF POSITION IN AN ORGANIZATION

Setting: Branch of a commercial bank.

Variables: Personal differences; type of job; management personnel may not be aware of their own limitations.

Relationships: At higher levels of management, the expectation of advancement is not as important as at lower levels. Conversely, at higher levels the people are more concerned with security—with keeping what they have.

Research Methods: Personal interviews were used to elicit answers which would imply how prevalent the respondents' feelings were concerning advancement and security. The data were analyzed statistically.

Findings: Middle management is significantly more advancement-minded than either top or lower management. Contrary to expectations, the lower management group was more security-minded than the middle management group. Furthermore, the lower management group was less advancement-minded than the middle management group.

15. A STUDY OF THE RELATIONSHIP OF A MANAGER'S PER-FORMANCE TO HIS OPINION OF THE EFFECTIVENESS OF HIS SUBORDINATES

Setting: A large firm with a sizable line organization.

Variables: Norms or standards for work performance of subordinates; measurement of manager's performance; length of time in position; number of supervisors reporting to each division head; type of work performed.

Relationships:.There is a relationship between a manager's performance and his opinion of the effectiveness of his subordinates. The manager's performance will be highest when his general opinion of his subordinate is neither high nor low.

Research Methods: Two kinds of questionnaires were used: (*a*) an objective one for section heads to rate division heads, and (*b*) a subjective one for division heads to rate line supervisors. The data were analyzed by a regression analysis and the *t* test.

Findings: The small sample of this research study failed to reveal the nature of this relationship.

16. A STUDY OF RUMOR IN ORGANIZATION

Setting: Large insurance company. Studied the Group Claims Division, which was located on three floors. Because of this, it was possible to analyze liaison between the three areas.

Variables: Type of rumor; person who receives the rumor; person who initiates the rumor; work space or seating arrangements.

Relationships: Rumor in organizations will tend to follow sociometric channels.

Research Methods: Two junior division leaders were to drop a selected rumor to three secretaries. A questionnaire was used to determine who had heard the rumor and from what source they had heard it.

Findings: The rumor failed to circulate. The supposed stooges also disclosed the design in order not to abuse confidence of secretaries.

17. PURCHASING DECISIONS BY RETAIL BUYERS

Setting: The purchasing agents in a large women's specialty store.

Variables: Information available to buyer; estimated sales; stock at the end of the period; stock on hand and on order; markdowns; general store policy; profit expectations; OTB performance.

Relationships: The quantity purchased by the individual buyers in a given period equals what is called the dollar "open-to-buy" control to insure that actual purchasing is done according to the plan (OTB Control). The buyer will adjust his OTB and hence the quantity to be purchased by manipulating the markdowns taken. The study is restricted to determine if a model can be developed to plausibly describe a decision process.

Research Methods: A search of the existing literature was conducted. Then the buyers were interviewed. The data obtained were analyzed statistically.

Findings: Experienced buyers tend to make purchases strictly according to the amount of OTB available to them; they consider it to be a valuable guide. Inexperienced buyers are less interested in meeting the calculated OTB—thus, they exercise a freer hand in the operation in their departments. Markdown manipulation to meet OTB is not practiced in this store. Buyers are evaluated according to net profit, not net volume.

18. A STUDY OF KNOWLEDGE OF COMPANY POLICY VS. FORE-MAN EFFECTIVENESS

Setting: A shoe manufacturing company employing over 1,000 people.

Variables: Knowledge of company policy; foreman effectiveness; company policy; personality differences.

Relationships: The most successful foremen will have a greater knowledge and understanding concerning the policies of the company than will those who are less successful. Effectiveness of foremen was measured by: superior's ratings;

rating by size of bonus; size of salary; level of responsibility; length of service with the company.

Research Methods: Questionnaire designed for foremen. The questionnaire was designed following conversations with general managers. Independent ratings of foremen by managers were obtained. The data were analyzed statistically.

Findings: .Hypothesis statistically substantiated. This experiment merely established the existence of the relationship in this case. It did not establish the direction of cause and effect.

19. FIELD STUDY IN A TELEPHONE EXCHANGE ROOM

Setting: Telephone exchange room.

Variables: Amount of interaction; informal organization; varying work load; personality differences of the workers and the supervisors.

Relationships: Does an informal organization develop when a work group deals with a varying work load?

Research Methods: Interviewed operators; observed operators in the exchange room and made interaction measurements. The data were analyzed statistically.

Findings: Only a weak informal organization was found to exist among the telephone operators' group. The formal organization of the group and the nature of the task suppresses teamwork or informal organization.

20. RELATION OF INTERACTION TO INFORMAL ORGANIZATION STRUCTURE

Setting: Work group in branch of large electrical manufacturing company.

Variables: Status differences; personality differences; nature of interaction.

Relationship: It is possible by observation of the verbal interaction of a small group in a face-to-face situation to deduce the informal organization structure of the group.

Research Method: Questionnaire—not enough data obtained to test statistically. Observed at meetings and scored on a matrix—units of interaction and initiation.

Findings: People of low rank tend to overestimate their communication with their leader. People of higher status originate more interactions. The data does not seem to indicate that there is a relationship between interaction in an *ad hoc* situation and the existence of an informal organization.

21. JOB SATISFACTION AS RELATED TO EXPECTATION OF PROMOTION

Setting: A medium-sized insurance company.

Variables: Job satisfaction; contents of job; identification with the company; financial and job status satisfaction; pride and group perfomance; expectancy of promotion; age; length of employment with the company; length of time on present job; marital status; sex.

Relationships: Job satisfaction decreases as expectation of promotion increases. Job satisfaction is correlated with productivity. The level of satisfaction is a combination of both level of aspiration and amount of return from environment. Job satisfaction cannot be described or predicted by any one variable. The stronger the need, the more closely will job satisfaction depend upon its fulfillment.

Research Methods: There were 56 respondents to a five-page questionnaire mailed to the insurance company. The data were analyzed statistically.

Findings: As expectation of promotion increases (the date of promotion being uncertain), there is a tendency for job satisfaction to decrease, but the relationship is curvilinear. Job satisfaction does not seem to be dependent significantly upon any of the four factors considered. It is noticeable that the low satisfaction scores occurred among the less educated. Job satisfaction tends to increase with age and with the number of years spent in the company. Job satisfaction tends to be much more variable in younger people than in older persons. Job satisfaction is found to be very high among 19 of the 21 subjects who were married.

22. INFORMATION TRANSFER FROM DESIGN TO PRODUCTION

Setting: A manufacturing company using advanced technology.

Variables: Blockage and flow of information; departmentation; status factors; work programs.

Relationships: Organizational and personal factors interact to block optimum transfer of design information from R & D units to production. Informal remedies tend to develop. (After T. Burns and G. M. Stalker, *The Management of Innovation,* Tavistock, London, Eng.; 1960.)

Research Methods: Extensive interviewing and flow charting of procedures.

Findings: Status barriers existed to transfer of design information. One unnecessary department had been created in the line of horizontal communication from design to production. Programs were structured as a handover of blueprints, thus insulating personnel from contact. At least one instance arose where the procedures were short-circuited, with direct transfer of design to shop floor.

REFERENCES

1. a. ADAMS, R. N., AND PREISS, J. J. *Human Organization Research.* Dorsey. 1960.
   b. KAHN, R. L., AND CANNELL, C. F. *The Dynamics of Interviewing.* John Wiley and Sons. 1957.
   c. SELLTIZ, C. X., JAHODA, M. DEUTSCH, M., AND COOK, S. *Research Methods in Social Relations.* Holt, Rinehart and Winston. 1959.
   d. FESTINGER, LEON, AND KATZ, DANIEL (editors). *Research Methods in the Behavioral Sciences.* Holt, Rinehart and Winston. 1953.
2. BALES, ROBERT F. *Interaction Process Analysis.* Addison-Wesley. Cambridge, Massachusetts. 1950.
3. BALES, R. F., AND HOUSEHOLDER, A. S. *Some Group Interaction Models.* RM 953. RAND Corporation. October 10, 1952.
4. BAVELAS, A. "Communication Patterns in Task-Oriented Groups." In *Group Dynamics.* D. Cartwright and A. Zander (editors). Row Peterson, 1953.
5. GUETZKOW, HAROLD. "A Use of Simulation in the Study of Inter-Nation Relations." *Behavioral Science.* Vol. 4. No. 3. 1959. pp 183–191.
6. GUETZKOW, HAROLD, Editor. *Groups, Leadership, and Men.* Carnegie Institute of Technology. 1951.
7. See issues of *Human Organization* over the past 20 years, formerly called *Applied Anthropology,* and the following:
   a. CHAPPLE, ELIOT D. "Applied Anthropology in Industry." *Anthropology Today.* A. L. KROEBER (editor). (Chicago: University of Chicago Press, 1953) pp 819–831.

b. CHAPPLE, ELIOT D. AND L. R. SAYLES. *The Measure of Management* (New York: The Macmillan Co., 1961).

c. RICHARDSON, F. L. W. *Talk, Work, and Action.* Monograph No. 3, 1961. The Society for Applied Anthropology, New York, State School of Industrial and Labor Relations, Cornell University, Ithaca, New York.

8. KAPLAN, ABRAHAM. "Sociology Learns the Language of Mathematics." *Commentary.* 1951.

9. ROETHLISBERGER, F. J., AND DICKSON, WILLIAM J. *Management and the Worker.* Harvard University Press. Cambridge. 1939.

10. SEASHORE, STANLEY E. "Field Experiments with Formal Organizations." *Human Organization.* Vol. 23. No. 2. Summer 1964. 164–170.

11. SIMON, HERBERT A. *Models of Man.* John Wiley and Sons. 1957. Chapter 6.

12. TORRANCE, E. PAUL. "Function of Expressed Disagreement in Small Group Processes." *Social Forces.* Vol. 35. No. 4. 1957.

Exercises

SECTION I

1. State "Theories" about the following phenomena in both verbal proposition form and symbolic or graphical form. Then give a verbal justification for your theory—it need not be from the papers you have read, but can be from your own experience and intuition. The purpose of this question is the form, not the substance of your statement, except that the justification should be reasonable and logical and not contradict common knowledge. Use this format:
   a. verbal proposition
   b. symbolic or graphical form
   c. justification
   The phenomena are:
   1. Basis for a management incentive system
   2. Sources of ideas for new R and D projects
   3. Efficiency (in terms of time-to-solution or percent of problems success-fully solved) of a small group communication net
   4. Policy on hiring members of a minority group
2. From the Articles in this Section, state five general propositions, in verbal form, about the nature of human behavior in organizations.

SECTION II

1. What does Weber (Article No. 4) mean by "monocratically organized, hierarchical office authority"?
2. Consider an organization of which you have been a member or which you have known very well—it can be an industrial, military, business, social or other kind of organization.
   a. Describe it briefly.
   b. State briefly what you believe are (or were) the goals of that organization. Use Selznick's (Article No. 8) notion of the evolving character of an organization to describe any changes in objectives.
   c. What characteristics of Weber's (Article No. 4) bureaucracy did your organization exhibit? What characteristics were lacking?
   d. Was an "informal" organization obvious in contrast to the "formal" organization (refer to Barnard—Article No. 6)?
3. Make a 15-minute interaction recording á la Horsfall and Arensberg (Article No. 9) of some group with which you have contact (e.g., fraternity, dis-cussion class, laboratory class, etc.)
4. Compare Selznick's research methods (Article No. 8) with those of Horsfall and Arensberg (Article No. 9): Can you defend the objectivity of these methods? How are they similar to or different from the methods used by a business executive to gather information?

5. Compare the cases of organization studied by Dalton (Article No. 10), Horsfall (Article No. 9), and RAND (Article No. 11):
   a. Were the systems efficient and effective? What evidence is presented?
   b. What environmental demands were responded to? How?
   c. Were there instances of informal organization, unanticipated consequence, or coöptation? Why did they occur?
6. Apply Lewin's "field theory" principles (Article No. 3) to the theory expounded in the RAND articles (Articles No. 11 and 12). How is each principle observed or violated in the theory?
7. Construct a "theory" of how an organization works, using these concepts from the readings:
   Task Environment (Weiner—Article No. 12)
   Unanticipated Consequences (Selznick—Article No. 8)
   Coöptation (Selznick—Article No. 8)
   Informal Organization (Barnard—Article No. 6)
   Bureaucratization (Weber—Article No. 4)
   Rationality (Udy—Article No. 5)
8. Explain the shoe factory case (Article No. 9) in terms of Barnard's theory of cooperation and organization. Identify each of Barnard's concepts (Article No. 6) and illustrate his principles from the case material.
9. Give an example of "uncertainty absorption" which could occur in the context of the RAND Air Defense Direction Center (Articles No. 11 and 12).

SECTION III

1. In Dalton's case (Article No. 10), the motivational basis for the actions of the various participants was briefly explored. Which of Maslow's (see Essay in Section III) categories of motives were predominant? Can you find evidence in support of McGregor's ideas on motivation (described in the same essay)?
2. In Chowdhry's case study (Article No. 14) what caused the differences in morale between A and B? Could the management have relieved the situation in A? How?
3. The readings provide a sample of the relatively large amount of research and writing in the complex area of human relations.
   a. Drawing from the readings in Section III, develop a conceptual scheme or "theory" to describe the relationships (in work groups such as those described in the readings) between:
      Patterns of supervision or leadership
      Interpersonal relationships
      Morale
      Productivity
   b. Be sure to point out any inconsistencies or direct conflicts between the readings.
   c. Drawing from your own experience and ideas, comment briefly on the reasonableness of the conceptual scheme or theory you have developed. Does it fit into your own beliefs about leadership, etc.?
4. Insofar as possible from the data reported by Chowdhry and Pal (Article No. 14), use Argyris' (Article No. 13) framework to describe the state of human relations in the two textile mills.
5. Which of Maslow's need categories (see Essay in Section III) were

prominent in motivating the shoe factory work teams of Horsfall and Arensberg (Article No. 9)? Explain.

6. Discuss the role of sanctions, attitudes of legitimacy, and authority in the Dalton case. (Article No. 10)

7. Make a check list of things to consider in designing an incentive scheme for division managers in large decentralized companies.

8. In the light of the nature of human personality, as discussed by Argyris (Article No. 13), how can a bureaucratic system of organization á la Weber (Article No. 4) realize Barnard's (Article No. 6) criterion of efficiency? (Make sure that your answer draws to the fullest on the relevant content of the articles in this Section, but do not limit your remarks to restating their findings; do some creative thinking.)

9. Selznick (Articles No. 7 and 8) refers to delegation of authority as a "hazardous venture"; Shepard (in the Essay in Section I) cites it as consistent with the newer administrative theory. What are the advantages and disadvantages of delegation according to these authors and the authors in Section III? Do you approve or disapprove of delegation? What qualifications would you impose?

10. For each of the following articles, indicate the major independent and dependent variables and parameters plus the major relationships each author was investigating. Use the following format:

a. Author b. Independent c. Dependent d. Parameter(s) e. Major
        Variable(s) Variable(s)   Relationship(s)

The articles are:
1. Dalton (Article No. 10)
2. Chowdhry and Pal (Article No. 14)
3. Hutchins and Feidler (Article No. 17)
4. Pelz (Article No. 19)
5. Argyris (Article No. 13)

SECTION IV

1. Reanalyze the case described by Sykes (Article No. 20) in terms of the model of superior-subordinate relations presented by Pelz (Article No. 19). Which approach is more helpful in explaining conflict between workers and foremen? Explain.

2. Discuss the role that a "change agent" might have played in the situations described by a) Dalton (Article No. 10) and b) Chowdhry and Pal (Article No. 14).

3. Develop a set of categories an investigator might use in studying the effects of technological change on organizational behavior. Use Articles No. 22 and 23 and the Essay of Section IV as a source of items for the set of categories. Combine related ideas.

SECTION V

1. What are the various constraints on control tower language found by Frick and Sumby (Article No. 31)?

2. Considering an individual in an organization as a communication link, outline the factors that affect the amount and kind of information he transmits. Construct a concrete example (from experience, imagination, or the readings) of the operation of each factor.

3. Three basic variables have been reported in the literature as affecting the transmission of a rumor. They are (1) importance; (2) ambiguity; and (3) the critical sense of the potential rumor transmitter. Based on Caplow's Article No. 30:

   a. Is this set of variables supported by Caplow's findings?

   b. Do Caplow's findings suggest any additional variables that should be included in a "law of rumor"?

4. What other operational methods of measuring upward communication might one use, in addition to that used by Read (Article No. 24)? Discuss the indicators you would use and the measurement problems you might encounter.

5. Find a spontaneous, on-going bull session. Gain entry and observe, but do not participate. Note instances of disagreement that arise, including a summary of the issues and a description of how each is resolved. In your write-up, interpret and explain your observations in terms of the kind of small group theories encountered in Articles No. 9, 16, 17, 18, 25, and 27.

6. List the theoretical variables (not the operational measures) studied by Blau (Article No. 25) and indicate which ones "cause" or affect which others and how.

7. For each of the following studies, indicate:

   a. The variables which were under investigation, stating:

   which were the independent variables,

   which were the dependent variables, and

   which were intervening or modifying parameters.

   b. The functional relationships being studied.

   The studies are:

   1. Pelz (Article No. 19)

   2. Guetzkow and Simon (Article No. 27)

   3. Walton (Article No. 28)

   4. Strauss (Article No. 29)

8. Using the ideas in mathematical communication theory or "information theory," (see Article No. 31) indicate the potential application of these ideas to:

   a. The inventory areas of a firm, and

   b. The cost accounting area of a firm.

   Be sure to define the terms you use.

SECTION VI

1. What criteria might be used to evaluate a Forest Service Unit? A hospital? A police department? A school system?

2. a. Select a specific kind of information group in a company, such as research, cost accounting, production control.

   b. Identify the significant "design variables" of such a group which may have an effect on its information-handling performance. This list of variables might include design variables like size, skill level of members, location, and so forth.

   c. Specify a number of significant behavior or performance variables which describe the information output and which might serve as control criteria for the performance of the group. A possible one might be total "amount" of information transferred per time period.

PORTION OF CONCEPTUAL SCHEME RELATING TO ASSIGNMENT

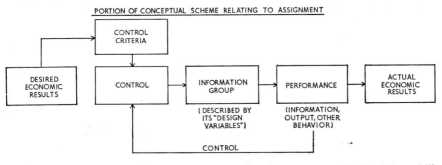

3. Construct a diagram of immediate effects for the system studied by Hemphill and Sechrest (Article No. 34).
4. Which of the three types of performance criteria discussed by Ridgway (Article No. 36) are reported or recommended by Haberstroh (Article No. 32), Williams and Wilson (Article No. 35), and Fey (Article No. 33)? Explain why you consider each example to be of that type.

SECTION VII

1. Outline an example of a two-person, constant-sum game in a business context to illustrate the ideas in Shubik (Article No. 43).
2. Comment on the findings of Wallach and Kogan (Article No. 41) in relation to your own experience with group and individual decision making.
3. Select one of the principal functional areas of the firm—production, marketing, finance, research and development. Based on the readings in the Section on decision making:
   a. Make an analysis of the decision-making process in the area. Include consideration of the kinds of decisions made; the decision makers and their characteristics; the decision process from the time the need for a decision is recognized through its implementation.
   b. Suggest a system for monitoring or "controlling" decision making in this area. What key variables would be used for this purpose?
4. Reread Figure 1 in the Essay of Section I. Construct a model for decisions on matters of internal administration for the "new direction in organization theory." Contrast this with the corresponding model for traditional theory.
5. Real organizations place limits on "rationality." As "rationality" is described by decision theory (Essay VII), what specific "limits" are treated in the empirical studies of Articles No. 37, 38, 39, and 40? Give some concrete examples.
6. Compare the definition of "rationality" given in the Essay in this Section or by Cyert, Simon, and Trow (Article No. 37) with the definition given by Udy (Article No. 5). How do the definitions and findings support or contradict each other?
7. Construct a flow chart of the decision process described by Dufty and Taylor (Article No. 38) that could be used to program a computer simulation thereof.

SECTION VIII

1. Design a field study for use in an operating organization. The study design should be simple, consisting of a single question or hypothesis arising out of the material covered in the course. It may be a question or hypothesis taken

directly from the literature, or one that you are interested in raising. The design should, where possible, allow for measurement and quantitative analysis of the data. The design should be general enough to be used in different kinds of organizations. The unique characteristics of any specific organization should not determine the question or hypothesis, but the data collection techniques should be adaptable to the circumstances of the kind of organization being studied.

The study design should include at least the following information:

    a. The hypothesis or question

    b. Reference to the underlying theory or previous work.

    c. The variables and their characteristics.

    d. The form of the relationships involved.

    e. Potential data collection methods.

    f. The mode of data analysis (e.g., correlation, regression, factor analysis, statistical test of hypothesis).

    g. Form of hoped-for or expected conclusions.

Index

This book has been set on the Linotype in 10 point Janson, leaded 2 points and 9 point Janson, leaded 1 point. Section numbers are in 18 point Janson italic caps and section titles in 24 point Janson italic caps and lower case. The size of the type page is 27 by 46 picas.

DATE DUE